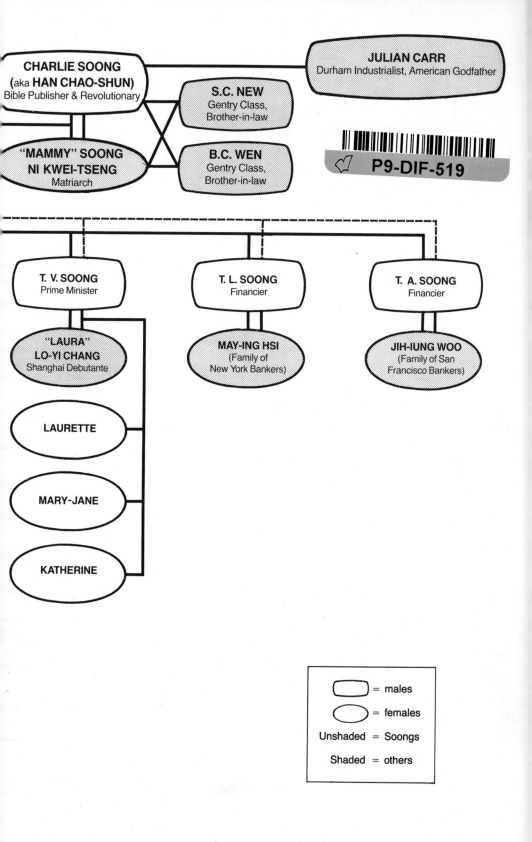

CHARLIE SOONG
(aka HAN CHAO-SHUN)
Bible Publisher & Revolutionary

JULIAN CARR
Durham Industrialist, American Godfather

S.C. NEW
Gentry Class,
Brother-in-law

B.C. WEN
Gentry Class,
Brother-in-law

"MAMMY" SOONG
NI KWEI-TSENG
Matriarch

P9-DIF-519

T. V. SOONG
Prime Minister

T. L. SOONG
Financier

T. A. SOONG
Financier

"LAURA"
LO-YI CHANG
Shanghai Debutante

MAY-ING HSI
(Family of
New York Bankers)

JIH-IUNG WOO
(Family of San
Francisco Bankers)

LAURETTE

MARY-JANE

KATHERINE

= males
= females
Unshaded = Soongs
Shaded = others

THE SOONG DYNASTY

Other books by Sterling Seagrave

Yellow Rain
Soldiers of Fortune

The Soong Dynasty

 STERLING SEAGRAVE

HARPER & ROW, PUBLISHERS, New York

1817

Cambridge, Philadelphia, San Francisco, London

Mexico City, São Paulo, Singapore, Sydney

THE SOONG DYNASTY. Copyright © 1985 by Sterling Seagrave. All rights reserved. Printed in the United States of America. No part of this book may be used or reproduced in any manner whatsoever without written permission except in the case of brief quotations embodied in critical articles and reviews. For information address Harper & Row, Publishers, Inc., 10 East 53rd Street, New York, N.Y. 10022. Published simultaneously in Canada by Fitzhenry & Whiteside Limited, Toronto.

Designer: Sidney Feinberg

Endpaper by Frank Ronan

Library of Congress Cataloging in Publication Data

Seagrave, Sterling.
  The Soong Dynasty

  Bibliography: p.
  Includes index.
  1. China—History—Republic, 1912–1949. 2. Soong
family. I. Title.
DS774.S393   1985   951.04   83-48802
ISBN 0-06-015308-3

FOR PEG

CONTENTS

Illustrations follow pages 208 and 358

The Soongs were made for China, not China for the Soongs.
　　　　　　　　　　　　—Soong Ching-ling
　　　　　　　　　　　　　(Madame Sun Yat-sen)

The most difficult problem in Sino-American publicity concerns the Soong family. They are . . . the head and front of a pro-American policy. It ill befits us, therefore, to go sour on them.
　　　　　　　　　　　　—Henry R. Luce
　　　　　　　　　　　　　(Time Inc.)

A NOTE ON NAMES AND SOURCES

To avoid confusing readers, the Chinese names in this book are rendered very casually in the way they were most familiar at the time. The new Pinyin system is used only for reference to locations on recent maps. Sources for the information on which the book is based are listed and described in the Notes, which begin on page 467. Readers seeking further elaboration may find the extensive Bibliography useful.

THE SOONG DYNASTY

Prologue

SHANGHAI TAPESTRY

Shanghai no longer smells like the Mysterious East. The realization came as a shock to my nostrils, which had expected to be indulged on the long drive out the Nanking Road—past the old British Concession race course, now the People's Park, through leafy tunnels of dappled sunlight from the canopy of plane trees, and into the vaulted arbor of the Avenue Joffre, once in the heart of the old French Concession, now called simply Huai Hai Middle Road. The tired sedan, built in one of Shanghai's ubiquitous people's factories, pulled up before the high wooden gate of a small brick villa, identified by Chinese characters on a plaque beside the gate. The gate cracked open cautiously to reveal the drowsy face of a young People's Liberation Army soldier, wearing forest green with vermilion flashes. His blank look was replaced instantly when he found himself confronted by a bearded round-eye. Two decades of militancy looked out, flanked by sentries of suspicion.

Yes, he admitted reluctantly, in a Shanghai whisper, this was once the home of Vice Chairman Soong Ching-ling, as clearly proclaimed by the plaque. But I was not permitted to enter. The mansion was now occupied by a senior party official.

When I suggested a stroll instead through its carefully tended gardens, where in my mind I could hear the click of croquet balls and the 1920 laughter of the little doctor Sun Yat-sen, the guard's eyes narrowed and he drew himself into the stance called Stork-Strides-to-Distant-Mountain. Old men practice it along the Bund during each morning's T'ai Ch'i exercises.

1

Disappointed, I stared over his shoulder, trying to memorize the bushes and flowers, the tidy gables, the turn of the window casements, hearing faraway voices through the foliage from the old servants' quarters in the back. He raised his shoulder to block my view. It was no use telling him that what I was looking for had not been there for half a century.

Nothing was there any longer, except the place where it all began. The old Shanghai, that "sink of iniquity" with its 668 brothels, was gone. The old British Club, home of the celebrated Long Bar, where the great taipans once sipped their "stengahs," and where the Japanese occupation forces had to cut down the legs on the tables and chairs for their bantam officers, was now a hostel for merchant seamen.

One night I went searching for the city's ghosts, to be sure they had left. If they were still around, they would be in the old Chinese city—the walled town now bounded by Chunghua Road. It was remarkably quiet. A century ago, even half a century, I could not have strolled the narrow alleys so peacefully. Once, the streets were crowded with people elbowing each other, constantly hawking to spit, while beggars sprawled in the gutters like wounded spider monkeys. A few "cash" could purchase a nine-year-old virgin for an hour of unnatural acts—or put a meat cleaver through the shoulder tendons to keep a man from ever again lifting anything for a livelihood.

But the ancient smells were not there and neither were the ghosts. Even the old Chinese city was scrubbed clean, tidy, healthy, attractive, unthreatening. I might as well have been in Lyon, Manchester, or Omaha. Except that the people of Shanghai were friendlier. Gone were the vigilante mobs of Red Guards who raced through the cities of China in the 1960s, tarring and feathering foreign diplomats in the streets of Shanghai, dragging members of the Communist party Politburo into Peking stadium with dunce hats on their heads, to confess their guilt for plotting against Chairman Mao. One man in a dunce hat was the former Minister of Public Security, General Lo, whom I had admired for his commendable aphorism "It is better to confess than not to confess." He was given a chance to practice what he preached, fulfilling the Orwellian prophecies. Those same hysterical mobs, stirred up by Madame Mao and the Gang of Four, had vandalized Vice Chairman Soong Ching-ling's house—the pretty little villa on the Avenue Joffre, where she had lived as a girl before she eloped with Dr. Sun, and which she had acquired after the Communist victory as a place for her old age.

Why was everybody now so friendly? In the Chinese villages along the border of Yunnan Province, where I had grown up, the poor people were always friendly and full of earthy humor. But it was hardly expected in Shanghai. While Russia and America vied to put the first man on the moon, the Chinese boasted that they would put a new man on the earth. Had they succeeded? If so, what better place to put him than in this city once considered the most sinful on the planet. Because it is the setting of our story, and its personality contributed so much to the Soong legend, the evolution of Shanghai requires a brief summary.

In the early 1800s, just before the Soongs came on stage, the old Chinese city was just a village on the muddy banks of the Whangpoo River, seventeen miles from the Yangtze River estuary. The name Shanghai means nothing more romantic than "by the sea." Along a towpath on the embankment, barge men pulled cargo junks upriver when the wind failed. For miles around, the countryside was flat, prone to flooding. But the site commanded all trade up the Yangtze for a thousand miles into the interior.

Foreigners were until then confined to trading at the southern port of Canton. Great Britain had been trading with China through the East India Company since the late 1700s. But early in the nineteenth century she had a severe cash-flow problem. Her imports of Chinese teas and silks were far greater than the value of her exports to China; there was little demand for expensive British manufactured goods such as woolens, cotton, and metal products. With the mercantile conquest of India behind them, British traders were confident that they could develop another vast market in China if a few ports other than Canton could be opened to foreign exploitation. The lever Britain used to pry them open was opium.

The primary source of opium then was India and the Middle East, monopolized by the British East India Company. Proper Englishmen like Dr. William Jardine, one of the greatest opium merchants, purchased raw opium from Indian growers for niggardly sums, and resold it to the Chinese through Hong Kong for ten times the amount.

For a while, the British were successful in financing their imports of tea by smuggling opium to China, but as tea consumption rose, opium traffic had to be increased accordingly. Since the Manchu regime had banned opium trading, British ships carried their loads to the Portuguese colony of Macao, at the mouth of the Pearl River, unloaded the drug there, then sailed innocently into Canton harbor with legal cargoes. Later, when enough Manchu officials had become partners in the illicit trade, the opium was shipped directly into Canton, where it was stored brazenly in warehouses along the riverside.

The Americans became involved in the 1820s, and dignified firms such as Perkins & Company and Russell & Company of Boston engaged in immense opium traffic by clipper ship. British and American traffic increased from 5,000 chests in 1821 to 39,000 chests in 1837. Britain's share of this growth again balanced her imports of silks and teas, and stemmed the outflow of her silver. But not without hazard to China. The increased consumption of opium, despite imperial bans, was causing social calamity. More and more people, from landlords and aristocrats down to soldiers and prostitutes, became addicted. The seduction of Manchu officials into the trade caused government corruption to spread. Eventually, the silver flow was reversed, and Chinese silver began to rush toward Great Britain in alarming quantities.

National pride and sovereignty were as much at stake as silver and opium. When Chinese officials crucified an opium smuggler in front of the Canton warehouses in December 1838, the foreign devils rushed out and broke up the wooden cross. Ten thousand Chinese rioted. The Westerners appealed to a powerful merchant they called Houqua—the Chinese kingpin of the opium traffic—and he bought off the local mandarins, setting a pattern for a century to come.

The Chinese government then insisted that all British captains must sign a bond that they would not carry opium into the country. Secretly, Americans began to carry British opium or to let British ships fly the Stars and Stripes into Canton. The last straw came when a crew of drunken British sailors killed a Chinese villager in an argument. Their consul refused to allow them to be tried by a Chinese court. To retaliate, the Manchu government ordered all provisions to the British cut off. Great Britain declared war on October 1, 1839.

British opium merchants had campaigned long and hard for this war, and they were its chief beneficiaries. A fleet led by the thirty-two-gun paddlewheeler *Nemesis* made short work of the Chinese navy. Humiliated, China paid a huge indemnity, opened five additional ports to British trade and residence, and exempted British subjects from Chinese justice.

Of all the new treaty ports, Shanghai was the gem. It was only a squalid coastal enclave when the British arrived in force. Captain George Balfour of the Madras Artillery was the first resident British consul; he was accompanied by a translator, a surgeon, and a clerk. Balfour selected a marshy site just north of the walled Chinese town because the river there provided the best anchorage.

"There our navy can float," he said, "and by our ships, our power can be seen and, if necessary, promptly felt. Our policy is the thorough command of this great river."

Not only did Shanghai command the mighty Yangtze for the movement of agricultural produce; it was connected by canals and lakes to the silk capital of Soochow, and by the Grand Canal to Peking. All the goods of China could easily flow out there, and all the goods of Europe and America could flow in.

Foreigners were slow to settle at first, but a handful of missionaries and merchants came up from Canton, accompanied by their shrewd Chinese business agents. The United States negotiated a separate treaty, allowing Yankees a concession of their own, plus most-favored-nation status and exemption from Chinese justice. An American consul, Henry Wolcott, raised the Stars and Stripes on the north side of Soochow Creek—the first foreign flag to fly in Shanghai because no British flagpole had yet been erected. Taken aback, Consul Balfour planted the Union Jack on the south side, and hastily built his consulate there. Eventually the Americans asked the British to handle police and other matters for them, and this led to the amalgamation of the two concessions as the International Settlement. The French remained aloof, establishing their own concession up the riverbank.

In the beginning, America was represented by zealous missionaries, not merchants. Many of them were puritan fundamentalists, full of New Testament virtues. "The Chinese are a hopeful race," they said optimistically, "and need only the transforming influence of Christianity to rise almost immeasurably above the rest of Asiatic nations."

Where once there had been just a towpath, a row of warehouses, or hongs, now stood, each in a handsome garden. Upstairs was the office of the taipan, or boss, and his assistants. These were hard men who came to Asia to make their personal fortunes first, and the profits of their companies and nations thereafter. No women accompanied them. Shanghai, in those days, was no place for a lady.

With no companionship but each other, the taipans led a life of leisure modeled on that of the English country squire. They rose late, breakfasted heavily, visited their hongs to go over accounts kept by Western office managers called *griffins,* then adjourned for a lavish lunch of Chinese delicacies washed down with English ale and Dutch gin. In the afternoon, they sipped whiskey on the verandah and observed the loading and unloading underway on the river, smoking cigars with amiable friends till supper. This repast featured Spanish sherries, French clarets and sauternes, exquisite Chinese fish and fowl, imported roast beef and mutton, augmented by Indian curries, pastries, cheeses, champagne, coffee, and more cigars. In everyone's mind was the urgent need for a club.

Shanghai began to boom. An atmosphere of freebooting capitalism took hold, and the role of cutthroat merchant gentleman was played to the hilt. Criminals and swindlers disembarked in great numbers. It was said that the only way to tell the criminal from the capitalist was by the size of his purse. Lancelot Dent and his partner, T. C. Beale, of Dent & Company were the first serious rivals to Jardine and his partner Matheson. Both firms used fast sailing ships to pick up their mail in Calcutta or Hong Kong and race north to Shanghai ahead of the sluggish British mail ships. In this manner they learned the latest commercial news from Europe a day or two ahead of would-be new rivals—and made fantastic killings. The leading American hongs were Russell & Company, Heard & Company, Wetmore's, Olyphant's, and Wolcott, Bates & Company. Among these, the most powerful was the established opium trader Russell & Company, linked to the famous Yankee merchant clans of Roosevelt, Delano, and Forbes.

But, if all was going brilliantly for the British and Americans, it was going very badly for the Manchus.

Britain's triumph in the First Opium War revealed the vulnerability of the Manchu dynasty, which had ruled China since 1644. The alien Manchus had never fully conquered South China. Conspiracy always simmered there, and anti-Manchu secret societies spread through the countryside. The brutal methods of the Manchus had long delayed a popular uprising, but the British opium victory disclosed that Manchu strength had rotted away over the centuries into profound weakness and corruption. It was only a matter of time before the anti-Manchu movement would pull together and topple the imperial government.

The Manchu throne was in a dilemma. If it devoted its energies and resources to resisting foreigners, it left itself exposed to internal revolt.

If it suppressed internal revolt, it left itself open to foreign demands. Both the Chinese secret societies and the Western nations took advantage of this dilemma. The West sought to keep the Manchu government off balance, but not enough to cause its downfall. The secret societies provoked trouble between the Manchus and the Westerners by attacking missionaries. Each outrage caused Western governments to bring new pressure on Peking.

Ironically, it was ferocious Old Testament Christianity that brought the matter to a head in one of history's great cataclysms—the Taiping Rebellion of 1850. In South China, a disappointed candidate for the Manchu civil service turned to Christianity for solace. He had visions that he was the younger brother of Jesus Christ. With him as its Messiah, a Society of God Worshippers (Christians, by their own estimation) rose up to smite the Manchus. Their objective was to put the government back in Chinese hands, and to establish common ownership of land. They also were hellbent on putting a crimp in prostitution, opium smoking, drinking, adultery, gambling, footbinding, slavery, and cruelty to women. They were quite ahead of their time. A mighty Christian army of famine-stricken peasants and workers swept north to establish the Heavenly Kingdom of Great Peace (T'aip'ing T'ien-kuo—hence simply the "Taipings").

This sort of Old Testament eye-for-an-eye violence was not really what the New Testament missionaries from the West had in mind for China. Some of them were also a bit offended by the suggestion that Jesus Christ could have a Chinese relative.

For fourteen years, the Taipings battled the Manchus, ravaging twenty provinces of China, while sending twenty millions souls to heaven. Then they made the mistake of attempting to seize Shanghai from the foreigners; they succeeded only in taking control of the native city for two years. They were driven out finally by the French, and then were set upon by an American soldier of fortune named Frederick Townsend Ward.

A ne'er-do-well from Salem, Massachusetts, Ward was bored working as a sailor on the Yangtze. The prospect of easy pillage appealed to him. In the pay of the Manchu throne, he organized a force of mercenaries to fight the Taipings. Ward called his troops the "Ever Victorious Army," but it accomplished little. Although Ward himself was no real danger, and he was soon killed in battle, he was succeeded by a peculiar and very dangerous military misfit, Charles George Gordon.

Gordon was a dashing, mustachioed hero of the Crimea, sent out to take part in the Second Opium War, when Western military forces occupied Peking in October 1860, burned down the magnificent Summer Palace, and dictated to the Dragon Throne the terms of humiliating new concessions. Afterward, Brevet Major Gordon was assigned to take over Ward's Ever Victorious Army in its "defense" of Shanghai. Disastrously for the Taipings, Gordon was a bent genius. When he was not in his tent sulking like Achilles, he waged brilliant attacks on the insurgents (and became a popular item in the British press, who gave him the nickname "Chinese Gordon"). His victories were the result of using surprise attack, cannon, high explosives, and modern rifles against rebels armed only with bows and arrows, spears, stink pots, and gongs. The Taipings were demoralized and lost the initiative. They had never dealt with Western military methods before. A Manchu army surrounded them at Nanking and, rather than be strangled slowly by a court executioner, the Younger Brother of Christ committed suicide. The Taiping Rebellion ended.

This did not mean the end, however, of the violent forces they had set in motion. It was the beginning of a great peasant upheaval that would climax nearly a century later under the leadership of Mao Tsetung. Two struggles would go on simultaneously—between the peasants and their feudal rulers, and between China and the predatory foreign powers. Shanghai would profit fantastically from both conflicts.

It is against this background of corruption, revolution, hypocrisy, and greed that the Soong legend begins.

Few families since the Borgias have played such a disturbing role in human destiny. For nearly a century they were key players in events that shaped the history of Asia and the world. Members of the Soong clan became household names—Dr. Sun Yat-sen, Madame Chiang Kai-shek, Generalissimo Chiang, Madame Sun. Others served as China's prime ministers, foreign ministers, finance ministers. They amassed some of the greatest fortunes of the age; T. V. Soong may have been the richest man on earth.

The "Soong Sisters"—Ai-ling, Ching-ling, and May-ling—provoked a now-famous Chinese saying: "Once upon a time there were three sisters: One loved money, one loved power, one loved China." Ai-ling Soong was notorious for her financial cunning, but most people were unaware that she was also the chief manipulator of the family destiny.

"If she had been born a man," it was said, "she would have been running China." May-ling Soong Chiang became one of the most famous and powerful women in history. She inspired two generations of Americans, who ranked her for years among the ten most popular and respected women on earth. For three decades, she influenced the decisions of American leaders and, through them, the world. She was the acknowledged power behind the throne of Nationalist China. The third sister, Ching-ling, remained loyal to the ideals of her husband, Sun Yat-sen, and became a Vice Chairman of Mao Tse-tung's People's Republic. She was generally condemned for this by popular opinion in America.

Their father, Charlie Soong, was famous as the man who financed the revolution of Sun Yat-sen, which finally led to the collapse of the Manchus. As a patriarch, Charlie Soong was without peer. He inspired his children to remarkable attainments, gave his daughters such grace and leverage that they could marry the top military, financial, and political leaders of the new China, and was himself one of China's most unusual entrepreneurs. Like many other legendary characters of Chinese history, he came out of obscurity to produce a dynasty. His son, Harvard-educated T. V. Soong, financed the rise to power of Chiang Kai-shek, and in World War II skillfully persuaded President Roosevelt to support "their" China—the China of Chiang Kai-shek and the Soongs —first against Japan and then against the Chinese Communists, at enormous cost.

The Soongs captivated publisher Henry Luce, of Time Inc., who enlarged their fame in his magazines. Luce, himself the child of American missionaries in China, helped to keep the Soongs in power as vestiges of his own lost horizon, symbols of a romantic China that had become a figment of his imagination. He provided the distorting lens through which many Americans came to see events in Asia. Scores of influential Americans fell under the Soong spell—operatic characters like Claire Chennault of the Flying Tigers, journalists such as Theodore White and Joseph Alsop, famous Washington lobbyists, such as Roosevelt's friend "Tommy the Cork" Corcoran. While FDR joked about letting himself be "vamped" by Madame Chiang, other Americans were nearly done in by the Soongs, especially those who argued for a more objective view of the Chinese quandary, men like General Joseph W. Stilwell, and diplomats John Service and John Paton Davies.

This is their story as well. It is also the story of the Russian secret agent Mikhail Borodin; of the tragic romance of the young American journalist Vincent Sheean; of writer Anna Louise Strong, who became Borodin's intimate ally; of the wildly independent Agnes Smedley, who came out of the dregs of a Colorado mining town to become a champion of lost causes.

The Soongs pose special difficulties. Some creatures in the wilderness have such effective camouflage that it is difficult to be certain of their presence. Like the Cheshire Cat, the Soongs were visible only when they wished to be. They hid by being obvious. They had a public plumage that was so praiseworthy it dazzled the eye. Once this image was established, it became practically impossible to observe their actual movements, to record their true habits and personalities, or other aspects of character easily discernible in ordinary people.

It is characteristic of the Chinese, rich and poor, to be reserved and private—even secretive. The Soongs were the most Westernized of all Chinese, but the appearance of openness and accessibility was merely an acquired manner, not a total transformation. Close associates could not penetrate this mask. Their public image was enhanced and propagated by a legion of publicists. The Chiang regime was known to have spent hundreds of millions of dollars *each year* in the 1940s, 1950s, and 1960s to guarantee its image in America and, thus, the continuance of the regime. At the same time, the regime suppressed negative publicity; for example, a critical biography of Chiang Kai-shek written by one of his ex-wives was purchased by Taiwan authorities for a sum said to be in excess of $1 million, and evidently was destroyed.

I found few people over the years who could seriously profess to know the Soongs intimately. Those who really did know them were members of the Chiang regime, and had reason to be silent. The Soongs were so powerful that they could punish anyone who was indiscreet. A few Westerners, like Claire Chennault, spent decades serving Madame Chiang personally, but were always guarded and hostile to questions because their careers depended on the continued success of their Soong patrons. Only the slanted perceptions of self-proclaimed intimates like Emily Hahn and Henry Luce were given credence and worldwide circulation. Others, like Theodore White, Jack Service, and Joseph Stilwell, criticized the Soongs and were ostracized; of the three, only White escaped having his career destroyed and his reputation ruined. It was customary for anyone who criticized the Soong clan to find himself branded a Communist sympathizer.

There have been biographies of Sun Yat-sen and Chiang Kai-shek, among them several that are mildly critical; there have been two highly-flattering hagiographies of the Soong sisters, and one fictionalized children's book about them by Pearl Buck's sister. But these have all stopped short of dealing with the darker side of the family history. This book is the first biography of the whole clan, and the first to examine both their positive contributions and their long-hidden, more sinister activities. When all the clan members are brought together in a single study, it is possible to see how they helped and hindered each other in the path to power, and to see in sharp relief their regime's long involvement with and dependence upon the Shanghai gangster underworld.

Such a biography did not exist earlier because the Soongs did not want it to. Until the reversal in American policy toward China in the 1970s, any "unwholesome" interest in the Soongs or a less than religious attitude toward the Chiangs, in particular, was enough to jeopardize a journalist's livelihood. The difficulties confronting *Time* Magazine correspondent Theodore White are a case in point, and are recounted, I hope with some justice, in these pages. Another outstanding journalist, Stanley Karnow, who for many years was based in Hong Kong for *Time,* once told me of a trip he made to Taiwan with his boss, Henry Luce. When they were whisked by limousine to the ornate Palace Hotel—a Soong property overlooking Taipei—Luce noticed that the car holding his luggage was no longer following. Beetling his brow, Luce remarked sourly, "I think they've lost our bags." Karnow, never one to endure pretense, cracked, "It won't be the first thing they've lost." Luce was not amused. Karnow's wisecrack helped break the spell of his relationship with Luce—a spell that was necessary if you wished to be one of his correspondents. ("Within a year," Karnow told me, "I was no longer working for *Time.* ")

For these and other reasons, I chose not to include the observations and "insights" of the most obvious sources—Soong family allies such as Clare Boothe Luce, Emily Hahn, Anna Chennault. Their points of view are well known. Emily Hahn's book *The Soong Sisters,* published in 1940, was drawn largely from her acquaintance with Ai-ling Soong while Hahn was a correspondent in Shanghai for *The New Yorker.* It had domestic details about the girls' early childhood and about May-ling's wedding, but proved too partisan to be useful in any other respect.

Instead, I have chosen a way of revealing the Soongs that is less subject to interpretation by friends or foes. Like Perseus, who avoided staring straight at Medusa, I have searched for the Soongs in the mirror of their times and in the lives of their close associates. Their plumage ceased to dazzle. (The methods used, the places where information was located in Asia and America, and the sources for major points in the text are all provided in detail at the back of the book.)

One example will suffice here: the dark side of Chiang Kai-shek's rise to power in the 1920s has been painted over by propagandists, and many of the more sordid details have been obscured or erased. About his youth there remains only an unctuous benediction. This has made it difficult to re-examine Chiang's actions and motives directly. However, a recent flurry of scholarship on China has brought to light the stories of a number of Chiang's early intimates, which I have included in the bibliography. By carefully piecing these elements together and showing how these cronies interacted with Chiang in the early 1920s, I have been able to reconstruct enough of the basic outlines of a major political conspiracy to show how it worked and who were the principals involved. Chiang's direct connection with the notorious Shanghai Green Gang after the winter of 1926–27 has been known for many years, but there has been only a vague understanding that those links went back much earlier, and of how they affected his career. It is now possible for the first time to see the "Divine Skein" linking them all the way back to his youth, before 1910, and the manner in which the Green Gang leaders used Chiang decisively (and were used by him) to snatch the revolution from the hands of Dr. Sun Yat-sen's coalition. Things that have only been rumored can now be seen rather starkly, and Chiang's takeover, which never made much sense in the official versions, begins to make sense now for the first time.

The same approach that reveals Chiang so clearly also reveals the rest of the Soong dynasty. Since the success of the Soongs depended upon shadowy characters who were not members of the family, the Soong story can only be understood by seeing the roles played by those shadows. While they are not Soongs, they must be considered allies of the clan. Foremost among them were the Green Gang boss, Tu Yueh-sheng, and a circle of men who did his bidding. Tu himself was almost a family member.

I hasten to add that I was never an old China hand, just a passerby. By the time I arrived on the scene, I was told that the past had already gone down the drain, the present was rushing after it, and the future was in jeopardy. After recovering from this disappointing news, I wondered who was responsible. While the choices perhaps were infinite, a few of the more interesting possibilities became my household pets. My fascination with the Soongs grew with each discovery that they were not what they seemed. One day in Singapore, I came upon a curious document entirely by chance. It was a British colonial administration copy of Generalissimo Chiang's old police record in Shanghai, listing assorted murders and indictments for armed robbery. These things were not widely known. There was an unspoken agreement among Americans in particular not to talk about the Soongs—especially the Chiang branch—with any realism; the way people are guarded about some terrible family secret, or about the locked door in the attic where Mrs. Rochester rattles her chains waiting for the big fire. They were part of America's adult fairy tale about China.

To start with, their name was not really Soong.

Chapter 1

A RUNAWAY CELESTIAL

The legend of Charlie Soong is a masterpiece of twentieth-century invention. With only the barest threads of fact, it was embroidered originally in the 1920s by China missionaries. Western journalists picked it up, adding their own enthusiastic exaggerations, and spread the legend in magazines and newspapers. At the time, it seemed just one of the charming fables of the Orient, no more true or false than many others.

Charlie Soong was said to be the son of impoverished peasants on South China's Hainan Island. In 1875, at age nine, he was adopted by an uncle and taken to Boston, Massachusetts, to toil as a clerk in a tea and silk shop. The boy longed to educate himself in the American manner, to fulfill his destiny. One day he ran away and stowed aboard a ship called the *Colfax* in Boston harbor. Fortunately, the skipper was a God-fearing Christian, named Captain Charles Jones, who took a liking to the lad. The good captain gave him a job as a cabin boy and tutored him in religion till the *Colfax* reached Wilmington, North Carolina. Captain Jones then led his grateful ward to a local Methodist church to be baptized. In honor of his patron, the youngster took the name Charles Jones Soong. The congregation of the church were impressed and arranged for Charlie to be educated. At their request, he was taken in by General Julian Carr, a hero of the Civil War. General Carr liked Charlie, put him through Trinity College (later Duke University) and then sent him to the divinity school of Vanderbilt University in Nashville, Tennessee. According to a grand scheme, in time Charlie

14

was sent back to China as a Methodist missionary carrying the gospel to his own people. In Shanghai, Charlie became rich printing Bibles, used the money to finance the revolution of Dr. Sun Yat-sen, and had six children who became the rulers of republican China.

Some of the legend is true, but much of it is sheer fantasy. The ship named *Colfax* never sailed into Boston. There was never a Charles Jones as its captain. "General" Carr never rose above the rank of private. Charlie's parents were not impoverished, and they had no idea that he was in the United States. For good measure, their name was Han, not Soong. These were only a few of the discrepancies.

The actual story is more interesting. The first clues to Charlie's clouded origins are in letters he wrote in 1881, when he had been away from home for six years. They were written because his parents did not know that he had left Asia. Journalist James Burke stumbled upon the letters in the late 1930s, while writing a biography of his missionary father, William Burke (a lifelong friend of Charlie Soong). They were composed in tortured, phonetic English by a young boy who had just begun to study the language, and the questions they raised could not be answered without knowing things that were not available to Jim Burke at the time.

In the letters, Charlie wrote that his father lived in "South East China in Canton state called monshou [sic] County." On the face of it, this made no sense. Canton state certainly meant Kwangtung Province, in which the big southern port city of Canton is situated. But no map of Kwangtung Province showed a place called Monshou County.

Charlie spelled his father's name as "Hann Hong Jos'k." He had no idea how to transliterate such a Chinese name into English. He simply spelled it the way the name in Hainan dialect sounded to him.

Fortunately, Charlie also wrote his father's name in Chinese characters at the bottom of one page. Properly rendered into English in the fashion used at the time, his father's name turned out to be Han Hung-i. From this it was clear that the family name must really be Han—not Soong. This was puzzling. How could a boy named Soong have a father named Han? Next to his father's name Charlie had written his own name in Chinese characters. Properly rendered into English, they came out as Han Chiao-shun. Evidently Charlie had two names. Since nobody really knew how he was given the name Soong in the first place, there was no way to make sense out of these contradictions, or to draw any conclusions from them. The letters were put away and forgotten. For many years, the origin of the name Soong remained a mystery.

In 1945, a researcher in the archives of the United States Coast Guard discovered another piece of the puzzle—Charlie Soong's service records on a U.S. revenue cutter. The riddle of the Soong name could have been solved then, if all the pieces of the puzzle had been in one place. But the Coast Guard researcher did not know about the old letters found by Jim Burke.

When I assembled those puzzling jigsaw pieces for the first time, the answer was obvious. Charlie's real name was garbled in America and the name Soong was attached to him entirely by accident aboard ship. Soong became the boy's American pseudonym. One of the most famous names in modern history was a fabrication. If Charlie Soong was not Charlie Soong at all, his children were not Soongs either. The maiden name of Madame Chiang Kai-shek was really not May-ling Soong, but May-ling Han. This discovery was an excellent signal to be cautious in scrutinizing every assertion about the Soongs. That caution was soon rewarded.

From meager scraps Charlie left behind, and bits and pieces culled from many other sources, we can reconstruct quite a bit of his early life.

He did come from Kwangtung Province, which includes the gum-drop-shaped island of Hainan in the South China Sea. About half the size of Ireland, Hainan at the time was an undeveloped mass of mountains and rainforest, surrounded by lowland rice paddies and a ring of coastal villages. In the cloud-soaked peaks of the interior, the Hmong and Li hill people, who inhabit much of the high ground along the southern edges of China, farmed precarious patches for food and grew opium poppies for enjoyment. The lowlands were farmed much more assiduously by Han Chinese from the mainland, who had migrated across the shallow strait over the last thousand years to escape plagues, famines, and political persecutions. In the coastal villages, along beaches shaded by palm trees and Australian pines, there were colonies of political refugees, many of them members of anti-Manchu secret societies, who had fled down the coast in creaking junks to find sanctuary. Even for the most ardent foreign missionaries, Hainan was a hardship post, far off the beaten path. Each year, the handful of foreign residents was depleted by bandits, who took advantage of open doors and windows to indulge in casual murder.

Aside from missionaries, there were always one or two young British customs officers sent there to mildew. The customs post was at Haikou, facing the strait. It was a harbor exposed to winds and seas, so prudent smugglers anchored their junks elsewhere. The best anchorages were all on the east coast, particularly the smugglers' haven of Wench'ang, on a large bay now called Qinglan Gang. The local residents pronounced Wench'ang in a guttural fashion that sounded something like a cross between "munching" and "one shoe," and from even the most cursory acquaintance with the Chinese language it is obvious that Charlie had simply misspelled it "Monshou." Indeed, a careful scrutiny of maps and geographic references makes it clear that this town, with its busy harbor, was the only possible location of Charlie's home. Wench'ang was the principal port for the famous Hainan junks that traded along the routes Charlie described.

Close to shore, junks were rafted together. Families spent their entire lives aboard. As in most Chinese harbors, there was a piercing smell of fish sauce and pork fat, the ripe stink of nightsoil, and the equally unmistakable aroma of wet, new-sawn teakwood. By local standards, the Hans were far from poor. Charlie's father was evidently quite a prosperous merchant, boat builder, secret society elder, and smuggler; from various references we know that he owned a number of big ocean-going junks. His fleet sailed as far as Sumatra, and traded regularly all the way from the Portuguese colony of Macao, near Canton, to Hanoi in Annam, a voyage that took a week at sea. (In one of his letters of 1881, Charlie wrote, "They have junks go from Macow to Hanhigh, six days water.")

Charlie's ancestors had lived far to the north in arid, mountain-girded Shansi Province, hundreds of miles from the sea. Like many other Chinese, they had been forced south to Kwangtung Province and across to the refuge of Hainan Island by upheavals following the Manchu conquest in 1644. Some of Charlie's ancestors were Hakkas who migrated southward even earlier, during the Southern Sung Dynasty (1126–1279), when North China was occupied by tribes from Central Asia. The name Hakka means "guest people," which was the label attached to these displaced northerners. The Hakkas were intensely clannish and, although they have now spread all over the world, remain clannish today. In this place of banishment, they had found an agreeable new livelihood among the boat people harbored at Wench'ang.

Much of this was confirmed by the discovery in obscure notations of the U.S. Department of State that Charlie's eldest son once presented a model of a Hainan junk to President Franklin Roosevelt. With the model, T. V. Soong enclosed this message:

> Knowing your interest in sailing vessels, I am taking the liberty of sending you through our Minister at Washington an accurate model of a Hainan sea-going junk, which has been carefully made according to scale under the supervision of our Customs. Hainan is an island off the coast of Kwang-tung where my family resided for generations and its hardy people have been known to trade regularly in these small vessels as far as India.

These big Hainan junks were unusually seaworthy three-masted vessels, distinctively curved from bow to stern like a banana, to ride the ocean troughs. They carried small cannons to ward off marauders, and big pairs of eyes were painted on their bows, staring far ahead at distant seas. The eyes, and the red patchwork sails rising like cocks' combs overhead, gave the junks the appearance and the nickname of "Big-eyed Chickens."

The Big-eyed Chickens of the Han family left Hainan each summer on a traditional annual migration. While the southwest monsoon blew, they sailed north with cargoes to Macao, Swatow, and Amoy. Then, as the seasonal winds changed for the rest of the year into the northeast monsoon, they sailed south loaded with Chinese goods toward Siam, the Malay States, and Java. Once in the South Seas, the crews were not above indulging in piracy, if they came upon a vessel sailing alone, or an undefended coastal town. (These waters are still avoided by yachts-men today.) Until spring, the junks would trade or prey among the islands. Then, with the new southwest monsoon, they would veer north and head home.

Charlie must have made brief voyages early in his life, crossing the short distance to Annam with his uncles and brothers, because it was customary for small children to be aboard. But, as he later recounted, when he turned nine in the summer of 1875, his father decided that the boy was ready to sail with an older brother to Java, where they would be apprenticed to distant branches of the family. This journey, begin-ning in such a familiar and comfortable pattern, would unexpectedly last a decade and take him to a new world.

With Charlie aboard, the Big-eyed Chicken sailed out of the bay that August, across the Hainan Strait to the mainland. As evident from his earliest photographs, Charlie was dark, short, and sturdy, like a block of teakwood, with bright eyes like a mynah bird about to learn to talk.

At this stage, his black hair was still shaved into a round skull cap with a long, heavy braid hanging down his back in the style dictated by China's Manchu rulers.

The coastline of South China was a succession of blue hills and headlands offset with islands. Squat Kwangtung fishing junks crowded the best anchorages. On their bows, the painted eyes looked down for fish, unlike those on Hainan junks, which searched the far horizon. It was an old joke that the same distinction could be made about the people of the two places. On the last of the fair winds at the end of August, the Hainan junks reached the Portuguese colony of Macao at the mouth of the Pearl River, its waterfront lined with Iberian bungalows, sprawling warehouses, and the towers of Catholic churches. Four months later, on the new monsoon in December, the traders traditionally finished selling their goods and loading new cargoes. Heaving southward from Macao in irregular squadrons, the Big-eyed Chickens cleared first Hanoi then Saigon, and stood across the Gulf of Siam to Malaya. In each of the ports there were industrious Overseas Chinese colonies. Farther south, in Malaya, Sumatra, Java, and Borneo, there were also large rural Chinese populations, working tin mines, running shops, or purchasing raw materials in the interior for transfer to the coast.

The Southeast Asian mercantile networks of the Hainan traders were linked by one of China's most powerful secret societies, the *chiu chao*. Originally, its members were refugee boat people from the Swatow area about 170 miles up the coast from Canton. The chiu chao had been deeply involved in the underground resistance to the Manchu invaders. When this organized resistance collapsed, the chiu chao dispersed and migrated far and wide over the next three centuries, taking their clandestine habits with them. Like sea gypsies, they kept their dialect and distinctiveness as a secret bond. Because they had this bond on top of their traditional Chinese extended family tradition, their trading networks were stronger and more closely knit than those of other Overseas Chinese. In time, the chiu chao dominated smuggling and opium traffic along the China coast. They were also on the ground floor in the British settlements at Hong Kong, Shanghai, and Singapore. Their secret association spawned exclusive guilds, and the guilds grew into syndicates and cartels with immense power and wealth. When Westerners imagined wicked Chinese pirates smuggling gold, drugs, and frightened maidens, and lurking in the dark recesses of the Spice

Islands, they were picturing the chiu chao. To this day chiu chao king-pins heading major banks in the region control the international narcotics trade from the Golden Triangle of Indochina through Bangkok to Amsterdam and other world drug centers. Western drug-enforcement agencies look the other way.

As in boxes within boxes, the chiu chao brotherhood contained many families with their own private smuggling networks. Outsiders were not tolerated and refugees or exiles from other parts of China had to find ways to merge into the chiu chao in order to survive. The Han family from Shansi, with its strong, equally clannish Hakka roots, to function at all in the Hainan commercial world of the nineteenth century and to prosper in its seagoing trade, had to become part of the chiu chao brotherhood by intermarriage. They had to become chiu chao themselves. Over the generations that the family had been in Hainan, it would only have been through marriage between Hakka clan and chiu chao brotherhood that the family's commercial ties spread, across Southeast Asia serving each other as trading agents. That was how it was done.

Charlie's elder brother was on his way to take up his apprenticeship with a branch of the family in the Indies. For three years, Charlie also became the indentured servant of a relative in the islands. But early in 1878 the restless boy found his chance to escape. Now age twelve, he met a distant relative, an "uncle" (Charlie never mentioned his name) —one of the Kwangtung emigrants who long ago had joined the exodus to build railroads in the United States.

Tens of thousands of Chinese from South China immigrated to America in the second half of the nineteenth century, to escape the disruptions of the Taiping Rebellion. For the most part, they were not coolies but skilled and ambitious workingmen, with their own money for tickets and enough left over for expenses till they got settled. In America, railroad foremen hired them to get around labor problems with European immigrants. "Celestials" were harder workers, with fewer complaints. Soon four out of five laborers on the Central Pacific Railway were Chinese, and the laying of track advanced rapidly. The Southern Pacific, Northern Pacific, and Canadian Pacific also turned to Chinese, and put them on the hardest jobs, hanging over the edges of cliffs in wicker baskets to chip roadbeds out of solid rock. Chinese were paid one third less than whites, and were not given free board. The Governor of California wrote President Andrew Johnson in 1865,

"Without them it would be impossible to complete the Western portion of this great national enterprise within the time required by Congress."

Charlie's newfound "uncle" remained in California only briefly, and then moved to New England. There, through perseverance and business acumen, he had saved enough to open his own shop in Boston, where he sold Chinese provisions. Now, after a brief trip home to show off his success, he was on his way back to Boston. During a stopover to change ships in Java, he made Charlie an offer—a voyage halfway around the world to the fabled land the Chinese called Fusang. It was a pitch that had seduced far more practical minds. Like Voltaire's Candide and Dr. Pangloss, Charlie set off with his "uncle." (As he wrote his father years later, "I left brother in East India.")

Passage to America was to be found at the western end of Java, at the port of Anyer Lor, where tea clippers put in for a last load of fresh water and provisions before dashing west across the Indian Ocean, around the Cape of Good Hope, to London or Boston. Charlie and his "uncle" apparently set sail in the spring of 1878, for they reached Boston early that summer.

The red-brick waterfront of Boston was cat's-cradled with the intricate rigging of tall ships in 1878, though the city no longer drew its wealth from the sea and the China trade. The Civil War had changed all that. Now old Boston money went into railroads, mills, and shoe factories. With new industries came labor disputes. Disbanded soldiers and immigrants from Europe demanded more pay and better conditions. In the aftermath of the war, the economy cooled off; by 1873 there was a major depression and ten thousand American businesses folded. Under the circumstances, strikes could not be tolerated. The answer was to bring in Chinese coolies from the Western states as strikebreakers. Charlie's relative had been one of them.

Boston had only a handful of other resident Celestials, living across the Charles River in Cambridge. These were the scions of wealthy Chinese families who had been sent abroad for a Western education. Two of these fortunates were Wen Bing-chung and New Shan-chow (now calling themselves B. C. Wen and S. C. New, in the Western style). New and Wen were from Shanghai, and they had the curious distinction of being mirror images of each other in nearly every way, down to the reversible Western spelling of their names—something that would have endeared them to Messrs. Gilbert and Sullivan. It was an oddity that persisted throughout their lives. In time they returned to Shanghai, married girls who were sisters, became Charlie's joint sponsors and brothers-in-law, rose to similar wealth and esteem, and were both instrumental in getting the first Western textbooks published in China. They had a profound, though indirect, effect upon the modern history of China, and upon the rise of the Soong dynasty.

Wen and New had come to America as members of the original Chinese Education Mission, organized by a Cantonese named Dr. Yung Wing, who was the first Chinese to graduate from an American college. While a student at Yale, he had decided that he could contribute to the reformation of his country by channeling promising Chinese youth through Western high schools and universities. In 1871, the Manchu rulers had approved his plan. The boys from Shanghai, Wen and New, were among the initial contingent.

They came to Charlie's shop frequently through the winter of 1878–79, to drink tea and haggle over how China could be recreated in the model of the West.

They became friendly with Charlie, and urged him to go to school and learn a significant profession. Finally, they prodded him into putting the matter up to his "uncle." That practical soul, obsessed with everyday concerns, was offended by the suggestion that there was a better life than to follow in his footsteps. He crushed Charlie's hopes. So the boy began nursing plans to run away.

In January, 1879, less than a year after leaving the East Indies, Charlie made a last but unsuccessful effort to obtain permission to enter school.

When he was again rebuffed, he took his meager possessions and made his way to the government wharf, where he slipped aboard the *Albert Gallatin* as a stowaway. He was not certain what he wanted to do, but he was certain that he wanted to do it. Like the eyes painted on Chinese junks, some look down for shoals of fish, others stare expectantly over the horizon.

The cutter put out to sea that evening. Charlie was found only after they had left land far behind and reached their blue-water station. He was taken immediately before the master.

Captain Eric Gabrielson was thirty-nine, a salty, God-fearing Norwegian from Stavanger, on the island-studded Bokn Fjord, one of the oldest seafaring communities in the Western world. As the child of shipbuilders, he had grown up aboard sailing vessels, and spent most of his life at sea. He had immigrated to America just before the outbreak of the Civil War in April 1861 and served in the Union Army. When the war was over, he went with considerable relief back to sea, as an officer in the Revenue Service. The home port to which he was assigned was Edgartown on Martha's Vineyard, in Nantucket Sound, a tidy community of puritanical ship captains and owners.

Eric Gabrielson was soon paying court to the daughter of Littleton Wimpenny, one of the grand maritime figures of Massachusetts. He became a dedicated member of the Edgartown Methodist Church, where the Wimpennys regularly raised their voices in hymn, and married Miss Wimpenny there on November 17, 1867.

Over the years, Captain Gabrielson established an exemplary record for resolute firmness in command, utter righteousness in judgment, and commendable compassion for his crew.

Charlie was most fortunate to fall into his hands.

There was just enough stuffed shirt in Gabrielson's wardrobe to give him the powerful conviction that the way of the Chinaman was inherently wrong. As a good Christian, an active, psalm-singing, deed-doing brother of a strong Methodist congregation, he was bound to make things right as God ordained. This boy had been a yellow slave in his uncle's shop. The Civil War had ended that sort of thing for blacks, and Gabrielson was not about to send this promising youth back to sweatshop imprisonment in the distinctly evil recesses of Boston's small Chinatown. Although their conversation was not recorded, the result was. When Gabrielson asked the boy what his name was, Charlie answered that his name was Chiao-shun. To American ears, this sounded exactly like "Chow Sun" or "Charles Sun." Gabrielson wrote it down that way in the ship's muster for January 8, 1879, along with the notation that Charlie was sixteen years old and of legal age to enlist. Charlie was then only fourteen, so we must assume that he thought it was necessary to lie about his age.

This was the first recorded instance of the use of the name Sun. When he eventually learned to read and write English, Charlie spelled it "Soon," probably because it sounded that way to him. Eventually, when he had been back in China for a while and felt under pressure to conform to Chinese rather than Western custom, he refined it to "Soong," which was one of the accepted English spellings of the dynastic name Sung.

Thanks to Captain Gabrielson, Charlie became the ship's boy of the *Albert Gallatin*, a paid crew member in the Revenue Service of the U.S. Treasury Department.

A new name was not all he got. He had his queue shorn and

received from ship's stores a spanking new suit of seafaring togs suitable for the cabin boy on an official vessel of the United States Government. In this new identity, Charlie was able to sail in and out of Boston harbor on the *Gallatin* for the next year and a half without fear of discovery, backed by the muscle of his crewmates and the awesome majesty of the Revenue Service. A photograph taken at the time shows that, with his short haircut and shipboard uniform, he looked remarkably un-Chinese.

A strong bond developed between Gabrielson and his Chinese ship's boy. When the *Gallatin* was in Edgartown, the captain introduced the lad about. Over the months, he schooled the heathen adolescent in the ways of Christianity. Long hours aboard ship were followed by days around the family hearth ashore and Sunday visits to the Methodist Church. Gabrielson outfitted Charlie with his first Western suit, a Scottish wool nailhead tweed with four buttons up the front. He wore it with a white wing-collar shirt and black cravat, when he went to church each Sunday morning. After church, as he recalled in a letter full of warm reminiscence, he played with Mrs. Gabrielson's nephew, eight-year-old Harry Wimpenny, in the yard of the Gabrielson home.

In January 1880, his future looked so promising that Charlie reenlisted for another term of duty. But four months later, unexpectedly, Captain Gabrielson was transferred to Wilmington, North Carolina.

For two months, Charlie moped about. He wrote to Captain Gabrielson and begged him to do something. The captain obligingly wrote to Washington and arranged with his superiors for the Chinese boy to be discharged from the service.

Charlie headed for the first ship in Boston harbor that was bound for Wilmington, stowed aboard, and was on his way south to rejoin his benefactor.

When the packet reached Wilmington, Charlie immediately went looking for Captain Gabrielson's new ship. Eric Gabrielson had been given command of a vessel that the Treasury Department referred to officially as "a second-class sidewheeler." The U.S. Revenue Service steamer *Schuyler Colfax* was one of those unfortunate hermaphrodite creations that came along at the end of the age of sail, with a clipper bow and champagne-glass transom, but only stubby, vestigial masts. She was a steamship, carrying no canvas. For propulsion, she was totally dependent on a paddle wheel. But this was what gave her the edge in hot pursuit of tax-evading smugglers who were dependent on the wind.

Charlie found the *Colfax* without difficulty, moored at the Customs House dock. Again Gabrielson took the boy under his wing. Although he could not offer Charlie his cozy old job of cabin boy, he had a place on the muster for a mess boy, and entered him as such in thᴄ log.

For a time, life resumed a familiar pattern. The *Colfax* steamed out of Wilmington, passed the light at Fort Caswell, the lightship at Frying Pan Shoals, and the lighthouse on Bald Hill, headed north to Body's Island, then south to Georgetown, aiding distressed vessels and capturing scofflaws.

To the crew of the *Colfax*, Charlie was a bizarre creature. In 1880 only a few Chinese had reached the South and most of those were taken to New Orleans to replace emancipated slaves in the cotton fields. A few started small stores or laundries; they were scattered around the southern states and none so far had settled in North Carolina. Charlie was the only Chinese anyone in this part of the state had ever seen.

The boy was almost fifteen, pretending to be seventeen. If he was to be educated, and launched properly on his way, no more time could be lost. Fortunately, Gabrielson's local church friends took an interest. One of them, Colonel Roger Moore, a Civil War veteran, was a leading figure at the Front Street Methodist Church, where he headed the men's Bible Class. Unlike many of his neighbors, Moore knew where China was and understood what Methodist missionaries were trying to achieve there. In the closing decades of the nineteenth century, church-going America was swept up with the White Man's Burden of civilizing and christianizing The Others. China, with one-quarter of the world's population, represented the largest potential harvest of souls.

According to Moore's descendants, who are still leading citizens of the community and enjoy telling the story, the colonel found the mess boy of the *Colfax* sitting on a bollard by the harbor one Saturday, and invited him to attend services the next morning at the Grace Methodist Church. Charlie was an immediate hit.

The next Sunday, Moore and his friends took Charlie to Fifth Street Church, where they introduced him to the Right Reverend Thomas Page Ricaud, a firebreather of Biblical stature.

Charlie was to meet a lot of revolutionaries in his life, but the Reverend Ricaud was the first and a man forged in the very heat of God's crucible. He was born a Catholic in Baltimore and was orphaned in childhood. An uncle adopted him and took him to Mexico City, where he attended the university and studied for the priesthood. Revolutionary violence in the 1830s swept him up and he became a guerrilla, lost his faith, was wounded and captured, before finally fleeing Mexico to France. Later, he returned to the United States and read law at the University of Virginia. One day at a revival meeting, he was overwhelmed and became a convert on the spot to the Protestant faith. When his Catholic uncle learned of this incredible reversal, the youth was summarily disowned. Ricaud rose to the occasion, however, becoming a Methodist preacher in Virginia in 1841, transferring later to North Carolina's tidewater country, a land of great solitudes and metaphysical shadows.

In the stark photographic plates of the day, Ricaud strikes a fearsome figure. He was small and gaunt, extremely haggard in mien, as though he had spent forty days and forty nights in a most uncomfortable place but had found a Bible there, which he brought back as evidence. His expression was haunted and he was bearded in the long, snaggly manner of the prophets that children stared at with suitable horror in Bible class illustrations. Above that formidable beard, Ricaud's eyes confirmed the worst. They were pale blue and watery, as vague as oysters, and could look through anyone to his innermost soul. It was apparent to all that he could discern the slightest hypocrisy, detect the smallest deceit or the least evasion. Under his stare, ladies squirmed until their knickers got twisted, and men's boiled collars got tight.

When he met Charlie, that well-traveled minister instantly recognized "an opportunity for Christ." He invited the lad to talk privately. A series of such meetings ensued in the preacher's parlor, where lemonade was served by Ricaud's comely daughter, Rosamond. If Charlie could be given a Western education to prepare him as a missionary, perhaps even as a medical missionary, he could take to China skills to heal the bodies and souls of his countrymen. His destiny, and perhaps the destiny of China, could be transformed. This was Ricaud's vision.

Wen and New had awakened Charlie's cravings. Gabrielson had shown him what an immigrant could accomplish. But it was Ricaud, the erstwhile Mexican bandit, who gave him a sense of purpose, a magnificent ambition.

At an evening church service in the first week of November 1880, Charlie got up and went forward to kneel. The whole congregation was riveted by the spectacle of a Celestial bowing at their altar. Back in one of the pews, a young woman watched Charlie as he became a convert.

When he arose, she noticed, "he seemed quite happy and his face was shining."

When the service ended, and the congregation emptied out into the twilight, Charlie proudly announced over and over that he had "found the Saviour." These open and enthusiastic people, by joining together, had an enormous power. They could do anything. They were his new family. He told them how he wanted to return to China as a missionary. Nothing could have pleased them more. Under the leadership of the Reverend Ricaud and Colonel Moore, they undertook their new cause. Charlie discussed the idea with Eric Gabrielson, who wrote personally to the Secretary of the Treasury requesting another discharge so that the Chinese boy could educate himself.

The following Sunday morning, November 7, 1880, a brief notice appeared under the heading "Fifth Street M.E. Church" in the pages of the Wilmington Star: "This morning the ordinance of Baptism will be administered at this church. A Chinese convert will be one of the subjects of the solemn right, being probably the first 'Celestial' that has ever submitted to the ordinance of Christian baptism in North Carolina. The pastor, Rev. T. Page Ricaud, will officiate."

It was an impressive scene at 11 A.M. that Sunday. The interior of the church was white plaster with the altar set back in an arched proscenium, faced by rows of dark-stained oak pews. Behind the altar hung a red velvet curtain. On either side were high-backed Tudor chairs. Just to the right there was an upright piano to accompany hymns, with a row of plain straight-back chairs beside it for the choir.

Dressed in his usual double-breasted Prince Albert frock coat, a conspicuous wig on his bald pate, Reverend Ricaud spread a handkerchief on the step before the altar and knelt in prayer. Then he stood and placed his hands on Charlie's carefully pomaded black hair. Solemnly, the preacher baptized him "Charles Jones Soon."

Where did Charlie find the name Jones? The explanations conflicted. The truth was really quite simple, and was clearly explained at the time by Rosamond Ricaud, the pastor's daughter. She said it was her father who urged Charlie to take the name Jones for his middle name. The boy was already known as Charles Sun aboard ship and Charles Soon ashore (because of the way he slurred the word). Ricaud had to complete a baptismal form with spaces for first, middle, and last names and needed a middle name for Charlie. According to Rosamond, her father simply plucked a name out of the air. But her explanation was not glamorous enough for the mythmakers who came along later.

The preferred version that would gain worldwide currency had Charlie adopt the name Charles Jones in honor of "the captain of the ship that brought him to Wilmington." (Depending upon who was telling it, that ship brought him straight from China, or only from Boston.) Another fanciful rendition made Charles Jones the captain of the *Colfax*, who originally introduced Charlie to the Reverend Ricaud and everybody in Wilmington. Oldtimers for years after swore they remembered Captain Charles Jones, who often attended their church. (Some said, if he was not the skipper, he was at least the boatswain.) This was the version institutionalizèd by the magazines at Time Inc.

The facts, however, demonstrate that the *Colfax* never steamed anywhere near Boston. Its home port was Wilmington, North Carolina. There never was a Captain Charles Jones on the *Colfax* or anywhere else in the Revenue Service during all the years of its existence, nor a boatswain of that name. For that matter, no Charles Jones appears on any muster in any position on any ship of the service.

Eric Gabrielson, on the other hand, did exist. Charlie was credited by his mythmakers with a gracious act of homage to a benefactor when he took the name of Charles Jones. Yet nowhere in the Soong archives does the name Eric Gabrielson even appear.

In the days following his baptism, Charlie found a job at a local printing shop, where he began learning the business. Meanwhile, greater things were afoot.

The idea of sending a saved heathen back to preach to his fellow heathens produced a predictable effect on the Methodists of Wilmington. Here was their chance, acting through Charlie, to alter history in a distant, dimly understood part of the world. The local congregation discussed what could be done about it, and a plan of action came into being.

First on the list was to get Charlie into school.

Trinity College was one of the few southern colleges to survive the Civil War. The administrator, Dr. Braxton Craven, kept going with a faculty of six, supported by wealthy individuals and Methodist congregations. In December of 1880, a few weeks after Charlie was baptized, the Reverend Ricaud put a proposition to Craven. Would he enroll a Chinese boy in Trinity and school him for great deeds?

For Charlie's tuition, Colonel Roger Moore wrote to Julian S. Carr of Durham, North Carolina, one of the richest men in the South. It was the sort of letter Carr received quite often in those dark days, from the widows of Confederate soldiers desperate to find schooling for their children. And, almost without exception, Carr helped them. Now he responded again.

Carr actually had no military rank. He did not rise above private during the war, although his admirers in later years insisted that he "carried a commission around in his pocket" but was too modest to accept it. His officer's rank had been bestowed as an honorary title by the North Carolina Confederate Veterans Association in appreciation of his generosity.

Julian Carr was a man of phenomenal substance. He was one of the leading capitalists of his time and place; he made and lost two great fortunes, in tobacco and textiles, was one of the founders of Duke University—and by sponsoring Charlie set in motion events that altered history.

The son of a successful merchant in Chapel Hill, Carr, wrote a biographer, "was reared under the lasting influence of pious and exemplary Methodist parents, who early instilled into the nature of their son the principles and precepts of morality, Christianity, and ambition."

After serving in the Confederate army, Julian Carr decided to court a young lady in nearby Durham and borrowed $4,000 from his father to purchase one-third interest in a small tobacco company in the town.

The war had made two articles indispensable to the soldiers, whiskey and tobacco, and the demand continued into the peace. Carr's firm was whimsically called Bull Durham, after the bull on the label of the popular British mustard, Coleman's, which was produced in a town with the same name—Durham, England. It was marketing a new, mild-smoking blond leaf that grew well in the poor soil of North Carolina and proved unusually popular with soldiers of both sides. Carr's main contribution was to make Bull Durham famous nationwide by having billboards painted on barns across America. He was soon a millionaire. He also developed machinery to mass produce and export Bull Durham worldwide. When American women went out behind the barn to roll their own smokes on any hectic day in 1880, the chances were they rolled a Bull Durham. Mark Twain joked that the only thing he remembered from seeing the Egyptian pyramids was the Bull Durham sign painted on them.

The company grew from assets of less than $30,000 in 1871 to an awesome $4 million in 1887. Carr became president or principal shareholder of other firms, including Durham's First National Bank, the Electric Lighting Company, the streetcar agency, and assorted land, milling, and mining companies. Despite this success, he continued to look after Confederate veterans and see that his own workers were able to raise money to start homes or school their children. It was characteristic of him to do this without attracting attention, and without seeking anything in return.

He was the proper man to underwrite the education of Charlie.

The train from Wilmington brought Charlie and the Reverend Ricaud into Durham late one warm, dusty evening in April 1881. It was a frontier town. There were only a few stores. Farmland began several blocks from the station. The red-light district was in the Edgemont section, but the ladies of pleasure were kept out of sight. Saloons were easy to find, and fistfights in the streets were common. There were only a few fine homes, out East Main Street, including Carr's mansion and a big one built by another tobacco man, Washington Duke, whose specialty was a new product called ready-made cigarettes. As Wilkes Caldwell, Carr's black manservant opined, Durham was "no place for an educated man."

Horse-drawn carriages were preferred over horseback by people of means. Julian Carr had a coach-and-four to meet the boy and the preacher at the station.

Carr proved to be a relaxed and agreeable man, with a high forehead, a full mustache, and calm, intelligent eyes. His receding hair was still dark at age thirty-six.

Nannie Carr, his wife of nine years, was a fresh, soft Durham girl, with cool gray eyes and translucent skin, who was happily engaged in motherhood. She was the reason why Julian Carr had become interested in a Durham investment in the first place. She produced two daughters and three sons and was, in the words of one admirer, "worthy to grace and adorn the family circle around any domestic fireside where female virtues shed their hallowed light and contribute the chief essentials to happiness."

The Carrs made Charlie at home in a room of his own. The only noteworthy possession he brought with him was a small wooden shuttle he had been using aboard ship to make string hammocks, a handicraft of the Outer Banks country taught to him by other sailors. He proposed to continue earning pocket money in Durham by making and selling hammocks, a demonstration of sound capitalist instincts.

The Carrs took Charlie to Trinity Church and introduced him to the congregation. He was now attired in a respectable and conservative beige linen suit with a vest, and wore a floppy four-in-hand tied for him by Mrs. Carr. His hair, parted on the right side, was short and slicked down, and his face was scrubbed and full of quick smiles. Without his Manchu queue, Charlie was surprisingly handsome by Western standards.

"You know," observed a girl his age, "he didn't look at all Chinese. He dressed well and had beautiful manners. In fact, he was very, very polite, as the Chinese gentleman is noted for being."

The Trinity Church Sunday school in Durham would provide for Charlie's upkeep at school (serving as a conduit for funds from Julian Carr). His tuition would be absorbed by Trinity College, using state Methodist funds. He would have a room with some of the other boys in the home of a professor.

Charlie made the acquaintance of nearly everybody in Durham that April, foremost among them big James Southgate and his daughter Annie. She was a little green apple of a girl, hard and tart and freckled and fun, about to ripen into a fragile puberty of flouncy smocks and mysterious illnesses. Growing up would kill her. But for the moment she was still a child, and she became Charlie's confidante and co-conspirator. Southgate was in the insurance business with his son, but he was full of ideas for starting a Young Men's Christian Association in Durham. Over suppers at the Southgate house, Charlie—who had never before heard of a Y—was soberly educated in the virtues of YMCA organizations.

Those pleasant weeks passed quickly, then Charlie was off to Trinity. It was housed in a single building, once a stately mansion of Randolph County, by a forest of softwoods three miles south of High Point. Two hundred students were enrolled that year. Once, the student body had included several American Indians, but no Chinese had ever been seen there till Charlie appeared. After only a few weeks, Dr. Braxton Craven was able to note in his annual report of June 9, 1881: "He is doing very well every way, studies closely and will be successful."

Unprepared for regular college studies, Charlie was considered a "special student" at Trinity—but this was not an unusual arrangement at that time in America. The professors had agreed to give him a compact preparatory education, cramming into mere months the schooling in reading, writing, and arithmetic that other students had been absorbing over a decade. It was understood by all that Charlie was to be prepared for a life as a missionary among his own people, so there were many aspects of normal schooling that could be bypassed. There was no need, for example, to teach him more than a smattering of Latin, Greek, and German, which were the specialties of most of the professors at the school. Instead, they concentrated on improving his English, and saturating him with the Bible.

He stayed in the home of Professor W. T. Gannaway, the "grand old man" and Latin instructor of the college. Most of his school work was carried out at the home of Dr. Craven. That fine and overworked gentleman was a master of metaphysics and rhetoric, who had to shoulder monumental burdens each morning in order to feel dressed for the day. Tutoring Charlie was a job Dr. Craven shared with his wife, who sat with the fifteen-year-old hour after hour, deciphering the runes of Western culture, which Charlie absorbed with an odd mixture of aptitude and rote memory. It was the Chinese custom for children to learn the classics by repetition, while rocking gently back and forth under the eyes of their tutors, repeating the lines of the masters again and again without comprehension and without asking for explanation, till they were inscribed in the memory. Charlie was therefore a quick mimic, able to repeat Biblical phrases he read and lines he heard in sermons as if he understood them. Like any child who recites Bible verses, he seemed to understand little; as his letters show, he scattered pious references helter-skelter. This did not trouble his tutors, who were impressed with his quick ability to mime, and took this as a demonstration of marked progress.

By summer, Charlie had learned enough English to write the first of several letters that contain some of the clues we have to his earliest childhood. There was a letter to his father in Hainan and a slightly garbled cover letter to the missionary Dr. Young J. Allen, head of the Southern Methodist Mission in Shanghai, asking Dr. Allen to forward the letter to his father:

United States America
Durham, North Carolina
June 25, 1881

Mr. Allen
Dear Sir.

I wish you to do me a favor, I been way from home about six years and I want my father to know where I am and what I doing, they living in South

East China in Canton state called monshou County, they have junks go from Macow to Hanhigh about 6 days water, my father name is "Hann Hong Jos'k" in Chinese. I hope you will be able to it out where they are, I was converted few months ago in Wilmington, North Carolina. and now the Durham Sunday School and Trinity are helping me, si [sic] I am in a great hurry to be educated so I can go back to China and tell them about our Saviour, please write to me when you get my letter, I ever so much thank you for it, good by.

Yours respectfully,
Charlie Jones Soon

The fact that the letter to his father was written in English is not surprising since Charlie had been away from China long enough to forget most of his childhood drills in Chinese composition. He was not yet very adept at English either, but he had been speaking it exclusively, and spending all his days at school learning how to write it.

United States America
Durham, North Carolina
June 25, 1881

Dear Father,

I will write this letter and let you know where I am. I left Brother in East India in 1878 and came to the United States and finely I had found Christ our Saviour. God for Christ sake has meet in the way. now the Durham Sunday School and Trinity are helping me and I am in a great hurry to be educated so I can go back to China and tell you about the kindness of the friends in Durham and the grace of God. he sent his begotten Son to died in the world for all sinners. I am a sinner but save by the grace of God. I remember when I was a little boy you took me to a great temple to worshipped the wooden Gods. oh, Father that is no help from wooden Gods. if you do worships all your life time would not do a bit goods. in our old times they know nothing about Christ. but now I had found a Saviour he is comforted me where ever I go to. please let your ears be open so you can hear what the spirit say and your eyes looks up so you may see the glory of God. I put my trust in God and hope to see you again in this earth by the will of God. now we have vacation and I stay in Mr. J. S. Carr house at Durham. Soon as you get my letter please answer me and I will be very glad to hear from you. give my loves to mother Brother and Sisters please and also to yourself. I will tell you more when I write again. Mr. and Mrs. Carr they are good Christian family and they had been kind to me before I know them. Will good by Father, write to Trinity College, N.C.

> Yours Son.
> Hann Cardson
> Charlie Jones Soon

For all his strangeness, Charlie was accepted enthusiastically by his schoolmates, who enjoyed playing pranks on him, teasing him as a "Chinee" and making jokes about his name. He dealt with this juvenile abuse in an appropriately juvenile manner, playing his own pranks, and sharpening his own tongue with rejoinders. On the matter of his odd adopted name, he grew accustomed to snapping: "I'd rudder be Soon den too late."

Lest he forget the serious destiny chosen for him by his benefactors, Charlie was conditioned and reconditioned for the role of preacher to the heathen. His mission was driven into him in public as well as private. One week before Christmas, 1881, an impressive ceremony was staged for his benefit at Trinity's small chapel. Dr. Craven was also the local pastor. His sermon that Sunday developed the theme "Go ye into all the world and preach the gospel to every creature." The sermon was directed at Charlie and set forth his task. As part of this Sunday's service, the boy's membership was officially transferred from the Wilmington congregation to the one at Trinity, with much hymn singing and handshaking.

Charlie spent his holidays visiting the Reverend Ricaud and his daughter Rosamond in Wilmington, or strolling with Annie Southgate in Durham after Sunday school, or crooning Nannie Carr's youngest boy to sleep on the porch of the big Carr house while five-year-old Liza sat on the steps, playing with her favorite dolls.

It is clear that the Chinese boy was deeply impressed by everything he learned from the man he took to calling "Father Carr," for he went on to copy or transplant many of the details of Carr's life and world into Shanghai decades later. These impart an interesting resonance as Charlie's own life unfolds, including the names of his children, his pet name for his wife, and the enterprises he pursued. Carr was also giving the boy a very effective education in commerce and business judgment, grooming his entrepreneurial instinct.

Charlie's interest in girls was becoming conspicuous. When his first year at Trinity was over, he wrote to a classmate, sixteen-year-old Gordon Hackett (Charlie called him "Golden"), who had gone home to

Wilkesboro for the summer vacation. The letter was written in a magnificently ornate engraver's script, which was one of Charlie's oddities, the result of learning at an early age how to wield a brush to write Chinese characters. The letter was full of news about summer days at Trinity:

> Both of Misses Field are here yet. They will go home next Friday morning. I tell you they are very pleasant Young Ladies I like them very much. . . . Trinity is very pleasant now, but I don't know what it will be like after the girls go off. . . . Miss Bidgood is here yet, I believed she will stay until next month. She looks as pretty as ever. I went to see her and Miss Cassie some time since. She talk right lively. . . . Golden, I been had good times with the grils [sic], all day long, never looked at the books hardly since Com [commencement] except the Bible. everything is quite now. Miss Mamie and two other grils gone to visiting last night we did had big time all the girls. . . . We went to called on Ella Carr, and we had the best time you ever heard of it.

It was Ella Carr, a gangling, leggy adolescent who received most of Charlie's attention. Her father was Professor O. W. Carr, one of Julian Carr's poorer cousins, who taught Greek and German at Trinity. The Chinese boy made friends with Professor Carr and his wife, then sat for hours in their parlor, listening to Ella play the piano.

There can be little doubt that Charlie's stay at Trinity came to an abrupt end because of his crush on Miss Ella, and the temptations of long warm afternoons and the breeze from the elms. It was evident from his letter to "Golden" that Charlie planned to continue at Trinity when summer ended, because he urged his friend to "come back to school if you can." If he did, Charlie promised, the two of them would "run things."

Suddenly in midsummer, Ella's mother threw Charlie out of her house and forbade him to return. We can only wonder what tender scene she interrupted, all arms and legs, and measure it by the severity of her response. There was a flurry of anxious activity, and Charlie unexpectedly found himself enrolled overnight at Vanderbilt University far away in Nashville, Tennessee.

To the outside world, the explanation offered by the Methodist Church was suitably pious, as shown by this extract from a church version of the Soong legend as it was recounted in the Raleigh *News and Observer* in 1936:

Dr. Craven, with whom [Charlie] had many long talks about his missionary career, took the matter up with the members of the Board of Missions of the Methodist Church and they advised him that the young Chinese would make more progress at Vanderbilt, where he could at the same time continue his education and receive training for the mission fields through contacts with members of the board and returned missionaries in Nashville.

Then, on a more revealing note, this account goes on to say:

Even though the move would speed him to his goal, Charlie had to discuss the step at some length with the Cravens before he would agree to leave North Carolina.

The position the Methodists had assumed in Charlie's life was beginning to exhibit the strains of a double standard. It was right and proper for Charlie to fill a role in the fantasy world of missionary endeavor. If he was willing to go preach the Southern Methodist gospel to the Chinese, and to help put things right in China after four thousand misguided years, his sponsors would provide him with an abbreviated education and feed and clothe him modestly for the duration. Both parties thus had their cravings gratified. He was their token Celestial, but they had to draw the line at intimacy between a Chinaman and one of their own daughters.

Woebegone on his last day at Trinity, Charlie brought Mrs. Craven a farewell present, the last of his hammocks. She confided to friends later that he gave it to her with a carefully prepared speech, then broke down, threw his arms around her and began to cry.

In Wilmington, there was a delicious scandal about the episode. Members of the congregation at Fifth Street Methodist Church whispered for years afterward that Charlie had run afoul of Julian Carr, by "getting caught with his daughter." The names were similar—Eliza Carr and Ella Carr—but Julian Carr's daughter was only five years old at the time. The gossips did have the last name right, however.

The moment he reached Nashville on the train, Charlie got himself shined up and went to a photographer's studio. There he had a formal portrait taken and mailed it through friends to Miss Ella Carr at Trinity. More than half a century later, in 1937, the original of that portrait was still one of Ella Carr's treasured possessions in her twilight years as the town of High Point's Mrs. Dred Peacock.

The sour breath of judgment surrounded Charlie from then on. Methodist elders who regarded themselves as intellectuals—like characters out of the pages of Dickens—condemned him as an opportunist, a fraud, and a freeloader. If the flock at large was euphoric, the intellectuals had to find flaws. The acting dean of the School of Religion at Vanderbilt University was one of the least charitable.

> Soong, or Soon as we called him, was here from '82 to '85. He was a harum-scarum little fellow, full of life and fun, but not a very good student. He gave no evidence of having any serious interest in religion, even less in preaching. As a matter of fact, when he went back to China, Soon became interested in some business enterprise. In the course of time he married a woman who must definitely have been his superior.

This was the observation of Dr. George B. Winton, the acting dean, and it was shared by his immediate circle of high church officials.

A much kinder appraisal was voiced by the Reverend John C. Orr, who was one of Charlie's classmates at Vanderbilt.

> At first the boys paid little or no attention to Soon. He was more of a curiosity than anything else. He was just a Chinaman. But this changed. He had a fine mind, learned to use the English language with accuracy and fluency, and was usually bubbling over with wit and humor and good nature. The boys became fond of him, and took him into all the social activities of the campus. His handwriting was like a copy-plate, with the hairline touch and the shading flourishes. He wrote the visiting cards for the boys. Although somewhat handicapped on account of his ignorance of the English language, he prepared his lessons well, passed all his examinations, and graduated with honor in his class of four in Theology.

The students were universally fond of him. "He was of a most genial and friendly nature," recalled classmate James C. Fink. Charlie's roommate was J. B. Wright, later a preacher in Cairo, Georgia. "He was jovial in his disposition and enjoyed a good laugh," Wright affirmed. "He was popular with all the students. He was a good average student with a bright mind." The Reverend D. H. Tuttle heard Charlie preach on several occasions and decided that it was "to the spiritual edification of all who heard him."

Whatever Charlie might have seemed on the surface, he was underneath just a boy far from home dependent on the kindness of strangers.

It was the custom of the more zealous of the boys [Orr recalled], to meet in the little chapel of Wesley Hall before breakfast on Sunday for a sort of religious experience. One morning Soon got up and stood for a while before he said anything. Then his lips trembled and he said: "I feel so little. I get so lonesome. So far from my people. So long among strangers. I feel just like I was a little chip floating down the Mississippi River." The tears were running down his cheeks and before he could say anything, more than a dozen of the boys were around him, with their arms about him, assuring him that they loved him as a brother. Soon broke up the meeting that morning.

The student who came to know Charlie best was William Burke. It was the beginning of a lifelong association. His opinion of Charlie was neither caustic nor sentimental, but frank. "Soon was chiefly remarkable to his collegemates," Jim Burke wrote in a biography of his father, "for the fact that he was neither a laundryman nor a cook."

One afternoon, Burke prepared a warm welcome for Charlie. It was an ordinary washbasin full of water, set upon a wooden writing table that was covered with a blanket in the middle of the room. In the water gleamed a silver dollar. Beside the basin lay a heavy flatiron with a metal handle. Hidden beneath the table was a set of wet-celled batteries, with almost invisibly thin copper wires running up under the blanket to the flatiron and the basin.

Burke, a husky six-footer who weighed over two hundred pounds, greeted Charlie and the others heartily as they burst into the room.

"I've got a little surprise for you all today," Burke announced. "It's that flatiron there on the table. It's an enchanted one. Came out of a witch's cave over in the Great Smokies. Anyone who touches it loses the power of his will. Just to prove it, I'll offer anyone of you that dollar if he'll pick it up while holding on to the iron."

There were several sly glances, but nobody moved.

"How about it, Charlie?" Burke drawled.

Charlie came forward cautiously and peered at the iron and the submerged silver dollar. Nothing seemed suspicious. He gripped the flatiron by the handle and reached for the coin. When his fingers touched the water, the shock jerked him backward, startled. Then, sheepishly, he realized that he had been taken. Burke guffawed, and Charlie joined in the collective whoop of laughter.

During summer vacations, the theology students went into the hustings to wage campaigns for the Lord. Charlie worked with circuit preachers and helped evangelists stage revival meetings across the South.

One of his favorite stops was Franklin, Tennessee, because he had become friendly with the Stockard family there, and they had a pretty niece named Sally. He made an extra print of the portrait originally taken for Miss Ella and gave the copy to Sally. But her friends teased her about having a romance with a "Chinee" and she threw the photograph in the fireplace. Her mother rescued it, slightly charred around the edges, and it remained the most widely published picture of Charlie till Mrs. Dred Peacock's much-loved original surfaced in 1937.

Exposure to the revival circuit gave Charlie greater poise and better English. After a couple of years, he was able to write to the church paper, the *Christian Advocate,* in Raleigh, North Carolina, with clear sincerity:

> Nashville people are now doing good work in this city. The revival meeting began the latter part of last month, and some of the churches had reached such result that never was known in the history of this city heretofore. The meeting is still going on in different churches, had 150 conversions already. In fact the success is greater than the expectation of the people. Rev. Mr. Sam Jones, of Ga., (the Southern evangelist) will be in Nashville this week, and will preach in a "gospel tent," which will be erected in an open place by the post office. This is a great blessing to the inhabitants of Nashville. We have not the least doubt, but that he will lead hundreds to Christ by the help and grace of God.

In a footnote reminding the readers of the *Advocate* who Charlie was, the newspaper's editor added, patronizingly, "His letter shows marked improvement."

Charlie was now certain of being sent to Shanghai when he finished at Vanderbilt in 1885. The decision had been made by Bishop Holland N. McTyeire, chancellor of Vanderbilt, who was also in charge of the Southern Methodist Mission in China. The bishop advised Dr. Allen in Shanghai of this decision, and Charlie received a brief formal letter of confirmation from Dr. Allen in the spring of 1883. Everything appeared to be set for him to become a teacher at the Anglo-Chinese University. When he replied, Charlie's letter was only a bit stilted:

Wesley Hall, Vanderbilt University
Nashville, Tennessee
July 27, 1883

My dear doctor Allen,

Your kind letter was received sometime since, and indeed I was very glad to get it. I see that you are fully consecrated your work, life and spirit in God's hand. I hope to see you all soon by the will of God. I do not know how long I shall remain in the States, but I will try to prepare myself as thouaghtly [sic] as the opportunity allow me. And when I ended my school days I hope that I will be able to carry the light to the Chinese. The object of my days is to do good, to honor man, to glorify God; to do good to others and save them from eternal punishment. God be my helper, I will. A few days ago there was a Methodist lady asked me an uncommon strange question, said she "well, brother Soon, you are a missionary, will you suffer in any convictions and die for the cause of Christ?" And I thought it was a strange question to me. But, for the sake of my heart I answered it according to my feeling. Replied I, yes, madam, I willing to suffer for Christ on any condition if God be my helper. Again said she "that is the way we ought to feel, for God will help us if we trust in him." May God help us all to lay our treasure in Heaven, and wait on him with great passion, and at last we may be able to say "I have kept the faith, I have fought the good fight, and henceforth I shall receive a crown of life." God bless you and all your labors.

Charles J. Soon

When the time came for commencement on May 28, 1885, the graduation of "the pious but somewhat ambitious young Celestial" was noted in the pages of the Wilmington *Star:*

... he graduated with high honors from the Vanderbilt University. He remains a few weeks with his friend and benefactor at Durham, and then, we understand, will go to China, where a professorship in the Anglo-Chinese University at Shanghai, King Si Province [sic], has been tendered him. His conduct all through, we understand, has been such as to afford the highest gratification to those who displayed such a warm interest in his welfare, while towards these good friends he has always seemed to feel the deepest gratitude.

Charlie was often said to have been a graduate of Vanderbilt, and here it is asserted that he was graduated with honors, but this was not the case. In order that he serve God's purpose in China as quickly as possible, he had been rushed through the system.

They did give him a diploma. But, in the end, Charlie did not want to go. Not to Shanghai. At least not for some time. He wanted first to go to medical school. Julian Carr was completely behind the boy. If Charlie wanted to go to medical school, Carr would finance him. But Bishop McTyeire was adamant. He claimed, rather preposterously, that there were "too many" medical missionaries in the field already. The real reason was hinted at in a letter the Bishop wrote to Dr. Allen in Shanghai:

> Vanderbilt University
> Nashville, Tennessee
> July 8, 1885
>
> My Dear Doctor Allen:
> We expect to send Soon out to you this fall, with Dr. Park. I trust you will put him, at once, to *circuit work*, walking if not riding. Soon wished to stay a year or two longer to study medicine to be equipped for higher usefulness, etc. And his generous patron, Mr. Julian Carr, was not unwilling to continue helping.
> But we thought better that the *Chinaman* that is in him should not be worked out before he labors among the Chinese. Already he has "felt the easy chair"—and is not averse to the comforts of higher civilization. No fault of his.
> Let our young man, on whom we have bestowed labor, begin to *labor*. Throw him into the ranks: *no side place*. His desire to study medicine was met by the information that we have already as many *doctors* as the Mission needed, and one more.
> I have good hope that, with your judicious handling, our Soon may do well. It will greatly encourage similar work here if he does. The destinies of many are bound up in his case. . . .
>
> Yr. bro. in Christ.
> H. N. McTyeire

This letter, plus Dean Winton's appraisal of Charlie as a "harum-scarum little fellow" reveals an unattractive side to the bishop and his associates. The bishop lied about a surfeit of doctors, and after newspapers were led to believe that Charlie was to teach at Dr. Allen's college, the bishop instructed Allen privately to banish the young man to the hinterlands.

No special considerations are to be given; he should be assigned the

lowest rung. He is to make his rounds from town to town on foot. This
was a move calculated to diminish Charlie among his own people; the
Chinese put a premium on such outward trappings as a sedan chair;
Charlie was to be reduced to peasant status. Charlie, the bishop be-
lieved, was getting soft, self-indulgent, the result of coddling by the
Methodists. But, once he was forced to develop a bit of humility, it
might be possible to get some useful toil out of this ambitious young
Chinaman.

At Charlotte, North Carolina, where the Methodist state conference met that summer, Charlie was ordained a deacon. He was now
nineteen years old. Normally, he would have received only a provisional appointment and waited two years for it to become official. But
Bishop McTyeire intervened. He wanted the Chinaman back in China
immediately. On page 53 of the conference minutes appears the entry:
"Missionary to China, Charles Jones Soon."

Charlie made a grand tour to say farewell to friends. The opportunity was provided by a string of revival meetings in Durham, Wilmington, and Washington, North Carolina.

There was no point in going to Trinity, the scene of his romantic
fiasco. After a final visit with the Carrs in Durham, Charlie returned to
his old church on Fifth Street in Wilmington and preached a farewell
sermon in honor of the Reverend Ricaud. Captain Gabrielson by now
had retired to his beloved Martha's Vineyard; Charlie kept in touch by
letter.

While he was staying with the Ricauds, local eyebrows were raised
by the way he and Rosamond flirted. The violet-eyed Rosamond, now
fifteen, had passed the coltish stage and was a lovely young lady. Poor
Ricaud, the gimlet-eyed old pistolero turned man of God, sent his frisky
daughter out of town to spend the rest of the summer under the protec-
tive eyes of her grownup sister.

To get Charlie out of Wilmington, before anything else went awry,
Ricaud took him along to the little country town of Washington, where
the minister was to teach a religious summer school. Charlie could not
have been happier when he discovered how many girls were attending,
a subject appropriate for discussion with his longtime comrade in Durham, Annie Southgate.

> I had a very pleasant time at Washington, although I know but a few
> girls as yet. They say there are seven girls to one boy. And some of them

are very beautiful. I have fallen in love with Miss Bell. Don't you think that is too bad, for I have to leave my heart in Washington and I go to China. There isn't any danger of my fall in love with one of uncle R's [Ricaud's] daughters. Miss Jennie is engaging to a young fellow, he is only seven feet and 9 inches in height, and Miss Rosa is too young, for she is only 15 and has gone to her sister's to spend summer. So you see there's no chance for me to fall in love, if I want to.

Then he confided, "Miss Annie, I must confess that I love you better and more than any girl at Durham."

The beautiful "Miss Bell" was blonde Eula Bell, a native bloom of Washington who was attending the summer school out of boredom. "I'm afraid," she admitted, many years later, "that we didn't go to obtain knowledge, but just to be going some place. . . . The young folks saw each other before and after school hours and at recess every day." Charlie was at a great disadvantage because he was Chinese, she said, so she had no formal dates with him. But she saw him every day while he was there.

It was December before Charlie boarded a train in Nashville with the medical missionary Dr. W. H. Park, and the two journeyed to Kansas City, where they changed to the transcontinental railway. The bench seats sat two passengers hip to hip, and had backs so low that it was impossible to doze. The newspapers and magazines on the train were full of dramatic accounts of events around the world. In Khartoum a few months earlier, they divulged to the edification of frontier readers, Britain's General "Chinese" Gordon (who had undone the Taiping rebels) had been torn to pieces by the fanatical warriors of the Mahdi; in Saskatchewan, Louis Riel had just been hanged for leading a rebellion against Ottawa; in England, Gladstone was in and out of power; in Paris, Louis Pasteur had developed a vaccine for rabies; and in the Pacific Northwest, anti-Chinese rioting had aroused so much horror around Seattle that President Cleveland was obliged to take action.

America's Wild West was on a rampage against Chinese. As Charlie crossed from sea to shining sea, Chinamen were getting scalped by whites on the fruited plains and on purple mountains' majesty. With the collapse of the silver boom, a recession had swept over the West Coast in the 1880s; jobs were hard to find. Manufacturers turned to Chinese labor because Celestials made fewer demands. In retaliation, unemployed whites were whipped into a "yellow peril" frenzy by unscrupulous editors and politicians. Chinatowns were put to the torch. White vigilantes staged "pigtail-cutting parties" in which they not only hacked off Chinamen's queues but ripped off their scalps as well. Beheading, which was not characteristic of America, occurred in places as far afield as Montana. In one of the most extreme and gruesome atrocities on record, a mob severed a Chinaman's genitals and took them to a saloon, where they were roasted and eaten as prairie oysters.

Thousands of Chinese fled the white peril and went home to China. In consequence, the population of Celestials in the American West dropped in the late 1800s from 110,000 to barely 60,000. The bloodbath reached a climax as Charlie headed back to Shanghai. At that very time, mobs in Rock Springs, Wyoming, hacked twenty-eight Chinese residents apart and burned others alive, while the town's proper ladies stood by clapping and laughing. They were following the advice of the editor of the *Montanian* who wrote: "We don't mind hearing of Chinamen being killed now and then, but it's been coming too thick of late. Don't kill them unless they deserve it, but when they do, why kill 'em lots."

In America, local laws and ordinances against Chinese were becoming so universal that Congress began to set limits on Chinese immigration—the first time that America had ever restricted the entrance of a particular nationality to its shores. In the beginning, the Manchus had prohibited Chinese from leaving their own country. But the foreign powers wanted cheap labor. One of the results of the Second Opium War was to force the Manchus to allow Chinese emigration. The Western powers, America in the forefront, then promoted and ran the coolie trade. In the Burlingame Treaty of 1868, Congress affirmed the right of free movement between China and America. But, when the railroads were finished, cheap Chinese labor was a burden rather than a blessing. Congress then revised the Burlingame Treaty drastically, and in 1882 passed the Exclusion Law, barring entry of all Chinese except teachers, students, merchants, and tourists. Chinese who were already in America were prevented from becoming naturalized U.S. citizens. Immigration from China plummeted from forty thousand in 1881, when Charlie was at Trinity, to only ten individuals in 1887, just after Charlie went home.

The response in China was bitter. Small mobs stormed American and European missions. In some parts of the countryside, foreigners traveled at high risk. In the Western press and history books, a great deal of attention is given to the indignities suffered by whites in China during that period, while ignoring the equally horrifying and much better organized anti-Chinese violence in America. This distortion allowed the Western Powers to bring new pressure on the weak imperial government in Peking. To appease the round eyes, Chinese troops were dispatched to put down local protests. Under diplomatic pressure, Peking issued proclamations calling on all Chinese to "live in peace with Christian missionaries." No similar effort was made by Washington to control yellow-peril mobs in America.

Without being aware of it, Charlie was taking his life into his hands crossing the country. Violent antagonisms were being set loose on both sides of the Pacific that would affect his life and his children. Fortunately, he reached San Francisco without incident, and sailed aboard a Pacific Mail Lines steamship for Yokohama and Shanghai—on his way home after ten years of wandering.

Chapter 2

THE HYBRID RETURNS

When Charlie's steamship crawled up the muddy Whangpoo River in January 1886, and tied up at the pier of the Shanghai Dock Company in Hongkew, the waterfront was jammed with Western ships and cargo junks. Among the vessels lying off the Bund were five notorious opium hulks. They had once been proud sailing vessels; now, with their masts cut down to stumps, they looked like ancient Roman galleys. Shed roofs were erected over their decks. In their holds lay a hoard of Indian opium, the well-guarded reserves of the Western trading houses.

It was customary not to go ashore in bustling, dirty Hongkew, but to take a sampan up the river a few hundred yards to the Bund, where passengers could disembark in style. As Charlie later described his homecoming to his divinity school friend Bill Burke, he and Dr. Park headed for the Bund together in a sampan. With a wiry hag pumping the single oar in the stern, the sampan crept past the mouth of Soochow Creek and approached the embankment in front of the British Consulate. By this time there were many photographic plates of the Bund, showing it to be an immaculate Victorian promenade. Through the gates of the consulate handsome gardens were visible, with flowering trees and shrubs shading brick buildings, and the Union Jack rippling lazily overhead. Directly in front of the consulate on the Bund was an orchestra shell, where white residents came with their ladies for drinks and band music at sundown. The Bund was now paved with stones and lined with shade trees. It was carefully policed to keep out Orientals, but here and there rickshaw pullers waited quietly, the rickshaws tipped forward on their poles, seats shaded by small, fringed awnings. Across the Bund was an imposing row of three- and four-story colonial buildings, with stately columns and broad verandahs overlooking the busy river.

Although the scene was entirely Western, the smell of China was unmistakable. It was an acknowledgment of flowers, a dollop of plum sauce, a nostrum of burnt garlic, a wriggle of squid, a remembrance of emptied loins, a prospect of beheadings, and a climax of nightsoil. It was like floating in amniotic fluid, and to be taken away from it was like being jerked from the womb.

There was a grand sweep to the skyline as the eye followed the river, the same Victorian majesty that greeted ships on the approach to Singapore or Bombay, and made you proud to be an Englishman during the Golden Age, if indeed you were.

Charlie went obediently to the far side of Hongkew to see Dr. Allen, the great mandarin of the Methodists. It was a meeting doomed in advance. Dr. Allen was a man who had no doubts about his own superiority. Although an American, he had come to China as many Englishmen had over the years, setting themselves up in Oriental ivory towers, orchid houses of the mind. Dr. Allen had arrived as a missionary before the American Civil War, only to have the conflict cut off all his funds from the home church. To support himself, he found a job teaching and translating at a Chinese institution connected to Shanghai's imperial arsenal, where he could deal exclusively with the privileged elite. In his case the term "missionary" was misleading. He was a high priest, in the tradition of Jesuit emissaries. He did not have it in him to preach Western religion to the unwashed Eastern masses, or to coerce ordinary Chinese into caring about the virtues of Christianity. He considered himself rather a missionary to the Chinese intelligentsia, rationalizing that if he could impress the elite with Western science they would be more receptive to Western culture, and to the subtler nuances of Christian ideology.

For forty years, Allen's main vehicle for conveying Western knowledge to his esoteric audience was a newspaper he produced in classical Chinese, called the *Review of the Times*. Filled with articles on politics, economics, science, religion, and social issues, it was devoured by the mandarins. The journal was a primary point of contact between the two cultures. Allen founded the Anglo-Chinese College in Shanghai, stocking it with bright young Chinese scholars, whom he groomed in his own image. He had his students write classical essays that embodied his ideas, and published these in the *Review.*

To him, Charlie was just an ambitious peasant.

In 1886, the Southern Methodist Mission consisted of only six missionaries, working under Allen's direct supervision. Three of the six considered his authority intolerable and requested a transfer to Japan.

Only two days before Charlie reached Shanghai, Dr. Allen had openly expressed his misgivings in a letter to Bishop McTyeire and the Board of Missions in Nashville. The people back home, he explained, had created a problem. Perhaps Charlie was Americanized, but he was still Chinese. He did not deserve special treatment. If any Chinese should be sponsored, and raised to glory, it should be one of those selected by Dr. Allen.

". . . There is yet one other item—" he wrote to the board,

> Item 10—which I should like to refer to—to wit the salary of Mr. Soon. He will be here in two days now and I have no information as to how the Board expects to treat him. What is to be his status and pay. There is much that is embarrassing in this case. The boys and young men in our Anglo-Chinese College are far his superiors in that they are—the advanced ones—both English and Chinese scholars, and can do and have done work here in the way of composition and translation that has won the encomiums of our eldest and ablest missionaries in public conference of missionaries when the work was presented and criticised. And Soon never will become a Chinese scholar, at best will only be a *denationalized* Chinaman, discontented and unhappy unless he is located and paid far beyond his deserts —and the consequence is I find none of our brotherin [sic] willing to take him.

Allen claimed that all three Southern Methodist missionaries who were to remain in China had refused to have Charlie as an assistant.

Dr. Allen set a monthly salary of less than $15 in American money. It was plenty to live on if you were a Chinese villager, with meek expectations. Charlie, neither ordinary nor meek, swallowed it for the time being. But he did ask Dr. Allen for permission to take several weeks before he settled down to work so that he could visit his family in Hainan. He had not been home in ten years, and had not seen his parents since he was nine years old. Dr. Allen refused, insisting that the trip must be delayed a month till the Chinese New Year holiday, when all the missionaries took time off. This was not an unreasonable delay, but Charlie took it badly, perhaps because of Dr. Allen's dictatorial manner. He revealed a deep resentment when he wrote to Annie Southgate's father:

No. I haven't been to see my parents as yet. Dr. Allen said I may go during the coming Chinese New Year and not before then. I am very much displeased with this sort of authority; but I must bear it patiently. If I were to take rash action the people at home (my Durham friends especially) might think that I am an unloyal Methodist and a lawbreaker; so I have kept silent as a mouse. But when the fullness of time has come, I will shake off all the assuming authority of the present superintendent in spite of all his protestation . . . and his detestation of native ministry. The great [Dr. Allen] was the man who wanted to dismiss all the native ministers from preaching a year ago. And he is the man who ignores my privileges and equality which I am entitled to. I don't like to work under him—I will apply for transmission to Japan.

Charlie did apply for transfer. The three American rebels were given permission to open a Southern Methodist mission in Japan, to escape Dr. Allen's clutches. Charlie was not.

Charlie's first assignment was at Woosung, beyond the outskirts of Shanghai, where the Whangpoo River emptied into the Yangtze, a horizonless expanse of brown water and hazy sky. It was low, flat country, ending in a long sandbar that jutted out into the mother river. The village houses were mostly one-story dwellings of mud brick and mortar with crumbling walls and wandering ducks, and small ponds filled with carp at the edge of rich black farmland. Charlie was to get his first experience here preaching to a small congregation of Chinese who were already loyal Methodists.

He was also to teach their children at the denominational school. The students were disorderly rustics, who delighted in bedeviling their teachers. According to one of them, Hu Shih (who later attended Cornell and eventually became one of China's most eminent philosophers), when Charlie appeared on the teacher's platform, his square body, short haircut, and homely South China face caused titters. He waited for the hubbub to subside, opened his books and began to talk. The students fell silent. It was not what Charlie said that won over the pupils, but the strong impression that he was one of them. Charlie had traveled to the West on his own, not on some imperial passport or as a ward of the missionaries. He had made his own way in America, at a time when Chinese there were being tormented. It was apparent that he came from the soil. Like farmers who spent their lives barefoot in the paddies, until their toes were splayed like duck feet, there was still mud between Charlie's toes. The very thing that Dr. Allen disliked about him—his common origin—was what made Charlie appeal to the students. He became the most popular teacher at the school. When his first term ended word spread and enrollment doubled from twelve students to twenty-four.

To Chinese on the streets, however, he was a joke. His dialect made no sense. He might as well have been a foreigner because he had to teach his pupils in English, the only language that they had in common. While everyone else was dressed in black cotton gowns or faded blue pants and jackets, with hair in queues, Charlie wore the suit of a foreign devil, and his hair was short and slicked down in Western style. Instead of hiding his feelings, his face was frank and animated in the Western manner. He was short and wedge-shaped in a part of China where people tended to be slim and tall. When children saw him on the street they shouted "Foreign Devil," and their parents barked "Siau a-ts" (Little Dwarf). He had even lost his taste for Chinese food. Instead, he craved ham steaks with red-eye gravy and grits.

Dr. Allen was determined to strip away this American veneer. To begin with, Charlie had to learn Shanghai dialect. His language teacher was a remarkable character known by his Christian name, Charlie Marshall. As a boy, Marshall had gone to America for fourteen years as a servant to Dr. D. C. Kelley, one of the original Southern Methodist missionaries. During the Civil War, Marshall followed his master into the Confederate Army, and was housed with the black slaves of other officers. Thanks to them, he developed a strong backwoods accent and an impressive stock of Southern idiom.

The language lessons between Charlie Marshall and Charlie Soon often turned into arguments over proper English equivalents for Chinese expressions. Charlie Soon, with his college education, was not above correcting his teacher's English. The small fraternity of Dixie missionaries were soon guffawing over an incident in which Marshall finally lost his temper:

"You, you upstart, you!" he burst out. "Why you come pesterin' me wid dat Yankee talk. I bin talkin' English 'fo you was ever born. Now go 'way and leave me 'lone."

Charlie also had to relearn his social graces. At church one Sunday, he saw a young Chinese girl who looked shyly at him for just a moment, and he made up his mind to introduce himself, as he would have in Durham or Nashville. He had forgotten that respectable boys and girls in China did not meet, or even see each other, till they were married. Although Western society in Shanghai brought Chinese together in situations where old moral codes were compromised, the Chinese continued to cling to such customs when it came to their daughters. Girls of marriageable age were whisked in and out of church under close family guard.

Charlie discovered that this girl was a teacher at a mission school in Nansiang, west of Shanghai. The school was run by the formidable Miss Lockie Rankin, the first Southern Methodist woman missionary in China; she had arrived in 1878, the year Charlie left the East Indies for Boston. Miss Lockie ran her school by the strictest moral codes from both cultures, plus a few that she thought up herself.

Unaware of this, Charlie went to Nansiang and politely asked Miss Lockie if he could call on the pretty teacher. Miss Lockie was horrified and said absolutely not. She threw Charlie out, and locked the young woman in her room until he was gone.

In one respect, at least, he did feel happier and more confident. He had been permitted, finally, to visit his parents. Charlie wrote the Southgates that he took a coastal steamer to Hainan and appeared unannounced on the family doorstep. His father and mother at first did not recognize him, but there followed a big family reunion. Mr. Han was the aging leader of the local chiu chao brotherhood, and Charlie's elder brother had taken over running their trading network across Southeast Asia. Although Charlie was now based far to the north, the chiu chao brotherhood had a powerful base in the Shanghai International Settlement, which allowed Charlie's family to provide him with many useful connections. It was only at this point, Charlie told the Southgates, that he discovered that Dr. Allen had never forwarded the letter he had written to his father six years earlier.

After six months of language training in Woosung, Charlie was sent into the hinterland to be a circuit preacher at Kunshan, on the road leading through the lake country to Suchow. Here was rich black soil deposited over the centuries by the Yangtze River, with raised footpaths criss-crossing green and yellow fields bursting with produce, tended by groups of blue-clad peasants kneeling in the dirt. It was an agricultural armory. Beside the waterways giant white radishes and striped watermelons were stacked like artillery rounds. Armies of ducks drilled in pens under trellises heavy with grenades of squash and bandoliers of green beans.

Kunshan was an old walled city four miles in circumference, with a threadbare population of 300,000. Besides the Southern Methodists represented by Charlie, there was a mission of Southern Baptists and one of French Catholics. Each had small congregations, but the majority of townspeople were Buddhists, Taoists, and Moslems.

On his pittance, Charlie rented a tiny cottage. This was a period of serious disenchantment. He found himself disliked and avoided by both Chinese and Westerners. The peasantry, gregarious and full of organic humor, were acutely wary of strangers. Charlie was a stranger because he was neither fish nor fowl. He felt even more conspicuous in Kunshan, because he was surrounded by traditional China, by people who had no knowledge of Westerners except to see them at a distance and to hear atrocity stories in teashops. White missionaries did not want to associate with him because he was Chinese—not a prospective convert, but a rival. To blend in better, he put away his American clothes and adopted Chinese robes and a skull cap.

Loneliness became his greatest burden. He sustained himself with memories of those who had been kind to him in America. It was a terrible blow when news came of Annie Southgate's death. Always fragile, she had finally succumbed to one of those vague but racking ailments that doctors treated with leeches and bleeding. Almost incoherently, he wrote back to James Southgate on February 4, 1887:

> It is a matter of great sorrow to learn of the death of Miss Annie, though on the contrary, do rejoice to know that she is happier in heaven than could possibly be on earth. And no doubt all things work for good to them that love God. May God comfort you all and sustain you with His tender love and grace and finally when our work is done in this life we may all meet her on that happy shore where there is no parting. Miss Annie was one of my best friends. Her Christian example is worthy of attention. When I left America I had no idea of such an event would have occurred so soon and that we are not permitted to meet again on this side of Jordan. O this is sad to think of the sweetest flower God has plucked off and took away from us; but that very identical flower is blooming in the garden of God in Heaven. Happy art thou who sleeps in the Lord. And thrice happy art thou who being translated from earthly sorrow to heavenly joy. May God

keep us from sin and weakness and finally translate us to His home where we will meet all our friends and loved ones and to live with Christ forever.

Then one day his luck changed. He was visiting Shanghai, strolling down a street, when he encountered a ghost from the past, the Boston student S. C. New.

Listening to Charlie's woes, New offered a simple solution. Charlie needed a wife. He volunteered to act as go-between and marriage broker in traditional Chinese fashion. New even had the perfect girl in mind—his nineteen-year-old sister-in-law.

S. C. New had just married into one of China's oldest and most illustrious Christian families, directly descended from the Ming Dynasty Prime Minister who was converted to Catholicism in 1601 by the pioneer Jesuit missionary, Matteo Ricci.

New's mother-in-law had been born at the Hsu family estate in the western outskirts of Shanghai. She was tutored by a scholar named Ni, an Episcopalian. In the fullness of time, she married Mr. Ni and became an Episcopalian herself. When the couple produced three daughters, Madame Ni bound the feet of each girl to preserve their childlike beauty. The youngest girl reacted badly, developing a high fever. Finally, her parents gave up. As the third daughter and therefore an insignificant candidate for marriage, her feet could remain unbound. However, no Chinese gentleman would consider marrying her after that.

The ugly duckling's name was Ni Kwei-tseng. As she grew up, her scholar father was pleased to discover that, even if she had big feet, she had an appetite for books. At age five, she was studying Chinese characters with a tutor. She learned calligraphy and read the classics while other girls were perfecting needlepoint. By age eight she was attending the Bridgman School for Girls, operated by the Woman's Union Mission of Shanghai. At age fourteen she had done well enough to be sent on to the Pei Wan Girls' High School at the West Gate in Shanghai, graduating at age seventeen. She excelled in mathematics and learned to play the piano, an alien instrument to most Chinese.

Miss Ni Kwei-tseng's eldest sister had been a highly eligible candidate for marriage when S. C. New returned from Boston. Through proper intermediaries, a society wedding was arranged. New's cousin and alter ego, B. C. Wen, also returned from Boston at this time. Shortly after New married the eldest sister, Wen married the next one. Only one sister remained—the one with big feet, a Western education, and the penchant for piano playing—all qualities that made her a poor candidate for a proper Chinese husband.

If she was not a proper candidate for marriage, neither was Charlie. Wen and New arranged for him to accompany them to church, where Miss Ni would be singing in the choir. That Sunday, Charlie saw before him a freshly-scrubbed vision of Christian contentment, a homely girl with plump cheeks and soft eyes, brow neatly plucked to give her a sweetly rounded hairline, straight black hair pulled to a knot at the nape of her neck, and a tiny cluster of seed pearls tucked over one ear. At age nineteen, Miss Ni Kwei-tseng was two years younger than Charlie. She was his size, as well, less than five feet tall. She radiated character and personality in the special way of young women who have not been cursed with beauty.

Miss Ni's mother that same afternoon received an elaborate account of Charlie's superior qualities, and after a suitable period for reflection, announced that she was pleased with the match.

The wedding took place in midsummer, 1887. It was a small affair performed by missionary Clarence Reid, followed by the traditional raucous Shanghai-style family banquet, with dozens of courses, quantities of sorghum whiskey called *kaoliang,* and hundreds of kinsmen and other powerful people Charlie did not know—people with links to his new in-laws through business, banking, the professions, the military, and imperial connections. The door to a new world was ajar. Unfortunately, there is no record whether any of Charlie's own family came up from Hainan for the occasion. Since the chiu chao brotherhood was very powerful in the Shanghai International Concession, it would not have been surprising if Charlie's father or elder brother was on hand, but distances were great. A few years earlier, it would have been characteristic for Charlie to mention his family openly in a letter to North Carolina friends, but by this point he was becoming increasingly secretive about his contacts. It soon becomes evident why.

After the celebration, Charlie took his bride to Kunshan, where they got to know each other for the first time. Life entered a mellow period, spoiled only by the salary, which, although there were now two mouths to feed, remained less than $15 a month. This was handsomely offset by a dowry (of a large but undisclosed amount) settled upon his bride by her wealthy family, in keeping with custom. It was valuable seed money. Her clan also gave Charlie something equivalent to entrée into the guarded circle of a British earldom. He now had status and visibility in Chinese society and was expected to make the most of the opportunities afforded by their intricate connections.

William Burke, his old schoolmate from Vanderbilt, witnessed Charlie's rebirth, and it is to him that we owe many details of this period. Burke's steamer arrived in Shanghai in October, 1887, in time for the second annual conference of the Southern Methodist Mission in Soochow. The towering, beefy Burke, unrecognizable in a bushy beard, found that his missionary colleagues included a Chinese, wearing a black silk gown and skull cap. Burke did not recognize him until Dr. Allen made the introductions.

Laughing, Charlie said, "You didn't bring that magic flatiron with you, did you?"

"No," chuckled Burke, "but I think I'll have to fix up another one."

When the conference ended five days later, Burke was assigned to Sungchiang, the prefectural capital of Shanghai district. They would be close enough to see each other from time to time. Charlie was ordered to resume his post in Kunshan, but was not dejected anymore by the prospect. He no longer felt vulnerable to Dr. Allen. He had secret plans. His next letter to the *Christian Advocate,* written November 4, 1887, was full of sap rising. Although on the surface he was speaking about missionary matters, he was actually referring between the lines to his own bright prospects:

> Well, the good Lord has been very gracious to us, and we feel very grateful to him. The outlook is very promising. The spirit of the Lord is rapidly making His way into the hearts of His benighted people. We pray and hope that the Lord will give us many souls during this year for Christ.
>
> Our China Mission Conference has met and closed. No change was made as to our appointments. Every man returned to his own charge. I returned to [Kunshan] for another year. By the grace and help of God, I hope to do better and more work for my Saviour than ever I did before.
>
> Our hospital for women in Soochow is completed. But the physician in charge, Dr. Phillips, is sick in Shanghai. Our new brick church in the English Concession at Shanghai is receiving its last finishing touch.
>
> China is about to turn over another new leaf. She has all sorts of plans and schemes on hand. The Government is contemplating building a long railway from Peking to Canton, as a western train, and another railroad is to be constructed in the island of Formosa for carrying the Imperial troops up and down the wilderness to subjugate the wild tribes of that island.

Well, I shall come to a close, but before I do so, I must tell you I am different from what I used to be—I am married. The ceremony was performed by C. F. Reid of our Mission.

At the Chinese New Year, Burke arrived in Kunshan to visit and later described the occasion in detail to his son. Charlie met him at the local teahouse. Fireworks were exploding everywhere. As they walked back through the market, a crowd of peasants gathered, peering with amazement at the huge white man and his abbreviated companion. One farmer could not contain himself.

"Two foreign devils—" he exclaimed in amazement, "a giant and a dwarf."

The parsonage was a two-story mud-brick dwelling with a tile roof. The lower floor had a tiny courtyard with a wooden gate. Crossing the courtyard, they stepped into a room that served both as parlor and dining room. An oil stove was lit in the corner, and the windows were sealed with two layers of waxed paper to keep in the warmth.

Charlie's bride entered with cups of hot green tea and was introduced. Burke was relieved to see that her feet were normal. He was still learning Chinese. Kwei-tseng spoke little English, and she was shy about using it, so Charlie interpreted. The conversation turned to his main grievance, the dismal salary and the misery of working for Allen. How could they have children when his pay would be increased only several dollars? Burke had a hunch that Charlie's days as a missionary were coming to an end.

In fairness, Dr. Allen may have been right. Charlie's genius was not in steadfast missionary endeavor. He was an unusual character, a runaway, full of charm, energy, restlessness, and mercurial adaptability. He was not cut out to be obedient. Captain Gabrielson, Julian Carr, and the Reverend Ricaud—all worldly men—had seen in him qualities of cleverness, resourcefulness, and alertness that brought them to his aid, as if they recognized a kindred spirit. Audacity was really what drew them to him, because each in his own way had been a tradition breaker. Charlie was, in the end, gifted at breaking rules, not at keeping them. China, at that moment of history, was in desperate need of men who could break rules. The old order had become a burden. Life was strangled by propriety. There is a time for fools to come forth, when only bandits can be kings. Such a time was at hand.

"Sometimes," said Charlie that night to Burke in Kunshan, "I think I could do more for my people if I were free of the mission, Bill. You know the way I feel about the spiritual and material burdens under which I labor. . . . But please believe me, if I do happen to leave the mission, it will never mean my giving up of preaching Christ and Him crucified. I will continue to work as much as I can for the mission always."

It was obvious to Burke that Charlie had something going, something afoot. What Charlie could not yet bring himself to reveal, but later did to Burke and others, was that he had already begun to make the break. Shortly before the 1888 Chinese New Year celebration, when his American friend noticed this dramatic change in Charlie's attitude, he had been initiated into a powerful secret society in Shanghai and had begun the transition from preacher to revolutionary. It is not possible to be precise about the exact date or circumstances, because these were all matters of utmost secrecy. But his association with the republican anti-Manchu conspiracy was well established by 1894 and, as it was for most of the other Shanghai revolutionaries, was based on membership in the most effective anti-Manchu triad, known as the Hung P'ang— Red Society or Red Gang. The color red was here a play on words identified with the reign title of the first Ming Emperor, Hung Wu, and was of course not associated at the time with Communism.

The Red Gang was the most influential and one of the most interesting organizations in China, and in Shanghai power circles you were nothing unless you were a member. It was evidently Charlie's ubiquitous brothers-in-law, New and Wen, who introduced him to its ranks, as they so generously had brought him into their family and fortune. Thanks to them, Charlie had broken into the real world. From this point on, most of his closest Chinese associates were patriotic members of the Red Gang. In time it became common knowledge that Charlie Soong printed all of the triad's secret papers and political broadsheets.

To Westerners, triads were part of an unsavory underworld comprehensible only to Chinese. But to many Chinese they were perfectly normal private associations of clan and business connections not unlike a Masonic order. Furthermore, in addition to providing moral and material support to members, these triads were dedicated to the ouster of the Manchus. This had been their purpose since the downfall of the Ming dynasty nearly three centuries earlier, and they were still obsessed with the mission. It bound them the way the Crucifixion and

Second Coming bound early Christians. It also lent an agreeable aura of mystery, secrecy, and magic to everything they did.

According to Shanghai police scuttlebutt and triad lore, the Red Gang's initiation ceremonies were conducted aboard an old opium junk anchored in the Whangpoo River off the French Concession. Initiates like Charlie were taken there late at night by three officers of the Red Gang—a councillor called a "White Paper Fan," responsible for legal and financial matters, an enforcer called a "Red Pole" skilled in the martial arts, and a messenger known as the "Straw Sandal." Deep in the hold, an altar was arranged on a table, decorated with long scrolls of red paper on which were written Chinese characters. On the altar was a bowl of uncooked rice, holding twenty-eight incense sticks and three red flags. In the shadows, a dozen elders and officers of the society watched the ceremony.

The initiates were told to kneel while the joss was lighted. As each stick began to smolder, it was passed to the Incense Master, who placed it back in the rice bowl. The initiates were then made to repeat certain phrases, and were given joss sticks to hold upside down in each hand. They were told to throw down the sticks, and to repeat thirty-six oaths, whereupon they were given new joss to throw down. Then the Incense Master took oaths of loyalty and secrecy, and held a large sword to a point between their shoulder blades. It was understood that betrayal would result in having the tendons severed so that they could never again raise their arms. The Incense Master pricked their fingers and made them blood brothers. Each was given a code number in the order, and learned secret recognition signals to make contact with other members in teahouses and other public places. The ceremony climaxed with the ritual burning of all decorations, flags, and scrolls.

Charlie's secret life had now begun. It was not until 1894 that he made the most important triad contact of his career. But he was on his way, helped by a brotherhood that provided access through the back door to everything Shanghai had to offer. It was up to him to capitalize on his good fortune.

The circumstances that made Charlie rich did not occur suddenly. They evolved from cross-pollination between his missionary career and his new secret life. Ironically, Charlie was beginning to succeed as a missionary. In 1888, he was promoted to full-fledged minister. The following year, he transferred to Shanghai district, where he was placed closer to the financial and revolutionary heart of China. In 1890, he was able to stop traveling the circuits and become a local preacher at Tse So, a Shanghai suburb. Word then got around that he was the proud owner of his own printing establishment and was resigning from preaching. Charlie no longer needed the Methodists.

At the end of 1889, while casting about for a way to make a bit of money on the side, Charlie had taken a part-time job as an agent or "colporteur" of the American Bible Society, an organization that made inexpensive editions of the Bible available in different languages around the world. The society sold and gave away Bibles, "without doctrinal note or comment." They were kept low in cost by subsidies from the society.

Charlie's job was to sell English-language Bibles and Chinese-language editions of the New Testament, as translated into classical Chinese by the missionaries Bridgman and Culbertson. He discovered that only middle-class Chinese could afford them or read them.

Most Chinese could not afford to buy books of any kind. Even subsidized Bibles were beyond reach. The one most widely available was published in China, but printed on foreign paper and bound in foreign leather. It sold for nearly three American dollars, which was astronomical by Chinese village standards. For that matter, it was one-fifth of Charlie's monthly starting salary as a preacher. The same edition bound in cheaper Chinese leather cost nearly two U.S. dollars. A staff member at the Presbyterian press in China in the 1890s once explained:

> Some think it best due to the sacred character of the volume that it be printed in the best style, on paper of a durable nature, and be more thoroughly bound than Chinese books generally are. Others feel that, as our books have to be, at best, so nearly given away, it is not wise to tempt those who care little or nothing for their contents, to desire to get them, either as ornamental prizes, or with mercenary intents. A medium position is generally taken, and there are editions of various degrees of expensiveness, suited to the various characters of readers.

The cheapest edition of the New Testament alone, using Chinese paper and substituting cardboard bindings for leather, cost one U.S. dollar.

Traditional Chinese printing was unsuitable. Wooden blocks were painstakingly carved by hand, and employed like Western woodcuts. The results were artistic rather than commercial. Furthermore, the language was classical Chinese, not the vernacular street language, and thus incomprehensible to ordinary citizens.

Charlie was in a position to help change this. Because of the job he once had as an apprentice in a Wilmington printing shop, he had a basic comprehension of mechanized Western printing methods. With Chinese ingenuity, that was all he needed. As a salesman for the American Bible Society, he learned the economics firsthand. If he could acquire several presses and run them full-time with cheap local paper, cardboard binding, and Chinese labor for typesetting, it would be practical to copy and mass produce Western books in English at prices all but the poorest Chinese could afford. Already, missionaries were making vernacular translations of the Old and New Testaments, which would make them comprehensible for the first time to any Chinese who could read.

On Bibles, a publisher would make only a modest profit. But such a commendable project would easily get financial and technical assistance from a number of Western missionary groups and religious organizations. Indeed, Charlie was soon doing job printing for several missionary societies, and was even able to get lucrative commissions from Dr. Allen's *Review*. By reprinting Western history, science, and technical books, he could greatly enlarge profits. He could also do discreet printing for the secret societies, including political tracts and membership materials. As a Taiwan government official once remarked to me proudly, "That Charlie Soong, he was China's first pirate publisher!"

His brother-in-law B. C. Wen was an educator, with excellent ties to the imperial court. He was also well connected with the aristocratic reformers who wished to arm China with Western knowledge and technology. Wen was quick to see that if Western textbooks could be produced cheaply in China, even in the English language, it would put Western education within the reach of millions, and contribute to the renaissance of the nation.

Charlie needed money. Kwei-tseng had become pregnant. Early in 1890, she delivered their first child, a girl. Charlie named her Ai-ling ("pleasant mood") and gave her the Christian name Nancy in honor of Nannie Carr. On January 27, 1892, Kwei-tseng gave birth to a second daughter, Ching-ling ("happy mood"). She was given the Christian name Rosamond in honor of the Reverend Ricaud's daughter.

By the time his second child was born, Charlie had turned the financial corner. Using his wife's dowry, a sizable contribution from each of his brothers-in-law, and a hefty investment of capital from his associates in the Red Gang, he bought additional printing presses and a small building in the French Concession to house them. For a long time, he had been discussing his project by mail with Julian Carr, and once the money for machinery was in hand the transaction apparently was arranged through his Durham patron. The building, acquired through the Red Gang, was a rundown warehouse on Shantung Road, where it was possible for patriotic individuals to come and go without attracting the attention of Manchu agents.

He called his company the Sino-American Press (Hua-Mei Shu Kuan) and in short order had contracts to print Bibles for the American Bible Society, tracts for the Methodists, and hymnals for other missionary groups. Typesetters were busy round the clock duplicating pages of Western textbooks. There was hardly time left to run off the secret society's inflammatory broadsheets. Already he had changed his missionary status to part time. In spring 1892, he resigned completely from the Southern Methodist China Mission.

In North Carolina, there was a spiteful reaction. Word went around that "Charlie Soon has gone back to worshipping wooden idols."

Angered, Charlie drafted a letter to the editor of the *Christian Advocate:*

> Shanghai, China
> September 8th, 1892

Dear Brother Reid:

Will you kindly permit me a space in your valuable columns to say a few words by way of correcting a false rumor which has been circulated in some quarters of North Carolina concerning me? I am informed by a letter from a friend that it was reported in his city that I "had gone back to the heathen custom of worshipping idols." I write this to say that there *is not a particle of truth in it.* The idea of giving up my precious Saviour Jesus, and returning to the worship of the lifeless gods of wood and stone, had never entered my head at any time ever since I was converted. It would be a foolish thing for a man to give up the eternal life for everlasting death.

But the originator of the false rumor may say Solomon was the wisest man that ever lived, and yet he afterwards worshipped idols. Why not any one else do the same? My answer is this, I am not so wise as Solomon was, nor am I so foolish as he has been. But the writer does claim to have sense enough to serve the Lord to the best of his ability. And he will continue to do so as long as he liveth.

My reason for leaving the Mission was it did not give me sufficient [income] to live upon. I could not support myself, wife and children with about fifteen dollars of United States money per month. I hope my friends will understand that my leaving the Mission does not mean the giving up of preaching Christ and Him crucified.

At present I am connected with the American Bible Society, but I am still doing mission work connected with our church. My co-laborers in the Lord, Brothers Hill and Bonnell, will bear testimony to this. So my leaving the Mission simply means that I am an independent worker of our Methodist Mission, or one who tries to do as much as he can for the Mission without depending on the church at home for his support.

I am now in charge of our new Methodist Church which is the gift of Brother Moore, of Kansas City (U.S.A.) and which is the finest native church in China.

We have a very large Sunday school in this church and a fine staff of teachers. I myself also have a nice Sunday school class which is composed of young men and old. We enjoy the "International Sunday school sessions" very much. Should any of you chance to call on some Sunday morning, we will give a never-to-be-forgotten welcome, and show you how well the children can say their lessons.

I hope those who have heard that I "had gone back to the heathen custom of worshipping idols," will kindly take the trouble to read these few lines and see for themselves wherein I stand. I am enjoying my religion and hope all my friends do theirs.

Finally, friends, I have a request to ask of you, that is, first, pray for me that I may be a useful instrument in winning souls to Christ. Second, pray for the Mission work in this benighted land, and third, pray to the Lord that He may send more laborers into the field for it is white unto harvest!

C. J. Soon

This was the last time that Charlie ever used the spelling "Soon." He now changed his name to Soong. No explanation of the curious change was ever offered by any member of the family, certainly not by Charlie himself.

After calling himself Charlie Soon for five years in North Carolina, and being assigned to China as the Reverend Charles Jones Soon, it would have been senseless to change his name back to Han when he reached Shanghai. Chinese men characteristically use a number of aliases or nicknames, to reflect a new state of mind or a new ambition. A boy might be called Noble Promise, then at school change his given name to Midnight Scholar. It was a matter of whimsy. In a country full of the lore of brigands and legends of heroism, names changed often according to the way a man saw his special circumstances. Charles Soon was a stage name. His closest Chinese friends in Shanghai always called him by his real name, Chiao-shun, to his face, without ever explaining why to Westerners.

When the time came to leave the China Mission and launch his career as a publisher, Charlie had to legitimize the odd name Soon. It might be acceptable to Americans, but it was not a prestigious name in China. The solution lay in a classical volume called the *Pak Ka Sing* (*Hundred Family Names*). This book lists the most distinguished names from Chinese history—the names of the original hundred great families of Chinese history. Anyone adopting a new name was wise to choose from it. The closest Charlie could come to Soon was the ideograph used by the Chinese dynasty called the Sung, which ruled from 960 to 1279.

Beginning in 1892, he began printing his own business cards with his family name represented by the character for Sung. In this way, he gave himself a new legitimacy among the traditional Chinese who were the upper class in Shanghai. It was fitting that he should adopt one of the great dynastic names of ancient China because he was founding one of the great dynasties of modern China.

Along with a new name, Charlie seemed to have much more income than even the most industrious publisher could make.

Times had changed.

He commuted to his publishing house in a rickshaw drawn by a bodyguard. The route home went by the tree-shaded park of the Shanghai Bund, along the riverfront of the British Concession, past the British Consulate, and across Soochow Creek to Hongkew District. In its outlying sectors (where Dr. Allen also lived), the suburbs spread out, homes became grander, interspersed with more countryside. Down a dirt lane between black-earth fields of vegetables, Charlie had just built his first real home.

It was suitably eccentric. To remind himself of Hainan, he planted coconut palms from South China around the property. By a brook in front, he built a low wall to keep his children from tumbling in. Beyond was a large entrance courtyard and the façade of a house common to Wilmington, New Orleans, Savannah, and other communities in the South in the nineteenth century. It had a full-length verandah on the ground floor, with another verandah above it, modeled on Julian Carr's first house in Durham. All that was missing from the antebellum image was hanging moss and wrought-iron work. Inside, there were Charlie's private study, a dining room, a parlor in Chinese style, and a second parlor in American style, with a piano for his wife and armchairs covered with lace antimacassars. Behind these were storerooms and a staircase.

Upstairs, four bedrooms faced the verandah, served by two large bathrooms with huge green-and-yellow-glazed Soochow tubs, decorated with dragons. They had plumbing for cold water; hot water was carried up from the kitchen. Beside the tubs were ornate commode chairs fitted with lifting lids and concealed chamber pots. Servants emptied them out back, where the accumulation was carried away on a trundle each morning by the local nightsoil collector for use in the nearby farm fields. All the rooms were lighted by kerosene lamps and heated with gas radiators. Guests found the beds a novelty because they had Western mattresses. (Chinese beds were hard wooden platforms, surrounded on three sides by carved railings, covered with a wood canopy. Poor people, if they were lucky, slept on *kangs,* or masonry platforms, built over cooking hearths. American mattresses were the height of indulgence. Charlie Soong's children grew up calling Western beds *kangs.)*

In back, across an inner courtyard, a small separate cottage contained the kitchen, pantry, and servants' quarters. The kitchen had brick ovens with charcoal pits, which held huge woks for universal cooking. At the back was a vegetable garden, big enough to provide fresh vegetables year round. Charlie tended the garden himself, though it added to his reputation as an odd character.

After living on $15 a month for years, Charlie was close-mouthed about his new prosperity. The secret society had given him a new perspective. Silence was both a game and a necessity. His triad associates were certain to be executed in the most grisly fashion if their activities came to light. Punishment for a loose tongue meant its removal. With Sunday school at one extreme, Red Gang at the other, Charlie led a tidy double life. Silence became his habit. More important, he cultivated the habit in his children, so their personal lives remain open through childhood then suddenly become opaque. Like their father, they worked hard to create a public image, but maintained an impenetrable silence about themselves.

There is still mystery surrounding his wealth. One possible explanation is that he supplemented his wife's dowry by borrowing a sum from Julian Carr. The tobacco millionaire, with his well-earned reputation for giving money to total strangers, considered Charlie "practically a member of the family." Although now on opposite sides of the earth, they kept up regular correspondence. If Charlie had approached Carr with a plan to set himself up as a publisher of Bibles in benighted China, nobody would have been more forthcoming.

There could have been other sources as well. Charlie had been welcomed home warmly in 1887 by the Han family, and other visits to Hainan followed as the years passed. Chiu chao brotherhood members in the service of British merchants had a stranglehold on all criminal activities in Shanghai's International Settlement until 1910, when they declared a truce and formed a syndicate with rival gangs based in the French Concession. This meant that Charlie's father and elder brother could have provided backing easily for Younger Son's first business enterprises. The Manchu regime followed the accepted Chinese principle that punishment for a crime should extend beyond the culprit to his entire family, giving Charlie every justification for secrecy. It was all very mysterious.

But the answer actually lies in a pedestrian sideline. The bulk of Charlie's money was coming from the noodle business. Printing was only the shoehorn that slipped him into the commercial world of Shanghai. Once he was involved in commerce, Charlie was a hot commodity as a broker, or comprador, between East and West.

By the 1890s, the Chinese gentry were launching their own industrial projects. At first, progressive members of the gentry believed that China's subservience to the West had come about because the West was stronger militarily. They sought to strengthen the nation by building a modern armaments industry and by adopting Western military methods. But they were succeeded by a new wave of Chinese reformers who claimed that the power of the West lay not in military might but in industrial power.

Western ideas, machines, industries, and trading houses were making fantastic inroads. A few wealthy Chinese decided to compete. It was not easy because Westerners dominated the markets. But, as recessions and financial crises thinned foreign ranks, Chinese entrepreneurs seized opportunities to fill the gaps. A native bourgeoisie began to grow as gentry money established cotton, tobacco, and food processing industries, shipping lines, banks, and trading houses. China was beginning to develop a significant middle class, and its heart pumped in Shanghai.

When Charlie set up as a publisher, the wealthy Fou Foong family —one of the leaders of the new middle class—approached him to become the manager of a flour mill, eventually one of the biggest in Asia. The Fou Foongs needed a front man with Charlie's ability to switch back and forth between the two cultures. He would be their comprador in negotiations with Westerners, advising on Western trends and attitudes and serving as middleman to buy American machinery for their mills. While South China depended on rice, North China depended on noodles, and Shanghai was the center for a new industry turning out pasta products for a market extending from Japan to Indonesia.

With assistance from Julian Carr, with his million-dollar grain-milling interests in America, Charlie became one of the first Chinese to import heavy industrial machinery for Chinese-owned factories. He was the chief English-language executive of the Fou Foong mills and held the lavishly-paid position for the rest of his life. He was rewarded with a major shareholding in the firm.

This role of comprador lies at the heart of hatreds that fired the revolutionary upheavals of the twentieth century. It was a complex role —somewhere between pimp and patrician—that linked the separate economic classes in the Orient and provided the lubrication between East and West. Shanghai was a city of compradors.

No British gentleman, and therefore no foreigner of any nationality hoping to pass as a gentleman, would have dreamed of engaging in direct business dealings with Chinese. Such a thing would have been debasing. It would also have been hard work, requiring a mastery of the Chinese language, Chinese social customs, and Chinese business practice, the latter a mystery unto itself. The British had engaged compradors in their opium trade, often Persians or Iraqi Jews, who became fabulously rich in the process and emerged as some of the great families of Shanghai, including the Sassoons, the Hardoons, and the Kadoories. It was said that they "came down from Baghdad to Shanghai on camels and left in Rolls-Royces."

Like them, many Chinese compradors also grew rich. Nothing could move without them. Skillful politicians, they made profits from both sides. Successful compradors were senior members of triads. The head of the Red Gang was the chief of detectives for the colonial government in the French Concession: a comprador of crime.

Charlie was perfectly equipped to enter this world. He now spoke both Hainan and Shanghai dialects fluently and was glib in English, seasoning his conversation with enough Biblical references to win over any puritan Yankee trader. He had lived in New England and the South, developing a disarming Dixie accent in the process. He had excellent business connections in America through the fabulously wealthy Carr. In Shanghai, where all the righteous foreigners went to church because it was important, and all the unrighteous went with them because it was a social essential, the church was a meeting place that brought men and money into fruitful contact. Charlie was that unusual commodity, an American-trained Chinese preacher turned comprador.

Out of obscurity, Charlie Soong emerged abruptly in 1893–94 as a figure to be reckoned with, a successful publisher and industrialist, as well as a prominent minister of a leading church in the International Settlement. Westerners ceased to regard him as a contemptible "native preacher," and he became instead something of a Shanghai celebrity. People talked about his success, and people who heard him talked about talked about him all the more. The legend was beginning to build.

For Charlie Soong himself, now that the years of poverty were over, a time of intrigue was about to begin.

Chapter 3

THE REVOLUTIONARIES

In 1894, Charlie Soong met a secret-society brother who became his closest friend and turned him into a revolutionary and a fugitive. Their names were permanently linked by marriage and mythology in one of history's great conspiracies. Together they bamboozled the Manchus and brought the Empire to the edge of collapse—when all that was needed was a final nudge.

His name was Sun Wen. As a rabble-rouser, hunted by Manchu agents, he adopted a number of aliases. But the name by which he became known to the world was Sun Yat-sen. His early years were a study in alienation and implacable ambition.

Sun's father was a village watchman in the farming community of Ts'ui-heng, in the Pearl River delta near Macao. In the 1870s, his older brother, Sun Mei, joined the exodus of Cantonese emigrants and sailed for Hawaii, where he worked as a laborer in the rice fields, then opened a store. He parlayed his profits into landholdings on the island of Maui, and sent money home faithfully.

Always loyal to tradition, Sun Mei returned to China in 1878 to wed a village girl chosen by his father. During this trip, he filled his younger brother's head with tales about life in the islands, where subjects of King Kalakaua enjoyed freedoms unheard-of in China. He persuaded his mother to bring Younger Brother to Hawaii, and a few months later twelve-year-old Sun Wen sailed across the Pacific.

The boy entered an Anglican school in Honolulu staffed by British teachers. For a peasant, excluded from possibilities of advancement in feudal China, a Western education fostered unrealizable ambitions. Sun went on to Oahu College, where he became interested in medicine, politics, and Christianity. His older brother could not allow him to be seduced by an alien religion. After a bitter quarrel, he took Sun Wen out of college and sent him home to China.

But it was too late. Transformed by his experience abroad, Sun Wen was now out of place in his ancestral village. Defiantly, he spent his time with local toughs, mastering the martial art known as *hsing-i* and joining a branch of a triad called the Three Harmonies Society.

A small, wiry youth, he still wore a queue and looked Chinese, but inside his head he was alienated from the seasonal rhythms of the community. In a show of contempt, one night he and a friend desecrated the wooden idol of the village deity. They were expelled and Sun took refuge with friends in Hong Kong, where he resumed his studies. In 1884, he was baptized there by the American Congregationalist missionary, Dr. Charles Hager, who bestowed upon him the mandarin name I-hsien. In Cantonese, it was pronounced "Yat-sen."

But the affair of the village deity was not over. When Sun's brother heard of the scandal, he ordered the boy back to Hawaii. He put Sun to work as a clerk in his store, determined to teach him respect. The effort failed. After only the briefest taste of discipline, Sun wheedled money from friends and sailed back to China. His brother, finally accepting the boy's independence, showed extraordinary strength of character, forgave him, and agreed to pay his way through college. Sun enrolled at Canton Hospital Medical School, then transferred to the new College of Medicine for Chinese in Hong Kong. There, he made contact with the leading Chinese liberals of the Crown Colony. One was Dr. Ho Kai, a British-trained lawyer and doctor of medicine, and an armchair political provocateur, who enjoyed considerable celebrity. Dr. James Cantlie, a British physician who later became world famous for his pioneering work in leprosy, was dean of the medical school, and the bright and imaginative Sun Yat-sen became his favorite student.

Filled with wild ideas and charismatic in his zest for action, Sun attracted young Chinese radicals. Young men with time on their hands, and a craving for recognition, they listened for hours to Dr. Ho Kai condemn the Manchus' "loose morality and evil habits." China had to be reformed, he declared, an end brought to corruption, her house set in order. Sun and his friends began to see themselves as revolutionaries in a great tradition. They started manufacturing bombs in the chemistry laboratory.

Sun did well enough to graduate in 1892. But his diploma was practically useless; the medical school's curriculum did not meet British standards. Sun opened an herbal medicine shop in Macao, but Portuguese doctors prevailed upon local authorities to close it down because he lacked a Portuguese diploma. Moving to Canton, Sun started a chain of apothecary shops, which were managed by friends, while he dispensed Western drugs and performed surgery. Meanwhile, Sun continued to experiment with explosives and to flirt with the idea of starting an anti-Manchu underground. But his commitment to revolution was not total, and he made one last attempt to break into the mandarin bureaucracy.

With exceptional audacity, he wrote an epistle to the most powerful official in the Empire, Li Hung-chang, the Grand Secretary to the Emperor. The Grand Secretary was a patron of the Hong Kong medical school that Sun had attended. If he could gain the great man's attention and favor, he might obtain a significant post in the government service.

His epistle was based on the argument of Dr. Ho Kai: that China could achieve the strength of the West by utilizing native human talent. Praising the Grand Secretary as a man renowned for encouraging people of talent, Sun outlined his qualifications:

> I have already passed the English medical examinations in Hong Kong. When I was young, I tasted the experience of overseas study. Western languages, literature, politics, customs, mathematics, geography, physics, and chemistry—these I have had an opportunity to study in the general sort of way. But I paid particular attention to their methods of achieving a prosperous country and a powerful army and to their laws for reforming the people and perfecting their customs.

Early in 1894, Sun headed north to make his case personally to the Grand Secretary in Tientsin. Along the way he stopped in Shanghai, where he met a triad brother named Charlie Soong.

The secret society Sun Yat-sen had joined as a boy—the Three Harmonies Society—was the same South China triad in which Charlie Soong's family was active on Hainan Island, a part of the chiu chao brotherhood. In the Shanghai International Settlement, it was one of the two triads that Charlie belonged to; the other being the Red Gang.

The first contact between Sun and Soong was at the Moore Methodist Church, where they were introduced after the Sunday service. Throughout his life, Sun regularly went to church to find recruits. He was fond of saying, "I do not belong to the Christianity of the churches, but to the Christianity of Jesus who was a revolutionary."

They had much in common besides their triad membership. Both were from Kwangtung Province, they spoke the same dialect and had learned colloquial English. Both had been educated abroad and were Christians. Both had wanted to study medicine. They were both intensely ambitious, and Confucian society had proved difficult to crack because they were both hybrids—Western-educated peasants. In each, the other certainly recognized a kindred ego.

Charlie did not hold out much hope for Sun's Tientsin undertaking, but he did all he could to further the venture, and assured Sun that if the mission was not a success he could count on Charlie to promote his cause in the Yangtze River area through the Red Gang. Charlie introduced Sun to two other important men, the powerful comprador Cheng Kuan-ying and the influential journalist Wang T'ao, who were senior officers of the Red Gang. The journalist provided Sun with an introduction to a minor bureaucrat in the office of the Grand Secretary. Armed with this bit of leverage, Sun proceeded on his journey.

Anyone who offended a Manchu court official even slightly could be beheaded. Other Chinese critics contented themselves with writing anonymous denunciations of the Manchu regime, and published them safely in the British Crown Colony or underground. The bold opinions of Sun's mentor, Dr. Ho Kai, had been published only under a pen name in Hong Kong's *China Mail.* Now, Dr. Sun planned to confront one of the most powerful men in the Empire personally with ideas that had been studiously ignored. Under the circumstances, this was an act of surpassing courage.

It was a bad moment to choose, however. The Grand Secretary had urgent matters requiring his full attention. War with Japan was looming, over Korea. For centuries, Korea had been China's vassal state. But when Japan was "opened up" by Commodore Perry, its isolation ended with a bang. The Japanese rapidly modernized their nation and sought to extend their hegemony over the mineral-rich Korean peninsula.

On reaching Tientsin, Sun left a draft of his letter with Wang T'ao's acquaintance, in the vain hope that it would reach the Grand Secretary. He waited fruitlessly. No interview was forthcoming. The Grand Secretary had no time to contemplate irrelevant social reforms proposed by an insignificant southern peasant herbalist.

Sun Yat-sen had come to the crossroads. Returning to Shanghai, he stayed at the home of Charlie Soong, who pulled strings as he had promised. He had Sun's letter to the Grand Secretary published as an essay on reform in the September-October issue of Dr. Allen's *Review of the Times*. This was the first occasion on which Sun's views were exposed to public attention.

During long discussions at Charlie's printing shop, Sun argued that social reform was hopeless. It was time to organize a new political movement along the lines of a secret society that could lead the way to revolution.

Thereafter, Dr. Sun regularly stayed in Charlie's home. He convened conspiratorial meetings in the study and became a godfather to the Soong children. Wherever Sun went to raise money and support for the cause, Charlie kept him informed and sent money out of his own pocket to pay expenses.

It was a friendship reinforced by the ancient Chinese tradition of banditry, embodied in the classic novel *The Water Margin*. In a fantastical setting of swamp country and a mountain lair called Liang Shan Po, the outlaw heroes of the novel established a "liberated" zone, a renegades' republic. In this twilight world of magic and genius, good deeds were done along with suitable knavery. Stories of these noble thieves and rebels were known to everyone in China through constant retelling and local dramatizations. One favorite tale told of a peasant who became a bandit and rose to be the first Ming Emperor.

There have always been such secret societies, piratical bands, and esoteric sects. But until the seventeenth century, they were fragmented and iconoclastic. The year of the Manchu conquest, 1644, was a watershed. After that a new network of secret societies spread across the landscape, dedicated to unhorsing the Manchus.

Aside from a collection of scholarly essays edited by the French historian Jean Chesneaux, there has been no popular and authoritative account in English of these societies and their evolution into the triads of the nineteenth and twentieth centuries. Everything the Soong dynasty became depended to some degree on these triad associations. So, while the subject is arcane and riddled with unanswered questions, making it a bit difficult to grasp, it is a vital part of the Soong story.

Initially the Manchus conquered only the northern half of China.

In the South, the pirate leader Coxinga remained loyal to the Ming Dynasty and battled the Manchus on land and sea. Coxinga was born in Nagasaki, the son of a famous Chinese pirate and his Japanese concubine; because of this, he remains a hero of Japanese puppet theater even today. When the Manchus overran Nanking, Coxinga and his father withdrew their forces to rugged Fukien Province, opposite the Dutch-controlled island of Taiwan, where they helped to maintain the Prince of T'ang as pretender to the Ming throne.

The Manchus were not able to defeat them, so they bribed Coxinga's father to turn traitor. Outraged, Coxinga gathered a hundred thousand warriors and, in 1659, marched into the heavily-fortified Yangtze delta. But he was a better admiral than general. He almost captured Nanking before he was turned back. He fought his way once more to his Fukien sanctuary, and then wrested the island of Taiwan from the Dutch to use it as a stronghold. For a while, Coxinga ruled both the big island and a substantial piece of the China coast around Amoy. But his rebellion came to an end in 1662, when he died suddenly of natural causes—possibly an epileptic seizure. It was his rebellion that gave birth to the new secret societies.

Although he is almost unknown in the West, Coxinga is one of China's greatest heroes, with striking similarities to Alexander the Great, and is so regarded by the Chinese Communist government. Coxinga's resistance movement included a powerful spy system and underground. After his death, this underground fragmented. But 128 militant Buddhist monks, who were part of the resistance, held out against the Manchu army at the Shaolin monastery near Foochow. They were unusually skilled at the martial art that is now called Kung Fu. A traitor betrayed them to the Manchus, and only eighteen escaped.

One by one, the heroic monks were tracked down until only five remained. These five Kung Fu masters became the nucleus of a new anti-Manchu resistance, which was organized along the lines of the ancient sects and pirate guilds of classical China. It was given the name Hung League after the first Ming Emperor, Hung Wu. The Hung League was dedicated to toppling the Manchu's Ch'ing Dynasty and to the restoration of the Ming Dynasty—a cause embodied in a patriotic slogan known to every child in China, "Fan Ch'ing fu Ming"—"Down with the Ch'ing and up with the Ming!"

Members of the Hung League spread down the coast from Foochow and Amoy to Swatow. Many of them were Hakkas who had gone into exile hundreds of years earlier. The old exiles and the new fugitives made common cause against the Manchus, and banded together to assure their collective survival. Engaging in trade and piracy and striking at the Manchus when they could, in time they reached Canton, a city deeply suspicious of strangers.

These wanderers spoke the peculiar chiu chao dialect, and kept to themselves. Since they were not accepted by the Cantonese, they formed guilds to provide themselves with shelter, assistance, and fraternity as they moved among their enemies. The guilds fulfilled both social and conspiratorial functions.

From these guilds, two main groups of secret societies evolved. In the North, where imperial control was severe, and there was less opportunity for public expression, the societies were intensely spiritual, in the form of sects. Among these were the Eight Trigrams Sect, or Fists of Harmony and Justice—whom Westerners came to call the Boxers.

In the South—far from such intensive Manchu scrutiny—the societies were less spiritual, more rambunctious. They were modeled on the bandit gangs of *The Water Margin*. They took the name "triads" after an equilateral triangle with sides representing the Chinese concept of Man, Heaven, and Earth. The triads were divided into three groups—the Heaven and Earth Society (T'ien-ti Hui), the Three Dots Society (San-tien Hui), and the Three Harmonies Society (San-ho Hui) —to which both Charlie and Dr. Sun belonged.

Membership grew rapidly. Because the Manchu conquest had fragmented Chinese life, the countryside for decades afterward was full of drifters, former soldiers, vagrants, beggars, thieves, desperadoes, murderers, journeymen, tradesmen, businessmen, itinerant craftsmen, artisans, students, and political exiles. To accommodate such diverse and growing membership, the triads multiplied until by the nineteenth century there were hundreds of secondary guilds that maintained only symbolic links to the parent orders. Some, like the widespread Society of Elders and Brothers, were Robin Hood bands of poor people, farmers, and canal boatmen, who built a complete underworld economy on smuggling. Many of the Communist guerrillas of the twentieth century came from this organization.

The triads attracted adventurers who found the upward path blocked in normal society. Through them, ambitious men could control secret funds and idle manpower, gaining extraordinary political and social leverage. Some triads were strictly patriotic, while others used patriotism to disguise purely criminal pursuits; still others combined both purposes, with an invisible "dark thread" criminal organization, on which was superimposed a patriotic and visible "light thread." Such was the Red Gang of Shanghai.

This fraternity of triads was waiting for anyone who felt alienated, outraged, or frustrated. For many it was sufficient just to be a member, with secret recognition signals—a particular way of holding a cup or rice bowl in a teashop—which made it possible to establish contact with fellow members anywhere. Like some labor unions in the West, in times of need the triad would always help. Once committed as a member, however, there was no backing out.

When Charlie Soong and Dr. Sun Yat-sen decided to combine forces with a tiny circle of other conspirators in Shanghai in 1894, their hopes of revolution depended entirely on rallying the enormous latent power of the triads. After the collapse of the Taiping Rebellion in the mid-nineteenth century, many triads had turned away from political action in favor of pure profit. It was time to lead them back to the cause for which they were first intended. Sun calculated that there were thirty-five million members of these societies throughout China, who might be drawn, once again, to the revolutionary cause. He made it clear that he intended to devote his life to the overthrow of the Manchus and the creation of an "Asia of opportunity." He invited his friends, and his secret-society brethren, to join him. Charlie Soong became one of the founding members of Sun's clandestine movement.

They immediately began plotting an armed insurrection.

In Charlie's Hongkew study, furnished in Western style with heavy black wooden chairs and a campaign-style desk, the plotters worked through the nights, preparing the uprising. Their attention was focused on Canton, where conspiracy was a part of life. In 1894, the surrounding countryside and Pearl River delta swarmed with pocket armies of brigands and smugglers, many of them known to Dr. Sun; they could be rallied against the imperial garrison. The city's underworld was ruled by triads, and their members could be counted on to support the insurrection, for a price. Once Canton was in Sun's hands, they reasoned, it would be possible to build a military force that could take back the entire nation from the Manchus.

While Sun was staying with the Soongs, a pro-Japanese Korean leader was lured to Shanghai and assassinated. Sun's small group had nothing to do with the assassination, and was in no position to capitalize on it. But there were others in the Red Gang who sought every opportunity to make trouble for the regime in Peking. The body was shipped on a Chinese naval vessel to Korea. There it was cut into pieces and put on display to discourage sedition. Japan was outraged. War seemed imminent, and it would keep the Manchus fully occupied in the north.

On August 1, 1894, hostilities began. Sun still had not started organizing men for his Canton coup. First he needed a broader political organization and a source of funds. Leaving Charlie Soong to keep him informed of developments, Sun departed for Hawaii. On November 24, 1894, he began recruiting for an organization to be called the Revive China Society (Hsing Chung Hui). One hundred and twenty Hawaiian Chinese came forward.

In December, 1894, while Sun was still searching for financial support in the islands, an urgent letter arrived from Charlie Soong: The Chinese government had suffered a series of humiliating setbacks at the hands of the Japanese. Public outrage toward the Manchus was intense. They had to move quickly. Sun was electrified. Early in January, he left Honolulu for Hong Kong. A handful of Hawaiian Chinese followed him to take part in the revolt. Charlie Soong remained in Shanghai to look after finances, and to serve as Sun's eyes and ears on the Yangtze.

In Hong Kong, Sun's group was joined by a faction headed by Yang Ch'u-wen. But they were still short of men. Time dragged on. Spring came and with it the news that China had suffered a resounding defeat in Korea. By summer 1895, only 153 fighters had been recruited. Sun and Yang, nevertheless, felt recklessly ready to launch their uprising.

To succeed, they would have to depend entirely on hired thugs— riffraff, bandits, secret-society strongarms, and demobilized Chinese soldiers.

The ninth day of the ninth month in the lunar calendar was chosen numerologically for the coup—October 26—an auspicious occasion when Chinese everywhere offered sacrifices at the graves of their ancestors. The commotion, as families milled about the countryside, would hide the movement of Sun's forces. The bulk, three thousand triad members, were to assemble in Hong Kong and sail for Canton as ordinary passengers aboard ferry boats. With them would go thousands of pistols, packed in drums marked "Portland Cement." Disembarking in Canton, this mercenary army would scatter to the homes of government officials and military commanders, murdering them or holding them prisoner till the coup succeeded.

The two organizers, Yang and Dr. Sun, divided responsibilities. Yang was to assemble the hired mercenaries in Hong Kong and dispatch them to Canton, where Sun was in charge of rallying the triads and overseeing military operations. Before setting events in motion, Sun sent a deputy to Shanghai to brief Charlie and others on final plans.

A sympathetic British journalist, Thomas A. Reid of the *China Mail* in Hong Kong, was allowed to sit in at planning sessions. To set the stage for the acceptance of the coup overseas, he began writing calculated articles. Reid portrayed South China as ripe for revolt. Once the Manchus were toppled, he claimed, a "responsible" new Chinese government would welcome the generous help and unselfish guidance of foreign governments and corporations. This bit of humbug was contrived to make foreign financial interests salivate.

"What they desire," wrote Reid grandly of the plotters, "although it seems impossible to realize any such feeling amongst a body of Chinamen, is a constitutional upheaval, to rid their country of the iniquitous system of misrule which has shut out China from Western influences, Western trade, and Western civilization."

The first hitch came two weeks before the coup. On October 9, a proclamation of war was drafted by one of Dr. Sun's Revive China party members, named Chu Ch'i. It was to be posted in Canton on the day of the uprising. By drafting this document, the man jeopardized his entire family. If the coup failed, everyone in his clan could be punished. Chu's elder brother, who was not involved in the scheme, but who by tradition was responsible for the safety of the family, decided to inform the officials.

Hearing from him of the plot, the Manchu authorities in Canton had a good laugh. Nobody believed that Sun Yat-sen was anything but a harmless dilettante and egocentric. Nevertheless, as a precaution, agents were assigned to watch his movements closely. Aware of being followed, Sun avoided doing anything suspicious. The agents reported that he was as usual up to nothing.

In the pre-dawn hours on October 26, trouble came from an unexpected quarter. In Hong Kong, where Yang's mercenaries had gathered, an argument began over who should get the choicest weapons. While they quarreled on the dock, the ferry boat sailed without them.

Frantic, Yang cabled Canton advising Dr. Sun that "the goods" would have to be sent the next day. Sun was in a terrible dilemma. His hired thugs and triad buckos were already in position to attack. If they proceeded without the Hong Kong contingent, it would mean certain failure. The sensible thing to do was to call everything off. Sun paid his goons and sent them home.

But, before his reply reached Hong Kong that the uprising had indeed been canceled, the quarrel over weapons was settled and Yang's mercenary force set sail aboard the *Powan* one day late. The Hong Kong police knew all about the conspiracy by then, and an inspector wired the Manchu authorities in Canton. When the *Powan* docked, a large contingent of imperial soldiers was waiting on the wharf. In the commotion, most of the mercenaries escaped, but the leaders were arrested along with fifty rebels.

In other parts of Canton, soldiers raided hideouts of the Revive China party, capturing plotters, weapons, uniforms, and rebel flags. Dr. Sun took refuge at the home of a Chinese Christian minister and then fled to Macao, disguised as a woman in a curtained sedan chair. From Macao he escaped to Hong Kong by boat.

The fate of the captured insurgents was typical of Manchu justice. Two of Sun's close comrades were beheaded. Another was beaten to death with six hundred strokes of a "military stick." Another was hacked to pieces in what was called "the Death of a Thousand Cuts"— the official punishment for treason.

In the aftermath of this fiasco, Sun Yat-sen became a fugitive. A reward was offered for his capture.

His plot had failed, but overnight he had become a celebrity—the acknowledged champion of the anti-Manchu cause.

For the next sixteen years, he would be a hunted criminal, living in exile, unable to return to Chinese soil. More than ever, he would come to depend on Charlie Soong for money and other party leaders to manage the revolution for him. He wandered from country to country, drawing support from Overseas Chinese, but always on the run.

To escape pursuit, Dr. Sun left Hong Kong immediately for Japan with two lieutenants. Disembarking in Kobe, they discovered that the Japanese were well informed of events in Canton and were calling the disastrous uprising part of a serious "revolution." Sun was flattered. His constituency was growing. He decided to go on to Hawaii, where his following was more substantial.

Before sailing, he concluded that the time had come for a disguise. He was too conspicuous wandering the globe in a Chinaman's robes with a long queue. He hacked off his queue, trimmed his hair evenly in the Western style, and acquired a business suit. For a final touch, he grew a mustache. The result was startling. He looked like a distinguished Japanese diplomat.

When he reached Hawaii in January 1896, Sun's family were already there in the care of his brother, Sun Mei. Sun's wife was a girl his father had chosen, the daughter of a village merchant. Her name was Lu Mu-chun. In the past, when he was traveling or studying in Hong Kong, he had left her in the village, and had seen her only infrequently. This reunion in Hawaii produced their third child, a girl born in November 1896.

After six months in the islands, Sun decided to seek support for the first time in Chinese communities on the American mainland. To smooth the way, he joined another Cantonese triad—the American wing of the Chih Kung Tong. Because of his mastery of the martial arts, he was given the high rank of Red Pole, or Enforcer.

The Chih Kung Tong was the most energetic triad in America at the time. It had its roots in Kwangtung Province, where its members were smugglers, pirates, and coastal traders. The tong had played a key role in the Taiping Rebellion of the 1850s, and when the Taipings were defeated, many tong members fled to America, where they established branches of the society. There were a number of other triads in America. The On Leong, based in New York City, held sway over Chinatowns as far west as Denver. On the West Coast, the Bing Kung Tong ruled Vancouver and San Francisco. The Hip Sing Tong was also strong in San Francisco and New York, while the Ying On Tong dominated the Southwest. Two smaller triads, the Hop Sing and the Suey Sing, were powerful in Los Angeles. Sun now had access to all of these associations through his membership in the Chih Kung Tong.

In San Francisco, however, Sun made a dangerous blunder. He posed for a photograph. A copy fell into the hands of Manchu agents and was sent to Peking. Descriptions of the "new" Dr. Sun were circulated immediately to Chinese legations around the world.

This first American tour produced little cash and few recruits. Life in the United States was difficult enough for Chinese without underwriting a revolution that would further distress Washington.

Sun sailed on to England to visit his friend Dr. Cantlie. The moment he arrived, he was spotted by plainclothesmen from the Slater Detective Agency, which had been hired by the Chinese Government to track him down. The gumshoes followed him to Cantlie's home in London's Devonshire Street, and watched as Sun moved into modest lodgings not far away at Grey's Inn Place.

Paradoxically, the Chinese legation was situated in Portland Place, just around the corner from Dr. Cantlie's home. Dr. Sun strolled past the legation every time he visited his friend. His ego soon got the best of him. He believed that his disguise was so effective that nobody at the legation would recognize him. He could walk right in and chat, and stroll out again without anyone's being the wiser.

Unable to resist the temptation, on Saturday, October 10, he sauntered up to the door of the legation, where he engaged a Chinese student in conversation. When Sun asked about other Cantonese, he was taken inside and introduced to a translator named Teng. Sun gave his name as Ch'en Tsai-chih, but the sharp-eyed translator noticed that the stranger's watch was inscribed with the name Sun. Coolly, Sun discussed the instability of the Manchu regime. Then, unaware that he had aroused suspicion, he left.

When he had gone, the translator alerted his superiors. They were startled, because Sun had given Slater's flatfoots the slip several days earlier. If he had been foolhardy enough to walk into their den once, he might try again. The legation assigned translator Teng to keep watch on the street and to lure Sun inside if he reappeared. Two sinewy Manchu security men were posted just inside the entrance.

The next day, Sunday, October 11, 1896, Sun left his rooms without awakening the dozing Slater man who was supposed to be keeping an eye on him, and walked again to Portland Place, bound for Cantlie's home. He saw a Chinese lounging by the legation entrance. It was translator Teng. While they talked, Teng maneuvered Sun closer to the entrance. The two Manchu goons came out, got between Sun and the street, and invited him inside for more "talk" over spicy Hunanese food. They had their gnarled hands on his arms, guiding him inside. The door slammed shut. Sun was hustled upstairs to a room specially emptied of furnishings for the occasion.

The Chinese legation in London was headed by Minister Kung Chao-yun, representative of the Ch'ing Dynasty in Peking. But daily operations were administered by an Englishman, Sir Halliday Macartney, who served as secretary of the legation. He was a descendant of Lord Macartney who led the first British mission to China in 1793. (The

Ch'ien Lung Emperor rebuffed the British famously: "Our Celestial Kingdom possesses all things in prolific abundance and lacks no product within our borders." Therefore, said the Emperor, there was "no need to import the manufactures of . . . barbarians.")

Sir Halliday Macartney had served as a military surgeon in the Crimea, and later enjoyed a distinguished career with British colonial administrations in India and China. There, he came to the attention of the Grand Secretary, and was hired by the Chinese government to handle diplomatic affairs with the Court of St. James's. He was another of those fastidious British mandarins whose Oriental natures were more inscrutable than the Chinese themselves.

Macartney had already applied to the British government to extradite Dr. Sun if he came to Great Britain. The request was turned down, but that did nothing to alter Macartney's determination to play havoc with this yellow mountebank. Once he had Sun captive in the legation, Macartney began making arrangements with the Glen Line to charter a ship and smuggle the hapless revolutionary illegally out of England to his certain and painful death.

Cooped up in his room, Dr. Sun tried everything to slip a message out to Dr. Cantlie. He threw notes out the barred window, only to have it nailed shut. He attempted to bribe the legation's English porter, George Cole, who was assigned to guard him. But the porter remained steadfast.

Meanwhile, Dr. Cantlie was alarmed by Sun's disappearance. He decided to call in detectives and (naturally) turned to the largest and most prestigious investigative agency in London at the time, Slater's. That worthy organization saw nothing wrong in serving two masters and gladly undertook to "find" Dr. Sun for Dr. Cantlie. (In point of fact, they did not know where Sun was, even after he had been captured by their other employer.)

While the porter stubbornly refused Sun's pleas for help, he did discuss the prisoner's pathetic predicament with the legation's housekeeper, an Englishwoman named Mrs. Howe. A woman of gumption, she decided that something must be done.

A week after Sun's capture, Mrs. Howe rang Dr. Cantlie's bell, stuffed a note into his mailbox, and hurried away. The note read:

> There is a friend of yours imprisoned in the Chinese Legation here, since last Sunday. They intend sending him out to China, where it is certain that they will hang him. It is very sad for the poor man, and unless

something is done at once he will be taken away and no one will know it. I dare not sign my name, but this is the truth, so believe what I say. Whatever you do must be done at once or it will be too late. His name, I believe, is Lin Yen Sen.

The next day, with Mrs. Howe's example burning his conscience, porter George Cole appeared at Cantlie's house bearing a secret message from Dr. Sun written on two business cards.

I was kidnapped into the Chinese Legation on Sunday, and shall be smuggled out from England to China for death. Pray rescue me quick; A ship is already charter by the C.L. [Chinese Legation] for the service to take me to China and I shall be locked up all the way without communication to anybody. . . . O! Woe to me!

Cantlie and a colleague, the famous expert on mosquito-borne diseases, Dr. Patrick Manson—also a friend of Sun's from Hong Kong school days—contacted Scotland Yard and the Foreign Office. Dr. Manson rushed to the legation and asked about Sun, but was told there was nobody by that name inside.

By Sunday night Cantlie was desperate. Neither the Foreign Office nor Scotland Yard had taken any action. He rushed to the *Times* and gave the story to their editors. But the Monday edition made no mention of Sun. The editors had chosen to be discreet until the government decided on a proper course of action. The editors of the *Globe* were less concerned about diplomatic protocol. When they got wind of the story, they ran a special edition. Reporters descended on the legation, and one warned translator Teng that if Sun was not released immediately there would be an angry mob outside by morning.

Indeed, by dawn the story was in every London paper and the public clamor was deafening in Sun's behalf. The Foreign Office, moved to action, issued an ultimatum to Macartney. At 4:30 P.M. October 23, twelve days after Sun's capture, Scotland Yard Chief Inspector Jarvis arrived at the legation with Dr. Cantlie and a Queen's home messenger sent by the Foreign Office to claim the hostage.

As spectators and newsmen swarmed around the entrance, Dr. Sun was brought out and driven away in a hansom to Scotland Yard, a free man.

Once again, a ludicrous blunder had catapulted Dr. Sun into prominence. He was now world famous. Journalists demanded interviews.

Sun enjoyed the celebrity. He hid the fact that he had brought the affair on his own head, and glamorized his role by claiming that he had been tricked and captured. His memoir, which was a clever exercise in thimblerigging, was published in England under the title *Kidnapped in London.* Sun Yat-sen became a household name. Copies of the book were reprinted and distributed in China with great glee by Charlie Soong and his friends.

Given Dr. Sun's propensity for disaster, we might be forgiven for wondering how he maintained his hold on his followers. What was his magic? In retrospect, with the advantage of hindsight and the collection of information over the years by many scholars, Sun's adventures take on a picaresque folly that would endear him to Viennese fans of *opéra bouffe.* But this was not apparent in Sun's day. The participants were too close to events. Revolutionary passion lent a terrible drama to each horrific setback. It was not possible to recognize the comic proportions of a fiasco when it resulted in gruesome beheadings, mutilations, and slow strangulation. Sun's pratfalls were not comic opera so much as *grand guignol,* taken with deadly seriousness by the participants, if not by all of the audience. (The British Foreign Office did not take him very seriously.)

Also, there were many conspirators involved, and Sun only appears to blame when his case is seen in isolation. He was unquestionably gifted. He was an impassioned orator, able to illuminate the cause he championed, and to inspire to action those who might otherwise have wasted their energy and ardor in drunken conspiratorial discussion, where most revolutions are stillborn. If he was in some respects superficial, it might have been this quality alone that kept him alive while other, better revolutionaries were being murdered. There was a great deal of carnage going on. Many firebrands and plotters died grisly deaths. Perhaps there were among them men and women of much greater nobility than Sun, but they were too engaged to last. Sun's quirks kept him slightly disengaged, so Sun always survived.

Those who survive also rewrite. History is constantly falsified, creating a perpetual struggle between propaganda and fact. Thus Sun's narrative of the kidnapping in London was heroic, mythic propaganda, and became the gospel. Many years later, after his death, a systematic program of deification raised his image to godlike stature. In the end Sun's true art was levitation, and his leadership endured, like that of many famous leaders, simply because he survived while all around him were dying. He had the intuition of Don Giovanni—to sense when it is time to leave by the balcony. He was, in a word, China's first modern politician.

Free to come and go as he pleased, Sun spent the next six months reading in the British Museum Library, making such provocative friends as the revolutionary exile Felix Volkhovsky, editor of the journal *Free Russia.*

At long last, in July 1897, Dr. Sun turned his back on London and sailed for Japan, which was to be his base of operations for the next few years. He was welcomed there by a group of powerful Japanese political ronin—energetic and dangerous men who would have been samurai in medieval Japan but now were freelance adventurers. These were impassioned men of the cut who founded the superpatriotic Black Dragon Society a few years later and thrust Japan into its headlong Asian military adventure. They became Sun's protectors, sponsors, and fellow conspirators. They saw him not only as a way to topple China's imperial government but, more important, as a means of expelling the Western powers from East Asia. The heady vision of Japan as the leader of a pan-Asian renaissance consumed them. Among these influential Japanese were Sugarawa Den, Miyazaki Torazo, Inukai Ki, Okuma Shigenobu, and Soejima Taneomi.

During the next eight years, Sun orchestrated several more unsuccessful revolts. He was now excluded from British Hong Kong as well as from the Chinese mainland, so he had to work through secret political agents from a distance. He was establishing revolutionary cells in each Chinese city and building his party organization. Charlie Soong kept all the financial records and membership rolls, invested every coin that came in to enlarge party coffers, and held regular planning meetings with other leaders at his printing press on Shantung Road. He was not the primary organizer, but one of the handful of leaders forming the inner circle. Their campaign depended heavily on the circulation of revolutionary literature produced secretly at his Sino-American Press.

The continuing humiliation of China by the West after the 1900 Boxer Rebellion eventually gave new momentum to Sun's cause. The Boxers are usually written off in the West as a bunch of fanatical Chinese who came out of nowhere, but they were driven into their rebellion by the mistreatment of Chinese workers by German colonial officials and mine owners in Shantung Province. Thus their protest was originally against the highhandedness of foreigners, and against an imperial government that was unable or unwilling to stand up to foreign pressure. When foreign troops marched into Peking to teach the Boxers and the imperial government a lesson, the Empress Dowager and her court fled. China's humiliation was complete. Angry Chinese students from then on came to Japan in ever-increasing numbers, seeking to master both scientific and military training. These students formed the core of a new and more radical revolutionary force. Many of them gathered around Dr. Sun, regarding him as the established revolutionary. To capitalize on this support, Sun persuaded leaders of a rival anti-Manchu faction to combine forces with him in a new organization called the Alliance party (Tung-men Hui).

The Alliance party brought together for the first time the traditional secret-society membership, composed mainly of merchants and working-class people, with radical intellectuals and young students. It was a volatile mixture.

An organizational meeting was held in Tokyo on July 30, 1905. Charlie Soong came from Shanghai. It was a closed session to plan political strategy. Most of the discussion, quite naturally, was about money. Dr. Sun asked Charlie Soong to shoulder the burden. To have any chance of success, they had to have more than a dribble of donations. A serious windfall was needed. They were all aware that Charlie had unusually wealthy connections in America of a personal kind beyond the reach of the rest of them. It was agreed to send him in search of millions.

Chapter 4

THE MONEYMAN

In the years since that first disastrous Canton uprising, Charlie's publishing ventures had sprouted like bamboo shoots. The Sino-American Press was turning out dozens of secular and religious titles, including the Soochow Colloquial Testament—one of the first Bibles in vernacular Chinese—devised by his old friend Dr. Park.

As Charlie's operations expanded, he became something of a Shanghai character, and was known to Westerners as "Charlie Soong, the Bible printer." He joined other investors in launching the Commercial Press of Shanghai, to produce Western textbooks for China and to do mass commercial printing. It became one of the biggest publishers in East Asia. Charlie Soong's growing empire covered the spectrum from political leaflets and Bibles to engineering texts, masterworks of Chinese literature, and noodles. Encouraged by Julian Carr, Charlie invested in tobacco and cotton factories, and imported industrial machinery for them. By 1904, his personal fortune was well established. His liquid assets went to the revolution.

As part of his contribution, Charlie brought the Shanghai Chinese YMCA into existence. Senior party leaders still met at his house in Hongkew or at his original printing shop on Shantung Road. But party rank-and-file used the YMCA as a safe house, where they could meet and mingle without attracting attention.

Charlie had put on weight and his eyes were a bit sad. Rumpled slacks and a white shirt and striped regimental tie tugged loose at the throat gave him the look of a harried Kansas City newspaper editor. His role as a revolutionary was known to only a few of his Western friends, including missionary William Burke and his wife, Addie. For the time being, he seemed safe from discovery. As a precaution, however, he purchased a Portuguese passport, claiming he had been born in Macao. Although passports were not yet in universal use and were not necessary for him to enter Japan, Portuguese citizenship would get around the new Chinese exclusion laws in America. If there was trouble, he and his family could take refuge in the United States.

In 1905, when Charlie sailed to America for Dr. Sun, he traveled as a man of means, with his own stateroom aboard a Pacific Mail steamer. When his ship docked in San Francisco he was welcomed by members of the Chih Kung Tong. The tong had its headquarters at 36 Spofford Alley, and Charlie was taken there for a round of introductions to Chinese bankers and businessmen. Although this triad was later one of the targets of a U.S. Treasury investigation into narcotics trafficking, opium was not illegal in 1905 and heroin had not been invented. The Chih Kung Tong was passing itself off amiably as "the Chinese Free Masons of the World," and a small sign to that effect hung over the Spofford Alley entrance. Among these wealthy Chinese-Americans, anxious to prove their patriotic fervor, Charlie's was a profitable stay in terms of fund raising for the party, but he remained in San Francisco only a few weeks. The main object of his trip was to see Julian Carr.

Carr was now the very personification of a Southern gentleman. His hair and mustache had gone white. He bore a striking resemblance to Mark Twain. In 1895 he had sold Bull Durham for $3 million, which was a magnificent sum in that day, putting Carr in the league of America's richest men. His total worth may have been three times that figure. He plunged into a new venture, launching the Durham Hosiery Mills to capitalize on his leverage in the cotton industry. The mills grew to be the largest manufacturer of hosiery in the world. At the Democratic National Convention in 1900, he was nominated for Vice President of the United States by delegates from North Carolina. He turned down the nomination. In the countryside, he started an experimental farm called Occoneechee, which became one of the leading agricultural and botanical research stations of its day.

It was during the Spanish-American War of 1898 that Carr gave his most spectacular display of generosity. As Durham men marched off to fight, Carr—who had a passion for just causes—announced that he would support any family left behind. He also asked the families of one white company of soldiers and one black company (consisting of 120 men each) from other towns in North Carolina to send their bills to him for all living expenses for the duration of the campaign. As a climax, he traveled to Florida, where troops were preparing for action against the Spaniards in Cuba. In Jacksonville, where he found the 1st North Carolina Regiment encamped, Carr saw to it that they were provided with every luxury possible without violating military regulations on camp life—and handed the commanding officer $25,000 to cover future expenses.

Julian Carr had a habit of backing his beliefs with money. He had taken up the cause of a young Chinese boy more than twenty years earlier because he believed in Charlie Soong, taken him into his home and paid for his education. Now Charlie was on his way to present Carr with a new cause.

This time, when Carr met Charlie at the station in Durham, it was a meeting of equals.

Charlie was no longer the gawky adolescent Celestial who had stepped off the train from Wilmington in 1881. He was now a wealthy panda bear of a man, wearing a three-piece blue serge and his favorite crumpled felt fedora.

The two men rode in an open carriage to the east end of Main Street, to a palatial mansion standing in five acres of gardens. This was Carr's famed Somerset Villa, named after an ancestor, Robert Carr, who was said to have been the Earl of Somerset. Carr was now so rich that he could not find adequate ways to use the money, and had become ostentatious. His Durham mansion was hailed as one of the nation's showplaces. Unlike mansions in Newport, Carr's was not a baronial chateau of carved stone. It was crafted of local pine in an elaborate Victorian gingerbread with turrets, gables, and ornate protuberances. Balconies were attached wherever the spirit moved, one stretching 220 feet. Atop a turret like a witch's hat on a plum pudding was a copper weathervane that cost a trifling $500. With the exception of Vanderbilt's Biltmore estate in Asheville, North Carolina, Carr's grounds were said to be "the most magnificent piece of landscape gardening in the South." Handyman John O'Daniels and landscape specialists from Holland, France, and Ireland had composed a symphony of dahlias, phlox, periwinkles, hydrangeas, sage, cannae, mallowmarble, calla lilies, roses, and percallas. One forty-foot bed of red, blue, and white blooms was cultivated into an American flag; another bed of gold and bronze blooms formed an American bald eagle with a thirty-foot wing span.

Inside, the opulence continued. Somerset has been called "one of the most beautiful and complete private houses in the world." Rays of color streamed from stained-glass windows, and cut crystal chandeliers had cost $5,000 apiece. This was one of the few homes in North Carolina that enjoyed both gas and electric lights. It also had a complete burglar and fire alarm. (Carr was a cautious man, who carried one million dollars' worth of insurance on his own life.) Forty thousand dollars' worth of carpets and furnishings adorned the rooms. The dominant feature of the main hall was a huge stained-glass portrayal of the poem "Curfew Must Not Ring Tonight." In it, a voluptuous maid, dressed only in flowing folds of cloth, clung erotically to the clapper of a huge bell —"There 'twixt heaven and earth suspended as the bell swung to and fro." To make the elegance complete, the ceilings were painted with cupids, and there were bathrooms of Italian marble.

In the following weeks, Charlie accompanied Julian Carr to the Old Club, Durham's private refuge for established merchants at the corner of Main and Market streets. In a setting of oak paneling and leather chairs stained with sour-mash bourbon, Charlie held long conversations with Carr and other old friends, including Miss Annie's brother, J. H. Southgate. Carr had rounded up old chums from Trinity and Vanderbilt, who were now preachers and shopkeepers. A couple of the professors from Trinity tottered by to catch up with the affairs of the little Chinaman who had been expelled for paying too much attention to the daughter of a faculty colleague. They found him prosperous, vigorous, and confident.

One of those present was T. M. Gorman, Carr's private secretary. Gorman observed later that Charlie seemed very much at home in the club, having many interests in common with the local rich men.

But Gorman was not present during subsequent weeks at Somerset, when Charlie and Julian Carr privately discussed the real purpose of his visit. In the study, furnished with leather-covered Chesterfields and lined with bookcases and paintings, Charlie gave a detailed accounting of the armed uprisings that went awry, and the cruelties and barbarities of the Manchus to captured revolutionaries. Given the type of man he was, Julian Carr must have been outraged at the contemplation of mass beheadings, live burials, slow strangulations, and deaths-of-a-thousand-slashes. As the person mainly responsible for looking after Dr. Sun's finances, Charlie believed that the uprisings had faltered largely because of inadequate funds. Organization suffered, shortcuts were taken, men acted in haste, with disastrous consequences. Their object was to free China of despotism. If they ever succeeded, the enormous human resources of China could be lifted from serfdom into a new life. Christianity would have a chance to flower. The odds against them were great. But, if they could liberate just one corner of Chinese territory, there would be a rush of native funds. Confidence in the revolution would spread among wealthy Overseas Chinese, millions of dollars would become available, and the revolution would become self-sustaining.

Julian Carr had his own bank down the street, and was in a position to place his hands upon a very large sum. His involvement in the Spanish-American War had cost him over $100,000 in a few months. Unlike the Spanish War, in which he had no personal connection, here was his lifelong protégé, Charlie Soong, a Christian leader of his own community, who was one of the principals of a struggle to free a quarter of the earth's population.

Although Gorman later failed to discover any record of financial transactions between Julian Carr and Charlie, not even a notation on a request for funds, he was convinced that the General gave Charlie a considerable sum. It was Carr's way.

When Charlie's Durham visit ended, he traveled north by train to New York City and vanished from view. He had business among the Overseas Chinese—fund-raising better done discreetly. He went about like a large carp in a muddy river, leaving a few surface ripples here and there to mark his coming and going, but no other sign.

In his New York ventures, brother-in-law B. C. Wen paved Charlie's way. It was a curious role Wen was playing in the revolution. Outwardly, he was a trusted educational advisor to the Empress Dowager. But he led a double life. Like his cousin, S. C. New, he opened doors for Charlie Soong and, by extension, for the republican plotters against the throne. Wen and New were part of the Shanghai ruling class. They occupied an enviable position not unlike the German banking families, the Fuggers and the Welsers, who financed Spain's conquest of the New World. In New York, Wen opened financial doors for Charlie and introduced him to the leaders of the Chinese community, and to Chinese bankers.

When he went home to Shanghai, Charlie turned over more than two million U.S. dollars to the treasury of the Alliance party. The figure is given by a variety of sources, including the Chinese Ambassador Alfred Sze in his address at Duke University in 1936. Certainly some of the money came from many people, but all the indications are that the lion's share came from his old friend and benefactor, Julian Carr.

Thanks to his success in raising cash during his 1905–1906 tour of North America, Charlie Soong was appointed Treasurer of the Revolutionary Alliance, a responsibility he had previously undertaken only informally. He was now officially responsible for financing the revolution. He continued to serve as Executive Secretary of Dr. Sun's party headquarters in Shanghai and to provide from his own pocket for Sun's personal expenses, essentially guaranteeing that the doctor could keep going no matter what.

After 1907 it became increasingly difficult to keep track of Dr. Sun, because he was constantly forced to leave one country for another, under diplomatic pressure from the Dragon Throne. The life of a fugitive was difficult, but he was wined and dined and favored by ladies. He was a master at rousing the passions of men who had been away too long from the Middle Kingdom. For a long time, Dr. Sun had been permitted to operate freely in Japan. But in 1907 the Japanese government, uneasy over the growing numbers of Chinese radicals on the islands, gave Sun money and asked him politely to leave. He went to Indochina, where he continued plotting in the big Chinese communities of Hanoi and Saigon. He had the support of sympathetic French authorities, who profited heavily in the opium trade with China, and who maintained lucrative ties with the secret societies in the Shanghai French Concession. Sino-French pocket armies roamed the upper reaches of the Red River and the Mekong River, along the back borders of China, smuggling goods and purchasing raw opium from the hill-tribe cultivators.

Sun Yat-sen saw these private opium armies as a means to harass the Manchu regime on its poorly-guarded rump, perhaps gaining control of a portion of Kwangsi or Yunnan Province. He accepted the generous offer of his Hanoi backers to put their "armies" to good use. A series of skirmishes ensued in which Dr. Sun's borrowed soldiers briefly held a piece of Manchu territory, before the startled Chinese garrison counterattacked. Sun's force then commandeered a train and fled back into French territory with their enemy in hot pursuit. The result was an international incident between China and France. Although the Manchus were clearly the injured party, the affair ended, as most did in those days, with China paying France an indemnity. In return, France obliged the Manchus by pressing Dr. Sun to leave Hanoi.

He went to Singapore and then to Bangkok, where he immediately stirred up another anthill. A remarkable letter from the flustered American Minister in Bangkok, Hamilton King—long buried in State Department archives—reveals Dr. Sun's complex character and slippery method of operation. It is addressed to Secretary of State Elihu Root and dated December 15, 1908:

> On his arrival in the city he very quietly went about his mission; but the local press both Chinese, Siamese and English immediately opened up on topics relating to The Chinese Revolution and The Revolutionists, using the Doctor's name, making mention of his work and reviewing his career up to the time of his coming to Siam. They called the attention of the Siamese Government to their duty as a government friendly to China, and the police were set to watch his movements and to report on his meetings.
>
> On December 4, Sun Yat Sen was summoned before the Mayor of the City and the Chief of the Police and during a conversation, in referring to which all speak of the Doctor as a courteous gentleman, he was told that his presence was causing a growing unrest among the large number of Chinamen in the city, and of the peculiar conditions that obtained in Siam, and was requested to leave the city in three days. He manifested much surprise, remarked that the notice given him was very short and said that he would have to beg an extension of time that he might arrange his business; and when asked how much time he would require said at least a week. On being urged he calmly replied that he would have to see his Minister before he gave the final word; asked who his Minister was he avoided the questions and courteously excused himself.
>
> It seems that up to this time, the idea of this Chinaman's being under the protection of another government had never occurred to any one in the Siamese Government, and to this day it is suspected by very few of any nationalities in the city. A few hours after, accompanied by his friend of The Chino-Siamese Daily News, he called at the American Legation. In this extended interview, during which time his friend remained outside, the Doctor revealed that this was the first time in the Orient that he had mentioned his relation to the American Government.—It will be observed that Siam was the first place in which he had found American jurisdiction. Dr. Sun Yat Sen is a graduate of the Hongkong Medical School; as a child he wished to be educated in America but, having professed Christianity with much of zeal, his father denied the request and sent him to China. He no longer professes the Christian faith. He speaks English excellently

with something of an accent, is intelligent, of mental strength and alertness and a man of decided character. He is fine looking, of rather distinguished bearing, mild in manner and at all times courteous. He wears no queue.
. . . .

Dr. Sun Yat Sen was born in Hawaii of Chinese mother and father— His passport and certificate of birth are enclosed—He had been twice in America the first time as a Chinaman and the last time in 1904 as an American citizen, when he had trouble in entering, as his papers show— He affirms that the question was raised because his status had changed and he bore an American passport at this time while he passed as a Chinaman before—He left America last on the 4th of December, 1904, since which time he has been traveling and lecturing on "Republican Institutions, educating the Chinese outside of China, advocating a republican form of government in place of the present form, the placing of the Chinamen in power, and China for the Chinese." He is an admirer of America and illustrates his lectures by examples from the government of the United States.

He was several months in Japan where he met with much of sympathy and assistance on all sides, but at a request from the government of China, Japan asked him to move on. In Japan he found a large and encouraging field for his work.

Later he was in French Indo-China and mixed in the rebellion on the Yunnan Province frontier. He said he found much of sympathy among the French officials, but at the request of the government at Peking the French government requested him to move on. In Cochin-China there are 160,-000 Chinamen, but few in Tonkin and Annam.

Previous to coming to Bangkok he had been at work in the Federated Malay States and in Singapore. He left Singapore on his own accord because he had learned that the Chinese Government had requested the British Government to ask him to move on. . . .
. . . .

His father was a wealthy planter in Hawaii; and Sun Yat Sen together with his brother owns estates there, which are worked by the brother. His wife and three children reside there.

At his request I am forwarding the Department his application for registration, which step also served me well in developing the case. Born in Territory not belonging to the United States at the time of his birth, but which later was made Territory of the United States by annexation, I presumed to use the application of a native born citizen—I shall be pleased to have the Department's ruling on this point—With the application I enclose his passport and also his certificate of birth.

This amusing letter demonstrates how easily Dr. Sun invented the truth to suit his purposes, how relaxed he was about taking oaths of allegiance. He carried a variety of sworn documents, including "affidavits" from "witnesses" claiming to have known him since he was "born" in Hawaii.

The U.S. government had no way of knowing whether his papers were counterfeit. Instead of confiscating them, the Department of State returned Sun's forged U.S. passport and fake birth certificate to Bangkok three months later. In a covering letter to King, the department went on record that Sun Yat-sen was indeed an American citizen, but had not been behaving like one.

> It appears that under section 4 of the Act of Congress of April 30, 1900 "providing a government for the Territory of Hawaii" Sun Yat Sen was made a citizen of the United States, but whether he is now entitled to protection as such is another question. Citizenship involves duties and obligations as well as rights. Sun Yat Sen had to choose between the duties involved in his political ties and the claims of blood. It seems clear that he has chosen the latter and has identified himself with the Chinese nation. He not only performs no duties of American citizenship, but is wholly engaged in the politics of China. Furthermore, he appears to be a leader in the agitation against a government with which this Government is on friendly terms.
>
> . . . there may be some question as to whether Sun Yat Sen has finally expatriated himself, but the Department does not consider that he is entitled to a passport or to registration as an American citizen, or to the protection of this Government, so long as he continues in his present course. Mr. Sun's papers are enclosed herewith.

In other words, Sun was an American citizen and would not lose his citizenship if he remained indefinitely abroad. But he could not expect protection if he continued rabble-rousing.

Had the department bothered to pass this correspondence on to its diplomatic mission in Peking, there would have been a howl of outrage. The American Minister in Peking considered Dr. Sun to be a "notorious revolutionist" and would have been astounded to hear him called an American citizen.

Unlike Don Quixote, Dr. Sun was a sly, wary, ever-shifting adversary—full of mercurial changes of personality. He lied frequently and flamboyantly, shifting blithely from one set of principles to another as the occasion required. He was a political chameleon.

Critics of the Soongs, on the other hand, have portrayed Charlie as a scheming climber who saw Sun Yat-sen as a means to gain power and prestige. One critic, Percy Chen, wrote:

> It was a matter of principle, in the old days before the liberation of China by the Chinese Communist party, that every Chinese would "look for the opportunity." When this opportunity came, it was essential to recognize it and seize it, for such an opportunity might never again come his way. Charles Soong probably saw in Dr. Sun Yat-sen just that opportunity. It was risky, but it still might be the means to fortune for himself and his family. The opportunity did not come in his lifetime, but it certainly did for his children.

How wrong Chen was. Dr. Sun was doing what he did best, taking his traveling road show from Singapore to Saskatoon. Charlie Soong was his manager. They were mutually dependent. When the two came to a parting of the ways, Charlie was the one injured.

On the other hand, Percy Chen was absolutely right about Charlie's children.

Chapter 5

THE PRODIGIES

In the fifteen years since Charlie had resigned from the Methodist Mission, he had fathered four more children, and the dynasty was nearly complete.

After the girls Ai-ling and Ching-ling, Kwei-tseng gave birth to their first son on December 4, 1894. He was given the Chinese name Tse-ven and was christened Paul, but became known simply as T. V.

Next came another girl. She was born in 1897, on the twelfth day of the second month in the old lunar calendar—March 5. She was a chubby child, with a moon face. In keeping with the style set with the other girls, Ai-ling and Ching-ling, Charlie called the new baby May-ling ("beautiful mood").

She was followed by two more boys—T. L. (Tse-liang) and T. A. (Tse-an). With three girls and three boys, the children were neatly balanced.

Madame Soong became more pious with the birth of the last of her brood, and began to run the house in Hongkew with a heavy hand. Charlie took to calling her Mammy, the way Julian Carr called his wife Nannie, but there the similarity ended. Prayers were said every day, and the children were strictly forbidden to indulge in such depravities as dancing or card playing. This transformation, from energetic young wife to pious dowager, occurred at the turn of the century, after the birth of May-ling. It was as if the year 1900 was the high noon in her life, and the revelry of morning was succeeded by the sober realities of afternoon. This change was also visible in the personalities of the children. The first four were full of life and mischief, spilling over with energy and invention. The last two—T. L. and T. A.—were subdued and wary.

Charlie had a great deal to do with it. He had encouraged his first children, catering to their moods, giving them everything they wanted, convincing them that anything in life was attainable, the world was at their feet. He enlarged their appetites, creating expectations that could only be fulfilled by the most extraordinary drive and rapacity. He was full of stories about his own adventures. He was a living example of how anything was possible to those who dared.

But by the time the last two boys were born, Charlie was too busy to devote the time he had lavished on the others. He was becoming a millionaire, and he had taken on the responsibility of Executive Secretary of the revolutionary party, maintaining close contact with Dr. Sun in exile. As a result, only the children born before 1900 were incandescent.

His favorite was Ai-ling. She was a tomboy, stocky and plain as a tree stump. But she was smart and quick, with a natural shrewdness that he fed by taking her everywhere with him, showing her the inner operations of the publishing house and the flour mill, the tobacco factories and textile plants, revealing the city and its predatory undercurrents as they rode about the streets in his private rickshaw, pulled by a man who doubled as his bodyguard. Ai-ling became a fixture in his offices. She sat watching coolly from the background, pie-pan face expressionless, while businessmen came to wheedle money from her father, or to engage him in murky investments.

When she pronounced herself ready for school at age five, her mother scoffed, but Charlie took Ai-ling to see Helen Richardson, the principal of McTyeire School for Girls. This was the most fashionable and exclusive foreign school in Shanghai, named for the same Bishop McTyeire who had made Charlie's life miserable as a missionary. Miss Richardson was an exceptional woman and an educator of no mean accomplishment. She was already well-acquainted with Charlie's children from Sunday school, and had been aware for some time that Charlie had an interesting problem on his hands. His eldest daughter was extremely precocious and much older than her years.

Miss Richardson listened to Charlie make his case, and agreed to take Ai-ling as a special student. She would be tutored by Miss Richardson personally. The arrangement was not unlike the circumstances that

Charlie had enjoyed at Trinity College. Miss Richardson appreciated the need to bend some rules.

When the term began, Ai-ling bade farewell to her mother and set out with Charlie for McTyeire School. Years later she told her friend Emily Hahn about that first day, and remembered it clearly. She was dressed neatly in green trousers and a plaid jacket, her hair in pigtails and ribbons. In her right pocket was a small box of Callard & Bowser's butterscotch, and in her left another of their bittersweet chocolate. A second rickshaw followed behind them, carrying a new black footlocker loaded with her clothing and personal effects, all neatly marked for boarding school.

It was only after Charlie had left her in Miss Richardson's study, and the heavy door closed behind him, that the tears came.

To everyone's surprise except Charlie's, Ai-ling was a great hit at McTyeire. She was the school mascot, Soong Tai-tai (Madame Soong). She spent her summers at home in Hongkew, and after two years of tutoring she was ready for regular classes with the other students. When she was old enough to stay on a bicycle by herself, Charlie took her riding along the Bund and up the Nanking Road, beneath the delicious shade of the broad-leafed sycamore trees. When she was ten, he bought her a bicycle of her own, and she would career down the Bund and ride circles around the Sikh constable who directed carriage traffic where the Nanking Road met the river.

In 1900, she was joined at McTyeire by her sister Ching-ling, who had just turned seven. Unlike the other Soong children, who had faces like dumplings and bodies to match, Ching-ling was a true beauty. Her features were delicate, fragile, and pensive. Her lower lip was set in a slight pout, and her eyes were soft, remote, and hurt. Like a hostage in a medieval tower, she seemed to be watching life sadly from a great distance. Instead of brushing her hair back impatiently in the manner of businesslike Ai-ling or thoroughly spoiled May-ling, she let it fall softly over her brow and held it at the nape of her neck with a curl of ribbon.

The imperious quality of her sisters was missing in Ching-ling, and in its place was something gentler, more gracious and endearing.

May-ling ruled the house. She was so rotund that they called her "Little Lantern." She was consumed with vanity, dazzled by her own power. Her egoism was unchallenged, and had little to do with external beauty. She was a born Brahmin, tightly wound, haughty and magisterial even as a young girl. She worshiped her industrious eldest sister, Ai-ling, did everything Ai-ling told her to do, and watched closely as Ai-ling played her commanding role in family affairs, as if May-ling were understudying for the part.

May-ling insisted on following Ai-ling to McTyeire when she turned five. Accordingly, she was packed off with steamer trunk and plaid jacket, amid many apprehensions. The experiment did not last. For weeks May-ling carried on beautifully during the days, winning hearts, bending elders to her will, breezing briskly through her studies. But after dark, lying alone in her dormitory bed while shadows swooped and darted about the eaves, she was racked by nightmares that left her shrieking, and shattered the virginal calm of the dorm.

They had to bring her home at last, and put her back to studying with her tutor. She was not another iron-willed Ai-ling. She was simply too high-strung. When she became that overwrought, she broke out in a rash of hives, with angry red bumps or "wheals" in all the nooks and crannies of her five-year-old body, making it impossible to be dignified.

May-ling's eldest brother, T. V., was the only one of the boys who benefited from Charlie's special handling. He was very much like Ailing—not as tough, by any means, or as single-minded, but sturdy and aggressive. T. V. had a gift for seeing through human pretense, and, unlike Ai-ling, was blessed by a sense of humor that made him good company. He was a short, jolly, beefy boy with an intense frown when he was studying, and he had an incredible knack for numbers.

Since there was no Methodist school like McTyeire for boys, T. V. was tutored privately at home for several years, then was sent to St. John's University, an Episcopalian institution in Shanghai that had classes for very young boys.

Towering William Burke and his petite missionary wife, Addie, had transferred to Shanghai in the autumn of 1899 from their small mission in Sungkiang. The Burkes now had four China-born sons. They maintained strong ties to Macon, Georgia, and had been home on furlough as recently as 1896. Burke was to be the new presiding elder of the Shanghai mission district, which meant that he would again be seeing a lot of Charlie Soong.

The parsonage was on Yunnan Road, near Moore Methodist Church, where Charlie ran the Sunday school. Next door was McTyeire

School. Burke's boys were in the habit of climbing the tree by the back wall of the parsonage to spy on the McTyeire girls at play.

It was Charlie's intention to send all his children to school in America. One day in 1903, he came to ask Burke's advice. Ai-ling was now thirteen and had announced that she was ready. Charlie had started at Trinity College when he was only fifteen, and Ai-ling was a great deal better prepared. After a year's tutoring in the States, Charlie argued, she should be able to enter regular college.

Burke offered to write to Judge DuPont Guerry at Wesleyan College in Macon, Georgia. Wesleyan was the first chartered college for women in America. Like Vanderbilt, Trinity, and Emory, it was a Southern Methodist institution. Unlike many other schools in the Confederacy, Wesleyan had not been destroyed during the Civil War. Macon had survived as a peaceful, genteel community, dozing among the magnolias.

Judge Guerry, the president of Wesleyan, was Burke's close friend. Burke wrote him a long letter explaining Charlie's background, and how he had become a Methodist minister at Vanderbilt, about Charlie's achievements in China, and about his exceptional children, foremost among them Ai-ling.

Judge Guerry's reply reached Burke at the end of summer 1903. The prospect of enrolling the daughter of a Chinese minister appealed to him. There had been several American Indian girls at the school over the years but never a Chinese. Guerry suggested that Ai-ling stay in his own home until she became adjusted (and until the Wesleyan girls became adjusted to her). Academic standards in that day were flexible, particularly in small, private colleges catering to the wealthy. Judge Guerry suggested that Ai-ling could enter as a subfreshman.

Charlie was concerned about how to get Ai-ling to Georgia. Burke expected to go there on furlough the next May and offered to take her with his family.

Ai-ling began to count the months. When winter rusted away in the fields and was overgrown by spring, she was already packed. Burke planned to sail with his family aboard the Pacific Mail steamer *Korea,* leaving Shanghai May 28. Charlie booked passage for Ai-ling aboard the same ship, then went to the Portuguese Consulate and paid a "special fee" to buy a passport for her, identical to the one he had carried as a safeguard since 1895. He claimed that he had been born in Macao, so Ai-ling was a citizen of the Portuguese colony by parentage. It was a routine deceit and a small sum of money. Charlie wanted to give her at least this nominal protection.

When the day came to sail, Addie Burke was not in good health. She was recovering from typhoid fever and was quite weak when they boarded the tender *Victoria* for the hour-and-a-half trip down the Whangpoo to the deepwater anchorage at the Yangtze. Ai-ling was to share a stateroom on the *Korea* with Miss Addie and her smallest son, Baby John. William Burke and his three older sons would share the next stateroom.

The whole Soong family did not come down to the waterfront to see Ai-ling off. They bade farewell to her at home in Hongkew. Only Charlie took her to the dock, and rode out on the tender. The *Korea* was a commodious liner of American ownership and registry. As a symbol of Western ingenuity in the dawn of the twentieth century, she was a floating palace of contrasts, with a cargo of 538 chests of strong-smelling black opium tar packed in her hold, and on deck a cargo of freshly-scrubbed missionaries perspiring in hot trickles from armpits to groins, clutching their Bibles and squirming in the muggy heat of May, watching Charlie pull away on the launch.

When Charlie waved, Ai-ling hid her feelings well. Two years would pass before they would see each other again. She watched from the promenade deck. She had her hair in a single, thick long braid, with a black silk bow at its tip and another large black bow on the top of her head. The ribbons were a grudging concession to femininity and to her mother. She wore a Western-style dress that had been made for her by one of the Methodist ladies in Shanghai, Mrs. J. W. Kline. A storm rumbled along the western horizon. Finally, she dug out a handkerchief. Standing beside her, William Burke realized that she was weeping.

The three-day passage to Japan was uneventful for those in cabin class, where Ai-ling was the only Oriental. But one day before the ship reached Kobe a Chinese passenger in steerage died from symptoms the ship's doctor identified as acute pneumonia. The Japanese quarantine officers who swarmed onto the ship in Kobe disagreed. To them it was clearly bubonic plague.

Japan lived in dread of the plague. The ship must be fumigated from bow to stern before proceeding to Yokohama, and everyone aboard was to go ashore for a total immersion in an evil-smelling and powerful medicated bath. Miss Addie as well.

William Burke protested that his wife was an invalid, just recovering her strength. But it did no good to argue with the Japanese officials.

The next day, Miss Addie like everyone else put on old clothes and trudged to the quarantine bathhouse. Men and women were segregated before being taken inside, where they found individual wooden tubs filled with disinfectant. They stripped and sat in the tubs and were drenched with ladles of the same hot brew. They were given cotton kimonos to wear while their clothes were decontaminated. By the time she returned to the ship, Miss Addie was running a high fever.

Ten days passed while the liner remained in quarantine. Finally, it sailed for Yokohama. By then Miss Addie was too weak to move. Worried, Burke made arrangements to take her ashore for emergency care at Yokohama General Hospital. He took her away in a horse-drawn ambulance. Then he returned for his children. They were going no farther, at least for the moment.

Burke explained the situation to Ai-ling. She had to get to Macon for the fall term. He did not want to delay her. She said she was willing to go on by herself. There was a Southern Methodist missionary couple aboard, friends of his, who agreed to keep an eye on her. It was settled. Burke rejoined his children at the hospital for their vigil over Miss Addie.

A few days later in Japan, unknown to Ai-ling, Miss Addie reached the end of her struggle. On June 30, 1904, one month after her thirty-ninth birthday, she died. Burke and his boys buried her there, in Yokohama.

Meanwhile, the *Korea* was on its way to Honolulu and San Francisco. As she later told Burke bitterly, Ai-ling was feeling a touch of loneliness, and went below to visit the missionary couple. As she approached their cabin, she heard voices down the passageway:

"It's certainly a relief to be getting out of this part of the world," the woman said. "I'm so tired of those dirty Chinamen and those awful Japs. We won't see any more for a long time, I hope."

Ai-ling retreated hastily to her own cabin.

The only distraction provided for the other passengers on the *Korea* was the presence of American journalist Jack London, who had rushed to cover the sensational new Russo-Japanese War in Manchuria. In a fit of bored ill-temper, he had struck a Japanese groom. For this the Japanese commander wanted him court-martialed but settled for his expulsion from Korea. The company of such a celebrity was no inspiration for Ai-ling. London's experience with the Japanese had only fueled his fear and loathing of Orientals, and confirmed his belief that the West faced a Yellow Peril. So far as Asians and all other races were concerned, he was "first of all a white man and only then a socialist."

His attitude unfortunately was typical of a growing number of Americans, particularly on the West Coast, especially in San Francisco.

Ai-ling spent the rest of the Pacific crossing by herself, except for conversations with a sympathetic young American woman, Anna Lanius, who had boarded the ship in Yokohama. She too was a Southern Methodist, so the young women had a bond and became friends. Anna Lanius had been in Japan as a missionary and was homeward bound on her first furlough. During a brief stopover in Honolulu, the two went ashore for sightseeing.

When they returned to the steamer, the ship's purser took Miss Lanius aside. Immigration officials had inspected everyone's papers before letting them go ashore. There had been some discussion of Ai-ling's papers afterward, the purser explained. It seemed that something was irregular with the Portuguese passport, and there was certain to be trouble when they reached San Francisco.

A huge, rolling fogbank obscured the entrance to San Francisco Bay when the *Korea* finally reached her destination. At the dock, immigration officers took up their places behind a table in the ship's lounge. The passengers lined up to present their documents. Ai-ling held out her Portuguese passport. The official took it from her and scowled. According to both Ai-ling and Anna Lanius, the following exchange took place:

"Trying to get by on one of those things, are you?" he snorted. "That's been tried by a lot of other Chinese, little sister. It won't work. You just stay here until we're ready to take you to the detention home."

Ai-ling stared at the passport. The immigration officer had no way of knowing where she had been born, so the only thing he could challenge was the authenticity of the passport itself. It was, however, a legitimate, official Portuguese passport, signed and sealed at the consulate in Shanghai. The information in it might be incorrect, but the document was most certainly not a fake.

She looked the official straight in the eye.

"You cannot put me in a detention home," she snapped. "I am a cabin-class passenger, not from the steerage."

The official looked startled.

Anna Lanius stepped forward. "You most certainly will not put her in a detention home!" she insisted. "I'm staying right here with her to see that you don't."

There was a hasty discussion among the officials. One sympathetic public-health inspector, a Dr. Gardner, protested. "That place is not fit for a self-respecting animal."

The detention home in question was a cellblock on the San Francisco waterfront, only a short distance from the sailors' prison, which was a notorious bin full of murderers, cutthroats, sodomists, and mutineers dredged from the leaky hulls that jammed the docks at the turn of the century. Few seaports had such a reputation for cruelty, vice, and corruption as San Francisco in the years between the Gold Rush and the 1907 earthquake.

Normally, Chinese immigration cases were confined in a shed at the Pacific Mail Steamship Company wharf, where conditions were sufficiently ugly to send many Chinese hurrying home in disgust as soon as they could extricate themselves from official clutches. Only the most belligerent or violent cases were taken to the detention home. Yet these officials were threatening to put a fifteen-year-old girl in with them.

The determination of Anna Lanius saved the day. Instead of locking Ai-ling in the detention center, they detained both young women on board the *Korea*—and promptly forgot them.

The ship was now scheduled for decontamination and refitting. As soon as the last passengers were ashore, workers arrived to strip carpets, linen, mattresses, and furnishings, so that the ship could be scoured from bridge to bilge. Anna Lanius and Ai-ling Soong were confined to a small cabin, and were fed identical meals of steak, potatoes, and bread three times a day.

No one knew of their plight, and there seemed to be nobody to turn to.

When the ship had docked, someone had come to meet Ai-ling. It was Dr. Clarence Reid, the missionary who had conducted Charlie's wedding ceremony. He was in San Francisco working with the Chinese. When Reid reached the steamer, he was unable to see Ai-ling immediately because of the immigration procedures. He waited for hours. When she did not appear, he had to rush away for a weekend engagement, unaware of what was befalling her.

After three days of this floating house arrest, Anna Lanius was so distressed that she was near collapse. A junior immigration official allowed her to go ashore to telephone Dr. Reid. After inquiring of a dozen places, she finally located Reid with help from a Presbyterian ministry in the city.

Early next day Reid arrived at the ship, accompanied by a nurse, who took Anna's place as guardian of the young Chinese girl. Miss Lanius hurried home to Missouri and put the frightening experience as far as possible behind her.

Ai-ling was confined for two more weeks. At whim, officials ordered her to transfer from the *Korea* to another ship in the harbor, then another and another. She was held a total of nineteen days.

She was not the kind of person to sit sniveling by her porthole. What tears she did shed were of frustration and rage. She had always been tough, shrewd, and inclined to keep her own counsel. The days passed in galling impotence. Meanwhile, Dr. Reid worked frantically to get word through religious channels to Washington, D.C. Somehow, his appeals succeeded, and Ai-ling was abruptly freed. There was no further question about her papers. Nobody challenged her passport. Although the document was real and the information faked, that had all become moot. The American government now accepted her.

Escorted ashore by Dr. Reid, Ai-ling stayed on with him in San Francisco for three days. She had learned about the death of Addie Burke, and knew that William Burke and his four sons were aboard the *China,* due to arrive in San Francisco on July 25.

When Burke disembarked, subdued and grief-stricken, Ai-ling rejoined him for the next stage of the journey by train to St. Louis, then to Macon. Ai-ling reached Wesleyan College after midnight on August 2, a good deal older and tougher than she had been in Shanghai.

The experience had left a deep wound.

On her first morning in Georgia, Ai-ling awakened to find herself featured prominently in the Macon *Telegraph:*

> Miss Eling Soon, the Chinese girl who was detained aboard ship at San Francisco while on her way to Wesleyan college, arrived in Macon at 12:30 this morning in company with Rev. W. B. Burke. Rev. Mr. Burke had been on his way for some time from Shanghai. It will be remembered that Mrs. W. B. Burke died at Yokohama on the trip home. The Chinese girl, when delayed at San Francisco, awaited the arrival of Rev. Mr. Burke.

Miss Soon is the daughter of a Chinese Christian mother and was reared at Shanghai. Her father desired to complete her education in America and qualify her for Christian work among her own people in China.

"As a child she was the product of our own missionary work," said President Guerry of Wesleyan yesterday. "Mr. Burke, our missionary, was glad to have her come to the United States with him on his visit home this summer. He, of course, preferred Wesleyan college for her, where so many of his sisters and nieces graduated."

Rev. Mr. Burke wrote to President Guerry and readily made arrangements for this girl to come as the daughter of a Christian minister and made provisions for her under the rules of the college.

When Rev. Mr. Burke reached San Francisco the Chinese girl was added to his company and she thus came to Wesleyan without traversing the continent alone. The girl is said to be quite a bright one.

"Of course she will not force herself or be forced upon any of the other young ladies as an associate," said President Guerry in speaking further. "They will be free and can conduct themselves as they see fit. I have no misgivings as to her kind and respectful treatment."

Miss Soon is the first Chinese girl to become a member of the student body, so far as President Guerry's information extends, but it is well known that at different times Indian girls have attended Wesleyan.

It was unfortunate that Judge Guerry felt it necessary to apologize in print for Ai-ling before she arrived. No young white lady would be forced to associate with her. She was given a small room at Judge Guerry's home, and began her studies as a "subfreshman" the following month.

The Macon she explored was a soft town of mellow woods and pastel shades, laid out along the Ocmulgee River in 1823 and named for the legislator Nathaniel Macon. It had survived the Civil War, although it had been a major arsenal and repository of Confederate gold. Thousands of rebel casualties were cared for in the buildings of Wesleyan College during the war.

The college sat on a hill above the town in those days, with a nice view over the pines. There was only one building, of the Greek Revival style, with a line of columns guarding the façade like Confederate Army pickets. Other Greek Revival confections were added as the campus grew. Then, just before the turn of the century, the main building was remodeled into a Victorian gingerbread of angular towers and mansard roofs, which the town decided was a "most elegant and complete edifice for educational purposes." The sleeping rooms for students were in the

THE PRODIGIES ⋅§ 107

attic, cozily furnished with large closets, dressing rooms—and one bathroom for each floor to house the tubs and all the porcelain chamberpots, "so constructed as to secure comfort, cleanliness and health." In 1900 an annex was added to accommodate an additional seventy-five boarders.

The students were predominantly children of well-to-do southerners, respectable if not wealthy. They dressed in lacy frocks with numerous petticoats, and piled up their hair in elaborate coifs. Although by the time Ai-ling arrived the Confederacy had long since gone under, the girls of Wesleyan managed to strike in every portrait an antebellum pose that must have made their fathers draw themselves erect and gruffly clear their throats.

Ai-ling's characteristic stubbornness paid off. In a matter of weeks, the other girls at Wesleyan decided that the short, stocky Chinese girl with the pie-pan face was not a threat of any kind that they understood. The firsthand impressions of her fellow students and faculty were collected in 1932 by an alumna, Eunice Thompson, who wrote a full-page feature article about the adolescent Soong girls for the Nashville *Tennessean* that year. It is full of quaint perceptions of the girls in a time of innocence.

Ai-ling was by all estimates a serious student, reserved and aloof, unsmiling, as if she were the only one present who could see beyond the laces and frills. She was probably the only young woman in the school who knew exactly the current market price for all of the pretensions on display, and who could calculate the net worth of each girl's father down to a penny and do it all in her head. Charlie Soong had a daughter who was nobody's fool. Ai-ling's schoolmates interpreted her reserve as shyness, and found it disarming.

Mrs. Guerry was a kind and warm-hearted woman, who tried hard to make Ai-ling feel at home. The frightened girl responded by developing a lifelong attachment to the judge and his wife. Charlie wrote to Ai-ling regularly of events in Shanghai, recommending books on Chinese history that she then dutifully digested. His influence kept Ai-ling's roots firmly in Chinese soil while outwardly she underwent superficial changes to adjust to her American surroundings. She wore nothing but American clothes. She developed a repertoire of American slang and made easy use of her adopted language. Before the first year was out, she cut most of her pigtail and began arranging her hair in a stylish pompadour.

Her appearance was misleading. One day, her school chums re-called, a Wesleyan professor looked her over and remarked that she had become "a fine American citizen." Infuriated, Ai-ling rebuked him in front of her classmates, reminding him that she was not an American citizen but a Chinese, and proud of it. The memory of her treatment in San Francisco still rankled. (For the sake of this particular argument, she forgot that she was claiming to be Portuguese.)

That January 1906, Ai-ling was given special leave from Wesleyan to go north. The excuse she provided was the arrival in Washington, D.C., of her uncle, B. C. Wen, who was dispatched to America by the Empress Dowager on an Imperial Educational Commission. College girls did not travel alone in those days, so Judge Guerry sent his wife as her chaperone. In Washington, Ai-ling accompanied her uncle to a White House reception, where she was introduced to President Theodore Roosevelt. In his blustery fashion, the President asked the sixteen-year-old Chinese girl what she thought of America.

"America is very beautiful," Ai-ling claimed she told him, "and I am very happy here, but why do you call it a free country?" She quickly described her reception in San Francisco the previous summer. "Why should a Chinese girl be kept out of a country if it is so free? We would never treat visitors to China like that. America is supposed to be the Land of Liberty!"

President Roosevelt, she said, was taken by surprise. After listening to her outburst, he simply muttered that he was sorry and turned to the next guest.

From Washington, Ai-ling proceeded with her uncle to New York. There she was reunited with her father, who had just seen Julian Carr in Durham. Charlie saw before him a girl no more. Ai-ling was now a sturdy young woman, done up in the latest fashion. After a round of socializing, Ai-ling returned to Macon.

If Ai-ling was less frivolous than her Georgia contemporaries, most of them local belles with limited horizons, she was not without comedy. In the college drama circle, she joined in poking mild fun at Wesleyan. A 1909 program for class activities listed the main event for that day as a play, *The Vicissitudes of College Life,* adapted from the books of Betty Wales by three young Wesleyan seniors, one of them Ai-ling Soong. At her graduation that year, she gave a reading adapted from the original libretto of Puccini's *Madama Butterfly,* in which she took the part of the virtuous Japanese woman Cio-Cio-San, who is betrayed by the callow American naval officer, Lieutenant Pinkerton. For the occasion, she wrote to her father asking for enough silk to make a proper Japanese costume. Charlie sent her forty yards of rose-colored brocade.

With her degree in hand, Ai-ling boarded the train for San Francisco as her father had nearly twenty-five years earlier. When she reached Shanghai, there was a desk for her in Charlie's Hongkew study —and another at his discreet political headquarters in the print shop on Shantung Road. Ai-ling was to be Dr. Sun Yat-sen's English-language secretary—handling his correspondence, polishing his speeches and declarations, and coding messages that were being sent to him wherever he was at the moment. This freed Charlie to concentrate on his responsibilities as treasurer of the revolution.

After Charlie had seen Ai-ling in New York in 1906, B. C. Wen had taken him across the Hudson to visit Miss Clara Potwin's modest school in the small town of Summit, New Jersey.

Clara Barton Potwin was a tall, energetic woman with a mass of chestnut hair. Her father had tutored some Chinese students at Yale before the turn of the century. These were wealthy young men. When they had returned to China, Clara Potwin had traveled to the Orient with her father to visit. Over the years she had come to know the Far East firsthand.

The Potwins were of White Russian ancestry, the name originally having been Potrovin. After her father passed on, Clara Potwin kept up his work by taking a small number of Chinese pupils into her little school in Summit to prepare them for American colleges.

The school was on Locust Drive in a rented house, a handsome white frame structure set off by brown cedar shakes.

B. C. Wen knew Clara Potwin through her father and another friend from Summit, an American educator named William Henry Grant. Harry Grant worked for years as a librarian in Manhattan, a short train ride from Summit. He was also active in the Presbyterian Church and was fascinated by its foreign mission work. Traveling to China to tour the missions and satisfy his curiosity, he met Wen and through him became one of the American founders of the Central Christian College in Canton.

Not far from the Grant home was a bigger mansion, the old Manley homestead, which had been turned into a boardinghouse called St. George's Hall. Harry Grant's Chinese friends always stayed there.

The purpose of Wen's visit to Summit in 1906 was to enroll his godson, "Ajax" Wang, in Miss Potwin's school. The boy was to be prepped for entrance to the University of Pennsylvania two years thence. Charlie Soong liked the atmosphere of the school and asked Clara Potwin if she would be willing to take his two daughters, Ching-ling and May-ling, the next year.

Since May-ling was only eight years old, Charlie's determination to place her in an American school might have seemed premature. But he was passing through a turbulent period in his life, a time of conspiracy and danger. It might be only a matter of time before he was discovered and had to flee for his life or face arrest and execution.

With Ai-ling at Wesleyan, and the two younger girls safe with Miss Potwin, the way would be cleared for emergencies. His oldest son, T. V., was finishing at St. John's Middle School in Shanghai, and would be ready to enter Harvard shortly. The other two boys—T. A. and T. L.—were still very young and presented less of a handicap in a crisis.

Clara Potwin was delighted to take the girls.

It was B. C. Wen who delivered them. In 1907, he headed another commission to America, and his diplomatic status would shield the children from a recurrence of Ai-ling's harrowing experience in San Francisco.

They embarked in the summer of 1907, Wen and his wife with Ching-ling and May-ling in tow, aboard the liner *Manchuria*. They were joined in the voyage by Harry Grant. In such company, the girls cleared immigration in San Francisco without incident.

One of Miss Potwin's other students, Emily Donner, recalled hearing that some Chinese girls were expected.

> This was a matter of interest in our little world, but for a long while nothing further was said, so we forgot about it until we came to school one morning and found them there.
>
> The older one, a very grave and quiet girl, must have been about fifteen. She seemed very aged to the rest of us, who were all about nine years old. Her Chinese name was Ching-ling, but for some reason we always called her Rosamond. . . . We did not see much of her, as she was naturally by age and disposition held away from our childish games and teasing.
>
> But there was also a delightful little girl, named May-ling, just our own age, and full of life and vitality, with more than a touch of mischief. . . .

May-ling was a jolly little round butter ball of a girl who wanted to know everything—all the new and different trees and flowers, all about the houses and people.

When the girls had been at Miss Potwin's for a little while, their older sister, named Ai-ling . . . came to visit them. She was quite grown up and very sweet and friendly. She startled our 1908 souls by wearing heavy rice powder with tinted lips and cheeks. We did realize that this was just as customary for Chinese girls of the same age as a discreet dab of powder would be for older American girls. I can see that she had done a beautiful job. But I remember hoping devoutly from my small-girl viewpoint that May-ling would never grow up to change her face so.

One day a package from China arrived. In it, among lots of lovely colorful things for the girls, was a darling little black silk suit for May-ling. It consisted of small black silk trousers and a coat with green dragons embroidered on it. May-ling put on the suit, and dressed in pants, proceeded to climb a tree. She went so high she could not get down by herself, so my brother went up after her while we stayed below hoping the suit would not get torn. It didn't.

The town librarian, Louise Morris, discovered that the two Chinese girls were avid readers. Ching-ling, "the serious one," devoured adult fiction and nonfiction that was "far beyond the taste of the average girl of that age." May-ling preferred "Peter Rabbit."

May-ling was often stricken by homesickness, and took refuge with Margaret Barnes, a teacher who lived at Miss Potwin's school.

Frequently in the evening she would come to my room to talk of her family or tell about life in China. Both girls disliked their Chinese hairdo, and begged to learn how to dress their hair in the American style. To this end some red ribbon was bought and regularly each morning May-ling appeared to have the ribbon tied in two big bows in her black hair.

Following that pleasant year in Summit, Ching-ling was old enough to enter Wesleyan College. She and May-ling spent the summer of 1908 with friends in the Georgia hill town of Demorest, the site of Piedmont School, founded in 1897 by a Methodist circuit rider known to posterity simply as Brother Spence. In the autumn, when it was time for Ching-ling to begin the fall term in Macon, May-ling stayed on in Demorest, attending a local school with her playmates.

Years later, she looked back fondly on the experience:

I was too small then to go to College, being eleven years of age, and as I liked the village and found my playmates among the little girls there, my sister [Ching-ling] decided to leave me with Mrs. Moss, the mother of one of my eldest sister's school mates.

I attended the eighth grade at Piedmont, and enjoyed my stay of nine months there very much. It interested me greatly to find that many of the students who attended the eighth grade with me were in reality grown men and women. They had come from far in the hills, many having taught primary school for years to get the funds to attend Piedmont. All these people were greatly interested in me, and, for my part, I began to get an insight into the lives of those who had to struggle for a living and for even the means to acquire an elementary education. I suppose my contact with these people as a girl influenced my interest in the lot of those who were not born with a silver spoon in their mouths, a contact which I may never have experienced otherwise. It made me see their sterling worth because, after all, they and their kind constitute the backbone of any nation.

It was at Piedmont that I was initiated into the mysteries of parsing sentences. My knowledge of English then was at best somewhat sketchy as I had only been in America two years and had many funny little tricks of phraseology which baffled my grammar teacher. To cure me of them she made me try to parse them. Her efforts must have been productive of some success, for people now say that I write very good English. . . . The village people used to look upon me as something of a curiosity, but curiosity or not, I thoroughly enjoyed the five-cent gum drops which I used to get at old Mr. Hunt's general merchandise store equally as much as any of my playmates enjoyed them. I remember that three or four of us little girls used to consider it a great treat when one of us had a nickel to enable us to invite others to share cheese crackers or all-day suckers, which were displayed so enticingly in Mr. Hunt's glass window. We knew little of the dangers of flies and microbes in those days, and cared less about them, even though speckled fly paper shared equal honors with the attractive merchandise displayed in the windows. However, I have lived to tell the tale.

Never in my life have I felt such a thrill of righteous charity as when Florence and Hattie Hendrickson, Flossie Additon and I decided a few days before Christmas that the true spirit of the season demanded the making of someone else happy. We each went the whole hog in our charitable intentions, produced twenty-five cents each, and with the sum of one dollar bought potatoes, milk, hamburg steak, apples and oranges for the destitute family across the railroad. We tried to be modest and keep to ourselves our noble deed, but so great was our excitement that Mr. Hunt, at the store, heard us chattering and arguing about the advisability of certain articles of food. I remember—physiology being my favorite subject —that I insisted that we should buy sugar and plenty of it so that the carbohydrate values could keep the puny youngsters warm, and give the mother plenty of energy, whereas one of the other charitably-minded contributors to the great investment was strongly for potatoes as the most filling and warmth-producing foods. Mr. Hunt was listening curiously and amusedly to the excited debate, and settled the matter by generously contributing some of each of the articles. . . . When we were trudging across the trestle with the parcels in our arms we felt like blossoming Joan of Arcs proceeding upon a sacred mission. However, when we reached the ramshackle wooden shack that the intended recipients called home, and faced the discouraged worn-out mother, with her brood clinging to her hands and peeking out from behind her skirts, we were stricken dumb and none of us could speak a word. We dropped the bundles and fled. When we had run sufficient distance to feel brave once more, one of us dared to shout out "Merry Christmas," and we ran faster than ever.

One of our favorite pastimes was to go hazel nutting. . . . I used to do a great deal of reading. A favorite place was on a wooden bench between two trees beside the house I lived in. It was Mrs. Moss' house. She was the head of the boys' dormitory. I lived with her in a suite downstairs—she, and her daughters, Rosina and Ruby. . . . When Mrs. Moss wanted to be very nice to me she used to let me make biscuits. They never came out right. I did not appear to be blessed with the instincts of a cook at all. . . .

I never went back to Piedmont, but I remember with pleasure the time I spent in its environment.

When May-ling turned twelve she was still too young to be even a "special student" at Wesleyan. But, when Judge Guerry retired, the rule prohibiting nonstudents from living in the dormitory was changed. The new college president, Bishop W. N. Ainsworth, arranged this so that May-ling could be near Ching-ling.

Each of the Soong sisters spent five years in Georgia, but May-ling was in the college officially only for one of those years. The rest of the time, people bent, broke, or rewrote the rules to accommodate her. She had free run of the college and was regarded as a mascot by the older girls. Although she had her own room in the dormitory, not far from the chamberpots, May-ling spent most of her time in President Ainsworth's home. The Ainsworths had a daughter, Eloise, a frail but lively spirit, who was only two years younger. They took fast to each other and were soon racing through the hallways of the Victorian main building, spying and playing tricks on the college girls. Her mother, Mrs. Ainsworth, later wrote an article filled with reminiscence of those days:

Eloise was overjoyed to have a playmate near her own age [she recalled]. From the very beginning she made herself completely at home with us, for most of her spare time was spent with Eloise. One day May-ling was pouting over a disagreement that had occurred between her and Eloise. They had made up, supposedly, but May-ling was still pouting. Because Eloise was so afraid her friend was hurt, I decided to speak to May-ling about the beauty of forgiveness. I asked her if she wasn't ashamed to show such an ugly spirit; but her reply, accompanied by a slight twinkle in her eyes, came back quickly. "Why, no, Mrs. Ainsworth, I rather enjoy it."

The two girls thoroughly enjoyed peeking through the blinds of the parlors where the college girls entertained their dates. They would giggle and come rushing back to tell me the things they'd seen. Two more romantic little souls could not be found, and they were as excited as anyone when one of the girls became engaged.

My sons, William and Malcolm, used to amuse the little girls by riding them up and down the long college verandahs in a wheelbarrow. May-ling's black braids would slip from her head and fly in the breezes. She was very good-natured when the boys would pull them.

May-ling was always a social triumph.

Special tutors were provided. They were Margie Burks and Lucy Lester, both young members of the faculty. Miss Burks's mother, Mrs. M. M. Burks, a professor of English, looked after May-ling's personal needs, making dresses for her and helping her buy shoes in town. While the Soong sisters dressed in American style, the fabrics used to make their clothes were Chinese, sent from Shanghai. When they were completely alone, each of the girls immediately reverted to Chinese gowns. Schoolmates would burst into May-ling's room only to see her bolt into her big closet to remain there till she could emerge in conventional Western garb.

May-ling was considered precocious. She was frantically active, often mischievous. But her quick tongue usually charmed her out of trouble. In a day when lipstick and rouge were regarded as shameful, she was once caught wearing Chinese flour makeup and lip rouge.

"Why, May-ling," exclaimed an older student, "I believe your face is painted!"

"Yes," snapped May-ling, "China painted."

During French classes, she was allowed to interrupt the proceedings at any point to run around the campus for a while—simply because she insisted that it was necessary.

When she finally became a college freshman in 1912, May-ling proved to be not especially hard-working. Instead of diligence, she relied on wit and flair. It was her older sister, Ching-ling, who became the serious scholar.

The silent Ching-ling dwelt on another plane, pondering the deeper meaning of events in China, weighing the moralities of the revolution that obsessed her father and his friend Dr. Sun. She was invariably described by classmates as "beautiful." But they might as well have said "somber" or "tragic." For what gave her face its transcendent beauty was a quality of sadness and brooding. In her heart she was already a dedicated conspirator.

Charlie kept his daughters informed with long letters and clippings. Ching-ling was able to piece together the tortured progress of Dr. Sun's revolution. She was too young to have the patience for failure that her father and godfather had learned after more than a decade of defeats. She could not know that the end was coming at last—in a way that nobody could predict.

Chapter 6

THE FATAL EUPHEMISM

It was a matter of tradition that each dynasty achieved power only when it received the Mandate of Heaven, and toppled from power when that mandate was lost. The Manchus had finally lost the mandate.

As if to signal its loss, there were ominous developments in Peking. In November 1908, the Empress Dowager died, possibly of poison. With a reptilian grip, the Old Buddha had ruled China directly or indirectly for half a century, coldly striking down anyone who dared to challenge her, sustaining the rule of the Manchus long after it might normally have collapsed. When reformers in China's leadership had rallied around her imperial rival, the young Kuang Hsu Emperor in 1898, she had imprisoned him in the Summer Palace and thwarted all their efforts. Now, on her deathbed, unwilling to let him survive her, she ordered her eunuchs to poison the young Emperor. He died the day before she did. When news of the Empress Dowager's death reached Ching-ling in Macon, she celebrated secretly for days.

With the Empress Dowager's passing the atmosphere of evil and corruption did not lift, however. Her successor was a child, her great-nephew Pu-yi, whom the court eunuchs would lead into a secret life of cruelty and dissipation. The power of the Dragon Throne was vested in the hands of his father, Prince Chun, as regent. But Prince Chun was ineffective. The powerful men who had guided China for the Empress Dowager over many years had died off one by one, preceding or immediately following her to the grave. The only strongman remaining, the cunning military chief Yuan Shih-k'ai, had been removed from his post and, under the guise of retirement, had withdrawn temporarily into the woodwork.

This diffusion of power left China without effective leadership. Given such striking signs of Manchu vulnerability, Dr. Sun Yat-sen was able to raise fresh funds from Overseas Chinese in the United States and Canada for another attempt to seize power in February, 1910. This uprising would be Sun's ninth since his bungled effort at Canton in 1895, and the seventh since the formation of the Revolutionary Alliance in Tokyo. In none of these except the first had Sun taken part directly, since he was barred from the Chinese mainland. He worked through secret agents. As in all the previous instances, this new uprising was badly organized, and the ill-trained men involved were unable to stick to schedule, derailing the entire effort. There was one encouraging note to come out of the débacle: For the first time since the revolution began, significant numbers of imperial troops were defecting to the ranks of the rebels, and a few gentry and merchants were pitching in, showing that disaffection with the imperial government was spreading across class barriers.

Sun traveled from Singapore to Europe and America, making speeches and raising money. In the name of the future republic, he offered to sell rights of citizenship, business concessions, terms of office in parliament, and statues and parks named after the biggest donors.

From Chinese in Penang and other parts of Southeast Asia, he raised about half of what he needed to organize yet another uprising. He was mightily encouraged. Sending the funds back to Charlie in Shanghai, Sun dashed off on another whirlwind world tour. It climaxed in Vancouver, British Columbia, where he raised the rest of the money he needed from the city's big Chinese community in a matter of days.

The new attack was scheduled for April 13, 1911. Once again Canton was the target. Five days before it was to begin, an overeager rebel recruit from Singapore took it upon himself to assassinate the Manchu garrison commander. Alarmed, the authorities clamped tight security on the city and confined unreliable military units to their barracks. Just as in 1895, when the ferry boat sailed from Hong Kong while Sun's revolutionaries argued over weapons, it was futile to continue but too late to turn back. Too late because so many financial backers were eagerly awaiting the results.

The leaders, after dragging their feet with indecision for two weeks beyond the originally scheduled coup date, at last attacked on April 27.

At 5:30 P.M., 130 revolutionaries, armed with pistols and homemade bombs, assaulted the governor-general's headquarters, or yamen. Nobody had bothered to alert mutinous units of the imperial government's so-called New Army, so they failed to appear. Only a few bandits turned out. When the revolutionaries broke through to the inner courtyard of the governor-general's yamen, they found that the Manchu officials already had fled. When they tried to leave, the rebels found themselves cut off by a large force of imperial troops. One of the revolutionaries, thinking that he could turn some of the soldiers against their masters, started to shout and was instantly cut down by a bullet. The rebel commander, realizing that the jig was up, slipped into a storefront, changed into civilian clothes, and escaped into the night.

Left to fend for themselves, nearly one hundred young revolutionaries were killed or captured. Those who were taken prisoner were either strangled or decapitated. Those who were already dead in the streets were beheaded anyway.

"Despite the martyrs' unmatched heroism," remarked historian Wu Yu-zhang, who took part in the uprising,

> an armed revolt without the participation of the broad masses of people could not escape failure. . . . All armed uprisings which are divorced from the revolutionary struggle of the masses are but military adventurism. Yet although the many armed uprisings launched under the leadership of the Revolutionary Alliance failed, they dealt a serious blow to the reactionary rule of the [Manchu] government. Countless numbers of people were encouraged to carry on the revolutionary struggle, and members of the reactionary ruling class became terrified.

During the soul searching that followed the Canton Massacre, the Australian journalist W. H. Donald visited Charlie Soong's Sino-American Press. Inside, he found the usual huddle of high-level revolutionaries.

Charlie greeted Donald heartily, and cracked, "How's Australia's gift to confusion of the enemy?"

Donald listened awhile to the discussion of the disorganization that had beset every uprising so far, then interrupted.

"After the job against the Manchus is done, what then? You people have dodged the matter of government. Government is big and should be an efficient business. It must be more than a dream and a hope. You must have men trained and capable. . . ."

One of the conspirators waved his hand. "Oh, those are practical matters," he said airily. "I suppose someone is looking after the details."

Charlie Soong looked distressed. Clearly, Dr. Sun was not alone in his impracticality.

But, by this point, it was a little late to worry about what to do with power once they had it.

Ching-ling was beginning her junior year at Wesleyan when it finally happened.

Far down the Yangtze River, in the triple city of Wuhan, a group of discontented army officers in the garrison were plotting their own uprising against the Manchus. On October 9, at a hideout, one of their homemade bombs accidentally exploded.

Police coming to the scene discovered documents, insignias, seals, and banners. Acting quickly, they stormed the nearby headquarters of the plotters in Xiao-chao Street and arrested large numbers of the conspirators. The gates of the city were sealed, the army barracks were surrounded, and police moved in with captured lists of rebel membership. Panic gripped the men. For the dissident military officers, the choice was simple: They could accept arrest and brutal punishment or they could risk everything and proceed with their long-planned insurrection. Four battalions of troops abruptly mutinied and took control of the city. The governor-general fled to a gunboat on the Yangtze. It was October 10, 1911—the auspicious tenth day of the tenth month, "Double Tenth."

The mutineers were disorganized. They were led by political unknowns, members of a local revolutionary faction called the Literary Association. They had no significant connection with any triad and no direct link with Dr. Sun's Alliance party. Yet they had done spontaneously what nobody else had been able to do in years of trying. On October 12, two days after the homemade bomb accidentally detonated, the rebels established a provisional republican government and named their local commander, Li Yuan-hong, as revolutionary military governor. In the days and weeks to follow, province after province joined the rebels, declaring themselves independent of the authority of the Manchus.

In a last effort to save themselves, the Manchus recalled from "retirement" the chief military advisor of the late Empress Dowager, the wily Yuan Shih-k'ai.

Yuan was a warlord who for years had exercised the real military power behind the Peking regime. When reforms were introduced in the 1890s, he had impressed foreigners by organizing the first "modern" army in China, and setting up the Peiyang Military Academy, where officers were groomed with Western training methods and taught how to use Western weapons instead of spears and bows and arrows. His career went into eclipse with the passing of the Dowager, but in 1911 he recognized this call to arms as a chance to seize power for himself. Yuan launched vigorous attacks on the rebels—attacks that deliberately stopped short of military victory. His object was to gain an advantage over the rebels, but without really strengthening the hand of the Manchus, and then to wait until both sides were exhausted.

The fate of the Dragon Throne ultimately rested with the foreign powers. There was little doubt among observers that the Manchus had come to the end of the road. Great Britain alone was so powerful in China that her backing, of the throne or of the rebels, would settle the outcome as it had half a century earlier during the Taiping Rebellion.

The British made it known that no action would be taken in support of the throne. When they saw how Britain was going to go, the other foreign powers fell into line. By deciding to sit on the fence, the West brought an end to the Manchu Dynasty. But, by also refusing to support the republicans, Britain deliberately placed China's fate in the hands of Yuan Shih-k'ai, making him the new strongman, and condemning the country to another period of despotism and turmoil.

Dr. Sun was in Denver, Colorado, when the revolution occurred. He was not aware of the momentous event until he opened a newspaper over breakfast one morning before catching a train to Kansas City. From newspaper speculation, he also saw that he was among those mentioned as potential leaders of the new China. He realized that the fate of this infant government could be decided by the foreign powers, particularly by Great Britain and the United States. If he could personally gain Western support, this might guarantee his position in the leadership. Instead of rushing back to China immediately, therefore, Sun hastened to Washington to seek a private interview with Secretary of State Knox. The secretary refused to see him. Undaunted, Sun hurried to New York and caught a ship for England.

In London, Sun was able to make contact with Sir Trevor Dawson, the head of the great armaments firm of Vickers' Sons and Maxim. In expectation of significant contracts from the new Chinese government,

Sir Trevor agreed to present Sun's case to the Foreign Minister. Among other things, Sun was prepared to offer Britain preferential treatment in China; he would place the Chinese Navy under British officers, and guarantee Britain the services of thirty-five million members of secret societies. These wild blandishments did no good. The Foreign Office had long ago concluded that Sun Yat-sen was a mere "windbag." In fact, the British Government's course of action had been determined— Whitehall was firmly behind strongman Yuan Shih-k'ai. The only assurance Sun received was that Britain would remain "neutral"—a decision that had already been revealed by its legation in Peking.

Disappointed, Sun traveled to Paris, where he obtained an interview with President Clemenceau, but again accomplished nothing. Empty-handed, he boarded ship in Marseilles and headed home.

Sun's failures kept him from being taken seriously by his most important political rivals, but did not diminish his public stature as a revolutionary. His followers believed that he had inspired the fall of the Manchus, even though he had not been physically present. When Sun reached Shanghai on December 25, 1911, he was accorded a hero's welcome by great throngs of party loyalists, among them Charlie and Ai-ling. He went straight to Charlie's house to confer with his lieutenants. The revolution was now an accomplished fact for much of South China, although the situation was far from clear-cut in the North. Delegates from all the liberated areas, including the powder keg at Wuhan, had descended on the old Ming capital of Nanking, just up the Yangtze River from Shanghai, which was proposed as the new capital of republican China. This move of the capital city was intended to symbolize the link with the pre-Manchu period—the payment of the old Ming blood debt—and to remove the fangs from Peking. In Nanking, the delegates were struggling to elect a republican President. So far they had failed to achieve a clear majority for any of the leading candidates. They were now searching for a man on whom they could compromise. There was an outside chance that Dr. Sun, who had missed the whole show, and who was coming on the scene rather late in the proceedings, might once again prove to have phenomenal luck and turn out to be just the compromise candidate to break the deadlock.

Ai-ling and Charlie accompanied Sun to Nanking. Once again he was accorded a wild reception, and he was unanimously elected Provisional President of the Republic of China.

Shortly after Sun's inauguration, Charlie sent Ching-ling one of the first five-barred republican flags. Her roommates later told how they watched in astonishment as she dragged a chair to the wall, climbed on it, ripped down the old imperial dragon flag and pinned the new flag in its place.

"Down with the dragon!" she shouted. "Up with the flag of the republic!" (The five horizontal stripes—red, yellow, blue, white, and black—represented the Han Chinese, the Manchus, the Mongols, the Moslems, and the Tibetans.)

Ching-ling had been exhilarated by the news of the empire's collapse. More vigorously than ever, she became absorbed in the events surrounding those violent changes and the people who had inspired them. The Wesleyan student magazine carried her article "The Greatest Event of the Twentieth Century." Because it anticipates so many of her later convictions, it is worth examining.

One of the greatest events of the twentieth century, the greatest even since Waterloo, in the opinion of many well-known educators and politicians, is the Chinese Revolution. It is a most glorious achievement. It means the emancipation of four hundred million souls from the thralldom of an absolute monarchy, which has been in existence for over four thousand years, and under whose rule "life, liberty, and the pursuit of happiness" have been denied. It also signifies the downfall of a dynasty whose cruel extortions and selfishness have reduced the once prosperous nation to a poverty-stricken country. The overthrowing of the Manchu Government means the destruction and expulsion of a court where the most barbaric customs and degrading morals were in existence.

Five months ago our wildest dream could not have been for a republic. To some, even the promise of an early constitutional government was received with scepticism. But deep down in the heart of every patriotic Chinese, were he a politician or a laborer, there was the anti-Manchu spirit. All the sufferings, such as famine, flood, and retrogression in every phase of life was traced to the tyrannical Manchus and their court of dishonest officials. Oppression was the cause of this wonderful revolution which came as a blessing in disguise. Already we are witnessing reforms that would never have been accomplished under a despot. We read in the papers of the queueless movement in China, and how thousands and thousands have sacrificed their appendages—the Chinese national disgrace. . . . There are innumerable other reforms that are now taking place. . . .

The Revolution has established in China Liberty and Equality, those two inalienable rights of the individual which have caused the loss of so

many noble and heroic lives, but there is still Fraternity to be acquired.
. . . Fraternity is the yet unrealized ideal of humanity, and that Liberty has
no safe foundation except human brotherhood, and that real Equality can
never be anything but a dream until men feel towards each other as
brothers.

In the Macon *Telegraph,* Ching-ling read that Sun's first official act
as Provisional President was to lead a procession bearing sacrificial
tribute to the tombs of the Ming emperors at Nanking. By this act, he
fulfilled his triad blood oath—"Fan Ch'ing fu Ming"—"Down with the
Ch'ing and up with the Ming!"

But one month later he resigned.

Although Sun held the title of Provisional President in Nanking, the
real power remained in Peking in the hands of strongman Yuan Shih-
k'ai. A master of palace intrigue, a skilled manipulator of assassins, Yuan
had China in his grip. He held Peking, which all foreign governments
acknowledged as the seat of power, he had Great Britain behind him,
his armies controlled North China, and without his cooperation the
Republic was impotent. The child Emperor, Pu-yi, remained on the
throne as Yuan's puppet and as a vestige of the Manchus. With China
so divided, the republicans could not speak for the nation. To drive this
point home, Yuan's supporters engineered a number of bloody riots in
the northern provinces that they controlled, and stood back to watch.
Dr. Sun was in no position to stop the riots without the cooperation of
Yuan's northern armies and police. He was made to seem incompetent.

Sun's Alliance party simply had not been prepared for the reality
of the revolution. The doctor himself still considered the Wuhan revolt
to have been "purely accidental." Representatives of his Alliance failed
even to win control of the republican leadership. As a result there were
two republican power bases—the revolutionaries headquartered at
Wuhan where the 1911 uprising had taken place, and Dr. Sun's Alliance
based in Shanghai and Nanking. In an effort to unify all the republican
factions, a new nationalist party was organized, called the Kuomintang,
or KMT. But it was not in control of the situation, and was being stymied
and opposed by scores of counterrevolutionary groups.

It took only days for Sun to realize that he was indeed powerless.
Behind his back, strongman Yuan was negotiating with leaders of various republican factions, offering himself as the only person able to end
the chaos and bring China under one clearcut authority. Yuan beguiled

them by offering to become a member of the Kuomintang himself, and to have each of his principal ministers join the KMT as well. He promised that he would dispose of the child Emperor the moment his terms were accepted and he replaced Dr. Sun as President.

Philosophically, Sun consoled himself that he had achieved his primary mission of leading China to freedom. But it must have pained him deeply when he finally acknowledged, "Yuan is the only man who can rule China today." Sun offered to resign in favor of Yuan on the condition that the child Emperor abdicate and that the strongman move the entire government to Nanking. Yuan accepted and the Emperor abdicated on February 12. Two days later Yuan was elected Provisional President. He was inaugurated on March 10, and on April 1 Dr. Sun Yat-sen moved out of the presidential offices in Nanking to make way. By September, the doctor was working for President Yuan as director of the national railroads.

It was a terrible disenchantment that followed. Once Yuan had control of the presidency, he began shifting his more sinister supporters into positions of leverage and appointing his most powerful followers to the presidential Cabinet. The several independent republican leaders who remained on the Cabinet found themselves isolated. It was only a matter of time before Yuan had them powerless, and seized dictatorial control. The pattern was a familiar one. But obvious as it must have been, many of the republicans did not immediately recognize the danger. In the euphoria following the Manchu downfall, they were preoccupied with other matters. Elections to a constituent assembly were being held in different parts of the country, and the more astute political leaders were involved in campaigning.

In Macon, Ching-ling could see more clearly than most that the real revolution had not yet taken place. She began to count the months until she could go home to play her role in it.

To Dr. Sun his job on the railways was something of a holiday—a time to lick wounds. Apparently it never occurred to him that this was Yuan's way of disposing of him by sending him on a fool's errand. He was given a salary of $30,000 Chinese a month, and traveled in style. At his insistence, Charlie Soong was appointed treasurer of the national railways and joined Sun's entourage, with Ai-ling acting as Sun's secretary.

It was a serious mistake. For the first time, Charlie Soong and his family were identified with Sun publicly, a change that was perilous for them all.

They traveled together on a grand tour of China, everywhere that existing railways could take them, flashing along the Yangtze, clattering through the kao liang grain belt of Manchuria, twisting around the ghostly karst formations of soft, green Kwangtung Province.

An entire train was provided with special cars. Dr. Sun's personal car was one previously used by the Old Buddha. The Empress Dowager had ordered a set of sixteen rail cars simply because other monarchs had them. Her personal car exceeded even the Fabergé elegance of the Romanovs' Trans-Siberian Railway coaches. No alterations had been made since the Dowager traveled with forty pairs of shoes and two thousand gowns. The imperial appointments—a rug of blue velvet etched with gold designs of the peony and the phoenix, complemented by imperial yellow silk window dressings—probably seemed suitable to the new railway director much as Stalin fancied the Tsar's décor when he traveled by train across Russia years after the imperial family was dead.

The Australian journalist Donald, who had attached himself to Dr. Sun, accompanied them on one trip to the north. The train was crowded with tag-alongs, henchmen, and office seekers, most of them there for a free ride, including the ubiquitous pretty girls. Donald noticed that assignations were routine at night, with sensual voices and bejeweled hands emerging unexpectedly from behind the heavy green velvet curtains of sleeper berths assigned to officers of the new government.

At each stop, bugles blared and Dr. Sun got down to greet dignitaries, have tea, and make a speech. Often, Sun would sit with Donald for long conversations about how to develop China, and sometimes Ai-ling would take a chair nearby to scribble notes and smile encouragingly.

From Sun's viewpoint, railways were the answer to China's poverty. Before railways, he insisted, the United States had been poor. But once it had borrowed money and built 200,000 miles of tracks, America had become the world's richest nation. Since China was a bit larger, she would have to build many more miles of track.

One morning, Donald was called to join the doctor. He found Sun peering at a large map of China mounted on the wall; he was wielding a writing brush. As Donald watched, Sun drew lines connecting various cities. When he realized what the man was doing, Donald thought to himself, "I saw evidence of a most convincing nature that Sun is not only mad as a hatter, but that he is madder." Donald's account of their conversation remains a classic.

"I want you to help me with this railway map," Sun said. "I propose to build two hundred thousand li [thirty-three thousand miles] of railways in ten years. I'm marking them on this map. You see the thick lines running from one provincial capital to another? Well, they will be trunk lines. The others are laterals and less important connections."

For the next few days, Donald appeared every morning at seven and watched while Sun drew his lines, wiped out the crooked ones, and drew them straight. Finally, as their train approached a major city where press interviews were scheduled, Donald spoke up.

"I wouldn't show your railway map to the correspondents," he said, casually. "You would be giving away your own special ideas."

"Oh, no," scoffed Sun. "I don't mind. I want people to know about them. My map will save China."

"A few days ago you said you'd build two hundred thousand li in ten years," Donald countered. "That might not be possible. It would take a lot of money, for one thing, and, for another, I don't think you'll have that many miles built in thirty years."

"It's very simple," Sun replied. "We shall get all the money we want. I'll build some of the lines with British capital, some with American, some with German, some with Japanese, and so on."

"Don't you know the Manchus tried to do the same thing? They tried to nationalize the railways and operate them on foreign capital. They got instead a railway revolt."

When Sun did not reply, Donald pointed to mountainous Tibet on the map. "Doctor, that line circling Tibet can never be built. You can build it with brush and ink—and that's all. Some of the passes over which your railway would run are fifteen thousand feet high."

"There are roads, aren't there," Sun stated rhetorically.

"Not roads, Doctor. Just narrow, rough trails. They go spiraling up into the sky. They're steep, so steep a strong yak can hardly climb them."

"Where there's a road, a railway can be built," Sun answered, dismissing the subject. Later, Donald recorded his private reaction to Sun's dream: "He is mad, not because he drew the map, for with money and an abundance of time, every line he drew, and more, could be built, but Sun has the audacity to think that because he drew the thing foreign

capitalists would give him sufficient money to build the whole lot within
. . . five to ten years!"

Sun's agents did solicit funds for these railways from financiers like
J. P. Morgan, but without success. Only one contract was signed before
the advent of World War I brought all such endeavors to an end, and
that contract—with George Pauling and Company of London—never
went beyond the surveying stage.

These were intoxicating moments for Dr. Sun, but Donald saw
signs that Sun's disappointment over the course of the revolution was
making him desperate, and in his desperation he was losing his grip on
reality. One day in Shanghai, Donald was visiting his office when Ai-ling
brought in some papers and then left the room. Sun studied her hips
as she departed, turned to Donald, and whispered that he wanted to
marry her.

"You'd better sublimate that desire," Donald said. "You're already
married."

"I will divorce my wife first," said Sun.

"But Ai-ling is Charlie Soong's daughter," protested Donald.
"Charlie has been your best friend. Without him, you'd have been in
the soup many a time. And as for Ai-ling and the rest of the children,
you've been their uncle. They've been almost your children."

"I know it, I know it," said Dr. Sun, "but I want to marry her just
the same."

Sun seemed quite serious. That night he insisted that Donald accompany him to Charlie's house, because he intended to ask him outright for Ai-ling's hand. Reluctantly, the Australian agreed, but only to
go as an observer—he had no intention of endorsing Sun's foolishness.

Charlie was stunned. He rocked back as if he had been struck. The
color drained from his face as he stared at the man who had been his
closest friend and fellow conspirator for two decades.

When he regained control of himself, Charlie spoke at last. "Yat-
sen, I am a Christian man. All the time, I thought you were, too. I did
not bring up my children to live in the sort of looseness you propose.
I will not accustom myself to people who trifle with marriage. We are
a Christian family and, Lord willing, we will go on that way."

Dr. Sun seemed confused, as if he had never expected this reaction.
He looked from Donald to Charlie and back again, his face darkening
with embarrassment.

"I want you to go, Yat-sen," Charlie said. "I want you to go, and I never want you to come back. My door is closed to you forever."

Donald's narrative of these events may have been exaggerated. Charlie and Dr. Sun shortly were back working together as usual. Whatever strain existed between them on a family level had been patched over with apologies. But the issue was far from dead. For Charlie, there were much bigger shocks to come.

More than likely it was Ai-ling who dampened Dr. Sun's ardor most effectively. He was a dreamer. She was a realist. As his secretary, she had been in a position to observe his frailties and to understand how thin was his veneer, how fragile his boasting. To a woman as practical as Ai-ling, it did not matter that Sun believed in what he was doing and never gave up. Conviction is not a tangible asset. Because she was so close to Charlie, she saw her father wring his hands over the continual setbacks of the conspirators. Perhaps she could not help blaming it all on Dr. Sun. But, for her sister Ching-ling, it was an entirely different story.

Early in 1913, the ambitious Yuan fulfilled the most dire predictions and launched his move for total power. It became apparent that he had visions of declaring himself Emperor. He assumed dictatorial control of the government and reversed his promise to relocate the administration to Nanking. In control of all the northern provinces were warlords loyal to him, the so-called Peiyang militarists trained in his Peiyang Academy. By keeping the administration in Peking, he had it under his thumb and within the protection of this northern military umbrella.

From his stronghold in the Forbidden City, Yuan dispatched assassins to eliminate his principal rivals. The targets were the republican leaders allied with Dr. Sun in the new nationalist party, the Kuomintang, or KMT. The party was winning elections by landslides. But before this could do much to strengthen their hand against Yuan, his hired killers began to take their toll.

It is one of the truisms of government by assassination that it removes the most promising leaders from competition. This was certainly true of the period that ensued in China, which stripped the field of flowers and left only weeds to grow.

Among the early victims was thirty-one-year-old Sung Chiao-jen, a leader of the new KMT party and one of only four independent republicans remaining in the strongman's Cabinet. This young politician had a capacity that was quite original for China—in addition to being a remarkable administrator, he was a grassroots campaigner, able to rouse popular support in the countryside, something even Dr. Sun had not attempted. Sun's immediate circle held that peasants needed to be led for a time by an educated elite, before they could be entrusted with a more direct role in the democratic process. By comparison, the popular appeal of Sung Chiao-jen was a political phenomenon. When Yuan began his power grab, Sung Chiao-jen and the three other independent Cabinet members resigned in protest, creating a direct confrontation. On March 20, 1913, while Sung was boarding a train in Shanghai, an assassin shot him twice in the stomach. The bullets were aimed to cause the greatest agony. It took two days for him to die.

An investigation of the murder led directly to the dictator's Prime Minister and a Cabinet secretary. A scandal raged around the strongman. But this was only the first of many assassinations—some carried out brazenly in public, others arranged with poison at banquets or private dinners.

Not in the least deterred by the scandal, Yuan continued his purge, dismissing KMT party governors from their posts, and replacing them with his own military loyalists. A long time passed before it dawned on the republicans what was afoot. Belatedly, they decided that the time had come for a showdown. On July 11, 1913, with the encouragement of Sun Yat-sen, the governor of Kiangsi declared his province independent of Peking. Dr. Sun followed this immediately by denouncing Yuan in public, saying: "Let all the people of the country attack anyone who dares make himself emperor." He was promptly dismissed from his post as head of railway development. The "Second Revolution" had begun.

Ching-ling had just returned from college in Macon, too late to observe Dr. Sun's brief but disturbing mental eclipse. Now that the "Second Revolution" was underway, the doctor seemed to be his old self again, plotting, organizing, and looking over his shoulder for pursuers. Once again he had a purpose, and once again he was a heroic figure. It was in this guise that Ching-ling found him when she returned from Wesleyan, full of passion and idealism.

When Yuan ordered Sun's arrest and execution, the doctor fled to Japan, reaching Tokyo late in 1913. Now that Charlie Soong was known to be one of those closest to Sun, he decided that it would be wise to leave China, and take his entire family. Charlie closed up the house in

Hongkew, and gathered his brood—Ai-ling, Ching-ling, and the two younger boys, T. A. and T. L. (May-ling and the oldest boy, T. V., were still at school in America). They accompanied him and "Mammy" Soong to the French Concession, then downriver at midnight on a Red Gang launch. At the Yangtze deepwater anchorage, they were taken aboard a steamship owned by the Red Gang, and sailed for Kobe on the next tide.

The Soongs had become political fugitives.

In Japan, they were heartily welcomed by local leaders of the KMT. Charlie and his family were housed temporarily in accommodations provided by Dr. Sun's powerful Japanese connections. Later they moved nearer to Tokyo, taking a mansion on the bluff in Yokohama, overlooking Tokyo Bay, an area fashionable with foreigners.

While Charlie and Dr. Sun revived the old conspiracies, Ai-ling resumed her duties as Sun's secretary. Ching-ling, ever the ardent romantic, began spending all her spare time in the party offices. Dr. Sun's wife, whom he had married in an arranged match many years ago in his father's village, was part of the exile group. Their one boy, Sun Fo, was fully grown and studying journalism in the United States.

One day, Charlie visited the Chinese YMCA in Tokyo, a popular meeting place for the exiles. There he was introduced to H. H. Kung (Kung Hsiang-hsi) a thirty-three-year-old native of Shansi Province, the rich opium-growing area where Charlie's own family had once lived, before resettling on Hainan Island. The Kungs had the curious distinction of being among the lineal descendants of the sage Confucius. More important, they were extraordinarily rich.

The family fortune had come from a string of pawnshops that spread all over China from the family seat at Taiku, in Shansi. These shops extended loans to peasants and both small and mid-level businessmen. At the time, the Chinese countryside had no banks in the Western sense. In good years, peasants were taxed heavily by their landlords, and when times were hard the landlords (if they were prudent) returned some of this tax money to the peasants in the form of loans and public works. In larger towns, where the straightforward equation between landlord and peasant was lost, such simple financial arrangements broke down. Pawnbrokers like the Kungs stepped in to fill the need. By managing their business wisely, they grew rich during seasons of plenty, and when disasters struck, were reasonably generous with small loans to farmers, landholders, and shopkeepers.

Through foreclosure, they acquired a great deal of property and shrewdly parlayed their profits into still greater sums. Eventually, the Kung moneylending network spread to Peking, to Canton, and even to Japan. The Kungs were in a position to underwrite or finance virtually any undertaking.

H. H. Kung's father had managed the family business in Peking, then returned to Taiku to help run the central branch. In the twilight years of the Manchus, the Kung pawnshops were overtaken by more modern regional banks. So the Kungs started their own banks, and converted their pawnshops into the Chinese equivalent of variety stores or five-and-dimes—and began to look elsewhere for big financial gains.

The Kungs were the most trusted advisors to the warlord Yen Hsi-shan, who had "liberated" Shansi Province from Manchu control and now was its military Governor. He was one of the few "enlightened" warlords in China, which meant that he cooperated with foreigners to their mutual profit. The Kungs guided him in financial matters, saw to his success in business ventures, backed Yen's own banking clan, and in return the Kungs were given choice opportunities in dealing with foreign corporations that were flocking to Shansi.

H. H. was born in Taiku at the family home. His mother died giving birth to his sister. Because his father was busy with high finance, the children were sent to a local American missionary school started by Dr. Charles Tenney. There H. H. secretly became a convert to Christianity. He remained at the school till 1896, when he transferred to North China Union College, a missionary institution near Peking. He then became involved in a very curious financial transaction apparently involving the transfer of a huge sum of money at the time of the Boxer Rebellion.

On their rampage across North China, the Boxers murdered more than two hundred missionaries and fifty of their children, and some twenty thousand "secondary devils"—Chinese Christians.

Kung was at home on vacation in Shansi in 1900 when the Boxers swept through his area. Both foreign and Chinese Christians were in grave danger. In a confrontation with his father and his uncle, H. H. announced that he was himself a Christian—the first that any of them had heard of it. They hid him till the Boxer threat passed. While he was in hiding, 159 foreigners in Shansi were executed, including 137 Protestant missionaries and their children—all his friends.

On July 9 at Taiyuan in Kung's home province, there was a particularly grisly scene witnessed by a Chinese convert:

The first to be led forth was Mr. Farthing [English Baptist]. His wife clung to him, but he gently put her aside, and going in front of the soldiers knelt down without saying a word, and his head was struck off with one blow of the executioner's knife. He was quickly followed by Mr. Hoddle and Mr. Beynon, Drs. Lovitt and Wilson, each of whom was beheaded by one blow of the executioner. Then the Governor, Yu Hsien, grew impatient and told his bodyguard, all of whom carried heavy swords with long handles, to help kill the others. Mr. Stokes, Mr. Simpson, and Mr. Whitehouse were next killed, the last by one blow only, the other two by several.

When the men were finished the ladies were taken. Mrs. Farthing had hold of the hands of her children who clung to her, but the soldiers parted them, and with one blow beheaded their mother. The executioner beheaded all the children and did it skilfully, needing only one blow, but the soldiers were clumsy, and some of the ladies suffered several cuts before death. Mrs. Lovitt was wearing her spectacles and held the hand of her little boy, even when she was killed. She spoke to the people, saying, "We all came to China to bring you the good news of the salvation by Jesus Christ; we have done you no harm, only good, why do you treat us so?" A soldier took off her spectacles before beheading her, which needed two blows.

When the Protestants had been killed, the Roman Catholics were led forward. The Bishop, an old man with a long white beard, asked the Governor why he was doing this wicked deed. I did not hear the Governor give him any answer, but he drew his sword and cut the Bishop across the face one heavy stroke; blood poured down his white beard, and he was beheaded.

The priests and nuns quickly followed him in death. Then Mr. Piggott and his party were led from the district jail which is close by. He was still handcuffed, and so was Mr. Robinson. He preached to the people till the very last, when he was beheaded with one blow. Mr. Robinson suffered death very calmly. Mrs. Piggott held the hand of her son, even when she was beheaded, and he was killed immediately after her. The ladies and two girls were also quickly killed.

On that day forty-five foreigners were beheaded in all, thirty-three Protestants and twelve Roman Catholics. A number of native Christians were also killed. The bodies of all were left where they fell till the next morning, as it was evening before the work was finished. During the night they had been stripped of their clothing, rings and watches. The next day they were removed to a place inside the great South Gate, except some of the heads, which were placed in cages on the city wall. All were surprised at the firmness and quietness of the foreigners, none of whom except two or three of the children cried, or made any noise.

By the time the red-sashed Boxers reached Peking and laid siege to the Legation Quarter, the Manchu government had decided to support the rebellion and declared war on the foreign powers. Six nations sent contingents of troops to relieve their legations, and made short work of Chinese resistance. Count Alfred von Waldersee, who commanded the German contingent, was given carte blanche by the Kaiser:

> When you meet the foe you will defeat him. No quarter will be given, no prisoners will be taken. Let all who fall into your hands be at your mercy. Just as the Huns a thousand years ago under the leadership of Attila gained a reputation by virtue of which they still live in historical tradition, so may the name of Germany become known in such a manner in China, that no Chinese will ever again even dare to look askance at a German.

Once they had taken Peking, the foreign force went on a binge. The repression that followed by the Western troops was far worse than anything perpetrated by the Boxers. Thousands of Chinese were massacred in Peking, and the Forbidden City's palaces were stripped. Pierre Loti, a French naval officer and a widely admired novelist, was stunned by the destruction:

> Silence and solitude within as well as without these walls. Nothing but rubbish and ruin, ruin. The land of rubbish and ashes, and little gray bricks —little bricks, all alike, scattered in countless myriads upon the sites of houses that have been destroyed, or upon the pavement of what once were streets . . . a city of which only a mass of curious debris is left, after fire and shell have crumbled away its flimsy materials.

Thousands more Chinese were slain in retribution at Tientsin. One punitive expedition by the Russians at the border village of Blagovetchensk, where the Chinese had fired a few shots, resulted in the butchery of thousands of Chinese men, women, and children, whose bodies were thrown in the Heilungkiang River.

While the Western armies were in control of Peking, H. H. Kung had a chance to perform a favor. The Westerners were certain to punish Shansi Province severely because most of the murdered missionaries had been slain there. Young Kung, as a Christian, had the delicate job of persuading the Western commanders to change their minds. These affairs were usually settled by the payment of large amounts of cash to the Western principals as "reparations," and the granting of significant commercial concessions to foreign firms eager to exploit China. In the case of H. H. Kung and Shansi Province, the terms struck were never revealed. Western financial interests suddenly became remarkably active in Shansi, including Standard Oil. The slaughter of the missionary families was relegated to the dustbin. No serious retribution was sought, or punishment exacted. Kung's miraculous negotiations so impressed the imperial throne that he was given honorary titles and a passport to go abroad in style for college in America. He chose to attend Oberlin, in Ohio.

When Dr. Sun Yat-sen came to Cleveland in 1905, Kung went to hear him speak at the meeting hall of the city's main Chinese tong. ·Kung was impressed, but he did not immediately join the Alliance party. He was bent to the task of acquiring an American education, and the following year, when he was graduated from Oberlin, he went on to Yale for a master's degree in economics.

Thanks to his upbringing in the midst of a household of bankers, moneymen, and pawnbrokers, Kung had an intuitive grasp of how money worked and how it could be caused to multiply rapidly under the right circumstances. Money to him was not magical, mysterious, or bewildering.

Back in Taiku after getting his degree from Yale, Kung plunged into the family business with enthusiasm. More pertinent, he became the primary advisor of warlord Yen Hsi-shan. Kung acted as the warlord's broker and as his eyes and ears in dealings with foreigners. Since the warlord was renowned for his avarice as well as for his guile and charm, it was an interesting and rewarding job. They remained close friends and mutual supporters for decades.

In 1910, Kung married a sweet-faced orphan girl, who had been taken in by the mission school in Taiyuan. They were happy together, but she was frail and consumptive. In August 1913, at the time Yuan Shih-k'ai seized dictatorial powers in Peking, Kung's young wife died of tuberculosis. Despondent, he joined the general exodus of "liberals" to Japan. He was appointed administrator of the Chinese YMCA in Tokyo just before Charlie Soong met him there that autumn.

To Charlie's surprise, he learned that Kung had met Ai-ling at a party in New York in 1906, when she had come north from Macon and Kung was a graduate student at Yale. Charlie could recognize an upwardly mobile young man if anybody could, and he immediately invited H. H. home for supper.

That night, after regaling the Soong family with a modest rendition of his adventures, H. H. Kung found himself the captive of Ai-ling Soong.

H. H. was the answer to her prayers. Chunky, puppylike, and humble in his manner, he was unprepossessing in the extreme. But, if he was far from glamorous, so was she. He was a link to reality in the midst of a traveling sideshow of political levitators. While others inhaled heady drafts of Utopia, Kung exhaled currency. To Ai-ling, idealism was frosting on the cake, the cake could only be baked with power, and power could only be purchased with money. She had seen it at work long enough to understand very well. It was money that had made Julian Carr's power, and it was money that had transformed Charlie Soong from an itinerant preacher into a dynamic force in the business world of Shanghai.

At the dinner table were Madame Soong, dewy-eyed Ching-ling, and the teenage boys, T. A. and T. L. On Charlie's right and left sat H. H. and Ai-ling, both totally homely and utterly galvanic about money.

In bazaars and marketplaces across China, stall keepers and fruit vendors were picking up coins and tapping them together to listen pensively to the sound. If the ring was clear, the coins were silver and the deal was made. If the coins rang false, they were counterfeit, and the deal was off. Millions of times a day as coins changed hands, the familiar routine was enacted from Yunnan to Manchuria. This night, Charlie Soong had taken two coins and tapped them lightly together. The sound was clear and sweet. The sound of pure profit.

They were married in the spring.

It rained furiously in Yokohama the morning of the wedding, flooding pink cherry blossoms down the streets and into the gutters, and sending floating islands of blossoms swirling out onto the pewter surface of Tokyo Bay. The air smelled of moist earth. Before the ceremony took place, the sky cleared and it became one of those soft, haiku Aprils. Like the cherry trees, Ai-ling wore pink, a pale satin jacket and skirt embroidered in plum blossoms. Her shiny black hair was decorated with a sprig of the same traditional flower.

The ceremony was conducted in a little church on a hill, the immediate members of Charlie's family present, along with Kung's cousins and a few friends. Afterward, Ai-ling changed into an apple-green satin dress decorated with golden birds, and the newlyweds drove off in a coach to the resort of Kamakura. Observing the clouds of pastel blooms and the delicate light filtering through the clearing sky, H. H. pronounced them "happy omens."

Sun Yat-sen's political omens were far from auspicious. In an effort to win the support he needed to challenge Yuan, he promised Japan special privileges in China, unaware that Tokyo was already dickering with the dictator under the table. With his usual extravagance, Sun offered political, military, and economic concessions equal to anything held by Great Britain. He succeeded in whetting Japan's appetite, but the time was not ripe for such deals. World War I had broken out in Europe and Tokyo's attentions were fixed there. The outcome of the European war could decide Britain's future role in East Asia and alter the ingredients of a bargain. Unable to make progress, Sun showed signs again of cracking under the strain. At one point, H. H. Kung wrote from Japan to an acquaintance: "Some think that his dangers and anxieties have affected his nervous system."

It was one of the rare times any member of the Soong clan let slip an opinion of the doctor, so tight-lipped were they about their personal lives. But, if H. H. thought Dr. Sun was losing his mind, he was probably quoting Charlie and Ai-ling.

It was a bad time for everyone who had hopes for China's destiny. The 1911 Revolution had brought the first promise of dawn after a millennium of darkness, only to have China plunged into blackness again by the dictatorship of Yuan Shih-k'ai. It was especially difficult for the revolutionaries, so close to achieving their goal. Wu Lao, who later became president of the China People's University, recalled: "The people's disappointment and despair was so great that they could hardly bear it, and a number committed suicide."

In this dismal state, Dr. Sun needed someone to lean on. Ching-ling took over her sister's duties as Dr. Sun's secretary. She believed as did no one else in his revolution. A grand passion consumed them. It was a winter-spring romance. He was nearly fifty, she was barely twenty.

They kept their affair secret as long as they could. Unexpectedly, Charlie announced that they were going back to Shanghai. He made arrangements to purchase a small mansion in the French Concession, the brick villa on the Avenue Joffre. Ching-ling resisted. Taking her practically as a hostage, the Soongs vanished from Japan. The newlywed Kungs went with them.

Charlie's choice of the French Concession was necessary for reasons of security. Most of China's revolutionary leaders lived in the French Concession because they were protected by being on French territory. More important, they were on Red Gang turf. The chief of detectives for the French Sûreté in Shanghai was "Pockmarked" Huang (Huang Chih-jung), the head of the Red Gang and the most powerful gang boss in the thousand-mile-long Yangtze Valley. As the man who handled all the Red Gang's printing, Charlie Soong had performed a lot of tasks for Pockmarked Huang over the years, and now that he considered his family to be in jeopardy it was natural for him to take cover by acquiring a house inside the magic circle.

Shortly after they returned to Shanghai, the Soongs announced the formal engagement of their daughter Ching-ling to a young man of good family. She fought stubbornly and insisted that she would not go through with it.

Charlie confined her to her upstairs bedroom. She wrote secretly to Dr. Sun, asking if she could come back to Japan. The letter was smuggled out of the house by her amah. At once, Sun wrote back asking her to come, saying he needed her.

Ching-ling explained the situation to her father, but Charlie was adamant; the very idea scandalized him. He ordered her back to her room. She warned him that she would run away, so he took the precaution of locking her bedroom door. That night, while her amah held the ladder, Ching-ling climbed out the window. She sailed that night for Kobe.

It was a daring thing for a respectable young Chinese girl to do, a transgression not only against filial piety but against the basic code of family first.

Dr. Sun, realizing that an ambiguous relationship would be foolhardy, made all the necessary preparations for a wedding. "I had no knowledge that he had gone through a divorce proceeding and that he intended to marry me," Ching-ling said years later, "until I arrived. When he explained his fear that I would otherwise be called his concubine and that the scandal would harm the revolution, I agreed. I never regretted it."

They were married the day after her arrival.

Shortly thereafter, Ching-ling wrote to a classmate at Wesleyan: "It was the simplest possible, for we both hate surplus ceremonies and the like. I am happy and try to help my husband as much as possible with his English correspondence. My French has greatly improved and I am now able to read French papers and translate by sight easily. So you see marriage for me is like going to school except that there are no 'exams' to trouble me."

It might have been less of a blow to the Soongs if Sun Yat-sen had actually divorced his original wife. Instead, he simply told everyone that he considered himself divorced. He had made his own rules and issued his own passports for so long that the truth had become flexible. If he had been a Confucian Chinese, it would have been acceptable to take a second wife providing that clan elders approved. But, as a Christian, he was committing bigamy. Strictly speaking, Ching-ling was an adultress. She was only Sun's mistress. For Mammy Soong in particular —a simple, straightforward woman, and religious fundamentalist in the classic sense—the elopement was a stunning shock.

When he discovered that Ching-ling was missing, Charlie made inquiries and learned that she had sailed on a Japanese liner. Grimly, he booked passage on a Pacific Mail steamer, and hurried after her. On reaching Kobe, he boarded a train and raced to Yokohama, but it was too late. The ceremony had already been performed.

According to Ching-ling, Charlie confronted the bride and groom. In a bitter quarrel, he accused Dr. Sun of betraying their friendship and acting insanely. He reminded Sun of the two decades they had struggled together. Now, so close to victory, how could his best friend let go of his wits and defile their mutual trust?

Sun remained composed. There was nothing he could say.

When Charlie saw that his appeal to loyalty had failed, he swore that he would have the marriage annulled on the grounds that Ching-ling was under age, and that she lacked parental consent. Still Sun refused to respond. He watched Charlie fume and sputter. If he needed Ching-ling with him to continue, that was all there was to it.

Charlie became bitter. This time Sun had gone too far. He vowed that he would never again have anything to do with Sun Yat-sen or his adventures, breaking off all relations with him and his party. His face growing black, Charlie told Ching-ling that he disowned her. He took the next ship back to Shanghai.

Later, whenever the subject of Ching-ling came up, the Soongs simply said that she had "formally joined Dr. Sun."

Months later, discussing the episode with his old friend, missionary William Burke, Charlie revealed his anguish in one terse outburst: "Bill, I was never so hurt in my life. My own daughter and my best friend."

In America, May-ling and her older brother, T. V., were absorbed in their studies when word came that Ching-ling had run away to marry a man old enough to be their father. By the time the news got to them months had passed. The news was too depressing to convey in a telegram.

Dr. Sun's family were equally stunned. Sun Fo, on his way to Japan for a reunion with his family, told a journalist who caught up with him in San Francisco that the news could not possibly be true.

Neither May-ling nor T. V. had taken much interest in Chinese affairs, or in the revolution, each being preoccupied with classes or social matters. Once Ching-ling had graduated from Wesleyan and gone back to China, May-ling had transferred to Wellesley College in Massachusetts, where she could be close to her brother at Harvard.

She attended Wellesley from the autumn of 1913 to the summer of 1917, and the four years transformed her from a chubby adolescent into a graceful young woman.

As a freshmen, she lived in the village of Wellesley, near the college campus, which she recalled years later as a place of "purfled walls [sic], enchanting woodlands and spacious grounds." Nearby in Cambridge, T. V. was in his second year at Harvard. He was listed in the Wellesley records as May-ling's guardian.

She had calling cards printed, MAYLING OLIVE SOONG, a middle name that she adopted in a moment of fancy. She spoke English with a lilting Georgia accent. Shortly after her arrival, May-ling decided that she did not like this new place, and went to the Dean of Residence, Edith Souther Tufts, and drawled, "Well, Ah reckon Ah shan't stay aroun' heah much longer."

She changed her mind, and was soon deep in studies, boys, and athletics. She majored in English literature and was especially fond of the Arthurian romances. She minored in philosophy, and among her electives took elocution.

After the first year, she moved onto the campus and lived at Wood Cottage for the rest of her stay. Not particularly athletic, she played on her class basketball team in a middy blouse and sateen bloomers, which came well below the knee. One Easter near Gloucester, she had to be rescued while swimming in a strong undertow. Other girls seized her by the hair and dragged her out of the water.

Boys appeared regularly on the doorstep of Wood Cottage, asking for May-ling. Most of them were Chinese students from Harvard and the Massachusetts Institute of Technology, with names the other girls remembered only as Mr. Li, Mr. Wang, and Mr. Peng—friends of T. V. When she learned of Ching-ling's crisis, she became obsessed with the possibility that she might have to accept an arranged marriage when she returned to China. Shortly afterward, May-ling announced her engagement to Peter Li, a Harvard student from Kiangsu Province. The engagement lasted only a few weeks till her anxiety passed, then she broke it off.

A member of the college faculty who knew May-ling intimately during those four years later wrote a confidential appraisal for the college files:

> My recollections of [May-ling] present a personality of more interest and more interior force than the rather sentimentalized figure we are getting along with the pietized propaganda. . . . She was, however, always to authority really docile, though the really interesting thing about her was her independence of thought—the fact that she kept up an awful thinking about everything. She was always questioning, asking the nature of ideas, rushing in one day to ask a definition of literature, the next day for a definition of religion. She thought about moral matters and discovered for herself some of the standards which people [who are] more conventionally brought up take ready-made, without inquiry. She was a stickler for truth, and resented in her past history any discovery that she had been fed conventional misinformation.
>
> I did not get the impression of wit and charm that others evidently speak of. . . . She was often in her mood sober and sombre (really moody and quite willing to show when she was bored). As the years went on, the return to China presented to her very hard problems, as she and T. V. both felt, I believe, and she wondered at difficulties ahead when she should return to a world and domestic standards from which she had grown away. She was, with all her sociability and considerable popularity, a little remote, watching us, questioning, criticising or liking, feeling herself a bit of an alien. She felt specially something unnatural in the whole life of Oriental students here, released from Chinese old rules which had kept the sexes separate and at the same time thrown them unnaturally together as young men and women by the fact that they are really an alien colony in a big American world.

She was, of course, much admired, not for beauty in those days, as were her sisters. But there was a fire about her and a genuineness, and always a possibility of interior forces. . . .

There was a real bond [with T. V.]. May-ling deferred to him. He was "brother," and his word was always desired for advice. . . . Of course it is just a strange accident that I never heard of the others [T. L. and T. A.]. May-ling was quite a family person, with great family pride and considerable family docility where no particular action was concerned. She talked and talked of her sisters, of her father, constantly of T. V. and sometimes of her mother, but never once did she mention those other two brothers.

By the time May-ling returned to Shanghai in 1917, the scandal over Ching-ling and Dr. Sun had subsided. May-ling was an instant celebrity. The Soongs were still living on the Avenue Joffre. It was a small house for gala parties, and May-ling berated her father for not having a more palatial home. The next time a Chinese friend sought his advice about sending a daughter to school in America, Charlie half-seriously advised against it. "Don't send your children abroad," he said ruefully. "Nothing's good enough for them when they come back. They want to turn everything upside down. . . . 'Father, why can't we have a bigger house? Father, why don't we have a modern bathroom?' Take my advice; keep your children at home!"

As a Shanghai socialite, May-ling was nominated for the usual committee posts. She accepted one on the Film Censorship Board and another at the YMCA. The Y had recently moved into a fine new building. Nearby was another handsome edifice, housing Charlie's booming Commercial Press.

May-ling came home from college in time to help her father entertain his old friend Julian Carr. Carr's wife Nannie had recently died and her passing left him melancholy. When Charlie had proposed a round-the-world ocean voyage with a leisurely stopover in Shanghai, Carr had resisted only briefly.

When Carr's ship reached Shanghai, Charlie, wearing his usual gray fedora, and with his paunch keeping his blue serge jacket from buttoning, met the General at the dock. He took Carr straight to the French Concession and introduced him to Mammy Soong and to all his children but one. In the days that followed, Charlie arranged for Carr to meet the Reverend William Burke, and showed him the old equipment at the Sino-American Press and the new Commercial Press building.

Julian Carr was now a spry old gentleman, but his legs were getting spindly. He was amazed by the industry of Asia's teeming millions: "Everything and everywhere around the cities seems like one vast shop. From the little fellow who peddles his wares on the sidewalk or the hole in the wall without a floor, to the large emporium vending silks and satins, everything is a shop and wide open, so as to be seen by the passersby."

Although Charlie had avoided Dr. Sun since the elopement, all animosity was set aside during General Carr's visit. Because of the extraordinary role that Carr had evidently played in financing the revolution, all the republican leadership joined ranks to entertain him. Ching-ling and Dr. Sun were now living in the French Concession at a house on the Rue Molière. Night after night, Carr was the honored guest at banquet after banquet. Two were hosted by Sun Yat-sen himself, with elaborate speeches of gratitude. Other political and financial leaders of China vied to throw the most extravagant celebration.

"They treated me like royalty—like a king," Carr wrote home. At Dr. Sun's personal orders, three magnificent porcelain vases were designed for Carr and handmade by Shanghai's finest artisans. They were presented as an official gift of the Chinese Government, even though Sun was not in office and the "government" was therefore a figment of their imagination. If any more proof were needed of Carr's help to the Chinese Revolution, this was it. The reception he received in Shanghai was like the one given to the Marquis de Lafayette by George Washington, in gratitude for his services during the American Revolution. Carr, like Lafayette, was a "hero of two worlds."

It was fortunate that Charlie and the general saw each other in Shanghai then—for only months after Carr's visit to China, Charlie Soong died in agony, the victim of what was called "stomach cancer." Three years after that, Carr succumbed to pneumonia.

The facts surrounding Charlie Soong's death are obscure. His friends were told that he died of stomach cancer—with the same utter conviction that they were told his name was Charlie Soong. But in Shanghai in the late spring of 1918, where Westerners sniffed nosegays or buried their nostrils in brandy while the morning collection of Chinese corpses was hauled out of the slums in tumbrils like so much nightsoil, nothing was as it seemed. Charlie had not been ill over a protracted period. There is no mention of anxiety about his health by any family members or friends in letters of the period. Only his oldest and youngest sons—T. V., fresh back from Harvard, and T. A.—were in Shanghai for the funeral, since there had not been enough warning for T. L. also to come home from America. So the possibility of foul play has always existed. In Edwardian society anywhere in the world, it was always fitting for men of note to die of a grand euphemism. Euphemistically, stomach cancer was as common in revolutionary Shanghai as lead poisoning was in Chicago and Marseille.

It was customary to publish tedious eulogies whenever someone died, but none appear to have been published or distributed about Charlie Soong. Although he once had been acclaimed for paying Dr. Sun's way, Charlie's name vanished from everyone's lips the moment he died—to be resurrected only when his children took power. In fact, he had become politically nonexistent the moment he raised an objection to Ching-ling's marriage. Sun's political supporters had to defend the doctor against Charlie's deprecations, so Charlie automatically ceased being a hero in the movement; when he died, he could not be celebrated. As a result, Charlie Soong's role in the revolution has been ignored by historians. At the time of Charlie's death, Dr. Sun was once more trying unsuccessfully to establish a foothold far to the south in Canton. He did not need just then to have the world reminded of how much he owed others.

Charlie's death passed so completely without notice that the dates given in ordinary library sources vary from 1918 to 1928—for example, Webster's Biographical Dictionary says 1927. Even Pearl Buck's sister, who wrote a children's book glorifying the Soong sisters, has Charlie alive and well in 1927 when May-ling's marriage to Chiang Kai-shek took place.

May-ling had been home less than a year when Charlie died on May 3, 1918, at the age of fifty-two. She joined Ching-ling and Ai-ling at his deathbed. Here was a show of sisterly unity that was to become exceedingly rare. Her older sisters then returned to their husbands, while May-ling set about moving with her mother into the bigger house on Seymour Road she had been craving since coming back from Wellesley, and which Charlie had refused to buy. There, while in mourning, May-ling and Ai-ling busied themselves "sorting" her father's personal papers—which thereafter could never be found.

If Charlie Soong was not poisoned by his enemies, he was certainly poisoned by his friends. For what probably killed him in the end was a broken heart.

Chapter 7

THE DRAGON'S TEETH

When Charlie Soong died in 1918, Shanghai was going through a remarkable transformation. We have seen the city in its earliest days and again in 1886 when Charlie Soong came home. Now, its appearance and personality were changing dramatically.

Industry was booming. As World War I drew the energy and attention of Western merchants back to Europe, Chinese money came out of hiding. Western firms were purchased by Chinese investors. New industries, backed by Chinese and Japanese money, made fat profits in rubber, coal, iron, soybean oil, flour, cotton, silk, cigarettes, and opium. Scores of Chinese banks came into existence to handle the enormous turnover of money. Shanghai bustled with overnight millionaires, looking for social affirmation. Other industrial cities boomed as well, including Canton and Wuhan, but the Yangtze Valley was the aorta, and Shanghai—the city of the capitalists, the compradors, and the gangsters —was the brain, the mouth, the wallet, the brothel, and the cesspit. European and American firms returned in force to Shanghai after World War I, displacing some Chinese companies in the process, but eventually the foreign and native merchants found a symbiotic relationship, scratching each other's backs while plundering the rest of China.

It was fashionable for prospering Chinese businessmen to talk about nationalism without meaning a word of it. The last thing the Shanghai capitalists really wanted was to cut their foreign umbilical cord. Thanks to the extraterritoriality of the International Settlement and the French Concession, Chinese could operate freely there, engaging in every illicit trade, reaping untaxable profits, without oversight or restraint. There was no other place in the world quite like Shanghai, and they meant to keep it that way.

The city grew along the river and sprawled across the countryside. It ate slums in its path and spat out more on its flanks. Small nineteenth-century buildings along the Bund were replaced by stone towers housing the Chartered Bank, the Hong Kong-Shanghai Bank, and banks from New York and London; other new buildings housed international oil companies, and the noble houses of the taipans. The first Chinese department stores came into existence, floor after floor jammed with dry goods and foreign luxuries. The Nanking Road glittered like Broadway at night. Motorcars replaced horse-drawn carriages and pushed through crowds like rhinos at a waterhole; around them rickshaws swirled like herds of long-horned antelope. The old British Club, with its gin-soaked verandah facing the river, was replaced by a stone club that would have pleased any West End Tory.

But there was another side to this prosperity—the long hours, the poor wages, and the grim conditions for the Chinese who lived and died in the factories. Boys and girls less than ten years old worked as slaves thirteen hours a day and dropped in exhaustion to sleep on rags beneath the machines. They were sold to factories and could not leave the guarded grounds night or day. Everywhere in the streets lay bodies of the destitute, corpses of starved children and unwanted babies. In any year from 1920 to 1940, as many as 29,000 bodies were picked out of the city's alleys, fished from the sewers, canals, and rivers.

None of this was hidden from sight. A travel writer of the time observed, "the hurried round-the-world tourist need not wander far from his luxurious hostelry to catch a hint, if his powers of perception are not totally atrophied."

For China as a whole, the ouster of the Manchus had not made life better. If anything, it was worse. Instead of a central government, however despised, the Middle Kingdom had broken up into fragments ruled by warlords and militarists. Skirmishes between their private armies laid waste the countryside. Farm production plummeted. Rice and wheat had to be imported, producing great profits for businessmen who hoarded to boost prices. Famine brought the people to their knees; they ate bark off trees and expired in city streets and country lanes. Rumors circulated of human flesh for sale in markets. Children were sold into slavery by hags along rural roads, and vanished into brothels and factories.

"It is Peking that really matters," observed the *Times* of London. Control of Peking did not mean control of China, but did mean possessing title to the nation. Foreign governments dealt only with Peking. If a warlord held the northern capital, he was automatically legitimate, received all benefits from foreign governments and commercial concessions, and reaped all taxes levied by the national government.

Yuan Shih-k'ai controlled Peking, while military governors of his so-called Peiyang Faction shielded him by controlling the surrounding northern provinces. To support themselves and their armies, the militarists secretly sold exploitation rights to foreign concerns, and exacted taxes from the peasantry many years in advance, wiping out the narrow margin of survival in rural towns and villages.

In 1918, there was still no Chinese Communist party, and the term "fascism" had not yet been coined. But ideologies now began to polarize. There had been two groups in Dr. Sun's Alliance party when it was formed in Tokyo in 1905—his original bourgeois supporters from the secret societies and his new supporters, the radical students. There was no boundary separating these groups in the beginning; but during World War I the students and the bourgeoisie began to see each other as adversaries. The students discovered the double standards of the middle class and turned against capitalism. They saw themselves as nationalists, with a utopian mixture of anarchy, democracy, Marxism, and agrarian reform. They wanted to complete the revolution by throwing out the foreign powers that had dominated China for more than a century, by redistributing land to the peasants, and by eliminating all economic privilege. The radicals saw their former allies in the Chinese middle class as anti-revolutionary and anti-national because businessmen profited from ties to the foreign powers. The breakup of the revolution into right and left wings was finally precipitated by the intervention of Japan.

When World War I broke Germany's grip on its distant colonial possessions, Japan quickly moved its forces to seize the German holdings in Shantung Province. The governments of Britain, France, and Italy, to enlist Japan's aid against Germany, secretly promised that she could keep Shantung after the war.

With this encouragement, Tokyo was emboldened to put a list of "21 Demands" before Yuan Shih-k'ai that would make China virtually its vassal state. In return for political and military support, Yuan must give Japan permanent control of Shantung, plus concessions in Manchuria and elsewhere. The demands were outrageous, but if he refused, Japan threatened to switch its support to his enemies. Yuan grudgingly accepted, on the condition that the terms be kept secret. Tokyo deliberately leaked the details. The result was a wave of public contempt toward Yuan and a bitter outcry against Japan.

Because they had helped the Allies in the war against Germany, the Chinese thought that they could turn to the Western powers, America in particular, to prevent Japan from taking such liberties. As China's contribution to World War I, hundreds of thousands of Celestials were sent to Europe and the Middle East, where they were assigned to work battalions. At the Versailles peace conference, the Chinese expected the Western leaders, particularly the idealistic President Woodrow Wilson, to help them regain their territory from Japan. They believed in the American President's grand design for a League of Nations, which seemed to offer a panacea for all the humiliations of the past.

Wilson was in a quandary. He badly wanted the League of Nations. He could simply declare at Versailles that he would not honor his Allies' secret Shantung agreement. But the Japanese let him know that in that case they would refuse to vote for his League. It was, said one diplomat, "a species of blackmail." Wilson finally gave in to the Japanese. His was not a popular decision; even those who had urged him to do it were disgusted. But, when the League of Nations covenant was signed on April 28, 1919, it was clear that Wilson had caved in to the Japanese.

The Chinese delegate at Versailles, Wellington Koo (a diplomat trained at Columbia University, who nonetheless was celebrated for keeping twenty-six concubines), would not sign the Versailles Treaty. "If I sign . . ." he told one of Wilson's aides, "—even under orders from Peking—I shall not have what you in New York call a Chinaman's chance."

When the news reached China and spread across the country by telegraph, six days later, on May 4, 1919, outraged students rioted. They targeted Chinese officials who were notorious for collaborating with Japan. In Peking, one bureaucrat had his house burned to the ground; another was beaten. The following morning, the Peking Students' Union was established to spread the May Fourth Movement across China. Teachers, journalists, liberal professionals, and some businessmen supported them. Demonstrations spread throughout the country and were met by severe police repression. Alarmed, Tokyo sent marines to China's port city concessions, including Shanghai, to intimidate the demonstrators. In Peking, the chancellor of the university, who had supported the students, was forced to resign, and more than one thousand others were arrested. Sixty thousand workers in Shanghai went on strike, till the Peking government agreed to fire its pro-Japanese ministers, and to release the arrested students. The capitulation of the government on these points did not satisfy the students and the intellectuals, but it did satisfy the merchants. The next day it was business as usual. To the merchants, enough was enough. But the student protest was just beginning. The line was drawn between those who wanted to go all the way and those who wanted to enjoy what they already had.

The May Fourth Movement was aimed not only at the foreign powers but at any Chinese who collaborated with foreigners. This was something new in the Chinese Revolution, and it made the merchants and the secret societies uneasy. From the point of view of the Shanghai capitalists, secure and comfortable in their villas in and around the foreign concessions, the revolution was taking a sinister path, one that threatened their livelihood and their stranglehold on the Chinese economy.

One of the leaders of the student movement in Peking was a mild intellectual named Ch'en Tu-hsiu, dean of the College of Letters at Peking University, where Mao Tse-tung worked in the library. During his two years at the University, Ch'en became a leader of China's intellectual vanguard. He spread the new ideas of the revolutionary left in a magazine called *The Weekly Critic,* which was written in vernacular Chinese to insure the widest possible readership. When the May Fourth riots exploded in Peking, he distributed pamphlets denouncing the Yuan dictatorship. For this he was imprisoned for three months and sorely treated. Following his release, he resigned his post at the university and departed for Shanghai. There, in the autumn of 1919, he became the rallying point for a group of young anarchists, socialists, and Marxists.

The Russian Revolution had drawn the close attention of Chinese students and the Chinese middle class for exactly opposite reasons. All over the world, leaders of government, commerce, industry, and the church reacted to the Red Terror of the Bolsheviks with horror and loathing while largely ignoring the equally grisly extremes of the Russian White Terror. It was the beginning of an era of intense worldwide political suspicion, when the fear of Communist conspiracy became epidemic and served to bring assorted fanatics to power in reaction, when the Ku Klux Klan boomed, when Jews were automatically reds, and when "labor" became a dirty word.

In Shanghai, Ch'en Tu-hsiu and his group of rather harmless and uncertain intellectuals decided that the doctrines of Lenin and Marx were appropriate for the situation that had developed in China, and that the next step in implementing them was to establish a Chinese Communist party. No doubt they were encouraged to reach this conclusion by the presence in their discussion group of Gregor Voitinsky, an agent of the Communist International. Marxist-Leninist study groups were organized across China with the help of Ch'en Tu-hsiu's former university colleagues and students. At Changsha, the capital of Hunan Province, the organizing was done by young Mao Tse-tung.

In the middle of July 1921, the hottest month in Shanghai, when there was little breeze down the Whangpoo to dissipate the heat hovering over the city, thirteen men gathered discreetly in the airless classrooms of the Boai Girls' School. The school, which was closed for the summer, was in a pink brick villa on Joyful Undertaking Street. The men were delegates to the First Congress of the Communist party of China. One of them was Mao Tse-tung, but there was not a single worker or peasant in their ranks. For nearly two weeks, the delegates debated their party platform. Two Russian envoys from the Comintern listened with growing irritation to these vague and indecisive Chinese.

Then a suspicious stranger was noticed lurking outside the black lacquer doors of the schoolhouse, and the meeting was hastily adjourned. The delegates were sufficiently alarmed by this ominous visitation to move their discussions to South Lake, a resort just outside the city. There the First Congress was reconvened aboard a gaudy pleasure boat while delegates fished, ate, and haggled over resolutions. The floating congress climaxed with the formal establishment of the Chinese Communist party.

It was a feeble and tentative beginning. Moscow regarded the Chinese Communists as bumblers and political adolescents. But their assembly was enough to alarm the Shanghai gangsters who were watching.

If the founders of the CCP had had any idea what was going to befall them, they would have been more alarmed by the mysterious figure watching the pink schoolhouse on Joyful Undertaking Street. The spy was not there merely for the French Sûreté, but for another of Pockmarked Huang's organizations—the Green Gang, a new gangster syndicate that would soon be the most militant anti-Communist force in China. Its leader was Tu Yueh-sheng.

Tu was that exotic creature, the pure criminal mastermind. He was born into desperate poverty in 1888 across the river from Shanghai, in a ramshackle village called Kaochiao in Pootung District, the most squalid slum in China. His father was a coolie in a grain shop. When his parents died, the boy became dependent upon his mother's brother, who treated him brutally. By the time Tu reached his teens, he was a sinewy and murderous youth, with narrow shoulders, unusually long arms, large yellow teeth, and the eyes of a successful rat. He decided to pursue a career pushing opium across the river in Shanghai. At first, he stayed alive by working as a helper to a fruit vendor, selling pears on the waterfront of the French Concession and doing homicidal favors for waterfront hooligans.

Tu's outstanding features were a big shaved head and ears that stood out like tree mushrooms. His face was lumpy and irregular, like a sack of potatoes—the result of childhood beatings. His lips were stretched taut over his protuberant teeth in a perpetual smirk, and his left eyelid drooped in a permanent wink, giving him a lascivious air. There was always fresh gravy on his gown. He fit in perfectly with the waterfront milieu. Around him were loitering toughs and pandering riffraff, low-end members of the famous Red Gang. Tu fell in with them and before he was fifteen became a member of the gang.

His closest pals were runners for the big man himself, Pockmarked Huang. Tu hung around the kitchen at Huang's heavily-guarded house, and eventually made the acquaintance of the great detective's well-thumped mistress. Through her he met the boss and was recognized as a valuable recruit, a young man of quick wits. Tu handled his assignments with energy and resourcefulness. He made friends everywhere by his easy manner, his generosity, and his genuine willingness to help. There was nothing he would rather do than aid a downtrodden street vendor by terrorizing the pawnbroker to whom the vendor was in debt.

Big-eared Tu was especially good at handling opium, which was Pockmarked Huang's main source of revenue. One day, Tu proposed that the rival gangs join in a cartel to move the opium to market, and then split the take. This would put them in control of most of the opium in China. They could dictate the price. Profits would rise dramatically.

Huang let Tu work out the details—which meant negotiating with some gang leaders and assassinating others. The leader of the Green Gang resisted and was disposed of; Big-eared Tu became the new boss of the Green Gang. The head of the Blue Gang—whose name was Chang Hsiao-lin—wisely decided to cooperate, and a troika was formed of the three gang leaders. Together they ruled the Shanghai underworld, the two adjacent provinces of Chekiang and Kiangsu, and the entire Yangtze Valley, far into the poppy-growing regions of China's interior.

In the International Settlement, bootleg opium had always been controlled by the chiu chao Three Harmonies Triad, headed for many years by the Cantonese Wong Sui. Big-eared Tu "persuaded" Wong to join the cartel also. This extended Tu's leverage into the International Settlement, where he gradually subverted and took over the Three Harmonies, absorbing it into the Green Gang. Eventually, the Green Gang completely displaced all other triads within its territory, except the deeply embedded peasant league, the Society of Elders and Brothers, in the countryside. Tu's worth increased fabulously, at one time conservatively estimated at over $40 million American. Never tight with funds, he gave money freely to friends and, if strangers offered him a plausible cause, he would give money to them as well. There were many legends about how Big-eared Tu helped widows, rescued men who had lost everything, and supported orphans. He also had a bottomless talent for inducing fear. People had a way of doing what Tu asked them to do.

He never tried to take the place of his patron, Pockmarked Huang. The Red Gang continued to exist as an exclusive social club for patriotic old revolutionaries, while criminal operations became the province of the Green Gang from 1910 on. Pockmarked Huang remained the head of the troika. But Big-eared Tu was the director of operations, and puppet master of Shanghai. When he pulled strings, the city danced to his tune. At his disposal were a large number of the urban workers, from longshoremen and street coolies to postal clerks and bank tellers. (The postal employees' guild allowed him to read people's mail.) Wherever possible, Tu took over the indirect control of companies by using extortion and terror to bully the boards of directors into submission; meanwhile, his men organized the employees of these same companies into guilds. It was carefully done for the most part to maintain an illusion of independence. But both the guilds and the management were powerless until Big-eared Tu jerked the strings.

This was why, in the summer of 1921, when the thirteen Marxist delegates gathered in the pink brick girls' school on Joyful Undertaking Street to establish the Chinese Communist party, there was a suspicious stranger lurking outside. The snoop had been sent by Pockmarked Huang and Big-eared Tu, to keep an eye on this odd collection of Chinese intellectuals and their rather more dangerous Russian friends. After what had happened in Russia, the presence of Bolshevik agents and organizers in China was a direct challenge to the growing dominion of the Green Gang.

As one might expect, Big-eared Tu had some very interesting friends. Of the few that he evidently considered his equal in guile and cunning there was a woman—one with a remarkable gift for high finance and backroom intrigue. Her name was Ai-ling Soong, now known to strangers as Madame Kung.

On many Sundays, after Ai-ling had been to the Young J. Allen Methodist Church, the gang leader arrived at her home on the Route de Seiyes for a quiet conversation while his bodyguards kept vigil on all sides. Their children grew up together.

This curious gathering on the Kung lawn combined the resources of the Kung banking empire, the leverage of the Soong family, and the mammoth clout of the Green Gang. They joined forces to make a series of stunning investments and takeovers during the years from 1916 to 1940. The Christian image of the Soong clan (with its collegiate veneer) was magic with foreigners, and the dark participation of Big-eared Tu intimidated any Chinese who might otherwise be stubborn. If the message was not clear, Big-eared Tu sent the offending party his usual warning—an ornate Chinese coffin. A positive change of heart could be expected momentarily.

At the opposite end of the Shanghai social scale, Big-eared Tu enjoyed visiting the famous Blue Villa and cruising the other Green Gang brothels in the Blue Chamber District with a young, ill-tempered bravo by the name of Chiang Kai-shek.

At precisely noon on October 31, 1887—one year before Big-eared Tu was born—Chiang entered the world on the second floor of the Yutai Salt Store in Chikow, a town west of Shanghai, beyond the Wuling Mountains in Chekiang Province. His mother was twenty-three years old, the third wife of a salt merchant nearly twice her age. She called her son Chiang Jui-yuan. Years later, a teacher gave him a courtesy name that was pronounced "Kai-shek" in Cantonese. It is by this name that he is known to history.

Chiang's father died when he was very young. The boy became unusually devoted to his mother, who was not a happy woman. He once said that she had "swallowed much bitterness."

He was an odd and sickly child, given to fits of ill temper, and became an object of ridicule in the village. A fortuneteller remarked that he had an abnormally-shaped head, and was "exceptionally strange." He grew up having bouts of weeping and seizures of uncontrolled rage, interspersed by long periods of withdrawal. A tutor who observed this erratic behavior remarked, "One would think he had two different personalities." When he was composed, he spoke rapidly in a high-pitched voice, in the sibilant Chekiang dialect.

Without a father in the house, the Chiangs were preyed upon by local authorities. Once, when a villager ran away without paying his rice tax, young Chiang was hauled into court and threatened with jail if he did not find the money to pay the other citizen's tax. Somehow he raised the money, but Chiang was embittered by the injustice. He called it "the first spark that kindled my revolutionary fire."

When he was fourteen, he was betrothed to a village girl named Mao Fu-mei, three years his senior. The marriage did nothing to settle him down; he was not inclined to remain in provincial Chikou or in the salt business. Four years after the marriage, using some of his mother's savings, he went to the town of Fenghua to study at a modest school called the Pavilion of Literature.

It was there that Chiang discovered a slim little Chinese military treatise, a classic called *The Art of War*, written by Sun Tzu in the fourth century B.C., during the Warring States period of ancient China. To Sun Tzu "the supreme art of war is to subdue the enemy without fighting." He favored cleverness over brute force, deceit and intrigue over combat.

"All warfare is based on deception," Sun Tzu observed. The most important ingredient was the "employment of secret agents," not troops. Any commander too stupid or avaricious to organize a corps of spies of the very best men was, according to Sun, "no general; no support to his sovereign," and was furthermore "completely devoid of humanity." Armed combat was a waste and horror that disrupted the economy and the lives of thousands. When the proper secret agents were put to work, "they are called the Divine Skein and are the treasure of a sovereign." But, Sun Tzu warned, "he who is not sage and just, humane and wise, cannot use secret agents. And he who is not delicate and subtle cannot get the truth out of them." It was all "delicate indeed! Truly delicate."

The Art of War, like other Chinese classics, attracted many commentators through the centuries. They added appendages to the original work. One commentator in the Sung Dynasty (960–1279), related an example of how an "expendable" agent might be properly used:

> In our Dynasty, Chief of Staff Ts'ao once pardoned a condemned man whom he then disguised as a monk and caused to swallow a ball of wax and enter Tangut. When the false monk arrived he was imprisoned. The monk told his captors about the ball of wax and soon discharged it in a stool. When the ball was opened, the Tanguts read a letter transmitted by Chief of Staff Ts'ao to the Tangut Director of Strategic Planning. The chieftain was enraged, put his minister to death, and executed the monk.

The commentator added laconically: "This is the idea."

Sun Tzu's ideas captured Chiang's imagination and gave shape to his future plans. It was also at the Pavilion that his tutor guided him into the austere Confucian sect of the Sung Dynasty scholar Chu Hsi, which prescribed self-denial, self-discipline, and moral endeavor as the proper means of achieving harmony. Chiang's life so far had been a struggle against poverty, a battle to endure ridicule because of his appearance, and a personal ordeal to overcome his own violent nature; this philosophy of self-denial held special significance for him and he tried without notable success to make it a central tenet of his life.

At the Pavilion he also developed the lifelong habit of rising before dawn, going to the verandah of his bedroom to stand and meditate for half an hour in his pajamas or undershorts, bolt upright, lips tight, arms folded across his chest.

Thanks to Sun Tzu, he was committed to a career as a man on horseback, a man who would command troops and secret agents. He left the Pavilion in 1906 to continue studies at the nearby Dragon River Middle School, but stayed only three months before giving it up to go to Japan for military training. He was nineteen. Japan's defeat of Imperial Russia the previous year made it clear that her arms were unsurpassed in Asia, and deserved to be studied as an example for development of the Chinese Army.

Chiang wrote to his mother for money for the trip. When she protested, he hacked off his Manchu queue and sent it to her, upsetting the whole village. She reluctantly agreed to pay his way.

When he arrived, Chiang discovered that Japanese military academies would accept only Chinese students recommended by the Manchu government. He remained in Japan for six months, becoming immersed in the heady atmosphere of the revolutionaries, enjoying their reckless style of life as much as their conspiratorial, gun-toting politics.

Sun Yat-sen's new Alliance party injected fresh excitement into the republican cause. One of Dr. Sun's most dynamic and promising followers was a thirty-year-old man from Chiang's own province. His name was Ch'en Ch'i-mei, and he was gifted with both high intelligence and extraordinary charisma. Here was a real man of action. He took Chiang Kai-shek under his wing, and they became fast friends.

This man of action, Ch'en Ch'i-mei, had arrived in Japan just a short while before Chiang. While working in Shanghai as a laborer in a silk company, he had been swept up by the revolution and joined the anti-Manchu Green Gang. His unusual imagination and resourcefulness had attracted the attention of the gang's leaders. Pockmarked Huang had urged him to go to Japan for military training, and Ch'en's older brother had agreed to pay his way. In Tokyo, Ch'en Ch'i-mei had enrolled in a police academy. He also had joined Dr. Sun's party and become an active recruiter.

In the winter of 1906–1907, Chiang went home for his sister's wedding. While on this trip, he put into action a scheme he had devised with the help of Ch'en Ch'i-mei to get around the problem of government sponsorship for military school. There was a competitive examination each year to select candidates for the Short-term National Army School in Hopei Province. Chiang sat for the exam and passed. He spent 1907 at the army school and was then given official permission to undergo military training in Japan. The ancient sage Sun Tzu might have been pleased; by this elaborate and single-minded detour, Chiang had overcome all obstacles and was back in Japan in 1908 for a three-year term at the renowned Shimbu Gakko academy.

Before he left for Japan, the village girl he had married at age fourteen bore him a son, Ching-kuo. Her life with Chiang and his severe, humorless mother had been difficult. According to the young woman's own testimony, Chiang treated her violently and frequently beat her. She was doubtless relieved when he left.

In company with his friend and patron Ch'en Ch'i-mei, Chiang early in 1908 went before the Alliance party and was invited to join the revolutionaries.

During the summers, Chiang returned to Chekiang for brief visits with his mother, then hurried on to Shanghai to join Ch'en Ch'i-mei in a number of armed robberies and gang murders, and began building his police record. These attacks combined revolutionaries and gangsters in such a way that they were indistinguishable. On one of these side trips, in 1908, he took part in a raid on a jail block to rescue Green Gang convicts and "imprisoned revolutionaries." It was probably then that Ch'en recommended him for membership in the gang, although the exact date has been obscured.

The following year, Chiang graduated from the Shimbu Gakko and began field training with the Japanese Army. In 1910, he participated in the gang slaying of a man described in the Shanghai police records as "a prominent Chinese resident of the Settlement." Chiang's police record in the British-administered International Settlement grew over the years to include murder, extortion, numerous armed robberies, and assorted other crimes. He was indicted on all the listed charges, but was never brought to trial, or jailed.

In the summer of 1911, Chiang helped set up another Shanghai assassination, and was just resuming his duties with the Japanese 19th Field Artillery Regiment when news came of the successful October 10 uprising. Chiang immediately rushed home and was commissioned by Ch'en Ch'i-mei to command the "83rd Brigade," a band of 3,000 Green Gang gunmen turned over to the revolutionaries by Pockmarked Huang.

Shanghai was still under Manchu government control, but Ch'en Ch'i-mei intended to take the city by force. In early November 1911, Ch'en led the brigade successfully against the Kiangnan Arsenal, and took personal control of the city, becoming the military governor of liberated Shanghai. It would have been natural for him then to appoint Chiang Kai-shek his chief of staff. He gave the post instead to another Japanese-trained military man who was more stable. Apparently, Ch'en had been put off by Chiang Kai-shek's violent temper tantrums, heavy drinking, and carousing.

But there were other jobs open. Ch'en put him in charge of a "Dare to Die" contingent of one hundred men, who rushed to Hangchow to help local revolutionaries liberate the city. The mission was a success,

and Chiang returned a hero. He was rewarded with command of the
5th Regiment of the Kiangsu Army.

The climax of Chiang's early career as a Green Gang bravo came
just before the end of 1911, when he took it upon himself to dispose of
one of Ch'en Ch'i-mei's republican rivals, an influential revolutionary
named T'ao Ch'eng-chang. He was the leader of the (Ming) Restoration
Society in Shanghai—another triad offshoot of the original Hung
League—and apparently intended to challenge Ch'en Ch'i-mei for the
political leadership of the city. Chiang Kai-shek decided that the time
had come to get rid of T'ao permanently, an act that presumably would
put him back in his mentor's good graces. He went to the Shanghai
hospital where T'ao was recovering from an illness, surprised him without bodyguards, and began a violent quarrel. Then, according to one
account, Chiang, "angry beyond control, yanked out his pistol and
killed [T'ao] with one shot."

Chiang eluded arrest and left hurriedly for Japan, where he remained discreetly out of the way for the better part of 1912. While
there, he published a small Chinese military journal, for which he wrote
his own passionate essays.

When he returned to China the next winter, however, he fell
right back into his old habits. According to one of his contemporaries:

> He abandoned himself to a life of intense dissipation. He would disap-
> pear for months from headquarters in the houses of sing-song girls, and for
> some reason or other he acquired a fiery, uncompromising temper which
> weighed very tryingly on his friends. . . . He also came into contact with
> the leaders of the secret societies of Shanghai, which later on became very
> useful to him in his dealings with the Shanghai capitalists.

Another put it more sympathetically:

> His work was light, taking, on the average, two or three hours a day;
> and with a comfortable income which he was receiving there was much
> chance for moral degeneration. His friends, knowing his temper, and that
> persuasion would be futile, deplored this. . . . But the results of his riotous
> living began to tell. Moreover, his hasty and violent temper rendered
> cooperation with others difficult. . . . Chiang is by nature obdurate. Not
> infrequently he would fly into storms of temper before which few human
> beings could stand. Above all he was self-opinionated, highly so. No one
> could endure him, and by degrees he became more and more disagreeable
> to his associates.

Chiang caroused with Big-eared Tu. According to an Englishmen who knew Tu well, the gangleader traveled in a manner reminiscent of Chicago mobsters:

> A carload of advance bodyguards came and "cased" the cabaret from kitchen to cloak-rooms, then took up stations to wait for the boss. Tu himself always traveled in a large, bullet-proof sedan. . . . Behind the leader's limousine a second carload of bodyguards travelled. Tu never got out until these had surrounded him. Then, with one at each elbow, he ventured to cross the footpath and enter the cabaret, where his men were posted at every door and turn. Inside, while he and his party sat at a front table, guards sat beside and behind, guns in plain view.

It was estimated that one out of every twelve Chinese houses in Shanghai was a brothel, which put the total number at 668 brothels for the International Settlement alone. One out of every 130 residents of the city was a prostitute. Of this number, more than half were owned by the Green Gang or owed allegiance to it. There were 121 prostitutes in the Blue Villa alone. In the French Concession, the gang's control of brothels was total. It was an arduous trade. No matter how attractive or skillful, the prostitutes were hard-pressed to lure men from their servant boys, or from the many male brothels. To even the odds, as it were, and compete for the attention of these sodomists, the more forthright young ladies were quick to offer themselves for games of "Playing with the Flower in the Back Garden."

Since this netherworld consumed so much of Chiang's and Tu's attention, it requires a closer look.

The Chinese brothels, almost without exception, were staffed by girls with bound feet—the ideal being less than three inches long. These were objects of extraordinary sexual excitement, and enjoyed a central role in any noisy evening. Although foot fetishes are common to many cultures (the Turk and Mongol women of Siberia, for example, go barebreasted on hot days but never show their bare feet to anyone but their husbands), in China it was institutionalized. As a nineteenth-century French scholar explained:

> My attention has been drawn . . . by a large number of pornographic engravings, of which the Chinese are very fond. In all these lascivious scenes we see the male voluptuously fondling the woman's foot. When a Celestial takes into his hand a woman's foot, especially if it is very small, the effect upon him is precisely the same as is provoked in a European by

a young and firm bosom. All the Celestials whom I have interrogated on this point have replied unanimously: "Oh, a little foot! You Europeans cannot understand how exquisite, how sweet, how exciting it is!" The contact of the genital organ with the little foot produces in the male an indescribable degree of voluptuous feeling, and women skilled in love know that to arouse the ardor of their lovers a better method than all Chinese aphrodisiacs is to take the penis between their feet. It is not rare to find Chinese Christians accusing themselves at confession of having had "evil thoughts on looking at a woman's foot."

The practice of footbinding began in the tenth century, made fashionable by palace dancers. There are no illustrations of Chinese with bound feet that date earlier. From court dancers, the fashion spread through the aristocracy, and eventually was imitated by the peasants. One purpose for the custom was to restrain women; Confucians barely tolerated females, and by crippling their feet it was certain that they could not stray far from their well-guarded quarters, or run from beatings. When the custom was occasionally condemned, it was not because of the pain and suffering it caused but because it aroused lewd behavior.

Bound feet demonstrated the lengths to which a woman would go to make her daughter a desirable sexual object. Footbinding usually began at age four. A ten-foot-long, two-inch bandage was wrapped around the toes to force them in against the sole. Each day the bandage was tightened until the foot was folded under with only the big toe sticking out, a shape called the "Golden Lotus" because it resembled a lotus pod with the petals removed. Flesh rotted and fell off, sometimes a toe or two, and the foot oozed pus, until the process of deformation was complete after two years, at which point the feet were practically dead.

Swaddled in exquisitely decorated silk boots, the feet were carefully hidden. It was commonplace for young rogues to go to great lengths to steal a maiden's tiny silk shoes, masturbate into them, and then return them, to her intense embarrassment and humiliation.

Thus hobbled, a girl grew up walking in a mincing step, not unlike a ballet dancer *en pointe*. This caused her limbs to remain undeveloped and spindly. By contrast, the girl's buttocks and "jade gate" were popularly believed to develop to such a degree that she could more tightly grip her lover's "jade spear." The Chinese intellectual Ku Hung-ming even argued that "the smaller the woman's foot, the more wondrous become the folds of her vagina." Chinese men cared little about breasts, but had visions of fondling and sucking deformed feet, with the result that the whorehouses of Shanghai each night saw thousands of performances of this extraordinary spectacle.

The prostitutes were very young, twelve to fourteen, kidnapped or sold into slavery by destitute parents. They dressed in loose silk trousers and jackets with high wing collars up to their cheekbones. Among their most popular games was Raft. A girl would surrender her tiny, embroidered shoes, which would be passed around the table for the fondling and perusal of all males present. A wineglass was put in one shoe and the other shoe was placed in a large bowl. The girl then hobbled around the table on her ruined feet and held the bowl an arm's length from each man. The patrons picked up lotus seeds from a bamboo box, and tried to toss them into the shoe within the bowl—the so-called Raft—following certain prescribed rules. After each guest had taken five turns, the girl who had donated the shoes would prescribe penalties, which ranged from downing one drink to five drinks, never more, to prevent them from becoming too drunk. Drinks were taken from the wineglass placed inside the other shoe, allowing the drinker to inhale the delicious fragrance of the perfumed foot.

At any point in the evening when so moved, one guest or another would go off with a girl. In a private chamber, it was customary to linger over the girl's feet, stroking, sniffing, and licking them, and even dipping them in tea before drinking it. A favorite delight was to eat almonds from between her crushed toes. When mounting passion could be contained no longer, the gasping customer would at last drive his jade spear into her jade gate and, raising her tiny feet to his shoulders, insert her Gold Lotus entirely into his mouth and suck noisily till the moment of "Clouds and Rain."

It is a matter of no small wonder, with all these peculiar goings-on night after night in Shanghai, that the young revolutionaries with Big-eared Tu had any energy or wits left to carry out their daily responsibilities. Perhaps here was one reason why the revolution did not succeed decades earlier.

"Everybody says that I am given to lust," Chiang Kai-shek wrote to friends in his own defense, "but they do not know that this is a thing of last resort, in a state of utter depression."

At one famous prostitute's home, Chiang exchanged torrid glances with a pretty chambermaid named Yao Yi-ching. The effect was explosive—and was not lost on his friends. At their urging, he took the girl as his concubine and installed her in his mother's home at Chikou. It was one big, happy family: his tyrannical mother, his forlorn wife and bullheaded son, and the exquisite Yao. That year Chiang Kai-shek turned twenty-five.

Apparently, his concubine cared deeply for him. Shortly thereafter, he brought home an infant boy named Wei-kuo. Originally, Chiang claimed that the child was the son of a friend in Japan who had not been able to care for him. Later, he said the boy was born in Shanghai. Some speculated that the child was his own, born out of wedlock in Tokyo. Whatever the case, the child was enthusiastically received by Concubine Yao, who set about looking after him as if he were her own. Many years later Wei-kuo was generally acknowledged as Chiang's second son by biographers.

In 1913, when the Second Revolution was launched to bring down Dictator Yuan, Chiang was asked to slip into the Kiangnan Arsenal and persuade his old army buddies to rise up against their commanders. Instead, Chiang blundered into the arms of an alert picket and only narrowly managed to escape. Rushing to Big-eared Tu, he obtained the loan of all the Green Gang hoods he could find, and launched an ill-prepared attack on the arsenal. His unruly force took heavy casualties and was obliged to retreat to the safety of the International Settlement, where they were disarmed embarrassingly by the British. Why Chiang was not jailed promptly by the British is best explained by mistaken identity. Chiang was not establishing a stellar record as a military officer.

Despite these misadventures, he was making crucial political and criminal contacts, which were to be of much greater importance on the road to power. Chiang Kai-shek, Ch'en Ch'i-mei, and Chief of Staff Huang Fu took a ritual oath becoming blood brothers, swearing to look after each other's kin as if they were of the same clan. The pact had fateful consequences for Chiang, because Ch'en's two nephews turned out to be a particularly zealous and efficient pair. Chiang also became extremely close with one of Big-eared Tu's intimates, a wealthy revolutionary named Chang Ching-chang, a banker, stockbroker, and international dealer in rare Chinese antiquities. The aura of menace surrounding this individual was heightened by a disease that crippled one of his feet and thereafter gave him the lurching gait of Shakespeare's Richard III. This sinister millionaire, whom some Westerners called Curio Chang and the French in Shanghai referred to as

Quasimodo, became one of Chiang Kai-shek's most important political patrons.

Hounded by Yuan's police, his secret agents and assassins, Chiang Kai-shek and Ch'en Ch'i-mei were finally forced to withdraw once again to Japan in 1915. They were right to fear for their lives.

For the next few months, they slipped in and out of Shanghai, staging uprisings, armed robberies, and assassinations. Ch'en had now risen to the rank of Chairman of the Central Committee in Sun Yat-sen's KMT party, putting him near the top of the republican movement. Until that spring, all efforts to murder him had failed. On May 18, 1916, in a quiet neighborhood of the French Concession, one of Yuan's assassins finally succeeded. The killers used a ruse to gain access to Ch'en's hideout at the secret party headquarters, and shot him to death.

His murder came as a terrible blow to Chiang Kai-shek. At age thirty, he had lost his sworn friend, boon companion, and role model. At the funeral, Chiang read a eulogy to which he added:

"Alas! From now on where can be found a man who knows me so well and loves me so deeply as you did?" Then, perhaps in reference to all the criticism of him for his wild rages, drinking, and whoring, he said, "I do not mind that you believed their lies about me when you were living. All I want is that I should have a clear conscience now that you are dead."

Chiang took his dead comrade's nephews under his wing. Ch'en Kuo-fu and to a lesser extent the quieter Ch'en Li-fu were both rising rapidly in the Green Gang thanks to their late uncle's influence. They remained close to Chiang the rest of their lives, personally and politically, and eventually made their Ch'en clan second only to the Soongs in China.

Chiang Kai-shek must have taken some bitter consolation when only a few weeks later Dictator Yuan, the man who had supposedly underwritten the murder of Ch'en Ch'i-mei, died of uremia, poisoned, some said, by his own ambitions.

In the KMT's reassignments following his mentor's murder, Chiang Kai-shek rose by default to become one of Sun Yat-sen's senior lieutenants. In the autumn of 1917, Dr. Sun and Ching-ling decided that the Second Revolution might have better results if they set up a new base far to the south in Canton, which was already in the hands of a warlord who had broken off successfully from Peking. That November, the doctor offered Chiang a post as his personal military advisor in Canton. When he reached the southern port city, Chiang was also named chief of the Field Operations Department of the Kwangtung army. His role was really to be Sun Yat-sen's security chief and liaison. He came and went on mysterious missions, dressed in civilian clothes, and was referred to as "Mister Chiang."

The Kwangtung army was commanded by warlord Ch'en Chiung-ming. His officers were southern men, all speaking Cantonese. They resented the intrusion of this odd fellow with the peanut-shaped head, who spoke only the incomprehensible dialect of Chekiang, and they had little to do with him. It was a difficult assignment for Chiang as a result.

Only a small area around the city of Canton was actually controlled by Dr. Sun's warlord ally. They were surrounded by hostile forces who were loyal to the northern warlords. Before he could do anything else, Dr. Sun had to secure his flanks, but the Kwangtung army was not sufficient in itself. To expand his army, Sun as usual hired shifty mercenaries from warlords, triads, and bandit chieftains, but these soldiers owed their loyalty only to a reliable paymaster, and money was a constant problem. Sun needed a real army, but there was no way he could get one unless he trained his own, which would require a large sum in foreign aid. Until then, he would be dependent on treacherous hirelings.

Preoccupied with these financial and military difficulties, Dr. Sun could give only divided attention to daily routine, and assigned administrative responsibilities to a claque of his followers, many of whom had a high opinion of themselves but little real ability. The few competent men in Sun's following were being killed off. In desperation, he began to turn more and more to Chiang Kai-shek, and brought Chiang down from Shanghai repeatedly in fruitless efforts to put things in order. Chiang resented these assignments, because they held no real authority. Time and again, he would arrive in Canton in response to Sun's latest plea, give his help for a few days or weeks, then go back to Shanghai in a huff.

In Shanghai, he was spending much of this time with his crippled friend Curio Chang. The millionaire art dealer owned shops in Paris and New York that sold ancient Chinese artifacts and imperial treasures to rich Western collectors. He joined Big-eared Tu in setting up a stock and commodity exchange in Shanghai under the cover of "legitimate" business friends. The exchange was portrayed as a clever way to raise political money for Dr. Sun and the revolution. But the participants were all right-wing extremists, and the money sent to Dr. Sun went not from the commodity exchange but directly from the bulging purses of Big-eared Tu and Curio Chang to build their standing in the KMT hierarchy. They gave Chiang Kai-shek a "job" on their exchange as a "broker," which was a modest position for a successful extortionist, bank robber, and hitman. The post involved no real work, and put him in a position to make quick and easy money. Chiang was said to have made and squandered a million Chinese dollars during this period, which was then equivalent in purchasing power to a hundred thousand U.S. dollars in New York.

He had again fallen madly in love—this time with a nimble harlot with unbound feet, named Ch'en Chieh-ju, who appears to have recognized Chiang as a high roller. So taken was he by this woman's diverting talents and unusual brains that he turned his whole life upside down. He divorced his original village wife, cast out the chambermaid concubine whom he had only recently installed at the family homestead in Chikou, and married Miss Ch'en. For the young woman, it turned out to be a stroke of incredible fortune.

In November 1921, Chiang wrote a letter to his first wife's brother, and asked him to help arrange a divorce:

> . . . for the past ten years, I have not been able to bear hearing the sound of her footsteps or seeing her shadow. To this day, there has been no home worthy of the name. My decision to divorce her is the result of ten years' painful experience. It has not been made lightly. Enlightened and wise as you are, I think you may be able to plan for my happiness, freeing me from the life-long suffering.

That November he married Miss Ch'en in a Buddhist ceremony. Big-eared Tu, who "owned" the young woman, literally gave the bride away. She became the second Madame Chiang Kai-shek, and traveled under that name both in China and abroad.

One night not long afterward (various dates are given but it was probably early December) Chiang attended a society Christmas soirée thrown by T. V. Soong at Dr. Sun Yat-sen's Rue Molière home, and met a vivacious young woman with extraordinary connections. She was T. V. Soong's little sister, the youngest daughter of the legendary Charlie Soong, and the sister of Madame Sun Yat-sen. Her name was

May-ling. She was also the kid sister of Big-eared Tu's pal Ai-ling. All at once Chiang's cup was overflowing.

Although he had a new bride, an old wife, and a recent concubine, Chiang by all accounts was so taken by May-ling Soong (and her remarkable connections) that he began immediately to plan a long-range courtship strategy.

When he traveled to Canton later in December in response to an urgent plea from Dr. Sun, Chiang brought up his introduction to the doctor's sister-in-law. He told Sun that he had "divorced" the Chikou village girl to whom he had been married in his youth. He went on to assert that he had tossed out Miss Yao, the chambermaid who was raising his Japanese-born son. But he completely avoided telling Sun about his new wife, Ch'en Chieh-ju—although they had then been married only one month. Chiang listed all of these items as evidence that he had now firmly put his life in order, turned over a new leaf, and was ready, as he put it, to undertake great responsibilities—"to dedicate my energy to the revolution with all my heart."

"I have no wife now, Teacher," insisted Chiang, according to Sun Yat-sen's celebrated memory of the conversation. "Do you think Miss Soong could be persuaded to accept me?"

The doctor reflected for a moment and then said, frankly, no. But he would consult his wife. When Sun brought up the matter to Ching-ling, she was scandalized. She would rather, she hissed, see her little sister dead than married to a man who, if he was not married, should have been to at least one or two women in Canton alone.

Chapter 8

THE DANCING BEAR

In the spring of 1922, Ching-ling and Dr. Sun were nearly murdered by their own military commander. The Suns were living in an exposed house on a hill in Canton, connected to his offices in the presidential Residency by an elevated wooden footbridge, roofed over and partially enclosed against monsoon rains.

The violent history of Canton had made it necessary for most warlords, military leaders, imperial magistrates, and rich pawnbrokers (like the Kungs) to build fortress-style dwellings in the city or on islands, where the Pearl River formed a natural moat. The hillside Residency had no such security. Perhaps deliberately, it was vulnerable to assault, especially to artillery or mortar barrage from the hill above. As ever, the doctor was casual about security precautions.

General Ch'en Chiung-ming, the bantam warlord of Kwangtung Province, was unrelated to the dynamic Shanghai revolutionary who had been Chiang Kai-shek's mentor. This Ch'en was a Hakka, one of the group of northern Chinese, speaking a distinct dialect, who had migrated to South China in the twelfth and thirteenth centuries. They were celebrated by foreigners for refusing to bind their women's feet, and were progressive in many other ways. They played a leading role in establishing the chiu chao brotherhood, and formed the nucleus of the Taiping revolutionary movement in the 1850s. As a young man, General Ch'en had played an important role in the 1911 capture of Canton that had made Kwangtung Province independent of the empire. He was now forty-four years old, and among China's warlords was regarded as uniquely progressive.

After Yuan's death, Dr. Sun had joined Ch'en in setting up a southern republic, which in reality was little more than a secret-society city-state in Canton, with boundaries that got larger or smaller depending on the shifting allegiances of warlords in neighboring provinces. During the honeymoon that followed, General Ch'en introduced liberal programs, including sending abroad promising students—Communists as well as conservatives. With the success of these social innovations, Ch'en became more concerned with the preservation and improvement of his southern republic than he was with the long-range goal of liberating the rest of China.

Sun Yat-sen, on the contrary, was so absorbed by his dream of leading the southern armies northward to "unify China" that he left administrative responsibilities to a group of sycophants, many of whom were quite incompetent at anything but conspiracy. Kwangtung Province fell into disarray and the city of Canton became unruly, unpoliced, crowded with brigands and stray bully bands of soldiers.

It became apparent to General Ch'en that his South China toehold was none too secure, and would be jeopardized completely if he were to embark prematurely on the Northern Expedition. Rival warlords could then move in. He soured on Sun's dream of a strong republican central government based far to the north in Nanking, and instead began to favor a loose federation of China's provinces, an idea that was being bruited about by the warlords as a way to retain their separate fiefdoms. Meantime, Ch'en's junior officers were becoming fat and corrupt; their interests were best served by staying put in the South while feeding parasitically on Canton's inhabitants.

Repeatedly, Sun ordered General Ch'en to battle, but Ch'en vacillated. It was finally agreed that Sun himself would lead the Northern Expedition armies, while Ch'en and his forces "looked after" Canton.

With the audacious Ching-ling beside him, Sun left Canton on May 6, 1922, and proceeded north to the town of Shaokuan to take command of his mercenary army. Escorting the Suns were a bodyguard of five hundred loyal Kuomintang soldiers—all that the KMT party could muster at that time as a genuine fighting force.

With Sun's departure, Canton immediately fell under the control of General Ch'en's troops. The warlord casually marched into the city and took over, displacing Sun. Hardly a shot was fired. The Kuomintang party leadership that remained in Canton was powerless. From Shanghai, Chiang Kai-shek and others had learned of the developing coup and telegraphed Sun urgently to "consolidate the rear" before proceeding with the Northern Expedition. Sun had not reacted.

On May 25, the doctor awakened to the peril. Leaving his hired army at the front, he took Ching-ling and his bodyguards and raced back to the city and the questionable security of the hillside Residency. As he watched Ch'en's forces take up assault positions around the hill, Dr. Sun sent a frantic telegram to Chiang Kai-shek in Chekiang: "HELP ME IN THIS MOMENT OF IMMINENT PERIL—THIRTY THOUSAND CATTIES HANG BY A SINGLE HAIR." (A catty is an Oriental unit of weight, slightly more than a pound, so this marketplace expression was like saying Sun was hanging by the skin of his teeth.)

What happened next was described by Ching-ling to a Chinese magazine:

About two o'clock on the morning of June sixteenth Dr. Sun roused me from my sweet dreams, telling me to hurry and dress, that we were in danger and must escape. He had received a phone call to the effect that Ch'en's troops were about to march on us. We must leave immediately for a gunboat, from where we could direct our men in resisting the rebels.

I thought it would be inconvenient for him to have a woman along with him, and urged him to leave me behind for the time being. There couldn't, I said, be much danger for me as a private person. At last he saw the sense of my argument, but he would not go even then until he had left all fifty of our bodyguard to protect the house. Then he departed, alone.

Half an hour after he had gone, at about half past two, rifle shots rang out in the vicinity. Our house was half way up the hill, connected with the President's Residency at Kuang Ying An by a passage about a li [one-third mile] in length, which stretched over the streets and houses like a bridge. It had formerly been the private mansion of Lun Chi-kuang. The enemy fired downhill at us from two sides, shouting, "Kill Sun Wen! Kill Sun Wen!" Pitch darkness covered them completely. Our small defense corps therefore kept quiet. I could just discern the crouching bodies of our guards in the darkness.

As day broke our men began to reply to the fire with their rifles and machine guns, while the enemy employed field guns. My bath was smashed to bits. One third of our handful of troops had been wiped out, but the remaining men resisted with more determination than ever. One of the servants climbed to a high place and succeeded in killing quite a number of the enemy. By eight o'clock our store of ammunition was running low, so we decided to stop shooting and preserve what was left until the last possible moment.

There seemed no use in remaining, now. Our Captain advised me to leave and the troops agreed with him, promising for their part to stay there in order to halt any possible pursuit by the enemy. . . . Later, all of the fifty were reported killed.

Four of us, Colonel Bow who was a foreign attendant of Dr. Sun's, two of the guards and myself, taking with us only the most necessary supplies for every day, crawled along the bridge passage to make our escape. The enemy soon concentrated fire on this passage and flying bullets whistled about our ears. Twice bullets brushed past my temple without injuring me, however, for at that time we were quite well protected by solid rails on both sides of the bridge. Soon, though, we came to a place where the rails had been smashed by the fire, and we were obliged to make a wild dash for it. Suddenly Colonel Bow cried out, and blood began to flow down his leg. He had been shot through the thigh; a large artery was broken. The two men carried him on.

We were several hours in the passage before we could manage to attain the back garden of the Residency. Half an hour after we had got there we saw a flash of fire, and one section of the bridge was completely demolished. Communication therefore was completely cut off. The enemy's fire was now concentrated on the Residency, and we could not return it because the building was surrounded by private houses.

We took Colonel Bow into one of the bedrooms and dressed his wound roughly. The sight of his agony greatly affected me, yet he never stopped consoling me, saying, "The victory will be ours some day!"

From eight in the morning till four that afternoon we were literally buried in a hell of constant gunfire. Bullets flew in all directions. Once the entire ceiling of a room I had left only a few minutes before collapsed.

At four o'clock Division-commander Wei Pang-ping, who had until then been neutral, sent down an officer to talk peace with us and to offer conditions of surrender. The first demand made by our guard was for my safety, which the officer refused to guarantee, saying that they had no power over the troops of another man. Even the enemy officers could do nothing with these soldiers, who had by this time gone completely mad. Our iron gates were soon smashed and we were confronted by the blood-thirsty bayonets and revolvers of the soldiers, who rushed, however, not for our persons but for the bundles in our hands. Quickly we seized our chance, and ran toward two currents of wild crowds of troops, rushing into each other's paths; one was a group of escaping soldiers and the other a batch of enemy looters. I succeeded in making an escape, wearing Colonel Bow's hat and Dr. Sun's raincoat.

A rush of enemy troops flashed by, attempting to loot the Ministry of Finance and the Customs Superintendent's office. We picked our way through the crowd in the savage mob, finding ourselves at last in a small lane, safe so far from the looters. I was absolutely exhausted, and begged the guards to shoot me. Instead they dragged me forward, one on each side supporting me. . . . Corpses lay about everywhere, some of the Party people and others of plain citizens. Their chests were caved in, their arms slashed, their legs severed. Once we saw two men squatting face to face under a roof. Closer observation revealed that they were dead, their eyes wide open. They must have been killed by stray bullets.

Again our way was cut off by a group of the mob running out of a little passage. The whisper ran through our party that we should lie flat in the street, pretending to be dead. In this way we were left unmolested; then we arose and continued our journey. My guards advised me to avoid looking at the corpses lest I should faint. Half an hour later, when the rifle shots were thinning out, we came to a small farmhouse. The owner tried to drive us out, fearing the consequences of sheltering us; his attempt was forestalled, however, by a timely swoon on my part.

I woke up to find the guards washing me with cold water, and fanning me. One of them went out to see what he could of the way things were going, when suddenly there came a tattoo of rifle shots. The guard indoors rushed to shut the door; he told me that the other one had been struck by a bullet and was probably dead by this time.

While the firing subsided I disguised myself as an old country woman, and with the guard in the guise of a pedlar we left the cottage. I picked up a basket and few vegetables on the way, and carried them with me. At last we reached the house of a friend which had already been searched that morning. To go on was absolutely impossible, so we spent the night there. Shelling never ceased the entire night, and our relief was enormous when we heard cannon shots at last from the gunboats. Dr. Sun, then, was safe. . . .

Next morning, still in my countrywoman outfit, I arrived at Shameen with the others, and there another friend, a foundry worker, arranged for a small motorboat for me, by which we got to another house in Linnan. The river was thronged with boats full of booty, both girls and goods. They were being sent away for safety. It was reported that two women unfortunate enough to answer to my description had been thrown into jail. That same afternoon I left Canton, the house in which I had stayed the night was searched again.

At last, that night, I succeeded in meeting Dr. Sun on board ship, after a life and death struggle. We soon went to Hongkong, disguised.

In his escape, Dr. Sun had walked by a rebel detachment unrecognized. With pistols drawn, his bodyguard took him to the sanctuary of the KMT gunboat *Yung Feng* (*Everlasting Prosperity*), where Ching-ling eventually joined him. For the time being, they were secure. Short of sailing away in defeat, which Sun was not yet prepared to do, he could only sit there. He needed help badly. His first telegram had not brought Chiang Kai-shek to the rescue. In growing desperation, on June 18, Sun sent another, less colorful appeal to Chiang: "MATTERS CRITICAL; HOPE FOR YOUR SPEEDY ARRIVAL."

Although Dr. Sun had landed himself in the mess, this time Chiang Kai-shek decided to go. Hurrying down from Shanghai, he joined his leader aboard the *Yung Feng*. It was their floating garrison for the next fifty-six days, while Chiang made as if to organize a counterattack. Learning that Chiang was back in town, Ch'en's face reportedly "turned blue"; the warlord beetled his brow and coined one of the memorable phrases of the revolution: "With him by the side of Mr. Sun, there will certainly be a great many devilish ideas." Indeed, but nothing came of them.

Aboard the gunboat the heat steamed the conspirators like dim sum. Their white tropical uniforms and gowns became tarnished with washing in the muddy river. For relaxation, Chiang read Sherlock Holmes. At night he slipped ashore with commando teams to get food (and, presumably, a little live entertainment). During the long days, to demonstrate that he was no longer given to tantrums, Chiang took his turn to sweep and scrub the deck.

It is hard to believe that he came to the aid of Dr. Sun and performed this uncharacteristic toil out of genuine chivalry. Up to this point he had walked out on Sun at every twist and turn. He did not respond to Sun's first urgent call for help, and took his time responding to the second. In view of what happened later, and from a careful appraisal of his letters, it is evident that Chiang was sent to Sun's rescue by his right-wing cronies in Shanghai, because they could see more clearly than he that this was the chance of a lifetime for him to step into the top echelon of the KMT. Whoever helped the quixotic old revolutionary by becoming his Sancho Panza at this dark moment of misfortune would earn his undying gratitude. Chiang's cronies were becoming deeply concerned about Dr. Sun's growing fascination with Soviet Russia, and with Marxism. Their alarm may have been exaggerated, but they soon had written evidence that they were correct.

Impressed as he was intended to be by Chiang's display of mulish steadfastness and humility, Dr. Sun decided that the young military man was ready for the big jobs of the revolution. Wearying eventually of life aboard the *Yung Feng,* they slipped out in disguise to Hong Kong, and from there the Suns went back to Shanghai to weigh their next move.

Chiang's meteoric rise was about to begin.

In their absence, General Ch'en's army burnt down Sun Yat-sen's Canton house and destroyed all his manuscripts—except for a few indiscreet papers making it clear that, with nowhere else to turn, Sun was about to ask Soviet Russia for aid for his revolution. When these inflammatory letters were published in the Hong Kong *Telegraph,* they caused a fearful hand wringing in conservative Overseas Chinese communities. Nobody knew much about Bolsheviks, but what was known was scary. The French newspaper in Hanoi, *L'Avenir du Tonkin,* summarized the shameful evidence this way on July 24, 1922: "The government of Ch'en Chiung-ming unveils the original documents establishing the plan of the Sino-Russian-German alliance prepared by Sun Yat-sen and the German minister to Moscow, M. von Hintze, former minister to Peking."

In San Francisco, Dr. Sun's old secret society, the Chih Kung Tong, announced indignantly that it was expelling him from the ranks because of his "secret conspiracy with the Bolsheviks."

There was also a nervous flap in Washington at the Bureau of Investigation (precursor of the FBI). The bureau was already in a swivet over the Bolsheviks in Russia, and the seamy prospect of an international Jewish conspiracy to overthrow industrial order by establishing labor unions. The bureau's unsophisticated director, William J. Burns, started a file on Dr. Sun and asked the Military Intelligence Division of the War Department who-in-the-deuce was this Yat-sen fellow, anyway? Burns was especially anxious to know if Sun Yat-sen was a Jew, if he had any Jewish connections or backing from any international Jewish interests. The director of naval intelligence replied with admirable restraint that no Jewish ties of any kind were discernible and added: "There is nothing . . . to indicate that he is in any way connected with Bolshevik or Radical movements. He has been termed a Radical and is called a Radical by conservative Chinese, but his radicalism consists in visionary schemes for the economic development of China far beyond her present requirements, the needs of the immediate future, and her financial resources." To the U.S. navy, at least, Dr. Sun was not a Bolshevik, just an eccentric.

Despite their victory in Russia, the Bolsheviks had failed to precipitate a worldwide revolution. Because of this, the Soviet leadership, in its search for opportunities abroad, was prepared to make expansive gestures. Immediately after taking power, the Bolsheviks addressed themselves to the Chinese masses, calling for their independence from imperialism, and renouncing all Czarist concessions in China. This made a deep impression on the Chinese, particularly after the disappointments of Versailles. Bolshevik emissaries were sent to Peking to assess the situation and to determine which revolutionaries were worth sponsorship. In 1922, a formal diplomatic mission under A. A. Joffe was dispatched to secure Peking's official recognition of the new Soviet government. The Peking militarists were busy courting London at the time and turned Joffe down. As an alternative, Joffe proceeded to Shanghai to see Sun Yat-sen.

The Russians had no illusions. Lenin once described Dr. Sun as a man of "inimitable—one might say virginal—naïveté." Sun's ideas were, from the Bolshevik viewpoint, utopian and reactionary. Nevertheless, they considered him malleable, and appreciated the potential of his Kuomintang party as a ready-made blunt instrument that could be wielded by more capable hands while Sun became a figurehead.

At the Rue Molière, Ching-ling and Dr. Sun (still licking his emotional wounds from the Canton débacle) entertained Joffe at dinner on January 18, 1923. The Soviet diplomat spent several more days at the house talking with Sun. Both spoke English throughout. Joffe succeeded in persuading the doctor that the Soviet Union had no grand design on China. This country was still feudal, and a proletariat was only beginning to take shape, so "the proper conditions" did not exist for a Communist revolution of the Soviet type. This was essentially a valid summary of the attitudes of Lenin and Trotsky, so Joffe was being quite forthright. But it was not the position of Stalin, as we shall see. Still, the Russian people felt the "warmest" sympathy for the Chinese people's predicament, and in their struggle they could count on Moscow's support. At Sun's request, Joffe reaffirmed in writing the principles expressed earlier by the new Soviet government, renouncing all Czarist concessions in China, including all treaties and agreements between Imperial Russia and Imperial China.

These points of agreement were summarized in a joint statement released in English on January 26, 1923, before Comrade Joffe left Shanghai for Tokyo.

It was not disclosed, however, that the Soviets promised to finance, guide, and support Sun and the Kuomintang in a new bid for power. But first Sun had to demonstrate his mandate by recovering control of his South China base at Canton, and then—in a show of political good faith—admit to Kuomintang ranks the fledgling Chinese Communist party.

Fortunately for Dr. Sun, there had been a dramatic change in South China during his absence. When his former associate, General Ch'en, had turned against him and ousted Dr. Sun from Canton, the doctor had struck a new alliance with the neighboring warlords of Yunnan and Kiangsi provinces, who were Ch'en's rivals. The armies of these two warlords, supplemented by remnants of Sun's own northern expeditionary force, and deserters from Ch'en's army, converged upon Canton and laid siege. General Ch'en wisely decided that he had had a stomachful of politics, and retired from office, making a smooth getaway to Hong Kong. All of this climaxed merely two days before Comrade Joffe appeared on the Rue Molière. So Sun could now return to Canton directly, resume his position as President Extraordinaire, and thereby fulfill Moscow's first condition for aid.

This time, caution prevailed and Dr. Sun and Ching-ling were ensconced for safety in a former factory on Honam Island, downriver from Canton. The river served as a moat, and the structure was solid enough to withstand an artillery barrage. The three-story building was surrounded by balconies on each floor, shaded by palms and bougainvillaea, and had been converted into spacious quarters upstairs, with tiny, transparent house lizards chattering and fornicating on the walls. The doctor had offices on the first floor. As another nod to security, visitors had to pass the scrutiny of Morris Cohen, Sun's Canadian-born bodyguard, who had once been a prizefighter. An American who paid a social call on the Suns remembered:

> Rarely during our months in Canton was the Generalissimo seen even in semi-public without Mrs. Sun the second at his side and the belligerent, or at least highly protective, face of Mr. Cohen in the immediate background. When we had the honor one Sunday morning to call upon Dr. Sun at his cement factory headquarters and residence, his Canadian shadow, tucked into a corner of the stairway at the entrance to the Doctor's study, scrutinized not only me but my wife as if to make sure that she had not come to wreak mischief on his chief.

In May, when enough time had passed for the Russians to be certain that Sun was sticking to his Canton commitment, Moscow telegraphed that aid was on its way.

Some years later, during a conversation in a chocolate shop, Chingling talked with Edgar Snow about the Russian alliance.

"Was Russia his last chance?" Snow asked.

"Well, you might say his last choice," she replied.

Mikhail Borodin arrived in Canton by Chinese coastal steamer on October 6, 1923, in the company of two hundred dead sheep killed by a violent squall. He was immediately taken to the cement factory on Honam Island.

> Sun Yat-sen welcomed me very warmly, made me sit with him and looked at me fixedly for several seconds. I conveyed to him the greetings of Moscow, and of the Political Representative, Comrade Karakhan, adding that the latter looked forward to an interview with him on the first favorable occasion. Then I shortly explained to him the aim of my coming to Canton and asked him several questions about the situation in the country and particularly in Kwangtung.

Dr. Sun's visitor was Mikhail Markovich Grusenberg. Borodin was an alias. He was sent to Canton by Lenin to be the chief Comintern agent in China. He was to reorganize Dr. Sun's Kuomintang into a centralized, Leninist-style organization, and to finance, train, and equip a powerful KMT army that would radically alter the balance of power in China.

Borodin had extraordinary presence, one reason for the success he had already achieved with the Bolsheviks. He was also charming. Even the restrained and conservative president of Canton Christian College, Dr. James Henry, found him "a very pleasing personality, [of] sincerity and deep earnestness. He puts one perfectly at ease. . . . I asked him if he liked the Chinese. He said that he had not given the matter any thought."

People who met him came away with the impression that he was very tall—a big, bearlike man. Borodin was only five feet ten, which was taller than most of the Moscow leadership, but less than he seemed. According to records of Barlinnie Prison in Scotland, where he was once interned, he had a "fresh" complexion, dark brown hair, gray eyes, and scars on the left side of his face and both sides of his body. A prison photo shows him looking as people often described him, like an angry banker who has caught a teller embezzling—his face ferocious, his hair close cut, his chin clean-shaven, for he had not yet adopted the Stalin mustache that he eventually grew in China.

He was born on July 9, 1884, in the village of Yanovichi, in Vitebsk Province, which became the Byelorussian S.S.R. His parents were Jews. A private man, not only as a secret agent, Borodin was reticent about details of his life. In answer to probes, he would answer only "I was born in the snow and lived in the sun."

As a brawny adolescent, he had worked floating logs down the ice jams of the Dvina River to Riga, Latvia, which may have accounted for some of his scars. His native tongue was Yiddish, and by the time he was sixteen he was showing his conspiratorial genius as a smuggler for the Jewish Bund on the Riga waterfront. But at age nineteen, he broke away to join Lenin in St. Petersburg. It was 1903.

Lenin found uses for the young man's underworld connections in Latvia, a region where the Communists had few contacts. The following year, Lenin sent him to Switzerland on a political mission, but news of the 1905 massacre of demonstrators at the Winter Palace brought him hurrying back to Russia. He was then assigned as Lenin's principal revolutionary agent in Riga. His star was rising. When he was sent to Stockholm in 1906 for a meeting of the Russian Social Democratic Labor party, he sat next to Stalin, who was impressed to find the tough Latvian voting with him on most key issues.

That July he was arrested by Czarist police, who generously offered him a choice between exile in Siberia or in the West. Borodin happily left for London. But, after a brush with Scotland Yard, he went on to Chicago, which was then a hotbed of American socialism. Borodin felt at home there, and married Fanya Orluk, a sweet-natured but tough Lithuanian immigrant. In 1908, he also began studying at Indiana's Valparaiso University.

In the Chicago slums he found justification for the proletarian revolution. He began to work there teaching English to immigrants at Hull House, the sprawling Jane Addams settlement house, which provided educational and social services for the big immigrant community. As a sideline, Borodin opened his own English-language school in Chicago's Russian-Jewish ghetto, and by 1914 was the director of the Progressive Preparatory School, a fixture of life in the Near Northside. Throughout these years of exile, he remained in close contact with the leaders of the

Bolshevik movement in Europe and Russia, serving as their agent-in-place in Chicago, and in 1918 they sent for him.

Back once more in Moscow, he was taken immediately to Lenin, who presented Borodin with a letter for American workers. In mid-September 1918, Borodin dutifully left for the United States by way of Petrograd's Finland Station, and was passing through Scandinavia when his orders were suddenly changed. He was to remain on the Baltic, gathering intelligence and pipelining funds for the revolution.

One of his contacts was the American poet Carl Sandburg, on assignment in Europe for the Newspaper Enterprise Association. Sandburg's strong socialist sympathies had caused trouble for him in America, and he had been able to obtain a passport to travel abroad only with the greatest of difficulty. As a result, he was trying to avoid radical friends, such as fellow journalist John Reed. Nevertheless Borodin prevailed upon him to take home a bundle of Bolshevik pamphlets, books, and newspapers for circulation in America. Sandburg also agreed to pigeon a check for $10,000 to Fanya in Chicago for distribution to Bolshevik agents, plus 400 Swedish kronor for Fanya herself. Suddenly, Sandburg got cold feet and rushed to the American embassy in Oslo, where he informed on Borodin and turned over the check. For some reason, he did not mention the pamphlets and books, and when he disembarked in New York an official search committee confiscated the Soviet literature. Through all this, Sandburg hung on to the 400 kronor for Fanya, and saw the money safely into her hands.

In 1920, Lenin appointed Borodin Soviet consul in Mexico City. When he left for Mexico, on a roundabout route via the Caribbean and New York, Borodin's baggage included a suitcase with a hidden compartment concealing a fortune in Czarist jewels to be sold in the United States to provide operating funds for Russian agents.

Arriving in Santo Domingo, he decided that it would be too risky for him to take the jewels through American Customs himself and decided to go directly to Mexico. He left the rigged suitcase in the care of an unwitting Austrian whom he had met on the crossing, exacting a promise that the Austrian would take the bag through U.S. Customs and deliver it to Fanya.

At his post in Mexico City, Borodin learned from Fanya that the jewels had never reached her. He sent an agent to Santo Domingo; the agent vanished. A second agent tracked the Austrian and the suitcase to Haiti. The hidden compartment was found empty, and the Austrian flew into a rage. He said he had discovered the treachery of the hidden compartment; instead of delivering the gems, he had put the suitcase in his closet. When Borodin's first agent had arrived, he had ripped out the jewels and disappeared with them.

Borodin's spy tracked the first agent down in Port-au-Prince and found him packing for New York. He professed to have no knowledge of the gems, insisting that the jewels had already been removed when he reached the Austrian's house.

The two agents went back to Mexico, where they were interrogated to no avail. Borodin returned to Moscow empty-handed. Some Communists were of the opinion that he was making it all up and had thrown the gems overboard or had tucked them away for his retirement. These innuendos temporarily cost him some of his standing in the party. But in the winter of 1920–21, Fanya, fairytale-like, appeared with the jewels and restored him to grace. What had really happened to the gems, and how she recovered them, was never revealed.

Borodin found himself once again a celebrity in his native land. His feats of daring and coolness of execution were legend, and Russian pedestrians again pointed him out as a "great man." He hobnobbed with Isadora Duncan, who was gadding about Russia, and was mentioned in the Western press by Winston Churchill's cousin, the liberated sculptor Clare Sheridan, who half-seriously suggested to Lenin that he should appoint Borodin as Russia's ambassador to the Court of Saint James's.

But this popular adulation, and his closeness with Lenin, provoked jealousy in other quarters.

His last assignment before China was as an agitator in Britain during the coal miners' strikes in 1921. Arrested in Glasgow a few months later, Borodin was thrown into Barlinnie Prison for half a year, then was deported.

When he arrived back at the Kremlin in February, 1923, Lenin was ready to send him to Canton.

Borodin traveled on the Trans-Siberian Railway to Lake Baikal, and thence to dusty Peking. Briefed by Soviet Ambassador Karakhan, he then traveled overland to Shanghai, where he met Soviet agents and leaders of the new Chinese Communist party before boarding a ship for Canton. Taking a normal passenger liner or freighter would have meant stopping at British Hong Kong, where police might have recognized him from his misadventure in Scotland. There was no alternative but to take a ship sailing straight to Canton. It was a small, rusty coastal vessel bearing a strong resemblance to a coal scuttle, carrying a cargo of sheep. Wallowing southward through the Formosa Strait, they ran into a typhoon and nearly foundered before taking shelter on the big island. All two hundred sheep in pens on deck had drowned, but their meat was sold a few days later when the boat limped into the Pearl River and dropped anchor off the Canton Bund.

It was Borodin's job to show Dr. Sun how to turn the KMT coalition into a disciplined party organization with a powerful mass movement behind it. The Chinese Communists were not to merge with the KMT but to coordinate with it and get behind its drive to become the central force of the national revolution. This was the decision of the Executive Committee of the Comintern on January 12, 1923. To provide the foundation for an entirely new army imbued with KMT ideals, one completely free of dependence on any warlord, the Russians planned to found a military academy for Dr. Sun and staff it with Russian officers. On his way to meet Sun in the cement factory, Borodin had an opportunity to appraise the city and to see firsthand just how precarious the KMT's position really was. Canton was jammed with soldiers, perhaps 40,000 of them—the capricious troops of various warlords; they were now in the pay of the KMT, costing Sun $26,000 Chinese a day. Of soldiers loyal to him personally, Dr. Sun now only had 200, serving as a bodyguard. The rest had been killed in the previous Canton fiasco.

General Ch'en had resumed his political life after a respite, and was again at the city gates, pressing to recapture the city. Sun's hired guns who roved the streets were bent on having a good time, not on putting up a defense.

Borodin immediately recruited a volunteer force of 540 streetwise cadres from the Chinese Communist party. On November 15, five weeks after his arrival, Borodin went to Sun to present him with this tough strike force, and discovered that the fleet-footed doctor thought General Ch'en was about to storm Canton. Sun was packing to leave, and wanted only to discuss the plan for his escape.

Disgusted, and forced to lead Canton's defense by himself, Borodin applied the proven, albeit bloody, methods of the Bolsheviks from the days of the Red Terror in St. Petersburg. His strike force attacked the enemy troops with a modern ferocity that was quite alien to traditional Chinese military posturing. There were always heavy casualties in Chinese battles, but these were most often the result of chaos and confusion or victimizing of civilians. Borodin introduced single-minded, well-organized military slaughter. Simultaneously, tough CCP organizers roused the ragtag warlord forces in the city from the brothels and gambling dens and forced them to join the fray at risk of being shot if they hesitated. This forthright and aggressive homicide so astonished General Ch'en that the warlord and his officers fled the city, with their foot soldiers hot behind them. With barely five hundred men in the vanguard, Borodin had won the day against thousands.

It was a lucky thing, his appearance on the scene; for Sun, who was beginning to suffer mysterious agues and illnesses, was so hypnotized by his lifelong objective of northern conquest that his position in Canton itself after five years was still no more than a wretched toehold. Dr. Sun was not considered a great asset by the Old Guard compradors and the commercial people of the city.

Despite Sun's on-again, off-again alliance with the warlords of Yunnan and Kwangsi, the authority of the "Southern Government" at Canton still extended little farther than the Pearl River estuary, except when a major campaign took soldiers into the distant countryside and opposing forces obligingly fell back in harmless reenactment of classical Chinese stink-bomb wars, in which gongs and evil smells played a major role.

Even in the heart of Canton, Sun's rule was tenuous because his mercenary troops were ungovernable, and shared the street with pirates, triads, and ruffians who bullied shopkeepers.

The town, as one Western traveler described it, was:

almost in the absolute power of these ragged, lazy, destructive bums and ex-bandits, who were quartered in almost every temple, in confiscated factories, commandeered houses, in anything without foreign protection that was capable of holding a few of them. Almost any day one could find the entrance to a military headquarters in some confiscated building along the Bund or elsewhere decorated with flags, streamers, flowers, with many colors and much pomp of naked bayonets and cocked automatics. . . . Chinese soldiers are bad enough anywhere, but I would much rather take my chances with those of the North than with these unsoaped, childish, yet often vicious and debauched, bullies of the South, who strutted the streets of Canton, often with powerful modern weapons. They not merely saw to it that gambling, opium-smoking, and prostitution flourished for their financial benefit, but they patronized all such vices themselves to the extent of their money or bullying. There was next to no drilling, discipline, or fixed duties—little to do but keep up their grafts.

Official automobiles with one weak-faced man of importance lolling inside and four, six, even eight soldiers in khaki on the running-boards, cocked rifle-handled automatics in hand, dash up to the Asia Hotel, follow close about the simple youth in flannel as he makes his way to the elevator, and descend with him to climb again all over the car as it leaves. Canton is particularly given to this parading with cocked pistols.

Canton in 1923 was running wild. Nobody missed an opportunity to meddle, including the Americans, who, upon learning that someone was actually helping Dr. Sun Yat-sen, went to him as Iago went to Othello, intending to poison the relationship with an anti-Semitic remark: "Do you know that 'Borodin' is a pseudonym? Do you know his real name?"

"Yes," answered the little doctor, a twinkle in his eyes, "Lafayette."

Fanya arrived with her two sons to join Borodin, and they moved into a gloomy, ugly yellow two-story building, which backed onto the Canton parade grounds and faced the equally ugly headquarters of the KMT ruling political body, the Central Executive Committee. Two armed Chinese sentries, wearing rumpled and undistinguished gray uniforms, guarded the entrance. Beyond there were a large, bare hall and stairs, where another sentry stood on the landing. The Borodins lived on the top floor, in a jumble of high-ceilinged rooms. There was a bare waiting room decorated only with a photographic portrait of Dr. Sun, opposite a similar likeness of Lenin.

The downstairs was stacked with files and crammed with busy translators. Borodin's chief Chinese aide lived in the house and supervised the work. Eventually a young Communist trained in Paris, named Chou En-lai, became Borodin's secretary.

There was a reason for choosing this house, aside from mere proximity to the Executive Committee. Borodin had a passion for horseback riding, and the parade grounds allowed him to exercise his mount when there was no time for longer rides. The gloomy rooms were also appropriate for games of chess that sometimes lasted days.

Dr. Sun had been greatly impressed by Borodin's forthright November defense of the city. His confidence in his Soviet advisor was apparent as new agreements were reached in subsequent weeks. In their conversations, Borodin carefully deferred to Sun, offering opinions only when asked, and listened as Sun's strategy emerged. If Sun

could establish control in Central China—a place such as Hankow—
with a second base in Mongolia, backed by the Soviets, he would be able
to deal firmly with the foreign powers. Mongolia, with Russia at its rear,
would put him within striking range of Peking. Until then, Borodin
agreed that a supply line by sea could be arranged. Under the pretense
of Russian trade for Cantonese timber, rice, and beans, military supplies
could be brought secretly from Siberian ports.

In these conversations, Borodin discovered Sun to be as Lenin had
characterized him—naïve. To the Russian agent, hardened by years of
intrigue, Sun was merely "an enlightened little satrap" who saw himself
as "the hero" and everyone else as "the mob."

However, Dr. Sun's vanity would not be the source of Borodin's
headaches. They would come, instead, from Chiang Kai-shek.

Chiang had begun to show interest in the Soviet Union in 1920,
probably at the instigation of Big-eared Tu and Curio Chang. He toyed
half-heartedly with the Russian language, and once wrote to Dr. Sun
that he thought Soviet policy was sound in concentrating on internal
security before external resistance.

Security meant discipline, which was something that interested
Chiang a great deal. In China Chiang believed, it was impossible to get
results because of lack of discipline, lack of security, and lack of organization; repeatedly, over the years, Chiang had given up assignments
because his comrades failed to enforce discipline or execute orders with
precision. He had refused to join the Canton government until he was
offered enough authority to command obedience.

Soviet discipline was the responsibility of the Bolshevik organ of
state security, then called the Cheka. The Cheka worked in harness
with the Red Army to enforce party rule throughout the Soviet Union,
to put down White Russian resistance and other reactionary or ideologi-
cal deviationism, and to silence all voices of dissent. Together the Red
Army, headed by Leon Trotsky, and the Cheka, directed by Feliks
Dzerzhinsky, co-authored the Red Terror.

During the Terror, Cheka agents shot, drowned, bayonetted, and
beat to death approximately 500,000 people, whose murders were authorized in one manner or another by the party. "We stand for organized terror," Dzerzhinsky proclaimed in 1918. "The Cheka is not a
court. . . . The Cheka is obliged to defend the Revolution and conquer
the enemy even if its sword does by chance sometimes fall upon the

heads of the innocent." His words were reinforced by Lenin, scornfully turning aside party idealists. "The energy and mass nature of terror must be encouraged," Lenin retorted. He sent telegrams to Cheka executioners, urging them to use "merciless mass terror."

Chiang was certainly aware of this because the Red Terror was widely reported in the world press, and Shanghai was a haven for fleeing White Russians who attested to horrific details.

Nevertheless, after badgering Dr. Sun to send him to Moscow and finally getting his way in August, 1923, there was something urgent and unrealistic about his expectation. He even boasted to friends before he left that he had toyed with the notion of staying in Russia "five or ten years"—although in retrospect this may have been said to make himself seem extravagantly liberal. He was disillusioned almost immediately by the discovery that Russia was an alien place.

The utter drabness, the dejection of the countryside, the terrible tedium of proletarian Moscow had all been made to seem glorious in propaganda renderings. After so many years in self-indulgent Shanghai, it is no wonder that Chiang felt out of place. He may also have sensed the traditional fear and hatred of Muscovites for Orientals.

Politically, if not personally, his visit was a success for the KMT. Soon after arriving in Moscow, on September 2, 1923, he addressed the executive committee of the Comintern, saying he was confident that the Chinese revolution would succeed within two or three years. He heard Chinese Communists in Moscow slandering Sun Yat-sen and his party, so Chiang insisted that the Comintern did not understand the revolutionary movement in China, and he urged it to send more agents to study the situation firsthand.

He inspected Red Army units, visited military schools and party organizations, toured the Kronstadt naval base near Petrograd, noting that the Soviet navy was still marked by the harsh suppression of a revolt by the sailors against the Bolsheviks two years earlier. He evidently spent most of his time with the Cheka, learning their methods.

While Chiang was in Moscow, Lenin was in the deep coma that preceded his death. Chiang had many long conversations instead with Trotsky, who assured him that Russia's role was to provide the maximum moral and material aid to liberation movements, but that she would never interfere in another nation's politics by sending in Soviet troops. Chiang also met Kamenev, Zinoviev, Radek, and Chicherin, and observed the growing power struggle between Trotsky and Stalin.

After only three months, Chiang was ready to go home. Many years later, in a memoir written for propaganda, he said, "From my observations and from my conversations, I perceived that fierce struggles were not only going on in Russia generally but also among the Communists themselves." The comment, intended to hold the Soviets up to ridicule, also reveals a certain disappointment. Between the lines and in other comments he made at the time, it is evident that Chiang hoped to witness firsthand the famous Soviet machine of discipline, and expected to find the party in absolute control of the nation and of itself. Instead, he found murderous rivalry and weakness inside the party, where he least expected it. His disillusionment was complete.

On his return to China he advised against trusting the Kremlin. "The Russian Communist Party," he cautioned a Kuomintang colleague, "in its dealings with China, has only one aim, namely to make the Chinese Communist Party its chosen instrument. It does not believe that our Party can really cooperate with it for long for the sake of ensuring success for both parties. It is the policy of the Russian Communist Party to turn the lands inhabited by the Manchus, Mongols, Moslems and Tibetans into parts of the Soviet domain; it may harbor sinister designs even on China proper."

On November 29, Chiang abruptly terminated his visit and hurried home.

Chiang knew that his experience of Russia would make him unique among the Kuomintang faithfuls. If Russian money was going to enable the KMT to set up a new military academy near Canton, where a real army could be trained and equipped with Soviet weapons, then Chiang had to be in a position to control the academy and, thus, the army. His firsthand experience in Russia gave him an edge over all his rivals for the post of Whampoa commandant.

Reaching Shanghai after an exhausting trip across Siberia, he withdrew to his home in Chekiang Province, which was near Big-eared Tu's country retreat in a monastery at Mokanshan, in the Wuling Mountains. There, while his conservative supporters lobbied furiously in Canton and Shanghai, Chiang waited for the party leadership to approach him. On December 26, 1923, he received a telegram promising him "full responsibility" for the academy. The organization of the military school, said the telegram, "cannot proceed without your proposals." This was followed on the 30th by a cable from Dr. Sun asking him to hurry to Canton "to report all matters and make plans for Sino-Soviet cooperation."

Chiang departed for Canton on January 16, 1924, a trip timed for a grand entrance at the First National Congress of the Kuomintang. As he had hoped, the Congress confirmed his appointment as chairman of the Preparatory Committee of the Whampoa Military Academy.

According to KMT insiders, the Russian advisors and the Chinese Communists, who recently had been allowed to join the Kuomintang as part of the Russian aid deal, ganged up on Chiang during an argument over the curriculum and management of the academy. When Chiang described his plans for Whampoa, the CCP members and the Russians objected and tried to outmaneuver him. Chiang threw one of his famous fits and walked out. Back in Chekiang Province, playing cat and mouse, Chiang wrote a long letter to Dr. Sun. In it he accepted blame for being "stubborn" at the Congress and "as restless as if I were sitting on a mat full of nails," but these, after all, were merely personal shortcomings. What really had caused his outburst, he said, was the factional strife stirred up by "new influences" in the Kuomintang—the reds and the Russians. He confessed to sharing conservative political views with others in the KMT. He argued that in admitting the "new influences" the KMT should not abandon its traditional system—"a central, undergirding force that can sustain it in each and every circumstance."

Many of those whom Dr. Sun considered able and loyal, Chiang wrote, were sycophants and opportunists. The doctor needed instead men who were really loyal and dependable—for example, himself. Chiang then reminded Sun that only he, Chiang Kai-shek, had stood by him during the Canton débacle and gunboat episode of 1922. Chiang could not direct the training of military cadets at the new Whampoa Academy without being involved in the broader political issues, in which case the "new influences" would have to defer to his judgment even if he held old-fashioned views. Chiang sanctified his "old-fashioned views" by invoking "traditional moral principles."

With this large herd of sacred cows blocking his path, Dr. Sun could hardly avoid the point. Sun gave way and agreed to support Chiang's right to overrule the political commissars at Whampoa.

It is always hazardous in one's thinking to see conspiracy playing too big a role in events, not because conspiracy is absent, but because events cannot be controlled so deliberately. In the case of Chiang Kai-shek's uncharacteristic rush to Dr. Sun's rescue aboard the gunboat, his peculiar love-hate visit to Russia, and his urgent pressure to become Whampoa's military commandant, there is at least a thread of conspiracy visible. Ham-handed as they sometimes were, the conservative members of the KMT party leadership, especially Chiang's right-wing cronies in Shanghai, were alarmed about Dr. Sun's swerve toward Moscow, and about the intrusion of leftists and Chinese Communist party members into the KMT ranks. There is little doubt that they influenced Chiang directly, urged him on, backed him, and guided him during this crucial period. His published letters show that he was in constant contact with them, continually seeking their guidance. They gave him stage directions, reminded him of his lines, and thrust him out for curtain calls. He was the cat's paw of the Shanghai right wing.

On May 3, 1924, Chiang was confirmed as commandant of Whampoa Military Academy and as chief of staff of the nascent Kuomintang army. The Russians, under orders from Borodin to risk nothing because of Chiang, kept their objections to themselves. By not blocking Chiang's appointment to the coveted position, they committed a fatal blunder. Borodin did not grasp the Chinese commitment to the student-teacher loyalty bond. By tradition, Chinese owed absolute loyalty first to the family, second to nonblood relatives through marriage, and third to the student-teacher bond. This was a bond warlords made use of; Chiang understood it perfectly. If he was commandant of Whampoa, every cadet was his student in the end. Borodin may have thought that Chiang could be disposed of later. He could not have been further from the truth. The mistake may have occurred because Borodin had left Canton in March for talks with Russian diplomats in Peking, and was not minding the store.

It had been agreed between Borodin and Sun Yat-sen that "the first task [was] to form an army on the Soviet model and to prepare a base for an expedition to the North." Russia would provide funds and advisors as necessary. Until 1924, the KMT had no adequate financial base and depended on loans from Overseas Chinese and domestic commercial circles. At the end of February 1924, Dr. Sun received a loan of sixty thousand Chinese dollars, apparently from Moscow. The Kuomintang leadership was so sensitive about the source of these funds that when Chiang Kai-shek asked about it he was told in a cable from leftist leader Liao Chung-k'ai to mind his own business: "As to funds for the military academy, I will not ask about disbursements and you will not ask about sources. There is no lack of funds, and you can proceed to administer with peace of mind." Moscow later confirmed that "This school was organized by us in 1924 and at first was maintained at our expense."

(Moscow spent about 2.7 million Chinese dollars in all on the academy.)

Once funds were in hand, training personnel had to be assembled. Borodin and the Soviet minister in Peking, Comrade Karakhan, sent a cable to Moscow asking for fifty "active military workers" headed by "a comrade who has considerable fighting experience and at the same time able to impress Sun Yat-sen."

The first Soviet officer to arrive in Canton, Comrade Palov, "accidentally drowned" while swimming in the Pearl River. His replacement arrived in October 1924. He was Vasily Konstantinovich Blyukher, known in China by his *nom de guerre,* Galen.

Whampoa was on an island in the Pearl River, ten miles south of Canton. In the 1870s, a Manchu fort and naval training school had been built there, and the old wooden buildings provided barracks for Chiang's cadets. Originally, the KMT planned to recruit students openly in Kwangtung Province, but the recruiters were jailed or murdered by opposing militarists. Instead, a clandestine search was conducted throughout all of China, and Sun was surprised to have three thousand qualified applicants, of whom only five hundred could be admitted in the first class. Chinese military schools ordinarily faced a high rate of illiteracy among students. At Whampoa all the first-year students, surprisingly, were graduates of middle school and were highly literate.

What Dr. Sun and Borodin did not know, and apparently never suspected, was that a very large number of these candidates came from the ranks of the Green Gang. The opportunity to stack the deck at Whampoa was not to be missed. The actual recruiting was carried out by Ch'en Kuo-fu, a nephew of the dead hero Ch'en Ch'i-mei, who had been a major figure in the Green Gang. Since his assassination, his two nephews had taken his place in the gang's hierarchy, and had been "adopted" by Chiang Kai-shek. In all, Ch'en Kuo-fu was credited with recruiting a total of seven thousand cadets for Whampoa drawn directly from the ranks of the Green Gang, or indirectly through family membership or dependency. He accomplished this almost without leaving the French Concession, obviously because he did not have to. These cadets formed the backbone of Chiang's personal officer staff. Not even the Chinese Communist party at that time was so well organized, and so well positioned to influence the course of events.

Classes began on May 5, 1924. When Borodin returned from his

Peking mission a month later, an official day-long opening celebration was held, with Ching-ling attending and Dr. Sun providing an emotional address:

> The foundation of our Republic scarcely exists. The reason is a simple one: Our Revolution has been carried on by the struggles of a revolutionary party but not a revolutionary army. Because of the lack of a revolutionary army, the Republic has been mismanaged by warlords and bureaucrats. Our Revolution will never succeed if this continues. With the establishment of this school a new hope is born for us today. From now on a new era has begun for our Revolution. This school is the basis of the Revolutionary Army of which you students form the nucleus.

Chiang Kai-shek, a member of the militant political right of the KMT, was the commandant. Liao Chung-k'ai, an American-educated leftist, was KMT party representative at Whampoa. In this way, Whampoa became a microcosm of the political polarization that had occurred in the KMT and in the Chinese Revolution. The militant right had a great advantage because it took the growing rivalry very seriously. Under Liao and Chiang there were six departments—a political department, a training department, an instruction department, and departments for management, military medicine, and military supplies. The teachers were all graduates of the Japanese Military Academy, the Paoting Military Academy, or the Yunnan Military Academy. Under the leftist Liao, Whampoa offered one of the best political curriculums in China, with courses on economics, the theory of imperialism, the history of China, and the history of the revolutionary movement in the West. Under Chiang, there was heavy emphasis on discipline and four martial qualities—bravery, daring, authority, and austerity. The law of collective responsibility was enforced—if you retreat, you die. But, if you kept the faith, the KMT showed genuine interest in your welfare as a soldier.

Whampoa put great emphasis on technical training, using Soviet instructors. For the first time in China, a completely modern, mechanically advanced army was being groomed.

Chinese warlords used modern weapons (including rifles and artillery) only for fireworks. Artillery rounds were to "fire for effect" only. Soldiers cared little whether they hit anything. Walls of Chinese towns were made of mud brick, so a single artillery round was enough to bring a town to surrender. Traditionally, the object was to make noise and then reach a political settlement. But, with the new Whampoa army, Chinese military strategy changed—Borodin and Chiang Kai-shek were not satisfied with scaring enemies. They wanted them dead.

The Russians found that the KMT arsenal consisted of only thirteen field pieces of incompatible models, a few rifles and machine guns of various types and calibers, and very little ammunition. The Versailles embargo agreements barred China from obtaining arms from signatory countries, but the Soviets, excluded from Versailles, were free to send weapons. The flood of arms from Russia to the KMT amounted to 2.5 million rubles' worth in 1925 alone, with much more waiting in Vladivostok.

That ancient master of intrigue Sun Tzu would have been interested in Chiang Kai-shek at age thirty-eight. He was letting the Russian Bolsheviks and the Chinese Communists build an unprecedented modern fighting army for him. It was almost as if the idea had been dreamed up by his pals Big-eared Tu and Curio Chang, perhaps while whooping it up over a game of Raft in a Shanghai brothel.

Before, money was needed to create an army. Now money—a lot of it—was needed to finance the Northern Campaign. Sun was at last taking appropriate action. At the suggestion of his wife, he decided to bring her brother down from Shanghai. T. V. Soong, the Harvard-trained economist, had some ideas on how to get money. As a proper capitalist, with excellent middle-class credentials—his father a well-known publisher and Methodist minister, and his older sister married into one of the oldest rural banking families in China—T. V. Soong could do much to offset the nervousness of the Canton merchants, who looked with increasing alarm at the Soviet advisors strolling the street and members of the Chinese Communist party taking up membership in "their" bourgeois Kuomintang. Indeed, while Whampoa Academy was getting under way, T. V. (still sporting his collegiate crew cut) was commissioned by Dr. Sun to reorganize the KMT's finances.

Here was a formidable challenge. The Chinese economy as a whole was a mess. The ground gained during World War I had been lost. The foreigners were back and once again gripped China by the purse strings. The first job given to Ching-ling's brother was to raise emergency funds for the KMT's daily operations. After that he was expected to reorganize the economy of Kwangtung Province and to bring its tax system into a semblance of order. That he succeeded on a provincial scale, compared to China as a whole, was, for many observers, nothing short of amazing.

T. V. Soong was a short, stocky young man with a face like a lucky dollar. His expression was genial but rigid, a tight smile engraved on a coin. He seemed aloof because he always had too much on his mind. This impression of sobriety was completed by a pair of spectacles with small round beady-eyed lenses like those worn by the Emperor of Japan and the novelist James Joyce. Here, they said, was a man who actually enjoyed searching ledger sheets for figures written in a tiny script, or referencing margin calls on pork bellies in the Chicago exchange. There always seemed to be a faint mist of perspiration on T. V.'s upper lip. He had a lot of American friends.

When he had graduated from Harvard in 1915, T. V. had moved to New York City to work for the International Banking Corporation, not as an executive, as was later implied, but as a clerk, shuffling through remittances to China. It was a rare opportunity to see how Overseas Chinese managed some of their most discreet financial arrangements with families and business interests at home. At night, he took courses at Columbia University. He had a fine mind and a robust sense of humor. Politically, he was a true Western liberal—able to hold two conflicting points of view simultaneously.

In 1917, the same year his little sister May-ling returned to China, T. V. went home to become secretary of the Han-Yeh-P'ing Company in Shanghai, an industrial complex of coal mines, iron mines, and steel mills. This was originally a Chinese company that had been coveted by Japanese businessmen. In compliance with the notorious "21 Demands," the Japanese had been given a controlling interest in the firm in 1915. With Charlie Soong's business connections, it was a simple matter to arrange a job for T. V. When he surprised everyone by straightening out its books and financial operations, word spread that he was something of a genius, who needed more than just the Shanghai financial world to test his talent. That test came when Ching-ling suggested that her brother could solve the KMT's financial worries in the South. He arrived in Canton in October 1923, and immediately went to work turning South China on its ear.

Because the Kuomintang urgently needed operating funds, T. V. suggested a series of Draconian "emergency measures" that went into effect in the opening months of 1924. These included special import duties on rubber, wood alcohol, and ammonium sulfate for fertilizer. In February, every merchant in Canton was called upon to "lend" the government sums ranging from $5 to $500. The following month, a 10 percent surcharge was levied on restaurant meals. In April, a tax was added to soft drinks. In May, taxes went into effect on patent medicines, cosmetics, weddings, funerals, religious celebrations, and even rickshaws.

For some time, Dr. Sun had dreamed of setting up a KMT government bank in Canton to centralize his control of the flow of capital in the region. In 1924, a Russian loan of $10 million provided the reserves needed, and the Central Bank came into existence with T. V. Soong as manager.

At the formal opening ceremony that August, Dr. Sun announced only that the bank's capital had been provided by a "foreign loan." It was never entirely clear whether the money was physically transferred to Canton from Moscow, or whether it was merely promised. But the Central Bank was off to a brisk start. Many Chinese banks had no more than 5 percent of their notes secured by silver reserves, but the Central Bank boasted 25 percent. Its reputation was so good that the Central Bank's freshly printed banknotes were accepted even in parts of China that were not under Kuomintang control. T. V. Soong scrupulously honored the bank's pledges and built up its credit. Private savings deposited in the bank increased sixfold in 1926. Before long, even ordinary Chinese began to see positive results from T. V.'s efforts.

Until T. V. came along, the feudal economy had persisted as it had for millennia. Local warlords and magistrates collected taxes on behalf of the central government, and kept a percentage for their trouble. Because of corrupt administration, these taxes were collected not once but many times, and the percentage kept by the collector each time was high. The salt gabelle, or salt monopoly, was equally corrupt, squeezing money from peasants for a dietary essential, with fiduciary hitchhikers taking cuts all along the line. The Billy Goat Gruff school of economics taxed dry goods and foodstuffs virtually every time they passed through a gate or crossed a bridge. This was the much-despised likin, or commodity tax. There was good reason for this loathing.

Traditionally, bureaucrats (including tax collectors) were paid salaries so low that they could not possibly live on them. The system worked on the basis of "prebendalism"—everyone started with a tiny base salary or "prebend," which could be increased only by graft—

"squeeze," or "tea" money. Take-home pay was therefore larger or smaller depending upon the individual's zeal—that is, his ability to collect "commissions." There was no other way out. Among tax collectors, the squeeze was taken out of each tax collected.

Because of his remarkable success in raising emergency funds and then getting the Central Bank on its feet, T. V. was appointed the KMT's Minister of Finance and set to work with extraordinary energy setting things right.

A special armed force (answerable personally to T. V.) was organized to police tax collection and often dispatched summary justice. It was not long before predatory country tax collectors and rural ruffians alike learned that collecting a tax more than once could mean their execution. T. V. never personally pulled the trigger, but he realized the value of the pen when backed by the sword.

He made KMT party officials personally responsible for revenues. However, as a precaution against too much zeal, it was decided that the new KMT army could not tax directly but had to go to civilian party representatives for supplies and funds. This was unprecedented restraint for a regime dependent on the military—a system of checks and balances.

During T. V.'s two years as Minister of Finance in South China, the revenues of Kwangtung Province grew to ten times their previous level —from $8 million Chinese at the end of 1924 to $80 million at the end of 1926, without any significant total increase in taxation. The gain came primarily from cutting "squeeze," and the endless repetition of it. The tax burden on peasants was somewhat lessened; ordinary consumers continued to pay about the same, wealthier classes paid slightly more, both in proportional and absolute terms.

T. V.'s efficiency was impressive but he alienated many people— from those who depended upon corruption to predatory merchants who felt comfortable with the old ways and did not want to see them changed. Although T. V. was a pure capitalist, the merchants, compradors, and tycoons of Canton soon regarded him as just another Bolshevik. They were already alarmed by Dr. Sun's friendship with Moscow. Members of the Chamber of Commerce began to argue for armed resistance to the Kuomintang. Quietly, they enlarged the Merchants' Volunteer Defense Force, a private militia organized in 1913 to protect them from intimidation by warlords. Sun Yat-sen was just another warlord in their eyes, and T. V. Soong was only his tax collector. The Canton merchants were tired of being bullied and were getting ready to fight back.

So it came to pass that it was T. V.'s liberal economic reforms that created the first armed challenge to Sun Yat-sen's Canton Republic.

Members of the Canton business community were evenly divided in their reasons for opposing Sun's alliance with the reds. The Old Guard capitalists—compradors, merchant princes, and bankers—were so far to the right that they despised both the KMT and the new middle class. They were terrified of Communists, but they also had no use for nationalists. T. V. Soong and his modern fiscal policies were overturning their applecart. The Whampoa Academy, they assumed, was turning out nothing more or less than a Bolshevik army. The overseas friendships of this Cantonese Old Guard lay with Great Britain. Their personal fortunes were kept in British bank vaults in Hong Kong, Singapore, or London.

The new middle-class leaders were horrified of Russia for entirely different reasons. These were the parvenus who, in an initial wave of nationalist fervor, had backed Dr. Sun, only to find him swerving left. They were ready to make some sacrifices if the result was "nationalistic"—meaning expanding Chinese participation in world markets. But they wanted stability to enjoy and enlarge their new-found wealth. Dr. Sun was going too far. There were Russians eating in their restaurants, and Chinese Communists were penetrating the work force, rabble-rousing, organizing and promoting strikes.

Both the new businessmen and the old tycoons watched the KMT army take shape at Whampoa. This modern army would soon be the dominant military force in the region, perhaps in all of South China. At that point, the merchants knew they would no longer be in a position to resist.

The Canton Chamber of Commerce was getting secret help from Great Britain to expand the Merchants' Volunteer Force. Locally, the volunteers were sponsored primarily by the powerful head of the Chamber, Comprador Ch'en Lien-po of the Hong Kong–Shanghai Bank. He was a snow leopard, a dangerous enemy; he owned silk factories and insurance companies, ten banks, and countless pawnshops; he had valuable properties in a dozen countries, and a score of mansions. He was also a senior figure in the South China triads. As comprador of the Hong Kong–Shanghai Bank, he was one of the most powerful Chinese financiers in the world. His personal empire extended around the

Pacific rim and into the Cantonese communities of Europe and the United States. By the autumn of 1923, he was pressuring every business firm in Canton to contribute $150—the cost of maintaining one full-time militiaman in the volunteers for six months. By the end of 1923, the militia had grown to fifty thousand men.

The volunteers received weapons and operating funds from sympathetic British commercial interests, with the quiet blessing of the British government. During the months when T. V. was introducing his emergency fund-raising measures, the volunteers stockpiled guns and ammunition. A slogan that circulated through the ranks had a chilling ring: "Save Canton from the Bolsheviks."

Someone at the Hong Kong–Shanghai Bank arranged with a German firm for the purchase of five thousand war surplus rifles and five thousand pistols and revolvers, with ammunition. They were shipped from Amsterdam aboard a Norwegian freighter. Dr. Sun's government actually was asked for and issued a permit for the shipment, but the permit turned out to be a charade. As the shipment came into the harbor on August 10, the KMT army seized it. Two gunboats escorted the freighter to Whampoa, where its cargo was unloaded.

At Whampoa, the cadets were alerted to trouble. Chiang's fledgling army was prepared for combat. Around the city, labor disputes were stirred up deliberately by CCP cadres to bring the confrontation to a head.

On August 26, the British consul general in Canton threatened Dr. Sun with British naval intervention if the KMT army attacked the Merchants' Volunteers. Outraged, Sun cabled a formal protest to Prime Minister Ramsay McDonald. He also appealed to the League of Nations, but received no reply.

The gun shipment had, in fact, been hijacked by the KMT army not at Sun Yat-sen's orders but by those of Borodin and Chiang Kai-shek.

The Chamber of Commerce demanded the guns back and staged a protest that forced up the price of rice. Borodin urged Sun to declare martial law, to seize all shops that remained closed, and to forbid the hasty removal of valuables from the city. Sun agreed. Canton was placed under martial law. Borodin, who was now orchestrating events, instructed the CCP to urge workers and peasants to rise up against the Merchants' Volunteer Force. As Canton's fate hung in the balance, Dr. Sun—determined not to let his grand scheme founder on a small point

—suddenly washed his hands of local matters and left the city to launch his long-awaited Northern Expedition. Borodin was furious. Chiang Kai-shek became nearly hysterical. With the city at flash point, the long-promised and overdue cargo of the first Soviet weapons—rifles, machine guns, and artillery—arrived from Vladivostok aboard the steamer *Vorovsky.*

Hearing this, Sun Yat-sen ordered Borodin to send the fresh weapons immediately to the front. Chiang Kai-shek, concerned only about the situation in Canton, persuaded Borodin that this was not the moment to humor Dr. Sun. Sun furiously telegraphed from the front ordering Chiang to join him at once. Chiang refused.

October came and the merchants offered to pay $200,000 for the return of their confiscated weapons. Sun decided that he could afford to relinquish some because of the timely arrival of the Soviet arms. He offered to return half. Chiang agreed to give them up, but without ammunition, and held off on the transfer until he had the new Soviet artillery in position.

On October 10—the mystical "Double Tenth"—the anniversary of the 1911 Revolution was to be celebrated by a great parade through Canton. Detachments of smartly-turned-out Whampoa cadets, among them young Lin Piao, set out for the parade. They were augmented by detachments of the KMT Labor Corps and Student Corps, waving revolutionary banners and shouting KMT slogans. To onlookers, it was not at all clear whether this was an anniversary celebration or a calculated provocation directed by Chiang Kai-shek and Borodin.

The parade followed the Canton waterfront to the place where the Merchants' Volunteers were unloading their ransomed weapons. The path of the marchers was blocked, and the two groups met and milled about. In the melee, marchers demanded that volunteers get out of the way. Pushing and shoving began. Shots rang out. A dozen KMT marchers fell, cut down by volunteers' bullets. Others were wounded.

Strangely, that was all there was to it, for a while. Following the skirmish, Sun rushed back to Canton, reaching the city on October 13. He found Borodin and Chiang preparing to launch a pre-midnight attack on the volunteers with a force of 800 Whampoa cadets, 220 cadets from the Hunan military school, 500 cadets from the Yunnan military school, 250 troops from armored trains, 2,000 policemen, all the available Soviet military advisors, and 320 Workers' Militia and

Peasants' Corps trained by instructor Mao Tse-tung. Approximately fifty thousand volunteers awaited them.

Just as a precaution, T. V. Soong quietly moved all KMT government funds aboard the *Vorovsky*. Provisions were made for the emergency evacuation of Dr. Sun Yat-sen, Ching-ling, T. V. Soong, and their combined retinues, along with Borodin and his Soviet aides.

At 10 P.M. on October 14, as planned, Chiang's Whampoa cadets struck all over Canton, supported by Communist cadres and workers. This time it was no mere skirmish. Whole sections of the city were put to the torch. Street fighting was so widespread that no clear description of the battle survived. The awesome destruction of property did as much to demoralize Canton's merchants as the killing. After twenty hours of chaos, the merchants sued for peace. Surviving volunteers were disarmed by Whampoa cadets.

It was known as Bloody Wednesday. By evening, it was all over except the fires. Large tracts of Canton still blazed. The western suburbs, where many foreigners lived, had been torched and looted. Canton lay disemboweled along the debris-strewn Pearl River.

For Chiang Kai-shek, it was a glorious victory. Neither he nor any of his Shanghai backers had any reason to mourn the losses of the capitalists of Canton. It was strictly dog eat dog. This gave the first blooding to a new army. It taught the merchants a lesson in twentieth-century politics. Henceforth, the KMT army was in charge.

Coolly and correctly, Borodin had assessed the situation, and he had guided the KMT's moves flawlessly. The new army that he had brought into being, and which Chiang Kai-shek and others had trained, had performed as ordered. The Soviet advisors had proven their worth. At a pivotal moment, Soviet arms had arrived. There had been no missteps. Chiang's defiance had disturbed Dr. Sun, but Sun could not argue with victory.

To demonstrate his pleasure, Sun had a triumphal arch erected on the Bund in front of the *Vorovsky*. Dressed in white uniforms and pith helmets, he and his staff accompanied Borodin to the ship for ceremonies of congratulations to the Soviet advisors, captain, and crew.

But Dr. Sun knew, if the others did not, that his base in Canton was finished. When he had left the city before the showdown—in what so many took to be an idiotic move—Sun had told his party leaders that

Canton was a dead issue. The city had already turned against them. Destroying Canton militarily proved nothing except the mettle of the Whampoa cadets. But Chiang and Borodin had ignored him, and made the city pay. It would never forgive them. Now Sun needed a new capital for his republic.

Chapter 9

SCRAMBLE FOR POWER

The *New York Times* announced the death of Sun Yat-sen on May 15, 1924. Sun was not dead. He was planning a trip to Peking, hoping to bypass the need to fight by joining in a coalition with the warlord then in control of the northern capital.

The warlord clique ruling North China had been ousted from Peking by "Christian General" Feng Yu-hsiang. Feng indicated that he was prepared to offer Sun the role of President of China at Peking, instead of merely President Extraordinaire at Canton. It was in this atmosphere of compromise that Dr. Sun was invited to Peking to "offer his advice on the new government"—a euphemism for private negotiations.

Feng was a rustic Pancho Villa. He baptized his troops with a fire hose, and, although nearly illiterate himself, forced his soldiers to memorize a new Chinese character each night before they were allowed to eat supper. He boasted that he taught his soldiers they were servants of the people. He also made a show of being strict about their moral behavior. But at the same time Feng also took part in conspiracies, palace coups, and conquests till he became a past master at duplicity. In 1924, tiring of these interminable rivalries, he seized the capital city for himself and turned to Soviet Russia for aid. Although Moscow was already supporting the KMT in South China, and was helping Sun Yat-sen plan an attack on the North, the Kremlin decided to back Feng as well. Russian instructors and advisors began to arrive in Peking along with weapons and other aid.

Feng fully understood the growing strength of the KMT and the widespread popularity of Dr. Sun. There were advantages in an alliance. Early in 1925, Feng held "long and successful talks" with Borodin, in which they came to terms. The next step was up to Dr. Sun.

But time was running out. Dr. Sun had turned fifty-eight years old on November 12, 1924. He suffered from digestive troubles and because of this did not drink alcohol. Before leaving Canton, as a precaution, he put his affairs in order. Key government posts were assigned to principal lieutenants. As a sop to the party's anxious conservative backers in Shanghai, he named as "deputy generalissimo" the rightist Hu Han-min, a top-ranking member of the KMT executive committee.

On his way to Peking, accompanied by Ching-ling, Borodin, and a retinue of eighteen KMT officials, Dr. Sun sailed to Shanghai aboard a Japanese steamer on November 17, and then sailed on to Kobe. In Japan, the Suns were given a warm public welcome, but the official reception was cold. The doctor was ignored by the Japanese government, which was displeased by his pact with Russia. He gave them a mild scolding in a memorable address at a Kobe school: "Now, the question remains whether Japan will be the hawk of the Western civilization . . . or the tower of strength of the Orient. This is the choice which lies before the people of Japan."

Empty-handed but full of heart, Sun disembarked at Tientsin on December 4, 1924. In the midst of a private talk with the current Manchurian warlord, the doctor collapsed in agony. For three weeks Ching-ling hovered beside his bed. On December 31 a special train rushed him to Peking, where a crowd of 100,000 well-wishers mobbed the station. He was too ill to address them. On January 26, he entered the hospital of Union Medical College, where specialists diagnosed a malignant tumor of the liver. The cancer was beyond treatment. He was moved to the spacious home of diplomat Wellington Koo, who had represented China at Versailles.

As news of Sun's terminal illness spread, close associates rushed to be at his side. His three most important lieutenants—rightist Hu Han-min, leftist Liao Chung-k'ai, and militarist Chiang Kai-shek—remained in Canton because their hold on the southern capital was shaky.

At Whampoa, Chiang went before the assembled cadets with the news:

Our Generalissimo, Dr. Sun Yat-sen, is now lying seriously ill in Peking, and he has not yet recovered. His disease is so serious that it is possible he is beyond recovery. Why is he stricken with this disease? Because for scores of years he has dedicated himself to the revolution, without any armies to put his plans into effect, and so he got cancer. Now we, who are the most reliable troops in the army of the Generalissimo, knowing that he is stricken with a mortal sickness and that the destiny of the country is at stake and the people are suffering—we are the ones who must struggle on bitterly to save the country and the people, and in so doing we may be able to cure the Generalissimo, who is already beyond all medical aid.

On his deathbed, Dr. Sun set up a Central Political Council to act on his behalf in Peking. The handsome, pomaded Wang Ching-wei was the senior member. Wang was famous for "attempting to assassinate" the Manchu Prince Regent in 1910, a plot that was little more than farce. The would-be assassins hid a homemade bomb in a ditch near the Prince's palace, then discovered they had cut the detonator wires too short. The bomb was found and traced by its casing to the plotters' hideout in Peking, where police found Wang. He had knowledge of the plot but had not actually participated. He was imprisoned a few months till the 1911 Revolution threw open the Manchu jails. Later, he claimed authorship of the assassination plot, and dined well thereafter. Wang's ability to compromise on virtually any principle gave him great staying power with the Kuomintang; he survived while all around him were getting killed. Now he had the good fortune to be at Dr. Sun's deathbed, where he stood an excellent chance of becoming the Generalissimo's successor.

As the great conspirator lay dying, there were two issues facing the KMT Central Political Council: whether to preserve Sun's alliance with Moscow and the CCP, and—most important—who would become the KMT's new Generalissimo or maximum leader to reap the rewards of Sun's long struggle. A scramble for power began.

Nobody seemed prepared. In Moscow, Lenin had died and Stalin and Trotsky were locked in their fateful struggle for power. When Borodin tried urgently to get instructions from the Kremlin, none were forthcoming.

Arrayed at Sun's bedside were the principal members of the Soong dynasty. Beside Ching-ling was her stepson, the ineffectual Sun Fo; her brother T. V. Soong, the financial *wunderkind;* the domineering elder sister, Ai-ling; and the latter's faithful husband, H. H. Kung, with his sad spaniel eyes and heart of gold.

All of those present—and some who were not—later claimed to have played a key role in the passing of the great man. Ai-ling let it be known that H. H. had made himself so indispensable that a "permanent bond" was formed between him and Ching-ling. Borodin claimed that Sun had the presence of mind to say, "If only the Russians continue to help . . ." Those who were anxious to placate the West claimed that he gasped, "Don't make trouble for the Christians. . . ." Even those who were many miles away—like Chiang Kai-shek—laid claim to some final benediction. The ambitious commandant of Whampoa Academy told everyone that Dr. Sun had used his last breath to pronounce the name "Chiang Kai-shek."

With everyone present listening intently, Wang Ching-wei read to Sun a political last will and testament drafted for his signature. Sun managed to say "Good, I thoroughly approve." Wang also read a personal will conveying to Ching-ling his books, papers, personal effects, and the house on the Rue Molière. After so many years of raising millions and spending them, this was all he had left. Both documents were signed on March 11, Ching-ling guiding his hand.

Sun's political will stated:

> For forty years, I have devoted myself to the cause of the National Revolution, the object of which is to raise China to a position of independence and equality. The experience of these forty years has convinced me that, to attain this goal, the people must be aroused and that we must associate ourselves in a common struggle with the peoples of the world who treat us as equals. The Revolution has not yet been successfully concluded. Let all our comrades follow my writings—The Plans of National Reconstruction, The Three Principles of the People, and the Manifesto of the First Congress of Representatives—and make every effort to carry them into effect. Above all, my recent declaration in favor of holding a National Convention of the People of China and abolishing the unequal treaties should be carried into effect as soon as possible. This is my last will and testament.

This document, know as "The Tsung-li Testament" (the testament of the Maximum Leader) was read in every KMT political meeting thereafter, and became the catechism of a growing Sun Yat-sen deification cult. A letter of farewell to the Soviet Union, prepared in English by Mikhail Borodin and Sun's Trinidad-born associate Eugene Chen, was read to the doctor by T. V. Soong and subsequently appeared in the Soviet party newspaper *Pravda*.

To the Central Executive Committee of the Union of Soviet Socialist Republics:

My Dear Comrades,

As I lie here, with a malady that is beyond men's skill, my thoughts turn to you and to the future of my party and my country. You are the head of a Union of free republics which is the real heritage that the immortal Lenin has left to the world of the oppressed peoples. Through this heritage, the victims of imperialism are destined to secure their freedom and deliverance from an international system whose foundations lie in ancient slaveries and wars and injustices. I am leaving behind me a party which I hoped would be associated with you in the historic work of completely liberating China and other exploited countries from this imperialist system. Fate decrees that I must leave the task unfinished and pass it on to those who, by remaining true to the principles and teachings of the Party, will constitute my real followers. I have, therefore, enjoined the KMT to carry on the work of the national revolutionary movement in order that China may be freed from the semi-colonial status which imperialism imposed upon her. To this end I have charged the party to keep in constant touch with you; and I look with confidence to the continuance of the support that your Government has heretofore extended to my country. In bidding farewell to you, dear comrades, I wish to express the fervent hope that the day may soon dawn when the U.S.S.R. will greet, as a friend and ally, a strong and independent China and the two allies may together advance to victory in the great struggle for the liberation of the oppressed peoples of the world. With fraternal greetings.

On Wednesday, March 11, Sun asked to be moved from the comfortable bed to an army field cot. At 9:30 in the morning of Thursday, March 12, he died.

The Russian legation immediately lowered its flag to half-mast, followed by all other Russian offices in China. In a calculated affront, no other embassy dipped its colors till the following day. The Russians also ordered a special coffin from Moscow, a steel box painted yellow, with a glass lid, of the type in which Lenin was originally displayed. It was a singularly ugly contraption and was not used. In China, coffins were carved from the trunk of a hardwood known as *nai moh,* or coffin tree, the best specimens coming from the western mountains of Yunnan Province. A traditional "number one" model was chosen by Ching-ling.

The private funeral on March 19 was a subdued Soong family affair. It was followed by a public funeral at the chapel of Peking's Union Medical College, featuring Comrade Karakhan as chief mourner. H. H.

Kung reported to the congregation that Dr. Sun had told him before his death, "Just as Christ was sent by God to the world, so also did God send me." The principal eulogy, delivered by former Minister of Justice George Hsu, was sprinkled with Sun's own words about his similarity to Christ:

"He was a revolutionist; so am I." "He came to save the poor, and the unfortunate, and those in bondage. So have I also tried to do." "He decried the traditions maintained by the lawmakers of Judea, and pleaded for universal brotherhood. It is because of similar shackles that bind China that I have made my crusade. It is because the organized Church has been so divided and divisive that I have long given up my membership in the church, but I believe in Christ and his teachings and have endeavored to make them my own."

American journalist Edna Lee Booker was at the funeral:

Out of the stillness came a surpliced choir of students from Yenching University, carrying tall lighted candles and singing a favorite song of Dr. Sun: "Sweet peace, the gift of God's love." [Leslie Severinghaus, the brother-in-law of *Time*'s Henry Luce, sang the solo parts.] They formed about the bier, stood there as the service, beautiful and impressive in its simplicity, continued. Outside . . . thousands waited, until the choir boys led the mourners from the chapel. Madame Sun . . . frail and appealing in her widow's dress, her enveloping veil, leaned on the arm of her younger sister, Soong May-ling, and of her stepson, Sun Fo; and there were Dr. and Mrs. H. H. Kung and others closely connected. Then came the great coffin borne by twenty-four pallbearers.

Sun's body lay in state for two weeks while half a million people filed past. Then the massive Chinese coffin was carried in a procession through streets lined by crowds and was taken to the Western Hills, where it was placed in a lofty chamber of the Azure Cloud Temple, set among white-barked pines. (The Russian coffin arrived in Peking at this inopportune moment. It was rushed to the temple, where the monks sensibly tucked it away in a side passage.)

It had been Sun's wish to be buried on the Purple Mountain outside Nanking, near the tomb of the first Ming Emperor. Plans were put into motion to build a mausoleum there. But five dark years were to pass before it was complete.

Borodin was not present at the funeral. Anticipating trouble, he had gone back to Canton, where trouble was indeed afoot.

Sun's death had come just as the KMT was launching a campaign to wipe out the irritating Kwangtung warlord, Ch'en Chiung-ming, who had driven Sun and Ching-ling from Canton in 1922. This punitive expedition was conceived by the new Soviet military advisor, General Galen.

Here was a dashing figure, who raced through Canton in an open touring car in the style of the Petrograd Bolsheviks, accompanied by armed bodyguards with cocked revolvers clinging to the running-boards. He was thought by some to be a renegade Frenchman, by others to be an Austrian noble captured by the Bolsheviks and converted to their homicidal communism. Actually, he was a Russian peasant who had joined the Bolsheviks in 1916. While the other Soviet advisors in China had attended Frunze Military Academy, Galen had had no formal military training. He was a natural tactician and received the highest Soviet military honor, the Order of the Red Banner, on four separate occasions. (To no avail; Stalin had the bloodthirsty dwarf Yezhov murder him in the 1937 purge.)

Galen was a martinet about military etiquette, which impressed Chiang Kai-shek. In everything he did, Galen made Chiang look good. He masterminded the 1925 campaign against Ch'en Chiung-ming with such flair that it gave Chiang leverage in the race for control of the KMT. To most onlookers at the time, Chiang was far from being a likely candidate. There were others who were far more prominent.

The leading public contenders were rightist Hu Han-min, centrist Wang Ching-wei, and leftist Liao Chung-k'ai. There was a fourth candidate in the wings who was unknown to the public but intimately acquainted with the party chiefs, the champion of the militant Shanghai right wing—Green Gang boss Tu Yueh-sheng.

There were two ways in which Tu could gain control of the KMT: by being named Sun's heir himself, which was highly unlikely by normal procedures, or by arranging for the election of a cat's-paw candidate who would act in his interests. As an opium addict and gang boss, Big-eared Tu must have realized early on that his ambitions could best be served by a proxy. He had two in mind—his military protégé Chiang Kai-shek, whom he had groomed for fifteen years, and his Shanghai business partner, the crippled millionaire Curio Chang. But Tu had to proceed indirectly. The presence of Borodin made the election of any obvious anti-Communist candidate unlikely.

The indecisive centrist candidate, ladies' man Wang Ching-wei, lacked a significant power base. At best, he could be a compromise, an interim pope. He and the thin, wiry rightist, Hu Han-min, were diametric opposites. They despised each other. It was expected that they would neutralize each other.

The clear front-runner was the American-born leftist Liao Chung-k'ai, who posed the greatest obstacle to an indirect takeover by Big-eared Tu. Liao was Borodin's favorite and Hu Han-min's close friend. Liao was well liked by everyone, particularly Dr. Sun's widow, Ching-ling.

He was the son of a San Francisco Chinese businessman. He had continued his studies in Japan and there become interested in Sun Yat-sen's movement. Liao, the budding leftist, fell in with Hu Han-min, the ambitious rightist, and the two became lifelong friends. While Hu Han-min argued for personal dictatorship, Liao favored drastic social reforms. Liao insisted that China had been exploited too long by selfish financial interests. He believed that capitalism should be restrained and that peasant farmers should be allowed to own their land and have access to manufactured goods through consumer cooperatives. He urged the widest possible democracy, but failed to persuade Dr. Sun to seek support directly from the peasants; the notion was too radical in the 1920s even for the Chinese Communists, who wanted instead a revolution on the Russian model, based on urban workers.

It was Liao who had finally persuaded Dr. Sun to seek Moscow's aid. Borodin liked him and preferred always to deal through Liao. At the time of Sun Yat-sen's death, Liao was the senior political officer at Whampoa, Chiang Kai-shek's political counterpart. He was also the KMT's Governor of Kwangtung Province. If matters had been allowed to take their natural course, Liao most certainly would have been Sun Yat-sen's heir.

In the weeks following Sun's death, two warlords who had previously been allied with the KMT took advantage of the confusion to attack and seize Canton. Borodin fled to Whampoa, and Chiang and Liao counterattacked with General Galen's help. The city was quickly recaptured. Within forty-eight hours the KMT took 17,000 prisoners, captured 16,000 guns, and the siege was over.

Once Canton was again secure, the KMT Central Committee met hastily to decide the matter of Sun's successor. It was concluded that there would be no individual successor. The national government would be led by a triumvirate of the left, right, and center—Hu, Wang, and Liao. Wang was given the largely ceremonial title of Acting Chairman while Hu was named Foreign Minister. Executive control remained with Liao. It was, in effect, a palace coup by the far left.

But the left in doing so was making powerful enemies. Spring and summer of 1925 had been filled with labor unrest. Communist party and KMT-leftwing agitators had stirred up workers and students. Their anti-foreign demonstrations throughout China had angered factory owners, bankers, and foreign taipans. In Shanghai on May 15, a Japanese foreman at a textile factory had shot and killed a worker during a strike. The CCP called a protest demonstration for May 30. There was a large turnout, and police from the International Settlement were called in. One British detachment fired into the crowd, killing twelve workers and wounding fifty others. This "May 30th Incident" precipitated strikes, boycotts, and demonstrations elsewhere. Fifty-two protestors in Canton were killed by French and British machine gunners. After the shooting, Vera Vladimirovna Vishnayakova Akimova, a Russian advisor in Canton, described the city's foreign settlement on Shameen Island as "a splinter in the living body of the city":

> It lay before us, hushed, on guard, separated from the Embankment by a small artificial canal and the wall of hatred and anger of the Chinese people. Some sort of sawhorse-like barrier draped with barbed wire stood on the bridge with its heavy cast-iron gates, leaving only a narrow passageway into the place of residence of all the foreign consulates. . . . Two British soldiers in colonial uniforms—cork helmet, short khaki pants, rifle in hand and a broad sword at the belt—were pacing evenly up and down by the barrier on the bridge. Not a sound was heard from the other side. It was as if the island were dead. In fact, very few inhabitants remained there. Even the missionaries who had fled from the mainland had gone away.

The incident brought on a protracted general strike in Hong Kong that aroused the deep enmity of the British. In Hong Kong's outspoken newspapers, articles appeared openly calling for the assassination of the leaders of the KMT left. The British offered T. V. Soong a "loan" of $10 million if the strikes ceased, but withdrew the offer when it became clear that the KMT right and left were engaged in a power struggle. These many negative consequences of leftist agitation galled Chiang

Kai-shek's backers, and furthered their determination to rid the party of its left wing.

In Shanghai, a new Communist-dominated General Federation of Labor helped organize more than five hundred strikes during the next year. The appearance of this new workers' union was a direct threat to the Green Gang workers' guilds. Big-eared Tu and Pockmarked Huang were not prepared to share their grip on workers. Already, Big-eared Tu was the most determined and methodical anti-Communist in China. Now he swung into action. In the first of a series of ominous initiatives, he sent Curio Chang to Canton to advise Chiang Kai-shek and to stage-manage a bid for power.

On the 20th of August 1925, in Canton, Liao Chung-k'ai arrived by car for a meeting of the KMT Central Committee. As he alighted from the sedan, five gunmen stepped out from behind columns at the front of the building and shot him down gangland style. Blame for Liao's murder was never formally established, but rumors were circulated that attempted to place responsibility on the moderate rightist Hu Han-min. It is unlikely that he was involved because, despite differing ideologies and lifestyles, Hu and Liao had been close friends since 1905. Nevertheless, Hu and his family and many other conservative KMT officials fled Canton to avoid the vendetta.

Borodin and Chiang set up a Cheka-style investigation to track down traitors in their midst. One suspect was brought to Chiang's office at Whampoa for interrogation. A quarrel began, Chiang became hysterical, took out his revolver, and shot the accused man dead.

Despite every effort to fix blame on right, left, and center, the method of Liao's execution had all the earmarks of the Green Gang. The murder disposed of the leader of the KMT's left, and the recoil disposed of the leader of the moderate right. It created a vacuum in the KMT leadership, opening the way for Chiang Kai-Shek. In the subsequent scramble to reorganize the chain of command, there were bizarre and unexpected developments.

Big-eared Tu's long-time business partner, Curio Chang—whom few previously had considered a serious possibility—was elected on May 19, 1926, to be Liao Chung-k'ai's successor as chairman of the KMT Standing Committee. He remained in that decisive position only a few weeks, just long enough to arrange for the election of Chiang Kai-shek as his replacement on July 7, 1926.

The Green Gang's well-disguised man in Canton—the irascible commandant of Whampoa Military Academy—had suddenly sprinted past all the front runners to become Sun Yat-sen's heir.

The way was now clear for Chiang to complete his takeover and make himself China's dictator. To guard against a premature backlash that could interfere with such plans, his moves had to be engineered with the utmost care.

Shorn of his Chinese pigtail and suited up for the Methodist ministry, Charlie Soong strikes a handsome figure in his days as a student at Trinity and Vanderbilt. He was the first Chinese many Southerners had seen. *(Fifth Avenue Methodist Church, Wilmington, N.C.)*

Charlie Soong's American benefactor, "General" Julian Carr of Durham, North Carolina, was a multi-millionaire tobaccoman known throughout the South for his philanthropy. He provided the footing for the Soong dynasty's great fortune. *(Durham Public Library, Durham, N.C.)*

Gentle and godfearing, Ni Kwei-tseng married Charlie Soong; she bore him three sons and three daughters, who were destined to rule China and dazzle the world. *(Private collection)*

Oldest of the Soong sisters, Ai-ling graduated from Georgia's Wesleyan College and became Sun Yat-sen's personal secretary. Fascinated by money, she married into one of China's richest banking families and became notorious for her wheeling-and-dealing. *(Wesleyan College, Macon, Ga.)*

Romantic and committed to revolution, Ching-ling Soong eloped with Sun Yat-sen and after his death became the guardian of his political legacy. Mao Tse-tung made her a Vice Chairman of the People's Republic. *(Wesleyan College, Macon, Ga.)*

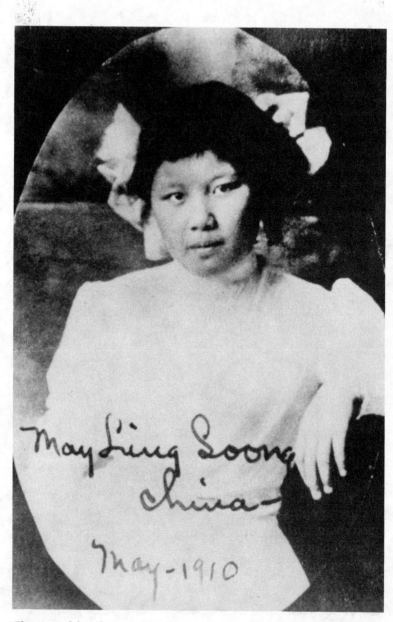

May Ling Soong
China —
May – 1910

Plump and headstrong May-ling, youngest of the Soong sisters, captivated America in her role as the ardent Christian Madame Chiang
Kai-shek. A favorite of *Time* magazine publisher Henry Luce, she was
regarded for decades as one of the world's Ten Most Admired Women.
(Wesleyan College, Macon, Ga.)

Charlie's closest friend until the bitter end when he eloped with daughter Ching-ling, Sun Yat-sen was the most effective Chinese revolutionary in exile. But his sudden death in 1924 led to a vicious scramble between Right and Left for control of China, which brought Chiang Kai-shek to power. *(National Archives)*

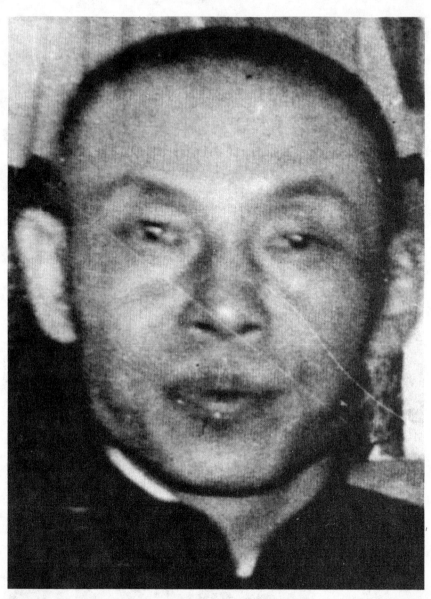

Leader of Shanghai's notorious Green Gang—a criminal cartel that dominated Chinese drug traffic and heroin exports—Big-eared Tu was Generalissimo Chiang's secret sponsor. Through drugs, extortion and strongarm political tactics, he brought Chiang to power and bolstered the Rightwing regime, eliminating all dissenters, particularly Communists, by the tens of thousands. *(Brian Crozier)*

Chapter 10

THE GREEN CONSPIRACY

Chiang Kai-shek had not simply blundered into power, and it did not fall like ripe fruit into his hands. How did this abrupt right-wing coup really take place? Why did nobody see it coming, and—more curious still—why did the KMT leftists, the CCP leadership, and the Russians fail to recognize where it would lead?

The notion became pervasive that Chiang Kai-shek was an acceptable leader for the KMT coalition because he did not represent any special power base or special interest group. This is often asserted in biographies and other books about that period, but it was dangerously inaccurate.

It was a basic rule of thumb in Chinese politics, understood by nearly every politically aware person, that promising military candidates usually represented provinces or districts, and therefore carried with them the virus of "warlordism." Although Chiang did not *seem* to have a power base in the familiar sense, he simply had a different kind of base, representing a different kind of power—a kind that thrived on secrecy. Even the CCP did not grasp that Chiang owed everything to the Green Gang.

In November 1925, three months after Liao's murder, a group of eight KMT rightists gathered secretly in the Western Hills outside Peking, at the Temple of the Azure Cloud, where Dr. Sun's remains reposed. They were meeting to decide the future of the KMT. These eight men agreed that all Communists and even the middle-roader Wang Ching-wei must be expelled from the KMT. The new leader was to be Chiang Kai-shek. This pact was the brainchild of three of Chiang's mentors. Big-eared Tu, Curio Chang, and Tai Ch'i-tao, Chiang's close political advisor, put the idea forward, assuring the others that Chiang was "a reasonable man"—he could be manipulated. The Western Hills meeting concluded by adopting the inevitable slogan, this time one that went "Ally with Chiang to overthrow Wang."

Ousting Wang Ching-wei was imperative because he was temporarily in charge of the Kuomintang government in the wake of Liao's murder, and he was too weak to prevent a Communist coup. He had just convened a Second Party Congress that placed most of the critical departments of the southern government in the hands of the CCP and other leftists—Mao Tse-tung, Chou En-lai, Madame Chou En-lai, and the newly-widowed Madame Liao. To the Shanghai conservatives, this was tantamount to handing over China to the Bolsheviks. It was imperative and urgent to "Ally with Chiang to overthrow Wang."

Masterminding the strategy, Chang Ching-chiang emerged into the political limelight in Canton. He was welcomed by the unwary Wang and others, because of his generosity to the KMT over the years, because he had loaned money to most of the republican revolutionary leaders when they had run short from time to time, and because he was one of Shanghai's leading power brokers. He was at this point crippled by his foot disease and generally confined to wheelchairs, in which he appears in photographs from that period. His face was gaunt and cadaverous, his cheeks hollow, his mouth half-open as if to wheeze, and his eyes behind thick-lens glasses cold and distinctly malignant. He bore a disturbing resemblance to certain photographs of Dr. Joseph Goebbels, Hitler's propaganda minister.

Curio Chang, observed historian Harold Isaacs,

> became Chiang Kai-shek's mentor, chief political aide, and counselor. . . . It was a question of stabilizing the leadership at the top by taking it out of the hands of vacillating liberals. For this a sharp blow had to be struck, damaging but not fatal, to the Communists and their petty bourgeois radical allies. . . . Their desires fused with [Chiang Kai-shek's] intense personal ambition, his cunning, his envy of political and military rivals, his flair for intrigue, his unmistakable lust for power. . . . [Chiang] became what Karl Marx, referring to Louis Napoleon, once called "a man who did not decide at night and act during the day but decided during the day and acted at night."

When Chiang struck, it was indeed at night.

In the humid, predawn hours of March 20, 1926, while Canton slept and even good Communists dreamed, Chiang ordered his most trusted Whampoa troops into action.

For weeks Chiang had been ready to pounce, waiting for the right provocation. The opportunity came when the gunboat *Chungshan* cruised downriver from the heart of Canton on the night of March 19, and anchored off Whampoa. Chiang decided that the gunboat—under the command of a skipper who was a Communist party member—was in a threatening position. It was possible that the reds had awakened to the Green conspiracy and were launching a preemptive strike against him.

Chiang's Whampoa units struck with precision. All political workers at the academy were arrested. All Soviet advisors in Canton were placed under house arrest. The Communist chief of the KMT Naval Bureau was seized. The party office responsible for directing labor agitation in Canton and Hong Kong was raided for documents and weapons. The pro-Communist political commissar of Whampoa, who had succeeded Liao Chung-k'ai, was arrested. Then there was a rash of bloody attacks on peasants by gangs of thugs in several parts of China. There was nothing to tie these peasant massacres directly to Chiang, or to the Green Gang, but the coincidence was provocative, like the reverberations caused by the impatient stirrings of a very large dragon.

By dawn, Chiang was in control of the city. The KMT leadership had been taken by surprise. In a state of utter confusion, there was a hasty meeting of the Central Committee, which lamely resolved: "Since Chiang Kai-shek has always struggled for the revolution, it is hoped that he will realize his mistake in this event."   •

Once again Borodin was not there to mind the store. He had left Canton on February 4, aboard the Russian steamer *Pamyat Lenina,* bound for talks in Peking followed by a visit to Moscow. In his absence, Wang Ching-wei crumpled to Chiang, announcing that he had been "taken ill." In a humiliating scene, he met Chiang at T. V. Soong's mint and handed over the KMT seals of office. He hurried away to a small village outside Canton, and then left for a "cure" in Europe.

Under orders from Chiang, all Russian advisors began packing to leave. Leading Chinese Communists went into hiding. Then, several days later, Chiang abruptly apologized, released all his prisoners, and said the whole thing had been a big "misunderstanding." He promised that the officers responsible would be reprimanded.

This kind of mischievous subtlety might have been typical of the sage Sun Tzu, but it was not characteristic of Chiang Kai-shek, nor was the language of his apology. Here were the hallmarks of Big-eared Tu, Pockmarked Huang, and Curio Chang. It was one of the signatures of the Green Gang that people who were kidnapped for extortion were always returned with profuse apologies (after the payoff had been made); and oblique threats of death, such as the delivery of a coffin to a man's home, were always followed by apologies and the explanation that it had all been the result of a terrible mistake—which, of course, the victim understood it was not. In this instance, although the voice was coming out of Chiang, Big-eared Tu's lips were moving.

It seems that the Green Gang leaders were surprised by the ease with which Chiang Kai-shek had succeeded. If the reds were so totally unprepared for a Green coup d'état, why not pay out more rope and let them hang themselves nationwide?

Chiang's backers had knocked the indecisive centrists of the KMT out of the saddle. But they were not yet ready for a China-wide confrontation with the hard-core leftists and the Chinese Communist party. Valuable ground had been gained and it was time to take advantage of the unexpected vulnerability of the left—time to consolidate the gains and prepare for a final showdown.

There was also no need under the circumstances to forfeit valuable Russian support and CCP organizational skills just as the long-awaited Northern Expedition was about to resume.

Chiang was now the de facto boss of the KMT, but his position needed to be confirmed formally by protocols. On May 15 the party leadership convened. The rattled KMT obligingly named Chiang Kai-shek head of the party. Chiang then briefly deputized Curio Chang as chairman of the Central Committee. Between the two of them, they could now control all party decisions.

Chiang's plans for the Northern Expedition were officially approved, and he was granted emergency powers for the duration. All KMT government offices were subordinated to his military headquarters. The arsenal, the Political Department, the general staff, the military and naval schools—all were placed at his disposal. The military coup was complete, Chiang's powers now absolute.

Strangely, the Communist leadership both in China and in Russia failed to react to Chiang's takeover. Lenin had warned in 1920 that true

Communists would have to be vigilant to preserve the leadership of the revolution from those who would lead it astray. But Lenin was dead. Trotsky, who had also understood this danger, was losing his power struggle. Stalin, instead of being alarmed by Chiang's takeover, decided to ignore it. The Kremlin inexplicably chose to deny that it had even taken place. All news of the coup was kept out of Soviet newspapers and the international Communist press. The Executive Committee of the Comintern, and even the presidium of the Executive Committee, had the information deliberately concealed from them. News reports of Chiang's coup in non-Communist journals were vehemently denied at Moscow's instructions by Communist organs everywhere in the world. They were all "lying reports." Said New York's *Daily Worker:* "There has been no insurrection in Canton."

On Borodin's return to Canton, it was not a triumphant, strident Chiang who greeted him, but a Chiang oozing humility, apologizing abjectly for the assorted "misunderstandings." To even the score, Chiang generously offered to stage a purge of the KMT right wing. This was nothing less than a self-serving proposal to eliminate the remaining moderate rightists in the government. If they were not members of the Green Gang, and if they had not paid the customary protection money, which even Chiang Kai-shek paid to Big-eared Tu, then they were fair game. As a demonstration to Borodin of his "good faith," Chiang proceeded on his own to purge the moderate right.

Borodin found himself confronted by an elusive target. Chiang at his best was pathologically devious, a man of mercurial nature, alternating between shrill outbursts of hysterics that terrified his subordinates and baffling interludes of self-condemnation and near groveling before his bewildered opponents. Borodin and the CCP leadership simply did not know what to make of Chiang's performance.

Two interpretations have been given to the fact that Chiang and Borodin now resumed their partnership. The American journalist George Sokolsky, who was in Canton at the time and who later worked for T. V. Soong in the Kuomintang government, maintained that Chiang had the Russians over a barrel: Moscow must either support him and his Northern Expedition, or the alliance was over and all Russians would be forced to leave. This argument is both naïve and unconvincing. Trotsky's losses were Stalin's gains in a much larger perspective. The other view is given by Stalin's biographer Louis Fischer: "Chiang, whose distinguishing characteristic was not courage, apparently had been frightened by his own action." Apparently, but not really. He apologized to Borodin categorically. "Both sides knew that the struggle between them was inevitable. But rather than engage now in bloodletting from which only the Cantonese militarists could gain, they tacitly agreed to postpone the issue until they reached the Yangtze." It was to the Green Gang's advantage, now that it had plumbed the weakness of the CCP and the curious inaction of Moscow, to set up a much bigger trap.

On orders from Stalin, Borodin went far to placate Chiang, agreeing to remove Soviet advisors that Chiang disliked. For the Trotskyites in China, it was all very confusing. One advisor later explained,

> We consider Chiang Kai-shek a peculiar person with peculiar characteristics, most prominent of these being his lust for glory and power and craving to be the hero of China. He claims that he stands not only for the Chinese National Revolution but for the World Revolution. Needless to say, the degree of his actual understanding of revolution is quite another matter. . . . He acts entirely according to his individuality without depending on the masses. However, in order to obtain glory, which is his goal, he sometimes wants to utilize the masses, the Chinese Communist Party, and ourselves.

More succinctly, Trotsky himself later observed: "In preparing himself for the role of an executioner [Chiang Kai-shek] wanted to have the cover of world communism—and got it."

Since Chiang planned to lead the Communists into a Green Gang trap, he was willing to negotiate just about anything until he was ready to trip the snare.

If further evidence was needed that Chiang was far from contrite about his past deeds, and far from modest about his future plans, it was provided when he sent a traditional Chinese intermediary—evidently Curio Chang—with a proposal of marriage to the widowed Ching-ling Soong. It was still fresh in her mind that Chiang had solicited the advice of her husband, Dr. Sun, on whether he stood a chance of marrying her sister, May-ling. Chiang and his backers were eager to cement his identification, one way or the other with the sainted doctor, as well as with the prestige and financial power of the Soong family.

Ching-ling recalled his proposal of marriage during a conversation with Edgar Snow, who recorded it tersely as follows: "Chiang proposed to her, after Dr. Sun's death in 1925, through a Chinese middleman. She thought it was politics, not love, and declined."

The Northern Expedition began in the summer of 1926; the goal was the Yangtze Valley, six hundred miles to the northeast. It was a two-pronged thrust, with a force consisting largely of leftists heading energetically northwestward toward Wuhan, while Chiang led a force of his favorite Whampoa units northeast toward Nanchang and Shanghai.

Galen, the Russian tactician, accompanied the northwestern thrust. Russian aviators reconnoitered enemy positions. In the army's path, CCP cadres roused peasants and workers in towns and countryside. The resistance of local warlords, and of the outposts of the northern militarists, was eroded from within by peasant spies and CCP saboteurs, while railway and telegraph workers interrupted communications. The Communists had made their preparations well, and tapped into the deep pool of bitterness against landlords and warlords alike. Atrocities occurred as peasants evened the score against local tyrants and "evil gentry." Conservatives in the KMT protested, but the CCP's answer was immortalized by Mao Tse-tung in his report on the peasant movement in Hunan Province:

> The peasants are clear-sighted. Who is bad and who is not, who is the worst and who is not quite so vicious, who deserves severe punishment and who deserves to be let off lightly—the peasants keep clear accounts, and very seldom has the punishment exceeded the crime. Secondly, a revolution is not a dinner party, or writing an essay, or painting a picture, or doing embroidery; it cannot be so refined, so leisurely and gentle, so temperate, kind, courteous, restrained and magnanimous. A revolution is an insurrection, an act of violence by which one class overthrows another.

For Chiang Kai-shek, however, "his" revolution was something of a dinner party. The CCP was fighting his Northern Campaign for him, while he kept his hands clean. Chiang, commanding the northeastern prong, seemed determined to get his personally-groomed army units to Shanghai unbruised and well rested. He proceeded slowly, avoiding engagements, restrained the CCP cadres that accompanied him, prevented peasants and workers from avenging themselves on landlords and gentry in their path. The victories of the western prong produced sufficient fear and excitement to create the impression that a vast Kuomintang army was sweeping inexorably northward. Chiang, having little to do with the northwestern forces, was credited erroneously by foreign observers as being the only "reasonable" and "responsible" military figure in the campaign; "irresponsible" acts were all blamed on the left.

By October 1926, Wuhan had fallen to the leftist force, and the KMT liberals and Communists were in control of both Hunan and Hupeh provinces. By December, they also had Kiangsi and Fukien provinces.

The KMT government moved up from Canton to Wuhan, the tricity on the Middle Yangtze, where the 1911 Revolution had taken place. The first group to leave Canton included Borodin and Ching-ling, her stepson Sun Fo, Eugene Chen and his two daughters, joined by T. V. Soong. They were accompanied by leftist military officers and a handful of Soviet advisors. Traveling first by train, they transferred at the end of the line to palanquins and struck overland, skirting hostile territory. Then they shifted to flatboats, river junks, and ponies. More than half the trip was made on foot through daily rainstorms, fording streams and negotiating muddy mountain trails.

Wuhan was waiting for them. Composed of three Yangtze cities—Wuchang, Hankow, and Hanyang—Wuhan was industrialized and full of restive labor. Support for the KMT left, and for the Communists, was strong. In a mass demonstration of popular support, 300,000 partisans welcomed the KMT leadership. Aircraft circled overhead, and great strings of fireworks crackled like machine-gun fire.

On January 3, 1927, in the frenzy of celebration, the Wuhan mobs spontaneously seized control of the British Concession in Hankow. Others took over the British Concession downriver at Kiukiang. The Wuhan government claimed these as victories, enhancing its prestige among leftist Chinese. The British government grudgingly relinquished both concessions. But, while giving in, the British were mobilizing a huge expeditionary force to defend their most important prize, Shanghai.

Compared to proletarian Wuhan, Chiang's temporary campaign base at Nanchang was a medieval stronghold of traditional values and landed gentry, with no significant industry—only an electric plant and an enamelware factory. The secret societies were strong there, and powerful conservatives came to Nanchang to retire. Borodin and the Wuhan leftists did not know it but Chiang Kai-shek had been staying in close touch there with the Green Gang bosses. The gangleaders knew that the Communists and other leftists were planning a Wuhan-style mass uprising for Shanghai. A Green reception was being prepared for the reds.

The Communists in Shanghai were not united in methods or purpose, and were continually being thrown into confusion by malignant and mischievous instructions from Stalin. Nonetheless, they naïvely planned an uprising of workers and Communist cadres in October 1926. It was foolishly intended to be a show of strength, months ahead of the scheduled arrival of Chiang's main force, when an even larger uprising was planned, and the city itself was to be seized.

After discussing the forthcoming red uprising with Pockmarked Huang and Big-eared Tu, Chiang sent a trusted staff officer named Niu Yung-chien to offer the leftists in Shanghai his "support" and the participation of a "special contingent" of Whampoa troops in the uprising. The leftists welcomed Chiang's participation and made the final details of their strategy known to Chiang's officers. The Green Gang bosses then tipped off the northern militarist who was in control of the Shanghai region—Sun Ch'uan-fang. When the red uprising began, the warlord's garrison was waiting. Chiang's "special contingent" failed to materialize. Caught by surprise by the warlord's well-armed mercenaries, large numbers of Communist cadres and workers were massacred. Incomprehensibly, the CCP organizers never suspected Chiang of betrayal.

It was immediately after this bloody fiasco that Chou En-lai arrived in Shanghai from Canton to take charge of reorganizing the battered and demoralized CCP strike forces. Chou had worked closely with Borodin, and had served as one of the political commissars at Whampoa under Chiang. He was an urban Bolshevik, with recent experience in the Paris Commune while a student in France.

Meanwhile Chiang went into another huddle with Pockmarked Huang in November 1926 at the town of Kiukiang. The senior member of the Shanghai troika usually delegated major operations to Big-eared Tu. But this meeting was important enough to bring the godfather out of his lair in the French Concession. The grand strategy that had been agreed upon at the Western Hills meeting the year before, and stage-managed in Canton meantime by Curio Chang, was now nearing its climax as the KMT army moved into the Green Gang heartland of the Yangtze Valley. Between them, Chiang's army and the gang would crush the reds for good.

Since the preliminary October massacre of leftists, tension in Shanghai had grown unbearable. The overwhelming impression was that Shanghai was about to be taken over by murderous Bolsheviks and that the approaching KMT army was a leftist legion that would take part in the Red Rape. Merchants took refuge with their families in the French Concession and the International Settlement. Around the perimeters, barbed-wire-covered barricades were erected, studded with pillboxes, braced with sandbags, patrolled by heavily-armed foreign police, Western soldiers, and militia. From various countries, a military force of no less than thirty thousand men was arriving "to protect foreign interests and foreign nationals." Of the British alone, there were soon two soldiers for each of His Majesty's subjects in Shanghai. British planes flew continual patrol missions over the port, and thirty warships from Great Britain, France, America, Japan, Italy, and Portugal rode at anchor in the Whangpoo ready for action. More were on the way.

Foreign residents were goading each other's fears with expectations of red barbarities. It was still very fresh in everyone's mind that, during the Russian Revolution and the civil war that followed, there had been appalling acts committed. The city's Western newspapers, notably the *North China Daily News,* maintained a shrill alarm that brought nerves to the breaking point.

Still unaware that Chiang Kai-shek was their Judas, the Shanghai Communists and KMT labor organizers were anxiously awaiting the arrival of "their" army. Its vanguard units were promised to reach Shanghai on February 22, 1927. To soften up the city for Chiang, the unions began a general strike on February 19, three days before the army was expected. Trams stopped running. Traffic on the Whangpoo grew still. Sampans stopped moving. Steamers could not sail. The doors of the post office were locked. All big department stores on the Nanking Road closed down. Factories were silent.

On February 19, however, Chiang was still far away in Nanchang. Lying in wait for the strikers were the heavily-armed police and mercenary soldiers of the local warlord, supported by foreign police. Since this was merely a work stoppage, the only targets available were students passing out leaflets, and a few strike pickets. Police and soldiers fell upon them, dragging them into the middle of streets and beheading them on the spot. In the presumed sanctuary of the International Settlement and French Concession, British, American, and French police arrested students handing out leaflets, and expelled them from the barricades into the waiting arms of warlord soldiers—who immediately beheaded them. Two hundred were decapitated that day. The following morning, February 20, 1927, the New York *Herald Tribune* reported: "After the heads of the victims were severed by swordsmen, they were displayed on the top of poles or placed upon platters and carried through the streets. Thousands fled in horror when the heads were stuck on sharp-pointed bamboo poles and were hoisted aloft and carried to the scene of the next execution."

In response to this wholesale decapitation, street fighting broke out for the next two days. The warlord forces were ready for it, and swiftly hacked their way into the ranks of the rioters, killing both workers and Communist cadres, who still expected Chiang's troops to arrive at any moment and even the odds. In an act of calculated treachery, Chiang ordered his army vanguard to stop twenty-five miles outside Shanghai. Some of the headless bodies that littered the streets of the city clutched handbills that read: "WELCOME CHIANG KAI-SHEK, GALLANT COMMANDER OF THE CANTONESE." The man whose troops carried out these beheadings, Li Pao-chang, was rewarded by Chiang a few weeks later with the command of the Eighth Nationalist Army.

Through January and February 1927, KMT emissaries of the right and left were hurrying between the government headquarters in Wuhan and Chiang's military headquarters in Nanchang, trying to mend the fences. Borodin's meetings with Chiang were little more than shouting matches. It was obvious that something was going terribly wrong, but nobody, not even Borodin, seemed certain what it was. Chiang had always been extremely difficult. Unless you knew what he was really up to—and nobody outside of the Green Gang knew that— his behavior revealed nothing.

Chiang's next surprise came on February 19, 1927, when he publicly announced his intention of eliminating the Communists inside and out of the KMT. In a speech, he explained that Dr. Sun Yat-sen's revolution had failed

> because . . . there were too many disparate elements . . . reactionaries and counter-revolutionaries who compromised the work. Of these people there are still now too many. The time has come to expel them since they are not true comrades. . . . Being known as a faithful believer in the doctrines of Sun . . . I have the right to say that every true member of the

party must be just that and nothing else. Whoever goes against the aims and methods indicated by [Dr. Sun] will not be a comrade but an enemy who must not remain among us.

By "counter-revolutionaries" Chiang, of course, meant Communists; they were counter to his way of revolution.

It took the government in Wuhan many days to frame a response. On March 10, Ching-ling and her colleagues on the Central Committee revoked all of Chiang's special emergency powers granted at the start of the Northern Expedition. Chiang immediately resigned as chairman of the Central Committee. For one fleeting moment he became illegal, politically betwixt and between. But, strangely, the Wuhan party leaders did not publicize his resignation. There were still many leaders of the left and center who refused to believe that Chiang had abandoned the revolution.

In Shanghai, there was a brief lull in the street fighting. Unable to grasp what had gone wrong, the workers went back to their jobs. Three Soviet agents in Shanghai—Trotskyites—wrote to Comintern headquarters in Moscow that they had been let down by the local leadership of the CCP and the senior Comintern agent, Gregor Voitinsky, who had been unable to decide whether to go all out and seize the city or wait for Chiang.

> We passed up an exceptionally favorable historical moment, an exceptional combination of circumstances. When the power was there in the streets, the party did not know how to take it. Worse, it did not want to take it, it feared to take it. . . . Had it intervened in a determined manner, it could have conquered Shanghai for the revolution and transformed the relationship of forces within the Kuomintang.

In other parts of China under his control, Chiang now began his own campaign of suppression. He ordered his soldiers to kill the chairman of the General Federation of Labor in the city of Kanchow. He began arresting Communist and left-wing leaders, student leaders, and union members, and closed down KMT newspapers that represented the left wing. In some instances, the leftists successfully resisted the gangsters till Chiang sent army reinforcements.

While his vanguard units remained outside Shanghai, Chiang and his headquarters staff were aboard a gunboat keeping even with the march of his main force down the Yangtze River. A third KMT group advanced from the west along the Soochow railway line. A fourth came from the southwest along the Hangchow railroad. These forces encountered no resistance. Aside from the massed foreign troops in the concessions, there was no longer any significant Chinese military command defending Shanghai from the KMT or, for that matter, from the leftist street mobs. The local warlord had wisely withdrawn.

It was at this time that Western officials of the International Settlement privately joined forces with the Green Gang. The chairman of the International Settlement, an American named Stirling Fessenden, the "Lord Mayor" of Shanghai, told the story in strict confidence to John Powell, editor of the *China Weekly Review*. Powell kept the story to himself till Fessenden's death years later. According to Fessenden, he began to cooperate with the Green Gang in the last days of February 1927.

The French chief of police phoned me one day and asked me to meet him for a confidential talk about the local situation. I went to the address he gave me and was surprised to find it was a Chinese residence surrounded by a high wall, with armed guards at the front gate. I was admitted and immediately ushered into a waiting room. I could not help but notice that the large entrance hall was lined on both sides with stacks of rifles and sub-machineguns. Soon I heard voices, and the French official entered with two Chinese. One was Tu Yueh-sheng and the other was an interpreter. We got down to business immediately, the French chief of police explaining that he had been discussing with Tu the matter of defending the foreign settlement against the Communists, as the local Chinese Government, which was composed of Northerners, had collapsed following the evacuation of the Northern defense commander and his troops. Tu went to the point in a businesslike manner. He was willing to move against the Reds, but he had two conditions: first, he wanted the French authorities to supply him with at least 5,000 rifles and ample ammunition. Then turning to me, he demanded permission to move his military trucks through the International Settlement, something which the Settlement authorities had never granted to any Chinese force. Tu said this was necessary in order to move arms and munitions from one section of the native city to the other. [Fessenden said he would agree providing he got the approval of the Municipal Council.]

I realized that we were taking a desperate chance in dealing with a man of Tu's reputation, but the situation was critical, as an attempt by the Communists to seize the Settlement and the French Concession was certain to result in widespread disorder and bloodshed, involving the lives of Americans, Britons, and other foreign residents as well as tens of thousands of Chinese who resided in the foreign-administered sections of the city. Since the Communists had plotted to seize the foreign areas and defend themselves against the Kuomintang troops, it would mean that the foreigners would be sandwiched between the contending forces. The result would have been international complications far more serious than anything which had occurred since the establishment of the Settlement nearly a century ago.

The French Concession authorities were under the French colonial administration in Hanoi. They were involved with Big-eared Tu and Pockmarked Huang in a full-scale intrigue. The French Concession was also the heart of Shanghai's illicit opium and heroin trade, which was controlled by the Green Gang. Each month Big-eared Tu was realizing profits of $6,500,000 and passing $150,000 of this on to French government officials and concession police to guarantee a happy working relationship between the Concessionaires and the Green Gang.

Unlike other foreigners, the French were not troubled by the advance of Chiang's army toward Shanghai. Various explanations were found for this attitude; newspaperman Powell thought it was because the French had some private understanding of Chiang's plans through Catholic missionaries along Chiang's line of march. Indeed they had, but through their own chief of detectives, Pockmarked Huang, not through missionaries.

The French were anxious about the growing danger of the CCP and the labor unions, and were doing everything they could to assist the Green Gang in exterminating the leftists. French authorities were about to turn over five thousand weapons to the gang, and were simply enlisting Fessenden in the scheme to enable gang goon squads to pass through the International Settlement and thus easily outflank the reds.

Fessenden went straight to the Municipal Council and got its approval. "It was at this point," said Powell, "that the shooting began; it continued without intermission for many days."

The left no longer expected Chiang's help. They had at last realized his treachery, and they were in a desperate hurry to seize Shanghai before Chiang arrived.

The KMT army approaching from Hangchow seemed likely to reach the city by March 22. The leftists planned their coup for the night of March 20. Since their opponents in the city now seemed few in number, there was no apparent reason why they should not succeed.

Chou En-lai was working out of a small apartment at 29 Rue Lafayette, a short distance from Big-eared Tu's house. Having painfully learned the lessons of street fighting in October, he had reorganized the five-thousand-man CCP force into squads of thirty each. These cadres were backed by shop workers, factory workers, and groups of unemployed. They were armed mainly with clubs, axes, and knives. Surprisingly, there were only about 150 guns, primarily Mauser pistols, in the Communist arsenal, one modern weapon for each force of thirty men.

Manpower, by contrast, was not a problem. On the evening of March 20, the coup began with a strike by nearly 800,000 workers, which paralyzed the city. Three hundred men personally led by Chou stormed police stations, and took over telephone and telegraph centers and power stations. By nightfall of March 21, the leftists controlled Hongkew, where Charlie Soong had built his first house; Woosung at the mouth of the Whangpoo, where Charlie had taught school briefly; Pootung across the river, where Big-eared Tu was born; a strip around the International Settlement; the native quarter south of the French Concession; and the densely populated working-class district of Chapei.

By midafternoon of March 22, Shanghai was to all intents and purposes completely in leftist hands. The last warlord soldiers surrendered at North Station at 6 P.M. Meantime, Chiang's troops had finally arrived. The KMT soldiers had been ordered by Chiang to halt outside the city, but they pressed their commander for a taste of the battle and he finally agreed. Ironically, these particular soldiers were sympathetic to the workers and wanted to lend them a hand.

As the first KMT soldiers marched down Markham Road, Shanghai grew remarkably silent.

It had all been a bit too easy.

Advancing down the Yangtze River meanwhile, the army under Chiang's direct command occupied the cities of Anking and Wuhu, then prepared to take the old Ming capital of Nanking. Each city was softened up in advance by mobs of Green Gang hooligans, who besieged union halls and other leftist sanctuaries. At Nanking, chaos reigned while the local warlord troops withdrew, gangsters attacked union halls, leftists fought back, and KMT soldiers moved in.

During the confusion, looting broke out and a handful of foreign missionaries and consular officials were killed by unidentified assailants. An American woman was surprised in her home by three nondescript soldiers, who dragged her upstairs and tried to rape her. They were frightened off before they could, but the rumor of "rape" spread through the foreign community, and an American missionary relayed it to Shanghai newspapers and through them to the world press. It was known thereafter as the infamous "Nanking Incident," and was blamed on the leftists. An American government investigation concluded eventually that the attacks on foreigners had been perpetrated by the soldiers of the northern warlords, who were attempting to provoke the foreign powers to intervene. This report was generally ignored. In the end, the Nanking Incident was a minor affair inflated to historic proportions by people who misunderstood what was unfolding.

Because of the turmoil in Nanking, Chiang stayed aboard his gunboat and proceeded downriver toward Shanghai. On Saturday, March 26, two days after the leftist takeover of Shanghai was completed and fighting in the city stopped, Chiang's gunboat tied up at the Bund. The city, except for the foreign concessions, was now under a transitional authority headed by Chou En-lai. Only a handful of Chiang's troops were in the city, and these were the ones sympathetic to the leftists. The rest were marking time in the distant outskirts. When Chiang stepped ashore with his staff officers, he was driven immediately to the old Foreign Ministry building on Route Ghisi, just outside the French Concession, where the first person he saw was Pockmarked Huang. They conferred privately for a long time.

Before the next group of important callers could enter, Chiang was interrupted by the chief of the Shanghai Municipal Police political branch, T. Patrick Givens, who gave Chiang a pass to enter the International Settlement with his own armed guard whenever he wished. No other KMT general was given such a privilege. This was one of the by-products of the deal struck with Stirling Fessenden by Big-eared Tu.

Chiang's Shanghai summit meetings then resumed. Curio Chang led in a group that included three of the millionaire's cronies—the eminent scholar and former chancellor of Peking University, Ts'ai Yuan-p'ei; the chairman of the Peking Palace Museum, Li Shih-tseng; and the arch anti-Communist scholar Wu Chih-hui, who recently had been tutoring Chiang's eldest son. The secret of Curio Chang's grip on so many otherwise enlightened men was that, in addition to being exceptionally clever and engaging himself, he had lent money freely to them while they were on their way up. This put them in his thrall, and he manipulated them to his own ends thereafter. Both Li and Wu had, at his urging, found posts on the government committee that inventoried the treasures of the Forbidden City—a significant asset for an international dealer in Chinese antiquities. In 1925, Li had become chairman of the Palace Museum.

During the Northern Expedition, these four cronies were appointed by Chiang Kai-shek as "special agents" for the region around Shanghai, to be his eyes and ears. Now they gathered in the command post on the Route Ghisi, giving him their reports. On the heels of this reptilian quartet, Chiang saw a group of bankers from his nearby home province of Chekiang, and another group of conservatives representing the Shanghai Chamber of Commerce. After hearing them out, Chiang pored over a map of the Shanghai area with his staff officers and contemplated the redisposition of his troops. There were only three thousand KMT soldiers in the city at this time, concentrated in the workers' stronghold of Chapei; Chiang did not trust them. He then sat down with Pockmarked Huang, Big-eared Tu, and the third member of the troika, Chang Hsiao-lin (of the Blue Gang) to lay final plans for the capture of Shanghai from the reds.

Contrary to the fears of the foreign Concessionaires, the leftist victory had not been followed by a Bolshevik bloodbath. The Communists maintained only the most tenuous control of the city, with less than three thousand armed workers patrolling in place of the deposed police forces. The provisional city government was dominated by the CCP, but many of these Communists and labor leaders still were not totally convinced that Chiang Kai-shek intended to turn on them. In the exhilaration of success, many in the CCP imagined a reunification with the Kuomintang, and a glorious future in coalition. Those who conceded that sharp differences existed were trying to find ways to placate Chiang politically, rather than bracing for a military confrontation.

In Hangchow, not far away, Chiang's army and the Green Gang struck on March 30, closing down the offices of the labor unions, beating or killing the defenders. Still the leftists in Shanghai were not alarmed. They did not see it as an omen.

Chiang insisted to interviewers, meantime, that "there was no split" and "the members of the Kuomintang were united." The next day, he imposed martial law in Shanghai. According to plan, a new "moderate" trade union was established by the Green Gang to create confusion and drain leftist strength among the workers.

For the next two weeks, Chiang wooed the Shanghai proletariat

and befuddled his leftist adversaries, making one declaration of solidar-
ity after another. As on the eve of his military coup in Canton the
previous year, his opponents were so confused by his conflicting statements that they were unable to anticipate his next move. The *North
China Daily News,* which on March 28 had raved, ". . . if Chiang is to
save his fellow-countrymen from the Reds, he must act swiftly and
relentlessly," on April 8 said, "his half-hearted, apologetic attacks on the
Communists leave uncertainty that the rift is irrevocable."

When the ousted KMT middle-roader Wang Ching-wei returned
from European exile on April 1, this gave Chiang yet another opportunity to confuse his enemies. Wang had come back to resume his chair-
manship of the KMT, succeeding Chiang Kai-shek. Chiang spent two
days obsequiously conferring with the man who had given in to him so
easily the previous year in Canton. They were joined by T. V. Soong,
the Finance Minister in the Wuhan government. The three men
debated the wisdom of expelling the Communists from the KMT government. Wang agreed to organize a party conference to "discuss" the
issue.

During these discussions, Chiang seemed remarkably compliant.
He made it appear as if the government at Wuhan was more worried
about the party rift than he. On April 3, the Wuhan government issued
a circular telegram announcing Chiang's complete submission to KMT
authority.

> I strongly believe [lied Chiang], that [Wang's] return will result in the
> real centralization of the party so that we may attain without a split the
> ultimate success of the Nationalist movement. . . . Hereafter all matters
> relating to the welfare of the country and the Kuomintang . . . will be
> handled by Chairman Wang or carried on under his guidance. . . . We will
> be guided by the Central Executive Committee and we must therefore
> show nothing but explicit obedience.

Chiang was only biding his time while he concluded a financial
transaction with the Shanghai capitalists. He and the Green Gang troika
were holding the whole city hostage for a massive ransom, the biggest
extortion in their long and busy careers. Their first objective, to be sure,
was to rescue their stronghold from a Communist seizure. But Pockmarked Huang and Big-eared Tu realized there was substantial profit
to be made in the process by charging the city the ultimate in protection money. A portion would go to their protégé Chiang Kai-shek for
operating expenses and for personal enrichment; the Green Gang

would keep the remainder. Hence the lengthy negotiations with the Chamber of Commerce, the bankers, and the numerous small guilds whose feet were held to the fire by the awful prospect of otherwise losing everything to a Communist regime. André Malraux, in his novel *Man's Fate,* explained it this way: " '. . . it's not because you pay [Chiang] that he is going to destroy the Communists; it's because he is going to destroy the Communists that you pay him.' "

Fifty of these terrified merchant groups were drawn into a federation under the thumb of one of Chiang's oldest friends, the comprador of a Japanese steamship company. Included in the federation were the Silk Merchants' Guild, the Flour Merchants' Guild, the Tea Merchants' Guild, the Bankers' Association, and the Native Banks' Guild. This federation represented Shanghai's richest men, and most of its Chinese commercial capital and property. A delegation from the federation was sent to Chiang to "lend" him three million Chinese dollars in return for protecting them from the reds. The money was turned over on April 4. This was only a down payment. A few days later, a "loan" of seven million dollars was made. Another delegation then negotiated with Chiang to put a "fund" of fifteen million dollars "at his disposal." And two weeks later a "loan" of thirty million dollars was floated to provide him with the necessary capital to set up a new "moderate" government at Nanking. Well over fifty million was now at Chiang's "disposal." This was only what became public knowledge. How much more actually changed hands is not a matter of record.

The political identity of the new Nanking government was no great secret or mystery to people who were politically aware in China in 1927. Chiang's faction was openly referred to as the "Western Hills" faction, after the site of the pivotal right-wing caucus.

"We are told that Chiang Kai-shek is making ready to turn against us again," said Stalin in Moscow on April 1, "I know that he is playing a cunning game with us, but it is he that will be crushed. We shall squeeze him like a lemon and then be rid of him."

Stalin was well informed on the Shanghai intrigues, but he was not permitting Chou En-lai or any of the CCP members in China to act. Publicly, the Kremlin and the Comintern expressed unity with Chiang Kai-shek. The French Communist daily *L'Humanité,* called Chiang's arrival in Shanghai "a new stage in the world revolution." *Pravda* carried a similar message.

Stalin ordered the Chinese Communists to rouse the workers. In the same breath, he ordered that all their weapons must be hidden, so that Chiang could not disarm them. Although it was not apparent to the CCP leadership at the time, Stalin was pushing the Chinese Communists forward to be martyred.

In the first week of April, Chiang ordered his only soldiers in Shanghai—the ones in sympathy with the workers—to leave the city. Their commander, Hsueh Yueh, hurried to the CCP Central Committee and offered to arrest Chiang as a counterrevolutionary. There was no other Chinese military force in Shanghai to prevent Chiang's arrest, aside from his small bodyguard force and martial-law patrols, which would have been outnumbered. But the CCP demurred and suggested that Hsueh feign illness to delay his departure. The moment of opportunity passed, and Hsueh's soldiers left the city.

In Peking on the morning of April 6, five hundred soldiers of the Manchurian warlord Chang Tso-lin, accompanied by city police and detectives, descended on the Soviet Legation and forced their way into the compound. The assault was later found to have been conducted with the prior approval of the diplomatic corps. The Russian staff hastily burned documents and ledgers, but the fires were extinguished and the papers seized. Twenty Chinese Communists trapped in the legation were arrested. Among them was one of the founders of the CCP, Li Ta-chao, the Peking University librarian who had once given a job to Mao Tse-tung. Li's two daughters were also arrested. After being tortured, the middle-aged librarian was held down and slowly strangled as an "example" to other Communists. His seventeen-year-old daughter, Phyllis Li, was tortured for three days, then she too was strangled.

Chiang Kai-shek sent a telegram to Moscow expressing his "outrage" and "regret" over these events in Peking. It was just another "misunderstanding." In Shanghai, foreign officials in the International Settlement threw a cordon ominously around the Soviet Consulate, searching all who passed. On April 11, British and Japanese troops raided leftist sanctuaries in the International Settlement, and ventured outside the perimeter at various points to arrest Chinese leftists whose hideouts were close by. These prisoners were turned over to Chiang's military tribunals outside Shanghai and were later executed.

At 4 A.M. on April 12, there was the sound of a bugle at Chiang's headquarters on the Route Ghisi, echoed by a loud blast on the siren of his gunboat lying off the Bund. Suddenly, the night was filled with machine-gun fire. The Green Gang had struck. In a coordinated attack planned long in advance, groups of civilian gunmen signaled by the bugle and the siren stormed Communist party cells and labor-union offices, private homes and working-class sections in every part of Shang-hai and on both sides of the river. Crack units of Chiang's most trusted Whampoa soldiers, those recruited from Green Gang ranks, infiltrated the city during the night, converged with the gangsters, and tried to blast their way into a union hall and a Communist-held police station. They had orders to shoot anybody carrying a weapon unless he wore a white armband with the Chinese ideograph for "labor." These white armbands had been passed out only to Green Gang gunmen the day before.

When the leftists at the guild hall fought back, Chiang's soldiers pretended to be on the leftist side, offering to mediate with the gang-sters. When the workers agreed and put down their guns, three hundred gangsters burst from hiding places in a nearby building and shot them down.

The CCP leadership scattered. Only a handful escaped—among them Chou En-lai. Many leftists taken prisoner were lashed together, dragged into the streets, and shot or beheaded. Others were driven in trucks to the KMT military base at Lunghua, where they were tried and executed by military tribunals. The White Terror had begun.

Chou En-lai took refuge in the Commercial Press building, once the pride of Charlie Soong, which had been a leftist headquarters since March. Four hundred reds held out there for hours against nearly a thousand gangsters. By noon most of the defenders were dead. Chou En-lai fled again, this time escaping from the city entirely. He made it safely to Hankow, where he was joined by the few other CCP leaders who had survived the massacre.

After nearly nine hours, the machine guns stopped firing. The death toll of gun battles and street executions that day was between four hundred and seven hundred. The Shanghai municipal police gave the lower figure. An additional, undisclosed number of leftist prisoners were executed at Chiang's military base. The executioners later trav-eled to other cities to conduct similar kangaroo courts. Chiang's soldiers and the Green Gang gradually spread the White Terror to the cities of Ningpo, Foochow, Amoy, Swatow, and even back to Canton.

Edgar Snow, who was in Shanghai writing for Powell's *China Weekly Review,* had kept score since the previous October. His tally of the dead for the White Terror in Shanghai was between five and ten thousand.

On April 13, the remnants of the Shanghai leftist leadership called a citywide work stoppage to protest the violence and deaths of the previous day. One hundred thousand workers walked off the job. The unarmed protestors planned to march to Chiang's headquarters, but when they were still some distance away soldiers on both sides of the route opened fire with heavy machine guns. As the marchers tried to escape, Chiang's soldiers charged with fixed bayonets. Many were pursued into private homes, dragged out, and bayonetted in the streets. The corpses filled eight trucks. At least three hundred people were slain.

A grim footnote to the terror of Black April was provided by author Han Suyin:

> Another eight thousand or so were killed in the next week. Six thousand women and adolescent girls, wives and daughters of workers, were sold into the brothels and factories of Shanghai. Tu Yueh-sheng, the deliverer, became a hero to the European women of Shanghai. He was also decorated by Chiang Kai-shek and acclaimed a pillar of society.

Shanghai was now in the hands of Chiang Kai-shek and the Green Gang, and in a matter of months, so was a significant part of the rest of China. By the end of April, it was apparent to nearly everyone that Chiang Kai-shek had struck a deal with the Green Gang—of course, Big-eared Tu had been methodically steering Chiang in this direction since as early as 1922.

After decades of playing with power, the Green Gang was in a far better position to capture the leadership of China's national revolution than any other force. It would be another decade before the Communists were in a similar position. In China, the Green Gang played a role similar to that of the Nazi Brown Shirts when national socialism brought Hitler to power in Germany. A parallel power struggle was occurring in the Soviet Union, expelling international communism in the form of Trotsky and his advocates, and replacing it with the narrower national socialism of Stalin.

In the stunned silence that followed the massacre of Black April, the Wuhan government could only bleat in protest. Ching-ling and her small circle of comrades on the Central Executive Committee issued a brave but impotent proclamation:

> Whereas Chiang Kai-shek is found guilty of massacre of the people and oppression of the Party, and Whereas he deliberately engages himself in reactionary acts and his crimes and outrages are so obvious . . . Chiang shall

be *expelled from the Party and dismissed from all his posts* ... commanders and soldiers shall effect his arrest and send him to the Central Government for punishment in accordance with the Law against counter-revolutionaries.

They were weeping into a windstorm. The government was in Wuhan, but military power was in Shanghai. Wuhan had no means to enforce orders, no way to carry out Chiang's arrest. The leftist army units still at its disposal—a mixture of rightists and leftists—were tied down in a campaign to defeat the northern warlords. Their loyalties in many cases were uncertain. Some of the more aggressive leftist commanders, like Hsueh Yueh, who had offered to arrest Chiang, would soon be bought out by him. The CCP was crippled.

Not all the Wuhan officials wanted to condemn Chiang. Some thought this was the time to compromise and let the Communists and other extremists take their lumps. Wang Ching-wei provided a rallying point for those eager to throw themselves into bed with Chiang. Ching-ling tried to stiffen their spines but found them nervous and uncertain.

Borodin attempted to launch an anti-Chiang propaganda campaign, but it was like trying to rekindle a doused campfire. He began burning his papers and making arrangements to get Soviet advisors and their families out of China.

The Wuhan government was not leftist in the classic sense, just a leaky boat full of moderates trying frantically to stay afloat. There had been no serious leftists in the Central Committee since the assassination of Liao Chung-k'ai in Canton two years earlier. Now, the so-called "leftists" included Ching-ling Soong, who was only a political visionary and a reformer; her stepson, Sun Fo, whom one foreign journalist immortalized as a "morose nonentity"; T. V. Soong, a Harvard liberal; the Victorian egoist Eugene Chen, who thought about no future except his own; finally, the fop, Wang Ching-wei.

They were no threat to anyone but themselves. Borodin captured the lot when he observed that Ching-ling was "the only man in the whole left wing of the Kuomintang."

What Borodin had come to do in harness with Dr. Sun had nearly succeeded, but Chiang and the Green Gang had hijacked the revolution. In Moscow there was a sullen silence. Chiang's betrayal of the CCP had fulfilled the dire predictions of Trotsky, and to Stalin the news of anything that made Trotsky look correct was better buried. As for

China, that had been Trotsky's project, and its collapse simply added to Trotsky's burden, even if he had correctly predicted the dangers. Stalin's agents had to make certain the Wuhan experiment remained a failure.

After quaking in expectation of a Red Terror, and getting a White Terror instead, Shanghai's foreigners began to crow. Any item of news that ridiculed the Chinese left was given heavy coverage in the city's mosquito press. According to one report, the leftists in Wuhan were so feeble-minded that the Women's Association of Hankow had staged a political procession of naked women "having snow-white bodies and perfect breasts." This fantasy, clearly Western in origin, appeared in *Time* Magazine in the April 25, 1927, issue as evidence of leftist degeneracy:

> Eight college-educated young Chinawomen, serious, zealous, patriotic, paraded solemnly down the bund . . . at [Wuhan], Nationalist capital, last week. The tallest walked first, carrying a placard atop a bamboo pole, and wearing only large shell-rimmed glasses. The seven others, were more scantily clad. The placard read: "Emancipate yourselves! We have Won Freedom From Christian Shame! Win Freedom for China from the Christian Powers!" . . . Chiang Kai-shek, who impeached the entire so-called "Red" Government of Hankow, last week . . . will do his best to discourage further extremism among Chinese students.

Publisher Luce, whose hand was frequently visible in the rewriting of copy on China, had filled in a few "missing facts" such as the precise wording of the nonexistent placards, and—for an alumnus of Yale to whom tortoise shell meant studiousness—the material from which the nonexistent eyeglasses were made. *Time* palmed off the Shanghai Massacre as simply an instance of Chiang "impeaching" the leftists. Chiang's authority to impeach anyone was apparently legislated by Luce himself.

When Chiang's oldest son condemned him publicly for betraying the revolution, *Time* was quick to assert that the lad was under the influence of the Kremlin. Chiang Ching-kuo—or CCK as he came to be called—was the child of Chiang's first marriage. After Chiang had "divorced" CCK's mother in 1922, the boy had gone off to school in Shanghai, where he became a leftist and took part in anti-imperialist street protests. Disturbed by his son's leftward plunge, Chiang sent CCK to a private school in Peking run by the anti-Communist Wu Chih-hui.

The boy refused to submit and was soon arrested for taking part in a student protest. He was determined to go to the Soviet Union, and after arguing at length with his father got Chiang's reluctant permission in August 1925. He was one of the first Chinese students at the newly-opened Sun Yat-sen University in Moscow, and joined Komsomol, the Communist Youth Corps.

CCK had just graduated from the university when the Shanghai Massacre took place. Shaken by accounts of the White Terror, the youth wrote to a Moscow paper:

> Chiang Kai-shek was my father and a revolutionary friend. He has now become my enemy. A few days ago he died as a revolutionary and arose as a counter-revolutionary. He used fine words about the revolution, but at the most convenient opportunity he betrayed it. . . . Down with Chiang Kai-shek! Down with the traitor!

Chapter 11

ALL IN THE FAMILY

Young, plump T. V. Soong had been practically a hostage in Shanghai since the beginning of April, when he left Wuhan to meet with Chiang Kai-shek. As Finance Minister of the Nationalist government in Wuhan, T. V. hoped to assert his authority over the financial community of Shanghai and the adjacent provinces of Chekiang and Kiangsu, which (because of their concentration of modern industry and foreign trade) generated 40 percent of the national revenue.

Before the massacre of Black April revealed Chiang's position and changed the rules, T. V. had invited business leaders to help him "balance the national budget" by buying Wuhan government bonds. As the KMT's top salesman, he was offering China's major capitalists influence in the new government and a chance to help define the government's role in banking and commerce.

But Chiang Kai-shek had other ideas. He had to replenish his army's bankroll. Shanghai's financiers had regarded him as their savior. Now they discovered to their everlasting dismay that he was to be their tormentor. The White Terror was turned against the wealthy merchants. According to journalist Sokolsky, "Every form of persecution was resorted to on the pretext of hunting Communists. Men were kidnapped and forced to make heavy contributions to military funds. . . . This anti-Communist terrorism has frightened the people of Shanghai and Kiangsu as nothing else in recent times."

The *New York Times* reported: "The plight of the Chinese merchant in and about Shanghai is pitiable. At the mercy of General Chiang

Kai-shek's dictatorship, the merchants do not know what the next day will bring, confiscations, compulsory loans, exile, or possible execution."

One of the richest men in Shanghai was Fu Tsung-yao, the head of the Chamber of Commerce, general manager of the Commercial Bank of China, and managing director of the China Merchants Steam Navigation Company. Chiang asked Fu for a loan of $10 million Chinese. When he refused, Chiang ordered his arrest and the seizure of all the banker's property. Fu fled into the International Settlement and for safekeeping made over all his holdings to foreigners. With help from Big-eared Tu, Chiang got his hands on most of it anyway. In the end, Fu realized there was no other way, and made a hefty, undisclosed personal donation to Chiang's coffers.

Chiang used this incident as an excuse to put the Chamber of Commerce under the supervision of his own friends.

Next, Chiang issued his own short-term "government" bonds, and used soldiers and Green Gang toughs to force everyone from small shopkeepers to bank presidents to buy them. When one millionaire refused, his son was kidnapped. Another youth, the son of a dye merchant, was arrested as a "counterrevolutionary," but released when his father "donated" $200,000 to Chiang. A cotton-mill owner paid nearly $700,000 to free his imprisoned son. Another merchant paid half a million when his three-year-old heir vanished. The boy promptly reappeared. This sort of extortion had been typical of the Green Gang for years, although at a more leisurely pace. Now Chiang Kai-shek was making it an instrument of government. It was still not enough.

The outflow of $20 million Chinese a month for Chiang's military expenses made it imperative for him to organize a self-sustaining tax base and new import duties. To do this, Chiang needed a "bagman"—which Webster's defines as "a person who on behalf of another collects or distributes illicitly gained money."

T. V. Soong, as Minister of Finance, knew that the "loans" Chiang was exacting were for his personal accounts. That is, once Chiang had the money, he would use it for his own personal enrichment, for the support of his own armies and commanders, and for whatever other administrative uses, bribes, and purposes he saw fit. None of it would be set aside for the treasury and administration of the coalition government in Wuhan.

The split between Wuhan and Chiang was not yet widely acknowledged, or even widely known. But it was known to bankers and businessmen, and they did not want simply to "give" money to Chiang. They hoped at least to get a written guarantee of repayment of the "loans" by having T. V. Soong countersign them as Finance Minister. In this way, if they could not get the money back later from Chiang, they might be able to get some of it from the financially respectable T. V. Soong. Sticking his neck out, T. V. refused to sign and thus legitimize Chiang's extortion. (T. V. was also acting out of concern for his family's investments in Shanghai flour and textile mills. The Soong wealth was just as vulnerable to economic chaos as any other in Shanghai.)

This brought an immediate confrontation with Chiang. On April 18, Chiang announced the establishment of his new (right-wing) Nationalist regime to be based upriver from Shanghai at Nanking. Chiang urged T. V. to accept a post as his Finance Minister and be done with Wuhan. For a few days in the middle of April 1927, T. V. wavered. But two days later, on April 20, T. V. let it be known that he would not countersign the extorted loans. Chiang closed T. V.'s Shanghai office and appointed a different Minister of Finance. At the same time, he cut T. V.'s legs out from under him by ordering his garrison in Canton to seize all T. V.'s assets at the government bank in the South. Now the financial wizard had no choice but to cooperate.

T. V. Soong was neither right nor left, but a frightened patrician who could be useful. Before T. V. had left Wuhan at the end of March, leftists fearing the Finance Minister's conservative sympathies had demonstrated in front of his house and mobbed him in the street. T. V. explained how he felt about the experience to American journalist Vincent Sheean, who was in Shanghai to cover Chiang's grab for power, arriving two days after the April massacre.

> . . . he [T.V.] had a . . . nervous dread of any genuine revolution; crowds frightened him, labor agitation and strikes made him ill, and the idea that the rich might ever be despoiled filled him with alarm. During a demonstration in Hankow one day his motorcar was engulfed by a mob and one of its windows was broken. He was, of course, promptly rescued by his guards and removed to safety, but the experience had a permanent effect on him—gave him the nervous dislike for mass action that controlled most of his political career and threw him at last, in spite of the sincerity of his idealism, into the camp of the reactionaries.

Chiang Kai-shek learned of T. V.'s horror of the common man at the home of Ai-ling and H. H. Kung on the Route de Seiyes, where

Chiang was assiduously courting May-ling Soong. Chiang had inveigled his way into the affection of Ai-ling and H. H. through their mutual friendship with Big-eared Tu. They were already Chiang partisans.

When they had first met, May-ling was engaged, so she had not been receptive. He was then, in any case, only an ambitious Chekiang upstart, the son of a salt merchant, a rude soldier with notorious gangster connections, and a string of painted ladies in Shanghai and Canton. But she had agreed to let him correspond with her, and Chiang turned out to be a persistent correspondent. Now, the upstart had become the "Ningpo Napoleon."

Visitors to the Kung house in the spring of 1927 encountered Chiang there, but only in the company of Ai-ling and H. H. Kung. Chiang and May-ling were never seen together in public, but there was gossip that Shanghai was not the only territory the young general had conquered.

The Kungs also pushed Chiang Kai-shek on T. V. at every turn. They browbeat T. V. mercilessly, playing on his liberal uncertainties. Each time T. V. visited the Route de Seiyes house, or the house on Seymour Road where May-ling lived with Mammy Soong, he came away brainwashed. He preferred to stay at Ching-ling's empty home on the Rue Molière, where he found refuge from Ai-ling's machinations. The fact that Green Gang thugs were keeping an eye on the house made him extremely nervous, and the constant pressure from Ai-ling and Chiang to give in—like the fondling of an unwanted bedfellow—was gradually eroding his self-esteem. He was no match for a military man whose troops enjoyed disemboweling young girls and winding their intestines around their naked bodies while they were still conscious.

While Chiang Kai-shek courted her little sister and bullied her younger brother, Ching-ling remained out of his reach six hundred miles up the Yangtze in Wuhan. Journalist Sheean went there to see her. Despite its reputation as a place of political hysteria crowded with revolutionaries and leftist blackguards, Sheean found Wuhan remarkably peaceful. "The nearest thing to an international incident that came under my observation," he said, "was the effort of a drunken American sailor to pick flowers in Mr. Eugene Chen's garden."

Wuhan was itself a peculiar flower, blooming in the worldwide despair and disenchantment that followed World War I. In the West, great expectations had collapsed. Idealism was in retreat. There seemed little to hope for. Even the Communists were tearing themselves apart in the struggle between Stalin and Trotsky. Yet here in this industrial city on the Yangtze River there was so much revolutionary promise that delegations came from all over the world to see for themselves.

At the center of this peculiar flower, Sheean found Ching-ling. She was the seed carrier of the revolution, its link to the dead leader.

> I had heard an enormous number of things about her, most of them lies. The American newspapers had surpassed themselves on the subject. According to them, Mme Sun was "China's Joan of Arc"; she was the leader of a Chinese "woman's battalion"; she was this, that and the other thing, depending on the fantasies of the headline writers. The notion that she had actually led troops in battle was so widespread that even in China some of the foreigners believed it. In Shanghai this grotesque legend was complicated by more offensive lies in which her personal character and motives were attacked—a favorite method of political argument in the treaty ports. Although I had sense enough not to believe most of the stories about her, they must have made, collectively, an impression; for I had certainly expected to meet something formidable. And instead, here I was face to face with a childlike figure of the most enchanting delicacy. . . . She had a dignity so natural and certain that it deserved the name of stateliness. The same quality can occasionally be observed in royal princes or princesses of Europe, especially in the older ones; but with them it is a clear result of lifelong training. Mme Sun's stateliness was of a different, a more intrinsic quality; it came from the inside out, instead of being put on like a harness. She also possessed moral courage to a rare degree, which could keep her steadfast in grave peril. Her loyalty to the name of Sun Yat-sen, to the duty she felt she owed it, was able to withstand trials without end . . . the fury of her own family and the calumnies of the world were unable to bend her will towards courses she felt to be wrong. She was, in a truer sense than the merely physical one intended by the headline writers, "China's Joan of Arc.". . . In the wreck of the Chinese Revolution . . . generals and orators fell to pieces, yielded, fled, or were silent, but the one revolutionary who could not be crushed and would not be still was the fragile little widow of Sun Yat-sen.

Sheean had many more encounters with Ching-ling and painted other stirring portraits, some tragic. Edgar Snow and Harold Isaacs were similarly impressed.

But the flower was already wilting. Wuhan was nearly finished. After expelling Chiang from the party, the KMT government was systematically crippled by the foreign powers. American and British gunboats patrolling the Yangtze River set up a blockade that interfered with shipments of rice, oil, and coal. In revolutionary Hunan Province, Mao's home and the most aggressively radical in peasant activity, there was a startling setback on May 22 when the city of Changsha was taken over by a reactionary general loyal to Chiang. Thousands of peasants marched on the city to take it back but were turned away with heavy losses.

Ching-ling's feebler colleagues like Wang Ching-wei expressed a growing anxiety: "The Communists propose to us to go together with the masses. . . . But where are the masses? Where are the highly praised forces of the Shanghai workers? Or Hunan peasants? There are no such forces. You see, Chiang Kai-shek maintains himself quite strongly without the masses. To go with the masses means to go against the army. No, we had better go without the masses but together with the army." Although Wang had spent the last year languishing in comfortable European exile, and had been back in China for less than a month, he was already urging his fellows to give up Wuhan and take shelter with Chiang—the man who had humiliated him in Canton. All that the softliners needed to bolt was another disappointment.

At this moment, Stalin decided to interfere. Moscow sent an extraordinary secret message to Borodin on May 31, ordering the confiscation of land, the purge of unreliable Wuhan generals, the arming of twenty thousand CCP members, and the creation of a new fifty-thousand-man worker-peasant army. Incredibly, one of the Comintern agents, an Indian named M. N. Roy, showed a transcript of the secret massage to Wang, on the pretext that he thought Wang would take heart when he saw that the Communists were at last taking action. Instead, Wang was astounded and horrified. Chiang had put the fear up Wang that the Communists secretly planned to take over, and here at last was tangible evidence of it, violating all Moscow's promises to the KMT since the Sun–Joffe agreement. Wang hurried off anxiously to see Borodin. From Roy's later activities, it is clear that he showed Wang the message at the express orders of Stalin.

Borodin also found the message incomprehensible. He tried to pacify Wang by stating flatly that these things would not be done, despite Stalin's orders. Meanwhile, Ching-ling, Eugene Chen, and others saw the cable. Stalin's brilliantly-timed intervention convinced the moderate leftists—all except Ching-ling and Eugene Chen—that Chiang Kai-shek was correct.

Next came crushing news from the battlefront. In an effort to reach Peking and claim the northern capital, Wuhan had dispatched its remaining troops. The army won a major victory over the northern militarists, but at a terrible cost in casualties. Fourteen thousand KMT soldiers were dead. There were not enough remaining to ward off Chiang Kai-shek.

For those who still hoped to hold Wuhan together, there was only one chance, Christian General Feng Yu-hsiang. If the Christian General could be persuaded to join them, he could provide a military barrier against Chiang.

Feng agreed to meet them in Chengchow to discuss a coalition. This was the same bearlike man, beloved of the foreign missionaries, who so recently had been wooed by Moscow. In theory, the Wuhan leftists had every reason to be optimistic about an alliance. The Christian General had just made a fruitful visit to Moscow, hitting it off so well with Stalin that his soldiers now had 200 pieces of Russian artillery, 200 new machine guns, and 200,000 rifles. An article had appeared in *Pravda* in which Feng promised that his army would "fight for the emancipation of the nation" and the "consummation of the national revolution." Feng made a dramatic entrance to Chengchow, arriving at the meeting in a freight car "since my brother soldiers also travel in freight cars." Later, it was discovered that Feng had boarded the freight car just before arriving in Chengchow, and had spent most of the trip in a private luxury coach.

When the talks ended, Ching-ling and her associates were full of hope. They had assurances from Feng that he would join them. Instead, the Christian General hurried on to secret talks with Chiang Kai-shek in Hsuchow, where he had his pot sweetened greatly, and sent the following message to Wuhan:

> When I met you gentlemen in Chengchow, we talked of the oppression of the merchants and other members of the gentry, of labor oppressing factory owners, and farmers oppressing landowners. The people wish to suppress this form of despotism. We also talked of the remedies for this situation. The only solution which we discussed is, as I see it, as follows: Borodin, who has already resigned, should return to his own country immediately. Secondly, those members of the Central Executive Committee of the [Wuhan] regime who wish to go abroad for a rest should be allowed to do so. Others may join the Nationalist Government at Nanking if they desire.... Both Nanking and [Wuhan], I believe, understand their mutual

problems. I do not need to remind you gentlemen that our country is now facing a severe crisis. But in view of this I feel constrained to insist that the present is a good time to unite the Nationalist faction in a fight against our common enemies. It is my desire that you accept the above solution and reach a conclusion immediately.

When Borodin read this telegram, he was so mystified by its convoluted sarcasm that he asked a Swedish journalist if his interpretation could be a mistake. In the end, Borodin accepted it with the same resignation that he had already accepted the Shanghai Massacre and M. N. Roy's devastating "secret message" from Stalin. The situation in China was no longer under his control. Borodin was now occupied with one goal—to get all his Soviet advisors safely out of China, and to get himself out as well. In Nanking, Chiang Kai-shek had put a price on Borodin's head, and wanted posters were appearing everywhere.

Journalist Sheean returned to Shanghai in June 1927, promising Ching-ling to do what he could to urge T. V. Soong to rejoin her. As a romantic and a bit of an adventurer, Sheean even saw himself smuggling T.V. through enemy lines.

> I thought the enterprise would be easy—all I had to do was to bring T. V. along with me under some kind of assumed name, as my interpreter. Travelling in my cabin on a British boat he would have been safe enough, for the boldest of Chiang Kai-shek's soldiers would never have dared break in. But in taking the idea so lightly I reckoned without T. V.
>
> When I went to see him in Shanghai he seemed ready to fall in with the plan. . . . He could see—or said he could see—that the true inheritor of the Kuomintang ideal was the [Wuhan] government, and not Chiang Kai-shek's military dictatorship. He had steadily refused to join Chiang Kai-shek's government in spite of persuasion and threats. The house was constantly watched by spies (it is one of the houses that are under observation at every hour of the day and night, as it has always been since it was built); and T. V. was very nervous. He did not dare go outside the French Concession and the International Settlement, for Chiang Kai-shek's soldiers were everywhere in the Chinese city, and they would have seized upon him in a moment. His alternatives, if Chiang Kai-shek ever caught him, were simple: the Ministry of Finance or the jail. I do not believe he would have been put to death, but he was not at all sure of it. He was, in fact, in a rare state of funk, and the suggestion I brought from [Wuhan] seemed to offer him a way out of all his troubles. He agreed almost at once, asked me to take a ticket for him in my cabin in the name of Mr. Wong

of Canton, and displayed a lively curiosity about the course of events at [Wuhan].

On the next day he had changed his mind. In the interim he had talked to his mother, his sisters, his brother-in-law, and they were a fundamentally reactionary family.

"There is no point in my going to [Wuhan]," he said, worried and nervous. "You see the truth is that I'm not a social revolutionary. I don't like revolution, and I don't believe in it. How can I balance a budget or keep a currency going if the labor policy frightens every merchant or factory owner into shutting up shop? I can't make the Central Executive Committee understand. . . . Look at what they've done with my bank notes, my beautiful bank notes! . . . They've been inflated out of existence. . . .

"Oh, my sister . . . ! My sister doesn't understand. Nobody understands how difficult it is. How do I know I won't be dragged out of the Ministry of Finance and torn to pieces by the mob the day after I get to Hankow? How do I know I can stop the currency from falling? Nothing can be done if they keep on encouraging strikes and mass meetings. They get the people into a state of excitement in which they expect everything, and they're bound to be disappointed. . . . And I'm not popular, mind you. I've never been popular. The mob doesn't like me. They would have killed me last winter if the soldiers hadn't come in time. . . . They all know I don't like strikes and mass meetings. . . . What could I do . . . ?"

On that day he was definitely anti-revolutionary. But on the next he had switched again—took a more hopeful view of the possibility of persuading the Central Executive Committee to modify the labor policy; yearned over his beautiful bank notes; agreed that the Nanking regime was only a disguised form of personal dictatorship, and that [Wuhan] still represented, in spite of the Communists, the pure party tradition of the Kuomintang.

Another Western journalist who arrived then was Anna Louise Strong, who had been in China before and knew many of the principal players. She went to the Rue Molière, and found T. V. changed.

Perhaps he was always Chiang's agent and a conscious hypocrite. Perhaps his past made him a social coward. Perhaps he thought reunion would save Chinese Nationalism. It is clear to me, from the talks I had with him, that he knew quite well that the Revolution and the party were in [Wuhan] and needed him for their work; but that, wavering between two paths, he did not choose that one.

Sheean tells us, in the end, what T. V. decided to do.

"I can't go," he said. . . . "I can't do it. I'm sorry I've caused you all this trouble, but I simply cannot do it."

He was excited and very jumpy. I sat down on a stair step in the hall and gaped with surprise. That very afternoon his mind had been conclusively made up, and now—!

"What am I to say to your sister?" I asked.

"Let's go talk to my family," he said.

We clambered into the Rolls-Royce and made a round of visits at about one o'clock in the morning. I took no part in the conversations with the Soong family, and can only imagine how they all urged T. V. not to cross the Rubicon. One of the persons to whom he spoke was his hyper-Americanized sister May-ling . . . another was Dr. H. H. Kung, his brother-in-law. After some hours of argument T. V. came out of the recesses of the Kung house and spoke—dejectedly, gloomily.

"It's all settled," he said. "I'm not going. Tell my sister I shall write to her. I'm sorry you were troubled for nothing."

I drove him home in the immense, hearse-like car, and neither of us said a word. I was exhausted from the sheer indecision of the proceedings, and he was very gloomy. I have never seen him since, and the events of that night were to give my final impression of Soong Tse-vung both as an individual and as a type, the honest Liberal at sea between opposing shores.

T. V. did go back to Wuhan in July, but only to deliver a message for his new boss, Chiang Kai-shek: There was hope for a coalition between Nanking and Wuhan—but only if Borodin and the Chinese Communist party were expelled from the Kuomintang formally and at once.

It had been apparent for weeks that the end could come momentarily. Borodin had sent Fanya off for Vladivostok, but along the way she was captured and imprisoned in Peking by the Manchurian warlord Chang Tso-lin, who was eagerly looking forward to Madame Borodin's strangulation. Death by strangulation in China did not mean garroting in the European manner, in which an executioner suddenly tightens an iron collar around the throat; in China the executioner used his bare hands to slowly wring the life out of the victim—a process an expert could drag out for fifteen minutes or longer. All the while the victim's enemies would be watching closely, as the victim lost control of bladder and colon. This was the kind of treatment the same warlord had accorded to those captured in the Soviet legation in April.

A scheme was afoot to rescue Fanya. But her capture drove home the nearness of the end. Pressure on the remaining KMT generals to side with Chiang was intense. The alternative was to go down with Wuhan, merely a social experiment. Already Chiang had secretly bought off General T'ang Sheng-chih, who was quietly moving soldiers into position to seize Wuhan on July 15—the date for the next KMT Political Council meeting.

Anna Louise Strong was then in Wuhan.

> I was invited to stay with Soong Ching-ling—Mrs. Sun Yat-sen . . . revolution had claimed her; she was dedicated to it, not only by her own devotion, but by the half-worship bestowed on her as Dr. Sun's widow by millions of simple Chinese. . . . Her friends sought vainly to induce her to desert the revolutionary government of Hankow, even placing at her disposal a Japanese ship for flight, on the theory that she was being held unwillingly. When she made it evident that she remained of her own free will, all the subtle weapons of slander were turned against her.

T. V. arrived on July 12, and went into conference with the Central Committee. His message from Chiang was blunt: Cast out the Communists and Borodin immediately and ally with Nanking, or else. Since Wuhan already had decided to expel the CCP formally on July 15, the major condition was already met. The rest of the ultimatum was intended to bully Ching-ling and others into submission.

By the end of the day, Ching-ling was exhausted and disgusted. But it was now her turn to listen to T. V. in private, while he relayed all the coercions, threats, and subversions that could be mustered by her mother, her two sharp-tongued sisters, and a Greek chorus of woe from H. H. She told her brother firmly and irrevocably, no. She would not cooperate. And if the Wuhan government finally collapsed, she would simply return to Shanghai and continue fighting Chiang Kai-shek there.

According to an FBI document that came to light many years later, based on remarks evidently made by Ching-ling to an American who befriended her, T. V. was horrified. He insisted that she leave the apartment above the bank and come outside with him for a walk. Once far from the flat and from the people who kept it always under surveillance, T. V. took his sister's hand and begged her not even to consider returning to Shanghai. He bent his head and whispered into her ear that her life was in danger, for she would certainly get a knife in her back.

She laughed. But T. V. insisted that Ai-ling had "planned her assassination exactly as she had several others before."

In spite of these chilling words, and the ominous threat of being murdered by her own sister, Ching-ling remained adamant.

T. V. sent a coded cable to Shanghai.

Correspondent Sheean went to see Borodin and found him fatalistic also:

> I shall remain until the last possible minute. When I am forced to go, I shall go. But do not suppose that the Chinese Revolution is ending, or that it has failed in any but the most temporary sense. It will go back underground. It will become an illegal movement, suppressed by counter-revolution and beaten down by reaction and imperialism; but it has learned how to organize, how to struggle. Sooner or later, a year, two years, five years from now, it will rise to the surface again. It may be defeated a dozen times, but in the end it must conquer. . . . What has happened here will not be forgotten.

The CCP had been pulling in its horns for weeks, "in order not to give grounds to support the charges made by reactionaries and counter-revolutionaries." A number of Communist officials in Wuhan discreetly asked for leaves of absence. Others resigned. The CCP told Borodin the party should offer to withdraw, rather than wait to be expelled. Borodin warned that Moscow would never agree.

In the middle of June, somebody attempted to poison General Galen at a banquet. One of the other Soviet advisors died, but Galen recovered.

Before everyone's eyes, the CCP was disintegrating. Young women comrades who had bobbed their hair as a sign of revolutionary commitment in early spring of 1927 were now letting it grow. As cadres vanished off streets, small CCP offices emptied, and the White Terror arrived in Wuhan in the form of small groups of security police and gangsters, who moved into CCP offices and arrested or shot whoever showed up.

T. V. went to Ching-ling again. She was working on a statement intended as a last rebuttal to Chiang. She would not abandon Wuhan. T. V. cabled Chiang in code through H. H. Kung on July 12, spelling out what face-saving devices had been set forth by Wang Ching-wei as the price for immediate capitulation. Late on July 13, T. V. received a reply from Kung. It read: "TELL THE SELLER THAT THE MERCHANT HAS

AGREED TO PAY THE PRICE DEMANDED. HE WILL EXPECT DELIVERY ON THE DATE AGREED."

"Now," said the acid Eugene Chen, "who do you think is the merchant? It is Chiang Kai-shek. And the merchandise being sold—it is the betrayal of the Wuhan government. This kind of language shows the mentality of H. H. and T. V. This is the language of the comprador, and they treat the fate of China as merchandise to be bought and sold."

This development was conveyed to Moscow by Borodin. The next day, he received from the Kremlin a solemn declaration: "The revolutionary role of the Wuhan government is played out; it is becoming a counterrevolutionary force." Moscow instructed the CCP to withdraw from the Wuhan government. In the time remaining on July 14, Mao Tse-tung and the other Communist party leaders still in Wuhan quietly left.

Ching-ling was virtually alone in standing firm. The only other KMT leader who stood by her was her friend General Teng Yen-ta. He had been a popular leader at the Whampoa Academy—not one of Chiang Kai-shek's men, but an independent. Because of his intelligence and popularity, he had become director of the General Political Department of the KMT during the Northern Expedition of 1926. Many of the political and military successes of the campaign had been credited to him.

If the selection process of the revolution had evolved without Green Gang interference, or Moscow's interference, General Teng might eventually have become China's leader instead of Chiang Kai-shek. During the Wuhan-Nanking split, General Teng had sided with Wuhan, calling Chiang Kai-shek a usurper and a traitor to the ideals of Dr. Sun. In return, Chiang had branded Teng a Communist. On the contrary, both Teng and Ching-ling believed that the Chinese Communists had some programs that were complementary to Dr. Sun's principles, but they disapproved of the CCP's subservience to the Comintern and to the dictates of Stalin. Now they had reason to wonder whether Stalin had not deliberately interfered to serve his own ends. With Chiang and the Green Gang on the one hand, and the machinations of Stalin and the Comintern on the other, the infant Wuhan experiment had been doomed before it could get on its feet.

It was now Ching-ling's turn to speak. On July 14, she released her statement on Chiang Kai-shek's usurpation of the revolution. She asserted that a revolution that excludes the workers and peasants was a sham:

some members of the party executive are so defining the principles and policies of Dr. Sun Yat-sen that they seem to me to do violence to Dr. Sun's ideas and ideals.

. . . all revolution must be . . . based upon fundamental changes in society; otherwise it is not a revolution, but merely a change of government.

To guide us in the Chinese revolution, Dr. Sun has given us his Three Principles. . . . It is the Third Principle, that of the livelihood of the people, that is at stake at the present time, the principle that answers the questions of fundamental social changes in China. . . .

In this principle we find his analysis of social values and the places of the labor and peasant classes defined. These classes become the basis of our strength in our struggle to overthrow imperialism, and cancel the unequal treaties that enslave us, and effectively unify our country. They are the new pillars for the building of a new, free China. . . . If we adopt any policy that weakens these supports, we shake the very foundations of our party, betray the masses, and are falsely loyal to our leader. . . .

But today it is being said that policies must be changed to fit the needs of the time. There is some truth in this statement, but change of policy must never be carried to the point where it becomes a reversal, so that a revolutionary party ceases to be revolutionary and becomes merely an organ, operating under the banner of revolution, but actually working in support of the social structure which the party was founded to alter.

. . . today the lot of the Chinese peasant is even more wretched than in those days when Dr. Sun was driven by his great sense of human wrongs into a life of revolution. And today men, who profess to follow his banner, talk of classes, think in terms of "revolution" that would virtually disregard the sufferings of those millions of poverty-stricken peasants of China.

Today also we hear condemnation of the peasant and labor movement as a recent, alien product. This is false. Twenty, thirty years ago, Dr. Sun was thinking and speaking in terms of a revolution that would change the status of the Chinese peasant. . . .

All these years, his purpose was clear. But today we talk of recent foreign influence. Was Sun Yat-sen—the leader who was voicing the agrarian revolution for China when Russia was still under the heel of the Czar —was he a tool of foreign scheming?

Dr. Sun's policies are clear. If certain leaders of the party do not carry them out consistently then they are no longer Dr. Sun's true followers, and the party is no longer a revolutionary party, but merely a tool in the hands of this or that militarist . . . a machine, the agent of oppression, a parasite fattening on the present enslaving system. . . .

Revolution in China is inevitable. . . . There is no despair in my heart for the revolution. My disheartenment is only for the path into which some of those who had been leading the revolution have strayed.

It was Madame Sun's final word. She had divorced, without question, Chiang Kai-shek's government. They could not use the name Sun through her to legitimize their policies. This withering blast from the "gentle" widow was quickly suppressed by her adversaries. But she arranged for its publication in the *China Weekly Review*.

The following day, July 15, according to plan, the Wuhan government expelled the CCP from its ranks. Those who wished to remain in the KMT must forfeit their CCP membership on pain of "punishment without leniency."

Borodin vanished. Although Ching-ling was not a member of the CCP, so did she. Others who had resisted the plunge to the right fled Wuhan, and, eventually, China. One of them was Ching-ling's friend General Teng Yen-ta. He resigned all his KMT posts and denounced the remaining Wuhan leaders for compromising with Chiang Kai-shek and betraying Dr. Sun Yat-sen. He then slipped out of the city disguised as a peasant. Several days later, executions began.

Thus ended the revolution that had started with such hope in Canton, and swept to the Yangtze. Not defeated by any outward enemy, but subverted by the Green Gang until it collapsed from within. Its northern enemies were fleeing before it; many foreign nations were preparing to grant it recognition; but the thousands of Green Gang recruits that had been stuffed secretly into Whampoa Academy under Chiang rose to dominate it in the lower ranks of the officer corps. Neither the unarmed peasants and workers, nor the would-be democrats and liberal intellectuals, had the strength to withstand their own militant right wing.

In disguise, Ching-ling was smuggled by boat down the Yangtze into Shanghai and paused at the Rue Molière to put her affairs hastily in order. For once she seemed to have eluded surveillance. Fearing that she would be murdered as T. V. had predicted if she remained in Shanghai longer than necessary, or would be held prisoner in her own home while Chiang used her name to sanctify a massacre across Central and South China, she had decided to carry her protest to the outside world. Borodin had suggested a dramatic gesture that would separate her clearly from Chiang—a public visit to Moscow.

After midnight, when the French Concession grew silent and the tree-lined streets were black with shadows, she slipped out of the house in a shabby disguise, in the company of red-haired Rayna Prohme, a vivacious young American Marxist who had been editing the KMT newspaper in Wuhan. (Vincent Sheean had fallen in love with her and was at this moment frantic about her safety.) The two women made their way like beggars to the riverfront. There, in a section dominated by the Green Gang underling Ku Tsu-chuan, they boarded a tiny sampan and were rowed out onto the garbage-strewn slurry of the Whangpoo. The unsteady craft passed between warships from a score of countries, drifted downriver silently by creaking junks, and after three tense hours reached a rusting Russian freighter. Before dawn they were joined on board by Eugene Chen and his two daughters. On the morning tide, the ship sailed for Vladivostok.

Fanya Borodin escaped from the clutches of the Manchurian warlord Chang Tso-lin by a masterful ruse. Borodin somehow put his hands on $200,000 Chinese for a bribe, apparently Soviet funds set aside in Peking for just such purposes. This was passed to A. I. Kantorovich, the legal attaché at the legation, who was to be Fanya's defense counsel at a "trial" set by the warlord to appease the sensibilities of the foreign diplomatic community before he had her strangled. Kantorovich went to see the judge assigned to the case. On the morning of July 12, at an hour so early the warlord was still fast asleep, a quick trial was convened; Fanya was found innocent and released. The defendant vanished suddenly and completely. The judge abandoned his wife and children in Peking to face the music, and went to Japan for an early, comfortable retirement.

Fuming with rage, the old Manchurian bandit, Chang Tso-lin, was forced to accept an embarrassing defeat. Right under his nose, Fanya was hiding in a Confucian temple in Peking that had been converted into living quarters for foreigners. When the manhunt subsided, she came out disguised as a Catholic nun and was spirited to Siberia.

Borodin also spent those last weeks of July hiding, in T. V. Soong's apartments above the bank in Hankow where Ching-ling had been living. Through a web of diplomatic guarantees, Chiang agreed to let the Russians leave, but not through his territory. Borodin and a small entourage were to go out overland, across the Gobi Desert. Anna Louise Strong, who had now come into Borodin's orbit, pleaded with him to let her go with him. He finally agreed.

T. V. Soong paved Borodin's path with a large sum of silver coins, rolled in rice paper affixed with the seal of the Kuomintang government and packed in wooden chests. This was part of the ransom to be paid by Wuhan for Borodin's safe retreat. It was intended for the turncoat Christian General Feng, who "guaranteed" Borodin's safe passage by train across his territory in North China to the terminus at Ling Pao, the end of the rail line. The Russians then had to cross the Gobi Desert by car and truck. Borodin in particular would find it grueling, for in addition to having chronic malaria picked up the past year, he had recently fallen from horseback and broken his arm.

Borodin and entourage of thirty, plus Chinese bodyguard, were provided with a special train at Hankow railway station on July 27. Among the "dignitaries" who came to see him off were T. V. Soong and Wang Ching-wei. While a Chinese band played vaguely recognizable marches, Wang, Soong, and Borodin drank tea and soda pop in one of the coaches. Wang, paying an idiotic gesture to Chinese etiquette, asked Borodin to reconsider and remain in China. Borodin, patience taxed to the limit, said no. Wang gave him a letter from the Central Committee, expressing its "friendly sentiments." Borodin thanked them and said goodbye. The train huffed out of sight. Some Chinese on the platform cried. Others made snide remarks. The band played the KMT anthem, set to the tune of "Frère Jacques."

Beside the rails as the train crossed Hupeh and Honan provinces, lay victims of war and famine. In the South, China's countryside was green and rich, but here the wasteland was burnt brown. Nothing grew. Trees and shrubs were stripped of leaves and bark. The people still alive were skeletons. In Chengchow, gateway to the deserts, Borodin's train was met by an effusive General Feng. Here was the man who, by throwing in his lot with Chiang, had doomed Borodin's long mission.

It was up to Percy Chen, age sixteen, to see how much bribe money Feng wanted.

> I was asked by General Feng to contribute to the repairs of the roads over which our caravan would have to travel [Chen recalled], to the repairs to bridges, and to the planting of trees along the roads. . . . The truth was that the roads were nonexistent, there were no bridges, and the trees that we saw had all been planted in the T'ang and Sung Dynasties. Still, Marshal Feng had maintained the proprieties. I paid his subordinate. . . . I will say that once the money was paid, there was no further demand from any other general along the route.

After three days of banquets with Feng, Borodin's procession left Chengchow while Feng's army band played "Onward, Christian Soldiers."

The train carried them to Loyang and finally into Ling Pao, the terminus. They transferred everything to four sturdy Dodge touring cars and a Buick that had a cloth top and mahogany-fitted interior. Borodin rode in the Buick. Here in the wheat belt the Yellow River had twice overflowed its banks and flooded the fields; when the floodwaters receded, they left behind a vast dust bowl. Leading the caravan was a Dodge with Borodin's bodyguard and Voroshin, an advisor who had worked with Feng Yu-hsiang. Then came the Buick, which had once belonged to a warlord; with Borodin rode his doctor, Orloff; his secretary, Kirishev; and Mrs. Orloff. They were followed by a Dodge filled with gasoline drums, suitcases, spare tires, and passengers—Percy Chen and brother Jack, a Chinese interpreter, and Anna Louise Strong. Two more Dodges and three trucks brought up the rear, loaded with wooden cases of documents, drums of fuel, tents, tinned food, tanks of water, and a folding canvas bath. Perched on top of one truck sat Borodin's Cantonese cook, ever cherubic.

Each night when they pitched camp, the Russians brought out an old Maxim machine gun, mounted on wheels, that they set up on the nearest knoll. Each morning the chef fixed breakfast of condensed milk, biscuits, sausage, and corned beef, eaten under the gaze of farmers, watching from their plots along the crumbling bank of the chocolate river. Each day's journey followed tracks cut by wagon wheels in the loess hills. They were stuck many times. When it rained they plowed through lentil soup. Reaching the hot-spring resort of Lin-t'ung, built by T'ang emperors near the city of Sian, the caravan paused to clean up.

After soaking all by himself in a steaming sulphur bath, Percy Chen wandered out to a discreetly placed side terrace and accidentally intruded upon a poignant scene. There was Borodin, freshly scrubbed, dozing contentedly in a chaise longue while Anna Louise Strong—looking flushed and radiant—sweetly crooned to him "While Shepherds Watched Their Flocks by Night." Anna stopped in mid note, and looked at Chen contemptuously. He felt he had made a significant discovery. (The romantic liaison between Mikhail Borodin and Anna Louise Strong was never remarked upon during their lives, although it went on side by side with a professional association for over twenty years.)

When the caravan reached T'ungkuan, north of Sian, they were astounded to come upon Ching-ling's friend General Teng Yen-ta, who had been waiting for them. After slipping out of Wuhan disguised as a peasant, he had proceeded north on foot along the Peking-Hankow railway line. With a price on his head, he had walked a great distance, over 250 miles, merging with refugees and famine victims, until he reached Chengchow. There, he had learned of Borodin's projected overland trek to Russia. Teng had struck off westward cross-country toward Sian, and north to T'ungkuan, to wait for them. He wanted to hitch a ride, and they took him aboard one of the sedans.

At last they crossed into Inner Mongolia. Here the steppes began. On the grassland, they were able to make sixty miles a day. With the heat of China behind them, they felt the autumn nip of the steppes. Borodin's health improved visibly as they came to the Great Wall. Beyond began the deserts. They had covered eight hundred miles. Seven hundred more lay before Ulan Bator, capital of Outer Mongolia. They skirted the territory of the Shansi warlord, the close associate of H. H. Kung. No roads existed from here on, and water was scarce. They knew that a Russian reception committee had set out from the west to meet Borodin's party halfway with fresh provisions and fuel.

One night, they almost lost Anna Louise Strong when she wandered off by herself. Borodin and the others searched, but decided she was lost for good. Just before noon, they sighted a speck in the distance. Purely by chance, she had walked in the route of their journey. When they pulled up beside her she was weeping in relief.

"Why on earth did you go off?" they asked.

"I got so cold, so I walked," she mumbled, tears streaming down her cheeks.

Four days out of Ulan Bator, they rendezvoused with the Russian relief caravan and feasted on caviar.

Borodin caught a Soviet aircraft to the Trans-Siberian Railway at Verkhneudhinsk, and was on his way to Moscow in austere style, to report to the Kremlin. General Teng, Percy Chen, and the others followed a few days later.

Ching-ling reached Moscow by special train from Vladivostok with Eugene Chen, his daughters, and the American Rayna Prohme, who was beginning to suffer peculiar dizzy spells. The teenage Chen girls, Yolanda and Sylvia, played a wind-up Victrola across the Siberian wastes. At each whistle stop from the taiga to the steppes, Eugene Chen and Ching-ling accepted bouquets from reception committees sent to greet the Chinese comrades. To these throngs Ching-ling murmured thanks for help to the revolution, and to her late husband. Eugene Chen, never at a loss for words, then gave the crowd its money's worth. The train chugged on.

They had come from Shanghai at a moment of great tragedy for China, and they reached Moscow just in time for another of the great tragedies of the century—the climax of the struggle between Trotsky and Stalin. With Lenin out of the way, the Russian leaders who had shown the most interest in China—Bukharin, Radek, and Trotsky— were under a cloud. With their defeat would come for Russia the beginning of a bloody inward turn, lasting a quarter of a century, until Stalin's death. The first blast of this hard political winter already gripped the Soviet capital. The Stalinists were not friendly to the Chinese, and before December was out the Chinese who managed to leave Russia considered themselves fortunate.

Less than three weeks after Ching-ling arrived, Trotsky was expelled from the executive of the International. As Trotsky's biographer Isaac Deutscher observed,

> These were grotesque assizes. The foreign Communists who sat in judgment over one of the founding fathers of the International and denied him all the merits of a revolutionary, were almost to a man pathetic failures as revolutionaries: instigators of abortive risings, almost professional losers of revolution, or heads of insignificant sects all basking in the glory of that October in which the accused man had played so outstanding a part.

These losers were also all staunch defenders of Stalinist policies, and they included the Indian troublemaker M. N. Roy.

Trotsky had supported Lenin's strategy for the spreading of the Communist revolution to the undeveloped nations, and had warned against too close or permanent an alliance with bourgeois liberation movements like the KMT, because they would inevitably turn on the Communists. M. N. Roy had argued strenuously against this restraint when Lenin first voiced it at the Second Congress of the Communist International in 1920. Seven years later, in Wuhan, it was M. N. Roy who had shown Stalin's secret message to Wang Ching-wei, and thereby struck the fatal blow to the Wuhan experiment. In view of the awful timing of Stalin's secret message, its exaggerated language, and the speed with which Roy acted to reveal it, it is irresistible to suspect that Stalin contrived it to bring down the roof.

The disaster in China, into which the CCP had been encouraged to blunder, had sealed Trotsky's fate in Moscow. He became the scapegoat. Stalin was victorious. Roy was his lickspittle. Deutscher described Roy as the man who "had done his best to induce the Chinese [Communist] party to lick the dust before Chiang Kai-shek." It was now Roy's pleasure to take part in striking the final political blow to Trotsky in Moscow.

The contemptuous attitude of Stalin's clique toward their Chinese comrades was apparent even in the Moscow theater, where Ching-ling saw a performance of the new jingoistic ballet "The Red Poppy," by Glière, a parody of the Chinese revolution, in which heroic Russians came to the aid of primitive yellow people with the demeanor of insects.

From the Metropole Hotel, Ching-ling and the strangely ill Rayna Prohme were moved to the Sugar Palace, a Czarist pastry built with profits from sugar beets. Once lavish, it had been picked bare. Vincent Sheean, who followed Rayna to Moscow, went to visit the two women there.

> I was led down a passage to another carved door, which admitted us to the room assigned to Mme. Sun Yat-sen. Like the rest of the overgrown house, it was on the grandest scale, and Soong Ching-ling looked like a child in the middle of it. She was dressed in European style for the first time in many years, and felt rather embarrassed in her short skirts; they did, actually, make her look about fifteen years old. . . . The room itself, so huge and gloomy that I could scarcely discern its opposite wall, might have been chosen to figure forth the scale of events against which this exquisite fragment of humanity was obliged to pit its hour of time.

There in a bed in that dismal, mirrored catacomb, the American girl was now in and out of consciousness, slipping away. Two months earlier, Rayna had been electrically alive. She was an audacious, unconventional young woman with a gamine face and a sensual presence that inspired Edgar Snow to describe her as "the improbable, red-haired rebel goddess." Sheean seemed to be able to think of nothing and nobody else. Even he now recognized that she was lost. Soviet doctors were uncertain what it was, possibly pneumonia, perhaps a tropical disease common in central China. Sheean hovered over her anxiously.

Ching-ling's gloom and sense of foreboding were deepened by the discovery that her other dear friend, General Teng Yen-ta, was now in grave peril. He had pressed the Kremlin to resolve its ambiguous stand on China, or to stop meddling. As one of the three KMT leftist leaders in Moscow—with Madame Sun and Eugene Chen—he had been invited to address the Third International. Boldly, he stated that the friendly assistance of the Comintern had been welcomed in the beginning by the Chinese people, but that the Chinese revolution was strictly a Chinese affair that could not be shaped to serve the Comintern's purposes. The Communist revolution, he said, was intrinsically a European phenomenon that could not be transplanted to Asia. Because China was a feudal, semicolonial country, agrarian reform was the most important issue to be resolved. Meddling by the international Communist movement would only derail the revolution and prolong China's agonies indefinitely.

Stalin reacted angrily to this speech, and orders went to the Cheka to arrest and dispose of Teng. Forewarned, he fled Moscow by night for the south, smuggled out of the city by Russian friends. Teng was to be spirited across the Caucasus and over the border into Turkey. Weeks passed, while Ching-ling waited anxiously for news.

Despite the efforts of Vincent Sheean to cheer her and to nurse Rayna Prohme, the atmosphere of dread deepened. They also had heard little from Borodin since his arrival. He seemed to be in political limbo and, on the few occasions when Sheean saw him, had become taciturn and noncommittal, as though he were waiting for the final judgment.

Another Russian who had befriended the cause of Sun Yat-sen's revolution was in Moscow gravely ill. It was the diplomat A. A. Joffe, who had concluded the pact of friendship with Dr. Sun in 1922, at the house in the Rue Molière. Joffe had tuberculosis. Trotsky had tried to intervene with the Kremlin to send Joffe abroad for a cure, but Stalin had refused. When Joffe learned later that Trotsky had been expelled from the party and was headed for exile, he wrote his friend of more than twenty years a last letter: "You are in the right, but the certainty of the victory of your truth lies precisely in a rigorous intransigence . . . in the repudiation of every compromise, exactly as that was always the secret of the victories of Ilyich [Lenin]. I have always wanted to tell you this, and have only brought myself to it now, at the moment of saying good-bye." Then Joffe put down his pen, picked up a revolver, and blew out his brains.

Borodin's fate was longer in coming. For him Moscow was the end of the line. Stalin was not pleased. After the parades on the celebration of the October Revolution, Sheean and Ching-ling never saw him again. He was consigned to a meaningless job as a newspaper editor under surveillance in Moscow, until he was arrested in the postwar purges of 1949. He died in 1951 in a Stalinist gulag, somewhere in the archipelago.

Borodin once put an epitaph to his whole experience with the Chinese Revolution when he remarked that the Kuomintang was "a toilet, which, as often as you flush it, still stinks."

Ching-ling was exhausted. In two years, she had plummeted from first lady to widow in exile, but she was still the most valuable commodity any Chinese revolutionary leader could acquire. It came as a stunning blow when she discovered a story in the *New York Times* saying she was about to marry Eugene Chen, and the Kremlin was going to give them a honeymoon. She learned of the story when she was congratulated by an Englishman in Moscow on her "forthcoming remarriage." Traditionally, a Chinese widow lost her virtue when she remarried. Someone in Chiang Kai-shek's camp—perhaps her sister Ai-ling—was determined to destroy Ching-ling's credibility.

She was so stunned she collapsed. She was ill for three weeks, and was just beginning to recover when the newspapers delivered another blow. Little Sister May-ling was to be married in a Shanghai society wedding to Chiang Kai-shek. It was now painfully apparent that the Eugene Chen slander was contrived to clear the way for Chiang's marriage to May-ling, to increase the significance of one Soong marriage by reducing the significance of another. The world could forget about Sun's widow because she was now the slattern of a "high yellow"—a mixture of Chinese and African blood was one of the gossip items about Chen—from Trinidad. The new matriarch of the Chinese Revolution would be the Soong wife of the Nanking Generalissimo.

Then came news of another kind that gave her heart. General Teng was alive. He had made it across the Soviet border to Turkey, and was now safe in Berlin. She decided immediately to get out of Moscow herself and to join him in Germany—as soon as her friend Rayna was well enough to travel.

Three weeks after the Shanghai Massacre, while Green Gang goon squads roamed Shanghai, and executions were taking place throughout

China on his orders, Chiang Kai-shek proposed to May-ling Soong. She accepted.

More is known about Chiang's motives than May-ling's. Brian Crozier, in his 1976 biography of Chiang, gives the analysis of Hu Lin, one of the founders of the newspaper *Ta Kung Pao.*

> Chiang's remarriage was a calculated political move. He hoped to win over Madame Sun Yat-sen . . . and T. V. Soong by becoming their brother-in-law. At that point, Chiang also began to contemplate the need to seek support from the West. With Mayling as his wife, he would have the "mouth and ears" to deal with Westerners. Besides, he thought very highly of T. V. as a financial expert. But it would be unfair to say that Chiang did not fall for Mayling. Chiang obviously considered himself as a hero. And in Chinese history, heroes tended to fall for beauties. For political considerations, Chiang would have done anything. To have a new wife would seem a logical move for Chiang to make in those circumstances.

This appraisal is reinforced by historian Tang Leang-li, who adds: "Chiang aspired to the *undivided* succession of Sun Yat-sen's heritage."

The importance of Sun's image cannot be taken lightly. Most Chinese knew him only as a semi-divine figure. Few ever came into contact with the little doctor directly. Now, propaganda identified everything magical with Sun. His photograph was everywhere. Even the most tenuous association with Sun endowed politicians or generals with some magic. Politicians, including Wang Ching-wei, were adorning themselves with Sun's image. In the Green conspiracy, it was essential that Chiang be able to portray himself as Dr. Sun's earthly delegate, with Sun's supernatural mandate.

If it was vital to lay claim to Sun's mystical authority by marriage into the Soong family, it was equally important that Chiang gain access to Western financial and material support, which he badly needed to underwrite his regime. The gang was hardly going to pay all his bills, and there were limits to extortion. Although he was rapidly expanding the area under his military control by conquest or by purchasing the loyalty of regional warlords, he commanded in practice little of China's generated wealth. So long as Peking continued to be the recognized capital, Chiang could not count on regular tax receipts or other central government revenues to keep his Nanking regime afloat. He was spending great sums on military campaigns, on hooligans hired to conduct repression, and on buying out rivals. The millions that he was able to extort were simply not enough. He needed an assured source of revenue. Although foreign assistance alone could never be sufficient to underpin his regime, it was one of several legs on which Nanking could stand.

The easiest way for Chiang to gain access to foreign wealth—private investment capital as well as official aid from foreign governments —was through the Soong family, particularly T. V. Soong. T. V. had standing with foreign banks, foreign corporations, foreign governments, and special groups such as American missionary societies, which had leverage in Washington, D.C. While he was a virtual captive at the Rue Molière house in April, May, and June of 1927, T. V. was being indoctrinated by Ai-ling and H. H. In the face of such family pressure, T. V.'s will had caved in. Now Chiang wanted to marry May-ling. T. V. himself had just married Laura Chang, a wealthy Shanghai debutante. He was fully aware that Chiang had been indicted in the past for murder, armed robbery, and extortion; there was also the matter of his multiple marriages. What stung T. V. the most personally as a banker was the way Chiang had seized the Central Bank silver reserves in Canton, paralyzing the financial structure that T. V. had so painstakingly developed. T. V. was in no position to resist.

"Who actually in the Soong family," asked author Han Suyin, rhetorically, "decided to put this 'grand alliance through marriage' into effect?" She pointed to Ai-ling as the mastermind, as did many others.

> She was always the matchmaker, planner and builder of the family wealth. Would it not be a brilliant coup to marry her youngest sister, May-ling, to the powerful Commander-in-Chief of the Nationalist armies? "We can use this man," she said. And immediately went about convincing the recalcitrant May-ling that such a marriage would be in the interest of all, especially the House of Soong.

The impression that the marriage to Chiang was "arranged" was reinforced by Ching-ling: "When I first met Ching-ling," reported Edgar Snow, "she said the marriage was opportunism on both sides, with no love involved." Ten years later, Ching-ling remarked to Snow again, "It wasn't love at the beginning, but I think it is now. May-ling is sincerely in love with Chiang and he with her." Then she added, "Without May-ling he might have been much worse."

What would be more natural than for Ai-ling to guarantee her influence at Nanking by offering Chiang marriage into the Soong clan, with its direct link to Sun Yat-sen and access to foreign financial support, plus the fiscal services of T. V. Soong and H. H. Kung?

Although some people were disarmed by her and thought of her as sweet-natured, Ai-ling was the dominant partner in all things. She had married H. H. Kung when they were both political refugees from the warlord Yuan Shih-k'ai in Japan in 1914. When they had returned to China after their marriage, Ai-ling had stayed with her parents at 139 Seymour Road until H. H. could make preparations for her safe journey to Shensi. When they finally departed by train for Taiku, H. H.'s hometown, Ai-ling had to disembark at Yutse, the end of the steel, and transfer to a sedan chair, while H. H. rode beside her the rest of the way on a Mongolian pony.

She may have been annoyed by the inconvenience, but Ai-ling was certainly not disappointed when she arrived at her new home. It was ugly but enormous. The house was a palace, set amid splendid gardens. There was a staff of no less than five hundred souls.

H. H. financed a local school called the Ming-hsien, which he was later able to link to his alma mater, Oberlin, to create a chain of Oberlin-in-China schools. Considerable effort was exerted to make it seem that he was actively involved with the school, but according to personal letters of Oberlin administrators it was decided not to make this assertion in America because it was untrue.

She bore her first child, Rosamond (Ling-i), in 1916 in Taiku. This child was followed by three siblings, all born in Shanghai, first David (L'ing-k'an), then Jeannette (Ling-wei), and finally Louis (Ling-chieh). They were all raised like hothouse orchids.

As Theodore White said of young David, "his conduct was outrageous." A famous Soong anecdote illustrates the point. After learning to drive when he was in his teens, David Kung was stopped by a Sikh traffic policeman at an intersection in Shanghai's International Settlement. When the policeman attempted to scold him for reckless driving, young Kung allegedly brandished a pistol. What happened next is unclear: in some versions, nobody was hurt, in another the policeman's thumb was shot off.

Jeannette Kung was remembered by one and all as being "inordinately arrogant," "unobliging and sulky." As she grew up, she took to wearing mannish clothes to such an extent that she was frequently mistaken for a man.

Emily Hahn described a domestic scene at the Kung family dinner table:

One of the family rules that had to be brought into existence, for example, dealt with the matter of after-dinner fruit. The dish was piled high with apples, pears, oranges or whatever was in season, and passed around the table; to avoid a general grab for the best piece, Madame Kung decreed that each child should take the fruit that happened to be on top, no matter how big or small it might be. One day the top fruit was a pear with a bad spot on it; the dish was placed first before David. "I don't think I'll have any fruit today, thanks," said that young man indifferently.

The dish passed on to Rosamond, who obeyed the family rule and took the spotted pear without a word of complaint. The fruit dish traveled farther, made the rounds, and was placed again in the center of the table with a nice unspotted pear reposing on the top. . . . David glanced at it and said, "I think I'll have some fruit, after all." Calmly he reached out, appropriated the pear, and began peeling it. The other children clamored shrilly; unfair, unfair, David had cheated!

David lifted his eyebrows as he peeled his pear. "Fruit politics," he explained.

In Shanghai, H. H. provided well for his little family, keeping them in a palatial home in the French Concession. The mansion had large public rooms furnished in a modernistic style. According to a foreigner who visited their home,

In this house, he kept a constant reminder of his importance: a large black screen standing at the diningroom doorway with a picture of a lion standing on a rocky promontory, head erect, mouth open evidently emitting a lusty roar. At one corner is a Chinese inscription: "The sleeping lion has awakened. This memento is presented to the man who more than any other has awakened the commercial lion of China, H. H. Kung." It was presented to him by the directors of the Shanghai Exposition.

In addition to this house, the family acquired other accommodations in Peking, Canton, Hong Kong, and Nanking. Much of Kung's attention was fixed on the family business and on his job as a principal agent of the Standard Oil Company in China, by which he conveyed another fortune to the family coffers.

H. H. Kung was wily rather than clever. He was often called in as an intermediary, or was appointed to boards of directors, or to commissions of negotiation, precisely for this reason. He served as perennial go-between for the northern warlords, all of whom knew him well and prospered from the acquaintance. During the Northern Expedition, Chiang gave H. H. the job of negotiating with Christian

General Feng and with Shansi warlord Yen Hsi-shan.

During the split between Chiang and the Wuhan leftists, it was H. H. Kung who brought the treacherous Feng into Chiang's camp by concluding "a financial settlement." Similarly, H. H. held fruitful negotiations with Yen Hsi-shan, whose territory put him within shooting distance of Peking. That bit of chicanery undermined the alliance of militarists and gave Chiang control of the northern capital. On the basis of these favors, Chiang Kai-shek owed a great deal to the Kungs. But H. H. was not the sort of fellow who could force Chiang to return favors, and hold his feet to the fire if he did not. H. H. could be counted on to do what he was told, and do it craftily, but there was apparently little danger of his doing much independent thinking. Nevertheless, there was a widespread impression that H. H. Kung's great financial leverage could be dangerous.

Ai-ling was the sting. After their marriage she took over administering the Kung fortune, working with teams of secretaries and accountants at her various mansions while H. H. chaired committees. She often kept her secretaries busy around the clock. In time, she became notorious in China for using her husband's position to obtain confidential financial information that she parlayed into a personal fortune. One of the darkest assertions about her was contained in testimony gathered by the FBI; its informant told the bureau that Ai-ling was reputed to have hired assassins to kill her enemies and uncooperative business rivals. Exactly how she went about this—if the assertion is true—is not spelled out in the FBI documents.

If she did engage in such extreme measures, it would have been simple for her to put such requests to her friend Big-eared Tu, who was in the trade. But there were other avenues as well. There had long been a female secret society in China, with branches throughout the rest of Asia, organized for the exclusive purpose of assassinating or otherwise punishing men. Its services would have been accessible. The FBI informant goes on to state: "The real brains of the group is reputed to be Madame Kung. . . . She is characterized as an evil and clever woman. She sits in the background and directs the family."

John Gunther, in his 1942 book *Inside Asia*, described Ai-ling as a "hard-willed creature, possessed of demonic energy and great will-to-power, violently able, cunning, and ambitious, she is as powerful a personality as any in China." Until the FBI reveals its source for these statements about Ai-ling, we may only judge their accuracy by the fact that the FBI cross-examined its source repeatedly and concluded that he was telling the truth. FBI agent L. B. Nichols said he believed the informant. A memorandum including these statements about Ai-ling was sent to the chief of the Special War Policies Unit, to the Attorney General of the United States, and to presidential advisor Harry Hopkins under the signature of FBI Director J. Edgar Hoover.

An illustration of Ai-ling's business methods provided in the same FBI document concerned a large real-estate deal purported to have happened in Hong Kong:

> Before the deal was consummated, two young Chinese, David Kung
> . . . and a younger brother of T. V. Soong [T. A.], went to Hong Kong and
> took an apartment where they set up a short wave transmitting set in a
> closet, made contact with Madame Kung, furnished her with detailed
> information daily which enabled her to manipulate herself into a position
> where she cleaned up $50,000,000 in the deal. [Apparently the sum re-
> ferred to was in American dollars, but would have been a fortune then
> even in Chinese currency.] David Kung and the younger brother of T. V.
> Soong, were allegedly "caught red-handed" by one of the British Intelli-
> gence Services and were given two hours to leave Hong Kong.

While Chinese blamed Japan for disrupting the Chinese economy, the U.S. Treasury Department agent in Shanghai, Martin R. Nicholson, said, "It's Mme. Kung, not Japan, who is killing the Chinese dollar."

In April 1927, Kung and his wife were helping Chiang squeeze money out of terrified merchants. The Generalissimo was a frequent visitor to the Kung household. When the Commander of the U.S. Asiatic Fleet, Admiral Mark Bristol, came to see Chiang, the meeting occurred in the Soong home on Seymour Road, with both the Kungs and T. V. Soong present. The admiral was impressed, later raving about his new acquaintances in his memorandum of the meeting, and joined the growing crowd of the Soong family's American admirers. During these sessions, Chiang had a chance to observe how smoothly the Soongs won over Westerners, and the ease with which they persuaded American officials in particular to share their views.

So when Chiang told H. H. early in May 1927 that he wanted to marry May-ling, it was simply the climax of a process set into motion long before by Ai-ling.

T. V., who was still a bit brash and feisty, gave in to the marriage when it was made clear to him that he would never be allowed to do anything in Shanghai if he balked. The capitulation altered him. Thereafter, he became a dedicated opportunist. He yielded in June in return for being reinstated as Minister of Finance, with a free hand in running the treasury and the economy. He also agreed to help Ai-ling and H. H. talk his mother into endorsing May-ling's marriage.

Charlie Soong's widow opposed the marriage because Chiang was not a Christian and she was aware of his previous marriages. She taught Sunday school at Charlie's church in the Settlement. Her generation now occupied the higher echelons in Shanghai; they owned banks and industries, built hospitals and schools.

The White Terror would hardly have turned Madame Soong in Chiang's favor. Possibly for this reason, Ai-ling persuaded her mother to take a holiday to Japan, to visit friends in Nagasaki, and take the cure at the baths in Kamakura, the resort where Ai-ling and H. H. had spent their honeymoon. The family would join her later. In Japan, Madame Soong would be conveniently out of touch.

At this moment, Chiang Kai-shek's ambitions were nearly derailed. The northern warlords made a secret offer to Chiang and the Green Gang bosses from which they artfully excluded Chiang's own trusted generals. Then, according to plan, the warlords double-crossed Chiang by tipping off his senior officers that the Generalissimo was negotiating with the enemy behind their backs. It was a ruse straight from Sun Tzu.

While Chiang furiously denied any duplicity, the northern warlords suddenly attacked and Chiang's distracted generals were driven back to the Yangtze. In disgust, three KMT generals announced that they would take no further orders from their Generalissimo. After consulting Curio Chang and Big-eared Tu, Chiang Kai-shek announced, "in the interests of [party] unity," that he was resigning from all posts in the KMT and retiring from political life. It was a classic tactic. Chiang left town, pretending he was giving up all his ambitions. This cleared the way for his rivals to tear at each other's throats.

Chiang took two hundred bodyguards and went off into the wilderness. His choice was the Buddhist monastery called Mokanshan in the Wuling Mountains, a favorite retreat of the Green Gang, which had been taken over by Big-eared Tu.

May-ling had already let it slip to friends that she was going to marry Chiang. By September, rumors were rife in Shanghai. When confirmation came, it was not from the Generalissimo but—curiously—from Big Sister Ai-ling. Taking charge of the whole business, Madame Kung called a press conference on September 16, at her mansion on the Route de Seiyes. There she "introduced" the Generalissimo and May-ling to the mob of reporters and photographers, and announced, "The General is going to marry my little sister." Everyone then adjourned to the formal garden to take pictures of the handsome couple; the pictures were carried in newspapers and magazines around the world. Nobody thought to wonder at the time what Ai-ling's role as marriage broker really had been, and nobody was inclined to ask what had become of the existing Madame Chiang Kai-shek to whom Chiang had been married since November, 1921. She was swept under the table. On September 17, the *New York Times* carried a story announcing: "CHIANG WILL WED MME. SUN'S SISTER." The story, from *Times* correspondent Misselwitz in Shanghai, said an English tailor was whipping up formal togs for Chiang.

"It is explained," Misselwitz went on, "that Chiang divorced his first wife . . . by the old Chinese custom of . . . proclaiming . . . she was no longer his wife. . . . Chiang has denied that the Mme. Chiang Kai-shek who is now in America is his wife at all, and it seems that he has sent away two other 'wives,' as well as his original wife, and is now ready to marry Miss Soong."

This confusion over which wife was which, and how many, had an interesting aside. The woman traveling as Madame Chiang Kai-shek in the United States then was none other than Ch'en Chieh-ju. Pictures taken of her in 1925 clearly show her to be pregnant—a tall, lanky, attractive woman with tosseled hair, a sharp-featured face, and a pronounced bulge in her abdomen—the outcome of the pregnancy is unknown. To get her out of the way for Chiang's wedding to May-ling, Big-eared Tu had arranged for her to go live in the United States. She enrolled at Columbia University in New York, persevering in her education until she obtained a doctorate, and later moved to the West Coast, where she bought a house near San Francisco and spent some time at Stanford.

Not put off by the existence of these various Madames Chiang, Misselwitz exclaimed that May-ling's forthcoming wedding was "a marriage based solely upon the love of the two parties principally concerned."

The news of Chiang's romance with the Soongs and the prospect of his becoming the "legitimate heir" of Dr. Sun Yat-sen upstaged all else. Everyone forgave Chiang for trying to make a secret deal with the northern militarists. Marriage to May-ling Soong was more pertinent.

The Generalissimo remained in Shanghai long enough to collect his freshly tailored English suits, and to confer again with his "chief political advisor," Curio Chang. His career was nearly back on track.

On September 28, 1927, Chiang sailed in sartorial splendor for Nagasaki to ask Madame Soong formally for Youngest Daughter's hand. Mammy Soong was at Kamakura, and Chiang caught up to her there.

Although Mammy had refused ever to grant Chiang a formal audience in Shanghai, she now received him, according to Emily Hahn.

> Chiang had provided himself with proof of his divorce from his childhood wife, and *had settled the other complications of which gossips had made much.* There remained, however, the matter of his religion. Mrs. Soong asked him if he were willing to become a Christian, and fortunately his answer pleased her. He would try, he said; he would study the Bible and do his best, but he could not promise, sight unseen, to accept Christianity. Mrs. Soong began to waver in her prejudice, and after a short time the engagement was announced. [The italics are mine.]

Madame Soong was in for some disappointments. She wanted her daughter married in Charlie Soong's church, by her own pastor, which had not been possible with Ai-ling's marriage in Japan or, naturally, when Ching-ling eloped. But the Methodist Church prohibited ministers from solemnizing rites between divorced persons, "except in case of innocent parties who have been divorced for the one scriptural cause" (adultery). Bishop Ainsworth, who had provided May-ling with a home in Georgia while he was president of Wesleyan, was now in China. But he was also bound by church law. So was the Soong pastor, Z. T. Kaung, of Young J. Allen Memorial Church. Madame Soong asked if he would at least come to the house on Seymour Road and pray with the couple. Yes, he would.

On December 1, 1927, the Soong family, friends, and relatives convened at Seymour Road. While Admiral Mark Bristol looked on approvingly with a squadron of U.S. Navy officers, the Reverend Kaung prayed with May-ling and the ex-Generalissimo, who knelt down in one of his new formal outfits of striped trousers, spats, black cutaway, and silver four-in-hand, his odd, peanut-shaped head freshly shaved.

The private ceremony was performed by David Yui, national secretary of the YMCA. Then, everyone adjourned to prepare for the public ceremony at the Majestic Hotel on the Bund.

By early afternoon, the ballroom of the Majestic was jammed with thirteen hundred people, and a thousand more packed the street outside. In the ballroom, round banquet tables were covered with linen and ringed with chairs filled with red-faced revelers. At the hotel entrance, guests were frisked by Green Gang thugs. At the entrance to the ballroom, the guests were stopped for another body search. Here guests were each given a pin bearing the ideographs of the bride and groom.

The ballroom was gaily decorated with bunting and white flowers arranged in huge wedding bells by the Lewis Nursery. On a makeshift stage there was a large portrait of Dr. Sun, flanked by the five-banded flag of the KMT and the red, white, and blue flag of the Nationalist Government. This altar, covered with white flowers, was dominated by two enormous shields carrying big Chinese characters for "happiness" and "long life." On a separate platform sat a White Russian orchestra.

At 4:15, the orchestra began playing. The man who would officiate took his place beneath Dr. Sun's portrait. It was one of the leading rightists, Dr. Ts'ai Yuan-p'ei, the former president of Peking National University, who had helped Curio Chang pave the way for Chiang Kai-shek's conquest of Shanghai. He had recently been appointed Minister of Education at Nanking. Among the guests were the consuls of Great Britain, Japan, Norway, France, and a dozen other nations. Representing the United States was Admiral Bristol. Big-eared Tu was in the crowd, his shaved head gleaming.

There was an abrupt hush as Chiang Kai-shek appeared, escorted by H. H. Kung and the best man, his chief secretary, in elegant European formal attire.

Suddenly there was a craning of necks. Guests climbed onto chairs. Newsreel cameras whirred. The White Russian orchestra played Mendelssohn. Into the ballroom came May-ling Soong, down an aisle lined with white flowers and carpeted in red, on the arm of T. V. Soong. May-ling was swathed in a gown of white and silver georgette, draped slightly at one side and caught with a spray of orange blossoms. She trailed a long train of white charmeuse embroidered in silver, from which peeked silver shoes. Her black hair was hidden by a veil of white Chantilly lace that fell down her back, creating a second train. She carried a bouquet of pink carnations and fern, tied in white and silver ribbons.

Behind May-ling came four bridesmaids dressed in peach charmeuse. After them came Jeannette and Louis Kung, dressed identically as pages in black velvet knee breeches and jackets with white satin frilly bibs, collars, and cuffs.

Before the altar to Dr. Sun, whose widow was shivering miserably in a Moscow winter, May-ling was joined by Chiang. They posed against the backdrop of Dr. Sun's portrait. Then bride and groom bowed to the portrait, bowed to the flag on the left, and bowed to the flag on the right. Cameras clicked, clattered, whirred, and popped. Dr. Ts'ai Yuan-p'ei read the certificate of marriage. When he was done a seal was affixed. The bride and groom faced each other and bowed. Then they bowed to the witnesses and again to the guests. There were no kisses or embraces. The orchestra began playing while an American tenor, E. L. Hall, sang "Oh Promise Me."

To thundering applause, the Generalissimo and his lady swept down the aisle to two chairs beneath a huge bell of flowers. A ribbon was pulled and out of the flower bell cascaded hundreds of rose petals, covering the bride and groom.

May-ling withdrew. She slipped out the back exit and was driven to Seymour Road to change. In the evening she left the city with Chiang and his two hundred bodyguards aboard a special train. They were heading for the Green Gang monastery on the mountain at Mokanshan.

The *New York Times* played the wedding at the top of page one the next day, noting that the KMT party plenary would convene that Saturday. "If the conference succeeds," the paper said, "Chiang will return formally to the revolt." Chiang issued a statement that he was ready to resume command. "After our wedding, the work of the Revolution will undoubtedly make greater progress, because I can henceforth bear the tremendous responsibility of the Revolution with peace at heart. . . . From now on, we two are determined to exert our utmost to the cause of the Chinese Revolution."

The presence at the wedding of the entire diplomatic corps was not lost on those watching from the wings. Nor was the presence of Admiral Bristol at both the family service in Seymour Road and the public ceremony in the Majestic Hotel, to which he brought his entire staff. The new member of the Soong family was being accorded international approbation: America was pleased.

When May-ling and her groom arrived at the monastery, Chiang was called away immediately for what was described as "an important party meeting." It lasted from eight in the morning till eight that night. The Green Gang bosses had accompanied him on his honeymoon.

The situation in China had deteriorated sharply following Chiang's resignation that summer. In the absence of the Generalissimo, the KMT's middle-road members made no headway. In desperation, the KMT asked Chiang to resume his position as head of state. On December 10, 1927, nine days after the wedding, Chiang was restored as Commander-in-Chief and, subsequently, elected chairman of the Central Executive Committee. Once again, he was, as *Time* Magazine labeled him, "China's strongman"—the Generalissimo.

Chiang's return to power was accompanied by a suitable show of force by his generals. Their confidence in his leadership restored, they pushed northward, and put the northern warlords into general retreat. The Japanese did not want the retreating warlords to cross the Great Wall and destabilize Manchuria, and issued severe warnings. Manchurian warlord Chang Tso-lin was assassinated by Japanese agents, who blew up his railway carriage. The armies of Chiang's new ally, Shansi warlord Yen Hsi-shan, swept into Peking and took possession of it for the KMT. On October 10, 1928—the anniversary of the "Double Tenth" of the Wuchang Uprising in 1911—Chiang Kai-shek's government at Nanking became China's national government.

Understanding May-ling's personal decision to marry Chiang is difficult in the absence of all but fawning profiles of "the woman behind China's great leader."

In 1927, May-ling claimed to be twenty-seven years old. She was already thirty, a woman of substantial self-esteem. She had turned down previous suitors, including many wealthy, ambitious young men. She claimed she would rather be an old maid than just the wife of another Chinese tycoon. In Chinese society she was pushing the limit. Lying about her age only emphasized her predicament.

May-ling was politically at home on the far right. She once described her sister Ching-ling as a mere romantic. Chiang's massacres brought suffering only to Communists and other members of the lower orders. "Excesses" were always due to the terrible zeal of common soldiers.

Chiang was now fabulously rich, beyond all but a few Chinese merchant princes. More important, Chiang had power. Money evidently interested her less than it did her eldest sister. Ai-ling had grown up while Charlie Soong was struggling to make his first million, so she was imprinted with his fixation on money. Ching-ling had turned away from Ai-ling's fixation, developing a compassion for the destitute.

May-ling grew up when the family fortune was secure, and she regarded money only as a convenience. Ennui was her greatest enemy and bred a lifelong impatience with people and things. She was full of ideas and energy, but there was a limit to what she could achieve by herself. Chiang proffered power. To him, power meant the ability to control circumstances and people. To her it meant leverage. He offered her the opportunity to implement historic changes, to alter the life of China according to her will. May-ling saw herself as a Medici able to alter destinies. The key, perhaps, was the observation of her house mother at Wellesley, that May-ling's most pronounced characteristic aside from vivacity was her total submission to authority. By this presumably she meant submission to power, not submissiveness in general, which May-ling never demonstrated. It would not be inconceivable if Ai-ling, however she painted the advantages for May-ling's benefit, had simply ordered her to marry Chiang.

The Chinese themselves put it best when they coined their celebrated aphorism mentioned earlier about the Soong sisters: "One loved money, one loved power, one loved China."

Anxious to wield her newly-acquired authority immediately as the Generalissimo's bride, May-ling got Chiang into trouble with the Green Gang the instant their honeymoon was over. Ilona Ralf Sues heard the details several years later from Soong family adviser W. H. Donald:

> It was customary in Shanghai for every important person to pay protection money to the Green Gang. Chiang had always paid his "dues." But May-ling, during their honeymoon, began working on him. She persuaded him that he was now the Generalissimo, the most important man in China, and above the paying of protection money.
>
> She was a wild and unruly young woman, often tosseled or unkempt, with flashing eyes and a way of cutting through all the rubbish to get to the point. She was proud of who she was, and if T. V. Soong had been quietly paying protection money for her all these years, she was not aware of it.
>
> Chiang let it go to his head. When he came down from the mountain again with his bride, they traveled incognito, slipped neatly into Shanghai. The Generalissimo had some pressing appointments to attend to. He would be home later in the day.
>
> Two hours later, a magnificent Rolls-Royce limousine pulled up at the

Seymour Road house, with a chauffeur and a pretty maid riding inside, come to deliver May-ling "to her sister."

May-ling got into the Rolls and drove off. She never reached Ai-ling's house. Hours passed. The Generalissimo returned and grew worried. He smelled a rat. He picked up the telephone. A direct approach was out of the question in this case. He dialed T. V.'s number.

It took Chiang's brother-in-law only a moment to understand what the Generalissimo was talking about. Then T. V. hung up and dialed again. He called a private number known only to a few. A second later a familiar and frightening voice came on the line. It was Tu Yueh-sheng.

Mme. Chiang was just fine. Not to worry. She was in excellent health. She had been found motoring alone through the dangerous streets of Shanghai with only a maid accompanying her, a very imprudent thing to do considering the ever-present hazards. For her safety she had been escorted to a comfortable villa, where she was being treated with every possible courtesy because of everyone's great esteem for her rank and station as wife of the new ruler of China. Although everyone had taken such pains to please her, she seemed displeased and refused to take any nourishment. Big-eared Tu sincerely regretted the fact that the Generalissimo had been too busy since the wedding to arrange for more suitable protection for himself and the Madame. This was careless indeed in a city as dangerous as Shanghai.

Perhaps Mr. Soong would care to come over and make appropriate arrangements for this contingency, a simple matter of a few customary formalities in the interests of his sister's security.

T. V. hurried over to Big-eared Tu's well-guarded mansion, took care of the "formalities," picked up May-ling at the villa where she was being "looked after," and took her to Chiang. The message was clear: Big-eared Tu was jerking the Generalissimo's leash.

May-ling did not realize when she married Chiang that she had also married into Chiang's "family." Ai-ling knew, H. H. knew, Ching-ling knew, and T. V. knew. But not till she was kidnapped did May-ling comprehend that Big-eared Tu was now her godfather.

Chapter 12

A TALE OF TWO SISTERS

One month before May-ling's wedding, Ching-ling stood in the bitter cold on Red Square for five hours while the Red Army marched past in celebration of the October Revolution. The Kremlin leaders saluted interminably. "We had not learned the trick of taking newspapers with us to put under our feet to stand on," recalled Percy Chen, "so our feet were frozen and very painful. I wore shoes with rubber soles, which to a certain extent insulated me from the cold. But my father and Madame Sun suffered since they were wearing thin-soled leather shoes inside rubber overshoes."

Ching-ling's life had gone bleak. On top of everything else, she was running out of money. Her family had set itself against her, so she could not draw upon any of its accumulated wealth. Her brother T. V., who later boasted that he had set up a small stipend for Ching-ling out of his own pocket, was preoccupied with serving his new master. All that Dr. Sun had left her was the house in the Rue Molière. The pittance she had from Wuhan was running out, but she was stubbornly determined to remain independent of the Kremlin and to escape to Berlin as soon as Rayna's fate was settled.

There were only a few brief reprieves. She was invited to the dachas of Soviet leaders outside Moscow, including the country villa of the Soviet President. There she went riding in a sleigh with Madame Kalinin. But such respites were touches of unreality. The reality was oppressive.

She had become gaunt—"a pathetic figure," Vincent Sheean told the Department of State,

> beset on all sides by importunate requests to commit herself publicly to different Communist proclamations and policies with regard to China. The opinion clearly is that in China the Russians were severely "stung." As a result, all the Chinese revolutionaries who went to Moscow are without money and without any prospect of obtaining money unless they go to America.

On November 21, Rayna Prohme died. Soviet doctors had been treating her for tuberculosis, but she had encephalitis, contracted in China. She was cremated on Thanksgiving Day, and all the Wuhan exiles gathered in a snowstorm for the funeral.

Heartsick, Sheean remembered:

> On the afternoon of the funeral, we all marched for hours across Moscow to the new crematorium. There were delegations of Chinese, Russian and American Communists, many of whom had never known Rayna. It was very cold, and as I walked along I became conscious of the shivering, bent figure of Mme. Sun Yat-sen. Her income had been cut off from China; she was too proud to accept the help of strangers; she had no winter clothing at all, and was walking through the dreary, frozen streets in a thin dark cloak. The motorcar loaned to her by the Soviet Foreign Office followed behind the procession; it was at least warm. I tried to persuade her to get into it, but she would not. She walked every step of the way across the city, her lovely face bent down towards her folded arms. She had recovered from her own illness only a few days before, and her pallor was extreme. Even through the cold haze in which everything moved on that day I was aware that Soong Ching-ling was now the loneliest of exiles, shivering through the early dark behind the bier of her most disinterested friend.

With Rayna gone, Ching-ling packed her few possessions in December 1927 and, using an international anti-imperialist convention in Brussels as an excuse, fled Moscow. She made her way eventually to Berlin. The contrast to Moscow was startling. Berlin in the twenties was a city overdosed and freaked-out by the defeat of World War I. The city's femme fatale was drug addict Anita Berber, the prototype for the "Blue Angel," who danced in the nude nightly at the White Mouse Cabaret, and made love with women as well as men. It was the rage at private parties to have waitresses, wearing only filmy panties, who were paid to be fondled. In the Kurfürstendamm, men dressed like women and women dressed like men. The world was upside down. What was usually done only in private was done in crowds, before spectators, and as a philosophy. Germany was already at sea in the Great Depression.

Berlin also sheltered artists, writers, musicians, and politicals. Communists vied with anarchists, while Fascists met secretly to rescue the Fatherland.

As one of Berlin's political exiles, Ching-ling devoted her time to the growing international anti-Fascist movement and the Anti-Imperialist League, with which she found common cause. She was elected honorary chairman of the league in December 1927, and again twenty months later. Most important, the courageous Teng Yen-ta was there in Berlin. Together they worked out plans to organize a new Third Force in China, a movement that would provide an alternative both to Chiang's reactionary Kuomintang and to the Communists.

Vincent Sheean found her in Berlin, and was dismayed at her impoverished circumstances, conveying his alarm to a friend at the U.S. Embassy. The diplomat passed this information to Washington in a confidential memorandum:

> I learn from an intimate common friend that Mrs. Sun Yat-sen has for three weeks been in hiding in Berlin and so closely that no one not even the police know of it.
>
> Her half year stay in Moscow has disillusioned her completely as to bolshevism and bolshevik propaganda in China.
>
> She has no hopes for China from the present Nationalist revolutionary government who she says are all corrupt including her own stepson Sun Fo who has grown rich in politics.
>
> Sun Fo in his world journey arrived in Berlin yesterday, his stepmother disappeared from her hiding place the day before probably having heard of his coming.
>
> She is in close touch with China and is studying how to save the country by the honest application of her husband's "three principles."
>
> She lives here most economically, even meanly.
>
> She has been offered five hundred dollars a night for thirty lectures in America but has not up to the present accepted.

In Nanking, a move was afoot to lure Ching-ling back and draw her into Chiang's web. It was planned to move Dr. Sun's remains from their resting place in the Western Hills near Peking to a permanent shrine on the Purple Mountain outside Nanking. It was to be a great show for Chiang Kai-shek's benefit, bringing the body of the venerated saint nearer to Chiang, endorsing his right-wing regime.

The Generalissimo and his wife were using part of his newly-acquired fortune to refurbish the decrepit city of Nanking. Chiang had no intention of allowing Peking to be identified any longer as the show-case of China. The name Peking (Northern Capital) was demoted to Peiping (Northern Peace). In keeping with the new image of Nanking, Chiang spent over a million dollars to build the marble mausoleum on Purple Mountain for Dr. Sun.

As mausoleums go, it was large and ugly, eighty thousand square meters of marble. At the entrance was an arch with the Chinese inscrip-tion "Philanthropic Love." Beyond was a large courtyard, then a tree-lined corridor ending in a stone three-arched gate bearing the inscrip-tion "The world belongs to the people." Next came eight tiers of steps in Soochow granite leading to the stele pavilion and then the mauso-leum itself. This was a marble structure with four cupolas and iridescent blue tile on the roof. Inside, the walls were covered with Dr. Sun's quotations, and on the ceiling was his flag. A place for his coffin was set aside at the back.

At Chiang's urging, the Soongs dispatched Younger Brother T. L. to fetch Ching-ling from Berlin. T. L. was the only member of the family who had not totally alienated Ching-ling. Ching-ling was aware of Chiang's ulterior motives, so, before she left Germany, she issued a public statement disassociating herself from Chiang and his govern-ment.

> I am proceeding to China for the purpose of attending to the removal of the remains of Dr. Sun Yat-sen to the Purple Mountain where he desired to be buried.
>
> In order to avoid any possible misunderstanding, I have to state that I emphatically adhere to my declaration made in Hankow on July 14, 1927, in which I announced my withdrawal from active participation in the work of the Kuomintang, on account of counter-revolutionary policy and activi-ties of the Central Executive Committee. . . .
>
> It must therefore be abundantly clear that my attendance at the burial will not mean and is not to be interpreted as in any sense implying a modification or reversal of my decision to abstain from any direct or indi-rect work of the Kuomintang so long as its leadership is opposed to the fundamental policies of Dr. Sun.

T. L. was horrified. He told his sister that she was a foolish woman. According to her Berlin associates, Ching-ling silenced him, saying, "The Soongs were made for China, not China for the Soongs."

She traveled by Trans-Siberian Railway first to Harbin. A reporter gave an account of the reception:

> All along the route from the frontier, there were demonstrations at each station. The train arrived at Harbin to the minute and a large crowd was waiting at the station, including Chinese officials, railway chiefs, commercial, financial and social representatives. The Soviet Consul-General and the Japanese Consul-General were amongst those who were present. Madame Sun passed quickly from the special car to the special waiting room where champagne and fruit were served, and after posing for a photograph, she left the station for the hotel. At 7 p.m. a banquet was served at the Moderne Hotel and at 10:40 she returned to the station and proceeded on her journey to Peking. The crowd on her leaving was much greater than when she arrived, and many flowers were presented to her. The train steamed out of the station amidst waving of flags and banners and martial music.

The Generalissimo had made sure that Ching-ling was being greeted warmly. Aware of the propaganda value of this for Chiang, Ching-ling reiterated her sentiments to every newsman she encountered:

> There have been betrayals and a complete distorting of the Nationalist movement. . . . The greatest blot upon China is that this shameful counter-revolution is being led by men who have been intimately associated in the public mind with the Nationalist movement. . . . These men . . . are trying again to drag China along the familiar road of petty wars for personal gain and power.

But her statements fell flat. Western news editors seem to have assumed that she was a dangerous red zealot. She was given little space.

In Peking she kept to herself till it was time to board the funeral train for Nanking. She avoided her family, because of their support for Chiang. Reaching hot, humid Nanking, she suffered through the long ceremonies, climbed the Purple Mountain to endure more, and finally saw her husband's casket put to rest. She escaped then to Shanghai and her house in the Rue Molière.

For two months she remained silent. Then, on August 1, which had been named International Anti-War Day, she published a new blast at

Chiang. To do so in Shanghai was an act of considerable daring. It took the form of a telegram to the Anti-Imperialist League in Berlin.

> . . . the reactionary Nanking Government is combining forces with the imperialists in brutal repressions against the Chinese masses. Never has the treacherous character of the counter-revolutionary Kuomintang leaders been so shamelessly exposed to the world as today. Having betrayed the Nationalist revolution, they have inevitably degenerated into imperialist tools and attempted to provoke war with Russia. But the Chinese masses, undaunted by repression and undeceived by lying propaganda, will fight only on the side of revolution. Terrorism will only serve to mobilize still broader masses and strengthen our determination to triumph over the present bloody reaction.

Although her language was cluttered with pink clichés, the content was sharp and penetrating. When Big-eared Tu read it, he must have reacted with even greater venom than the Generalissimo. For the next few days, Madame Sun was probably as close to death as she had ever been.

When efforts were made to circulate her message in Chinese leaflets, the distributor was arrested. Somebody tossed an armload of the handbills off the roof of the Sincere Department Store in the Nanking Road. When a friend asked Madame Sun how she felt about her outburst, she touched her breast and said, "I feel good inside since I sent that telegram. . . . What happens to me personally as a result is not important." Her house was watched, her visitors followed, and the rumor spread that the clacking of her typewriter at night was really "a secret wireless to Moscow." Ching-ling remained serene. "There is no despair in my heart for the revolution," she told friends. "My disheartenment is only for the path into which some of those who had been leading the revolution have strayed."

One of those who had helped to lead the revolution astray came to scold her about the handbill, under the pretext of a social call. He brought his wife, to demonstrate that it was strictly social.

He was the fanatic Tai Ch'i-tao, a one-time leftist who had served for years as Dr. Sun Yat-sen's secretary and knew Ching-ling from the old days. His ancestral home was Chekiang Province, the same as Chiang Kai-shek's, and the base of Green Gang strength. He had toyed briefly with Marxism and had written a Chinese introduction to *Das Kapital.* He had encouraged his friends to form the Chinese Communist party, and had almost joined it himself, but decided that he had his hands full with Dr. Sun.

In 1922, Tai Ch'i-tao was on a mission to Szechuan Province when he went through a mysterious psychiatric crisis. It happened in Hankow, and might have involved a traumatic confrontation with one of that city's more fanatical Communist cells. He tried to commit suicide by throwing himself into the river. He was rescued, and turned for comfort to one of the ascetic schools of Buddhism. When he came back to Shanghai, in the autumn of 1923, he despised all Communists and radicals. Big-eared Tu and Curio Chang took Tai into their confidence and convinced him that the key to salvation was a right-wing coup with Chiang Kai-shek as its military figurehead, because Chiang was "reliable."

Suddenly, Tai stopped protesting against Communists and accepted a post in Dr. Sun's Canton coalition as head of the Political Department at Whampoa, where he could act as Chiang's counterpart. Between the two, they controlled the academy and carefully selected and groomed cadets.

As right-wing anxiety increased over the CCP and the Russian alliance, Tai Ch'i-tao organized the Western Hills meeting that brought the party's hard-core rightists together behind Chiang Kai-shek and bundled them neatly into the pocket of Big-eared Tu.

After Chiang's takeover, Tai became president of the Examination Yuan, which controlled all civil service appointments—a powerful slot for a Torquemada. When he came to the Rue Molière on August 10th, the following conversation took place, as transcribed by Madame Sun from her notes.

> After some sentimental references, Tai stated that his health was poor and that he had sought to go abroad many times and in fact was on the point of leaving for Europe last year, when the appeals of Chiang Kai-shek and his other friends to assist them in the reconstruction work of the country prevented him from carrying out his cherished plan. Tai added that he cared neither for money nor for position, and had no other motive for joining the government than to bear his share of the responsibilities in the difficult tasks of the "party and the country." Sensing that Tai had come on a "mission" from Chiang and was trying to "break the news" to me, I cut it short by remarking that it indeed was a great pity that he had not succeeded in leaving the country. He became embarrassed and silent. . . .

At this point, Tai straightened up from his seat and mumbled about having something to show me and began fumbling in his pocket. Finally, a folded paper was extracted from his purse. He was about to hand it over to me when I assured him that it looked like a copy of my telegram to the Anti-Imperialist League which Nanking had suppressed. . . .

Tai: "Then it is really from you. I could hardly believe that! It is incredible for a person of your position to assume such an attitude. This is a very serious matter indeed!"

Soong: "It is the only honest attitude and the one which Dr. Sun would take were he under the same circumstances. It was foolish of you to spread the rumour that my telegram was a forgery of the Communists, for I have it in my power to prove that every word of it was from me."

Tai: "The Communists have been responsible for all sorts of crimes. Just how could you issue such a telegram attacking the government, especially at this time when the Communists are creating havoc all over the country, murdering, pillaging and burning, all under the direction of Moscow? It is a very grave offense that cannot be overlooked by the government, in spite of personal considerations. Even if the government had committed a mistake, you had no right to speak openly! You must abide by Party discipline. And the worst of it is the telegram is addressed to foreigners! *It amounts to disgracing the government and the people, your own people!*"

Soong: "Regarding Party discipline, I do not belong to your 'party,' although I am 'indebted' to you for packing my name on your Central Executive Committee. Now you have the nerve to tell me that I have no right to speak! Did you put me on your Party Committee as a trade-mark then, to deceive the public? Your insinuations are insulting, but rest assured that no one considers the Nanking Government as representative of the Chinese people! I speak for the suppressed masses of China and you know it! . . . is it not disgraceful . . . to accuse me before the French police of having installed a secret wireless? Is it not disgraceful to set foreign spies against me? You have brought stains upon China's revolutionary history for which the masses of China will call you to account one day!"

Tai: "You are too impatient, Mrs. Sun. Revolution cannot be accomplished in one day. Instead of wasting your energies in destructive causes, in attacking the government and the leaders, it is your duty to co-operate with us. Your indignation and feelings, I can quite understand. They are the result of these last years of painful experience. But Dr. Sun was not an ordinary mortal. He was far superior to all human beings. Heaven endowed him with extraordinary wisdom and talents. . . ."

Soong: ". . . I must warn you against interpreting Dr. Sun as an idol, as another Confucius and Saint. It . . . is insulting to Dr. Sun's memory, thought and . . . action. I am sorry but your mind has degenerated!"

Tai: "On the contrary, my mind has progressed with the years. To better the social conditions, to reform the livelihood of the people, is this not revolutionary?"

Soong: "The Kuomintang was created as a revolutionary organization. It was never meant to be a Reform Society, otherwise it would be called that."

Tai: "May I ask what is your idea of a revolutionist? There seem to be various definitions!"

Soong: "One who is dissatisified with the present system and works to create a new social order in the stead that will benefit society at large. And may I ask what are your revolutionary achievements since?"

Tai: "Have you failed to notice the great progress made in every department of the government—the reconstruction that is going on, new buildings that are springing up to replace the rotten structures, new railway lines proposed that will transform the communication of the country and relieve the people's sufferings? . . ."

Soong: "I have noticed nothing but the wanton killing of tens of thousands of revolutionary youths who would one day replace the rotten officials. Nothing, but the hopeless misery of the people, nothing but the selfish struggling of the militarists for power, nothing but extortion upon the already starving masses, in fact, nothing but counter-revolutionary activities. . . .

"Do you suppose for one moment that Dr. Sun organised the Kuomintang as a tool for the rich to get still richer and suck the blood of the starving millions of China? . . ."

Tai: "Kai-shek is exerting himself to his utmost to carry out Dr. Sun's program. He has tremendous responsibilities on his shoulders and there are overwhelming obstacles for him to overcome. It behooves all loyal comrades to asisst him therein. But the situation is very difficult and complicated. Indeed, even if Kai-shek were to hand over the government to you or to Wang Ching-wei, I am certain that conditions would not improve the least, if not become worse."

Soong: "Rest assured that I do not aspire to substitute Mr. Chiang! . . ."

Tai: "Why couldn't you come to Nanking for a while? You will have the pleasant company of your family members and will be happier there amidst such environments. We are all human beings and entertain goodwill and sympathy for each other."

Soong: "If happiness were my object, I would not return to painful scenes to witness the burial of our hopes and sacrifices. And I prefer to sympathize with masses rather than with individuals."

Tai: "I hope that you will not make any more statements, Mrs. Sun."

Soong: "There is only one way to silence me Mr. Tai. Shoot me or imprison me. If you don't then it simply means that you admit you are not wrongly accused. But whatever you do, do it openly like me, don't . . . surround me with spies."

Tai: "I shall call again upon my return from Nanking."

Soong: "Further conversations would be useless—the gulf between us is too wide."

As Tai Ch'i-tao and his wife left, the old man turned and—his tongue flicking over dry lips (he was a very nervous man)—hissed out a parting bit of venom: "If you were anyone but Madame Sun, we would cut your head off."

Ching-ling smiled. "If you were the revolutionaries you pretend to be, you'd cut it off anyway."

It did not matter that the story about the transmitter in her bedroom was ludicrous. If the Kremlin wanted secret communications from Shanghai, the Soviet secret service had three senior spies in Shanghai, Comrades Diamant, Dribensky, and Sorge. There was also a Tass correspondent, Comrade Rover, and a Foreign Ministry representative, Comrad Krymsky.

In town at the time was the American writer and activist Agnes Smedley. She was a stocky, square-jawed woman, not unattractive, with the short-cropped, no-nonsense haircut of a revolutionary. She was lively and energetic, with a sense of humor and playfulness that prompted her much later during a party at red headquarters in Yenan to teach Mao Tse-tung how to dance. But, she explained good-naturedly afterward, "pride prevented him." Eventually she would travel with Mao's forces and write at length about the heroism and sacrifices of the red armies. She was accustomed to a hard life. Said John Fairbank about her, "She had grown up on the bottom level of Colorado mining towns, where the American dream turned nightmare. Her father died of drink, her mother of overwork, her aunt became a prostitute. Agnes survived by sheer force of intellect and personality." She was energized by injustice whether in the cause of India's independence or the civil liberties of the Chinese peasant. She had been introduced to revolution through a love affair with an Indian anarchist. Now, at age thirty-six, she had come out from Germany as the China correspondent of the *Frankfurter Zeitung*.

Smedley was on the Generalissimo's blacklist because she fraternized with Ching-ling and the CCP. American military intelligence was also suspicious of her, and linked her to the Soviet spy ring headed by Richard Sorge. This was evidently based simply on the fact that Smedley was casual about acting as a mail drop in Shanghai for people she barely knew, which included a number of Russians in Sorge's twilight world. Smedley lived only a short distance from Ching-ling at 85 Avenue Dubail in the French Concession, so she was under the constant scrutiny of Green Gang goons.

Agnes and Ching-ling had many things in common, including their links to the Anti-Imperialist League. They had a lot of Chinese friends in common as well, including members of the new Third Force and members of the CCP. The fact that they both loathed Chiang and did not keep their contempt hidden drew the enmity of Chiang's admirers. From there it was only one step further to accusing both ladies of espionage.

The Nanking dictatorship was not above inventing such misconduct. There had been a whispering campaign against newspaper editor John Powell, suggesting that he, too, was in the pay of the Kremlin.

Although Ching-ling was being muzzled, and her memorable argument with Tai Ch'i-tao did not become widely known in China, there were other ways in which her message got through. A scandalous leaflet was in circulation that does not seem to have been penned by Madame Sun, but only a member of the Soong family could have known such details about her younger sister's toilet:

TEARFUL ANNOUNCEMENT TO FOUR HUNDRED MILLION COMPATRIOTS

After the success of the Anti-Northern Campaign of the Revolutionary Forces last year, Chiang Kai-shek, who originated in a gang of blackmailers, turned to his advantage the opportunity of grasping governmental authority . . . in the name of the Kuomintang and of Leader Sun. . . .

[Chiang] behaves as Emperors Chieh and Chow, two tyrants, who killed whoever whispered. . . . [D]ifferent kinds of public credit bonds have been arbitrarily issued to serve as the private property of Chiang, the individual. His deposits in certain banks run by foreigners of the white race have amounted to a total of fifty million dollars. . . . The fixed annual amount of toilet articles ordered from France by his illegitimate wife, Soong May-ling, is four million dollars, and each piece of her toilet paper manufactured with a foreign medici-

> nal solution costs $20. Likewise a pair of her shoes made of
> diamonds costs $800,000, and one garment costs $500,000.
> Such luxurious ease and licentious extravagance have never
> been heard of before.

The leaflet could be regarded as pure propaganda except for the curious remarks about May-ling's wardrobe and cosmetics. Only someone intimately acquainted with her could have known that she suffered from urticaria, a chronic skin ailment that produced angry red patches all over her body whenever she was nervous. Since she was extremely high-strung, this occurred frequently. Accordingly, she was obsessive about silk sheets and lingerie. It was not unusual for her to have servants change her silk sheets three or four times in a single afternoon.

This may have been an underhanded way to attack the Generalissimo's wife, but the odds were already unfair in the war between the Soongs and their wayward sister. Ching-ling was fighting a solitary battle, holding out against the intimidations of the Nanking regime, the Green Gang, and her own sisters and brothers. Her most dangerous enemies in the Nationalist government were the Soongs, and as she knew better than most, they stopped at nothing. Said Anna Louise Strong:

> . . . her former associates try to blacken her name and prestige with
> slander. She is rumored married to various persons in Russia and Germany;
> any prominent Chinese revolutionist who seeks her out to work with her
> may be alleged her new husband. . . . Even these slanders are perhaps not
> so annoying to her as other rumors which constantly deny her the possibil-
> ity of independent judgment. . . . "When I make a statement," she said to
> me in Paris, "they will not concede that I, a woman, can have an opinion.
> All my opinions have been influenced, it seems, and usually by Moscow."

Ching-ling went to Europe briefly for a council of war with Teng Yen-ta in Berlin. He had been working at a distance, building the Third Force movement inside China through friends and agents who acted for him. Ching-ling convinced him that he should return to Shanghai with her to join the struggle against Chiang directly. They agreed to work together to build the Third Force underground until it was strong enough to confront Chiang openly. A few weeks later, when Ching-ling was back in Shanghai, Teng slipped into the International Settlement, where he set up headquarters in a safe house and began contacting and drawing together the diverse membership of the Third Force through-out the country.

From the scant evidence available, it appears that Ching-ling, five years after Dr. Sun's death, had at last found another soulmate, and that, in growing closer to the tough and audacious Teng Yen-ta, might have been in love with him. This is implicit in observations made by Agnes Smedley and Harold Isaacs, who were both in Shanghai then, spending a good deal of their time in the circle of friends around Ching-ling. Whether it was purely platonic, or a full romance, may never be certain. It is more a suspicion than a fact. But whatever existed was short-lived.

With the Third Force underground alive and growing, for a brief period China again had an alternative to the Communist party and the Nanking dictatorship. Surfacing from time to time, Teng publicly accused Nanking of betraying the people and becoming the tool of militarists, bureaucrats, landlords, and financiers. He also attacked the CCP for putting the interests of the Chinese peasantry second to those of the Kremlin. He called for a complete social upheaval supported by all the oppressed "common citizens," to turn away from both capitalism and communism in favor of a socialist state.

Working through Big-eared Tu, Chiang Kai-shek secretly arranged to have Teng Yen-ta arrested by the British and American police authorities inside the sanctuary of the International Settlement. Without bothering with formal charges, they tracked Teng to his sanctuary, took him into custody, and turned him over to the Nanking secret police. Chiang imprisoned him outside Nanking, and had him tortured for many months.

Ching-ling tried desperately to free him. She made repeated appeals. Although the story may be apocryphal, Agnes Smedley told Harold Isaacs that Ching-ling took the extraordinary step of going to Nanking herself to see her detested brother-in-law. Given an audience by the Generalissimo in his office, Smedley said, Ching-ling broke her own vow never to ask anything of Chiang. She tried every appeal to the point of begging for Teng's life. Chiang listened to her for a long time without expression, without a word, till she was exhausted. Then, looking at her closely, he said simply: "I ordered him put to death."

Days earlier, on November 29, 1931, nearly a year after his arrest, Teng Yen-ta had been taken from his cell at Chiang's command and was slowly strangled with a wire. The executioner was said to be famous for keeping victims alive for half an hour while he tightened his grip. In his office, Chiang had remained silent while Ching-ling pleaded for a man already dead, enjoying the spectacle of her momentary vulnerability.

Ching-ling was deeply shocked. When she returned to Shanghai, she denounced the political murder:

> It is no longer possible today to hide the fact that the Kuomintang has lost its standing as a revolutionary body. It has been liquidated not by its opponents outside the Party, but by its own leaders. . . . The [real] Revolution was driven underground by frightful slaughter and terrorism. Using anti-Communism as a screen for its treachery, the Kuomintang continued its reactionary activities. In the Central Government, Party members strove for the highest and most lucrative posts, forming personal cliques to fortify their positions. . . . But faithful and true revolutionaries have been deliberately tortured to death in many cruel ways, the latest example of which is the murder of Teng Yen-ta, who was firm, patient, loyal and brave. . . .
>
> I for one cannot bear to witness the work of 40 years by Sun Yat-sen being destroyed by a handful of self-seeking and scheming Kuomintang militarists and politicians. . . . I am convinced that, despite the terroristic activities carried on by the reactionary forces in power today, millions of true revolutionaries in China will not shrink from their duty, but, urged by the critical situation facing the country, will intensify their work and march on triumphantly toward the goal set by the revolution.

By contrast to Ching-ling, who was hounded and hectored in every way, Little Sister May-ling had become a power behind the throne. She was now even more a woman of violent energy and imperious ego. Chiang's followers, wary of her quick temper and arrogance, gave her a wide berth and treated her with elaborate ceremony. May-ling's influence over Chiang in the first two decades of their marriage waxed and waned depending on his fidelity, and her success in promoting foreign support for his regime. In *Life* Magazine, Henry Luce intentionally caricatured the Generalissimo and his lady, turning them into romantic stereotypes that became hot commodities at the newsstands. As part of this process, Luce always chose nicknames for his celebrities. He christened Generalissimo Chiang the "Gissimo" and May-ling, the "Missimo." In China, journalists truncated Chiang's label to "the Gimo" and called May-ling "the Madame"—or, sometimes, "the Dragonlady." The U.S. Army attaché at the American legation in Peking, a wiry, nononsense field officer named Joseph Stilwell, coined his own name for China's Maximum Leader: "Peanut."

May-ling became "Peanut's" interpreter to the Western world. She gave "semi-official" interviews and wrote long letters, magazine articles, and books for publication in the United States. To Americans the effect was dangerously fascinating. It was as if a brainy American college girl had taken over China and was providing a running commentary on what was true and false in the affairs of that mysterious and complicated nation. Although she looked Oriental, she was reassuringly American in every other way. As she said, "The only thing Chinese about me is my face." It was also nice to know that she was Christian.

Less than two years after their wedding, May-ling collected on Chiang's promise by pushing him into a public baptism. The time for such a gesture was running out. Madame Soong, now sixty-one years old, was in ill health. To everyone's surprise, the matriarch of the Soongs had taken a liking to her new son-in-law. In the small world of Mammy Soong, the figure of the dapper Generalissimo, trim as a swagger stick in his neat uniform, followed by well-groomed aides, bodyguards, and groveling bureaucrats, was symbolic of the arrival of the Soong Dynasty. Through him, the Mandate of Heaven had been bestowed upon the fruit of Mammy's womb. Although the Soongs would not acknowledge it, they would not have had the mandate if Ching-ling had not eloped with Dr. Sun.

Chiang was baptized by the Reverend Z. T. Kaung at Charlie Soong's church, on October 23, 1930. News of the event was received with astonishment in China, followed by snide disbelief. But among foreigners, especially Americans, there was an audible sigh of approval. After eight years of severe anti-Christian agitation in China, here was a sign that the work of the missionaries was going to be made easier, the cross lighter to bear. May-ling, whose most distinctive characteristic was the capacity to believe whatever she wanted to believe, evidently took the baptism as an act of sincerity.

While Chiang's motives were in doubt, Mammy Soong apparently was content with this gesture. She died at her summer home in the port of Tsingtao on July 23, 1931.

Not everyone was taken in by Chiang's conversion. *The Christian Century,* an American periodical, editorialized:

> Chiang is at the head of a government which, through its educational and other edicts, has been widely regarded as opposed to the program of the Christian churches in China. . . . Christian leaders . . . are seriously debating whether it is possible . . . to carry on. . . . [T]he entrance of Chiang Kai-shek into the enrolled Christian community will be greeted with re-

strained enthusiasm. Certainly the Church outside China will wish to watch developments for a considerable period before concluding that this baptism represents an important victory. . . . [M]ost thinking Christians will admit that the conversion of Constantine constituted one of the most dire misfortunes that ever befell the western church. Similarly, the conversion of Vladimir is not remembered as a triumph but as a defeat for genuine Christianity in the world of eastern Europe. . . . [T]here are other factors in the present Chinese situation . . . for example, the obvious and pressing need for foreign support, especially in the form of loans . . . so pressing has been the need of funds that there have been persistent rumors of a revival of the opium traffic with official or semi-official connivance. . . . [T]he leaders of the Nanking government . . . know that it will not lessen western interest in their government to have a baptized Christian at its head. . . . [T]hey must have had very immediate and practical advantages in mind in encouraging the president to take this step. . . . Christians everywhere will be well advised not to greet the announcement . . . as any sure indication of a forward stride in China on the part of the kingdom of God.

Confidently, May-ling increased her output of letters to well-placed friends; many of them were later published (as she apparently expected them to be). Often, they were accompanied by snapshots of May-ling, for example, "Picnicking with the Generalissimo." Her letters covered affairs of state, battles against feudal warlords and Communists, homes for orphans, and uplifting campaigns. Her style fitted comfortably into the conciousness of Middle America. Here was China as Americans wished to see it.

One of the first of May-ling's published letters was written in 1928 to a college classmate, who passed it on to the Wellesley College alumni association. It appeared in *The Wellesley Magazine*:

> As you doubtless see from the papers, the warlords in China have not yet been crushed. They defied the Central Government in order to satisfy their selfish desires for spheres of interest, regardless of the fact that a united China is the only salvation of our country. As Chairman of the National Government and as Generalissimo of the Nationalist Army, my husband did all he could to prevent the insurrection of the rebel generals Yen and Feng. But these generals, with their feudal ideas, couldn't see other than their selfish interests. The result was inevitable. The Central Government issued orders for their suppression, and my husband as Generalissimo led the army. . . . My heart bleeds at the thought of the disasters which our country has faced. Famines from droughts and floods,

bandits at the instigation of communism, and now again bloody war to satisfy the greediness [of] unscrupulous militarists.

The metamorphosis of May-ling into consummate propagandist grew out of a suggestion made by that perennial meddler in Chinese affairs W. H. Donald. The Australian had been called in to advise the Kuomintang leadership again. He frankly criticized Chiang and May-ling for their parochial knowledge of China. The Generalissimo, he pointed out, knew little about his own country; he had not traveled through the provinces. Chiang might be adept at handling warlords and running his army, but he had no idea what the people of China were thinking. He depended dangerously upon what he was told by subordinates. He stayed in his office and issued orders.

Down in the mountainous border region of Kiangsi and Fukien provinces, on the other hand, Mao Tse-tung was building a Chinese Soviet Republic with the support of the peasantry. Mao lived with the peasants, understood their problems and cravings, believed in their potential, and sought their support. The Generalissimo, Donald argued, could not wage an effective campaign against the Communists, or hope to unify the nation, without also knowing "his" people. He should travel. Although he did not like airplanes, he should use them to venture into the countryside. He could take May-ling with him, and let her speak to the missionaries.

During the long and sometimes adventurous journeys that resulted, Chiang remained woodenly incapable of arousing popular support. One story told by Donald illustrates Chiang's sensibility:

> Somewhere in a remote village they met a man who had the national flag tied round his hips like an apron. Astonished at the indignation of the strangers, he explained placidly that he was a butcher and that this piece of cloth came in very handy, as blood showed less on a red background. Chiang foamed and wanted the man hanged there and then. Donald chipped in: The hanging of one butcher was not enough. Something more had to be done to rehabilitate the flag. Instead of a hair-raising performance which would have only local effect, Chiang might use his power to order obligatory flag raising ceremonies throughout the country. Not the butcher but the Government was to blame for his ignorance. . . . Chiang saw the point and issued the order. After that day, every morning and night, school children, students, soldiers, officials and organizations rallied round the flagpoles to salute the symbol of China.

May-ling had negligible impact on the Chinese people, but attracted enormous attention among foreigners. Wherever she went, she spoke to foreign missionaries and to women's clubs. She was already the foremost clubwoman of Shanghai; now she became the foremost clubwoman of China. She marshaled the foreign wives, the church groups, and the missionary men to her side. The missionaries were quite naturally grateful for any increase in their influence at court, no matter how illusory, and began to see May-ling as the champion of Christianity.

At the end of 1933, she insisted on going to the front in the mountains of Kiangsi. The Communists had suffered heavy losses during Chiang's various "extermination campaigns," but his army failed to oust the guerrillas from their sanctuary. Peasants who were in the way were punished for supporting the "bandits." Out of sight of foreign observers, the KMT destroyed villages, burnt fields, and executed any peasants who were foolish enough to remain. May-ling was told that this destruction was the work of the reds. She never got close enough to learn otherwise.

Exposed to raw weather, rough terrain, and primitive conditions, she came down with a cold and in mid-January 1934 took to bed. She used the opportunity to dictate her adventures to a secretary, in a letter to one of her former teachers at Wellesley:

> I arrived in Kien-Ur on the ninth instant after a four days' sampan trip from our last field headquarters. As you probably know, I have been with my husband at the front lines in Kiangsi in the campaign against the communist-bandits in that province. I was heading the Soldiers Relief and working with all my heart to direct the Kiangsi women in their attempts to comfort and cheer our wounded. While life was hard, moving with our army as it advanced further into the interior, still I was happy that I had good health and endurance so that I could be with him and help, for were I to sit quietly at home until such time when peace has really come to China, we would have to wait a long time till we could be together. And so I have always chosen to be with him. We never stay in any one spot more than two weeks for our army penetrates quickly. Whatever material comforts we have to forego, however, we do not mind because we have each other and our work.
>
> ... I am thinking of an incident which happened last month in Fuchou, Kiangsi, where the Field Headquarters were, in the campaign against the communist bandits there. In the dead of night suddenly we heard the crack crack of several hundred shots from the direction of the city wall.

What had happened? My husband called me hurriedly to get dressed. He ordered the secret service men to investigate. Meanwhile the shots became more insistent, more frequent. Shivering with the bitter cold, in the feeble candlelight I threw on my clothes and sorted out certain papers which must not fall into enemy hands, and kept them within reach to be burnt in the stove if it should happen that we had to leave the house. I then took my revolver and sat down to wait for what might come. I heard my husband giving orders to have all our available guards form a cordon so that we could shoot our way out if we were actually surrounded by communists. We did not know what was happening outside but we knew that the enemy was desperate because we had won so many victories that their complete annihilation was in sight, and they were goaded to try anything to kill us. My husband had sent all our men to active service except a small body of guards, and so we were practically unguarded. My husband never keeps many guards around anyway, and it is a well-known fact that he takes terrific risks with his own life. When I am around he is a little more careful, but he often tells me that a real leader must not value his own life too highly, because to be too concerned with individual safety lowers the fighting morale of the army and that since we are fighting for the country, Heaven will protect us. And should we be killed, what more glorious than to die in action?

. . . But to return to Fouchou, after an hour reports came that the sentries at the city wall gate had mistook several trucks of our men in the dark for the enemy and an altercation had arisen causing one of the men to fire which enraged the others so that all the sentries around the wall returned the firing at the supposed enemy. The men responsible for the trouble were court-martialed the next morning. I was sorry, but I suppose it is necessary to maintain discipline. While we were in doubt as to the nature of the trouble I was not the least bit frightened. I had only two things on my mind; first, the papers giving information of our troop movements and positions must not fall into enemy hands; second, should I find myself about to be taken captive, I must shoot myself, for death would be clean, honourable and preferable, since women who have been captured by the communist-bandits suffered untold brutalities and indignities.

On New Year's eve my husband and I took a walk in the surrounding mountains. We discovered a tree of white plum blossoms flowering profusely. What an omen of good luck! . . . He carefully plucked a few branches, and when we returned home and lit the evening candles, he presented them to me in a little bamboo basket. A real New Year gift! I think from this perhaps you will understand why I am so willing to share life with him. He has the courage of a soldier and the sensitiveness of a poet!

The military campaign May-ling described was engineered for Chiang Kai-shek by one of the best-known strategists of Nazi Germany —General Hans von Seeckt. When Hitler came to power in 1933, Chiang asked for military help. Hitler sent von Seeckt and Lieutenant General Georg Wetzell. The Generalissimo's determination to fight Communists, rather than Japanese, was to Hitler's liking. Von Seeckt worked out an expensive strategy, which obliged Chiang to dip deeper than expected into T. V. Soong's bank vault, leading to a bitter quarrel in August 1934.

It was von Seeckt who asked Chiang to have hundreds of miles of roads built into the red sanctuary in Kiangsi. And it was von Seeckt who had thousands of concrete fortifications built, and moved in tanks and armored cars under cover of heavy air and artillery bombardment. As the KMT ground forces inched forward, more concrete bunkers were built, and Chiang's enemies were gradually encircled. Von Seeckt's strategy brought famine to the mountain populations and his scorched-earth tactics devastated the towns and villages. Estimates of the dead varied widely. Edmund Clubb said 700,000 KMT troops participated, against 150,000 Communist guerrillas. Edgar Snow said the Communists suffered 60,000 casualties, and that in all a million people were killed or starved to death. Of that million dead, therefore, at least 940,000 were not "Communist bandits."

Up the Yangtze at the cool pine-fringed resort of Kuling where she went on holiday with the Generalissimo in 1934, May-ling held court with vacationing British and American missionaries. According to the missionaries, none of the benefits of Chiang's government were trickling down to the common people. The Generalissimo now "controlled" a sizable chunk of China. But all the talk of unification and progress passed over the heads of the masses. If Nanking expected support from foreign governments and foreign loans, the missionaries said, Chiang must first impress foreigners inside China with tangible social-welfare programs. This was, after all, the era of the New Deal.

May-ling was quick to grasp their point. She went to Chiang with an idea, and he agreed with surprising speed. May-ling sat down with the missionaries to work out the details of China's "new deal." She called it the "New Life Movement." She started with four Chinese virtues—courtesy, service, honesty, and honor—refashioning them in the style of sturdy Middle America. Her way of New Life was embodied in familiar American credos: "Don't spit; safety first; good roads; watch your step; keep to the right; line up here; fresh air and sunshine; swat the fly; brush your teeth; take your vitamins; love thy neighbor; push; pull; save; go slow; stop, look, and listen; better babies; clean up, paint up, fix up."

May-ling proclaimed, " 'Except a man be born again' he cannot see New Life."

Bizarre things began to happen. Chinese Boy Scouts, armed with wooden boxes, stationed themselves along the streets of Chinese cities. When a man approached with his hat on crooked, or a smoldering cigarette dangling from his lips, a Scout stopped him, climbed onto the box, straightened the man's hat, removed his cigarette, and threw it into the gutter, saluted, stepped down, and waited for another victim.

The Chinese did not like it at all, but foreigners loved it. Government officials, realizing the importance of pleasing the Generalissimo's wife, got behind the campaign. Overzealous military commanders, anxious to win favor with Madame, sent terror squads to beat up anybody who spat in the street. Men who shuffled when they walked, and restaurant diners who drank wines and spirits with their meals or who ordered more than four dishes and a soup or who gave tips, were dragged out and clubbed. (Brandy and wine were served thereafter in teapots, to fool the Boy Scouts who stood watch everywhere.)

Girls who used rouge and lipstick, or who wore Western coats and hats, were grabbed unceremoniously by police and had the ideographs "Queer Clothing" stamped in indelible red ink on their skin. Barbers who gave permanent waves and shopkeepers who sold immodest bathing suits were humiliated before crowds of onlookers. New Life slogans were splashed on the walls of alleyways, and big-character posters, announcing news in giant-sized ideographs, were plastered everywhere.

Some practical projects also got underway, including public hygiene campaigns, sewer construction, and improvements to water supplies. Funerals were overhauled to make them less gaudy. Mass marriages were conducted, to eliminate the cost of separate celebrations. Superstition was attacked, including the ancient customs of lighting joss sticks, setting off firecrackers, or burning fake money at funerals to pay the way for the departed. Everyone was "encouraged" to wash hands and face three times a day, to bathe once a week, to wash and boil vegetables before eating, and to stop smoking.

May-ling made an effort not to smoke in public, but she was addicted to mentholated English cigarettes and chain-smoked in private.

The Generalissimo got behind the crusade with an article (written in "May-ling" English) for a Shanghai journal:

> The attitude of mind of the great majority of Chinese today is marked by drift and insipidity. This expresses itself in acts which do not distinguish between good and evil, right and wrong, and private interests and public welfare. Hence, our officials are hypocritical, greedy and corrupt, our people are disorganized and indifferent to the welfare of the nation; our youths are degenerate and irresponsible; and our adults are vicious and ignorant. The rich are given to pleasure and extravagance, while the poor are low, filthy and groping in the dark. All this has led to a complete breakdown of authority and discipline, resulting in social unrest, which has in turn made us helpless in the face of natural calamity and foreign aggression.

Like Mussolini, Chiang was determined to scrub his nation clean, teach the peasants not to spit, and make the trains run on time. Like Hitler, he was determined to get rid of all social and political perverts, and discipline the citizens, even if it took a few severe beatings. Chiang believed that fascism stood on three legs—nationalism, absolute faith in the Maximum Leader, and the spartan militarization of the citizens.

The New Life Movement was the popular manifestation of Chiang's fascism—a toy for his wife and the missionaries—and it was comic enough not to be taken seriously by foreigners in general. The missionaries, ignoring the warnings expressed by their own periodicals at the time of Chiang's baptism, were now eagerly climbing aboard the New Life bandwagon. Forgotten were the days when Chiang's regime had been perceived as an adversary of missionary endeavor.

Chiang's fascination with Hitler resulted in the creation of a new secret society modeled on Hitler's Brown Shirts and Mussolini's Black Shirts. Chiang called his the Blue Shirts, though he denied their existence repeatedly. They were an offshoot of his two secret services, the party gestapo under the Ch'en brothers, and the military secret police under Tai Li.

Chiang came to depend heavily on the two nephews of his Green Gang mentor, the assassinated revolutionary hero Ch'en Ch'i-mei. The older nephew, Ch'en Kuo-fu, who had organized and headed the drive that recruited seven thousand Green Gang youths for the Whampoa Military Academy, had since then been given the responsibility of setting up a gestapo organization within the KMT. As head of the KMT's Organization Department, his job was to purify the party and the Nanking government continually.

To guarantee the loyalty of each party member, Ch'en Kuo-fu built a spy network that touched every government agency. To run this new apparatus he selected his younger brother, Ch'en Li-fu. Both the Ch'en brothers were "blood brothers" of Chiang Kai-shek, having taken part in a Green Gang ceremony after the death of their uncle. Of the two, Elder Brother Kuo-fu was considered the more intelligent, cunning, and diversified. He wrote plays and songs for his own amusement. He paid Li-fu's way to America, where Younger Brother studied mining at the University of Pittsburgh. But Li-fu abandoned mining in 1928 to become the director of Chiang's secret service—the Central Bureau of Investigation and Statistics (CBIS), the euphemism chosen for the KMT's political secret police.

While the CBIS spied, conducted purges and political executions within the party, large-scale public terrorism was the province of its military counterpart, the Military Bureau of Investigation and Statistics (MBIS) run by "China's Himmler," Tai Li—for twenty years the most dreaded man in China. Here was yet another of the Generalissimo's Chekiang comrades. Born in 1895, Tai Li had spent his youth as a Green Gang aide to Big-eared Tu and was educated at Tu's personal expense. In 1926 he was one of the Green Gang recruits enrolled at Whampoa Academy. During the Northern Expedition, he was the principal contact between Chiang Kai-shek and the small-town hoodlums of the Green Gang. As the army approached each district on its way north, CCP cadres went ahead to rouse the peasants to attack the local warlord garrison, and Tai Li went ahead to alert the Green Gang death squads to attack the CCP cadres from behind. With the establishment of the Nanking regime, Tai Li was given responsibility for counterespionage against Japanese agents in China, and for orchestrating the White Terror against Communist cells. All clandestine operations in China, except those conducted by the Ch'ens, were his responsibility during the

1930s. He was a deceptively mild-looking man with a high rounded brow and a pleasant smile, but he was regarded by connoisseurs as extremely treacherous. Tai Li commanded more than 100,000 government agents, and possibly twice that number were at his disposal from Green Gang ranks.

Both of these secret police organizations were supplemented by Chiang's Blue Shirts. Although it was a replica of the European fascist cults, the Blue Shirts also emulated Japan's dreaded Black Dragon Society, the most militant secret cult of the Imperial Army. The Blue Shirts' job was to reform China the hard way, by knocking heads together, carrying out political assassinations, liquidating corrupt bureaucrats and "enemies of the state." Its members numbered 10,000. They were officered by old Green Gang classmates from Whampoa. All of the powerful cliques in the Nanking regime were represented in the Blue Shirts' membership. Included were members of the C-C Clique, headed by the Ch'en brothers and named after the initials of the Central Club at Nanking, and the so-called Whampoa Clique, headed by Defense Minister Ho Ying-chin. Finally, among the Blue Shirts were professional killers who owed loyalty not to the party or the army, but to Tai Li and Big-eared Tu. Chiang made them all take part in the ceremony of blood brotherhood, pricking hands and mingling chromosomes.

"The whole country was to be militarized," wrote Brian Crozier, for many years China correspondent of the *Economist*, "from the kindergarten to the grave. . . . Their aim was unabashedly totalitarian, and although Chiang Kai-shek continued to the end, with apparent sincerity, to protest his devotion to democracy, there can be no doubt that he identified himself with the Blue Shirts, whose members included many of his Whampoa Academy cadets."

The New Life Movement, of which Soong May-ling was so proud, and to which her husband had agreed so readily, was merely a public extension of the Blue Shirts, a way of involving the Boy Scouts, the YMCA, and the foreign mission societies in Chiang's drive to discipline China. By 1936, the Blue Shirts were running amok, driven by excesses of zeal and brutality, giving the New Life Movement a bad name. *The Literary Digest* observed that year, "Most likely to upset the teacups were Chiang's own civilian, antiforeign, bombing, stabbing, shooting 'Blue Shirt' terrorists, who once useful, now unmanageable, have become something of a Frankenstein monster."

When the Ch'en brothers' secret political police, the CBIS, tortured and strangled General Teng Yen-ta, Ching-ling was not the only one shocked.

One of Chiang Kai-shek's oldest and staunchest supporters now had had enough. He was the former head of Peking University, Ts'ai Yuan-p'ei, who had been the right-wing leader of the Restoration League. Until now, he had faithfully served Chiang and his Green Gang godfathers, and had read the certificate of marriage at the wedding of Chiang and May-ling. Ts'ai had been rewarded with the job of president of the Control Yuan—one of the five branches of the Nanking government. He had also been Minister of Education, in charge of reorganizing the nation's university system. But, as he watched the new regime in action, Ts'ai began to suspect that he had helped midwife a monster. Everywhere, he saw human rights being violated.

Unlike many other rightists, Ts'ai was an accomplished scholar and a humanist; it was impossible for him to wear blinders indefinitely. After lengthy soul searching, he resigned his principal government posts and established the Academia Sinica—the highest institution of advanced study and research in China. Ts'ai openly sided with Ching-ling against Chiang Kai-shek, joining her in founding the China League for Civil Rights. The primary purpose of the league was to fight Chiang's insidious campaign to portray all his opponents as Communists. By so doing, Chiang was able to arrest, imprison, torture, purge, or execute anyone he wished, with the apparent blessing of all "reasonable and decent people," thanks to the prevailing paranoia about reds.

One of the league's first efforts was to free from prison the former head of the Chinese Communist party, Ch'en Tu-hsiu, a harmless and now rather pathetic figure who had once been dean of the Peking University college of letters. All their efforts failed.

When the league was less than a year old, one of the Ts'ai Yuan-p'ei's closest associates at the Academia Sinica, the politically-active, Cornell-trained engineer Yang Ch'uan, was murdered by the Blue Shirts. He had been dangerously outspoken. Well-acquainted with everyone from Chiang Kai-shek to Big-eared Tu, he knew the inner workings of the Nanking regime. In 1933 he apparently discovered the secret reason why Chiang and Defense Minister Ho were not protesting the Japanese invasion of Manchuria, the invasion of Jehol and the breaching of the Great Wall. It was enough to get Yang murdered immediately. Ts'ai Yuan-p'ei was shocked. He resigned all his remaining government posts, issued a public statement expressing disgust with the regime, and withdrew completely from public life.

The extreme was soon reached with the horrific end of six of China's foremost writers, all followers of the leading literary figure of the revolution, Lu Hsun. He was a short, dark figure with warm eyes and a tragic sense of the nation's grief. His most famous story was the "True Story of Ah Q." In it, an illiterate coolie baffled by the 1911 Revolution is continually humiliated in life, but always rationalizes his defeats. As he is about to be executed for a crime that he did not commit, he goes to his death singing cheerfully a popular Chinese opera song proclaiming, "After twenty years I will be reborn again a hero." It was an allegory about the degradation of the individual and the nation by powers that drugged their victims with useless fantasies. Lu Hsun's message was that China would recover her lost greatness only when the peasants themselves shook off this narcotic trance and carried out their own revolution. "Before the republic," complained Lu Hsun, "we were slaves. Afterward, we became the slaves of ex-slaves."

(There is a photograph of Ching-ling sitting with her hands folded, surrounded by George Bernard Shaw, Agnes Smedley, Ts'ai Yuan-p'ei, Harold Isaacs, Lin Yu-t'ang, and Lu Hsun. They are all smiling except Lu Hsun, who was then fifty and wasting away with consumption, which killed him three years later in 1936. Shaw was by then an octogenarian, and was visiting Shanghai only briefly. Ching-ling and the others had spent the day trying to interest the playwright in the outrages and atrocities of the Chiang regime, but had found it fruitless. His mind was too busy flitting about in its characteristic fashion to be dragged into such political depths.)

Lu Hsun had been unrestrained in criticism of the Nanking regime, and he was always in hiding, in fear of arrest. Although friendly with many of the leading Chinese Communists, he was too skeptical to become a Communist himself. He and Ching-ling were soulmates and perennial outsiders; it was not a healthy position to take.

Chiang Kai-shek finally had had enough of Ching-ling, Lu Hsun, and the circle of writers around them, who called themselves the League of Left Writers. He ordered his secret police to arrest the writers. Lu Hsun eluded arrest but six young leaders of the group—including Feng Kung, China's best-known woman writer—were taken into custody and forced to dig a large pit. They were tied hand and foot, thrown into the pit, and buried alive.

"That," said Ching-ling bitterly, "is our Generalissimo—burying our best young people alive. Evidently in his Bible studies he has not yet reached the Corinthians."

Chapter 13

THE SUGAR PLUM FAIRIES

When T. V. Soong agreed to join Chiang Kai-shek's regime in Nanking, visions of sugar plums danced in his head. Despite the sinister goings-on, he believed he could do something about China's economy. After the extortion of millions from the Shanghai merchants to pay Chiang's bills and set up the Nanking dictatorship, T. V. was eager to right the wrongs—to establish a modern and legitimate revenue base to underwrite the new China. He had sound ideas and, as Minister of Finance, he theoretically had the power to put them into practice.

But he was both right and wrong at the same time. Everything he did came back to bite him. It was a litany of woes. When he created a very attractive bond market, investors became convinced that buying government bonds was a better investment than any other, which was good. But this took capital reserves away from infant Chinese industry, which was bad. Banks and brokerage houses poured money into T. V.'s bonds; Chinese investors came to identify him as their Fort Knox; bonds were secured simply by his reputation. All this was good, particularly for his ego. The other side of the coin, however, was that whenever T. V. had a falling-out with Chiang the bond market instantly faltered. When he brought China's capitalists into line in support of Nanking, T. V. did such a mercilessly thorough job that he destroyed their role as an independent force, making them slaves of the dictatorship. When, eventually, he was succeeded as Minister of Finance by his brother-in-law H. H. Kung, all fiscal restraint was abandoned. The machinery that T. V. had set up was allowed to run wild.

The gangster fund-raising tactics of 1927 were never repeated to the same flagrant degree, but extortion did define the relationship of the Nanking government to the Chinese business community. This was hidden from foreign eyes by T. V.'s Western-style economic flair. He thought he spoke for China, but to Chiang he was simply a captive sorcerer, an alchemist useful only so long as he could turn lead into gold.

At the beginning of 1928, the government was collecting monthly revenues of $3 million Chinese, while its expenditures were nearly four times as much. (Officially there were at the time three Chinese dollars to one U.S. dollar.) The bulk of these revenues was bullied out of "investors" in China's richest provinces of Kiangsu and Chekiang, adjacent to Shanghai. T. V.'s first method was simply to eliminate middlemen who exacted a "squeeze" each time taxes passed through their hands—a technique he had first enforced successfully in Canton for Sun Yat-sen's southern government. However, each province fell back into its old habits the moment T. V. stopped policing the system.

T. V. then shifted his tactics from interfering with corruption to a direct courtship of the Shanghai capitalists. In June 1928 he called a conference of seventy Shanghai bankers, businessmen, and industrialists, and forty-five representatives of national, provincial, and city governments. He reassured them that the extortion of the previous year occurred only because of the extraordinary military needs of Chiang's Northern Campaign. Then he came to his point:

> No government can enjoy the confidence of the people unless the people share in the formulating of its policy. . . . The Ministry of Finance has not waited until high-flown plans are formulated for the participation of the people in the government. We have called together responsible non-political persons, representatives of the tax-payers, to criticize us, to help us, and to guide us.

This, he insisted, was to be "a step forward for democratic institutions in China."

T. V. proposed limitations on military spending, adoption of a budget, establishment of a strong central bank, the elimination of the tael as a standard of measurement, the creation of a central mint, and the nationwide abolition of the feudal tax known as the likin. The delegates, in turn, asked for the return of their confiscated properties. They also petitioned "that the government should enact Labour Laws governing the organization of labour unions so that trouble-makers can be prevented from utilizing such organizations for fomenting troubles." This might have been a hedge against Communist agitators, or a veiled plea for protection from the "labor unions" of Big-eared Tu.

At a similar economic conference in Nanking the following month, T. V. pressed again for a reduction in military expenditure. This could best be accomplished, he argued, by cutting the number of men employed by Chiang and his fellow militarists. (Many military leaders padded their musters in order to collect the pay of nonexistent soldiers.) Now that the Northern Expedition had reached Peking and "unified China," T. V. suggested that the time had come for such cutbacks. In the *North China Herald,* T. V. brashly urged Chiang to accept his proposals for "after July 31, not one cent will be lent to the Nationalist government by the Shanghai bankers, who control the wealth of China."

John Macmurray of the American legation in Peking explained how the bankers hoped to induce the generals to cooperate: "funds for disbandment will be advanced by Chinese bankers . . . in installments, and . . . the continuation of advances will depend upon the actual . . . disbandment."

Playing out his daring gambit, T. V. then warned the KMT Central Executive Committee that it faced imminent bankruptcy. A delegation of one hundred Shanghai capitalists lobbied for Soong's proposals. Under this pressure, Chiang agreed to establish a National Budget Committee. But he packed its board of directors with warlords—Chiang Kai-shek, Feng Yu-hsiang, Yen Hsi-shan, and Li Tsung-jen. T. V. Soong was the only nonmilitary member.

The appetites of these military leaders had only increased with victory. The Generalissimo found other ways to undercut T. V. Instead of making more demands on Shanghai bankers at that point, Chiang turned for the first time to the Peking Bankers Association and forced it to lend him $3 million Chinese. He humiliated T. V. by ordering him to go to Peking to raise another $50 million by the sale of government bonds to the same infuriated bankers.

T. V. tried again at the Military Reorganization and Disbandment Conference on January 15, 1929. Surprisingly, the conference accepted T. V.'s condition limiting military expenditures to $192 million Chinese annually, cutting numbers of troops accordingly. But this proved to be only a public-relations charade, for the budget changes were never implemented.

When all was said and done, China was still a collection of feudal fiefdoms paying only nominal loyalty to Chiang's KMT. They were held together by Chiang through financial payoffs and lavish military expenditures to support private armies on ghost campaigns. The only way army payrolls and expenditures could be cut was to have Chiang and his fellow militarists empty out their bloated wallets and go on half rations. They would rather have slit their own throats.

The Nanking government was quite simply a Trojan horse, painted in bright colors by the Soong clan. In its belly were hidden the generals, secret policemen, and Green Gang leaders who actually wielded power in China. It was skillfully done, and one of T. V.'s major accomplishments. Americans, more so than other Westerners, were taken in.

But T. V.'s skills at persuasion sometimes did damage to the people he was claiming to represent. He was, at times, too smart for his own good. By seeking an alliance with the Shanghai merchants in his own interests, T. V. defied Chiang and dangerously encouraged the financiers to attack the Nanking regime. At times he may have believed sincerely that he was fostering democracy by inviting the moneymen to advise and consent; this would impress the merchants, who would in turn treat the nation's economy as a sacred responsibility. However, democracy in China was only an illusion. By encouraging the capitalists to defy Chiang, T. V. put them in grave danger.

The capitalists in Shanghai disregarded government orders to disband the Chapei Merchants' Volunteer Corps (similar to the merchants' militia that Chiang had put down ruthlessly in Canton in 1924), and announced plans to increase the budget for their corps. The Generalissimo responded by launching a propaganda campaign against the bankers. The Shanghai Chamber of Commerce came under physical attack. Chiang sent Green Gang thugs to the Chamber building. The building was inside the International Settlement but predated the terms of concession, so it was not under the protection of foreign police. On the 24th of April 1929, a mob stormed the gates, ransacked the building, seized documents and property, and sent four employees to the hospital. The Chamber protested to Nanking to no avail. The regime suppressed all news of the incident in Shanghai papers. Unable to resist, the Chamber was forced to reorganize under the control of Big-earned Tu's man, Yu Hsia-ch'ing, and became totally subordinate to the Green Gang and the KMT.

T. V. had failed miserably in his initial bid to create a power base
for himself around the merchants of Shanghai. The first fiscal year of the
Nanking government had been a disaster. Not only was 87 percent of
government revenue spent on the military, but nearly half the revenues were outright loans, meaning another large portion of the budget
had to be designated for interest and loan payments.

Most of the wealth of China was still in the hands of Shanghai
bankers. From Chiang's viewpoint, a way was needed to pry it out of
them, but T. V. was determined that coercion and extortion were not
the way. He tried bonds, instead.

His technique was irresistible. He offered the bankers government
bonds at fire-sale terms, selling them at nearly 50 percent discount. The
government would deposit the securities with the banks before the date
of formal issue in return for a cash advance of 50 percent of their face
value. After the formal date of issue, the bonds would be marketed by
the Shanghai Stock Exchange and the Shanghai Chartered Stock and
Produce Exchange, or retained by the banks, which could negotiate the
final sale price and make an instant profit. Unloading the bonds was easy
because of their attractive yield. Even at their low point of 12.44 percent, the interest was well above industrial yields or straight interest
payments on savings accounts.

It is estimated, from the murky evidence available, that the Shanghai banks directly held one-half to two-thirds of the Nanking government bonds and notes by the end of 1931. The majority of these holdings were concentrated in the big commercial banks that belonged to
the Shanghai Bankers Association. Because of interlocking directorates,
most of these bonds came into the control of a handful of very powerful
tycoons.

A giveaway bond market like this was too tempting for Shanghai's
get-rich-quick climate. Wild speculation in bonds began. Anything from
a change in weather to rumors of a domestic quarrel inside the Soong
family could affect the market value, creating irresistible opportunities
for the banks and the bankers themselves to profit from manipulations
of the market. The sensitivity was greatest where T. V. himself was
concerned. A spat between T. V. and Chiang Kai-shek could cause
serious fluctuations. Who would know better about the government's
domestic health than members of its leadership—particularly the
Soongs themselves?

"A major instrument for this speculation by government-connected personnel," observed Parks Coble in his landmark study of *The Shanghai Capitalists*,

> was the Shanghai based Ch'i-hsing Company. T. V. Soong's younger brother T. L. Soong, his sister Madame H. H. Kung and two officials of the Ministry of Finance . . . created the firm. It was closely connected with Green Gang leader Tu Yueh-sheng, who was a member of the board of directors of the Shanghai Stock Exchange and a director of a number of commodity exchanges. Tu maintained a close relationship with the Kungs and was reportedly their representative in handling bond manipulation. . . . Armed with advance knowledge of market trends and a large supply of capital, the leaders of the firm stimulated wild swings in market prices creating a virtual battlefield on the Shanghai exchanges.

Perhaps unwittingly, T. V. had guided the Shanghai bankers into a terrible trap. His success in tendering government bonds to the bankers locked them to the Nanking regime in a unnatural embrace. As the bankers' portfolios filled with government bonds, they became politically committed to the survival of the dictatorship.

Chiang was pleased. At the end of 1931, during a major crisis over Japan's seizure of Manchuria in September of that year, he took T. V. into his confidence.

Manchuria had been dominated by Japan since the Russo-Japanese War. The Manchurian warlord, Chang Tso-lin, had maintained a delicate relationship with Japan until his railway coach was blown up by militant Japanese officers. Tokyo waited patiently to see whether the warlord's son would ally himself with them or with the Nanking regime. When the "Young Marshal" Chang Hsueh-liang allied with Nanking, the Japanese army seized the rich industrial region in September, adding it to Korea, which it had taken from China in 1895, and set up new positions deeper in China facing Peking.

The invasion elicited from the League of Nations nothing more than a tepid promise of "investigation." The United States refused to play any role in negotiating a settlement. But the Chinese were outraged when Chiang Kai-shek inexplicably refused to take arms against the Japanese invaders, merely exhorting his people to "maintain a dignified calm."

Rioters in Shanghai attacked Japanese business establishments and demanded that war be declared. The Generalissimo's standing sank to an abysmal low. There was unsavory gossip that a secret "deal" existed between Chiang and Tokyo—possibly a pact struck originally at the time of the Shanghai Massacre to assure Japanese support for Chiang's takeover. According to this rumor, Chiang could not act against Japan, or Tokyo would reveal the secret pact. Other gossip singled out Chiang's Defense Minister, General Ho Ying-chin, and Chiang's chief political advisor, Tai Ch'i-tao, as leaders of a pro-Japanese faction with a suspiciously strong hold on the Generalissimo. It was also whispered that Chiang and members of Madame Chiang's family were linked to powerful Japanese cartels with industrial and business holdings in Shanghai, many of them involving Big-eared Tu. (It was the discovery of some especially sordid aspect of this presumed secret pact that led to the murder of Yang Ch'uan by the Blue Shirts, mentioned earlier.)

In deteriorating situations like this, Chiang had always found it effective to apply the principles of T'ai Ch'i exercises. When the aggressor pressed hard, the defender stepped aside, and the assailant was carried off balance into a fall.

After speaking to T. V. Soong, Chiang chose the critical moment. On December 15, 1931, he resigned and flew off with May-ling to his mountain monastery retreat. In the vacuum, Sun Fo became China's new Premier and Eugene Chen was named Foreign Minister. But they found the national treasury empty and the army uncooperative. Although the Generalissimo had resigned as chairman, he still controlled the army, which would not lift a spear for Sun Fo.

After talking with Chiang Kai-shek, T. V. Soong resigned as Finance Minister, and retired to Shanghai. Before he left, he had the foresight to take with him—as Chiang had apparently instructed—all the documents and archives from the Finance Ministry, and made certain that the treasury's coffers were empty.

Most of the provincial governments were loyal to Chiang and withheld their likin and salt-tax revenues from Sun Fo's government. Suddenly, military commanders in Chekiang and Kiangsu began to make heavy demands on Sun Fo's accounts for payrolls. The new government had only just taken office, but it was already bankrupt and powerless. The coup de grâce came when T. V. Soong predicted in public that Sun Fo's government would collapse in three months. With these words from the wizard of Shanghai's Wall Street, all new loans and bond offers were smothered in their cribs by nervous Shanghai brokers.

The hard-pressed Sun Fo announced that he was suspending all bond payments for six months. The next day, January 13, 1932, a run began on the Shanghai banks. Government securities were dumped as investors attempted to save a portion of their profits before the bond market and China's economy collapsed. Nanking was barraged with telegrams of protest from members of the Domestic Bondholders Association, headed by Big-eared Tu. Within days, talks between the Sun Fo government, the Green Gang bosses, and Curio Chang resulted in the promise that certain loans would be made to the government in exchange for the resumption of bond payments. The government kept its part of the bargain, reopening the bond market and paying off investors. But the loans promised by Big-eared Tu and his brethren never materialized.

Big-eared Tu was not a man you could force to pay up. Sun Fo's failure was complete. Just three weeks after the establishment of his government, Chiang Kai-shek conferred with his brothers-in-law T. V. Soong and H. H. Kung and consented to return to Nanking. T. V. became Vice Premier and Finance Minister. It was a promotion.

Tempers were still short in Shanghai because of the invasion of Manchuria. A boycott of Japanese goods was a great success. Many small merchants in the Japanese sector of the city faced bankruptcy. In mid-January 1932, five Japanese priests of a particularly noisy sect were mobbed by angry Chinese on a Shanghai street. One of the priests died of injuries. A crowd of Japanese residents rioted in revenge, resulting in the death of a Chinese policeman and one of the Japanese. On January 18, five Japanese were attacked outside a Chinese towel factory. In retaliation two days later, fifty members of the Japanese Youth Protection Society, armed with daggers and clubs, set fire to the towel factory, and two Chinese died in the conflagration.

The Japanese government officially demanded apologies, reparations for hospital bills, and guarantees that all anti-Japanese organizations would be disbanded. The Japanese navy steamed into Shanghai on the evening of January 24. Two days later, still waiting for a response from the Mayor of Shanghai, the Japanese consul-general issued an ultimatum, and advised commanders of the other foreign defense forces that he would take action the morning of January 28, if no satisfactory reply had been received from the mayor. The Shanghai Municipal Council declared a state of emergency.

The League of Nations committee report described the next sequence of events.

... the Imperial Navy, feeling extremely anxious about the situation in Chapei, where Japanese nationals resided in great numbers, had decided to send out troops to this section for the enforcement of law and order. ... Japanese marines and armed civilians, having mobilized ... advanced along the North Szechuan Road ... dropping parties at the entrance of alley ways as they went along, and at midnight, at a given signal, all these parties advanced ... in the direction of the railway. ... The Japanese marines ... met with resistance on the part of the Chinese regular troops. ... The Japanese during the course of January 29 bombed the station and destroyed the train with airplanes. Other buildings along the Paoshan Road were also set on fire by incendiary bombs.

At no point did Chiang Kai-shek challenge the Japanese, although his armies vastly outnumbered the invaders. He simply cabled an appeal to the League of Nations, then withdrew his government from Nanking to Loyang for safety.

The only Chinese troops defending Shanghai were technically acting without authorization from the Generalissimo. This was the seasoned Nineteenth Route Army, which had come up from Canton and had been allowed by Chiang Kai-shek to remain in the Shanghai area running dope and doing other odd jobs for "Major General" Tu Yueh-sheng. "Everyone, including the Chinese and Japanese, was surprised at the heroic fight put up by the Chinese 19th Army," said American journalist Sokolsky. But the soldiers were taking casualties and were in urgent need of reinforcement.

There were two million men under arms in China, looking on. Chiang finally sent in a small group. They were described by Eugene Chen: "On January 31 Chiang Kai-shek solemnly promised the 19th Route Army 100,000 reinforcements within a week. ... The only assistance [that arrived] was the 88th Division of 9,000 men and the 87th of 6,000. These troops, green and unused to modern warfare, availed little ... sustaining losses of two-thirds their strength."

Big-eared Tu provided much of the financial support for the Nineteenth Route Army during its defense of Shanghai. The Green Gang underworld supplied the logistical support. Tu's motives may have been entirely self-serving, since the Nineteenth had been running his errands and was defending his turf. But there may be another explanation, in light of the curious fact that T. V. Soong's 30,000-man brigade organized to protect salt taxes was also fighting alongside the Nineteenth in the unofficial city defense. Since T. V. could not have authorized their participation without the approval of his brother-in-law, this suggests that Chiang was trying to stave off the Japanese marines without formally declaring war and bringing down a wholesale invasion of China. Whatever the reason, it was understood in Shanghai that the Generalissimo was playing some mysterious game.

Harvard's John Fairbank, then a Rhodes scholar in his twenties, arrived in Shanghai on his first trip to China in time to observe the action. "We landed on the bund of the International Settlement a few hundred yards beyond the Japanese cruiser *Idzumo* and other vessels that were bombarding Chapei. . . . The 19th Route Army from Canton, dug in under the rubble of bombarded buildings, was being supplied at night across the [Suchow] creek, a hundred yards wide, and Japan's naval forces could not dislodge it."

What Fairbank could not see from the river, Edgar Snow observed from the smoldering ruins of Chapei. "It was dark midnight, January 28, 1932. Suddenly Japanese rifle and machine-gun fire laced Jurong Road. . . . I saw a figure stop and fall. Beyond, a Chinese soldier dropped to his knees, crawled inside a doorway, and commenced firing. The street emptied like a drain; iron shutters closed as if clams lived inside, and the last light disappeared."

By the time of the ceasefire on March 3, 1932, nearly 600,000 people were refugees, trade was at a dead stop and customs revenues were down 75 percent. Some 900 factories and businesses were destroyed or closed—a capital loss of $170 million.

Shaken by what he had observed of the Japanese assault, T. V. Soong began to draw some dangerous conclusions. "If China is placed before the alternative of communism and Japanese militarism with its military domination, then China will choose communism." This rather daring statement, given during an interview with Karl H. von Wiegand in March, 1932, placed T. V. in direct opposition to Chiang Kai-shek. It was all the more iconoclastic for being made by a rich financier and Finance Minister. Von Wiegand began his article by pointing out that T. V.'s wealth made him the "Pierpont Morgan of China."

> We were sitting in the drawingroom of his magnificent villa in the French Concession of Shanghai. The villa is surrounded by a twelve-foot wall. The two gates are of heavy sheet-iron. There isn't even a peephole in them to look through from the outside.
>
> Within the grounds I counted eight "gunmen" guards. Two of them

had riot guns slung over their backs. The pockets of the other bulged. I was quite certain they did not contain apples.

Mr. Soong's voice vibrated with feeling and bitterness. He is a man who does not talk much least of all for publication.

"And after all, is China not being driven into . . . desperation, while the world looks on and does nothing to help us?"

By the "world" in this instance, it was obvious that he meant the League of Nations.

"China has been invaded—invaded in Manchuria and invaded here in Shanghai—by a foreign power, that power a member of the League of Nations, one of the signatories of the Kellogg Pact renouncing war as an instrument of national policy, and a signatory of the Nine-Power Treaty as well.

"No demands were presented, either in Manchuria or here in Shanghai. None of the machinery provided in the League of Nations, in the Kellogg Anti-War Pact or in the Nine-Power Treaty, was relied upon or set in motion prior to hostilities.

"There was no declaration of war, but war there was—in Manchuria under the thin veil of 'Bandit Suppression,' in Shanghai in the almost cynical guise of alleged 'Protection of our Nationals.' Later, even that dwindled to the 'Shanghai Incident' in the language of the invader. For a little time it was called 'a state of emergency.'

"So now we know some of the names that future wars will be called.

"The 'Shanghai Incident'—yes, an 'incident' that has cost more than 12,000 in dead or wounded, destroyed values aggregating hundreds of millions of dollars, paralyzed the great commerce of Shanghai for weeks. The League and the big powers looked on. They even permitted the International Settlement to be used as a base of operations.

"Can you be surprised that China would turn to Communism or Sovietism, if that were to unite the country, rather than submit to foreign military domination?"

While others bit their nails, Chiang's preoccupation was exclusively with the Communists, and it was growing more obsessive. He continued to demand funds for his "bandit suppression campaigns."

T. V.'s concern that this fixation on the Communists was distracting Chiang from the real danger posed by Japan was shared by many of his fellow tycoons and Western-trained professionals. In the spring of 1932, they formed a group in Shanghai called the Anti–Civil War League. While T. V. did not participate directly in its meetings, he remarked that it was "composed of the sound elements of the nation" and that it was "rapidly gaining in power and strength and will soon become an important factor in outlawing the use of military force to solve political problems." The League pledged to cut off all funds to the Nanking government if they were used to conduct civil war rather than to resist foreign (Japanese) aggression.

This was in many respects an old and troublesome issue, dating back long before there was such a thing as a Communist or a Chiang regime. Whether the internal enemies of a government were reds, Boxers, Taipings, or "bandits" of any stripe, they were still Chinese. Any regime's responsibility presumably was to protect China first from foreign invasion. But it was over the definition of what constituted foreignness that the league was divided. The league was composed of all sectors of the Shanghai elite. There were some who regarded the CCP as an extension of Soviet Russia, rather than as a native Chinese movement. So the debate—were they Communist Chinese or Chinese Communists?—was referred to a standing committee. The standing committee was dominated by those wealthy philanthropists Big-eared Tu and Chang Hsiao-lin, the third member of the Green Gang troika. The Generalissimo had just appointed Big-eared Tu as chief of Communist suppression. For some reason, this standing committee was unable to resolve the issue. And, out of frustration, the league itself dropped dead in its traces.

T. V. was so disgusted that, after ruminating like Hamlet for a few weeks, he took the next opportunity to resign. The opportunity came almost immediately.

Just as King David got Bathsheba's husband out of the way, the Generalissimo dispatched the valiant Nineteenth Army to fight Communists in far-off Fukien—to rid himself of this very popular fighting force that had attracted so much acclaim during its defense of Shanghai. Apparently jealous and resentful of its heroism, he intended the force to be swallowed up at the front in his new drive against the red guerrillas' mountain stronghold.

The removal of the Nineteenth was very unpopular in Shanghai financial circles because it weakened the city's defenses. This gave T. V. a ready-made cause that would impress his financial peers, and he resigned on June 4, 1932.

For the moment, he had the upper hand. His skills as a fundraiser were too important for Chiang to let him go. They reached a compromise. T. V. agreed to go back to work as Finance Minister providing he was also raised from Vice Premier to full Premier. This meant that Wang Ching-wei would have to be sacked. T. V. also wangled a dark concession from Chiang having to do with the use of secret opium revenues to defray some of the regime's heavy military expenditures.

Accordingly, in October, the ever-flexible Wang Ching-wei announced that he was ill and would go abroad for "medical treatment." T. V. became China's Acting Premier. He had more clout than ever before, and immediately used it to regenerate his anti-Japanese campaign.

With the Japanese in control of Manchuria, it seemed likely that they would next try to seize the adjacent Chinese provinces of Jehol, Chahar, and Hopei on the pretext of putting down "bandits" (Communists). T. V. called for resistance to any such aggression. He also called for another nationwide boycott of Japanese goods and again condemned the League of Nations for its desultory response to the Japanese invasions of Manchuria and Shanghai. When the Japanese soon did attack Jehol, it was T. V. Soong, not Chiang Kai-shek, who flew to Jehol in February to rally the troops. The Young Marshal, Chang Hsueh-liang, accompanied him.

Conservative as he was financially, T. V. did not hesitate on his return to go to the bankers of Shanghai to raise another bond issue, this time for arms and payrolls to fight the Japanese. He was quickly thwarted by the Generalissimo, who simply withdrew all Chinese troops from Jehol's capital without a fight. Then, to put T. V. in his place, Wang Ching-wei was magically "cured" of his political illness and returned to China to resume the post of Premier—and to sign a new truce with Tokyo. Once again, merely the Vice Premier and Finance Minister, T. V. found that his gains were illusory and Chiang had merely been duping him. The Tangku Truce of May 31, 1933, was also a virtual surrender to Japan of neighboring Hopei Province.

T. V. had many economic successes to his credit, but he was a failure at Chinese politics. His peers were fond of saying that he ran into trouble because he refused to do things "the Chinese way." Among his achievements, in the first half of 1932, was a balanced national budget for the first time in the history of the republic. For reasons unknown, the Generalissimo briefly restrained his military spending, possibly as a gesture to Japan to demonstrate that he was not arming against them. But as soon as a truce was reached, Chiang allowed his military budget to float wildly again, and T. V.'s brief and illusory triumph came to an end.

T. V. was compared to Alexander Hamilton because he had established a national bank to serve as the government treasury. In 1928 he had approached the two leading Shanghai financial institutions, the Bank of China and the Bank of Communications. Both of these banks originally had been established as government banks but during the turmoil of the 1920s had fallen under the control of Shanghai financiers. The officers were reluctant to turn their banks over to T. V. Rather than antagonize the community when it was the most important market for government bonds, T. V. took the simple expedient of borrowing money from these two banks to set up the Central Bank of China, formally established on November 1, 1928, as the state bank. The head office was in Shanghai on the site of the old German Club.

It was obvious by May 1933 that T. V. was not going to be able to make further progress if he was continually sabotaged by Chiang. Instead of beating his head against the Great Wall, it would be more constructive to work outside of Chinese politics in an area where he was without peer. Already fortune was on his doorstep, in this case an advance copy of the June 1933 issue of *Fortune*, Henry Luce's magazine, which arrived in Shanghai and was largely devoted to China's fabulous Finance Minister, T. V. Soong.

Henry Luce was paying off on a promise given the previous year, when he had come personally to Shanghai to interview T. V. During those long conversations at T. V.'s house in the French Concession, Luce had urged Soong to come to the United States, where he would find a warm reception in the American financial community and among U.S. Government leaders. (The chance for such a trip materialized with an invitation to attend the World Economic Conference in London. T. V. would proceed from London to New York and Washington. Luce had timed the lavish *Fortune* profile for the eve of Soong's arrival; it was also arranged for T. V. to make a major radio address to Americans over the NBC network from London.)

Henry Luce's trip in May 1932 had been his first time in China since his missionary boyhood, twenty years earlier. The publisher went out on the town with American friends, touring the Blue Chamber District and dancing at cabarets till 2 A.M. with the White Russian dime-a-dance girls. He flew to Nanking and Hankow, huddling with bankers, American oilmen, and missionaries. In Peking he visited

Yenching University, which his missionary father had helped finance. Everywhere he went, the stupefying misery of daily life in China appeared in his mind in romantic, glorious color, the way it had in childhood memories. The drabbest, most depressing scenes were not drab or depressing to him.

"The trouble with Harry," observed the writer Laura Z. Hobson, wife of one of his classmates at Yale, "is that he's torn between wanting to be a Chinese missionary like his parents and a Chinese warlord like Chiang Kai-shek."

He could not be either, but he could do the next best thing—he could adopt the Soongs and make Chiang over into a missionary-warlord. If anybody could carry off this transformation, Henry Luce could. As one of his less docile employees, writer Alexander King, discerned,

> I felt at once that there was a great deal of dangerous integrity in the man. I mean, the sort of integrity I generally associate with the head of the Women's Christian Temperance Union. An almost unbribable pig-headedness. It was also instantly obvious that he didn't have a shred of humor to cover any part of his almost frenzied intensity.

The editorial control of *Time* at first had been in the hands of co-founder Briton Hadden, but Hadden had died in 1929, opening the way for Luce to launch strenuous offensives against Russia, and in favor of Mussolini and Chiang. The Generalissmo first appeared on *Time*'s cover in April 1927. It was only the first of many cover appearances.

T. V. flew down from Nanking to see Luce at the Seymour Road residence. Luce noted that T. V. was feverish with a touch of malaria. "He refused to see anyone—except the Editor of *Time* and *Fortune*, to both of which he subscribes," boasted Luce. He also noted with satisfaction that T. V.'s children had a nanny "dressed just like the amah I used to have 30 years ago."

By the spring of 1933, when T. V. was ready to visit America, Luce was rapidly becoming the world's most powerful publisher. With him to take care of their public relations and image building in America, the Soongs, Chiangs, and Kungs were in for a sensational ride. The *Fortune* treatment of T. V. showed how it would be done.

According to the article, T. V. Soong shuttled

> by air between Shanghai and Nanking, a hundred miles away. When Chiang Kai-shek wanted funds for his army, as frequently happened, T. V. would board his amphibian in Shanghai and zoom up the endless valley of

the Yangtze. In the capital, Chiang would meet him and insist he was "losing face" because he couldn't afford a gesture toward the upstart ruler of a certain province. Soong would rage and roar, swear the money was not to be found, bully and badger his brother-in-law into getting along with what he had. But for all that, Soong would leap into his plane and fly back to Shanghai there to discuss the whole matter with the bankers.

Luce characterized T. V. as a cartoon super-tycoon. Luce had a soft spot for superheroes that enabled him practically to venerate Chiang Kai-shek. "The hero-worshipper in him," said his biographer, W. A. Swanberg,

> responded to the Fascist superman who could inspire the allegiance and cooperation of the masses. . . . He pointed to the success of Mussolini in revitalizing the aristocratic principle in Italy, "a state reborn by virtue of Fascist symbols, Fascist rank and hence Fascist enterprise." . . . Luce admired strong regimes in which the "best people" ruled for the good of all. . . . Communism, in his view, was the deliberate elimination of the best to permit government by the worst. In Mussolini he saw such greatness and in Fascism such dramatic political innovations that he could not contain his excitement.

The business tycoon, Luce believed, was America's answer to the need for fascism. If the good were successful, it followed that the unsuccessful were not good. He found justice in the survival of the fittest, and saw quite clearly that a society built on greed was more dynamic than one built on charity. "The moral force of Fascism," Luce pronounced, "appearing in totally different forms in different nations, may be the inspiration for the next general march of mankind."

Certainly many of T. V.'s new fiscal policies had come as a blessing to China, but others had been a curse, and neither Luce nor *Fortune* seemed able to tell which was which. For example, T. V. had paid Chiang's way to power by victimizing the Canton merchants and helping to extort funds from the merchants of Shanghai and Peking. His bond drives had put China's capitalists at Chiang's mercy. The abolition of the likin meant that the central government collected a consolidated tax in areas controlled by government troops, while petty bureaucrats in other parts of China continued to collect likin tariffs. Internal commerce was burdened therefore with both the old and the new taxes. In many respects, T. V. had needlessly complicated matters.

Nevertheless, *Fortune* characterized this consolidated tax as being immensely popular with Chinese merchants. Wrote Luce (he was the author of the profile, although it was unsigned),

> He has endeared himself to the merchants by every encouragement to trade: specifically, he abolished the likin, a city-to-city tax which hampered and delayed shipments and cost the merchants untold sums in bribery or unfair appraisals. The merchants know that formerly the likin brought heavy revenue to the treasury; they appreciate Soong's sacrifice.

Luce also lauded T. V.'s sweeping reforms in the collection of salt revenues.

> The Salt Gabelle . . . has always reeked of squeeze. Determined not to be cheated, Soong lifted his lantern's ray to find an honest man. There was an obvious candidate, for besides his three famous sisters, Soong has two less-publicized brothers. The younger of these, "T. A.," he picked to administer the Salt Gabelle. T. V. thoroughly appreciated the difficulties that T. A. would encounter in the way of tax evaders and of bandits holding up the little gray donkeys that trip along under panniers heavy with taxes in silver dollars. He therefore organized a military unit which is commonly known as "Soong's Brigade." For Brigadier General of this Salt Tax Collecting Brigade, there was also an obvious candidate, since T. V. has a beautiful wife, and she has a brother named Chang.

Luce acknowledged the nepotism in these appointments, but justified it by editorial policy. He told his staff once in a confidential memo: "The most difficult problem in Sino-American publicity concerns the Soong family. They are . . . the head and front of a pro-American policy. It ill befits us therefore, to go sour on them." But, to unwary American readers, this exaggerated praise made T. V. seem like the answer to China's prayers.

On the evening of May 16, 1933, American radio audiences were treated to an address from T. V. Soong himself, speaking from London. The tangent he took in his remarks, which were quoted the next day in the *New York Times,* set the course of T. V.'s life for the next decade as he waxed eloquent about the special relationship between China and America. It was an argument that turned out to have great appeal in Washington. There were a lot of Americans—businessmen, politicians, and generals as well as missionaries—who liked to think of the United States as China's savior, natural ally, and proper romance. In combination with the calculated press campaign of Henry Luce, this was the sort of unabashed flattery that would cause Americans to open their pocketbooks and pour the contents into the China of the Soongs.

"During the years immediately following the American Revolution," he said, "your trade with England was at a standstill. As a result, a severe depression set in. Then suddenly the depression vanished, and your nation embarked on its greatest expansion of the early 1800's. American merchants had discovered the China trade.

"Some of your most distinguished families were engaged in the China trade. The family of President Roosevelt, in both the Roosevelt and Delano branches, was prominent in the early commerce between the two countries.

"Millions of dollars changed hands without one word being put down in writing. It was a superb example of trust and mutual respect.

"You did not seek to ram goods down our throats at the point of a gun, but sold your merchandise because we wanted it for its own sake. At first we thought it was too good to believe, but gradually it dawned on us that we had come into contact with a new kind of people working for and believing in a new deal in international justice.

"Do you realize that over half the present Cabinet of our government are graduates of your colleges? I have the honor of being an alumnus of Harvard.

"In my immediate family, one of my sisters, Mrs. Chiang Kai-shek, went to Wellesley. Two sisters, Mrs. Sun Yat-sen and Mrs. H. H. Kung, whose husband was Minister of Commerce and Labor, attended Wesleyan College in Macon, Ga."

So T. V. began his operatic courtship of America. The Soong family would serve as the courtiers, the handmaidens, and the compradors. They would set the terms, carry the moneybags, keep the accounting ledgers, and be responsible for identifying all enemies and villains. America's role would be to provide the funds. In return for their money, Americans would be in charge of feeling virtuous.

It worked like magic. Before he returned to China from Washington in August, 1933, T. V. had successfully negotiated a loan worth fifty million hard American dollars from the United States Farm Board in the form of wheat and cotton. These commodities were to stimulate native Chinese milling industries, in which the Soongs, purely by coincidence, had major investments.

Such a coup was unprecedented for China. But T. V. underestimated the influence of rival Japanese industry on British and American financiers. One by one, the House of Morgan, the Bank of England, and other centers of financial leverage turned deaf ears to T. V.'s plan for an international consulting committee that would help China in her struggle for industrial development. The financial world had a nagging fear of offending militant Japan.

Once T. V. was back in China, the Japanese press intensified its campaign against him. Messages were sent by Japanese diplomats to Chiang Kai-shek and Wang Ching-wei warning that T. V. must be removed from office.

A worse shock still was the discovery that Chiang, during T. V.'s three-month absence, had run up an unanticipated debt of $60 million Chinese at the Shanghai banks. The Generalissimo apparently had spent the money on his latest crusade against the reds. It was left to T. V. to cover these debts.

On the 25th of October 1933, after negotiating another emergency bond deal for that purpose, T. V. had a violent quarrel with the Generalissimo. Chiang's most recent Communist Suppression Campaign had been another costly failure. But this time Chiang accused T. V. of being responsible. Chiang flew into a rage, his voice rising to a high-pitched squeal. If T. V. had provided adequate funds, the campaign would have succeeded. When T. V. responded in his own defense, Chiang slapped his face. (This version, though never verified with either of the participants, was generally believed in China to be accurate.)

Face burning, T. V. left Chiang's office and submitted his resignation as Minister of Finance and Vice Premier. As the reason for his abrupt retirement, the government press cited "health."

Speaking to the press, T. V. ridiculed reports that he had a "Far Eastern illness." In private, he confided that "being Minister of Finance is no different from being Chiang Kai-shek's dog."

For getting his face slapped by Chiang, T. V. really had H. H. Kung to thank. It came about in a convoluted fashion.

When the lineal descendant of the sage Confucius in the seventy-fifth generation was appointed to replace T. V. as Finance Minister and Vice Premier of China on October 29, 1933, nobody seriously expected sagacity. H. H. Kung was fifty-two years old, and some things never change. He did make dramatic moves, but they were all backward. For the next eleven years, he was Chiang Kai-shek's imperial "chop"—his rubber stamp. By doing Chiang's bidding, plus a few small favors for his wife, Ai-ling Soong, "Daddy" Kung completely undid T. V.'s efforts to establish an independent financial base for the Chinese economy. By the time World War II was over, the cost of living had risen 2,500 percent since H. H. took office, and the new Chinese paper money that H. H. introduced in 1935 (fa-pi) was nearly worthless. News photos showed Chinese carrying baskets of money to market to buy a few eggs.

According to Edgar Snow,

> Chiang obviously preferred Dr. Kung, who had no party prestige and never openly opposed Chiang's demands; but Dr. Kung knew nothing about modern banking. "He has the mentality of a child of twelve," Cyril Rogers [the Bank of England representative in China] once told me in disgust. "If I were to record his conversations with me about banking and play it back abroad nobody would ever take Chiang's government seriously again."

Theodore White described H. H. at the time as a

> round man with a soft face draped with pendulous flabby chins . . . a cartoonist's delight. . . . An amiable man, he disliked quarrels or crises, and he could be coaxed into almost anything with a smile or a sob story. He was a favorite target of American salesmen for high-pressure campaigns. His one great desire was to be loved, and those who knew him well found him so lovable that they called him Daddy.

It was commonly said that Kung was thoroughly Chinese and that T. V. by comparison was thoroughly Westernized, especially with his brusque manners and curt conversation. The New Republic recalled that when T. V. was Finance Minister,

> the employees of the department were in a constant state of alarm; they could make no personal appointments because they never knew whether the big boss would allow them to leave the office for so much as a luncheon date . . . his Chinese employees worked out a system by which they could avoid falling in disgrace: while they had their little chat in the morning, they posted a spy outside who announced the arrival of T. V.'s car; when he entered the office, they were all at their desks, busily adding figures, and not even looking up to say hello.

By contrast, Kung's work force was made up of cronies and hangers-on of the Soong extended family. Kung, as portrayed by Y. C. Wang, was the "bonhomme of Chinese politics [who] tried to be as amiable as possible with all politicians and warlords." While Soong spoke idomatic

English almost without accent, Kung preferred old Chinese ways and language. He was a man of China's interior.

T. V. had run the Finance Ministry like a New York tycoon, which made him popular in the West—but in Nanking it made him many enemies. Kung, with his easy ways, his good-natured patience, and his rack of rubber stamps, cheerfully applied whatever hairbrained manipulation would solve the problem of China's finances for the moment. Much more could be said of him, but Ching-ling's nickname for her brother-in-law perhaps is enough; when she learned of his claim to be a direct descendant of Confucius, she henceforth called him simply "The Sage."

Until 1927, H. H. had served the Soongs primarily as a go-between. He provided Chiang Kai-shek with an inside track to the northern warlords, especially to Yen Hsi-shan and Feng Yu-hsiang, and appears to have been the key instrument in striking the financial deals that brought them over to Chiang's side and delivered Peking on a platter. When Chiang formally inaugurated the Nanking regime, H. H. was rewarded with the job of Minister of Industry, Commerce and Labor.

He remained Minister of Industry until 1932. During that time his contributions to the development of a strong Chinese economy were summed up by this example of the textile industry's plight, in the journal *Chinese Critic.*

> For one picul of fine cotton worth $20.00 at Louhokow, the militarists there collected no less than $16.00 of taxes. Because of their extraterritoriality the Japanese can evade such levies and buy cotton from the interior not only for their own use in China, but also for [resale to] the Chinese mills. In this respect, the Japanese are not only making considerable profit for their mills in selling cotton to Chinese mills, but they also enjoy a lower cost of raw materials for their own mills. If the Chinese mills use foreign cotton, they must first pay from $14.00 to $15.00 import duty on cotton, and after the cotton is spun into yarn, they again have to pay from $8.50 to $11.63 of the consolidated tax per bale for production. The cost of production of Chinese mills is therefore $22.00 to $26.00 more than that of the Japanese mills.

Obviously, Chinese manufacturers were in urgent need of protection from Japanese competition, and of improvement of their tax and tariff burden. Rather than deal with the problem, Kung sat on it like a frog. When T. V. got around the problem temporarily by negotiating his $50 million U.S. wheat and cotton package, the Chinese producers had a decent chance of competing with Japan for a while. At that moment, Finance Minister Kung stepped in, eliminated tariffs for Japanese producers, and nullified all the precious gains made by his countrymen.

In the spring of 1932, H. H. was appointed special commissioner to study Western industrial organization "with a view toward modernizing China's own industries." His schedule included a journey abroad and a visit to President Herbert Hoover in Washington.

He was accompanied on his tour by Madame Kung and David, then fifteen years old. This was Ai-ling's first trip to America since college days. Because Chiang Kai-shek's propaganda department was not yet totally effective in laundering the Soong linens, some of the sordid Shanghai gossip about the Chiangs, the Soongs, and the Kungs reached American ears. Apparently, Ai-ling discovered that her reputation for avarice preceded her. She wanted to visit Wesleyan College, but the prospect of being embarrassed in front of old schoolmates was too much. According to Eunice Thompson, the alumni magazine editor at Wesleyan, who saw Ai-ling during this trip:

> I have seen Madame Kung shed very real tears of feminine vexation and have myself fetched her spirits of ammonia to calm her nerves. . . . She was afraid that even at the last minute she might find it too much to face the possible notoriety. But we promised her that no trumpets would be sounded and were able, with the co-operation of friends who could understand her need for a little peace and privacy, to keep that promise. Her classmates were notified and came from far and wide to join her at Wesleyan. For two whole days she saw none except familiar faces and was able to lay down for a few hours her country's burdens.

Ai-ling was so touched by "the familiar grounds and . . . faces of those I have loved," that she established a $10,000 scholarship fund in memory of Judge DuPont Guerry, president of the school when she was a student.

The Kungs then sailed to Europe and the most important part of their trip, the booming German arms industry. H. H. arranged to purchase $25 million U.S. in weapons from Germany. Then, since fascism was fashionable, and his brother-in-law was one of its leading exponents, H. H. decided to visit Benito Mussolini.

He was preceded into Venice by Ai-ling. Mussolini's welcoming party greeted her ship in a launch completely covered with flowers; Ai-ling remarked demurely, "It was lovely, but I was nervous at having such a fuss made over me." When H. H. arrived he cut a deal whereby the $2 million U.S. balance of Boxer indemnities still owed to Italy would be used to buy Fiat war planes. Mussolini left it to his handsome, swarthy son-in-law, Count Ciano, his Minister to China, to arrange the details. Italian assistance to the infant Chinese air force was expanded to include a school to train pilots at Loyang and a Fiat aircraft assembly plant in Nanchang.

Kung's "success" in Germany and Italy was not surprising. Hitler's Third Reich was just getting started and wanted suitable right-wing customers for its arms. Italy was the leading light among fascist nations; compared to the established Mussolini, Hitler was a mere tyro, who visited Italy in an ill-fitting suit and scuffed shoes. Mussolini by then had already leveled the streets of Rome, cleaned out its slums, and returned the ancient capital to its classical open grandeur.

While T. V. Soong was trying to persuade Chiang to forget the Chinese Communists and defend China against Japanese aggression, the Japanese, Germans, and Italians were all encouraging Chiang to love Japan and kill reds. Both Italy and Germany were anxious to cultivate allies. China was particularly important, because it formed the eastern border of Soviet Russia. It was axiomatic that if Russia could be kept busy on the east, she was less of a threat in the west. The Generalissimo daily became more enamored of the Nazi military and police state. Eventually, he sent his younger son, Wei-kuo, to be schooled by the Nazis, possibly to make up for the disappointment of his first son's defection to Russia. (Wei-kuo became a second lieutenant in the 98th Jaeger Regiment and before returning to China took part in the invasion of Austria in 1938.)

When the Kungs returned to China at the end of their European sojourn, the stage was set for the face slapping—one of those truly edifying moments in the history of the Soong dynasty when the interests of various members of the family clashed with harrowing consequences.

The sequence in which it happened is important. H. H. returned to China in April 1933, just after T. V. had left for his trip to Europe and America. Here was a ripe opportunity for the Kung financial mice to play while the Soong cat was away.

T. V. had always tried to keep Chiang Kai-shek on a tight budget in financing his anti-Communist drives. But, with T. V. temporarily out of the way, Chiang craftily appointed H. H. Kung governor of the Central Bank of China and ordered him to produce more money. Four months later when T. V. returned from America, he found that Chiang had overdrawn his budget by $60 million Chinese, and spent it on his latest anti-red military adventure. Furthermore, it was brother-in-law Kung who had enabled brother-in-law Chiang to get away with it—one member of the tribe had used another to outfox a third. In a fury against H. H. and outraged by the duplicity of Chiang, T. V. rushed to see the Generalissimo. It was this confrontation that climaxed in the sensational shouting match that ended with Chiang slapping T. V. in the face, T. V. resigning, and H. H. taking his place as Finance Minister and Vice Premier.

But to what extent was H. H. blameworthy? It was never settled at the Long Bar whether H. H. Kung was simply a bumbler, a kind-hearted oaf used by Chiang to mischievous ends (and used similarly by Ai-ling)—or whether he was fully aware of the consequences of his actions. Even W. H. Donald was never quite certain. "His swears were not worth a continental damn," Donald griped in a letter to a friend after being stung by H. H. in 1928. "He meant well, but God save us from the people who mean well!"

If Daddy Kung was a fool, however, he was foolish like a ferret.

Taking over from T. V. Soong was a grand elevation for The Sage, but with it came headaches that would have daunted a lesser man. At his inauguration on November 6, 1933, Kung's first act as Finance Minister was to ask the nation to contribute liberally to the anti-Communist campaign, declaring flatly that the success of the "bandit suppression" drive was more important than a balanced budget. With these words, Kung struck his first blow to destroy the fiscal restraints T. V. had labored for five years to establish.

On December 16, Kung upped cigarette taxes by 50 percent. Twelve Shanghai tobacco factories folded.

As T. V. had before him, H. H. financed the budget largely through bond issues, with the same attractive terms that T. V. had offered. By the middle of 1934 more than one-third of the income-earning ability of the Shanghai banks was tied to the government. This had a disastrous effect on the rural and industrial economies. Money that normally would have gone into bank loans to industry and agriculture was going instead through bonds to Chiang and the army. There simply was not a more attractive yield than what could be derived from Kung's bonds. The money the banks used to purchase the bonds came in the form of Chinese silver, which made its way through the domestic money market down the Yangtze to the polluted financial harbor of Shanghai. By spending these silver reserves on Nanking bonds, the banks prospered for two dizzy years while China's farmers and countryside fell deep into depression.

This brief Eden for the bankers was a fool's paradise. The rest of the world for some time had been in the coils of the Great Depression, a serpent now slithering into Shanghai. The United States had abandoned the gold standard in 1933 and to satisfy Western mining states hit by the slump had begun to stock U.S. Treasury reserves with silver. Congress set the silver price at fifty cents per ounce. To financiers in Shanghai this meant that instead of buying Nanking bonds their silver holdings could now be sold to the United States for a clear profit of 10 percent. The consequence for the Chinese economy was catastrophic. Chinese silver left the country in a great rush and bond sales plummeted. Without bond sales, Chiang's anti-red military operations halted, and in October Mao's Red Army was able to break through the weakened Nationalist blockade and begin the Long March to a safe new base in Yenan. The outflux of Chinese silver created a tight money market in China, so interest rates on bank loans rose sharply. These trends threatened the deficit financing of the government. The very survival of the Nanking regime was now in question.

Kung was at a loss. The only way he could think of to keep the silver in China was to announce an embargo. The Ministry of Finance proclaimed, "Until further notice, purchases and sales of foreign exchange shall be prohibited." The embargo was ignored. Sterner measures followed. If silver outflow could not be blocked, it could be taxed. The Nanking Government issued a statement on the 15th of October, 1934: "In view of the undue rise of silver out of relation to the level of general commodity price, the National Government, in order to safeguard China's economic interests and protect its currency, has fixed the customs duty on exports of silver, effective October 15." The result was a 10 percent tax on silver exports. While there was substantial smuggling to bypass the tax, when it was paid the tax equalized the price of silver in China with that offered by the British and American markets. So the outflow of silver stopped. But by then silver reserves in Shanghai had fallen by half. At the same time, Kung's embargo threw off the Chinese dollar nearly 20 percent.

Faced with a drastically reduced market for government bonds, and an emergency need for funds, Kung turned first to the government-controlled Central Bank. When T. V. had been Finance Minister, he had kept a $13 million ceiling on the bank's investment in Nanking bonds. H. H. increased this to $173 million in 1934. Chiang Kai-shek's coffers thus were filled by Kung's using the government's bank to buy the government's bonds, to purchase government notes, and to extend loans to the government. It was straightforward fiscal incest.

The 10 percent tariff barrier that Kung had slapped on the silver trade had caused silver trading to slump, but it had caused a corresponding jump in gold prices as speculators shifted to the other precious metal. Kung saw to it that the Central Bank, as the exclusive agent for gold trading in China, profited heavily in the new gold market. He also exempted the bank from the silver export tax, so that the Central Bank alone was able to sell great quantities of Chinese silver overseas at a substantial profit. Even so, the Central Bank could not keep the Nanking regime afloat by itself.

Once again the regime had to take emergency measures to avoid bankruptcy, and find a way to avoid it in the future by bringing the banking community to heel once and for all. Grudgingly, Chiang Kai-shek recognized that he needed the help once again of the best financial brain in China. Gritting his ill-fitting false teeth, he called for T. V. Soong. There was an elaborate pretense of friendship and brotherhood, but the deal struck was a cold, "straightforward" business arrangement.

T. V. was simply too full of energy and ideas to be content. After his face-slapping showdown with Chiang Kai-shek, he could have moved his private base of operation to Hong Kong, or to New York, and devoted his energies to becoming a global tycoon. But he was still young, still patriotic, still involved with China, and could not forget the success he had achieved, however brief, in his efforts to revolutionize the ancient nation.

T. V. had been keeping himself busy in Shanghai with a private venture he called the China Development Finance Corporation, which encouraged foreign investment in Chinese industry and commerce. He was also wheeling and dealing on his own bond market, and was charming American firms into introducing rayon, fertilizer, paper, rubber, and truck manufacturing to China.

Chiang had power, but no purse. T. V. knew how to fill a purse, but could no longer stomach Chiang. The deal they hashed out was that H. H. Kung would serve as a buffer between them, and would do Chiang's bidding as Finance Minister. T. V. would continue as a private financier but would be available to Chiang and Kung for consultation. As always, the brothers-in-law would be helped behind the scenes by Big-eared Tu, who sat on the boards of several banks and had flunkies on the boards of most of the others. Together, they would force the Shanghai banks into line permanently, climaxing in their nationalization. T. V. then would be given control of the nationalized banks. In that position, he would be able to counterbalance H. H. Kung's eccentricities at the Finance Ministry, and serve as a restraint on any fiscal extremes by Chiang. This came to be called the Great Shanghai Banking Coup. The villain in the plot was to be H. H. Kung. He was already regarded as such by the private bankers in Shanghai. T. V. remained in the background, but gave H. H. instructions.

First, in July 1934, the government passed the Savings Bank Law, which required all banks to invest one-quarter of their assets in government bonds or securities. These bonds and securities were to be held "in trust" for them by the Central Bank. The Generalissimo might just as well have marched troops in to seize a quarter of their vaults. There was a storm of protests. But protests did no good.

In practice, Nanking did not enforce the new Savings Bank Law across the board. It was used selectively and punitively.

The Shanghai Bankers Association (made up of Chekiang and Kiangsu province tycoons) privately controlled nearly three-quarters of China's banking assets, while the Nanking regime directly administered only two banks—the official Central Bank and Chiang's more or less personally-controlled Farmers Bank.

Some private bankers saw what was coming, particularly the enormously rich, feisty Chang Kia-ngau. He was general manager of the original Bank of China and also controlled the other great Shanghai bank, the Bank of Communications. Together, they were three times as large as the government's recently-created Central Bank, and represented nearly a third of all the money in all Chinese banks. This maverick banker was now saying what T. V. Soong had been saying all along: Japan was the real enemy, too much money was being squandered on the army's Communist Suppression campaigns, and Nanking bonds were worthless.

In a last-ditch maneuver to save his bank's independence, to which he had devoted much of his life, Chang Kia-ngau tried to fight back by dumping his holdings of Nanking bonds. His move interfered just as H. H. Kung was also trying to unload $40 million Chinese in government bonds to unwary and unwilling investors. The troublesome Chang Kia-ngau had to go.

For once, Kung moved cautiously. A government takeover of the Bank of China and the Bank of Communications would be wasted if the public lost confidence in the bank notes circulated by these two institutions. On the 28th of February, 1935, at a meeting that included T. V. Soong, H. H. Kung, and Chiang Kai-shek, the Generalissimo insisted that the coup proceed.

Kung immediately launched a whispering campaign against the two big banks. Speaking one at a time to unhappy businessmen, H. H. insinuated that all of the problems besetting China were the doing of the big bankers, that was why businessmen were unable to get loans, why money was so tight, and why interest rates were so high. He and Ai-ling spent their own money lavishly to entertain these gullible Babbitts of Shanghai, their minds clouded by dismal financial worries, and drove a wedge of suspicion between them and their own bankers. T. V. Soong chimed in; so did Big-eared Tu.

Banking magnate Tu Yueh-sheng sponsored a series of conferences that February for Shanghai business leaders. Tu and H. H. promised that business in general would be greatly improved and easy low-interest loans would be forthcoming if a three-bank consortium could be formed combining the Central Bank, the Bank of China, and the Bank of Communications. It was carefully made to seem as if this was just their private pipe dream. Many bankers were lulled by the tone of the meetings.

Suddenly and without warning, Nanking announced on March 23, 1935, that it would immediately take over the Bank of China and the Bank of Communications. Kung justified the move by saying, speciously, that it was necessary to increase the credit capacity of the banks so they could make more loans to businessmen, to fight the Depression. Once the takeover was complete, Kung "forgot" about relief loans for Chinese businesses.

As reward for his part in the coup, T. V. Soong was made chairman of the board of the Bank of China, replacing Chang Kia-ngau. Keeping a straight face, T. V. informed the press that "the object of the Government" in seizing the two biggest private banks was simply "to coordinate . . . on policy." Chang Kia-ngau was demoted to the post of second assistant manager of the Central Bank of China, a position directly under H. H. Kung. He pleaded with Chiang Kai-shek. The banker who had stood up to the Peking warlords was humiliated by the Ningpo Napoleon; he announced that he was too "fatigued" to accept the government appointment at the Central Bank. The coup was complete. (Chang Kia-ngau eventually retired to Los Angeles, where he taught at Loyola.)

Kung then completed the formalities with the banks' stockholders —by the use of pressure, intimidation, and compromise. The Bank of China's new board was elected on March 30. Among the new directors were T. V. Soong, T. L. Soong, and Big-eared Tu. When the Bank of Communications held its first stockholders meeting after the coup, T. L. Soong was on its board. Both T. V. and T. L. acquired seats on the board of the Central Bank.

The bank coup of March was followed by the methodical subversion of three other important Shanghai commercial banks that June. The Ningpo Commercial and Savings Bank, the Commercial Bank of China, and the National Industrial Bank of China suddenly found that their credit had "collapsed" and that they were unable to redeem their bank notes. The government forced the managers to resign. All three banks were placed under the supervision of H. H. Kung's Manufacturers' Bank, on the board of which sat T. L. Soong, T. A. Soong, and T. V. Soong. Big-eared Tu became the new chairman of the board of the Commercial Bank.

Nanking also gained control of the Sin Hua Trust and Savings Bank. T. V. Soong was named to its board. The Bank of Canton, which according to a whispering campaign was "running into financial difficulties," was "saved" by T. V. and reopened with him as chairman of the board and T. A. Soong as a director. T. L. Soong became the new director of the Agricultural and Industrial Bank of China. When banks in Kwangtung Province then fell under Nanking's control, T. L. Soong was named director of the Kwangtung Provincial Bank and the Canton Municipal Bank. The list went on and on, as bank after bank, then company after company, came under control of the clan.

These were not the only interesting posts held by T. V. Soong's younger brothers. The youngest, T. A., who also had attended Harvard, getting his B.A. in 1928, was in charge of the salt monopoly, and its army of thirty thousand was commanded by the brother of T. V.'s wife, Laura. T. L. Soong, the Vanderbilt graduate, was managing director of H. H. Kung's Manufacturers' Bank. T. L. was also the head of the Whangpoo Conservancy Board with jurisdiction over Shanghai harbor, which was dominated by the Green Gang. Everything that happened on the waterfront was the business of Big-eared Tu's man Ku Tsu-chuan. The mere mention of his name was said to strike terror into the hearts of the worst cutthroats on the China Sea coast. Although it was not widely known, and certainly not talked about, this waterfront gangster was the older brother of one of Generalissimo Chiang Kai-shek's senior military officers—General Ku Chu-t'ung, who eventually rose to be chief of the general staff and, because of the New Fourth Army Incident, one of the most hated men in China.

T. V. seemed content with this new public role as head of the Bank of China, wielding his scepter over stocks, bonds, and international loan agreements, which were becoming his new specialty. He was in his element, securing multi-million-dollar hard currency investments in Chinese industry and commerce, carefully enlarging his own investments in a growing portfolio of international blue-chip stocks. It was rumored that he was amassing large personal holdings in General Motors and DuPont, among others. Wisely, he now avoided politics, confining himself to manipulating developments behind the scenes. Publicly, he supported H. H. Kung's policies. For a time, he was able to swallow this rich feast, but it was not the end of his quarrels with Chiang Kaishek and that branch of the Soong dynasty.

The next move H. H. Kung made seemed uncharacteristically sound and legitimate. Because China's economy suffered from wild swings in the price of silver, Nanking planned to go off the silver standard and make government-issued notes the legal tender, or fa-pi, of the nation. But, on closer scrutiny, it is evident that Kung was merely trading silver, which he could not control, for paper, which he could control simply by speeding up the printing press. By decree on November 3, 1935, all silver held by banks or individuals was to be exchanged within three months. Four banks were empowered to issue the new paper currency. They were the Central Bank of China, the Bank of China, the Bank of Communications, and the Farmers Bank of China.

The procedure was to be supervised by the Currency Reserve Board, which would guarantee silver reserves as a hedge against the anticipated inflation. While a number of respected bankers were on the Currency Reserve Board, so were H. H. Kung, T. V. Soong, T. L. Soong, and the distinguished philanthropist and humanitarian Big-eared Tu.

When H. H. next found his treasury pressed by deficits, the opportunity to abuse the new currency was too great a temptation. Between November 1935 and June 1937 the total circulation of fa-pi shot up from $453 million Chinese to $1,477 million, and only about half of this was backed by the silver exchanged for the paper currency. The rest, over $500 million, was simply worthless paper manufactured by the government to pay its debts. Exact figures for the years after fiscal 1935 are unknown since that was the last year the Nanking regime published a budget or reported its expenditures. Kung was certainly not exclusively to blame for the amazing inflation that followed, but his printing-press approach to the economy was certainly a major factor.

It was obvious that government officials, particularly those highest in government, made a personal killing off Kung's economic policies and currency manipulations. The banks of China were now being run by one big (if not happy) family.

Chapter 14

THE HIGH PRIEST

Big-eared Tu was now respectable, the director of many banks, companies, and exchanges, including the Bank of China. He was everywhere. It was no great surprise that Tu's own Chung Wai Bank in the French Concession was one of the few private banks that enjoyed steady profits after 1935.

However, as economist Parks Coble pointed out,

> despite his prominence in "legitimate" business circles, Tu remained a ruthless, underworld chieftain as well. Even H. H. Kung, who had significant business contact with Tu, was wary of his power. At the time of the fa-pi reform, Kung had included Tu on the Currency Reserve Board. The British advisor Sir Frederick Leith-Ross objected to this appointment because of Tu's notorious reputation. Kung acknowledged the problem but candidly told Leith-Ross that Tu was "undoubtedly a speculator; he was also leader of the gangsters, but," Kung noted, "a hundred thousand men in Shanghai obeyed his orders; he could create a disturbance at any moment."

This discreet financial discussion between H. H. and Leith-Ross was taking place at the Kung mansion, with Ai-ling present simply because she was the lady of the manor. (This apparently was standard operating procedure for the Kungs, because it enabled Ai-ling to capitalize on what she overheard.) As the two men dickered over various potential silver reform measures, Ai-ling began to insinuate her "suggestions." Leith-Ross began to realize that he was being manipulated. Becoming incensed, he broke off the discussion and stalked out of the Kung mansion. What happened next was related in his memoirs.

From what she had heard in the conversation, Ai-ling gave Tu the inside word on an upcoming government policy shift with regard to foreign-exchange transactions. Tu misunderstood what she told him. He invested improperly, was caught short, and lost 50,000 pounds sterling—equivalent then to $250,000 U.S. Unwilling to absorb the loss, he complained to Kung and suggested that the Central Bank make good his losses. Kung refused. "That evening," recounts Leith-Ross, "a No. 1 style coffin was deposited on Dr. Kung's doorstep by half a dozen funeral attendants." The following day, Kung called a hasty meeting of the Central Bank board, which agreed to reimburse fully a "patriotic citizen" who had recently suffered losses in the foreign-exchange market.

Leith-Ross stumbled upon another financial curiosity while he was overseeing the shift from silver to paper currency. It involved the Farmers Bank, which had been established in April 1933. This bank was closely linked to, if not personally controlled by, Generalissimo Chiang Kai-shek for his private use. It was known colloquially as "The (Opium) Farmers Bank." The Farmers Bank was a conduit for opium and heroin revenues, which were under Chiang's direct control as head of the Military Affairs Commission. The bank issued its own notes whenever Chiang found himself short of funds. Its reserves were free of any kind of audit and Chiang flew into a rage when Leith-Ross requested that this bank comply with an audit before it was authorized to issue the new government fa-pi. The Farmers Bank was not required to open its books.

Chiang Kai-shek always seemed to squeak by financially despite Kung's horrific economic blunders and strangulation of the Chinese economy. This was because Chiang, although personally uninterested in economics, had a source of giant revenues that guaranteed him great amounts of secure foreign currency. The source of Chiang's comfort was narcotics. Keeping in mind that Green Gang domination of the Chinese underworld originated in its virtual monopoly of opium traffic, that Shanghai itself had been founded on a great brown swamp of opium tar, and that the only exportable resource for some provinces like Yunnan was opium, it can come as no surprise that Nanking was quietly paying many of its bills with narcotics revenues.

The opium trade, which had been inflicted on China by the British, had fallen into the hands of the Chinese underworld after the turn of the century, when Britain withdrew from the trade in a moralistic turnabout. During the warlord era that followed, opium was also the main source of revenue for the military rulers who controlled China province by province; taxes on its cultivation and transportation, opium dens and paraphernalia provided the sums to meet both military and civilian needs of these pocket dictatorships. Sun Yat-sen had taxed Canton opium dens to raise revenues for his hard-pressed treasury, and Chiang Kai-shek saw opium in much the same practical light—only on a grander scale.

If Chiang's regime could control China's entire illicit opium trade, it would provide a vast source of sustaining revenue for his armies. There was nothing original in the idea. This was precisely the same reasoning that Big-eared Tu gave to Pockmarked Huang two decades earlier, leading to the amalgamation of all the Yangtze Valley triads into an opium cartel dominated by the Green Gang. Chiang simply wanted to "elevate" this principle to national policy. In 1927, before T. V. Soong agreed to join the Nanking regime, the Finance Ministry had started to organize an official opium monopoly to raise revenues within areas occupied by Chiang's armies. All was well until the National Anti-Opium Bureau (as it was facetiously called) tried to extend the official monopoly into Big-eared Tu's home provinces of Chekiang and Kiangsu. Foolishly, the overeager bureaucrats had blundered into the territory of the Da Gong Si, the company set up by Big-eared Tu to handle opium sales in the sprawling region around Shanghai. In record time, Nanking suddenly canceled its official opium program and dismantled the government monopoly. Tu's syndicate was left undisturbed in its control over the transport and marketing of all opium in the Yangtze basin.

It was not just Tu's murderous presence, and his bloodcurdling influence, that made Chiang back away from the opium-control issue at that point. There was a serious outcry by Chinese intellectuals and Westerners alike on the widespread use of the narcotic in China. By 1928, opium had penetrated into every aspect of Chinese life. The Kweichow Chamber of Commerce even adopted the drug as the official standard of exchange. In Yunnan, one of many major growing areas, where poppies in various combinations of red, white, and mauve blanketed the hillsides, 90 percent of adult males smoked, and many new-born infants were addicts, having acquired their dependency in the wombs of addicted mothers.

In response to international protest, on August 20, 1928—one year after blundering into Tu's personal poppy territory and having to close down the Anti-Opium Bureau—Chiang organized a new National Opium Suppression Committee as a public-relations charade under the Ministry of Public Health. Its announced purpose was to eliminate opium addiction in China. With suspicious boldness, the Generalissimo announced that "The National government will not attempt to get one cent from the opium tax. It would not be worthy of your confidence if it should be found to make an opium tax one of its chief sources of income." During the following year, 1929, Nanking was able to raise (from three provinces alone) some $17 million Chinese in what was grandly called "opium prohibition revenue." Compared to revenues from the salt tax, the potential proceeds from opium were mind-boggling.

To minimize confrontations between the Green Gang and Nanking, there had to be careful liaison between their opium field personnel. Nanking sanctioned the close cooperation of its navy and police forces with the Green Gang. Demand even then outstripped domestic supply. Shanghai police reports indicate that in 1930 T. V. Soong personally arranged with Tu to deliver 700 cases of Persian opium to Shanghai under KMT military protection to supplement depleted Chinese stocks. All parties involved in setting up the shipment and protecting it during transit—including T. V.—received fees.

Time Magazine carried a breezy little squib in April 1931 about T. V.'s plans for opium and the Nanking treasury:

> Finance Minister T. V. Soong cheerfully declared last week that China will soon have "a new and realistic opium policy." . . . a "realistic" opium policy, according to Minister Soong, cannot be one of prohibition. Consequently Chinese Treasury officials have been sent to Formosa to study Japan's opium system: restricted sales under government monopoly. If shrewd Minister Soong does harness opium to his Treasury chariot, he may find a way to balance the Chinese budget for some time to come.

Because of the complexity of trying to divide the sources, growing areas, transportation, processing responsibilities, and so forth, the only sensible solution was to split the overall take with Tu. Accordingly, the Generalissimo had a long meeting with Tu in which he began by appointing the gang boss as Chief Communist Suppression Agent for Shanghai, which gave Tu an official sanction to spill all the blood he wanted legally. This was something Tu needed very badly because he was in the midst of a campaign to clean up his public image. Chiang cut a deal with Tu to team up on opium. The Green Gang would be given full government protection for all shipments and all processing factory operations. The gang would also have veto power over the selection of government monopoly officials, and would take a lion's share of the proceeds. In return, the gang agreed to pay Nanking $6 million Chinese as a down payment on the government's anticipated share of the next take.

Apparently even Tu Yueh-sheng could make a mistake. For, after he paid the $6 million to T. V. and went home to Shanghai, he talked the deal over with Pockmarked Huang and abruptly changed his mind. He demanded the money back. Unwisely, T. V. then tried to pull a fast one. He sent Tu the money in government bonds instead of cash. From Tu's viewpoint, knowing the government as intimately as he did, the bonds were worthless. He wasted no time in reminding the Harvard economist of the depth of his folly.

"BULLETS MISS SOONG" was the headline in the *New York Times* on the 23rd of July, 1931. The *Times* printed T. V.'s own account of the assassination attempt.

> I was coming out of the station and was about fifteen feet from the exit when firing broke out simultaneously on both sides of me. Realizing I was the target, I threw away my white sun helmet, which was conspicuous in the gloomy station, ran into the crowd and dodged behind a pillar.
>
> Soon the station was filled with smoke from the revolvers of the attackers, and there was confused firing from all sides, to which my guards replied.
>
> It was fully five minutes before the station was cleared. At least four would-be assassins were seen by my guards to be firing, but there may have been more. When the smoke cleared my secretary, who had been walking by my side, was found shot in the stomach, hip and arm. Bullets had entered his body from both sides. His hat and document case were riddled, and it was a miracle that I was unscathed, as I towered above him.

Doubtless the assassins could have hit T. V. if they had wanted, because all their "stray" bullets were neatly placed into his secretary, killing him. But they apparently had instructions only to scare T. V. out of his wits. Now T. V. had no illusions of any special immunity if he tried to cheat Tu.

One of the richest opium-producing areas was in North China, and when Japan overran these territories in the early 1930s, Chiang took a heavy loss financially. The problem was twofold: he lost revenues from his share in the opium trade in that area, and the Japanese were running a very profitable international heroin trade using the raw opium from the conquered Chinese territory.

Chiang solved the problem by making it illegal for Chinese to use the refined drugs morphine and heroin, and then concluded a trade treaty with Japan to purchase opium from them. As illogical as this may sound, Chiang preferred to pay the Japanese a basic price for raw opium from North China rather than to forfeit all the revenues he could make from it. Otherwise Japan would smuggle it into KMT-controlled China anyway.

By the early 1930s, opium was taking a back seat to its more powerful products, morphine and heroin. The evolution was gradual. Morphine had been widely used by Western missionaries in the late 1800s to cure Chinese opium addicts; so in China the drug became known as "Jesus opium." Then heroin, first derived from opium in 1874 by chemists at Bayer pharmaceuticals in Germany, and launched by Bayer as a patent medicine in 1898, showed promise as a treatment for morphine addicts. Chinese first became opium addicts, then graduated to morphine, then to heroin. By 1924, China was importing enough heroin from Japan each year to provide four strong doses of the drug to every one of the nation's 400 million inhabitants. In that same year, however, the U.S. Congress, which had only recently banned alcohol, banned heroin as a patent medicine. Immediately, American mobsters who were doing a thriving trade in bootlegging, plunged into the heroin trade. While European criminal syndicates drew their supplies of opium from the poppy fields of Persia and the so-called Golden Crescent, American mobs found it easier and cheaper to buy from China.

In 1931, the League of Nations established international quotas for the production of heroin designed to reduce the supply to strictly medicinal needs. The same year, Big-eared Tu held a great celebration in his own honor, to inaugurate an ancestral temple in his native village of Kaochiao in Pootung, across the river from Shanghai. Acrobats and operatic troupes performed. Fireworks exploded for hours on end. Eighty thousand people turned out for the celebration, thousands of them government officials and national dignitaries invited personally by Tu. He gave them over half a million Chinese dollars' worth of gifts as tokens of the occasion. They reciprocated with equal extravagance. A few, including Generalissimo Chiang Kai-shek, gave Tu scrolls on which they had personally brushed flowing Chinese calligraphy, eulogizing him for his great services to humanity. The pageant went on for three days. After everyone went home, the ancestral temple Tu had built became his largest clandestine morphine and heroin factory.

The Chinese were blessed by a constant supply of the very finest heroin, thanks to Tu Yueh-sheng. It was customary in the streets of any Chinese city simply to buy and swallow pills of relatively pure heroin, or sometimes to smoke it in pipes in the form of pink tablets. In America it was necessary to inject heroin directly into the veins because the drug, by then, was so ruinously diluted by dealers in order to increase their profit margin; it was impossible to get an effect from the drug any other way. Big-eared Tu used heroin tablets to cure his own opium and morphine addiction, something he bragged about, but in doing so became a heroin junky for the rest of his life.

By the mid-1930s the Right Honorable Tu Yueh-sheng was lauded in Shanghai's *Who's Who* in glowing terms:

> At present most influential resident, French Concession, Shanghai. Well-known public welfare worker . . . councillor, French Municipal Council. President, Chung Wai Bank, and Tung Wai Bank, Shanghai. Founder and Chairman, board of directors, Cheng Shih Middle School. President, Shanghai Emergency Hospital. Member, supervisory committee, General Chamber of Commerce. Managing director, Hua Feng Paper Mill, Hangchow. Director, Commercial Bank of China, Kiangsu and Chekiang Bank, Great China University, Chinese Cotton Goods Exchange, and China Merchants Steam Navigation Co., Shanghai, etc. President, Jen Chi Hospital, Ningpo.

Here was a fine collection of titles and honors. They had accumulated with amazing speed after Chiang Kai-shek took over the KMT and became China's Generalissimo. Immediately following the Shanghai Massacre, Chiang had made Big-eared Tu, Pockmarked Huang, and the third member of that Green Gang troika, Chang Hsiao-lin, "Honorary Advisors" with the rank of Major General in the KMT army.

Tu's dealings with the civil authorities of the French Concession were straightforward. Much of Tu's heroin went out to metropolitan France through official channels. Since the French Concession in

Shanghai was administered by Hanoi rather than directly by Paris, this created a web of intrigue leading from Shanghai to Hanoi and Saigon, and thence to the Marseilles underworld dominated by Corsicans of the powerful criminal syndicate, the Union Corse. In France there were rivalries between the security services and politicians of Paris, and the Corsican mobsters. Big-eared Tu played off these rivals. The French Concession's police captain Étienne Fiori and Consul-General Koechlin became deeply beholden to Huang and Tu. Fiori was a Corsican and a key figure in the Chinese drug operations of the Union Corse. Tu paid large sums of narcotics profits into French government pockets in Paris to block periodic efforts in the General Assembly to investigate the scandalous situation in Shanghai.

Trouble came in 1933, however, when a new French administration took office in Paris and dispatched an admiral to Shanghai to purge the concession of corruption. Under the guns of French navy units, a new police chief was appointed, many Green Gang "detectives" were fired, and Consul-General Koechlin was replaced—after first being obliged to "remove" Tu's name from the Municipal Council. To correct this situation, Tu sent new bribes to Paris, carried by a flying squad of dapper "diplomats." Such an august personage as Madame Wellington Koo, wife of the diplomat who had represented China at the Versailles peace talks, joined in appealing to the French government to allow free passage of Tu's opium shipments.

It was transparent to Tu that Fiori and Koechlin had betrayed him in order to save what was left of their own political skins. They were now ready to sail for France to spend the rest of their days in luxury on the Riviera. Before their Messageries Maritimes liner sailed from the Yangtze, Tu invited them to a farewell banquet at his home. The dishes were poisoned. Consul-General Koechlin died in agony, along with several other guests, and the Corsican Fiori only barely survived after being violently ill for weeks.

The poisonings sent such a shock through the French colonial administration that the new Consul-General, Meyrier, immediately volunteered to provide police escort for all of Big-eared Tu's narcotics shipments thereafter. Apparently as a gesture to Meyrier, Tu's operations never again became as blatant in the French Concession as they had been. But there was no need for him to depend on the cooperation of the French when Tu now had carte blanche through Chiang Kai-shek to operate openly throughout KMT-controlled China.

From time to time, Tu Yueh-sheng would remind Nanking that he could be very generous. Between 1932 and 1934, while T. V. Soong and H. H. Kung bailed furiously to keep the ship of state afloat, the Nanking government was able to make purchases totaling an impressive $5 million U.S. from the United States. Foreign observers with knowledge of the precarious state of Nanking's treasury were knocked flat. As Willys Peck, head of the American legation in Nanking commented in 1936:

> I was somewhat "floored" by [Pan American Airways official] Mr. Bixby's information that within the last three weeks Dr. Kung had signed orders with the Curtis Wright Company for 120 military air planes. It is possible that I have overlooked information reaching this office reporting this important transaction. Not only did Mr. Bixby assert that there is no doubt about the matter, but since my conversation with him I have obtained partial confirmation from a person close to Dr. Kung, who has told me that two weeks ago a contract for the first eighty Curtis Wright planes, of two varieties costing about $20,000 U.S. currency per plane, was ready for signing. . . .
>
> How Dr. Kung has managed to finance it seems a mystery, for the price must amount to roughly $8,000,000 in Chinese currency. . . . We have seen reports from Shanghai that General Chiang is straining every effort to further his preparations to put China in condition for military resistance to all forms of foreign aggression, but this caps the climax.

The source of this financial help was Tu Yueh-sheng, who personally spent millions of dollars to purchase American airplanes one after another, and once outdid himself and donated a whole squadron to the government. For Chiang Kai-shek's fiftieth birthday in 1936 (when he was that age by Chinese reckoning), Tu proudly presented him with an airplane emblazoned with the name "OPIUM SUPPRESSION OF SHANG-HAI." This prompted wags at the Long Bar to observe, "a way at last has been found to get Opium Suppression off the ground."

But to some Westerners it still came as a shock to find his eminence Tu Yueh-sheng thriving openly in the Shanghai of 1934. Ilona Ralf Sues, a Polish-born member of a Geneva-based private organization called the Anti-Opium Information Bureau, which worked with the League of Nations, was not content dealing with paper facts and penciled figures at a distance in Switzerland. She decided to see for herself if Shanghai's opium-suppression campaign was on the up and up. With remarkable audacity, she obtained a rare interview with Big-eared Tu, so rare in fact that it appears to have been the only one he ever gave to an Occidental. Her account of that meeting was published in 1944 in a journal of her China adventure, *Shark Fins and Millet.* Perhaps because it was published during the war, the book attracted little attention. It remains a gem:

> He is by far the most powerful man in China, and the government itself had to count with this power. . . . Tu was a combination of Al Capone and Rockefeller. . . . Tu financed opium production in China, imported Iranian opium by the shipload, financed narcotics manufacture, and had a rake-off from practically every dope transaction in the country. In addition, he was the Chinese partner to the powerful international drug ring which had begun to extend its activities to the Pacific Coast of Canada, the United States and Latin America.

Even though she had heard tales of Tu's enormous power in Shanghai, particularly in the French Concession, where she was staying, she had a difficult time believing that he even had censors in the postal union reading all outgoing mail. Friends advised her that the only way to convey uncensored messages to Geneva would be by posting them personally on a departing steamer. To test the system, Sues wrote two letters—both highly critical of Tu, attacking him for being the chief dope dealer in China while simultaneously occupying the position of chief of opium suppression. Sure enough, the letters were intercepted and Sues received an invitation to interview the great man himself about his fine civic activities in Shanghai.

In return for this interview, Sues would be obliged to write an article for international distribution lauding Shanghai's most benevolent gangster. With her to the interview went her companion Aimee Millican, a gentle soul who frequently prayed that Tu Yueh-sheng "might see the light someday and become a power for God." They were escorted by a clean-cut young man named Wang Kwei-son, "a young social worker to whom Tu Yueh-sheng had entrusted his model rural center and eight orphanages." It was stipulated that Sues ask only three predetermined questions and that she avoid the issue of opium altogether.

Miss Sues, Aimee, and Kwei-son were taken to 143 Avenue Edward VII in the French Concession, a small, elegant red brick building with gold lettering above the entrance: THE CHUNG WAI BANK. They were taken up to the second floor in an elevator that seemed armor-plated.

The elevator operator, a powerfully-built thug, pressed a hidden button. A pale green wall slid apart, unveiling what Sues described as "two of the toughest guys I had ever laid eyes on—huge fellows with bulging pockets, bulging muscles and fierce, brutal faces—and the one on our left who bent over to inspect us was one eye short." The situation was so grotesque that, after being petrified all morning, Sues suddenly felt like bursting out laughing, until she saw that her companions were pale with terror.

They were led into a big reception hall furnished like a hotel lobby with armchairs, potted palms, and nests of tables. A group of well-tailored Chinese businessmen sat talking in one corner. The twelve other men standing around the room were obviously gunmen, bodyguards.

One of the men present stiffened, his eyes fixed on a door behind Sues, and announced respectfully, "Mr. Tu Yueh-sheng."

> I turned, and we all watched the man approach ... a gaunt, shoulderless figure with long, aimlessly swinging arms, clad in a soiled, spotted blue gown; flat feet shod in untidy old slippers; a long, egg-shaped head, short-cropped hair, receding forehead, no chin, huge, batlike ears, cold, cruel lips uncovering big yellow decayed teeth, the sickly complexion of an addict. ... He came shuffling along, listlessly turning his head right and left to look whether anyone was following him.
>
> We were presented. I had never seen such eyes before. Eyes so dark that they seemed to have no pupils, blurred and dull—dead, impenetrable eyes. ... I shuddered.
>
> He gave me his limp, cold hand. A huge, bony hand with two-inches-long, brown, opium-stained claws.
>
> Mr. Tu assured us of his pleasure in our visit. I said the pleasure was entirely on our side. Then we sat down.

Worried that she had only fifteen minutes with Tu, Sues went boldly to the point, while Kwei-son acted as interpreter. Although she said there were many questions she wanted to ask about China's reconstruction problem, in which Mr. Tu was playing so significant a part, there was another matter of pressing importance. As Mr. Tu was fully aware, she had worked seven years with the Anti-Opium Information Bureau in Geneva and could not resist the temptation of asking his authoritative opinion on the opium situation in China.

Tu frowned for a fraction of a second, looked at each of them in turn, as if disbelieving his own ears. With complete composure, he replied that he was not an authority but a mere government servant on Generalissimo Chiang's Opium Suppression Committee. The Generalissimo was the sole authority as Inspector General. Tu summarized the official line: that a properly run monopoly, with every addict registered and rationed, and opium sold only to holders of government opium certificates, afforded the best means of control. The Indian opium monopoly gave ample proof that opium trade could be fully regulated, to the best interest of the state.

"India," Sues retorted, "is ruled by white men who consider themselves superior to every other race and sell the drug exclusively to natives and to local Chinese. No white man can be registered as a smoker! From their point of view, they are selling poison to an inferior race." In China, on the other hand, she said, the monopoly was under Chinese officials and meant the legalized poisoning of China's own nationals! No parallel could be drawn with India. Furthermore, India ran her monopoly like a straightforward excise bureau, yielding up to 23 percent of the nation's annual gross revenues, and there was no pretense of running it for only a short period. In China, Chiang had promised to set a time limit. But, if revenues were big, what assurance was there that the opium monopoly would not be extended indefinitely? One of the four Chinese banks empowered to print and distribute currency, she said—the Farmers Bank—was guaranteed only by opium revenues and Chiang Kai-shek's word. How could such things be taken on trust?

Tu's eyes searched hers with curiosity. He was obviously surprised and amused that she spoke so freely of a fact that the Nanking regime tried to hide. He asked her if this, too, had been discussed in Geneva. She replied that the information about the funding and management of the Farmers Bank did not seem to have leaked out abroad.

Tu then launched into a defense of the Generalissimo. Chiang, he said, had earnestly tried to eradicate poppy production by military force, but had met with armed resistance from the "poor peasants," who defended their precious crop "for fear of starvation." Chiang finally was "persuaded" that gradual reduction under an opium monopoly was the only solution. There was no doubt, insisted Big-eared Tu, that Chiang's intentions were sincere.

"I said I was sure Mr. Tu would agree with me that no poor peasant earned money enough in his lifetime to buy a machine gun. To my knowledge, the armed clashes had occurred at the outskirts of huge estates owned by wealthy landowners who had armed and trained their own farmhands."

Tu had merely been revealing how he had bullied Chiang Kai-shek into sharing the opium monopoly with the Green Gang. Such a revelation was extraordinary for Tu to make, even inadvertently. The fact is, Tu was not accustomed to being interviewed by anyone, much less a shrewd and well-informed young European woman. Normally, he was shielded from contact with investigators of any kind, and he would ordinarily never have responded to cross-examination. He was in this clumsy and unaccustomed position only because of his late craving to clean up his public image.

Realizing that she had him at a disadvantage, Sues rushed on. The Chinese opium monopoly, she assured him in a flattering but double-edged way, was better organized than any government institution, probably because it was financed and marketed by Shanghai's most efficient big businessmen—bankers and opium merchants.

> I had a great admiration for the Opium Merchants' Association, but I only wished they would concentrate upon organizing China's export trade of silk, tea, tin, tungsten, tung-oil, in the same efficient manner. It would be more patriotic. I was very sceptical of their co-operation in Chiang's Opium Suppression project, and Chiang was certainly not equipped financially and militarily to force their hands.

Big-eared Tu paused to drink his tea out of the spout of a small golden teapot. The cover was kept tight by a little golden chain, and the spout was so narrow and curved that nothing could be inserted into it from without. It flashed through Sues's mind that he was afraid of being poisoned.

> I . . . described to him how the whole of Geneva was in uproar when Generalissimo had appointed the Opium Tsar head of the Shanghai Suppression Bureau! A fleeting smile made Tu's face quite human. He himself must have considered the appointment a huge joke.
>
> There were pessimists, I continued, who maintained that Chiang's whole Opium Suppression was nothing but window dressing. Geneva experts had plucked his first financial statement to pieces. They had multiplied the number of addicts by the quantity of their daily opium ration, then by the price per ounce, and proved it in black on white that China's opium revenue must have been five times the amount alleged.

The accusation was unjust, retorted Tu. Chiang had told the truth. He got only $20 million Chinese. He did not handle or control operations. It was the opium merchants themselves who handled production, purchasing, and pooling of stocks, transportation, refining, packing, distribution—the business end. They collected the gross revenue and assessed a percentage, which they considered appropriate, for Chiang's Opium Suppression Inspectorate.

Here was the rest of the secret picture confirmed by the horse's mouth. Again Sues was stunned by the oblique admission. She hid her astonishment and hurried on. She told Tu she was more concerned about morphine and heroin than about opium. The Japanese, having taken control of poppy-growing regions in Manchuria, were free to subvert China by flooding it with morphine and heroin. And in the foreign concessions, where the Chinese government had no jurisdiction, both Chinese merchants and foreigners could conduct their illicit trade in the white drugs with impunity. One consequence of Chiang's opium-suppression campaign was that, when it deprived some opium smokers of their ration, it drove them to the more expensive morphine and heroin. She stopped short of suggesting that this was one of Chiang and Tu's ulterior motives.

Warming to this opportunity to shift the blame to the Japanese, Tu agreed that Japan's dope traffic was formidable and had spread its tentacles far inside China. It was true that opium was far less harmful. He said a gigantic smuggling campaign was being waged by Japan against China. Trains and shiploads of contraband goods of every description were entering under heavily armed military escort, without paying customs duties, swamping Chinese markets.

I said I had seen the last two seizures at the Custom House. Could Mr. Tu enlighten me as to what happened to such seizures? I turned my head to see his face, and met his eyes ablaze with anger. I had drawn blood. The dead eyes had come to life—they were intelligent, passionate, cruel. A thrilling sensation to look into them . . . beginning of a duel. I did not flinch. The eyes dulled down again, as he turned to Kwei-son [the interpreter] with the government's line: that seized narcotics were burned under official supervision in public places. He was astonished that I had not seen the many photographs of such destruction, which had received wide publicity in the world press.

"That was past history," Sues protested. According to the latest regulations, Shanghai seizures were turned over to the local Opium Suppression Committee under Tu himself. How did he dispose of them?

Tu said he shipped them to Nanking, where they were destroyed by the National Government.

This might pacify the League of Nations, Sues conceded, but Mr. Tu knew perfectly well that it was not true. Every grain of heroin seized and turned over to Tu went back into the illicit traffic.

"And this," she snapped, "is by a damn sight worse than the opium monopoly."

Tu smashed a clenched fist down on the table. Their tea cups clattered. All around the big room, bodyguards craned their necks from behind their potted palms.

"I protest," he bellowed. "That is a lie! Everything is being destroyed except a small part, which the Government keeps for emergency stocks."

"Emergency stocks!" Sues exclaimed. "If there's a war there won't be a grain of morphine available for the wounded."

Before Big-eared Tu could explode again, Sues was told that her time was up. The interview was over. As everyone made polite noises and rose from the chairs, Sues "apologized" to Big-eared Tu for talking so much about opium, and proposed that she return another time to discuss his civic activities. Walking them to the elevator door, Tu chatted pleasantly and promised to consider her request.

At the time, very few people were aware that Big-eared Tu had shifted much of his energies over to heroin production. Hence the public clamor over Japan's massive heroin trade inside China. Sues herself spoke of the "Japanese who were free to flood the country with . . . heroin." Throughout Chiang's administration, the official government line was to blame those who smuggled the white drugs into China, not those in China who controlled most opium production and were using a larger and larger portion of it each year to produce heroin. The Japanese heroin traffic was big, but the Chinese heroin traffic was bigger, and getting much bigger still as it moved into American and European markets. Madame Chiang Kai-shek gave this stilted official version of the Chinese drug problem in a speech in September, 1937.

> Just contemplate the terrible and loathsome efforts of the Japanese and their agents to drench a land with opium and narcotics with the primary object of so demoralizing the people that they would be physically unfit to defend their country, and mentally and morally so depraved that

they could easily be bought and bribed with drugs to act as spies when the time came in order that their craving might be satisfied.

The Japanese worked with diabolical cunning in this direction, and we find spies in various parts of the country doing the bidding of their drug-providing masters. . . .

If ever humanity was confronted with a horrible crime it now has one to contemplate, and when the so-called "free citizens" are assembled by the Japanese to parade in alleged support of their schemes, the world witnesses not a procession of men but a parade of drug-steeped unfortunates who know not what they are doing. But Geneva knows the tragically sordid story and so do the Governments of all countries.

Shanghai had always been the heart of the import-export trade for China and it was no less true of heroin than of silks or tea. As May-ling spoke, seven-eighths of the world's heroin supply was coming from China. In the late 1930s it became all too apparent even to the U.S. government that large amounts of heroin were being smuggled into America through diplomatic channels from China. One of the ways Tu kept track of his associates was to provide them with bodyguards, who served also as traveling companions on overseas trips. For many years, the person who filled this role with T. V. Soong was "Tommy" Tong (Tong Hai-ong). He became Soong's "bodyguard" and "chauffeur" and went along on T. V.'s foreign travels. As demonstrated by State Department archives, whenever Chinese government officials journeyed to the United States, the Chinese embassy in Washington prudently went through the exercise of writing a letter to the State Department, double-checking to make certain that "the usual diplomatic privileges" would be observed about not inspecting their baggage at customs. Tommy Tong supervised T. V.'s baggage handling personally. According to Bureau of Narcotics records, Tong was a major link to the U.S. heroin trade run by the crime syndicate of Charles "Lucky" Luciano. Chinese heroin smuggled into San Francisco came through Tong and the chiu chao leader in Shanghai's International Concession, Wong Sui. Tommy Tong was later appointed China's Chief of Customs for Shanghai, which gave him the best of all possible covers for narcotics smuggling. "Tong," reported one Treasury Department source at the time, "is acting as agent for Chiang Kai-shek in arranging for the preparation and shipment of the stuff into the United States."

Heroin also moved through the mails. N. S. Wong, the Director General of Chinese Posts, was one of Big-eared Tu's lieutenants. Wong met regularly with America's West Coast narcotics bosses individually, and in 1934 attended a summit meeting with all of them in San Francisco.

When American narcotics officials occasionally intercepted a shipment, they found that the five-ounce tins of heroin invariably carried the official stamps of the Chinese government's National Anti-Opium Bureau, which confirmed that the bureau was merely a cover for China's international heroin trade. The heroin problem finally became so severe in the United States that in the late 1930s a number of prominent Chinese officials were indicted. The Chinese consul general in San Francisco was spared conviction for diplomatic reasons, but the president of the Hip Sing Tong in New York was sent to prison when Treasury agents of the Bureau of Narcotics cracked his ring in 1937.

May-ling's gullibility about Japan's evil narcotics traffic can be measured by her judgment in 1936, when Big-eared Tu decided to follow Chiang's lead and become a Christian. May-ling was impressed. She found reason to take heart. Tu was so much a member of the Soong family that he took his "religious instruction" under Methodist ministers at the home of Ai-ling and H. H. Kung, attending regular prayer meetings and Bible classes at the mansion on the Route de Seiyes. When Big-eared Tu was ready to "take-up the cross," the baptism was performed at Charlie Soong's church. There is no record of lightning immediately striking the church, or of the baptismal water turning green, but May-ling is reported to have said earnestly a few weeks after the ceremony: "Tu Yueh-sheng is becoming a real Christian because ever since he was baptized there has been a marked decrease in kidnapping cases in Shanghai." Her observation evidently elicited dry witticisms throughout the French Concession.

Chapter 15

TOOTHLESS AT TIGER ROCK

Even Chinese who preferred dictatorship to the anarchy of the warlord era were now panicky at Japan's encroachments. When Chiang's supporters pressed him as they did periodically to make a dramatic gesture toward Japan, what they had in mind was not armed confrontation but appeasement. In 1935, the Generalissimo outdid himself when he offered to conclude a treaty of friendship with Tokyo, promising to force all Western interests out of China and to turn over to Japan all Western commercial rights and territorial concessions. Here was a stunning capitulation. The Japanese Foreign Ministry was agreeable, but the imperial army now was committed to military conquest and turned down Chiang's offer.

Chiang knew that Japan was about to attack. As far back as spring, 1931, his chief analyst of Japanese strategy, scholar Wang P'eng-sheng, had warned of Japan's plans to seize Manchuria—many months before the takeover took place. Chiang was not taken by surprise this time either. He was also not short of arms. H. H. Kung had made another trip to Germany to buy large quantities of weapons from the Krupp works, with the understanding that they would be used exclusively against Communists. In October 1936, China also became the largest buyer of American arms and aircraft for the second consecutive month.

As predicted, the Japanese seized Chahar Province, and proceeded to demand the withdrawal of all KMT troops and Blue Shirts from Hopei Province next door. When that demand was met, the Japanese immediately merged the five Chinese provinces of Hopei, Shantung,

Shansi, Chahar, and Suiyuan into an "autonomous" region under their control. Japan possessed all northeastern China to the outskirts of Peking, which sat like an island in a sea of Japanese armies.

Meanwhile, Mao Tse-tung's Communist forces reached Yenan at the end of the Long March, and began rallying anti-Japanese nationalists to their side. To many students, the authentic heroism of the Red Army combined with this blunt stand against Tokyo was a siren call. On December 9, 1935, ten thousand Peking students demonstrated against Japan. The protest drew nationwide attention, and Madame Sun Yat-sen emerged from seclusion in Shanghai to support the students by launching a National Salvation League.

Apprehensive of Japan, Moscow ordered the CCP to stop its anti-Chiang propaganda and seek a united front with the KMT. Mao resisted but was overruled, and reluctantly agreed to approach Chiang through the Young Marshal, Chang Hsueh-liang, who was now based with his army on the northwestern frontier.

The Young Marshal was an intelligent man in the midst of venal, single-minded warlords. After a playboy youth in Manchuria and Europe, he had become addicted to opium and the morphine derivative Pavernal. There were indications that his drugs might have been doctored to demoralize him, the sort of thing at which Chiang's secret police chief, Tai Li, was expert. After the death of his father, Old Marshal Chang Tso-lin, at the hands of Japanese assassins in 1928, the Young Marshal in a fit of patriotism had chosen to join Chiang Kai-shek. The Generalissimo prevented him from defending Manchuria, then saw that he was blamed by the Chinese public for the loss. Thereafter, the Generalissimo used him as a scapegoat for each Japanese advance. In disgrace, the Young Marshal resigned all his posts and sank into oblivion with Pavernal.

He was rescued by the indefatigable W. H. Donald, who persuaded him to take the cure in Europe, and went along to make certain that drug treatments were followed to the letter. When the Young Marshal returned to China in 1934 he was transformed. Gone were the narcotics, and in their place was a tough new nationalism. He decided that China's salvation lay in persuading Chiang to stand firm against Tokyo. He had long talks with T. V. Soong in Shanghai about how to engineer this, and T. V., who must have realized that a powerful military lever had fallen into his hands, burned the midnight oil with the dapper Manchurian general, exploring all possible maneuvers against Chiang, short of an outright coup. No quick solution seemed at hand.

Early in 1936, the Young Marshal quietly instructed his troops on the frontier to stop shooting at red guerrillas. He had reached the conclusion that most of China's Communists were driven into the arms of the CCP by the degradation of the country at the hands of Chiang and the foreign powers. Chinese, he decided, should no longer fight Chinese while the nation was being ravished by foreign invaders.

That June he met privately with Chou En-lai to see if they could put aside differences and develop a joint strategy. He came away with his conviction reaffirmed that the answer lay in a united front. He was good to his word. All military action halted, liaison was set up between their two headquarters, and bureaus of the National Salvation League were organized throughout northwestern China.

Word of this "treachery" reached Chiang Kai-shek at Nanking. But Tai Li's spies neglected to plumb the depth of what had transpired. They told the Generalissimo only that the northwestern command had become unreliable, at a time when his latest "Communist annihilation" was about to begin. Chiang decided to fly to the Young Marshal's headquarters at Sian, and bully him into line.

When the Generalissimo arrived, the Young Marshal told Chiang that his anti-red campaign should be scrapped and a united front formed with Mao Tse-tung. The time had come for a patriotic war, not a civil war. Chiang hotly rejected the argument and stormed off to his field headquarters at Loyang two hundred miles away. When the Young Marshal followed him to argue further, he was rebuked angrily.

On December 4, 1936, the Generalissimo returned to Sian to announce that he was going ahead with the annihilation campaign, to begin December 12. A new commander would lead the offensive, and the Young Marshal was to be transferred to South China with all his soldiers and his fellow conspirator, the northwestern territory strongman, General Yang Hu-cheng. The two generals tried to reason with Chiang, but the Generalissimo grew hysterical, slammed the door, and drove off with his bodyguard to the T'ang Dynasty hot springs resort by the Lishan Hills twelve miles north. This was the same spa, called Lin-t'ung, where Borodin had stopped to cool his heels while escaping to Russia overland in 1927.

The Young Marshal and local strongman Yang were now in deep jeopardy. If they did nothing, their cause was lost and they would be sent south and rendered impotent. It was Yang who came up with the solution. He had suggested it weeks earlier: "We can hold the emperor hostage," he said metaphorically in mandarin, "to demand submission of all the feudal princes in the realm."

The Generalissimo was in the habit of rising before dawn, leaving his full set of false teeth on the bedside table, and standing for an hour before the window in his nightshirt. The pavilion was protected by fifty bodyguards, headed by an officer who was a notorious student killer. At 5:30 in the morning of December 12—the day the new annihilation campaign was to begin—Chiang Kai-shek was staring out the back window of his bedroom at the mountain beyond the garden wall. In the darkness, four trucks loaded with 120 armed soldiers rumbled to a halt at the gates. The battalion commander in the lead truck demanded that the gates be opened. The sentries refused. The men in the trucks opened fire.

Chiang was startled by the shots. He wondered if there had been a mutiny inspired by the Communists. When the shooting intensified, followed by shouts and the sounds of forced entry, three aides burst into his room urging him to flee. Forgetting his dentures, Chiang hiked up his nightshirt and sprinted for the back door, followed by his aides. They boosted him too forcefully up the garden wall and he fell down the other side, twisting his spine and spraining his ankle. The hillside was rocky, sparsely covered with thorny scrub. There was no place to hide. Chiang scuttled up the slope, his feet pierced by thorns. His ankle could barely support him, and his back was causing him severe pain.

In the pavilion, the coup proceeded. One by one bodyguards were shot to death and rooms were searched for Chiang. When it was certain that he had fled, the hated student killer was dragged out, driven twelve miles to Sian, and crucified on the city gates.

There was no question that the Generalissimo must have fled up the hill. The mountain was completely surrounded. Twice the battalion spread out, and twice they failed to find him. Back in his room, they found his teeth, his diary, and some documents.

It was not until nearly four hours later, at 9 A.M., that a squad on the hillside discovered a shallow cave behind a boulder called Tiger Rock. Inside, Chiang was making himself as flat as possible against the rock. He was cold, exhausted, and in pain. A soldier hitched him up piggyback, and they all took turns carrying him down the hill. A car was waiting. They drove him to the new city hall, where strongman Yang had his headquarters. Incongruously, there was a full military band waiting in the courtyard, flanked by senior officers. The band struck up the KMT's "Frère Jacques" anthem and the officers saluted their captive as he hobbled out of the sedan, nightshirt flapping. The Young Marshal came forward and helped Chiang to a room, where the Generalissimo took to bed, while a doctor tended his injuries.

The coup was now complete. Troops of strongman Yang celebrated with three days' looting, which was halted by the execution of three soldiers.

It was outside Sian that problems arose. The most important objective was the taking of the airbase at Loyang—the Generalissimo's field headquarters two hundred miles to the east. The Young Marshal had telegraphed Loyang before 5 A.M. to issue instructions to his brigade commander there, but the brigadier balked and turned over the telegram to the Generalissimo's garrison commander, who clamped tight security on the airfield and alerted Nanking. This meant that the one airbase near enough to allow Nanking planes to bomb the rebels was still in Chiang's camp. This failure also permitted news of the coup to leak prematurely, enabling Chiang loyalists to counterattack and capture Tungkuan, which controlled the pass between Shensi and neighboring Shansi Province to the north.

In the west, the capital of Kansu Province was seized successfully by rebel supporters, protecting their rear. The Young Marshal then issued a circular telegram over the signatures of the rebel leaders, listing eight demands: reorganize the Nanking government to include all factions; stop the civil war; release all political prisoners; permit free demonstrations of patriotism; allow political gatherings to take place freely; carry out the will of Dr. Sun Yat-sen; and immediately summon a National Salvation Conference.

The Generalissimo had been completely unstrung by his experiences that morning. He refused to eat or to get out of bed. The Young Marshal offered to move Chiang to a more comfortable residence, but he refused to stir or speak. On December 14, when W. H. Donald (now working for Madame Chiang) arrived in Sian to mediate, Chiang agreed to shift to a private home. There, the Australian did not pull punches. The Generalissimo, he said, must realize that the Young Marshal was not a Benedict Arnold but a Patrick Henry. He must realize that there was a clique in his own Nanking regime that was obsessively pro-Japanese—referring to Defense Minister Ho's army clique. At this very moment, Donald said, Ho was determined to take advantage of the Sian incident to attack the city with troops, artillery, and bombers. Under the pretext of rescuing the Generalissimo, Ho's followers would cause his death and seize power for themselves and Japan. Already, Donald warned urgently, there were government forces moving on Sian.

In Shanghai, Madame Chiang fainted when told of her husband's kidnapping. According to *Time* Magazine: "Mme. Chiang, her brother T. V. Soong, who is the financial kingpin of China, and her brother-in-law, Dr. H. H. Kung, who took on the functions of Premier in China's awful emergency, held the destiny of Eastern Asia in their hands."

Indeed, Kung had stepped in as acting Premier during the crisis, but there was some doubt whose side he was on. Defense Minister Ho demanded a show of force with an immediate attack on Sian. Joining him in this demand was Tai Ch'i-tao and other members of the group who had brought Chiang to power in collaboration with the Green Gang. They now appeared ready to sacrifice the Generalissimo and take control themselves.

But they underestimated Madame Chiang. Racing to Nanking by train, May-ling Soong flew into a fury at Defense Minister Ho. First, she had to overcome the conviction that a woman could not be rational under such circumstances. Then she had to persuade the generals to delay their attack, which had already been set in motion. She later said she presented her case as follows:

> I am making this appeal to you, not as a woman thinking of the safety of her husband, but as a citizen taking a dispassionate and realistic attitude to secure the least costly solution to a grave national problem. . . . But what you are proposing today actually endangers the life of the Generalissimo, and since in the mind of the people, as well as in my own mind, the Generalissimo's safety is inseparable from the continued unity, and even existence, of the nation itself at this critical period of our history, no effort should be spared to secure his release by peaceful means.

It was at this delicate juncture that H. H. Kung demonstrated that nobody could be too certain of his loyalty at any given moment. In a national broadcast revealing plans to bomb Sian, he said tactlessly: "While we are all anxious that Generalissimo Chiang may be rescued . . . our attitude is that the personal safety of one man should not be allowed to interfere. . . . It gives one a pain in the heart that this extraordinary development should have taken place in Sian." How tragic to destroy ancient Sian, of all places.

The Generalissimo heard these words over the radio with a sinking heart. Donald had warned him of this. Chiang asked for one of his closest aides, and hurried him off by plane to Nanking with strong orders to halt the attack. H. H. Kung had just told the nation that it would not be halted. This placed the Soongs in an exquisite predicament—"a dilemma," as *Time* phrased it a few days later, "calling for the talents of Brother T. V. Soong." And going on: "Great Mr. Soong has been called 'the Morgan of China,' and it is stockbroker gossip in Shanghai that Brother Soong is not always on the best of terms with his little sister, Mme. Chiang. The Soong family tie binds them and it always will, but sometimes the bonds chafe."

There was speculation that the whole Sian incident might have been engineered by T. V. Soong in order to put his brother-in-law in a bind. Eleven KMT divisions were converging on Sian, and all the aircraft in the Nanking air force were at Loyang awaiting orders to proceed.

At Sian, Chiang stubbornly resisted the Eight Demands. "He refused to turn our guns against the enemy," the Young Marshal explained in a public address to a huge crowd in a Sian park on December 16, "but reserved them for use against our own people."

Other rebel chiefs, including strongman Yang, were now convinced that the only way to deal with Chiang Kai-shek was to shoot him. But the Young Marshal restrained them.

At Communist headquarters two hundred miles north, Mao Tse-tung heard the first news of Chiang's kidnapping with great excitement. "Since April 12, 1927 [the date of the Shanghai Massacre]," Mao told a meeting of three hundred comrades in his cave, "Chiang has owed us a blood debt as high as a mountain. Now is the time to liquidate the blood debt. Chiang must be brought to Pao-an for a public trial by the people of the whole country."

It was agreed that Chou En-lai would go to Sian to represent the CCP. But first they must await instructions from Moscow. Mao was not yet strong enough to do otherwise. When instructions from Moscow did come the next day, they ruled out anything but compromise. Chou En-lai was to arrange it. Stalin insisted on a united front. Chiang was to go free. Mao was overruled.

As to Japan, its position was correctly described to London in a diplomatic cable from Ambassador Clive in Tokyo:

JAPANESE ATTITUDE IS WAIT AND SEE, COMBINED WITH SCARCELY
DISGUISED FEELING OF SATISFACTION THAT THE WORLD MUST NOW
RECOGNIZE THAT CHINESE ARE HOPELESS, AS JAPANESE ALWAYS
KNEW.

Defense Minister Ho assured the Japanese ambassador in a meeting
that the punitive expedition to Sian would proceed according to plan.
Ho angrily ordered T. V. Soong to keep his nose out of the affair. But
T. V. replied coldly that he was a private citizen, not a soldier. Madame
Chiang quieted the argument by agreeing not to go with T. V. on this
trip if Ho stopped interfering.

Without further delay, T. V. boarded a chartered plane.

When Chiang looked up from his bed and saw T. V. enter his room,
he was so overwhelmed that he could not speak. T. V. handed him a
letter from Madame Chiang. It read: "If at the end of three days T. V.
does not return to Nanking, I must come to Sian to live or die with you."
The Generalissimo was overcome. He burst into tears. T. V. gestured
for the Young Marshal and Donald to leave them alone.

They talked in private for half an hour.

Among other things, Chiang told T. V. that his captors had changed
their attitude toward him since reading his captured diary, with its
assertions of intent to defend China against Japan eventually. Then he
repeated Donald's warning that the gravest threat was not from the
rebels but from the pro-Japan clique that was at this moment making
final preparations to blast Sian and Chiang with it.

That night, T. V. came back to Chiang's chamber with the Young
Marshal for some hard-nosed dickering. It was agreed that time was
running out, and that, if anything were to be salvaged, it would have
to be while T. V. was there. Afterward might be too late for all of them.

T. V. had brought one bit of cheering news. At his intercession, the
Nanking cliques had agreed to a three-day truce. But that was all the
time they would allow. Whatever else T. V. had in his briefcase to bring
pressure on his brother-in-law has never surfaced. But it took only
twenty-four hours—not three days—to get Chiang's grudging agreement to the most important rebel demands: a reorganization of the
regime to create a united front against Japan, and a suspension of the
civil war. Chiang insisted only that he must be released before his
agreement took effect.

Whether or not T. V. had conspired to get the Generalissimo into this crisis, he had certainly encouraged the Young Marshal to "do something." And the outcome was exactly what T. V. had been seeking for more than three years, since Chiang had slapped his face in 1933. But the clock was still ticking and other complex matters remained to be settled before the Generalissimo could be sprung. T. V. and Donald hurried back to Nanking. There, they picked up Madame Chiang and secret police chief Tai Li, and flew back to Sian.

The scene at Sian on their arrival that night was truly memorable, captured forever in the murky black-and-white exposures of a Chinese photographer. Their Fokker tri-motor, guy wires singing, rolled to a stop in the mud, and the weary passengers tumbled out into a circle of torches held high by Manchurian soldiers in sheepskin caps. Madame Chiang was bundled to her ears against the wind from Mongolia. T. V. had put on a lot of weight in recent years; it was difficult to tell where his chins ended and his scarf began. On his head sat a great black bearskin hat with ear flaps. His plump face was a mass of dimples like a rumpled grapefruit, decorated with a pursed mouth and two dark pips. Beside him, Donald was gray-haired, ashen-faced, and somber, eyes bloodshot and swimming in the wind. Behind them hovered the wary, well-dressed Tai Li, klieg lights on inside his head, his soft face handsome and highly intelligent, his hard eyes flicking over the rooftops looking for the hidden shapes of people like himself.

The last two figures out of the plane were Madame Chiang's maid and her cook. She never traveled without a cook, for there was always the danger of being poisoned. A few years earlier, the Young Marshal had been poisoned during a dinner at the Generalissimo's own table, barely surviving the episode, and there was no reason to take a chance that he might return the compliment in a repast at Sian.

Stepping out from behind the ring of torches, in a neatly pressed uniform, the Young Marshal greeted May-ling with a deep bow; long ago, he had been one of her more accomplished suitors. Now, he was her husband's kidnapper.

Escorted by the wool-hatted Manchurian soldiers, the group were driven through the city gates, where the student killer drooped on his nails. The procession rolled through back alleys to the bungalow where Chiang was detained. Entering the room where he waited, the others paused and turned their backs politely while Madame Chiang went to the Generalissimo and passed him something that was small enough to be hidden in his hand. Raising his hand to his face in a fumbling gesture, Chiang then turned to his guests and gave them a big, toothy grin—the first since he had fled eleven days earlier without his dentures. May-ling had brought his spares.

The next morning, December 23, Madame Chiang's cook brewed tea while the Generalissimo sat at a low table with T. V. Soong, W. H. Donald, May-ling, Tai Li, and the Young Marshal. For hours that day and the next and the next, warlords and delegations from warlords came and went. The biggest worry was local strongman Yang, and the commanders of adjacent areas who had supported the kidnapping coup. On Christmas Eve, the Young Marshal reported to May-ling that "Yang and his men are not willing to release the Generalissimo. They say that since T. V. and Madame are friendly toward me, my head would be safe, but what about theirs? They now blame me for getting them into this affair, and say that since none of our conditions are [irrevocably] granted they would be in a worse fix than ever if they now release the Generalissimo."

Even Yang might be persuaded by Chou En-lai. It was a matter of trade-offs. Tai Li agreed to release certain political prisoners, and sent out telegrams giving those instructions. Other secret guarantees of safety for Yang and his officers were met and secured. Substantial sums of money were moved between foreign bank accounts. Large quantities of Napoleon brandy were poured, and many cartons of British cigarettes were smoked from round tins of fifty placed on tables near porcelain spittoons. The rough shape of a new Cabinet was agreed. It was conceded that the Whampoa Clique and the C-C Clique were too pro-Japanese. It was agreed that Defense Minister Ho should be replaced by one of Chiang Kai-shek's best cadets, General Ch'en Ch'eng. It was argued that T. V. Soong should head the new Cabinet. The Generalissimo acceded in principle to all Eight Demands, though he refused to put it in writing, insisting on only a verbal promise in front of his wife and brother-in-law. He was in effect saying that those two were the last people on earth that he would ever betray, once having made a promise, but T. V. must have heard the oath with a bit of exasperation. (Very little of what Chiang promised ever was put into effect.)

One of those who entered the room was Chou En-lai. He was polished and urbane as the Young Marshal introduced him to Madame Chiang. Chou conferred with the Generalissimo for two hours on the

24th and the 25th, doing most of the talking. Because of their Whampoa association, he addressed Chiang as "Commandant." Chiang later described Chou during this encounter as "the most reasonable Communist" he knew, and on another occasion thanked Chou with deep emotion for "what you did for me." He referred to Chou's intercession with strongman Yang to gain the Generalissimo's release, convincing Yang he should take T. V.'s money and go abroad in exile. By this, Chou was instrumental in saving the life of the man who had launched the Shanghai Massacre. Apparently Chou accepted the premise of CCP policy that, if a united front against Japan was going to work, it had to involve the largest possible number of KMT right-wing factions, and this could be achieved only with Chiang's participation as figurehead.

Madame Chiang also was impressed with Chou's grasp of national issues. At one point he is said to have assured her that "apart from the Generalissimo there was no one capable of being the leader of the country at this period of [its] existence." Chou, ever the elastic Bolshevik, then added, "We do not say that the Generalissimo does not resist aggression, but we say that he does not resist definitely enough or sufficiently fast." Madame Chiang replied that all internal problems in the future must be solved by political means, not by force. "We are all Chinese," she assured him.

How much money changed hands at Sian was never revealed, and was not important. T. V. Soong was now the richest man in China, next to Big-eared Tu, with the Kungs and Chiangs in third and fourth places. Money was less important to them than perhaps it was to some of Chiang's captors.

At 3 P.M., the Generalissimo and his entourage left the bungalow freely, drove to the airport, and—taking the Young Marshal with them —roared off into the blustery sky. They were back in Nanking in time to celebrate the new year, 1937.

In the months that followed, Chiang's survival was interpreted by his admirers as a great victory for all the things that were good in life. Henry Luce announced in due course that the Generalissimo and Madame Chiang were the outstanding figures of 1937. He put them on the cover of *Time*'s first issue of 1938 as "Man and Wife of the Year." May-ling Soong Chiang now became an even bigger international celebrity. At Sian, according to American diplomat John Paton Davies, China's first lady had shown that she was "endowed with a temperament which in an earlier epoch would have propelled her to the Dragon Throne." It was not the sort of remark that got wide circulation in the Lucepress.

There is an epilogue to this extraordinary affair. By going back to Nanking with the Generalissimo, the Young Marshal was performing a drastically quixotic act. Cynics regarded him as a fool, but Mao conceded to Agnes Smedley that it was the only thing that made the deal work. Mao was scornful of the way the Generalissimo and Madame Chiang subsequently described the incident, making themselves look good by elaborately rewriting their accounts. He called their narrative "an interesting specimen" of ambiguity and evasiveness.

By surrendering himself to Nanking, the Young Marshal shifted attention away from Sian, helping to avert any residual clash, and by subjugating himself helped to restore the face Chiang had lost by being kidnapped.

The Young Marshal gallantly accepted all blame for the Sian Incident, allowing Chiang to wash his hands in public and wipe them on him. (Interestingly, he was put up at T. V. Soong's home in Nanking.) He had done China a historic service by bringing about the long-sought united front, whatever its later failings. In the course of the Sian Incident, he had become more intimately acquainted with Chiang than anyone else in China outside of the Soongs and Big-eared Tu. He had also become unusually close to T. V. and May-ling. But Chiang Kai-shek never forgave him for the humiliation, or for wrecking his dream of crushing the Communists. This event continued to haunt the Nationalists for decades, and they pointed to the Sian Incident as the beginning of the Communist victory. It also must have haunted Chiang that this young Manchurian general showed so many qualities of leadership that might displace him in time. So, instead of letting him go, Chiang placed the Young Marshal under house arrest and turned the key over to Tai Li.

In his Good Friday message to China that spring of 1937, Chiang referred to the Sian Incident and said piously, "Remembering that Christ enjoined us to forgive those who sin against us until seventy times seven and upon their repentance I felt that they should be allowed to start life anew."

Efforts by his friends, including T. V., to gain the Young Marshal's release failed. The Generalissimo kept his kidnapper under modified house arrest and close surveillance for the remainder of his life, in the

charge of his secret police, who followed the usual procedure of ac-
quainting the captive with heroin. Chang Hsueh-liang, we are told,
spent those decades studying the history of the Ming Dynasty.

The Young Marshal's co-conspirator, General Yang, despite the
Good Friday amnesty, was imprisoned when he came back from European exile and languished for eleven years in one of Tai Li's special
detention camps near Chungking. His wife went on a hunger strike in
protest and was allowed to starve herself to death.

Years later Ching-ling Soong summed up Chiang's kidnapping this
way: "What Chang Hsueh-liang did was right. I would have done the
same thing if I had been in his place. *Only I would have gone farther!*"

Innovative financier of the
revolution,   Harvard-educated T. V. Soong brought
Western genius to China's
chaotic economy and paid
Chiang's bills as dictator. In
the process, T. V. made himself, for a time, the richest
man on earth. *(National Archives)*

Masking their intense political rivalries, leaders of the revolutionary Right and Left pose before a train at the start of the Northern Expedition. From far left, the Russian agent Mikhail Borodin, a Chinese secretary, Borodin's wife Fanya, Madame Liao Chung-k'ai, the second Madame Chiang Kai-shek (apparently enceinte), Moscow's General Galen, Chiang Kai-shek himself, his son Wei-kuo, and Rightist Tai Ch'i-tao. Seated is Chiang's "evil genius," the crippled millionaire Chang Ching-chang. *(Asia Magazine)*

Rich, jovial Finance Minister H. H. Kung provided the levers of power manipulated by his intense, secretive wife Ai-ling Soong. Here they are seen with Generalissimo Chiang, whose marriage to younger sister May-ling they arranged. *(National Archives)*

Support for the Soong dynasty in America came from China-born Henry Luce, co-founder of *Time,* Inc., here with his celebrated wife Clare Boothe Luce. A child of missionaries, Luce had a romantic image of China that prevented him from acknowledging the dark side of the Chiang regime. *(Historical Picture Service, Chicago, Ill.)*

In a rare moment of conviviality, Generalissimo and Madame Chiang pose with General Joseph W. Stilwell, senior American military commander in the China-Burma-India Theater, who was one of Chiang's most astute and severe critics. Said Stilwell of Chiang, "He's a vacillating, tricky, undependable old scoundrel who never keeps his word." *(National Archives)*

Wowing the generals and the politicians in typical Soong style, T. V.'s wife Laura basks in the admiration of U.S. Air Corps General "Hap" Arnold and former Republican presidential candidate Wendell Willkie at a wartime New York rally for United China Relief. Meanwhile, millions of dollars in American aid to China went astray. *(National Archives)*

With Auntie May-ling, the Kung children Louis, Jeannette, and David pose for photographers during Madame Chiang's fabulous 1943 American tour. Louis (far left) became a Dallas oilman, while David, a New York tycoon, provided a Long Island sanctuary for the twilight seclusion of May-ling Soong. (*National Archives*)

A stellar climax for Madame Chiang's U.S. tour brought Jeannette Kung into the company of Claudette Colbert, Marlene Dietrich, and Mary Pickford. Miss Kung's attire prompted President Roosevelt to call her "my boy." *(National Archives)*

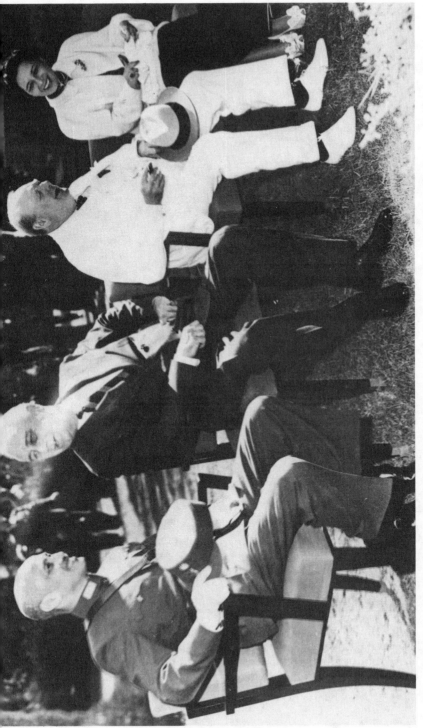

Most often reproduced of the famous Cairo Conference publicity photos, this staged picture made it seem that Churchill and May-ling were on good terms and that FDR and Chiang were swapping a private joke. In fact, Chiang spoke no English and Churchill had vigorously objected to the Chiangs' presence at the talks. *(National Archives)*

Ambassador Hurley approached China's problems with all the finesse of General Custer at the Little Bighorn. In contempt, Mao called him "that turtle egg" and Hurley returned the compliment twice over, calling Mao "moose dung" and "motherfucker." *(National Archives)*

Chapter 16

ON FAMILY BUSINESS

Claire Chennault arrived in China for the first time in May 1937, five
months after the Generalissimo had hidden behind Tiger Rock. He
came on a secret mission to find out for Madame Chiang why the
Chinese air force could not fly.

During the Sian Incident, a number of the Generalissimo's closest
associates in Nanking had conspired to bomb him into oblivion, so it was
unwise to leave the air force in their hands. Madame Chiang told her
husband that she would enjoy running it herself, and would see that it
was turned into an effective weapon against their enemies, rather than
merely serve as a political pawn. Chiang agreed and put her in charge.

One of her first acts was to hire a former U.S. air corps pilot, Roy
Holbrook, as her advisor. She asked Holbrook who could get the air
force into shape; Holbrook knew just the man.

Nobody was neutral about Claire Lee Chennault. He was either
hated or loved. He was a chronic failure who made his way through life
at top speed, leaning on his horn. His violent energy and overheated
opinions guaranteed him a place in history as a madman or a genius, it
was not certain which. As a young man, he was too belligerent to endure
the discipline of the U.S. Naval Academy, which he thought of entering,
too old for flight training when he enlisted in World War I, and too late
to be in the last air support units going to Europe. He spent the war
quelling rowdy black construction workers at Langley Field, Virginia,
and tending victims of the worldwide influenza epidemic.

When the war ended, he got his wings in the peacetime military and showed a flair for aerobatics and tactics. Becoming an air corps instructor, he pushed the wild idea that teams of small fighter planes could clear the sky of bombers. (The idea was not original; it had been practiced first by Baron Manfred von Richthofen with his Flying Circus in World War I.) The U.S. air corps was now dominated by "bomber generals" who did not appreciate Chennault's challenge. They believed heavy bombers were invincible. Chennault circulated a monograph telling how wrong they were. He demonstrated the point by showing how men with binoculars placed in watchtowers could telephone advance warning of bombers in time for large numbers of fighters to take to the air. Using aerobatic skills, the nimble fighters could then fall on the clumsy bombers and pick them off with teamwork.

"Who is this damned fellow Chennault?" asked one lieutenant colonel, whose name was "Hap" Arnold. Before long, Arnold became commander of the U.S. air corps, and the abrasive Chennault remained in official disfavor. He was no longer "useful" as an instructor, so he was assigned to lead a precision flying team. For three years he and his wing men made a name as the "Three Men on a Flying Trapeze." By 1937, Chennault was grounded with chronic bronchitis from smoking, low blood pressure, exhaustion, and a severe hearing loss caused by too many earsplitting power dives. He decided to look for a civilian job. The Soviet Union was searching for someone like him—a job that would have involved him with the Russian pilots flying in the Spanish Civil War. Chennault turned it down. Then came the offer from Madame Chiang.

Chennault was bowled over by Madame Chiang. He wrote in his diary, "She will always be a princess to me." He had been waiting all his life for a sponsor, and a chance to do everything his way. He remained in the service of the Chiangs for the rest of his life.

He did not like what he saw of the Chinese air force in 1937. It was more danger to itself than to an enemy. There were supposed to be five hundred airplanes; but fewer than a hundred could fly. Corruption was rife.

The Italian training program arranged by H. H. Kung made a deep impression on Chennault. With his usual lack of humor, he said the "Italians did all they could to sabotage China." He went on to note some specifics:

> The Italian flying school at Loyang . . . graduated every Chinese cadet who survived the training course . . . regardless of his ability. . . . However, the Generalissimo was pleased with the Italian method. Chinese aviation

cadets were carefully selected from the top social strata, and when they were washed out at the American-style Hanchow school, protests from their influential families caused the Generalissimo acute embarrassment. The Italian method solved this social problem and all but wrecked the air force. . . .

The Italian assembly plant at Nanchang was also a fraud. It turned out large quantities of a Fiat fighter that proved to be a firetrap in combat. The Savoia-Marchetti bombers were of such obsolete vintage that the Chinese could use them only as transport.

Italians were also responsible for encouraging some quaint practices by the Chinese Aero Commission. No plane was ever removed from the official roster for any cause. . . . As a result, when war came the Aero Commission roster listed five hundred planes but only ninety-one were fit for combat.

Two months after Chennault's arrival, in July 1937, Japan challenged the new United Front by attacking Peking. Swept up by the excitement and indignation, Chennault rallied Madame Chiang's novice air force. The Japanese assault spread quickly down the coast to Tientsin and Shanghai. Under Chennault's command, the poorly-prepared Chinese pilots flew courageous missions, but few came back alive.

The Japanese thrust was slowed with the help of Russian planes and pilots—some of them with combat experience in Spain. Madame Chiang asked Chennault to hire more Western mercenaries till Chinese pilots could be given proper training. An American entrepreneur named William Pawley was prepared to sell China two-dozen long-range Vultee V-11 bombers. Chennault agreed.

He knew the men available were misfits and adventurers. There were exceptions, among them Texan Jim Allison, who had been flying for the Republicans in Spain; Cornelius Burmood, who chauffeured May-ling's own plane; and hot pilot George Weigel. But the rest, Chennault said bitterly, "subsisted almost entirely on high-octane beverages."

His mercenaries boozed and bragged at public bars in Hankow till one day Japanese spies knew everything they needed to know about the International Squadron, their Vultees, and the attack planned on Tsinan the following day. That evening Japanese bombers appeared and destroyed all the new Vultees. Chennault's mission was a washout. But, now that he had almost no planes, the Chinese people began responding to his "Jing Bow" (alarm) system. Whenever enemy planes were spotted, Chinese civilians spread the alarm by telephone, telegraph, and radio. At his headquarters, Chennault had time to scramble his handful of pilots. So long as Russian aid continued, he could carry on, but Moscow was increasingly distracted by the war in Europe. Only America could help China.

Mercenary hirelings were one thing, but Chiang Kai-shek wanted more. The Generalissimo made a direct appeal to President Franklin D. Roosevelt in the summer of 1939, writing, "China looks forward with great earnestness to further timely material assistance from the American Government and financiers. Substantial amounts granted at this juncture would be of inestimable value to us in view of Japan's attempt to undermine our currency and economic fabric."

May-ling wrote articles making it clear to American readers that neither Chiang nor China was to blame for the situation—Westerners were letting China down.

> We hope to be able to secure supplies to enable us to keep on indefinitely. If the Democratic States do not see to it that provision is made to this end, then a time will come when they will regret allowing Japan to defeat China. . . . When one thinks how the Democracies are allowing . . . China to be ruined one can be excused for wondering what is the matter with their mentalities.

W. H. Donald also tightened the screws on the American conscience, identifying war profiteering as America's greatest sin:

> The Japanese are doing their best to lure financiers to support them in the exploitation of China. They promise all kinds of profits. . . . If American financiers are wise they will consider the whole proposition very carefully before they allow themselves to be intrigued into an effort to "get rich quick" with the aid of the Japanese and at the expense of the Chinese. On the other hand, support of China will open a tremendous field for foreign investment, and a market of immense value, in time. . . . If the democratic Powers refuse to give China any aid, they will commit the greatest crime in history if they, in any way, succor or give tangible support to the Japanese.

On June 26, 1939, *Time* talked about the exhausted state of European powers that were "in no position to take part of the White Man's Burden in Asia on . . . [their] sagging shoulders." *Life* Magazine chimed in, saying,

> The world waits now to see whether China and its Generalissimo . . . have the moral and material stamina to go on fighting Japan. Not many people

have the courage to be a "Lost Cause." And Chiang's prospects are now worse than were ever those of the American Revolution's George Washington. Chiang Kai-shek has heretofore shown himself a man of remarkable courage and resolution. He proved, while kidnapped by Communists at Sian two years ago, that he is not afraid of death. He is a converted Methodist who has now for solace the examples of tribulation in the Christian Bible.

Chiang's only similarity to George Washington was false teeth. But in this pious campaign he was portrayed as a heroic Christian soldier, holding the Bible in one hand while fighting off reds and Japs with the other. Americans could not resist the appeal of a Christian underdog, particularly one who had looked death in the eye, and defied "Communists" at Sian. The Generalissimo was fighting the good fight, and needed help. It was time, Luce implied, to send in the U.S. cavalry.

When Japan attacked China's northeastern cities, T. V. Soong said, "I predict that within three months . . . Japan will be on the verge of bankruptcy and facing revolution!" Instead, within three months, T. V. was asking the U.S. navy to smuggle him out of Shanghai in disguise; the city was in Japanese hands. While Washington thought over his request, he got the Green Gang to smuggle him out instead, for a pretty penny.

Before 1938 was over, the Japanese had not only frightened Chiang and his regime into bolting from Nanking (and massacred 300,000 people thereby left undefended), but chased the Generalissimo unceremoniously out of Wuhan and five hundred miles farther up the Yangtze River to mountainous Szechuan Province—traditionally out of reach for even the most determined conqueror. There, Chiang set up his wartime government in the shabby Yangtze river town of Chungking, and told the world that he still ruled China. Because this had been the prevailing American mythology since 1927, he was believed there, more so than elsewhere. In the course of escaping to Chungking, the KMT regime had "rescued," "liberated," and "seized" enough funds from various private sources and institutions to staunch its bowels for a few months till the spasms quieted. But by spring 1940 Chiang was again craving operating capital. H. H. Kung was printing hundreds of millions of Chinese fa-pi dollars in Hong Kong and flying the money to Chungking. But some things could not be purchased with money that just about everybody knew was worthless. Hard currency was needed for foreign arms purchases, and for domestic negotiations that had to be conducted in real coin. More to the point, the Japanese conquest had temporarily disrupted opium and heroin traffic, cutting severely into Chiang's most reliable source of revenue.

So in June, 1940, T. V. Soong was dispatched to the United States as Chiang's "personal representative" on what he called "family business." When his Pan Am Clipper reached San Francisco, he was asked by reporters whether he was going to Washington to negotiate war loans. T. V. replied: "I wish it were true. As a matter of fact, I am going to New York on private business. . . . The war has been very exhausting to the Japanese. China is holding out exceedingly well, and the morale of the army and the people remains excellent. Industrially, we are going ahead as well as possible under war conditions. Materials are, of course, more scarce than manpower."

T. V., who had no appetite for what Chiang was really doing, was to remain in the United States with his wife and children for nearly two and a half years. His first job was to secure a credit of $50 million U.S. against exports of Chinese tungsten. America's attention was riveted on Europe, where Hitler's Wehrmacht was driving deep into France and Goering's Luftwaffe was bombing London. Roosevelt was running for a third term and the outcome was not at all certain. T. V. moved through Washington as quietly as a nanny in a nursery.

With his pretty wife, Laura (described by a Chinese embassy official confidentially as a "honey"), T. V. set up housekeeping first in a two-bedroom suite at Washington's yellow brick Shoreham Hotel, overlooking Rock Creek Park. A personal secretary took phone calls and borrowed best-sellers from the hotel library. Looking like an overweight walrus, T. V. swam the hotel pool in blue trunks, borrowed from the Shoreham gym, embroidered with a large "S" that people mistook to mean "Soong." Most guests were unaware that the Chinaman snorfling in the pool was single-handedly keeping China afloat.

Because a third term was unprecedented, T. V.'s trip was timed to plead for as many concessions as possible before the Roosevelt administration left office. The President's cronies were too busy getting FDR reelected to be much help just then to China. When it became apparent to T. V. that he would be staying longer than expected, he moved from the Shoreham to a small shingled house out Connecticut Avenue in a fashionable part of Chevy Chase, Maryland. There, T. V. and Laura regularly entertained Cabinet and "kitchen cabinet" officials of FDR's Administration, including Jesse Jones, head of the Federal Loan Agency, who later became Secretary of Commerce; Treasury Secretary

Henry Morgenthau, and Warren Lee Pierson of the Export-Import Bank. As a genial host, T. V. overcame his preference for steak to serve Chinese food for his important guests, who seemed to expect it. That was the extent of the Celestial trappings. T. V. ate quickly and then served cigars, ripping the cellophane off decks of cards for games of bridge or poker. He was good at bridge and successful at poker.

Dr. Soong (as he now preferred to be called) had made his first official contact with the U.S. government when he met Treasury Secretary Morgenthau on August 15. At that time, Soong described China as "nearing the breaking point on the material side and . . . desperately in need of assistance." He was not at all shy about pressing his case. John Fairbank, who came to Washington a few months later to organize a corps of China Watchers for the war effort, once encountered T. V. in the company of OSS chief William Donovan. "T. V.," Fairbank observed, "reminds me of . . . the star Wisconsin halfback, very quick on the ball and inclined to plow through between guard and tackle rather than waste time going around end."

Morgenthau turned Dr. Soong over to Jesse Jones, who talked of a loan of $5 million. With the election still uncertain, no one seemed willing just yet to take T. V.'s appeal to the top. Morgenthau remarked that autumn to Secretary of War Stimson, "Well, poor old T. V. Soong is here and we can't do a damn thing for him."

But, with Japan's next rush down the Chinese coast to seize Indochina, Congress agreed on September 25 to lend Chiang $25 million U.S. More would be forthcoming. But Chiang was not willing to let this opportunity pass. He pressed Ambassador Johnson for more, and Johnson advised the State Department that the "failure of the United States . . . to afford timely aid . . . may in the end result in Communist ascendancy in China."

If FDR was elected to a third term, T. V. would be in a much better position to reach into the White House. He knew how things worked in Washington, and he had cultivated his own cronies, including the influential journalists Joseph Alsop and Edgar Ansel Mowrer, who had powerful connections throughout the establishment. Alsop, who was yet another of President Roosevelt's many relatives, had benefited somewhat professionally from his tie to the imperial presidency, but was not inclined to credit anything or anyone but destiny for his own success. He was once described by David Halberstam as "American's most imperial and imperious journalist." Alsop and Mowrer were lobbying American political leaders and members of Congress to rescue China. Others cultivated by T. V. were the President's special assistant Harry Hopkins, and Assistant Secretary of War John J. McCloy.

T. V.'s most influential crony was Roosevelt's close aide Thomas G. Corcoran, nicknamed "Tommy the Cork." During FDR's first two terms, Corcoran had become one of the most powerful men in the administration. Although he was not officially on the White House staff, Corcoran was FDR's top speechwriter, drafted much of the New Deal legislation, and helped push it through Congress. He was one of those backstairs operators that Presidents find so useful to have around the White House; once they become wizards at invoking the President's supernatural power they are set for life. Since FDR was in the White House for an unusually long time, Corcoran's leverage became somewhat greater than that of most cronies. In 1941, after making numerous enemies on Capitol Hill, Corcoran left the federal government (but not FDR's inner circle) and went private. He continued to do favors for FDR, and became involved with the President's relatives and friends in manifold business ventures. Corcoran acquired a reputation as a high-priced lawyer peddling inside government information to big business, and there were widespread assertions of impropriety, though none of the formal investigations into his activities ever resulted in an indictment. It was Harry Hopkins who succeeded Corcoran as FDR's principal domestic advisor and all-purpose agent.

All these men knew that FDR was recklessly predisposed to help China. Because of his family's old ties to the Shanghai opium trade, which his relatives never tired of resurrecting as evidence of their worldliness and sagacity, the President seemed to think he had a comprehension of China transcending the need for facts, experience, and details. Like many other Americans who imagined themselves to be old China hands, not least among them Henry Luce, FDR had a highly colored and idealized image of the Orient. Knowing this through their diplomatic representatives in Washington, both T. V. Soong and H. H. Kung had taken advantage of their government posts in Nanking over the years to write letters to Roosevelt, cultivating him, sending him gifts of tea that—with shrewd calculation—were not sufficiently ostentatious to be turned down as a bribe. T. V. had also sent Roosevelt the wooden model of a Hainan junk. These contacts had had the desired effect. T. V. was a foreign identity that the White House recognized. Now that he had adopted FDR's cronies as his own, and was cultivating them shrewdly and lavishly, T. V. had a direct pipeline into the Oval Office.

The November election confirmed FDR in his third term, and wheels began turning with extraordinary speed. On December 2, 1940, barely a month after the election, Roosevelt asked for and Congress approved a $100 million U.S. loan that, *Life* Magazine reassured Americans, was the bargain of the year. "For $100,000,000 China promised to keep 1,125,000 Japanese troops pinned in the field; to keep Japan's formidable Fleet blockading the China shore; to retard the aggressors' march in the direction of immediate U.S. interests. The merchandise was fantastically cheap at the price." Luce knew Americans could never resist a bargain.

The loan consisted of two $50 million U.S. parcels, one provided by Warren Lee Pierson's Export-Import Bank and the other from Morgenthau's U.S. Treasury—that is, from two of T. V.'s poker pals. The Treasury loan was to "help stabilize" China's currency, wildly inflated by H. H. Kung's uncontrolled paper-money-printing operations, while the Export-Import Bank loan would cover food, gasoline, tanks, and trucks purchased by T. V. from General Motors and elsewhere, in the name of the Chinese government.

In order to administer this huge sum, and to handle the complex transactions entailed, T. V. set up a number of companies, foremost the Universal Trading Corporation, headquartered in New York's Rockefeller Center, and China Defense Supplies in Washington. The movement of U.S. aid passed through several stages. Funds were solicited by China Defense Supplies, then were used by Universal Trading to make purchases of matériel, and thereafter, presumably, these purchases were shipped to China.

China Defense Supplies was headed by Tommy Corcoran's brother, David. Tommy served as its general counsel. Company secretary was Whiting Willauer, a Washington jack-of-all-trades with links to the OSS (and later to the CIA); Willauer eventually became Chennault's "business partner" in China at the time a controlling interest in his aviation operations was taken over by the CIA. One of the directors of China Defense Supplies was Frederic Delano, the President's uncle from one of the family branches that had traded in Shanghai. When T. V. had remarked once that he was going to America on family business, it turned out that he meant Soong family, Roosevelt family, and Corcoran family.

There would appear to be no trace of T. V. Soong's name or that of any other Soong anywhere in Treasury's archives, although he was a recipient of hundreds of millions in Treasury's funds, was unusually close to one Treasury Secretary and several other senior officials of the department. According to FBI documents at the Justice Department, it emerges that in 1940 an investigation of T. V. was undertaken by the Treasury Department and by the FBI at the initiation of Secretary Morgenthau. This is described simply as "an analysis of his financial operations" for reasons of "internal security." Morgenthau must have been satisfied with the results, because after this he and T. V. became close friends. But Treasury's own records of that inquiry appear to have vaporized.

It has been noted that the problem of heroin addiction in the United States largely evaporated during World War II; this was attributed to the disruption of trade caused by the war. However, there was no real disruption of narcotics traffic and production inside China during the war, as KMT generals and Green Gang leaders continued operations with only brief interruptions, and carried on a brisk trade in narcotics with the Japanese across the lines. Coming on the heels of the 1937 U.S. government crackdowns on Chinese diplomats, the $100 million Lend-Lease loan was tantamount to an outright American subsidy of Chiang's regime, replacing narcotics exports as Chiang's main source of foreign nourishment.

The rapidity with which Chinese narcotics ceased to be a major problem in America after the loan was approved raises provocative questions. It is a subject on which the archives of the Treasury Department failed to produce a single document in response to a Freedom of Information inquiry.

On the subject of narcotics, there were in fact many reports from China over the years by U.S. Treasury agents, and duplicate copies of these reports were preserved in a special archive of the State Department. Why the Treasury Department and the Drug Enforcement Agency profess to have no knowledge of these files creates an interesting situation. In none of them is T. V. Soong mentioned, except indirectly, so there was never any suggestion of his being involved in narcotics traffic overseas. T. V. is mentioned indirectly because his employee and traveling companion who went abroad with him frequently, was said to have been actively engaged in heroin smuggling to America on a large scale.

Seen against current policies of the U.S. government, in which opium-producing nations are given "alternative crops" and heavy economic aid to compensate them for the loss in drug profit, it may be that American drug policy germinated in that first package deal with Chiang's China.

In October, the Generalissimo sent Chennault to join T. V. in Washington; China needed planes for her air force. Chennault spent a lot of time with T. V.'s friends preparing a shopping list, and trying to discover just where he could put his hands on fighters. In his spare time, he made the rounds with Joseph Alsop and economist Lauchlin Currie, another of FDR's kitchen cabinet.

T. V. had told Secretary Morgenthau that China needed five hundred airplanes; Morgenthau had replied that this was like asking for five hundred stars. The United States was already committed to supply large numbers of fighters and bombers to Britain. But Chennault learned that Curtiss-Wright was about to ship to Britain one hundred P-40 fighters that London did not want. These were heavy, slow fighters burdened with armor plate, and the British were eying newer, faster American planes. Chennault told T. V. about the P-40s, and in no time at all the British were promised better planes if they would let these go to China.

The Japanese had sealed the China coast. The Burma Road was being built to carry supplies to China through the back door from British Burma over more than 600 miles of impossible mountains. Chennault's aircraft would be shipped to Rangoon in crates and assembled there. They would fly cover for Burma Road convoys—and provide air defense for Chungking.

To get the planes ready, T. V. hired William Pawley, who had sold the ill-fated Vultees to Madame Chiang. Pawley set up a company called Central Aircraft Manufacturing Company (CAMCO) to do the work.

Next, pilots had to be found. It was not a simple matter to recruit U.S. combat pilots to fly for China without violating a 1907 law that stripped citizenship from any American who "has taken an oath of allegiance to any foreign state." This law had been dusted off in 1936 by the Department of State as a weapon to use against Americans rushing to fight for the Spanish Republicans. More than one American flier had his passport yanked because he was flying, or on his way to fly, for "the wrong side" in Spain. The enormously popular American ace Frank Tinker, who was in Spain because he was a romantic, not a political animal, and who was so good he was allowed to fly side by side with Russian pilots in the latest Soviet fighter aircraft, was hounded by State Department and FBI agents on his return until he committed suicide in a Little Rock hotel room. It would be embarrassing indeed if it got out that, only a year or so later, Washington was recruiting its own air corps pilots to serve Asia's answer to Generalissimo Franco.

On April 15, 1941, FDR quietly issued an executive order permitting military personnel to resign, sign contracts with Pawley's CAMCO, and go with Chennault to fight Japan for one year, after which they could regain their former positions in the American armed forces. Recruiters went to army, navy, and marine air bases offering contracts up to $750 U.S. a month, plus travel allowances, housing, and thirty days' paid holiday. CAMCO agreed to pay a $500 U.S. bonus for each Japanese plane shot down. The State Department, overcoming any squeamishness it might have felt after confiscating citizens' passports for meddling in Spain, set to work preparing falsified passports for the pilots going off to meedle in China. According to the passports, the American Volunteer Group (AVG) were tourists, students, salesmen, entertainers, bankers, and missionaries.

One of the "missionaries" was Gregory ("Pappy") Boyington, a marine corps pilot with a terrible thirst and fists the size of tree trunks, who took an immediate dislike to Chennault and found real joy in persecuting the Gimo and the Dragonlady whenever they visited an AVG base. Another was Eric Shilling, who, after seeing a photograph of Luftwaffe fighters painted with gaping shark's teeth, decorated his P-40 the same way. Chennault liked it so much he had all the planes in the three squadrons so embellished.

After bombing Kunming and Chungking for a year without resistance, the Japanese were taken by surprise on December 20, 1941, when they ran into shark-nosed P-40s guarding Kunming. Making use of the impressive diving speed of their heavy planes, the AVG pilots wreaked havoc on the Mitsubishi Ki-21 twin-engine bombers, and sent them scurrying back toward their base at Hanoi. Three days later the AVG was also in action in southern Burma as the Battle of Rangoon began with a major Japanese air assault by Nakajima bombers and fighters. In the months that followed, the AVG became world famous for its exploits. The Chinese in Kunming called them "tigers," and the name caught on.

It was front-page news in America whenever the Gimo paid a call on the Flying Tigers. On a typical visit in Kunming early in 1942,

Madame and the Gimo praised the AVG at a banquet. The following morning, as Chennault escorted Generalissimo and Madame Chiang up the steps to a DC-2 that would carry them back to Chungking, seven well-oiled Tigers led by Boyington roared out of the sky and flew upside down over the DC-2, missing it by a hair and sending Chiang and May-ling sprawling on their bellies in the dust.

It was this unorthodoxy that gave the Tigers their winning unpredictability in the air. But it was also what brought their mission to an abrupt end. That part of the story was successfully hidden from the public. Less than a year after their recruitment, some of the pilots had become suspicious of the great discrepancy between myth and reality in their mission. Boyington was shocked by the disinterest, arrogance, and fraud blatantly visible in the Nationalist leadership. He made it known far and wide that he had no intention of dying in a P-40, glamour or no glamour, as a pawn of American propagandists and a corrupt tyrant.

With America now in the war, the role of the AVG was about to change, obliging the pilots to go back to regular military status, regular routine, regular pay, regular uniforms. Chennault was reinstated as a brigadier general in the army air force, subject to a new pecking order. His wild bunch were ordered to fly hazardous low-level strafing missions to provide cover for Chinese foot soldiers, and low-level reconnaissance with terrifying risks from Japanese ground fire, and to escort stodgy RAF Blenheim bombers. The Tigers mutinied. A petition was circulated asking for signatures to support a mass resignation. If they were civilians, it was a resignation; if they were military, it was mutiny. The War Department considered them to be military. Out of thirty-four pilots, twenty-eight signed. One of those who refused, Tex Hill, urged his comrades not to turn their backs on their own nation at a time of peril. With this emotional appeal to their lagging sense of virtue, the mutiny fizzled. But, when it was announced that the entire unit would become part of the army air force on July 4, 1942, the bitterness rushed out again. Brigadier General Clayton Bissell, who had never liked Chennault and outranked him by one day of service, ordered the Tigers to sign up.

"If you don't sign up," Bissell bellowed, "you'll be inducted anyway, as privates if need be!"

The Tigers appealed to Chennault. He told them: "I know all the troubles we'll have, and more too. But that doesn't count. All that counts is getting the Japanese out of China and winning this war. That's our job, that's our sacred duty."

The pilots did not agree. Chennault had been in Chiang's pay a long time, even though he now wore a U.S. general's star. It was different for him. All but five Tigers resigned, and on July 4, 1942, the most famous American fighting unit since the Minutemen of the Revolution ceased to exist. To cover up, and to capitalize on the AVG's extraordinary press image, hundreds of other U.S. aviators who came to China were called Flying Tigers. They were only Tigers on paper. America now had too great a commitment to Chiang Kai-shek to let it be challenged.

Chiang's defense of China was being portrayed by T. V. Soong as a valiant defiance against Japanese hordes, carried out assiduously by KMT generals. If so, it was proceeding in a curious fashion. Chiang was engaging in as little actual fighting as possible. On only one occasion, a KMT army under General Li Tsung-jen proved that Chinese soldiers could whip the Japanese when they had the will to do so, in the battle at Taierchuang in April 1938. The Japanese in this instance were badly beaten and the people of China were elated. But Chiang ordered his army not to pursue, and within weeks of Taierchuang the Japanese had recovered the initiative.

Chiang was husbanding his resources for a renewal of his war with the Communists. Once holed up in Chungking, he let the people fend for themselves. "The suffering caused by Japanese brutality," observed French historian Jean Chesneaux, "and the disasters resulting from the incompetence of the Kuomintang were staggering." One of Chiang's few attempts to slow the advance of the Japanese led him to dynamite the dikes on the Yellow River. Without warning of any kind, three provinces, eleven cities, and four thousand villages were flooded, two million people were made homeless, and all their crops were destroyed. The Japanese were only bogged down for three months. Although the demolition of the dikes was witnessed by correspondent Jack Belden, Chiang's government tried to put the blame on the Japanese and the Taiwan government continues to do so today. Militarily, Chiang demonstrated what Chesneaux called "overwhelming incompetence, impulsiveness, and authoritarianism." But he was careful to look after his own, and to intervene every time the Chinese Communist forces seemed to be nudging into "his" territory. What resulted was one of the worst atrocities of the war, one in which the Japanese were not even involved.

By 1940–41, Chiang's sphere of influence had shrunk while the Communists' area had expanded at the expense of the Japanese. In the red area, soldiers, guerrillas, and peasants were fighting furiously and with results. But, each time the reds enlarged their perimeter, Chiang had his army attack the Communists instead of the Japanese, to keep his rivals from making territorial gains. It was a war within a war. Chiang had half a million soldiers occupied blockading the red area in the Northwest.

Part of the United Front agreement involved putting Mao's Red Army under joint KMT command. The existing Red Army was renamed the Eighth Army, and a fresh Communist force was christened the New Fourth Army. In 1941, the New Fourth Army was assigned to operate under joint KMT-CCP command along the south bank of the Yangtze River within the orbit of the Green Gang.

The gang's operations had not seriously diminished because of the war. The gang operated under the Japanese occupation much as it had before, although Big-eared Tu, bearing the rank of general in the KMT, wisely moved to Chungking. In his absence, the Shanghai gang headquarters was left in the hands of Tu's harbor boss, Ku Tsu-chuan. As a complement, Generalissimo Chiang gave all military responsibilities for the lower Yangtze River region to Ku's brother, General Ku Chu-t'ung.

The New Fourth Army was probing into the Ku brothers' domain in December 1940, in order to raid the main enemy-held railway leading to Nanking and Shanghai and the road linking Nanking and Hankow. This was an area in which there was cooperation between the Green Gang and the Japanese. In return for permitting its opium smuggling and underworld operations to go on uninterrupted, the Green Gang guaranteed the security of Japanese garrisons and enterprises in the Yangtze Valley.

General Ku in consultation with Chiang Kai-shek, decided that the New Fourth Army was a threat to this fiefdom. He ordered it to move immediately across the Yangtze to a specified location on the north bank. The New Fourth commanders protested that this would lead them straight into a heavy concentration of Japanese, which was the point. On its own initiative, the bulk of the New Fourth took a safer route, leaving behind its high command, staff, nurses, women political cadres, and support personnel, with only a small force of five thousand soldiers to protect them. This mixed group that had been left behind was attempting to follow the main force when suddenly, early in January, 1941, General Ku fell upon it with a much greater force and massacred all but the headquarters contingent and its women cadres and nurses. All five thousand combat soldiers left behind as a guard were slain. According to survivors, the men of the headquarters staff were then butchered. The KMT general who had been commanding the New Fourth was arrested, while the CCP political commissar of the unit —who had escaped the 1927 Shanghai Massacre—was brutally murdered. Meanwhile, the Communist nurses and women political cadres, many of them schoolgirls, were being raped repeatedly by hundreds of soldiers. They were kept in army brothels near the attack site for a year and a half. The women contracted venereal diseases and some committed suicide, singly and with each other's help. Eventually they were forced to carry the baggage of the soldiers overland to a new concentration camp.

The New Fourth Army Incident became what Theodore White called "the King Charles's head of the Chinese civil war."

General Ku Chu-t'ung, the author of the atrocity, was eventually promoted to commander-in-chief of all KMT armies.

When the details of the massacre became known in Yenan, Mao Tse-tung cabled Chungking a message for Chiang: "Those who play with fire ought to be careful. . . . If things continue to develop this way, the whole people of the whole country will throw you into the gutter."

Although both sides, thereafter, maintained the pretense of a United Front whenever it served their immediate interests, it was over. Theodore White later interviewed Chiang Kai-shek on the incident. The Generalissimo was blunt: "The Japanese are a disease of the skin, the Communists are a disease of the heart."

Regardless of Chiang's suspicious handling of the war, once the Japanese attacked Pearl Harbor, China's status in America changed overnight. When T. V. Soong was talking with Secretary Knox the day after the attack, Knox—forgetting who he was with—slammed his clenched fist to the table and bellowed: "By God, T. V., we are going to kill every one of those yellow bastards."

Less than three weeks later, T. V. was named China's new Foreign Minister. It was a surprise to some, who thought that this would distract him from his specialty of financial politics. They were mistaken. The new title only gave him additional leverage to bargain for Chungking.

Early in January 1942, T. V. went to Treasury's Morgenthau with the Generalissimo's request for a new loan of $500 million U.S. Morgenthau was curious what plans existed for this money, pointing out that China already had $630 million in Lend-Lease goods stacked to the rafters in Burma. T. V. patiently explained "that the Generalissimo wants a billion dollars [half from the U.S. and half from Britain] in reserve to use when he sees fit." Although there was some muttering in Washington, the loan was recommended by the President to Congress, which authorized the full amount on February 7, 1942. Whereupon Chiang telegraphed additional instructions to his new Foreign Minister. The Generalissimo insisted that there should be no specific security on the loan, no interest, no terms of repayment, and no conditions for the use of the money. Chiang got the money on his terms.

Certainly the Generalissimo was pleased with the deal. He now had the assurance of bottomless resources, for once having made such commitments, America would have to stand behind Chiang. He had carte blanche to spend it any way he wished, without answering to Congressmen or to private citizens. But Joseph Stilwell, who had now become the senior American military officer for the China-Burma-India Theater, and who was intimately acquainted with the Soongs, had his own opinion about Chiang and American aid:

> I never heard Chiang Kai-shek say a single thing that indicated gratitude to the President or to our country for the help we were extending to him. Invariably, when anything was promised, he would want more. Invariably, he would complain about the small amount of material that was being furnished. . . . He would complain that the Chinese had been fighting for six or seven years and yet we gave them practically nothing. It would of course have been undiplomatic to go into the nature of the military effort Chiang Kai-shek had made since 1938. It was practically zero.

Chapter 17

LITTLE SISTER WOOS AMERICA

Before May-ling took her turn to vamp America again she tested her charms on Wendell Willkie, who had lost to Roosevelt at the end of 1940 and was given the consolation prize of a goodwill tour to China in the fall of 1942. They made an interesting picture in Chungking, he with dark locks tousled over a boyish face looking like an overweight school lad on the verge of midlife crisis, she with her Georgia accent acting like a fading Oriental Scarlett O'Hara at her most impudent. John Paton Davies, then a U.S. Foreign Service officer in Chungking, watched May-ling work her magic:

> There is little doubt that Little Sister has accomplished one of her easiest conquests. Presiding at a relief organization tea, with the cloak of an air marshal thrown over her shoulders, she admitted with disarming feminine frailty that Mr. W. was a very "disturbing influence," a confession which visibly gratified the president's personal representative. . . . It's interesting the influence which enforced celibacy has on judgment—and the course of political events.

According to Willkie, backpedaling furiously, it did not happen that way at all:

> Just before we were to leave, Madame Chiang said to Dr. and Madame Kung: "Last night at dinner Mr. Willkie suggested that I should go to America on a good-will tour." The Kungs looked at me as if questioning. I said: "That is correct, and I know I am right in suggesting it."

Then Dr. Kung spoke, seriously. "Mr. Willkie, do you really mean that, and if so, why?"

I said to him, "Dr. Kung, you know from our conversation how strongly I believe that it is vital for my fellow countrymen to understand the problems of Asia and the viewpoint of its people, how sure I am that the future peace of the world probably lies in a just solution of the problems of the Orient after the war.

"Someone from this section with brains and persuasiveness and moral force must help educate us about China and India and their people. Madame would be the perfect ambassador. Her great ability—and I know she will excuse me for speaking so personally—her great devotion to China, are well known in the United States. She would find herself not only beloved, but immensely effective. We would listen to her as to no one else. With wit and charm, a generous and understanding heart, a gracious and beautiful manner and appearance, and a burning conviction, she is just what we need as a visitor."

However it happened, Willkie was electrified by May-ling and dazzled by the Generalissimo, and rushed back to share his insights with his fellow Americans on radio and in newspapers.

During the war years, a new comic strip called "Terry and the Pirates" became popular in the United States, full of the adventures in China of a young American pilot modeled on the heroes of the AVG. The strip was populated with characters based on real and often recognizable people in the news, and introduced more than a few Oriental archetypes who became a permanent part of American folklore, such as the useful coolie Big Stoop, and the mysterious Dragonlady. In moments of crisis, young Terry Lee would be rescued from evil clutches or certain death by the Dragonlady, who appeared and disappeared like a sinister fairy godmother. Although it was essentially a contradiction in terms, or oxymoron, the image of a slinky, sinister, possibly even faintly evil fairy godmother was so tantalizing that it must have gratified deep puritan cravings. Of course the name Dragonlady, originally applied by foreigners to the poisonous old Dowager Empress Tzu Hsi, had been used more than once in recent times as a sobriquet for Madame Chiang. It was conspicuous that she was the model for the comic-strip Dragonlady, in her role as godmother to the AVG. So it was not surprising that, when America listened to Wendell Willkie report on his trip to China, complex issues took on cartoon simplicity.

K. C. Li, a perceptive multi-millionaire in the Chinese rubber business who had come to America in 1941 and settled in New York, reported to T. V. Soong how Americans responded:

> The odyssey of Wendell Willkie to the East has struck a popular chord. His visit to China has made a deep impression on the American people. His report, impressive for its sincerity and deep conviction, was widely heard. Indeed, no private citizen has ever commanded so huge an audience as when Mr. Willkie broadcast his report to the American people over all stations on the evening of October 26, 1942.
>
> The New York Herald-Tribune expressed national sentiment when it said the following morning: "It is a noble gospel that Mr. Willkie preaches, both with respect to American duty in the world and with respect to American duty at home." . . .
>
> . . . some of Mr. Willkie's pro-China statements have inspired objections. Mr. Willkie referred to the reservoir of goodwill to the American people that is leaking because of holes punched in it by American "bungling." . . . The reaction . . . has been unmistakable. . . .
>
> Mr. Walter Lippmann, in his widely read column on "Mr. Willkie in Asia," . . . warned: "The Chinese people are the last people on earth who have the right to question our good faith, and what we did in refusing to sell out China in the darkest hour is more important than all the words that can be pronounced on the subject of war aims or liberty and justice." . . .
>
> The reaction indicates that, even when differences need to be submerged for the sake of unity, American opinion is sensitive about any question of her loyalty or aid to China. . . .
>
> Certainly we should clear up our position, and do all we can to clarify the American mind, and reach an understanding with public spokesmen as to the real cause of America's entry into the war. . . . It seems a job well worth assigning to the China propagandists and China propaganda organizations in this country.

This was clearly a job for the Dragonlady.

When T. V. Soong learned in Washington about May-ling's forthcoming visit he was strenuously opposed. America was his territory; only one Soong at a time could dance on the head of this pin.

May-ling had no trouble convincing Chiang that she should go. Rumors were rife in Chungking that the Generalissimo and "Darling" (as May-ling demanded that Chiang call her), were having severe marital difficulties. Jack Service cautiously summarized the scuttlebutt as a political observer in Chungking for the State Department:

Chungking is literally seething with stories of the domestic troubles of the Chiang household. Almost everyone has new details and versions to add to the now generally accepted story that the Generalissimo has taken a mistress and as a result his relations with the Madame are—to say the least—strained. There is so much smoke, it would seem that there must be some fire.

Normally, such gossip about the private lives of government leaders would not be considered as within the scope of political reporting. This is hardly the case, however, in China where the person concerned is a dictator and where the relationship between him and his wife's family is so all-important. That relationship is already weakened by the strained relations between the Generalissimo and T. V. Soong. If the Madame, whose nature is both proud and puritanical, should openly break with her husband, the dynasty would be split and the effects both in China and abroad might be serious. Even if the present situation becomes generally known abroad, as it almost certainly and eventually will, there will be a great loss of prestige to both the Generalissimo and the Madame. . . .

The Madame now refers to the Generalissimo only as "that Man."

The Madame complains that the Generalissimo now only puts his teeth in when he is going to see "that woman."

The Madame went into the Generalissimo's bedroom one day, found a pair of high-heeled shoes under the bed, threw them out of the window and hit a guard on the head. . . .

The Generalissimo at one time did not receive callers for four days because he had been bruised on the side of the head with a flower vase in a spat with the Madame. . . .

Nonetheless, most observers believe that the stakes of power are so important to the Soong family that they (with the exception of Madame Sun but the important addition of H. H. Kung) will do everything possible to prevent an open break and that she will swallow her pride and put up with the situation.

The rumors were not all frivolous. Other women were identified with the Generalissimo during the 1940s, including his original concubine, Miss Yao. In 1942 Chiang was understood to have taken up again with his previous wife (wife number two), Ch'en Chieh-ju, who had been paid off and sent away to America in 1927 to clear the way for his marriage to May-ling. She was back in China secretly. In due course, Chiang was understood to have gotten her pregnant again, and she was expecting to deliver in the late spring of 1944. Apparently, Chiang had never lost his grand passion for Miss Ch'en, although their marriage had become politically inconvenient.

It was also possible that the social, financial, and political advantages of marriage to the Soong Dynasty were now taken for granted; that the marriage to May-ling, as a marriage of convenience, really had little to sustain it; that Chiang had gained all the advantages, and was now beginning to lose them in ways that the Soongs could not fix; and that May-ling herself had become disenchanted by Chiang's ineptitude and empty posturing. As his world closed in, May-ling's was expanding; she was an international celebrity, one of the most influential women on the planet. The constant reminders of her enormous financial and political value must have stung him to the quick.

May-ling, for whatever reasons, also had not borne Chiang an heir. His own two sons were growing older. Wei-kuo was back from his training with the Wehrmacht, and had never got along with his step-mother. Meanwhile the older son, CCK, had returned from Moscow at long last in 1937, bringing a Russian wife. At the airport to meet him, the Generalissimo had turned and said, "Now come meet your new mother."

"That's not my mother," CCK snapped, and stalked away in outrage to his birthplace at Chikou, where his real mother awaited him. This was the beginning of a contest between CCK and May-ling for the succession to Chiang's throne that would provoke moments of high drama over the years.

To complicate matters for her, May-ling's health was deteriorating. By 1942, she was in urgent need of medical care. She suffered from wrenched ribs, a twisted back, nervous exhaustion resulting in weakness and insomnia, sinus trouble from heavy smoking, impacted wisdom teeth, and her chronic hives or urticaria. The rib and spine injuries had occurred while she was touring the Japanese front in 1937. As she was speeding along in a bulletproof sedan, under heavy fire, a tire blew out, the car flipped over and rolled, and May-ling was thrown out a sprung door. She suffered a fractured rib, a wrenched spine, and shock. Her back continued to bother her five years later because of nervous tension, which kept her muscles rigid in the lumbar region of her lower back. These were tense times, and any kind of anxiety caused her to break out in angry red "wheals." Simply put, the princess was a nervous wreck from sleeping on the dried pea.

The prospect of a period of medical care in the United States therefore outweighed any objections from T. V. May-ling was forty-five.

It was known to insiders also that Chiang suspected she had cancer, so this would afford an opportunity to run tests.

One hundred miles northwest of Chungking, outside the old city of Chengtu, coolies were building the Americans a sprawling airbase for long-range bombers that could strike the Japanese home islands. At 4 A.M. one chill November morning in 1942, a Boeing 307 Stratoliner named *Apache*, on lease from TWA, was serviced and ready for takeoff at Chengtu when headlights flashed over the hangars and a fleet of cars led an ambulance onto the runway. Out of the cars climbed Generalissimo Chiang; Brigadier General Clayton Bissell, commander of the U.S. Tenth Air Force; and fifteen other generals and colonels, both Chinese and American. From the ambulance, a stretcher bearing Madame Chiang was extracted and carried carefully onto the plane. The skipper of the Stratoliner, a former Central American bush pilot named Cornell Newton Shelton, had flown all the way from the United States to pick up a secret passenger. Even now he did not know who. Two American nurses and May-ling's eighteen-year-old niece Jeannette Kung also boarded, and C. N. was ordered to take off. The engines had given him trouble all the way out from America, across the South Atlantic, through Africa and India, but as he now flew south over the Hump on the return trip, they ran smoothly in the cold air.

This was the first four-engined airliner with a pressurized cabin and nobody else was aboard but Madame Chiang's small party and the crew, so it was a comfortable flight. Nevertheless, the usually hyperactive Madame Chiang was in such poor condition that she did not exchange a single word with Shelton the entire trip. For reasons never explained to him, he was ordered not to speak to her. The implication was that she had been through some grave crisis that was not to be made public for any reason.

When they reached Palm Beach, May-ling had recovered enough to insist on stopping overnight. Then Shelton switched planes for safety and flew her on in a C-54 to Mitchell Field, New York. Despite her silence, May-ling thereafter insisted on having Shelton as her pilot whenever she flew out of China. When she later discovered that his dream was to start his own airline in Latin America, she lent him a quarter of a million U.S. dollars to set up a company making removable seats for airplanes, with Louis Kung in financial control, and kept 50 percent share for herself.

As a consequence of the overnight stop in Palm Beach, May-ling arrived in New York a day late, on November 27. But Harry Hopkins was at Mitchell Field anyway to greet her as the President's representative. He recorded the events of that day:

> I had previously arranged that planes land only at military fields so there would be little probability of her entrance being discovered, because the Chinese were anxious to get her into the hospital before it became known. . . . I met Madame Chiang Kai-shek and drove back to the Harkness Pavilion with her where they had arranged for her to occupy all of the twelfth floor.
>
> On the trip in she told me that she wanted to make it clear to the President she was here for no other purpose than medical treatment and rest. However, in the same breath she proceeded to raise many questions relating to China and the United States. . . .
>
> She expressed more forcibly than I had heard anyone express it before her belief that the two wars against Germany and Japan can both be won but that the way to do it is to put all our strength into defeating Japan. . . .
>
> She thinks Stilwell does not understand the Chinese people and that he made a tragic mistake in forcing Chiang Kai-shek to put one of his best divisions in Burma where it was later lost. [When it came under Japanese pressure, the Chinese 55th Division literally vanished into the rainforest and was never seen again. "It's the god-damnedest thing I ever saw," Stilwell exclaimed.] She said Chiang Kai-shek did this against his best judgment. . . .
>
> It is pretty clear she does not like Stilwell and expressed the greatest admiration for Chennault. She spent a good deal of her time in explaining an article in LIFE magazine, which attacked the British Government vigorously. She wanted me particularly to read that article as being her point of view.
>
> I told her Mrs. Roosevelt wanted to see her and arranged for an appointment with Mrs. Roosevelt at the hospital the next morning.

This was quite assertive for a woman who was to spend the next eleven weeks in a hospital bed. When she saw Eleanor Roosevelt the next day, May-ling was again in good form, for the First Lady declared that "I had a desire to help her and take care of her as if she had been my own daughter."

May-ling did undergo medical treatments. She also had her wisdom teeth extracted and her sinusitis relieved. It was all very secretive. She was listed in the Harkness Pavilion of the Columbia Presbyterian Medical Center under a false name, but was guarded by a phalanx of federal agents. Harry Hopkins had made the arrangements at Harkness in cooperation with T. A. Soong's bride, Jih-iung, the daughter of Y. C. Woo, who ran the San Francisco branch of the Soong family's Bank of Canton. May-ling was attended by Dr. Robert F. Loeb. For company at Harkness she had both her niece Jeannette and her nephew David Kung, on leave of absence from Yale to cheer up Auntie. Younger nephew Louis Kung was flying around America setting up May-ling's public tour.

While she was in Manhattan, May-ling learned that Winston Churchill was going to Washington to visit President Roosevelt, so she wrote the Prime Minister suggesting that he drop in on her in New York on his way. Churchill replied suggesting that Madame Chiang instead join him at lunch with Roosevelt in the White House. His invitation, Churchill recalled, "was refused with some hauteur." Nonetheless, "in the regrettable absence of Madame Chiang Kai-shek, the President and I lunched alone in his room and made the best of things."

May-ling wasted no time taking advantage of other presidential perks. After her release from the hospital, she spent two weeks at Roosevelt's retreat at Hyde Park, where she amused herself with the resident canines and drafted her address for Congress. John Fairbank told this story about her stay there:

> It was Pearl Buck who particularly tried to counter the hyperbole of the fleeting vogue of Mme. Chiang. As the guest of President Roosevelt she had in fact behaved like a petulant princess. Pearl Buck, whose Nobel Prize for *The Good Earth* in 1934 had made her the best-known American China watcher, later told us one symptomatic incident. She received a hurry-up call from Madame's entourage at Hyde Park, saying, "Please come right away. Madame wants to see you." Pearl Buck therefore hastened from Perkasie, Pennsylvania, to Hyde Park but found herself embarrassingly unexpected. Mme. Chiang had actually wanted to see her attendant Pearl Ch'en. So Sorry!

When May-ling arrived at the White House early in February as the guest of Eleanor and Franklin, she made a deep impression on the household staff. Although she required that her bed be made with silk sheets, she had thoughtfully brought her own from China. However, the sheets had to be changed at least once a day—more often if Madame napped or sat on her "kang." According to the White House butler, Alonzo Field, the sheets were changed four or five times a day. When she wanted a maid or butler, wherever she was in the executive mansion, she did not use the buzzers or bell ringers provided, but clapped her hands in Chinese fashion, which aroused expressions of sentiment from the staff. She insisted on having meals served in her quarters for her two nurses and for Jeannette and David. Jeannette impressed everyone with attire that prompted the President to address her mischievously as "my boy."

When May-ling dined with the Roosevelts, the President asked how she and the Generalissimo would deal with a wartime strike of coal miners. Everyone at the table gasped when May-ling silently drew a long lacquered nail across her throat. Roosevelt laughed hollowly and —catching Eleanor's attention—asked, "Did you see that?" Eleanor privately remarked, "She can talk beautifully about democracy, but does not know how to live democracy." When this remark got around and May-ling was asked about it by reporters, she refused to comment.

May-ling also drove the White House secretarial staff to distraction because she rewrote her speeches and articles seven or eight times. The congressional address was to be her most important public statement, and she repeated its essential points time and again during her blitz of North America. For she was now sufficiently cured to step out "from behind her official incognito and reveal another larger reason for her presence in this country."

To the American public she was hardly an unknown quantity. Henry Luce had spared no effort promoting her image in his magazines, and in 1941, Doubleday, Doran & Company had published Emily Hahn's *The Soong Sisters*. Hahn had lived in Shanghai, where she was a friend of Ai-ling. Apparently, she had no difficulty reconciling the Soongs' complex personalities, ambidextrous economics, and ambiguous politics. Ching-ling took exception to Hahn's interpretation of her relationship with the Chinese Communists. When Hahn received the message from Sun Yat-sen's aging bodyguard, Morris Cohen, that Madame Sun is "no Communist, and she doesn't want you to say she is," Hahn became indignant. She later explained "I was horrified that anybody could so patently lie to me."

According to the headline writers of America, who took May-ling to their withered dugs, she "invaded" the United States, "taking the country by charm." Bent over their copy desk rims like the crones in *Macbeth*, they shrieked her praises and proclaimed "Mme. Chiang a

Hit Everywhere." *Newsweek*'s coverage of her February address before Congress was enthralled: "The effect was enchanting. The lady was dark and petite. She wore a long, tight-fitting black gown, the skirt slit almost to the knee. Her smooth, black hair was coiled simply at the nape of her neck. Her jewels were of priceless jade. Her slim fingers were red-tipped. She wore sheer hose and frivolous high-heeled slippers."

May-ling's material was equally florid, and was leaked to the press weeks ahead of time in bits and pieces. On the kinship of America and China: "The 160 years of traditional friendship between our two great peoples . . . which has never been marred by misunderstandings, is unsurpassed in the annals of the world."

On the issue of Japanese belligerency:

> There has been a tendency to belittle the strength of our opponent. When Japan thrust total war on China in 1937, military experts of every nation did not give China a ghost of a chance. But, when Japan failed to bring China cringing to her knees as she vaunted, the world took solace in the phenomenon by declaring that they had over-estimated Japan's military strength. Nevertheless, when the greedy flames of war inexorably spread in the Pacific following the perfidious attack on Pearl Harbor . . . the pendulum swung to the other extreme. . . . Let us not forget that during the first four and a half years of total aggression China has borne Japan's sadistic fury unaided and alone.

Despite her "purfled" prose, May-ling's address to Congress was a great success. She had one more significant contact with the Washington press, at a conference in the White House Oval Office, where 172 journalists crammed in for another look. She wore a dress cunningly adorned with the wings of the Chinese Air Force. The newsmen came closer to subjects sensitive for both Madame Chiang and the President:

> Is there any truth in reports that China is not using her manpower to the fullest? Madame Chiang showed a touch of anger. China, she said, is using her manpower to the extent that she has munitions. The President had said the need was for more munitions. China has trained pilots, but she has not enough planes or gasoline.
>
> How is she going to get them? Madame Chiang turned deferentially to Franklin Roosevelt. He had solved so many important questions and come through so many crises, she could safely, she felt, leave that question to him.
>
> The reporters smiled at how she had neatly tossed the ball to Franklin Roosevelt. Undeterred, the President picked it up and ran—ran hard.

There are immense difficulties in getting planes and supplies to China, he said, but the U.S. is working hard to get them there. If he were a member of the Chinese Government, the President added, he would certainly ask: But when and why not a little more? As a member of the American Government he would have to reply: As fast as the Lord will let us. The President settled contentedly back in his chair.

Next question for Madame Chiang: Did she have any suggestions on how U.S. aid to China could be stepped up? She rose, stared straight ahead, then turned to the President. He had just said as soon as the Lord will let us. But she remembered, the Lord helps those who help themselves.

Dazed by the show, one columnist remarked, "Some day they may put Helen Hayes in the part, but she'll never do it any better than Madame Chiang." On March 1, May-ling again graced the cover of *Time*.

But all was not well in the White House. Eleanor Roosevelt, who had treated her like a daughter, was disenchanted. The staff concurred that she was the most troublesome guest in all the years of the Roosevelt administration. In February, the chief White House usher telephoned Treasury Secretary Morgenthau's office. May-ling had learned that a shipment of a special brand of mentholated English cigarettes had just arrived for her in New York. She wished to have the Secretary of the Treasury instruct the Collector of Customs to release the shipment immediately. Morgenthau's staff discovered that the cigarettes were still aboard ship. But calls from the White House persisted. In annoyance, Morgenthau's office sent a Treasury agent to get the cigarettes and fly them down to Washington.

It came as no surprise when Morgenthau told his staff, "The President . . . is just crazy to get her out of the country."

Despite his exasperation, Roosevelt had to guard May-ling's public reputation because it reflected on his China policy. There were still grand plans for Madame Chiang, plans laid by that master stagecrafter, Henry R. Luce.

Henry Luce was very busy helping one-time missionary B. A. Garside consolidate the eight charitable agencies aiding China into what would become United China Relief, cutting down overhead so more money would reach the Chinese people. Luce contributed $60,000 and assigned two *Time* publicity men, Otis Swift and Douglas Auchincloss, to the effort. Then Luce persuaded Thomas W. Lamont, Paul Hoffman, Wendell Willkie, David O. Selznick, and other prominent figures to share the UCR board of directors with him. Luce also sent a personal appeal to all *Time* subscribers, which netted the campaign nearly a quarter of a million dollars.

By the end of 1942, remittances of $17 million U.S. were committed to UCR. Some came from the rich and powerful like Henry Luce, but other sums poured in from small-town America. One gift was accompanied by a letter that read: "This is a small offering from the Stacy Bible class in Chapel Hill, North Carolina. The Stacy Bible Class is made up of mature women, mothers and grandmothers, and they have collected this money. We are none of us rich people, but we know about children and what they must have to grow up well and bright." Unfortunately, the widow's mite from Stacy Bible class, and more formidable sums from others, vaporized on contact with H. H. Kung's superheated currency market. China's inflation was becoming ridiculous. Prices rose in 1938 by 49 percent; in 1939 by 83 percent; 1940, by 124 percent; 1941, by 173 percent; 1942 by 235 percent. While foreign currency coming to China had to be converted at the official rate of $20 Chinese to $1 U.S., prices for goods and services were determined by the black market, where a single U.S. dollar could bring up to $3,250 Chinese. At the official rate, a pack of American cigarettes in Chungking cost $5 U.S.; on the black market, $5 U.S. would buy 162 packs. Therefore, the millions donated for China relief became almost worthless when exchanged at the official rate. It was Chungking's idea of a joke that, at the official rate, building a latrine in China cost $10,000 U.S. What was less amusing was that Chinese officials could exchange the aid money on the black market and realize extraordinary profits.

Luce's correspondent in Chungking, Theodore White, was reporting some of these unappetizing realities, but Luce was not letting them into his publications, or possibly into his own consciousness. Because of his blind spot toward the Chiangs and Soongs, Luce seemed totally unaware of the uses to which American private aid was being put. He struggled to raise more and more, with May-ling's help. He arranged banquets and speaking engagements coast to coast. The six-week itinerary included New York, Chicago, and Los Angeles.

May-ling's first stop was New York, where Luce had persuaded John D. Rockefeller to chair the Citizens' Committee to Welcome Madame Chiang Kai-shek. The committee totaled some 270 influential, fashionable New Yorkers, and was co-chaired by Henry Luce. Wanting nothing but the best, May-ling took a suite on the forty-second floor of the Waldorf-Astoria Towers a few floors below the Luces. Every time she prepared to leave her suite, the Secret Service was required to clear the entire floor. On more than one occasion, May-ling dawdled for hours before deciding to cancel an outing, causing no small amount of ill-feeling among guests who were obliged to twiddle thumbs while Madame Chiang came to a decision.

On the evening of March 2, she was guest of honor at a mass rally in Madison Square Garden. There was a wartime blackout the same evening, and May-ling, according to one account, "had to dress in the dark by the inadequate circle of light cast by a flashlight which her nurse held for her." The reporter then added, with the peculiar toadying that Americans lavished on the Chiangs, "But she had been drilled in sterner blackouts than any of us have experienced."

Prior to her speech at the Garden, Luce was to introduce May-ling at an elaborate "private" banquet at the Waldorf for sixty special guests, including Wendell Willkie, General Hap Arnold, Paul G. Hoffman, David Dubinsky, New York Governor Thomas E. Dewey, plus the governers of New Jersey, Pennsylvania, Connecticut, Massachusetts, Rhode Island, Maine, Vermont, and New Hampshire. T. V. was also among the guests.

The first ladies of the North Atlantic states toyed with dishes of tepid *tournedos sautés aux champignons* as their menfolk cleared their throats, and Luce finally sent a nervous message to May-ling's suite. Apparently May-ling was indisposed and could not make it down the corridor to the elevators even for after-dinner coffee. She was saving herself for the address that was to follow the dinner.

If Luce was infuriated by this behavior, there was no sign of it in the *Life* coverage of May-ling's appearance later that night at Madison Square Garden. "Mass Tribute to Mme. Chiang" rang the headline. The story described the "vast, enthusiastic audience [that] roared approval as Wendell Willkie called Madame 'an avenging angel . . . a soldier unafraid to fight for justice.'"

Her New York stops also included a tour of Chinatown, where thousands lined the narrow streets. Some estimates placed the crowd at 50,000. May-ling worked in a long weekend at her alma mater, Wellesley, with a reunion of the class of 1917. The next day, she took a well-publicized Sunday stroll across the campus, wearing slacks in a day when such mannish attire was shunned in proper girls' schools. One student remarked: "Golly, what a break she gave us! Now they'll stop razzing us about the way we look in dungarees." Wellesley's President McAfee graciously replied, "Anyone who can look as smart as Madame Chiang in slacks may wear them."

Then she was off for six weeks by train cross-country. In Chicago, the local United China Relief Committee offered Madame half a floor of the Palmer House for herself and her entourage. The hotel management had been persuaded to donate the space in behalf of Madame's China cause. But Louis Kung, who served as advance man for the tour, decided that the Palmer House was not the best that Chicago had to offer. At a cost of many thousands of dollars to United China Relief, Madame was ensconced instead at the Drake.

The relief officials also were hard-pressed to explain May-ling's opulent attire in light of her plea for impoverished China. Some of the pearls she wore in her shoes may have been those stripped from the Phoenix Crown of the Dowager Empress when grave robbers looted her tomb and defiled her corpse in 1928. These pearls, according to the boy emperor Pu-yi, had then been presented to the Generalissimo and his wife as a gift. But part of her impact came from being anachronistic. To Americans, she was the princess of the Chinese paupers, the American empress of China, Snow White at the court of the Seven Oriental Dwarfs. (The State Department actually referred to her in code as "Snow White.") She was not the real China but what Americans were fond of calling "a reasonable facsimile." Like chop suey.

Her role as a fantasy stand-in was nowhere more clearly revealed than at a little town in Utah, where every inhabitant, including fifty village schoolchildren, turned out in the dawn hours hoping to catch a glimpse of the famous Madame Chiang Kai-shek. As the train clattered and shrieked to a stop, May-ling was still in bed. Instead of appearing herself, her Chinese maid, who spoke and understood a little English, came out on the platform. Dressed in May-ling's cape, the maid, who had watched the procedure countless times, and was well coached, nodded her head graciously at the excited crowd and smiled benignly in acknowledgment of the choruses of "There she is! There she is!" P. T. Barnum would have been pleased.

New York and Chicago could hardly compare with what Henry Luce arranged in Los Angeles. Following a huge banquet on March 31 at the Ambassador Hotel, there was a full house waiting at the Hollywood Bowl. The Committee to Receive Madame Chiang included Mary

Pickford, Rita Hayworth, Marlene Dietrich, Ingrid Bergman, Ginger Rogers, and Shirley Temple. She was escorted by the governor and the mayor, and introduced by Spencer Tracy and Henry Fonda. "The Madame Chiang Kai-shek March" (composed for the occasion by Herbert Stothart) was played by the Los Angeles Philharmonic Orchestra, and a symphonic narrative about China was delivered soberly by Walter Huston and Edward G. Robinson. It was all "Arranged and Supervised by David O. Selznick," better remembered for *Gone With the Wind*.

Rising to the occasion, May-ling recalled particularly brutal highlights of Japanese warfare in China, especially the Rape of Nanking, when "The invaders plundered and stripped the crucified populace of all means of livelihood, molested our women and rounded up all able-bodied men, tied them together like animals, forced them to dig their own graves and finally kicked them in and buried them alive." She sounded every bit as outraged as had been her sister Ching-ling, in 1936, when the Generalissimo had ordered that China's six leading young writers be buried alive.

One of the chief commitments of United China Relief was to help the millions of Chinese suffering from famine in Honan Province. It was *Time*'s Theodore White who drew the situation in Honan forcefully to the attention of Chiang Kai-shek and then to the American public when *Time* at last covered the story in March 1943.

This is how White described the incident many years later:

What we saw, I now no longer believe—except that my scribbled notes insist I saw what I saw. There were the bodies: the first, no more than an hour out of Loyang, lying in the snow, a day or two dead, her face shriveled about her skull; she must have been young; and the snow fell on her eyes; and she would lie unburied until the birds or the dogs cleaned her bones. The dogs were also there along the road . . . and they were sleek, well fed. We stopped to take a picture of dogs digging bodies from sand piles; some were half-eaten. . . .

I was invited to visit [an orphanage]. It stank worse than anything else I have ever smelled. Even the escorting officer could not stand the odor and, holding his handkerchief to his nose, asked to be excused. These were abandoned babies. They were inserted four to a crib. Those who could not fit in cribs were simply laid on the straw. I forget what they were fed. But they smelled of baby vomit and baby shit, and when they were dead, they were cleared out.

So I saw these things, but the worst was what I heard, which was about cannibalism. I never saw any man kill another person for meat. . . . But it seemed irrefutably true that people were eating people meat. . . .

What [Chiang's] army had done in Honan was to collect more in grain taxes than the land had raised in grain. They had emptied the countryside of food; they had shipped in no grain from grain-surplus areas, they had ignored the need of the people. . . .

I was uncontrollably indignant as I tried to reach Chiang Kai-shek with the story: I ran about screaming, in almost insane fashion. . . . So impatient had I been to get the story out from the famine area that I had filed it raw from Honan, from the first telegraph station en route home—Loyang. By regulation, like any press dispatch, it should have been sent back via Chungking to be censored by my old companions in the ministry, who would certainly have stopped it. This telegram, however, was flashed from Loyang to New York, via the commercial radio system in Chengtu. Either the system had broken down, or some unknown telegraph key-tapper at the Loyang telegraph office had been pushed by conscience to scoff at regulations and route the dispatch to New York, direct and uncensored. Thus, when the story broke, it broke in TIME magazine, of all places—the magazine most committed to the Chinese cause in all America. Madame Chiang Kai-shek was then in the United States, and the story infuriated her; she asked my publisher, Harry Luce, to fire me; but he refused, for which I honor him. Our own quarrel would come later.

May-ling returned to Chungking on July 4, 1943.

Graham Peck, who was working in China for the Office of War Information, noticed that, although Americans at home were fooled about China, American GIs were not. When May-ling's luggage was taken off at an airfield in Assam, to lighten her airliner for the dangerous flight over the Hump, the luggage was put aboard a U.S. army transport plane.

This was done [Peck said] in a rather remote part of the field, and the GI's who were doing it happened to drop one crate. It split open and its contents rolled out . . . it was full of cosmetics, lingerie, and fancy groceries with which Madame Chiang planned to see herself through the rest of the war. The GIs were furious, for this was one of the times when the Hump transport was in a bad state, with many American fliers losing their lives to get war supplies to China. The soldiers dropped and broke all the other crates they transshipped. When they had kicked every fur coat and trick clock around in the dust as thoroughly as time would permit they threw the mess into the waiting planes.

Back in America three months after May-ling went home, a large stained-glass window was installed in the St. John's Episcopal Church in Massena, New York, a quiet town on the St. Lawrence River. The window, executed by Pennsylvania artist Valentine d'Ogries, depicts the Heavenly Life, with Jesus Christ at the top, Mary and various saints below, moving forward chronologically to the present. The figure representing the present has an Oriental countenance. It is Madame Chiang Kai-shek, "the First Lady of Christendom." She is holding a scroll bearing her Christian plea to all Americans: *We must try to forgive.*

Chapter 18

A HOUSE DIVIDED

The 1943 Cairo summit was the apex of May-ling's political career, and the beginning of the end for Chiang. Along the Nile, protocol officers arranged the four famous leaders in a row for a photograph designed to lend Chiang historic stature. There are many versions of the picture. The Generalissimo was on camera left. Next to him sat President Roosevelt, then Prime Minister Churchill, and finally Madame Chiang. Churchill was dressed in a white three-piece suit worn with black socks and a cigar; on his plump lap perched a gray homburg. Beside him, May-ling was in her usual cheong-sam, wearing a short white coat and shoes adorned with net butterfly bows. (Churchill was studiously ignoring her, exchanging witticisms with someone out of camera range; the Chiangs were never taken very seriously in Great Britain, where a popular wartime radio comedy featured a character named "General Cash My-check.") At the far end, the Generalissimo was in his usual crisp uniform with three stars at the high collar. In his gloved hands he held a képi bearing the disk emblem of the KMT sun. Beside him, FDR looked puffy and weary in a double-breasted gabardine, his crippled legs set at a jaunty angle for the cameras. With consummate skill, FDR leaned over toward the Generalissimo and seemed to be sharing with him some wry observation. Chiang wore a tight grin as if he understood. But of course he did not. Whatever Roosevelt was pretending to say was said only as a petty deceit for the benefit of the American people. It had a greater impact than FDR could have imagined.

It had been Roosevelt's idea to invite Chiang to Cairo. Churchill

had resisted stubbornly, but the President insisted. A few months earlier, Roosevelt had also obliged General Stilwell to stifle his indignation
and pin America's Legion of Merit on the Generalissimo. After invest-
ing so much money and matériel in China, FDR wanted the world to
see Chiang as a great international statesman, a member of the Big
Four, who shared private jokes with the American President. In Cairo,
he held frustrating discussions with Chiang through interpreters and
promised to divert Japanese pressure from China by staging an Allied
assault in Burma and the Bay of Bengal in 1944.

Churchill's opinion was that these China talks were "lengthy, complicated and minor." The Prime Minister believed that the Americans
were greatly exaggerating the ability of Chiang's government to play
a role in the war. He was more concerned with keeping the Japanese
out of British India, and with recapturing the lost bastion of Singapore,
which remained "the supreme British objective" in Asia. Churchill and
Roosevelt proceeded from Cairo to confer with Stalin in Teheran,
where FDR was finally persuaded to give up those Asian battle plans
to devote attention to the Allied invasion of Europe. When word of this
reversal reached Chungking, Chiang Kai-shek was incensed. Angrily,
he advised the U.S. ambassador that nothing but a loan of a billion U.S.
dollars could "assure the Chinese people and army of your serious
concern." T. V. Soong had just obtained a loan of half that amount from
Washington, and another five hundred million from Britain. Now
Chiang wanted Washington to double the ante. General Cash My-check
had struck again.

As often as different versions of the Cairo photograph were reproduced in history books for schoolchildren and for the general public in
the popular press, they continued to give the deceptive impression of
rapport. The truth was exactly the opposite. Not only could Roosevelt
and Chiang not speak face to face, or see eye to eye; not only was
May-ling's presence an irritant both to the Prime Minister and the
President (who so recently had been desperate to get her out of his
house and country)—but at that moment the Chiangs themselves were
not on the way up but on the way down. The year the Soong Dynasty
lost the Mandate of Heaven was not 1949 when Mao Tse-tung took
power in Peking, as is so often asserted, but 1943—*before* the United
States became inextricably entangled with its fate.

This historic change of tide was noticed and reported by those
watching China for the press and the State Department, but they were

ignored. A question that is now a sour joke was then being asked for the
first time: How could Chiang begin to lose power just when the United
States was really getting behind him? It was an example of judgment
so bad that Washington for decades would resist admitting its mistake.
For such bad news are messengers shot.

The Chinese Communists were still in no position to challenge
Chiang; they were sealed off from southern China by a 500,000-man
KMT blockade. But, bottled up as they were in northern China, the reds
were waging a remarkably effective guerrilla war against the Japanese.
The Imperial Army tried to force the Communists back with a
scorched-earth policy that ravaged the countryside and drove more
people into Mao's ranks. Along the KMT-Japanese front in the South
there was little action, because Chiang's armies were under orders to
keep a safe distance between them and the enemy. Opposing commanders engaged in trade across that no-man's-land, bartering American Lend-Lease materials for Japanese consumer goods. Fortunes were
made.

The only KMT armies that did fight were those under Stilwell's
control in Burma, particularly those under General Sun Li-jen. They
fought only occasionally, but when they could be coerced into fighting,
as in the Myitkyina campaign, they did well. Everything Vinegar Joe
accomplished he did over the strenuous objections of Chiang Kai-shek,
who was joined by Chennault in a campaign to vilify and get rid of
Stilwell.

Within the Chinese territory nominally under Chiang's control,
conditions were deteriorating at an alarming rate. Currency was worthless, although H. H. Kung kept up his paper-money pantomime. Manufactured goods were unattainable except to corrupt bureaucrats and
military officers, who, with few exception, hoarded and profiteered.
Foolishly, Chiang backed Kung's latest plan to fight inflation by fixing
prices. Immediately, producers withheld all meat and cooking oil from
the marketplace, awaiting better prices. In Chungking, even the middle class grew gaunt, and saw their children die. Many educated Chinese who had once supported the Kuomintang now realized that it was
preoccupied only with maintaining its grip, and turned against it. Some
were permanently alienated. Others restrained themselves to mildly
condemning the policies of the regime, only to become targets of secret
police repression. Absurdly, the regime did not fight the war but

dragged into Tai Li's headquarters any loyal subjects who dared to criticize. They were beaten, beheaded, starved, or turned into heroin addicts at KMT concentration camps run by Tai Li.

The loyalty of Chiang's officer corps was a thin crust on top of a huge standing army that had been dragooned into service. There was no anatomy of loyalty running down into the ranks. This was not new in China; but in the past, when dynasties fell, the mandarin bureaucracy usually carried over to the new dynasty, providing a vital continuity of administration. When classical Chinese regimes changed, they changed only at the top. This mandarinate no longer existed. It had been one of the targets of the 1911 Revolution. Nothing had since grown in its place.

The "right" to govern now depended entirely upon the *believability* of the KMT, which is to say its prestige, by definition "a conjuror's trick or illusion." This was the essence of the Mandate of Heaven. As Chiang's believability evaporated, those who drew attention to the fact, as to the emperor's lack of clothes, were in terrible danger.

Chiang was becoming more tyrannical. He shifted more and more control away from members of the Soong family (who had always been an indulgence), to the C-C Clique of the Ch'en brothers (who had always been a necessity). He could not survive without the Ch'ens, because they directly represented the people who had put him in power—the hierarchy of the Green Gang—and survival was now at issue. Big-eared Tu was aging and no longer in a position to guarantee Chiang's position entirely on his own. In the end, Chiang's ties to the blood brotherhood of the Green Gang as a whole were proving stronger than his ties to his dynastic family.

The influence of the Soongs was not immediately eclipsed. They stayed where they were, and kept their titles, while the Ch'en Clique leapfrogged over them. Liberalism, such as it was, represented by the Soongs, ceased to be the national façade. As Chiang leaned more on the Ch'ens and Tai Li, he drifted, like Hitler, into megalomania. He showed increasing arrogance toward Washington. This did not cost him its support. American officials were not interested in whether Chiang violated human rights and ruled by charade. Washington—not as represented by Chief-of-Staff General George C. Marshall but as typified by FDR's political advisor Harry Hopkins—increasingly shared Chiang's fixation with the postwar threat of Communism. To please the Generalissimo and his supporters in America, the Washington of Hopkins and the Department of State was prepared to sacrifice any number of its own people.

American aid to Tai Li was stepped up through U.S. Navy Commander Milton E. "Mary" Miles, who had been sent out to run "black," or covert, operations against the Japanese along the China coast. Miles by his own admission figured that the best way to accomplish this in a strange land was to put everything in the hands of the man who knew where all the bodies were buried—the secret police boss. They set up a joint operation code-named SACO. As a consequence, Miles ended up doing little against the Japanese but a lot for Tai Li, and Tai Li nothing whatever for the U.S. This led to a memorable confrontation with America's spymaster William J. "Wild Bill" Donovan.

It was apparent to Donovan that Tai Li was doing everything possible to keep the OSS from knowing what was going on in China, and that Tai Li and Miles were altogether too friendly. Flying to Chungking, Donovan found his opportunity in the midst of a banquet for him that included as guests the American ambassador, assorted generals of both sides, Tai Li, and T. V. Soong. Everybody drank too much except Donovan and his counterpart, who remained cold-eyed as toast followed toast into the wee hours. The others were startled when Donovan suddenly told Tai Li that if he was going to obstruct the intelligence gathering of OSS agents in China, the OSS agents would operate separately.

Smiling, Tai Li said, "If OSS tries to operate outside SACO, I will kill your agents."

"For every one of our agents you kill," replied Donovan, "we will kill one of your generals."

"You can't talk to me like that," said Tai Li.

"I am talking to you like that," Donovan answered.

But such frankness was rare. America failed to understand the trap it was falling into because the State Department was not listening to its China Watchers. Very few of their secret reports actually reached the Secretary of State, because the rest were being intercepted by partisans inside the department hierarchy. Although the Secretary of State was not reading them, the Chinese were. According to information gathered by the FBI at the time, someone high in the department was passing this secret information straight over to China Defense Supplies, to be read by T. V. Soong and to be acted upon as he saw fit. So the Americans sent to China to watch Chiang's regime were reporting to the Soong family, not to President Roosevelt.

At the War Department, the situation was quite different. General Marshall was suspicious of Chiang, and listened to Stilwell's warnings. But it was difficult to persuade FDR to share this suspicion. The President's ear was monopolized by politicals like Harry Hopkins and the China cronies around Tommy Corcoran and T. V. Soong. There were now so many well-connected people muddling things up that no rational discussion of China could take place. Joe Alsop added his considerable skill to the confusion of matters on the spot in Chungking. First, Alsop had himself posted to China as Chennault's "press aide" in charge of public relations. Then, when he was captured by the Japanese in Hong Kong and later repatriated, Alsop used his influence to get a new assignment as Lend-Lease representative in Chungking, where he threw his weight again into the campaign to destroy Stilwell.

The Stilwell issue came to a head in 1944, right after the Japanese launched Operation Ichigo in eastern China. This was their first big drive since the capture of Wuhan in 1938. It was made necessary because American submarines had penetrated into Japanese home waters, interrupting the seaborne supply route used to maintain the conquered empire in Southeast Asia. Those distant outposts were now short of matériel and vulnerable to Allied assault. Japan's only alternative supply route was the main north-south railway line in China, the capture of which had not been necessary before. At the same time they planned to destroy the new forward air bases being established by Chennault's Fourteenth Air Force.

Chennault had impressed FDR by boasting that his planes could sink a million tons of Japanese shipping if he had those forward bases, and if he had the planes—and if Stilwell did not get the best part of the war supplies. These same bases, he said, could be used for B–29s to strike at Japan's home islands. To the contrary, argued Stilwell; he predicted that the Japanese would simply destroy the bases. As usual, Stilwell was right.

Fifteen Japanese divisions plus five other brigades struck in April 1944, and the defending Chinese army of 300,000 men simply evaporated. Japanese units of as little as five hundred men routed thousands of Chinese troups. The Chinese commanders commandeered trucks to flee with their families and possessions into the interior. Chennault claimed none of this would have happened if Stilwell had allowed enough Lend-Lease to go to those particular Chinese units. In truth some of the armies in question were so lavishly provided with U.S. equipment that their commanders were selling it on the black market and to the Japanese. In places where the Generalissimo claimed that a bold defense was planned, Theodore White found only two ill-equipped

regiments of dragooned peasant soldiers, who were going to be sacrificed beneath a huge Japanese steamroller.

> The men walked quietly, with the curious bitterness of Chinese sol-
> diers who expect nothing but disaster. . . . They were wiry and brown but
> thin; their guns were old, their yellow-and-brown uniforms threadbare.
> Each carried two grenades tucked in his belt; about the neck of each was
> a long blue stocking inflated like a roll of bologna with dry rice kernels, the
> Chinese soldier's only field rations. Their feet were broken and puffed
> above their straw sandals; their heads were covered with birds' nests of
> leaves woven together to give shade from the sun and supposedly to supply
> camouflage. The sweat rolled from them; dust rose about them; the heat
> clutched the entire country, and giddy, glistening waves rose from the rice
> paddies.

When the battle began it was soon over. "All that flesh and blood
could do the Chinese soldiers were doing," White wrote. "They were
walking up hills and dying in the sun, but they had no support, no
directions. They were doomed."

With the loss of the airfields, Chennault and Chiang stepped up
their efforts to make Stilwell the scapegoat. In June, when Vice President Henry Wallace arrived to spend several days in Chungking, Stilwell was not around to speak in his own behalf. He was at the Burmese
front, involved in the long, bloody drive on Myitkyina, the biggest and
most successful American military operation on the Asian mainland in
all of World War II, and the only one that included American combat
troops—Merrill's Marauders.

For cosmetic reasons, the Generalissimo ordered all beggars
rounded up, roped together, and sent far out of Chungking. Wallace
was taken in tow by T. V. Soong and Joe Alsop. Before the Vice President's ears had stopped ringing from the aircraft engines, they were
being filled with all of Stilwell's sins.

At meetings with the Generalissimo, Wallace was successful in
pressing him to allow a team of American observers to go to the Communist headquarters at Yenan. But Chiang wanted tit for tat. When he
drove Wallace to the airport to see him off, Chiang pressed him in
return to see that Stilwell was replaced by Major General Albert C.
Wedemeyer, a more agreeable and flexible man on Lord Mountbatten's
staff in Delhi. The Generalissimo also wanted Roosevelt to send out a
new personal representative to replace the troublesome Ambassador

Clarence Gauss. After reflecting overnight, Wallace sent the following report to the President from his next stop, Kunming: "Chiang, at best, is a short-term investment. It is not believed that he has the intelligence or political strength to run post-war China. The leaders of post-war China will be brought forward by evolution, or revolution, and it now seems more likely the latter."

Ironically, as political pressure against Stilwell increased in Chungking, the War Department got more firmly behind him and urged Roosevelt to promote Vinegar Joe to four-star general, and to insist that Chiang put him in charge of all Chinese forces in China as well as in Burma and India. "We are fully aware of the Generalissimo's feeling regarding Stilwell," said a Joint Chiefs' memo to the President, ". . . but the fact remains that he has proven his case or contentions on the field of battle in opposition to the highly negative attitudes of both the British and the Chinese authorities."

Thus prompted by his senior commanders, Roosevelt sent the Generalissimo a message saying that Stilwell was being promoted and urging Chiang to put the entire Chinese army at his command, because "the future of all Asia is at stake."

Chiang could not refuse outright, so he hedged, insisting that Roosevelt first send a special emissary to "adjust" relations with Stilwell, and give Chiang time to get his armies accustomed to the idea of being commanded by an American. Before the matter could be settled, there was a brief Japanese attack along the Burma Road and Chiang became so nervous about the chance the Japanese might press all the way to Kunming that he threatened to withdraw all his soldiers from the Burma front to safety behind the Salween River.

Roosevelt sent an urgent note to Chiang, warning that all U.S. aid would cease if the Generalissimo withdrew his troops from Burma and if he did not give Stilwell overall command. The note from FDR. Stilwell realized, was "a hot firecracker." Stilwell got an audience with Chiang, "handed this bundle of paprika to the Peanut and then sank back with a sigh. The harpoon hit the little bugger right in the solar plexus and went right through him."

Chiang was mortified and infuriated by Roosevelt's blunt demand. Putting Stilwell in charge of the KMT armies raised questions that were political, not military, and would jeopardize the vast web of corruption on which Chiang's survival depended. Stilwell's delight was premature.

When the crunch finally came, Stilwell was not defeated by Chiang, by Chennault, or by the Soongs. He was defeated by Washington's refusal to trust its own observers in the field, and by its predisposition to resolve Chinese dilemmas with Oklahoma logic. Stilwell was defeated by someone who knew nothing about China—by Roosevelt's new "personal representative" Patrick Hurley.

As the new man in town, Hurley got off on the wrong foot immediately by promising the Generalissimo that America was "behind Chiang personally all the way." In other words, anything the Generalissimo craved he could now have. Chiang decided to test Hurley's boast; he turned his back on Roosevelt's demand and, in a message dated September 24, 1944, insisted once again that Stilwell be recalled: "General Stilwell is unfitted for the vast, complex and delicate duties which the new command will entail," Chiang wrote. Before Roosevelt could reply, Chiang announced formally to his Central Executive Committee that he would not give the command to Stilwell. This put President Roosevelt in a predicament. He could not force Chiang's hand without doing so before the whole KMT leadership. In fact, this was only a facile and transparent political maneuver on Chiang's part, but it gave Stilwell's American enemies, including Harry Hopkins, a point of leverage. The time had come for the American government to stand firm if it was ever going to be firm with Chiang. And, as just about everybody knew in his bones, it was really not going to be firm.

Major General Patrick J. Hurley carried a disproportionate amount of political weight. He was a tall, wealthy Oklahoman who had been Secretary of War in the Hoover Administration, and FDR occasionally used him as a troubleshooter. His solution to handling the Chungking snakepit was to play the fool with Choctaw war whoops, gladhanding the men he called "Chancre Jack" and "Moose Dung," and brandishing a loaded revolver in the face of an old China hand at the embassy when he filed memoranda that Hurley did not like. Hurley was the proverbial bull in a China shop. He sent a note to Roosevelt urging FDR to do what Chiang wanted. From Hurley's simple-minded point of view, if it was a choice between Chiang and Stilwell then the only choice was Chiang. Roosevelt, putting out of his mind everything he had been told by General Marshall and others, decided to let America's bet ride on Hurley. He ordered Stilwell's immediate recall.

"THE AX FALLS," Stilwell wrote in his diary.

After Stilwell's recall, Roosevelt rewarded Hurley with Ambassador Gauss's job. Dangerously encouraged, Hurley trimmed his jaunty mustache and decided to attempt the single-handed overnight settlement of China's civil war. First, he went to Yenan and startled the Communist leadership by asking under what terms they would agree to work with Chiang. Armed with Mao's straightforward terms of settlement, Hurley hastened back to Chungking, only to discover how wrong he was. The Generalissimo would not even consider Mao's terms. Thereafter, even Chiang Kai-shek referred to Hurley as "a damned fool."

Rushing off to Yenan again with a new plan, Hurley tried to get Mao to accept domination by Chiang Kai-shek—to which Mao shouted: "That turtle's egg Chiang!" From then on, the Communists referred to Hurley contemptuously as "Little Whiskers." To make the name calling complete, Hurley thereafter referred to Mao as "Motherfucker!"

Harold Isaacs, who was now covering the war for *Newsweek*, concluded that Hurley "had fallen among men whose brand of politics is a little too finely spun." But *Time*'s Annalee Jacoby was less charitable. Hurley, she noted, "forgot where he was, with whom he was, and even what he had just said."

The eyes and ears of the U.S. Government in Chungking were a handful of old China hands, several of them the children of missionaries. While some went on to have long and distinguished careers in the Foreign Service, for our purposes the most important were those whose careers were short-lived, Jack Service, O. Edmund Clubb, John Paton Davies, and John Carter Vincent. They were among those who were forced out of government and otherwise were persecuted during the McCarthy era for reporting unwelcome news about China. According to the witch hunters, these were the Americans who "lost China."

The China Watchers' message essentially was that no matter how much Washington wanted Chiang Kai-shek to "run" China, he was about to lose it to the Communists. This was something that their immediate superiors at the State Department simply did not want to hear. It was contrary to the prevailing myth. The observers in Chungking were accused of being in favor of what they predicted—in favor of communism. In fact, they were only warning their government of a course of events that now seemed certain, so that a realistic policy could be developed. Washington reacted with deep suspicion and hostility, and insisted on nailing the American flag the more tightly to the mast of Chiang's sinking ship.

"China is in a mess," reported Jack Service in a typical memorandum on March 20, 1944.

... for the sorry situation as a whole Chiang, and only Chiang, is responsible. . . . Chiang will cooperate if the U.S., upon which he is dependent, makes up its mind exactly what it wants from him and then gets hard-boiled about it. . . . This may mean taking an active part in Chinese affairs. But unless we do it, China will not be of much use as an ally. And, in doing it, we may save China.

Davies, assigned to work with Stilwell, wrote to Harry Hopkins that "The Generalissimo is probably the only Chinese who shares the popular American misconception that Chiang Kai-shek is China."

Rather than being hard-boiled, Washington coddled Chiang. It became routine for the Generalissimo (or T. V. Soong speaking for Chiang) to threaten a separate peace with Japan unless their latest demands were met. One variation of this threat was for T. V. or Chiang to warn that they would get help from Moscow if they could not get it from Washington, which, if anyone thought about it, was a curious threat from a government whose usual theme was anti-Communism.

Roosevelt was bulldozed. He imagined himself to have a serious grasp of the Chinese mentality. The truth was he had firsthand contact only with Americanized Chinese like May-ling and T. V.—the kind other Chinese call "bananas" because they are only yellow on the outside, white on the inside. When the President met Chiang in Cairo, it was FDR's first glimpse, he admitted, of a "real Oriental." Roosevelt confided to Sumner Welles that he had encountered "innumerable difficulties" dealing with Chiang, found him "highly temperamental" and personally was affronted "with the regime's apparent lack of sympathy for the abject misery of the masses of the Chinese people." Nevertheless, Roosevelt instructed General Marshall to give Chiang special consideration:

> All of us must remember that the Generalissimo came up the hard way to become the undisputed leader of four hundred million people—an enormously difficult job to attain any kind of unity from a diverse group of all kinds of leaders—military men, educators, scientists, public health people, engineers, all of them struggling for power and mastery, local or national, and to create in a very short time throughout China what it took us a couple of centuries to attain.
>
> Besides that the Generalissimo finds it necessary to maintain his position of supremacy. You and I would do the same thing under the circumstances. He is the chief executive as well as the commander-in-chief, and one cannot speak sternly to a man like that or exact commitments from him the way we might do from the Sultan of Morocco.

This portrayal of Chiang was ridiculously inaccurate. Roosevelt seemed to be talking about himself rather than about Chiang. He confessed during an interview with Edgar Snow early in 1945, "I was never able to form any opinion of Chiang at Cairo. When I thought about it later I realized that all I knew was what Madame Chiang told me about her husband and what he thought."

American policy was thus based upon the personalities of the Chiangs, the Soongs, and the Kungs, rather than upon the events, the nation, or the people. This was a tribute to the Soongs' extraordinary stagecraft. The man officially responsible for making U.S. China policy —Stanley Hornbeck, the doyen of State's Far Eastern Division—had only the most abbreviated and stilted knowledge of China, and had been out of touch personally for many years.

Hornbeck was one of those basking hamadryads of the State Department who, having reached a place in the sun, lie coiled in wait for any creature that might disturb its repose. He had spent only four years of his life in China, teaching in government colleges at the time of the 1911 Revolution. He had scant knowledge of the language, even less of the country or its people. What little he knew he published in 1916 in an opaque book titled *Contemporary Politics in the Far East,* which quickly found its way to oblivion. As an army captain during World War I, he attained a role of "expert" on the Far East, lent his insight to the dismal resolution of Asian matters in the peace settlement of 1919, and at the Washington Conference in 1921, which further resolved the world's balance of power and set the stage for World War II. On this dubious basis Hornbeck got a job as a lecturer on Asia at Harvard in the twenties, published another book that did not stand up to serious scrutiny, and parlayed the book and his Harvard position into an appointment in 1928 as chief of Far Eastern Affairs at the Department of State.

This incredible stroke of misfortune for the nation gave Hornbeck control of the flow of information from Foreign Service officers to policy planners at State and to the presidential Cabinet. He withheld cables from the Secretary of State that were critical of Chiang, and once stated that "the United States Far Eastern policy is like a train running on a railroad track. It has been clearly laid out and where it is going is plain to all." It was in fact bound for Saigon in 1975, with whistle stops along the way at Peking, Quemoy, Matsu, and the Yalu River.

Hornbeck hid his ignorance behind a moralistic front. He relied on the venerable old State Department ploy of using legalisms and technicalities to counter the proposals of better-informed junior officers. He claimed to have special, esoteric knowledge of the Mysterious East that was beyond the reach of ordinary mortals. Hornbeck and his drab protégé Maxwell Hamilton were dangerously out of touch with reality. But when his staff finally rebelled in 1944, calling attention to Hornbeck's withholding of vital information from Secretary Hull, he was simply reposted as ambassador to the Netherlands, and evaded all blame for the next three decades of disastrous consequences. Other, better men had their careers ruined and their lives wrecked because of the way Hornbeck had run his shop, but Hornbeck blithely eluded it all.

It was too late in any case, for Hornbeck's express was already hurtling down the wrong track. When Jack Service returned to Washington for consultations at the beginning of January 1943, he discovered that he was the first American Foreign Service officer to return from Chungking since Pearl Harbor. "There was Spanish Moss hanging from the rafters," he reported. Professionally, Service had concentrated on Chinese Communist affairs, and achieved a keen understanding during a journey through the region under Mao's control.

While he was in Washington, he wrote a long memorandum urging that "the most careful study should be given to the internal political situation in China, particularly the growing rift between the Kuomintang and the Communists." He warned that the KMT was veering away from "even the outward forms of democracy" and was obsessed by the coming resumption of civil war. If this resumption occurred before the defeat of Japan, it could be "disastrous." The importance to America's war effort, he said, should not be underestimated. The political implications were also serious, because the Communists controlled a very large area in which they had been able to mobilize and indoctrinate the population. When the Japanese were defeated, the reds would be firmly entrenched, ready to move into the vacuum in other parts of China as the Japanese occupation collapsed. The Chinese Communist leaders believed that Washington could, if it wanted, force Chiang to behave; they regarded continued, unrestrained American aid to Chiang as an indication of Washington's intention to support him against them when the civil war resumed, and therefore they considered U.S. aid to be a provocation forcing them to turn toward Moscow for equivalent backing.

This memo, dated January 23, 1943, concisely anticipated what did happen historically. But the comments scribbled in the margins when it was ready by Stanley Hornbeck, were "Ridiculous," "Preposterous," and "Scandalous." According to Hornbeck, Service's views were "rash, exaggerated, and immature."

Service understood Chiang clearly. "Chiang's experience as a young man in Shanghai is important to an understanding of his methods," he wrote in a memorandum to the department on another occasion.

> From his contact with the gangster underworld he learned the usefulness of threats and blackmail. To these he adds the traditional Chinese habits of bargaining and of playing off one opponent against another. . . . Chiang shows these traits in everything he does. He has achieved and maintained his position in China by his supreme skill in balancing man against man and group against group, by his adroitness as a military politician rather than a military commander, and by reliance on a gangster secret police.

Service could not have been more clear.

There is another aspect to this unfortunate handling of American policy toward Chiang's China, which has come to light only because hitherto secret FBI documents were declassified in 1983 in the course of a Freedom of Information inquiry for this book. Among the one thousand pages of documents is a portion of a memorandum for the FBI Director, J. Edgar Hoover, dated January 9, 1943, only a few days after Service reached Washington. Although the memo had been "laundered" in a half-hearted attempt to disguise the identity of the source referred to, with all key names blacked out, it may have been either author John Gunther, who had just come back from China, or Jack Service because of the nature of the information he gave and the fact that he was the only China Watcher to return from Chungking in over a year. It sounds like Service, and includes details and observations that parallel his published memoirs. But Gunther had just spent a lot of time with Service in Chungking and had met the people described in the memo. The memo demonstrates a personal knowledge or intimate understanding of the Soongs, and contains a brutal anecdote that could only have been told by Ching-ling to someone she trusted.

The interview was conducted and transcribed by the bureau's L. B. Nichols. Nichols told Hoover in an introduction that he had gone to great pains to satisfy himself that the source knew what he was talking about and was telling the truth.

The Soong family, the informant pointed out by way of introduction, was the most influential in China and "practically had a death grip." The Soongs "have always been money mad and every move they made was prompted by their desire to secure funds." Because of this "there was a gigantic conspiracy afoot to defraud the Chinese from materials they would ordinarily receive through [Lend-Lease] and to divert considerable of this money to the Soong family."

He pointed out that Chiang had been legally married before, and therefore in his opinion Madame Chiang was "not the legal wife." However, she was, of course, closely associated with T. V. Soong, who "is one of the motivating forces in the Soong family to further their own ends." When T. V. came to America, he set up the Universal Trading Corporation, staffed with Chinese, to handle the flow of Lend-Lease materials. "So far," the informant asserted, "approximately $500,000,-000 has been allocated to China from Lend-Lease and . . . a large part of that will ultimately be diverted to the Soong family."

> The Soong organization [he said] is very closely knit. It is ruthlessly operated. If anybody gets out of line they are either bought off or exterminated. . . . The real brains of the group is reputed to be Madame Kung . . . an evil and clever woman. She sits in the background and directs the family. T. V. Soong is the actual manipulator and carries out many of her ideas. They have so closely welded their organization that today everything that happens in China must go through at least one member of the Soong family. Madame Kung is reputed to have hired assassins in China. Many Chinese officials who are high up know of her and her activities but have not said anything. Their fury at the Soong manipulations is equalled only by their contempt for the laxity by which the Americans have allowed themselves to be hoodwinked. Whenever anybody goes to China, such as Wendell Willkie, Lauchlin Currie, and others, they are taken into camp by the Soong family, they are taught what the Soong family wants them to know and ordinarily do not talk to others who would be in a position to know. . . . An official of the Treasury Department, is very close to the "Soong Gang" [evidently a reference to Arthur N. Young, who was in Chungking as an economic advisor to Chiang, and wrote a book after the war whitewashing the regime], and is entertained by them constantly. He should be in a position to know what the situation is although he has probably been taken in by the Soongs.

The informant then told the FBI that one of the ways T. V. diverted Lend-Lease funds into his own pocket was illustrated by reports reaching Chungking that a freighter carrying sixty new American battle tanks and other very expensive war matériel furnished by Lend-Lease had been sunk. As a matter of fact this

> freighter never left the West Coast with any tanks; the tanks were never made . . . this is a positive illustration of the manner in which the Soongs have been diverting funds from Lend-Lease inasmuch as the money was allocated for the 60 tanks.

The memorandum goes on to say that Dr. Hu Shih, who had been the Chinese ambassador to Washington before T. V.'s arrival—the same Hu Shih who had been a pupil of Charlie Soong as a boy in Woosung —had been recalled because he had begun to suspect that these diversions were taking place.

In Service's published memoirs, he tells about one of the visits he paid to Ching-ling at her wartime home in Chungking, and provides a little essential background to her perilous situation:

> She has recently been invited by several organizations to visit the United States. . . . She has, however, been bluntly told that she will not be permitted to go abroad. . . . She mentioned that her family was "very annoyed." . . . I could not help getting the impression that Madame Sun's position is now a strained and difficult one, and that she is more than ever a prisoner.

In the FBI memorandum, the source I presume to be either Service or Gunther relates that Ching-ling

> would like to come to Washington, but she is afraid to, for fear that the "Soong Gang" will kill [her]. . . . She wants to stop the [Lend-Lease] diversions at their source and told [the informant] that the President alone has the power to do this, that she hoped some method could be worked out by the American government to put a check on the distribution and allocations of funds and to investigate the Universal Trading Corporation.

Although the next passage of the FBI memo was chopped up by the censor before its release to me, it appears that the informant was trying to characterize the real danger posed by Ai-ling if any member of the Soong clan defied her—for example, if Ching-ling were to go to America despite being warned not to. The example he gives apparently refers to the occasion in 1927 when T. V. came to see Ching-ling at his apartment over the bank in Wuhan—at the time of the collapse of the KMT-leftist government—to talk her into compromising with Chiang

and, if she refused, to warn her not to go back to Shanghai. The FBI
paragraph as I reconstruct it then reads:

> . . . she had a long talk with [T. V. Soong] away from his home. At that time
> [T. V. Soong] warned [Mme. Sun] not to go to Shanghai alone. He was very
> much agitated and he held her hand and whispered his words of warning
> to her. He made the direct statement that he hardly expected to see her
> alive again as she would get a knife in her back. [Madame Sun Yat-sen]
> laughed at this. [Soong] stated he could prove it if necessary, that he knew
> she was in danger because [their sister, Madame Kung] had planned her
> assassination exactly as she had planned several others before.

Even taken with a grain of salt, usually advisable with FBI materials
because of their bias, this anecdote is clearly coming from someone who
is surprisingly well-informed, and fits with other clues to Ai-ling's nature
and method of operation. There is no direct evidence of such assassinations taking place, but there is no reason why there should be. In China
they were part of the Soong folklore, were widely believed to have
occurred, and help to explain the fear of Ai-ling that was part of her
reputation as "the most hated woman in China." It takes a lot to earn
such a reputation. Of course, it must be acknowledged that this is the
more extreme view of Charlie Soong's children, not the American but
the Asian view. It is all the more perplexing, by contrast, to listen to the
inflated piety and oversweet admiration being voiced at the time in
Washington by the chorus of cronies immediately surrounding President Roosevelt. The truth may lie somewhere between.

A few months later, when the battle between Stilwell and Chiang
was nearing its climax, Jack Service was correct in noting the beginning of a separate battle between T. V. Soong and his sisters Ai-ling
and May-ling—with fateful consequences for the dynasty. This sibling
quarrel apparently turned on the issue of T. V.'s growing independence, wealth, and power on the other side of the Pacific Ocean. The
picture that begins to emerge from the FBI documents and from the
reports of the China Watchers suggests that perhaps T. V. was keeping more of Lend-Lease than the other members of the family
thought he should. And far off in America, where it was difficult for
them to interfere or to punish him, he had been building his own
independent empire. In the beginning of 1944, Service suddenly

warned the Department of State of what at first seemed to be "the dramatic eclipse of T. V. Soong."

> As Foreign Minister, Soong was too independent to please the Chiangs (both Mr. and Mrs.), who prefer to manage their own foreign relations. . . . Soong enraged Chiang and alarmed H. H. and Madame Kung (commonly spoken of as the "most powerful person in China") by caustic criticism of Chinese mishandling of economic problems. . . . The story is widely told that after the initial break, which apparently was in November [1943], the family arranged a meeting late in December at which it was hoped that a reconciliation could take place. Unfortunately Chiang asked Soong for his ideas on how to deal with the economic situation. Soong replied that one reason for lack of effective control was that there were too many agencies, each without power to cope with all economic problems. [T. V. urged Chiang to let him set up a single agency to oversee all the others.] Chiang countered that the setting up of such an agency . . . would upset the whole government structure and would be unconstitutional. To which Soong retorted: "You've always been able to change the Constitution whenever you wished, as for instance when you decided to be President." This interview is supposed to have ended with Chiang throwing a teacup at Soong's head, and, of course, the abandonment of hope for any immediate reconciliation.

Ai-ling and May-ling, it seems, were not the only ones who thought T. V. was getting too independent. The Generalissimo and the Ch'en brothers also were anxious to pry the jealously-guarded foreign-aid portfolio out of T. V.'s hands and put it in Kung's hands, where it would always be accessible. But T. V. would not give it up without a fight. One of the ways he fought back was by putting a big chunk of his foreign financial empire out of Chiang's reach.

Immediately after the teacup-throwing incident in Chungking, T. V. used his position as Foreign Minister to issue his brother T. L. Soong a special diplomatic passport, and sent him hurriedly to Washington and New York. T. L. was actually being whisked out of China to take over as chief purchasing agent and administrator of all U.S. Lend-Lease supplies before they left for China. Since the very beginning, T. L. had been in charge of Lend-Lease at the Chinese end. It was a period of intense scandal when warehouse fires and sabotage were blamed for the disappearance of large quantities of U.S. war supplies. Little was reaching soldiers in the field, and Stilwell—as the senior American Lend-Lease administrator—protested that it was being siphoned off through official corruption. One Chinese general, in charge of the fleet of army trucks that carried Lend-Lease supplies up the Burma Road, was famous for having his trucks disappear only when they were fully loaded, until his private warehouses were bulging.

The director of the Southwest Transportation Company, which provided the six hundred trucks carrying Lend-Lease supplies, was T. L. Soong. Less than two hours after reaching China, the goods were sometimes for sale on the black market. At other times they were not seen again. In all, some $3.5 billion U.S. worth of Lend-Lease supplies were supposed to have passed through T. V.'s and T. L.'s hands during the war, either on the Chinese end of the pipeline, or before it left Universal Trading Corporation in New York. Little reached its destination. A senior official of the British Foreign Office once speculated that "The Soongs diverted billions of U.S. dollars to their own pockets and much of the money never did get out of the U.S."

By moving T. L.'s base of operations from China to America, T. V. put his brother out of the Generalissimo's reach, out of the reach of the Ch'en brothers and Tai Li, and out of the immediate reach of Ai-ling. No matter what happened to T. V.'s political fortunes in Chungking, control of the U.S. cornucopia was retained in T. V.'s hands through T. L. This placed T. L. in a position of extraordinary leverage, negotiating contracts worth many millions of dollars to the biggest corporations in America. He set up office in New York City, the home of his wife's wealthy Chinese family, and lived at the Kung mansion in Riverdale, which had been seeing little use.

The other way T. V. fought back was by convincing the Ch'en brothers that it was May-ling and the Kungs they had to fear, not him. The Ch'en brothers had always detested Ai-ling and perhaps feared her as well. One of the Soongs, apparently Ching-ling, once remarked: "If Elder Sister had been a man, the Generalissimo would have been dead, and she would have been ruling China, fifteen years ago." It is not difficult to believe that her opponents would stop at nothing to wrest power from her. To be sure, events and conspiracies began to take an ominous turn in that "Cairo December" of 1943 that suggested Ai-ling —or somebody in the family—might be involved in a coup plot.

For her part, May-ling's ability to play a role in any power struggle was fading fast. In the months since her return to Chungking from her American tour, nothing had changed in her marriage. The Generalissimo continued to put his teeth in only for the other woman. But

May-ling kept up a brave front. When John Fairbank came to see her in the fall of 1943, just before she went to Cairo, he noticed that "she was tired and her head shook a bit as old men's do."

"She is trying so hard to be a great lady," Fairbank decided.

> Conversation too cosmic to be real. An actress, with a lot of admirable qualities, great charm, quick intuition, intelligence; but underneath, emotions that are unhappy . . . bitterness about something, a penchant for acting a part which produces falsity. Usually the beautiful but sad expression and the well-modulated tones with pauses for effect, upper lip pulled down in a strained way; but occasionally a real laugh, with a round relaxed face and higher-pitched voice, which seemed natural and at ease and made all the rest seem forced and tragic.

Later, he added, "I got the impression that pride led her to play-acting."

At one point, May-ling slipped from the tragic to the cosmic pose:

> Looking into the distance [said Fairbank], she said that Life is a combination of keeping your ideals, keeping your sense of humor, and meeting the circumstances that come up; and she also said something about seeing ourselves as actors in a great experiment of which we do not know the denouement.

Fairbank found himself wishing that she had stayed with the role of the tragic heroine besieged by fate, and "left out the phony part."

During the Cairo talks, she collapsed and was seen by Churchill's physician, Lord Moran. He found her in bed. "She is no longer young," he wrote in his diary that evening, "but there is about her an air of distinction; there is still left a certain cadaverous charm."

When he finished his examination, she interrogated him. "Well, what is wrong?"

"Nothing," he said.

"Nothing?" She smiled faintly. "I shall soon get well, you think?"

"Madame," Lord Moran said, drawing himself up, "you will only get better when the strain of your life is relaxed."

The strain was not going to relax.

In Chungking, she was living with the Kungs instead of with Chiang, avoiding social life and public appearances. She was seen with the Generalissimo only on rare occasions, when they appeared very cool toward each other. She was bothered constantly by her skin rash, so she avoided photographers. The lines in her face were hardening, and she was constantly irritable. Six months after the teacup-throwing incident between T. V. and Chiang, Service concluded that there had been a pronounced change in the fortunes of all the Soongs. He was fairly sure that they were on the way out.

"The most obvious fact at present is that Dr. H. H. Kung, the Minister of Finance, is under attack from almost all factions. Joined with him as the targets of the attack are his wife and sister-in-law, Madame Chiang." Service speculated that some of the gossip about May-ling's marriage might have been politically motivated; once she was discredited, it would be easier to get rid of her. As for Daddy Kung, the Ch'en Clique protested that he had become "too powerful"—meaning he had outlived his usefulness. "Rumors in this connection," reported Service, "are that Kung will give up the ministership of finance, that he will go abroad." Then Service added, "The Madame seems to be becoming a less active factor in internal politics and may leave the country for a long summer vacation."

As usual, Service was on the button. He had predicted that T. V. would seek revenge and become a magnet attracting other vengeful people (the Ch'ens) to his side—now here were the consequences. In June, 1944, two months after he wrote this memo, May-ling "took the advice of doctors" and left China for—of all places—Brazil. For the first time in anyone's memory, Ai-ling traveled with her, as did son Louis and his wife, tending to confirm rumors that Ai-ling had been forced out in a power struggle. The two Chinese matrons were guests in a Norman-style mansion on the Brazilian government's pint-sized VIP island called Brocoió, in the middle of Guanabara Bay. They remained in seclusion there for two months, May-ling under medical care, while Ai-ling wheeled and dealt with Brazilian strongman Getulio Vargas, transferred sums of money, and acquired unspecified properties in rich, industrial São Paulo. The Kungs and Soongs all along had spread some of their fortune around South America, including what were reputed to be megalithic deposits in Caracas, Buenos Aires, and São Paulo banks. Their holdings reportedly covered a broad spectrum of oil, minerals, shipping, and other transportation stocks, with heaviest emphasis on rails and airlines vital in a continent of great distances and few roads. If the Kung financial position in China was now in jeopardy, then Ai-ling's trip with May-ling to Brazil was understandable, and probably signified a geologic shift in dynastic funds.

Brocoió also was a fine, out-of-the-way place to recover from nervous fatigue. The sisters were rarely seen in Rio itself. On September 6, they flew to New York, where May-ling again took over an entire floor of the Harkness Pavilion. She was listed as suffering from nervous exhaustion, under the care of Dr. Robert F. Loeb and Dr. Dana Atchley, who said only that she needed a long rest. May-ling remained at Harkness barely a month this time, then moved on October 9 to the Kung mansion in Riverdale. Hibernating there with Ai-ling and Younger Brother T. L., May-ling stayed out of public sight for many months.

On November 11, 1944, the Calcutta correspondent of the London *Daily Mail,* falling upon an indiscreet source in Lord Mountbatten's staff, reported that Madame Chiang had "definitely" separated from her husband and would establish a permanent residence in America. The published report was hastily discounted by Chinese diplomatic spokesmen. Nevertheless, a secret U.S. intelligence message from Chungking put it this way: "Mme. Chiang will probably remain in the U.S. but they will not be divorced because of repercussions which might result in [damage to] Chinese morale; source said he understood that the Generalissimo's former wife and their son were at present living in the family home." This referred to his second wife, Ch'en Chieh-ju, and the Generalissimo's residence in Chungking. The son referred to apparently was the child Miss Ch'en was due to deliver in Spring 1944 just before May-ling left for Brazil. The Generalissimo's other sons—CCK and Wei-Kuo—were on active military duty.

This time, Henry Luce did not publish a word during May-ling's entire stay in New York, although Time Inc. files reveal that Luce was kept informed. In twelve months, ten spent in the United States, she was seen in public on only one occasion, when she visited the women's prison at Bedford Hills, New York, on June 14, 1945. She told prison authorities that she wanted to gather information that might be useful in managing China's prisons.

The two sisters stayed away from China for the remainder of World War II. May-ling did not return to Chungking until July 1945, more than a year after leaving for Rio.

In June 1944, when Ai-ling and May-ling left so mysteriously, and H. H. was fired from his post as Minister of Finance, he also left China under a cloud. For public consumption, he was given a "special assignment" to attend the international economic conference at Bretton Woods, New Hampshire. He too was gone for a full twelve months, returning to China one month after May-ling, in August 1945. He spent most of that year of exile at the Riverdale mansion, going out only to drop by the New York branch of his Chinese bank—or to pay courtesy calls on "friends of China" in Washington.

What was the event in China that precipitated all these astonishing changes in the fortunes of so many members of the Soong dynasty?

In the closing months of 1943, younger Chinese generals, who had risen to command during the war and were not a part of the old system of cliques, decided that if China was to be saved Chiang Kai-shek and his corrupt inner circle had to be overthrown immediately. These young generals approached U.S. Army Brigadier General Thomas S. Timberman, in charge of training Chinese troops in East China, and pleaded with him for American support. Officially, America said no, but apparently the OSS took more than a passing interest in the plot, particularly since the confrontation between Donovan and Tai Li.

Preparations for the coup proceeded. It was scheduled to take place on the anniversary of Chiang's kidnapping in the Sian Incident, while the Generalissimo was away from Chungking at the Cairo talks. He would be confronted with a fait accompli.

Somehow Tai Li got wind of the plot, and provided the Generalissimo with enough evidence to convince him that members of his own family might be involved. Whether they were or were not, it would have been an irresistible opportunity for Tai Li and the Ch'en brothers to plant the idea and thereby undermine their Soong family rivals. The role played by T. V. Soong was unclear, but he came out of it not only unscathed but completely restored to positions of power.

With the Generalissimo's approval, Tai Li arrested more than six hundred army officers, and on Chiang Kai-shek's return from Cairo sixteen of the most promising young generals in the Chinese army were executed. Shortly thereafter, Chiang completely reinstated T. V., fired H. H. Kung, and ordered him to get out of China, taking Ai-ling and May-ling with him.

Certainly a power struggle had been taking place. Anyone who listened closely could hear scuffling and grunting behind the throne. Chungking was alive with plots. Brooks Atkinson of the *New York Times* called it a "witches' fairgrounds of anxieties, suspicions and intrigue."

The Kungs lost the struggle and T. V. Soong won, evidently by casting his lot with the Ch'en brothers and Tai Li. By the end of 1944, T. V. was again Acting Premier, while continuing to be Foreign Minister. Six months later, in May 1945, he was given the full title of Premier, concurrent with Foreign Minister. For good measure, he was also given Kung's post of Finance Minister. Once again, on paper at least, T. V. was one of the most powerful men in China.

It was a bitter moment in the affairs of the Soong Dynasty, now a house divided. From 1944 on, all of them except Ching-ling became more involved in America than they were in China, devoting their full attention to building what was probably the largest fortune, collectively, on the planet, a fortune probably well in excess of $2 billion U.S., perhaps more than $3 billion. The *Encyclopedia Britannica* was moved to say that T. V. alone was "reputed to have been the richest man in the world."

Taking another look at the famous Cairo summit photograph, in the light of all this, gives a slightly different significance to the scene and its players.

Chapter 19

ASHES, ASHES, ALL FALL DOWN

Theodore White posted the following sign in the shack that served as the *Time* office in Chungking: "Any resemblance to what is written here and what is printed in *Time* Magazine is purely coincidental."

This reflected his increasingly pessimistic attitude about his ability, if not to change the course of China's destiny, at least to keep the American public informed of the events as he and observers like Stilwell, Service, and Davies saw them.

White had been buoyed briefly by Luce's publication of his report on the Honan famine. Harry Luce had actually stood up for him when the outraged Madame Chiang demanded that White be fired. When White made a trip to the United States in the spring of 1944 for a bit of rest, he wrote an article that was to be a test. Here he was free of Chinese censorship and could find out, once and for all, if Luce was interested in the facts. Put to him this way, Luce had no choice but to make a show of objectivity.

"Life Looks at China" appeared in the May 1, 1944, issue. It was a collaborative effort that carried White's by-line. It was surprisingly frank and, according to White, "He published my piece much as I wrote it—after a remarkable intellectual volleying between us."

You have to live in Chungking to feel the weight of the party in men's personal lives. Censorship hangs over authors, playwrights, movie makers and all participants in public expression. The press lives in a shadow world of gossip, handouts and agency dispatches. None of the great problems of

417

China—famine, inflation, blockade, foreign relations or public personalities—can be honestly discussed in public. . . .

The gray atmosphere of Chungking eats into the lives of all who live there. There are not one, but two, secret police outfits in China. One secret police operates for the National Military Council, another for the party itself. Their spies and agents are everywhere. Men can be arrested in China and thrown into jail or concentration camps for any fancied offense. . . .

Today the Nationalist Party is dominated by a corrupt political clique that combines some of the worst features of Tammany Hall and the Spanish Inquisition. Two silent and mysterious brothers, Ch'en Li-fu and Ch'en Kuo-fu, known to all the foreigners of Chungking as the "CC clique" . . . practically control the thought of the nation through a combination of patronage, secret police, espionage and administrative authority. Ch'en Kuo-fu, the elder . . . controls almost all entrance to the Great Presence. Paper work and memoranda to the Generalissimo . . . filter through this man.

His younger brother, Ch'en Li-fu, a frail and handsome man, is even more important. He is an indefatigable worker, an ascetic, and fiscally honest. His mystic, Olympian and pseudophilosophic writings almost defy understanding.

When he went back to China that summer, White was heartened by Luce's willingness to publish his frank account of Chungking politics. But in no time at all he had reason to wonder if he had been right in his doubts about Luce all along. It began to look as though Luce had published "Life Looks at China" just to score a journalistic point with his New York staff. White wrote a hard-hitting report setting forth some of the real circumstances behind the Stilwell crisis. The report was turned over by Luce to the new foreign editor at *Time*, Whittaker Chambers, to be ground into oatmeal and "edited into a lie." Chambers had no difficulty in using doublespeak and triplethink to turn the whole Stilwell crucifixion upside down, so that the issues at stake were all presented from the point of view of Chiang and Chennault. Stilwell was made to look like a country bumpkin who could not grasp the larger issues involved. Chiang became the hero of the affair, and it was proclaimed that America had made a simple choice between a happy, democratic, prosperous, Christian China under Chiang—and a sinister Communist China under Russian domination.

White drafted a forty-five-page letter to Luce angrily protesting this deliberate distortion of the record. Luce calmly replied that "supporting" Chiang in Time Inc. publications was no different from backing Winston Churchill. The argument raged over the wires. Three times White resigned. But Luce responded with soothing words and a salary raise, like a father to an errant and naïve son. Luce was a deity, and when you walked away from Time Inc. all paths led downhill. Or so folklore had it. Sucking hind teat at Time Inc. was miles ahead of where everybody else in journalism had to find nourishment. Anyway, by then Stilwell's career had collapsed, Luce's Gissimo had won, and other issues had come and gone. White stayed on—grieved but hoping that all this would someday change.

Without May-ling around to "interpret" what he was "saying" for his worldwide audience, Chiang was reverting to his pre-Soong state— to the petulant demeanor of his early twenties, when he had been the *enfant terrible* of the Shanghai underworld. He was spending all his private time with old flames and old Green Gang cronies. Chiang was aging and now preferred the public role of Confucian ascetic, aloof from worldly matters. He was encouraged in this by the Ch'en brothers, who relieved the Generalissimo of the awful burden of decision making. Chungking retrogressed to a medieval mentality of Chinese court intrigue, dark assignations, and furtive alliances. Meanwhile, those who saw what was coming were preparing for disaster.

So totally removed from reality did Chiang become that he was struck with disbelief one day by rumors that his own soldiers were dropping dead of starvation in the streets. Corruption was keeping them from being fed the barest rations. He sent his eldest son, CCK, to investigate. When CCK reported back that it was true, Chiang insisted on seeing for himself. CCK showed him army conscripts who had died in their bedrolls because of neglect. Chiang was enraged and used his cane to lash the face of the officer in charge of conscripts. The culprit was jailed and another loyal officer given the post. The starvation deaths continued. In August 1944, the corpses of 138 starved soldiers were removed from the streets of Chungking. Chiang did not come out again to see.

The Generalissimo's own *Mein Kampf* had now been published, giving glimpses of his increasingly precarious mental state. Called *China's Destiny*, its pages twisted history out of joint to blame the foreign powers for all of China's woes, including those that were peculiarly Chiang's own doing. It oozed so much bigotry and dementia that those translating it into English began taking sick leave, rather than face foreigners who were reading it.

Of the Soong clan members who had sided with Chiang long ago, T. V. was the only one remaining in Chungking the last year of the war. T. V. had changed also. In Washington in 1941–42 he had seen how the game was played, and he had discovered that he could play it better than anyone else. T. V. had grown up. There was no longer any Harvard liberal confusion or moralizing. Now he had more real power than Chiang and more real money than all but a handful of the world's super-rich, an imbalance that he was about to correct in his favor.

In Chungking each evening, when journalists were not around, he dined on Kansas City steaks flown in exclusively for him. He was fond of his wife, Laura, whom he called by the nickname Ding-Ding. Once, when she was ill, he was said to have sent a plane all the way to Connecticut to hurry back with a sprig of dogwood bloom for her. She had a soft spot for dogwood, and was suitably touched.

T. V. could now do May-ling's job better than May-ling. He was her "faggot," the old British army term meaning to stand in for somebody else at muster. He interpreted for Chiang, had tea with politicians and diplomats he detested, made Chiang feel good, said patriotic things when called upon, and portrayed the regime as a staunch supporter of human rights and social progress. He was totally absorbed with the discovery that if he concentrated he too could make Chiang's lips move.

Employed by Chiang's government were a great many people— Chinese, Europeans, and Americans—involved exclusively in image protection, public relations, and propaganda. One of their jobs was to keep scandals out of the papers. But there were occasional blunders, like the ugly news that broke in the American press in May 1945, when T. V. Soong, then Acting Premier and Foreign Minister, was attending a United Nations conference in San Francisco. T. V. was nonplused when radio commentator Raymond Gram Swing reported:

China is going through its worst scandal of the war. It is a gold scandal, and arises from insiders, with high Government connections, making a cleanup when the price of gold was officially raised on March 28. . . . The gold involved . . . is part of the $500,000,000 this country loaned to China. . . . Fortunes have been made. . . . There is strong pressure on the Government . . . by public opinion.

The United States had been lending gold to China since 1943, at the urging of T. V. Soong and H. H. Kung. Theoretically, the gold was to be sold by the government-controlled banks of China in order to help stabilize inflation, like an injection of vitamins for an anemic patient. Chiang complained that the United States was slow in transporting the promised gold. Because of this alleged slowness, H. H. Kung, at the time still Minister of Finance, announced that the banks would sell "gold certificates," which could be redeemed for the real gold when it actually arrived. In other words, the gold that was intended to halt the wild inflation of the Chinese market (an inflation that was largely the result of Kung's own funny money and Ai-ling's profiteering) now provided a new commodity futures market that could be manipulated for further profit.

But no alarms were sounded until Swing's radio report. The reason for this delay was simple. Suspicions were normally focused on the Kungs and Soongs, but by this time all of the Kungs were gone except one of the children, and the only Soong remaining was T. V., who was too busy to get involved in such small-scale chicanery. It took a while before anything peculiar was noticed. When it was discovered, no official charges were immediately brought. The object was first to hush it up if possible. But word slipped out that somebody in Chungking with access to official secrets was trying to manipulate the new gold futures market. Broadcaster Swing jumped to the conclusion—because he had the story exclusively—that this was the "worst scandal of the war." It was hardly the worst. The culprit was never revealed officially; there were those in China who suspected that the Soong family was behind it. The only Kung still left in China in March 1945 was David. His associate in various ventures at the time evidently was Big-eared Tu's son, Tu Wei-p'ing. No charges were ever brought against these two.

Confronted by reporters in San Francisco, T. V. claimed that his "own suspicions" had been aroused by the peculiar behavior of the gold market. He explained that when the government decided on Friday, March 28, to raise the official price of gold effective Monday, March 30, it had been agreed that strict secrecy would be maintained. But, in going over trading figures, T. V. noticed that gold sales on Friday were double the recent daily averages. Such a thing could happen only if somebody close to power had tipped associates that the gold price would go up dramatically over the weekend, allowing them to buy cheap on Friday and sell dear on Monday. T. V. might have thought that he had treed a Kung, and Kungs were in season. He said he hurried to Chiang Kai-shek with his suspicions.

On orders from Chiang, a speedy investigation was conducted that turned up the true "guilty parties"—two junior clerks of the Central Trust Bank. This bank included on its board of directors both H. H. Kung and T. L. Soong. Apparently no fault was found among the management of the Bank of Communications or the Central Bank of China (both Kung operations) although, curiously enough, both those banks had extended their normal closing time that Friday from 5 P.M. until 9 P.M. to "handle the sudden demand" from gold purchasers.

Sentenced to the firing squad, the two hapless clerks were taken hastily before its muzzles, but not before one of the condemned shouted the obvious—they were "scapegoats."

T. V. saw their execution as a necessity "because at the slightest suspicion of corruption in the Government, immediate and thorough investigation and punishment should follow. This could only result in strengthening . . . the authority of Government . . . [and] enhance the confidence of the people."

The profits from the Gold Scandal, as it came to be called, sounded big. News reports spoke of "forty-five billion dollars," but these were inflated Chinese dollars. The unnamed "high officials" actually responsible for the Gold Scandal had only made about $20,000 U.S.

H. H. Kung in his role of "the Sage" had once pronounced that "war is bad business for everyone," but he overstated the case. It was bad business for everyone in China except those associated with the Soong dynasty. As Dr. Francis Hsu of Northwestern University observed, "Official position in China brought such large economic returns that it was the most lucrative industry of the country."

A case in point was General T'ang En-po, who was somehow able to participate in the war's most appalling scandals, and whose story embodies the Chiang regime's worst qualities. "Paper Tiger" T'ang began life as a rural tough in the Generalissimo's own Chekiang Province, his education limited to martial arts. In Shanghai, he won favor with the Green Gang as an aggressive bodyguard, and talked a local warlord into paying his way to military school in Japan. When World War II began, he was one of Chiang's favorite field commanders, a member of the Whampoa Clique. His first achievement was to be among the senior officers who blew up the Yellow River dikes. He was then put in charge of the army that controlled Honan Province. There, T'ang was instrumental in bullying the peasants to cough up their last handfuls of grain as a "special tax," bringing on the great Honan famine of 1942–43 which so deeply moved Theodore White.

"He was a relatively pleasant man," White recalled, "gracious, good-humored, energetic. . . . [T]he peasants and civilians accepted him . . . as the true author of their ills, and they mouthed deep and bitter curses. 'Honan has two sorrows,' they quipped, 'the Yellow River and T'ang En-po.' "

While the peasants starved, General T'ang found countless ways to make his own life more pleasant. His territory was just up the Yangtze from the Ku brothers' wartime stronghold around Shanghai—bestowed upon them by Big-eared Tu for safekeeping while he spent the war years in Chungking. This enabled T'ang to purchase bootleg Japanese consumer goods from the Green Gang downriver, and pipeline it in U.S. Lend-Lease army trucks to inland cities, including Chungking, where it was sold on the black market. What he could not get from the Ku brothers he obtained directly from the Japanese, in straight trade for American Lend-Lease goods. He also traded Swiss watches, French perfumes, and British woolens, and forced peasants to grow tobacco, which he sold to inland cigarette manufacturers, and opium, which he sold to the Green Gang. Since even this was never enough, T'ang withheld pay from his troops, kept them on short rations, sold all the U.S. equipment provided for them, and filled one-third of his ranks only on paper, which allowed him to collect the wages of the nonexistent men.

When Operation Ichigo began in 1944, General T'ang absented himself from the front. His troops panicked, broke, and ran. Staff officers abandoned their men, commandeered six hundred of their eight hundred trucks, loaded aboard their wives and families, household possessions, and all the loot they could manage, and fled. In order to eat, the abandoned foot soldiers pillaged the peasants and confiscated the oxen that farmers depended upon to plant grain. In outrage, the peasants armed themselves with wooden pitchforks and disarmed fifty thousand Chinese soldiers.

As a reward, T'ang was given command of fourteen U.S.-equipped divisions as chief of the Third Front Army. And, with the war's end, he was given the bonus assignment of taking the surrender of the Japanese throughout the Lower Yangtze-Shanghai region, and disarming them.

As soon as he had finished, he was instructed to repatriate all Japanese troops and civilians through the port of Shanghai. He gathered a group of twenty high-ranking Japanese commanders and gave them a touching farewell address:

> China and Japan occupy the opposite shores of the same sea and mutually support each other. Their people are of the same race; the languages are the same. Joined they can both survive; asunder they must perish. Eight years of bloody warfare have brought grievous wounds to both. Recalling past sufferings we brothers should hold our heads and weep bitterly. Today we cast aside our arms and send you gentlemen home. Some other time we shall welcome your return holding jade and brocades in our arms.

The peasants of Honan would have been warmed by these fine sentiments.

The Generalissimo, pleased with T'ang's performance throughout, rewarded him yet again after the war by making him commander-in-chief of the Ku brothers' Nanking-Shanghai garrison, and deputy commander-in-chief of the entire Chinese Army—second only to that other venerable military leader, General Ku Chu-t'ung, hero of the New Fourth Army Incident. "T'ang En-po," judged one historian mildly, "was one of the most disreputable Kuomintang military men."

There was plenty for everyone. On V-J Day, China had (on paper at least) six million ounces of gold and U.S. dollar reserves of more than $900 million, all from American taxpayers. Despite this great reserve of hard currency and gold, the China Lobby was so energetic that foreign aid continued to pour into China at an astonishing rate. The United Nations Relief and Rehabilitation Administration (UNRRA) shipped more than $685 million U.S. worth of goods, food, clothing, and equipment to China between 1945 and 1947. Added to this was an $83 million U.S. loan from T. V.'s old friends at the Export-Import Bank and a long-term loan of $60 million U.S. from Canada.

In order, as he put it, to "preserve the dignity of the Chinese people," T. V. Soong insisted that the full legal control of these foreign aid supplies must rest with the Chinese. Chiang had tried this gambit before, in 1944, and there was no harm in asking. Incomprehensibly, the loan agencies agreed. They agreed even though it was scuttlebutt at high levels in Washington and London that, by the end of the war, T. V. was one of the richest men on earth, with huge holdings in some of the world's biggest corporations, from which he had found creative ways to buy war matériel. Felix Greene quoted a friend of T. V.'s that his assets in America alone were over $47 million U.S. by 1944. A high-level source in the British Foreign Office alleged in a 1953 interview that "T. V. Soong owns the controlling interest in your General Motors, doesn't he?" When told that American officials generally assumed it was not GM but DuPont, the Foreign Office official snapped, "Well, there are ways to disguise ownership, aren't there?"

After T. V. was named Premier, he created a special agency, the Chinese National Relief and Rehabilitation Administration (CNRRA) to oversee the distribution of UN relief goods. The deal he struck with the U.S. government and the United Nations was that UNRRA would relinquish all title to supplies the moment the goods touched down on any Chinese wharf. (In other countries, UN officials stayed with the goods throughout, to see to their proper distribution.) The wharfs where most of these goods landed, the warehouses where the goods were stored, and the transportation companies that moved them (including China Merchants Steam Navigation Company) were owned by Big-eared Tu. This was a situation ready-made for abuse.

As relief goods began to arrive, they were immediately diverted into black-market channels. When blood plasma donated by the America Red Cross showed up for sale in Shanghai drugstores for $25 a pint, the U.S. navy shore patrol seized the rest of the 3,500 cases, which were sitting in a Shanghai warehouse.

After giving all this money to China for humanitarian purposes, and meeting T. V.'s unusual terms, UNRRA discovered that it had to foot the bill for all shipping, unloading, storage, and transportation. This was no small amount. When T. V. presented the "administrative" bill for these costs to the UNRRA accountants, it came to a choking $190 million U.S.

Chiang and Big-eared Tu had used the fear of communism to extort millions from the Shanghai merchants in 1927. Now Chiang was using the fear of a Communist takeover to obtain millions from the United States. Fear served him well.

With hyperinflation soon to hit the incredible exchange rate of $11 million Chinese to $1 U.S., the Chiang regime secretly prepared to issue a new form of currency with new banknotes "backed" by gold—a so-called "gold yuan." The plan called for all Chinese to turn in all their discredited old-style fa-pi banknotes, and all their personal holdings of silver and gold, in exchange for the new banknotes. The gold and silver would be redeemed at an artificial rate set by the government. This is one of the oldest cons on earth. This meant that people who had managed to hang on to any gold or silver through the war would be forced to accept new banknotes of doubtful value at a ridiculous rate of exchange. Anyone able to survive a day as a small shopkeeper in China could see through it, but nobody was to be given any choice.

The opportunity to take advantage of this "currency reform" existed for anyone who knew what date the change would take place. Here was the sort of large-scale scam for which the famous Gold Scandal had been only a warmup. This time the leak of secret information came from T. V. Soong himself.

T. V. apparently alerted a number of his favorite KMT army officers —293 of them in Shanghai alone—to withdraw their gold from Shanghai banks before the date in question. Ungraciously, somebody in that group spread the word around. Panic struck Shanghai. There was a gold rush as hundreds of important depositors withdrew their gold from the banks. Millions of dollars in private gold was yanked out of the government's grasp by its rightful owners. The panic spread to other cities. The Generalissimo was infuriated. He had been made a laughingstock in front of the nation. This time he had had enough of T. V. Soong.

T. V. was officially charged with causing the "gold rush." Chiang ordered him to resign as Premier, removed him from all other government posts, and told the Ch'en brothers to conduct a secret investigation of all T. V.'s financial dealings. Until the investigation was complete, Chiang pressed upon T. V. a "consolation" post as governor and "pacification commissioner" of Kwangtung Province. This gave T. V. a period of grace to clear his immense wealth out of China through his branch banks in Canton and Hong Kong, and time to liquidate most of his properties.

In his resignation speech before the Executive Yuan, which he had headed as Premier, T. V. spoke familiar words: "The truth can be told in one sentence. The present economic crisis is the cumulative result of heavily unbalanced budgets carried through eight years of war and one year of illusory peace, accentuated to some degree by speculative activities."

In the fall of 1947, the Ch'en brothers completed the investigation they had been ordered to conduct, and submitted a 15,000-word report charging T. V. with "mismanagement of foreign . . . funds." The report stated that a certain group of privileged corporations had expended funds and supplies for "purposes other than the import of materials for reconstruction." The privileged group included Dr. Soong and his China Development Finance Corporation, T. L. Soong's Fu Chung Trading Corporation, and the Yangtze Development Corporation headed by David Kung. Once T. V. had been relieved of his posts and packed off to Kwangtung Province, investigators had discovered that roughly half of China's reserves of hard foreign currency and gold bullion was missing, including half of $900 million U.S. currency and half of the six million ounces of gold that were supposed to be in China's treasury while T. V. had the key.

Where had it all gone?

Gardner Cowles, the plain-talking publisher of the Des Moines *Register* went to China on a tour after the war and came back with this story, which appeared in September, 1947:

> At a dinner party in Shanghai, an irate critic of the present government said to me, "China will never find herself until she gets rid of the Soong family. Why, they have more than a billion dollars in their personal accounts in Washington, London and Amsterdam banks." When he walked away a moment later, a high official of the Bank of China said to me: "Don't believe such foolishness. They don't have more than 800-million dollars on deposit."

With H. H. in America and T. V. Soong in provincial exile as governor in Canton, and with Mao's Red Army moving irresistibly across North China, Generalissimo Chiang still toyed with the pretense of government. In the calm before the storm, he was determined to proceed with the introduction of the gold yuan. After more delays, the official date for issuance of the new currency became August 19, 1948. All old banknotes were to be returned by September 30, along with all gold, silver, or foreign currency. This time, in order to see that the job was done right, Chiang appointed his son CCK—General Chiang Ching-kuo—to enforce the new currency regulations, working with the new Finance Minister, O. K. Yui.

The Generalissimo gave CCK special instructions to first clean house in Shanghai. He evidently wanted everyone to know that Chiang Kai-shek was back in town. CCK was ordered to erase all vestiges of the Kung family, and remove any Kung flunkies still around. While at it, he was to boot out all corrupt elements (who were not part of the exclusive Green Gang), close down the black market, jail all unscrupulous speculators, and assist in the economic "reformation" of Shanghai's underworld. A tall order. CCK seems to have taken his father quite literally. He waged a ruthless war against corruption, against black marketeers and currency speculators, ranging far and wide with his Moscow-style security cadres, holding street-corner tribunals and sidewalk executions. But then CCK made two terrible mistakes. He arrested stockbroker Tu Wei-p'ing. The young broker was accused of having dumped thirty million shares of stock on the market just before the currency reform was to take effect. Apparently he had been given advance word by his father, Tu Yueh-sheng.

The son of Big-eared Tu, a graduate of the Massachusetts Institute of Technology, was tried and sentenced by CCK so fast that it was all over before anyone was dimly aware even that he had been arrested. Young Tu was given a relatively mild jail sentence of eight months— not for the fact that he had illegally obtained information about the currency reform but on a technicality of having sold the shares outside of the regular exchange. He did not serve the time, for that would have been pressing his father a bit much. But his arrest, trial, and conviction were a clear sign that times had changed.

After the war, Big-Eared Tu's grip slipped because of his age and bad health from years of drug addiction. He was also under pressure from war-profiteering rivals who wanted to break the Green Gang hold. Now in his sixties and not at all well, Tu was in no mood to take up again the daily administration of the gang's operations. It was hard to concentrate on reorganizing the old Shanghai operations when the reds were steamrolling across Manchuria and moving ever southward. Tu began shifting his assets to Hong Kong.

CCK's second mistake was even bigger.

When he went snooping about Shanghai, he came upon large quantities of purloined American and European goods on the premises of the Yangtze Development Corporation. Being wise by now to all the inner workings of the black market, CCK immediately arrested the general manager of Yangtze Development—none other than his cousin by marriage, David Kung.

Chapter 20

THE SOONG LEGACY

May-ling was home again in Nanking when she received an anonymous phone call from Shanghai, advising her of David Kung's arrest. She was outraged. She confronted the Generalissimo, but Chiang washed his hands of the whole business. Flying down to Shanghai, May-ling confronted CCK and demanded that David be released into her custody. Her errant nephew reluctantly came back to Nanking to get a scolding from Uncle Chiang. Prudently, May-ling then hurried David onto a plane for Hong Kong, with continuing connections to Florida. He was not to come back. Yangtze Development Corporation's offices in China were closed down overnight and reopened in Miami Beach.

CCK got chilly instructions from the Generalissimo then to cease and desist. For CCK, it was a serious loss of face, one he chalked up to his stepmother. He angrily resigned from his enforcement job. He apologized to "the citizens of Shanghai" and invited them "to use their own strength to prevent unscrupulous merchants, bureaucrats, politicians and racketeers from controlling" their city.

After collecting her wits for a year in New York City in 1944–45, Madame Chiang had come back to China after the war to see if there were any pieces left worth putting back together. She had identified herself so totally with her country's fate that it seemed incongruous for her to be anywhere else while China was being overwhelmed by a sea of Communists. The issue at hand was, as her American friends were so fond of putting it, a battle to the death against the reds.

429

Because of the effectiveness of the propaganda machine, most people had no idea that there had been a crisis in the Chiang marriage. To the vast body of her admirers, to the press, to most of the American government, her rule had continued unbroken. May-ling went back to Chungking, resumed her place at Chiang's side (presumably after a bit of private negotiation), and picked up the strings of power.

At May-ling's insistence, the Generalissimo moved out of his palace, which he had insisted on calling Eagle's Nest and where the Other Woman had left traces, and resettled in a small villa near the Kungs. Miss Ch'en, the second Madame Chiang, was not around anymore. The exact timing of May-ling's return may have had something to do with Miss Ch'en's departure. That, in turn, may have had something to do with the fate of Miss Ch'en's child. There were reports that she gave birth to a boy, but the child may not have survived. Chiang had apparently lost interest. Miss Ch'en in fact had gone back to California. Eventually she retired to Hong Kong and died there in old age, taking many mysteries with her.

In October 1945, the reconciled Missimo and Gissimo lavishly entertained Henry Luce in Chungking. At that time H. H. Kung was also back briefly, with Ai-ling, to clean up some tag ends of family business. Luce had tea in the palatial Kung home while H. H. shamelessly complimented the publisher for his perspicacity in predicting in July 1945 that the "end of the war [would come] in the very near future." Luce then dined with the Chiangs. Another fête was hosted for him separately by T. V. Soong.

The publisher also had a chance to talk with one of his avowed enemies, that arch red Chou En-lai. In no mood to be courted by Communists, Luce recorded in his diary that "We had a nice talk—and completely frank from the moment we sat down. He said we [the Lucepress] hadn't been very nice to them recently. I said that was too bad because we had a world-wide battle on our hands with world-wide left-wing propaganda—and it was just as nasty as a skunk." When he called on Ch'en Li-fu, the Pittsburgh-educated head of Chiang's secret police, Luce remembered him as a "man of great charm."

Chennault was still there after the war, filling his role as chain-smoking, trench-coated soldier of fortune, bustling briskly back and forth, running his new outfit, Civil Air Transport (CAT). He was being paid well to rush planeloads of weapons and troops here and there in a fruitless effort to block the tide of the Red Army. At one point after the war, he tried briefly to retire to his childhood bayous of Louisiana, but a new deal was soon struck with the Chiangs and he disengaged himself from wife and children and went back to China again, this time for good.

The American attitude toward China was going through a curious transformation. President Truman was at a low ebb in popularity in 1946, a slump that stemmed as much perhaps from the war fatigue of the electorate as anything else. His Republican rivals, who had been out of power through four Democratic presidential terms, were at last making gains in Congress on the argument that it was time for a change. The GOP hoped to capitalize on the national mood further and win the next presidential election in 1948. One of the Republicans' favorite themes, now that fascism had been vanquished, was the threat of communism. In harmony with Luce they harped on the fact that the Democrats were not providing Chiang Kai-shek with the money he needed to beat Mao's hordes.

Generals Marshall and Wedemeyer, who had become acquainted with the Generalissimo the hard way, proposed that further aid be carefully limited, and strictly supervised by American officials. Any loan should be contingent on Chiang's purging his regime of corruption and establishing a broader political base—in effect taking steps toward the old fantasy of a coalition with the reds. It was not that the backers of this policy had any affection for the CCP. Marshall had simply realized long ago that Mao's greatest asset was the Chiang regime's dismal corruption. During a fact-finding trip to China in the summer of 1946, Wedemeyer toured the major cities, then frankly told Chiang and other Nationalist officials that, unless the KMT cleaned up its act, it would be impossible to stop the reds. Wedemeyer also pointed out that Chiang could raise at least $1 billion U.S. immediately by liquidating some Nationalist Chinese investments abroad.

Chiang and the Republicans in Washington would hear none of this. The first shot at Marshall's policy of limited aid was fired by no less than GOP Representative Clare Boothe Luce, who inserted into the Congressional Record a letter of protest dated July 24, 1946, signed by thirty-eight distinguished American champions of the Chiang cause. These stalwarts included Chinese-goods importer Alfred Kohlberg, who later helped Clare Luce set up the American China Policy Association, one of the more active lobbying groups that made up the China Lobby.

It was clear to Chiang's advisors that a Republican victory in the 1948 elections would practically guarantee a change of heart in the White House. Instead of the tight-fisted Truman hostility, once again there would be billions in aid with no strings attached. Accordingly, Chinese agents hit the road in America, helping Republicans win elections, pushing the GOP cause in expensive ways. One of the more prominent political activists was Louis Kung. What they accomplished was summarized years later by Harry Truman: "They had a great many Congressmen and Senators lined up to do pretty much what they were told, and they had billions of dollars to spend. . . . I'm not saying that they bought anybody out, but there was a lot of money floating around, and a lot of people in Washington were following . . . the China Lobby."

The Chiangs and the Luces considered New York Governor Thomas Dewey certain to win the presidency, so Ambassador Wellington Koo made a point of decorating Dewey with the Special Cravat of the Order of the Auspicious Star. In further expectation of Dewey's triumph, the Generalissimo arranged for May-ling to visit Washington again, to charm America as she had in Roosevelt's day, and to appeal personally for urgent military and financial assistance against the Red Menace. Specifically, she was to ask for $3 billion.

Meantime, there was heartening news from "China's friends," as they called themselves, in Washington. While the presidential primaries were still under way in April 1948, the pro-Chiang campaign, backed by all the muscle of the China Lobby and a large number of Republican leaders, pushed a rich aid package through. To stem the red tide, Congress by a narrow vote gave the Generalissimo over $1 billion. But Chiang at once let it be known that this was not enough. He needed $3 billion more.

While the United States was indulging in the luxury of the democratic process, China was being lost. Through the months of 1948, the Red Army won victory after victory, while Chiang's KMT forces scattered in disarray. If Chiang was going to be rescued it had to be fast. A mere $1 billion was hardly enough. Chiang's defeat was in sight as Americans went to the polls on November 7.

That very day, the Communists attacked a large concentration of Nationalist regulars defending the central China plain. The battle lasted two months, until January 10, 1949, and ended in the complete defeat of the Kuomintang. The Battle of Huai-hai, as it was called, was the last great clash between Chiang and the Communists. Out of some 550,000

KMT soldiers, 325,000 were taken prisoner. In the final moments, Chiang ordered his air force to bomb his own troops to keep their supplies and weapons from falling into the hands of the Communists. The charade on the mainland was almost over.

During this last battle, Chiang found that the powerful sleeping pills he had been using for years to knock himself out at night no longer worked. He began drinking himself into a stupor, downing one-and-a-half water glasses of whiskey each evening. His anxiety was aggravated by the news of Truman's narrow but decisive victory at the polls. There would be no more charity at the White House.

Chiang hurried May-ling off to Washington anyway. When her plane took off at the end of November 1948, it was the last time she would ever touch the Chinese mainland.

This time, Washington's red carpets were at the cleaners. There were no invitations for Madame Chiang to overnight at the White House or to speak to Congress. Since Congress had only recently given Chiang $1 billion, and a bitter election had just been won, President Truman was in no mood to pander to Lucean foreign policy or to the China Lobby.

"She came to the United States for some more handouts," Truman recalled caustically. "I wouldn't let her stay in the White House like Roosevelt did. I don't think she liked it very much, but I didn't care one way or the other about what she liked and what she didn't like."

Madame Chiang's presence was an official embarrassment. Only the Republicans, the China Lobby, and Luce showed any sympathy for her plea for help "in the present struggle." The trip was a disaster. Not only did Truman turn her down, he ungallantly issued a statement to the press disclosing that American aid to Chiang already totaled more than $3.8 billion. The dragon's teeth sown by the Soong dynasty were sprouting with a vengeance.

With World War II over, and Chiang's regime collapsing like a rotted log, it became fashionable in Washington to remember many things. It was recalled by intelligence circles, for example, that H. H. Kung had used $200 million in U.S. loans to purchase goods from the merchants of occupied Shanghai in 1942—from businesses owned or controlled by Big-eared Tu and the Soongs in joint ventures with the Japanese. These and other novelties were pulled like maggots out of the log by the sharp beaks of gossip, and passed around Washington for everyone to cluck and sigh over, and shake their feathered heads, and do a little hop.

Shaken by the President's rejection, and by her inability to work the old magic, May-ling left Washington in a dudgeon and went into seclusion again on the Kung estate in Riverdale.

Truman all the while was speaking frankly to his aides about "grafters and crooks" in the Chinese government, adding, "I'll bet you that a billion dollars of [American loans] is in New York today" (in Chinese bank accounts). The President soon learned that his estimate was conservative. In May 1949, a few months after May-ling's visit, Truman heard of allegations made by banking sources to members of Congress that the Soongs and Kungs actually had $2 billion salted away in Manhattan. The President immediately ordered the FBI to make a secret investigation of these reports, to establish precisely how much money was involved and where it was deposited. So sensitive was the inquiry, and its findings, that the details were only declassified thirty-four years later, in 1983, still heavily censored.

First, the FBI dug out its wartime dossiers on the Soongs, rediscovering information that T. V. Soong had "started out his public career with rather limited resources and [by January 1943] had amassed over seventy million dollars." During the war, the bureau noted, Japan had charged that T. V. had $70 million either in Chase National Bank or National City Bank in New York; that Madame Kung had $80 million in one of those banks; that Madame Chiang Kai-shek had $150 million deposited in either or both of them. These allegations had been regarded originally as mere Japanese propaganda.

Instructions were sent by J. Edgar Hoover to FBI field offices throughout the United States, saying: "BUREAU DESIRES TO IMMEDIATELY DETERMINE EXTENT OF DOMESTIC BANK ACCOUNTS OF CAPTIONED INDIVIDUALS, AS WELL AS INDUSTRIES, CORPORATIONS OR ENTERPRISES UNDER THEIR CONTROL." Banks in San Francisco, New York, and elsewhere in the country responded, some stating that they had no business with the Soongs whatever, others agreeing to provide "information concerning accounts . . . on confidential basis if Bureau desires." Other clan accounts turned up that were not on the list, belonging to younger brothers T. L. and T. A. (chairman of the Bank of Canton in San Francisco at the time).

The two banks mentioned in the Japanese charges—Chase and National City—agreed to cooperate on a "highly discreet and strictly confidential basis." This was necessary to avoid stampeding big depositors, who might object to the bank's betraying the confidentiality of transactions.

But the bureau hit a snag when it came to the Manhattan Company, a major New York bank that later merged with Chase National to become Chase Manhattan. Senior officers of the Manhattan Company initially cooperated with the FBI, disclosing some Soong accounts, including a personal trust fund belonging to T. V. But when the agents went back a few days later with a request for further elaboration, they were met by a totally different attitude. To every question their source at the bank replied that "There was nothing available to him." He also refused to acknowledge previous information in any way, or to add to it. He asked if the bureau was in a position to furnish the bank with subpoenas. The FBI could not provide subpoenas without risking public disclosure of the presidential investigation, which Truman had strictly forbidden. (If the probe became known to the China Lobby, there would be a violent political backlash.)

"It would appear," an FBI agent noted laconically, "that high bank officials had prepared a flat statement for issuance to the Bureau in this matter."

The FBI did uncover a few nuggets. It conjectured that a large part of the Kungs' liquid assets in America were in H. H. Kung's Bank of China in New York, while much of T. V.'s liquid assets were in his Bank of Canton in San Francisco. But, with the family directly involved in the management of the two banks, it was deemed unwise to ask either bank for details. Other large accounts turned up in Seattle and Boston banks.

It was discovered that various members of the family, including May-ling, owned apartment buildings and office complexes in cities from coast to coast. A number of companies were found to be owned or controlled by the Soong clan, including a foreign manufacturer's representative at 1 Wall Street called Fu Chung International Corporation, and Mono Chemical Company. But these were small fry. What about the long-standing rumor in British and American financial circles that T. V. owned a huge block of General Motors, or DuPont, or both? If such discoveries were made, they were among the FBI documents still blacked out or withheld by the censors.

The bureau was told that some of the information it was seeking was in the files of the Federal Reserve Bank and the Treasury Department, which contained, among other things, Form TFR-300 (required of all aliens). This presumably listed all Soong family assets in America or was the place where such information was supposed to be filed by aliens. The FBI was reluctant to ask Treasury for a copy because it believed that senior Treasury officials were close to T. V. and might reveal the investigation to him. When copies of the TFR-300 were obtained indirectly, they were found to contain almost nothing. The form filed by May-ling, for example, was blank regarding all property holdings. Apparently the Treasury Department had been too chivalrous to press her for details.

FBI agents tried surveillance of the Kung mansion at 4904 Independence Avenue in Riverdale. This was exceedingly difficult, complained an agent, because it was one of the most exclusive communities in the country, with the big houses hidden by trees, at some distance from each other. Interrogating the neighbors was also a delicate matter. (The FBI did get a glimmer of strange goings-on inside the Kung mansion when a scandal broke in New York's Chinese press in the summer of 1955. According to those newspapers, several Chinese servants who had been brought from Hong Kong ostensibly to work in the Chinese Embassy found themselves virtual prisoners of the Kungs in Riverdale. They claimed they were not paid promised salaries or allowed to leave the grounds at any time. They were even forbidden to write home. In desperation, they escaped together, but were captured and brought back. According to their statements published in the *China Daily News*, the hapless servants were taught a lesson when they were hung from the ceiling and whipped. Although H. H. Kung wrote to the paper denying its allegation that he was engaging in the coolie trade, he did not deny any of his servants' other charges.)

On the West Coast, other agents discovered the cold trail of a Chinese plot to fly huge quantities of gold from China to an out-of-the-way private airport in the Los Angeles suburb of Van Nuys.

The FBI investigation, which was never carried out with noteworthy enthusiasm, finally ground to a halt because of the peculiar circumstances under which the Soongs and Kungs were in America. They were not U.S. citizens, and they were not registered foreign agents. They had come to America originally as prominent officials of the government of China and still carried diplomatic passports. Obviously, they were no longer officials of that government. But exactly what were they?

Sooner or later, even dethroned kings have to fill out forms, especially in the democratic West, where things do not exist until they are recorded on paper. But the Soongs and Kungs were in America in a special status of celebrity that absolved them of such requirements. Their situation was so ambiguous that the clan apparently was under no obligation to spell out any financial holdings or activities. Nearly twenty years later, as a very old man, H. H. Kung arrived in Seattle after a brief visit to Taiwan, and at the airport was listed by a cooperative functionary of the U.S. Immigration and Naturalization Service simply as "government official." H. H. was assigned "A-1" status and cleared through immediately.

The Soongs always seemed to slip through the cracks. They were free to come and go in America as they wished, live there, bank there, invest there, do whatever they wished there, encumbered by none of the usual burdens of daily life.

Deciding that it was politically dangerous to pursue the investigation further, the FBI finally closed it down with the old bureaucratic device of passing the decision over to somebody else—in this case the politically sensitive chiefs of the Justice Department, where the matter quickly and predictably sank into oblivion.

President Truman was given a certain amount of hard information to answer his original question. It was only a peek into the world of the Soongs. Years later, during an interview with writer Merle Miller, Truman said, "They're all thieves, every damn one of them. . . . They stole seven hundred and fifty million dollars out of the [$3.8] billion that we sent to Chiang. They stole it, and it's invested in real estate down in São Paulo and some right here in New York. . . . And that's the money that was used and is still being used for the so-called China Lobby."

In China, while this FBI investigation was getting under way, the Generalissimo was very busy planning his escape to Taiwan. A man who bombed his own troops to prevent a few weapons and supplies from falling into Communist hands was not about to leave far more significant treasures to the "bandits." Chiang set his most trusted men to systematically emptying China's banks, her arsenals, and her museums. Across the countryside there were scenes reminiscent of the last frenzied days in Nazi Germany when stolen Rembrandts were being spirited away to private vaults for recovery at a more suitable time.

Years earlier, at the suggestion of Curio Chang, long-range plans had been put into action for the "evacuation" of the Palace Museum treasures collected by Ch'ien Lung, the fourth Emperor of the Manchu Dynasty. His reign, from 1735–96, had been a golden age of the arts. Frugal personally, but anxious to display his fine taste, the Emperor furnished his residences with a magnificent collection of art masterworks that later formed the nucleus of China's national museum. It was this collection that long had been coveted by Curio Chang and his art world friends.

The Generalissimo regarded these treasures as his dynastic heritage. In the early 1930s, he had them moved from Peking to Nanking. As the Japanese advanced, Chiang's agents hauled the art works around the country in thousands of crates, "to keep them away from the Japanese" or (alternatively) "the Communists." They were finally taken into the remote reaches of western China till the war ended. That many of the masterpieces meanwhile disappeared overseas to wealthy connoisseurs has always been the subject of tantalizing speculation, but the way in which the treasures were shuffled around over twenty years made it impossible to be certain what, or how much, was missing. Curio Chang left China in 1938 for Europe, where he maintained galleries in Paris, London, and Geneva. He spent the war in New York City, where he had another well-stocked gallery, and died there on September 3, 1950 unremarked by the *Times*.

Nearly a quarter of a million paintings, porcelains, jades, and bronzes ultimately were spirited away to Taipei before the conclusion of the Battle of Huai-hai. Eleven days after the battle ended, on January 21, 1949, Chiang Kai-shek resigned as President of Nationalist China.

Certainly he resigned to spare himself the humiliation of defeat. But he took with him, as he always did whenever he resigned, the authority of command. There were still troops, bureaucrats, Lend-Lease materials, airplanes, all sitting awaiting Chiang's orders. There were political generals clamoring for a chance to take over the regime. The presidency fell to Chiang's old KMT rival, General Li Tsung-jen, whose first move was to try to negotiate with Mao Tse-tung. Mao's first condition was that the Generalissimo and Madame Chiang Kai-shek—who were listed as the people's number one war criminals, followed by T. V. Soong and the Kungs—be turned over for trial.

H. H. Kung never resumed his career. When the war ended, he was sixty-five years old. He and Ai-ling together were worth (by modest estimates) somewhere close to $1 billion U.S., most of it moved with considerable foresight outside China. In 1946, they paid a last brief visit to Shanghai, to liquidate their holdings and transfer everything they could to Hong Kong or abroad. In 1947, they visited the Kung estate in Taiku, Shansi, to close down the palace before it was overrun by the Red Army. H. H. then informed his friends that he was taking Ai-ling back to America because she was "not feeling well" and it was necessary for her to be close to New York medical centers.

T. V. Soong did not stick around either for the bitter end. He was on the reds' list of top war criminals, and his enemies in the Nationalist government, claiming to have documented vast embezzlements, were demanding that T. V. return at least half of his entire fortune. On January 24, 1949, fearing for his life, T. V. resigned as governor of Kwangtung and fled with Laura to Hong Kong. He stepped off the plane at Kai Tak airport wearing a double-breasted business suit and a gray homburg, carrying his favorite cane. On his lapel were two rows of medals from the Nationalist government and the Kuomintang party. Ding-Ding walked beside him swathed in mink, wearing dark glasses to hide eyes puffy from weeping. T. V. had never looked so grim. Both sides were after him—the reds and the greens. He asked for a British police guard in Hong Kong, and got it. By May 16, he was in Paris for "medical treatment." He touched down on American soil on June 10, 1949, entering on a diplomatic passport, again strictly "on family business."

That February, although he was no longer President of Nationalist China, Chiang Kai-shek arranged for the government's remaining gold reserves to be removed urgently to Taipei. If he was to leave President Li holding the bag, Chiang evidently wanted to be sure the bag was empty. This meant no payroll for Li's dwindling armies, no food for the soldiers still holding out. When Li discovered that his treasury had been emptied, he pleaded with U.S. Ambassador John Leighton Stuart for American aid, to allow him to negotiate with Mao from a position of strength. Ambassador Stuart advised him to ask for patriotic contributions from the KMT officials who had salted away billions of American aid in their foreign bank accounts.

Chiang Kai-shek summoned Sun Fo, and made the kind of suggestion that was certain to electrify the poor fellow into folly. Chiang suggested that this was the time to establish a separatist government in Canton, just as Dr. Sun had done so many years before. The Generalissimo promised the doctor's son that if he did this Chiang would be able to launch a new Northern Expedition. Sun Fo hurried off to Canton. But, before the month was out, even the lackluster Sun Fo came to his senses and left quickly for exile in France. Chiang began shipping his remaining loyal troops across the Formosa Strait to Taiwan. With enough money and soldiers, and with all the riches of mainland China that could be transported, perhaps even he could hold out there indefinitely. His next-to-last stop was Shanghai.

In Shanghai that April, Big-eared Tu saw Chiang one last time. The Generalissimo was conferring with General T'ang En-po, who proposed to make Shanghai a "second Stalingrad." Paper Tiger T'ang, the hero of the Yellow River dikes, made wild declarations of patriotism and now forecast total victory over the reds. He had thousands of coolies dig a great moat and build a ten-foot-high bamboo palisade, to no apparent military end. It was understood that he had a relative in the lumber business.

Chiang's real reason for coming to town was to get Big-eared Tu and the Green Gang to help him rob the Bank of China. He wanted the money badly. He had no intention of fleeing to Taiwan without it. His hopes for the gold yuan had collapsed after only a few months, when word got out that there really was no gold to back the new currency. The gold had been there at one time—six million ounces of it. While half of that had vanished with the Soongs and Kungs, according to official charges, the remaining half had just vanished. What gold there was left in China was private gold still in this bank.

The gold yuan hoax was Chiang's parting shot at history. Five months after the gold yuan was introduced at an artificial exchange rate of four gold yuan to one U.S. dollar, the rate plummeted to one million to one. After that it went crazy.

The people who suffered most were those earnest souls who somehow had managed to save one or two thousand U.S. dollars' worth of gold in the course of a lifetime, and obeyed Chiang's orders and brought it to government banks on the prescribed day to trade for gold yuans. When their gold yuans became worthless overnight, they could be seen sitting in teashops in Shanghai or Hankow or Canton, in a state of shock, abandoned by the Kuomintang, certain to be persecuted as capitalists by the Communists, sitting there without even enough coppers to spirit the wife and children out of the country to Macao or Hong Kong before the roof caved in. They were the last of Chiang's constituents.

Chiang's plans for the Bank of China had been laid with considerable care. A dingy freighter was tied up on the Bund, opposite the Cathay Hotel. Its coolie crew, dressed in filthy rags, were hand-picked naval ratings in disguise. Several executives of the Bank of China had been given large bribes and a promise of passage to safety on the waiting freighter, in return for opening the vaults. Nationalist troops cordoned off an area of several blocks around the bank, including part of the Nanking Road and the Bund. Out of the darkness came the steady chant of "coolies" as they carried their heavy loads. Each man carried two parcels on a bamboo pole. They were ghoulish in the light of arc lamps illuminating the way from bank to freighter. Amazed, George Vine, a British correspondent, watched the proceedings unnoticed from his office, where he had been working late on a dispatch. When he realized what was happening, he cabled his London office with an oddly philosophic message that "all the gold in China was being carried away in the traditional manner—coolies."

With this, Tu Yueh-sheng pulled his last heist. He slipped out of Shanghai just days before the Communists entered the city triumphant on May 25. He lived the last two years of his life in Hong Kong. The decades of hard drugs caught up with him. He could no longer walk, paralysis set in, and on the 16th of August 1951, he died. Chiang Kai-shek sent a message from Taipei commending Big-eared Tu to posterity for his "loyalty and integrity."

Chiang fled to Taiwan himself aboard a gunboat early in May 1949. Defense Minister Ch'en Ch'eng had been taking care of preparations in Taiwan since October of the previous year. When he arrived in Taipei, Chiang was offered the former Viceroy's residence but declined in favor of setting up housekeeping in the guest quarters on the Taiwan Sugar Company plantation eight miles north of the city. It was in this wooded retreat, among lush green hills, that he was informed Shanghai had fallen with hardly a shot being fired, and secret police records in Nanking had been handed over to the Communists, giving them details on many of Chiang's underworld dealings for the past thirty years. These files were taken to Peking and kept initially at 15 Bowstring Alley, the CCP's secret service headquarters, and later housed in the Central Party Building West.

Remoter parts of western China were still in KMT hands. In August 1949, Chiang and CCK flew from Taiwan to Chengtu to pay their respects at the grave of T'ai Ch'i-tao. T'ai, the born-again anti-Communist who had helped stage-manage Chiang's rise to power, had realized in February that the end was near. He took a fatal overdose of sleeping pills on the night of February 11. As long as he was in Chungking anyway, the Generalissimo stopped by police headquarters to finish off one remaining bit of "personal" business. In a Chungking prison compound there was still a prisoner who was very special. It was Yang Hu-Cheng, the warlord who had joined the Young Marshal to kidnap Chiang in the Sian Incident. Though allowed to go into European exile, Yang had so antagonized the Generalissimo that in 1938, when he returned to China following an amnesty, Chiang ordered his immediate arrest. For eleven years, Yang, a son, and a daughter (along with a loyal secretary and his wife) languished in Tai Li's concentration camp outside Chungking. Now, before leaving China for good, Chiang made this special trip just to sign Yang's death warrant. The old man, his son, his daughter, his secretary, and the secretary's wife were all taken out and shot.

In January 1950, Madame Chiang arrived in Taiwan from New York to set up housekeeping. The island did not welcome the KMT. It was driven into submission by terror. Here was one of the world's truly fortunate islands, fertile, temperate, with cliff-lined seascapes and misty peaks that unrolled each dawn from the scroll of night. During decades of Japanese rule, the island had become economically self-reliant. But, after World War II, the Allies had turned it over to Chiang as part of a secret agreement made during the Cairo talks. Chiang forced Taiwan to heel. There were massacres; in the first, ten thousand Taiwanese were slain by KMT troops in riots in downtown Taipei. Twenty thousand more were put to death before Chiang was firmly established. Taiwanese leaders who were still alive went underground or slipped out to Tokyo. On an island of such moderate proportions, Chiang's secret police and armed forces were effective in a way they never had been on the mainland. They gave Taiwan the treatment that Chiang had given Shanghai in Black April, 1927.

Few thought Chiang would survive on Taiwan more than a year. The smell of defeat was strong. Britain had recognized Peking. It seemed only a matter of time before the United States would follow suit. The State Department notified its diplomatic posts to expect the fall of Taiwan to the Communists and said the United States would not provide Chiang with military aid or advice. American conservatives were shocked, and counterattacked. Senator Joseph McCarthy made the first of many accusations that the State Department was full of Communists. President Truman retaliated that McCarthy and a handful of other Republican Senators, including New Hampshire's Styles Bridges, were "the Kremlin's greatest asset" in the Cold War. This new China debate was driven to the edge of hysteria on June 25, 1950, when North Korea invaded South Korea, and the United States plunged into one of the darker periods in its history. Fear of the witch hunt paralyzed debate. Before the first year of the Korean War was over, policy was reversed, and Washington decided to defend Taiwan. The CIA made the Chiang regime its principal operational base in Asia, became a partner in Chennault's airline, and the dictatorship was given precious time to find its footing and remodel its image.

The American press at the end of the 1940s was just getting accustomed to the sound of a new editorial policy—"Tell Chiang he is finished, and that the U.S. is finished with him"—when the Chiang government poured millions of dollars into a counteroffensive. Zealous Americans who joined the pro-Taiwan crusade became the fund raisers, the organizers, the telephoners, the legmen, the gofers, the publicists, the congressmen, the tycoons, the hosts and hostesses of the shadowy society that was called "the China Lobby." Its management, its direction, and its primary finances were not American. The China Lobby belonged to the Soong clan and the Nationalist Chinese government. The people involved thought they were working for the greater glory of God, or for "the survival of the democratic system." They were really working for a Chinese public-relations campaign .

Everybody in the 1950s heard the term "China Lobby" but nobody knew exactly what it encompassed and who was involved. "If it had been run by Moscow rather than Taipei," said a French diplomat, "everyone involved could have been hung for treason."

Marquis Childs wrote, "No one who knows anything about the way things work here doubts that a powerful China lobby has brought extraordinary influence to bear on Congress and the Executive. It would be hard to find any parallel in diplomatic history for the agents and diplomatic representatives of a foreign power exerting such pressures —Nationalist China has used the techniques of direct intervention on a scale rarely, if ever, seen." Part of this campaign was to pour gasoline on the McCarthy witch hunts.

Chiang's government used existing American corporations headed by men who shared its viewpoint; it hired advertising agencies; it created dummy corporations as blinds for propaganda; it set up a "propaganda ministry" of its own in the United States; it cultivated influential, sympathetic Americans who set up bipartisan, "nonprofit" committees that served as pressure groups. Few activities were directed personally by the Soongs. That was no longer necessary. The Chinese technocrats who guided daily operations were a new generation of Soong protégés slickly groomed on Soong techniques.

The New York public-relations firm Allied Syndicates, Inc., counted among its major clients the Bank of China (with H. H. Kung as director). Another public-relations firm, Hamilton Wright, worked for six years as a registered agent for Nationalist China, writing and distributing stories, news articles, photographs, and movies to create a favorable image of Chiang Kai-shek and his regime. One clause of the Wright organization's contract with the Nationalist government guaranteed that: "In 75 per cent of the releases, neither the editor of the newspaper—nor the newspaper reader—HAS ANY KNOWLEDGE WHERE THE MATERIAL ORIGINATED." (Original emphasis.) The Herald Tribune Service, for one, owned by Henry Luce's Republican friend Jock Whitney, fed this spurious material to unsuspecting American newspapers for years without ever identifying the source.

T. V.'s wartime Universal Trading Corporation was listed in 1949 as a foreign agent working for the Chinese government, with assets of nearly $22 million. The Chinese News Service based in Taiwan established branches in Washington, New York, Chicago, and San Francisco, and distributed millions of copies of a journal called *This Week in Free China*. It also circulated news stories and feature articles, thinly-disguised propaganda, to fill the columns of American papers. Taiwan's Central News Agency, which went to great lengths to emulate the Associated Press, spent $654 million U.S. in only three years, 1946–49, producing articles on Chiang's anti-Communist struggle, and on lavishly entertaining American editors and correspondents in the U.S. and the Far East—more than $200 million each year. Small wonder that a large segment of the American public believed that Chiang was the essence of virtue and his cause a just one. Similar amounts were spent during the Korean War and the periodic crises over the defense of the Formosa Strait. Guesses at the grand total spent by Taiwan to stupefy Americans ran as high as $1 billion each year.

Taiwan exercised a particularly strong influence on American newspapers of the far right, notably the influential Oakland *Tribune,* owned by Senator William F. Knowland, a dominant figure in West Coast politics and one of the most powerful Republicans in Washington. His Capitol Hill colleagues called him "the Senator from Formosa." Another unabashed Chiang supporter was New Hampshire's William Loeb, far-right publisher of the Manchester *Union Leader,* who backed Senator Bridges in the China Lobby. Others were Roy Howard of the Scripps-Howard Newspapers, John Daly of ABC News, and, of course, Henry Luce. Biographer Swanberg gives an assessment:

> Luce now saw the most grandiose project of his lifetime in danger of ruin. Wrapped up in the ruin was not only the fate of China and of Christianity and the Asian hegemony of the United States but also his own peace of mind and reputation. Chiang-in-China was to have been the crowning of a decade and a half of planning in the Chrysler Building and Rockefeller Center and of countless thousands of words of Lucepress propaganda. The nightmare rise of Mao-in-China brought a powerful Luce counter-strategy. For one thing, his China Institute of America, founded as a haven for Chinese students, now was registered (with Luce as trustee) as a foreign agent working for the Nationalists.

Newscaster Robert S. Allen reported,

> One of the most remarkable aspects of this remarkable foreign raid . . . is the fact that it's being masterminded by certain well-known Americans. . . . Luce has been propagandizing and agitating for another two-billion-dollar U.S. handout for Chiang for a long time. . . . And in Washington practically the whole Luce bureau has been working full blast as part of the Chiang lobby.

Many of the activists in the lobby were people whose families had worked in China as missionaries, and now thought their heritage was being thrown away. Among them were the directors of the American China Policy Association and the Committee to Defend America by Aiding Anti-Communist China, which issued blizzards of paper urging the U.S. government to provide more aid to China. There were powerful people on the committee's board of directors: David Dubinsky of the International Ladies' Garment Workers' Union and second vice-president of the American Federation of Labor; James Farley, chairman of the board of Coca-Cola Export Corporation and former Postmaster General. The American China Policy Association was headed by Alfred Kohlberg, that wealthy importer of Nationalist textiles and friend of

Clare Luce. Last but far from least was the Committee of One Million (which included Henry Luce in its membership). It was created in 1953 to keep Communist China out of the United Nations; later it was reborn as the Committee for Free China. It was still lobbying for grassroots support for Taiwan even after U.S. relations with Peking were normalized in 1979. Among its members were twenty-three senators, including Knowland, Mike Mansfield, Everett Dirksen, and Jacob Javits, plus eighty-three congressmen, a number of generals and admirals, and a plethora of tycoons.

These groups were periodically supported by campaigns waged in Chiang's behalf by the executive council of the AFL-CIO, the American Legion, the American Security Council, the American Conservative Union, and Young Americans for Freedom. To many conservative organizations, Taiwan became synonymous with anti-Communism. In the atmosphere of the 1950s, the fear of Red China kept normally sensible people from wondering where all the money was coming from.

Despite the ebb and flow of their personal relationship with the Chiang regime, the Kungs and Soongs remained the primary pipeline connecting American special interests with Taiwan. Ai-ling and H. H. Kung, T. V. Soong, and May-ling Soong Chiang devoted considerable energies to the lobby and sometimes gathered for strategy sessions at the Kung estate in Riverdale.

Ai-ling and H. H. stayed in exile in Riverdale from 1948 on. As principal director of the Bank of China's New York City branch, H. H. was driven in to Wall Street two or three days a week. He spent the rest of his time working at home. Columnist Drew Pearson, one of the few journalists who maintained an interest in the Soongs after they went into exile, called the Bank of China the "nerve center of the China Lobby." Through its offices, Pearson reminded his readers, many millions of dollars were transferred from the Nationalist government to underwrite the propaganda blitz.

> Dr. Kung's knowledge of American politics is almost as astute as his knowledge of Chinese finance; and well before he entered the Truman cabinet, Kung picked Louis Johnson as his personal attorney.
>
> It may or may not be significant that, later, when Johnson became Secretary of Defense, he was one of the stanchest advocates of American support for Formosa. . . . Dr. Kung has been a caller upon popular Sen. Styles Bridges of New Hampshire, and the Senator likewise has been active in urging aid to Formosa and the Chiang Kai-shek exiles.

When Bridges ran for re-election in 1948 he listed a $2000 campaign contribution from Alfred Kohlberg of New York, the front man for the China Lobby and a friend of Dr. Kung.

It is significant that Senator Bridges not only has voted and made speeches in favor of China Lobby policies, but extended one of the greatest possible favors to the Kung-Soong dynasty. . . .

In 1948, the same year that Bridges received his contributions from Kohlberg of the China Lobby, Bridges appointed ex-Sen. Worth Clark of Idaho as an impartial representative of the Senate Appropriations Committee to go to China and make an "impartial" report on the Nationalist Government. Bridges at that time occupied the potent post of Chairman of the Appropriations Committee.

The purpose of the survey was to recommend whether more U.S. aid to Chiang was justified.

What most people didn't realize about the supposedly impartial survey, however, was that Clark was not exactly in a position to be impartial. For the ex-Senator from Idaho had long been a member of the law firm which represented T. V. Soong, the other brother-in-law of Chiang Kai-shek. In brief, Clark was a paid lobbyist for the China Lobby.

Furthermore, part of Clark's expenses were paid by the Chinese Nationalists, despite the fact that he was supposed to be working for the U.S. Senate and the American taxpayers.

Clark came back with a vigorous recommendation that more aid be sent to Chiang.

A few weeks later, Pearson declared that these policies were still being practiced to the great benefit of the Soong family fortune.

A move by a Chiang brother-in-law, with other wealthy Chinese, to corner the soybean market at the expense of the American public . . . The brother-in-law is T. L. Soong, brother of Foreign Minister T. V. Soong, who formerly handled much of the three and a half billion dollars worth of supplies which the United States sent to China during the War. The soybean pool netted a profit of $30,000,000 and shot up the cost to the American consumer $1 a bushel.

One of the strange things about the soybean manipulation was that its operators knew exactly the right time to buy up the world's soybean supply —a few weeks before the communists invaded Korea.

Recently this column told how Eugene Soong, son of T. L. Soong, together with L. K. [Louis] Kung, son of Dr. H. H. Kung, another brother-in-law, sold a huge quantity of precious tin to the Chinese Communists. . . .

Operations like this may be one reason why the disillusioned Chinese people threw out the Soong-Kung Dynasty and accepted Communism as a lesser evil.

Louis Kung had become one of the busiest members of the clan. During Richard Nixon's 1950 senatorial campaign, Daddy Kung dispatched Younger Son to Los Angeles to give the senator donations and encouragement. He also persuaded California's large Chinese constituency to help elect Nixon. Louis's helping hand forged a bond between the Kungs and the Nixons, who visited the Riverdale mansion from time to time over the years.

Louis took an active role in the Soong-Kung petroleum holdings, with oil properties across Texas, Oklahoma, and Louisiana. At the (Nationalist) Chinese embassy in Washington in 1956, Louis organized the Cheyenne Oil Company, which controlled Magnatrust Company, Westland Oil Development Corporation, and the Atoka Drilling Company. Cheyenne Oil made it a practice to solicit investments from important politicians, journalists, and movie stars. If one of Louis's wells (leased for example, to John Daly, then vice-president for news of the ABC Network), did poorly, Louis guaranteed that Daly would have his investment back; if the well turned out to be a success, then the profits were divided with Daly. Some of the investors who were offered this type of deal did not know that Chinese money controlled Cheyenne Oil. In this fashion, powerful men could invest without appreciable risk and make handsome profits.

When May-ling returned to Taiwan in 1950, she found herself embroiled in a final struggle for the succession and for her own political survival. In May-ling's periodic absences, CCK had been given a job as Chiang Kai-shek's personal assistant, and was then promoted to be chief of security as head of the Political Department of the Taiwan Defense Ministry. Over the next two decades, it seemed, each time May-ling turned her back to visit the United States, CCK moved another rung up the political ladder, one step closer to replacing her as his father's heir.

May-ling was too intense to sit around Sun-Moon Lake painting the simple pictures of flowers that she gave to everyone, including CCK. (His was a painting of bamboo, autographed "To Son.") She had always involved herself in social work, particularly orphanages—although the orphans were almost without exception those special ones left by the untimely deaths of her husband's officers. (Even Tai Li had run orphanages. In China it was necessary to guarantee the welfare of a man's children to get secret agents to work for you. So orphanages proliferated under the KMT.)

When Taiwan became oppressive, May-ling hurried off to the United States to lend her presence to the China Lobby. On one trip she stayed from August 1952 until March 1953. When she returned to Taiwan, she learned that CCK had received an invitation to be the guest of the Pentagon and State Department. Washington was becoming curious about the heir apparent. CCK was invited to talks with President Eisenhower, treatment that May-ling had not received since 1943.

While she held no official position in Taiwan, May-ling was still in close contact with the Generalissimo, as close as it was possible to be as he began to turn senile. She spoke for him at audiences with American officials. He would mumble a few words, then she would talk for five minutes, then he would mumble again and she would launch into another long discourse. The impression was one of a store-window mannequin dressed up to look like Chiang, sitting on his throne while Luce's world-famous Missimo held sway.

Few of Chiang's generals or bureaucrats dared to offend her. Even her stepson was circumspect in handling her. She was quick to take offense, and certain to exact retribution. The story is told by friends of Clare Boothe Luce of a shopping trip the two ladies made by limousine in Taipei. After making their purchases, they returned to the car and each urged the other to get in first. After three turns of "No, after you," Mrs. Luce gave up and climbed in first. Madame Chiang then got in beside her and sulked all the way back to her residence in the northern outskirts. After May-ling had stalked off to her rooms, Mrs. Luce asked a secretary what she had done wrong. "I offered three times," she said.

"You should have offered four," the secretary answered.

The hard core of the China Lobby—the senators, the Pentagon generals, the American tycoons who built paper mills and aluminum plants and electronic assembly lines across the Taiwan landscape—knew little about Asia. At mid-century there was still a bit of nostalgia and melancholy for James Hilton's *Lost Horizon* in every American's fantasy about the Orient. Madame Chiang had immortalized the role of the lost cause in real life. In her advancing years, there was mingled in her an air of sadness and loss. She swept visitors off their feet with gestures of the most outrageous flattery. She always had at hand little expensive gifts—silver boxes, silver trays, miniature teak chests inlaid with mother-of-pearl. With the help of a large but invisible staff, these tokens were engraved ahead of time with a man's name and a brief enigmatic message. It was enough to impress Western men, who never encountered such ingratiating Oriental niceties in their normal life.

In April, 1954, May-ling went to Washington for six months to stir up action against the proposal to seat the People's Republic in the UN. When she returned to Taiwan to celebrate Chiang Kai-shek's sixty-seventh birthday, her homecoming at Sungshan airport was marred by another sign that power was slipping out of her grasp. While the elderly, white-haired Generalissimo stayed out of sight in the terminal, CCK and his own small son walked out to the plane to greet May-ling. As a presumption, it was unprecedented, and May-ling was icy as CCK escorted her to a cluster of VIPs and a covey of ladies from the Chinese Women's Anti-Aggression League. Brushing past them, May-ling strode into the terminal, muttered an inaudible comment to the senile old fascist, and then walked on tight-lipped to their waiting limousine. Perhaps, like Mao Tse-tung, she called him Turtle Egg.

She hung on tenaciously as what some unchivalrous newsmen privately called "the foremost clubwoman of the world," even if the only audiences she could command now were luncheons at the Taiwan Rotary Club. In 1958, CCK was promoted once more and Madame Chiang went off in apparent disgust for a fourteen-month stay in America. She was sixty-one years old, claiming to be fifty-eight. As a courtesy, CCK's appointment to the presidential cabinet as Minister Without Portfolio was announced two months after her departure. When May-ling eventually gritted her teeth and went back to Taipei, she remained stubbornly there for the next six years.

As H. H. Kung grew very old, he did not neglect his philanthropic image. In 1959, at the age of seventy-seven, he went back to Oberlin for the fifth anniversary of the Oberlin Shansi Memorial Association, and set up a scholarship at the college. A reporter asked him about his rumored U.S. fortune of "over five hundred million dollars." His eyes growing moist, the old pawnbroker shook his head, looked befuddled, and said that he had lost all of his investments with the collapse of the Nationalist government and was now living off his meager savings. The young reporter nodded in genuine sympathy and took notes.

In 1966, at age eighty-four, H. H. stepped down at last from the directorship of the Bank of China and moved into a new mansion with Ai-ling, on Feeks Lane in Locust Valley, Long Island. His health was deteriorating rapidly, with a severe heart condition. In August 1967, he was rushed to New York Hospital, where he died on August 15, at the age of eighty-seven. The *New York Times* tried to give some appraisal of him as a politician, but limped through the column by saying only:

> Mr. Kung was a controversial figure. One of his former subordinates said recently that "he was a very difficult person to work with. He liked to talk and gossip but he would never hand down definite instructions. As for his ability, he was a smart operator like all those Shansi bankers, but he was not a financier in the sense of statesmanship!"

The funeral was at the Marble Collegiate Church on Fifth Avenue. Madame Chiang flew in from Taiwan with a five-man color guard and General Chiang Wei-kuo, the Generalissimo's younger son. Among the mourners were such pillars of the China Lobby as Richard M. Nixon, Cardinal Spellman, Senator Everett Dirksen, James A. Farley, and Miami Beach millionaire William Pawley, owner of the Miami Transit Company—the same Pawley of CAMCO who went on from the Flying Tigers to become U. S. Ambassador to Brazil, one of the Soongs' favorite countries for investment.

T. V. Soong did not attend Kung's funeral. In those later years, there was no love lost.

Ai-ling survived H. H. by six years, but never went back to China or to Taiwan. In Asia, there was a persistent rumor that the Soong sisters had a family reunion every year in Hong Kong, but this was folklore. In spite of the fact that she had been ill since 1949, apparently suffering from intermittent bouts of some form of cancer, Ai-ling reached age eighty-five before succumbing at last in New York City. She was remembered only tersely in a perfunctory *New York Times* obituary.

Thus was lost to the world, lips tightly sealed, one of its more interesting and predatory inhabitants. A woman of enormous financial accomplishment, whose wealth was exceeded only by her brother T. V.'s, perhaps the wealthiest woman ever to put it all together with her own cunning, the broker of May-ling Soong's marriage to Chiang Kai-shek, the principal contriver of the Soong legend, and the true architect of the dynasty's rise to power.

Exile for T. V. Soong was a bit more turbulent because he was on the lam. Early in 1950, he and Laura had just settled into a luxurious apartment at 1133 Park Avenue in Manhattan, when an urgent invitation arrived from Chiang Kai-shek for T. V. to come to Taiwan—like an invitation from the Cosa Nostra to come back to Sorrento, or to "see Naples and die." Understandably, T. V. was in no mood to go. The Generalissimo persisted and threatened to expel him from the inner circle of the KMT if he did not come "to take up his official government functions," so to speak. Again, T. V. refused. The *New York Times* reported the strange affair this way:

> The Kuomintang said that Dr. Soong, one of the wealthiest men in the world, had chosen to resign rather than come to this Communist-threatened island, refuge of all that Generalissimo Chiang has left of his once populous nation.
>
> Dr. Soong left China shortly before the Government fled to Canton from Nanking a year ago. At that time there was a move afoot to have him donate to the Nationalist cause a part of his fortune, reputedly scattered in French, British, North and South American, Indian, South African and way point banks.
>
> So far as is publicly known here he ignored the requests and left Canton hurriedly.

T. V. was much too shrewd to take chances at this point. He had plans of his own. They included buying a large stash of guns, 45,000 Enfield rifles plus ammunition, owned by the American Machinery Company and stored in warehouses in Canada. In January 1950, the same time Chiang was trying to get T. V. to pack his toothbrush and his checkbook, Robert Bigelow, the Washington representative of the Brako Company, asked the State Department for a permit to export the guns. He said the head of Brako, William Brailowsky, was a "personal friend" of T. V. Soong and wanted to ship the guns from Vancouver to Taiwan. State was suspicious that the approach was not made by the Taiwan embassy, and by the odd detail that a U. S. permit was requested instead of one from Canada, where the guns were. The implication was that T. V. might be involved in plans to stage a coup by elements sympathetic to him in the Nationalist army, to overthrow his brother-in-law and install a new government with T. V. Soong as its head. An informant, however, told the FBI that T. V.'s role was really as "a purchasing agent for an outfit selling to a Chinese Communist purchaser." As in many of T. V.'s enterprises, only the dorsal fin was visible. It was not possible to know the upshot.

Although T. V. avoided Taiwan, and devoted most of his attention to his expanding financial empire, he did back the China Lobby financially, because it was in his interest to do so. The levers of the China Lobby could be worked in many directions. Moving out of Manhattan, he purchased a palatial home on Long Island, which he had decorated with paintings selected by people who he admitted knew more about art than he did. He had a rich collection of Chinese bronzes as well, although he acknowledged that they, too, were chosen for him. His mansion was heavily guarded and had an elaborate alarm system.

It was ordinary street lore in the Chinese-American communities of the United States that T. V. Soong's Long Island home contained an "unbelievable" fortune, and that T. V. was an "extremely dangerous" man because he was the most powerful Chinese tycoon in America and a lot of "bad people" were dependent on him. A variation of this was repeated to me by a Chinese scholar employed as an analyst by the CIA. It was not so much implied that T. V. himself was dangerous but that the slightest word from him could bring about terrible consequences from the Chinese tongs or syndicates, the Chinese banks, and nameless other objects of fear.

T. V. was frenetically busy wheeling and dealing in oil stocks, commodity futures, and new technology. He energetically pursued the reputation he was earning as the "richest man in the world."

He dropped in on Averell Harriman now and then, either in Washington or at Harriman's cottage at Sands Point, to chat about the Sino-Soviet dispute and check the Washington mood. He hardly saw Henry Luce, though they exchanged letters now and then, and sent each other cordial invitations that they failed to accept. The Luces were close to May-ling, and this precluded seeing T. V. His real friends were his powerful financial contacts in Singapore, Hong Kong, Tokyo, and London, and the directors of the banks he controlled.

The KMT old guard who hated T. V. for enriching himself were themselves in no position to throw stones, but they were gradually dying off. Tai Li's plane disappeared mysteriously after the war—apparently blown up by explosives hidden aboard. T. V.'s worst enemy next to Chiang and his own relatives, Ch'en Kuo-fu, died in Taipei in August 1951 at age sixty. Once his older brother was dead, Ch'en Li-fu gave up running the Taiwan secret police and became a gentleman farmer in America. After a while, he abandoned farming and retired in Taiwan, living to a ripe old age.

In February, 1963, when tempers had cooled for over a decade, T. V. finally did accept an invitation from the Generalissimo to visit Taiwan. He stayed with the Chiangs a few days at their retreat north of Taipei, where he conferred with "unnamed officials." On his return, when he reported to Harriman about this visit, T. V. seemed to be fishing to see if the United States had changed its mind about backing Chiang in an effort to "recover" the mainland. Joseph Alsop told Harriman that "the Generalissimo and Madame Chiang intensely disliked T. V. Soong and would only have asked him to come because they believe he is probably the best analyst of U.S. Administration opinion." Apparently, Chiang had decided that, if he couldn't pry money out of T. V., he could at least have T. V. work his old magic on Washington. He was wrong. T. V. still had well-placed friends, but he no longer had the will to give it the effort required. Nothing came of the Generalissimo's aspirations then, and nothing came of them later.

T. V.'s youngest brother, T. A., was listed by Harvard, his alma mater, as a "Lost Man" after 1950, meaning that they had lost track of him. He was in San Francisco, where he was chairman of the board of the well-endowed Bank of Canton until he died in February 1969.

The middle brother, T. L., who had been in charge of Lend-Lease during World War II, and whose American roots were in New York City, became something of an enigma. Sources in Washington said T. L. worked as a secret consultant to the Treasury Department in the 1950s, engaged in what they would not say. Treasury claims it has no record of a T. L. Soong whatever.

Two years after T. A. died, in April 1971, when T. V. was seventy-seven years old, he and Laura visited San Francisco once more to see friends and relatives. On the evening of April 24, they were honored by old friend Edward Eu of the Bank of Canton, at a dinner party in his San Francisco home. Despite the elegance of the evening, T. V. was hurrying through the various courses in his usual fashion when he suddenly stopped, looked startled, rose to his feet choking, and collapsed. A moment later he was dead. The autopsy showed that a bit of food had lodged in his windpipe, and the nerves in his neck had sent emergency signals to his heart that his heart was too weak to support.

Inappropriately, or mischievously, Henry Kissinger had President Nixon send a message of condolence to Madame Chiang and the Generalissimo: "His brilliant career in the service of his country, particularly during our great common efforts in World War II, will long be remembered by his friends in America. We share with you the sense of loss which his passing brings."

Although May-ling was in the United States when T. V. died, she lamely excused herself from attending the New York funeral.

The New York papers disclosed that T. V.'s estate consisted of only "one million dollars," which would be divided among his wife and children. There was a lot of chuckling and shaking of heads in London and Paris and Moscow and Tokyo, and in Rio and Hong Kong and Singapore and Johannesburg, and in Manila and Taipei and Peking.

The red carpets were finally rolled out again for May-ling when she went back to Washington in 1965, amid an unusual flurry of diplomatic activity. The Nationalist embassy threw a party for fifteen hundred leading politicians and China Lobbyists. Madame Chiang was the guest of honor. She arrived from New York on a private train, and was greeted by Mrs. Dean Rusk. She was driven to a fine mansion rented for her in the fashionable Kalorama Road section within walking distance of Defense Secretary Robert McNamara's own house. She hobnobbed with J. Edgar Hoover, Supreme Court Justice Byron White, Senator Thomas Dodd, had tea at the White House with Lady Bird and a tête-à-tête with LBJ. It was like the old days.

A minor detail that received little attention by the press was that Madame Chiang was accompanied by her stepson. CCK, now Taiwan's Minister of Defense, was the guest of May-ling's neighbor, Secretary McNamara. He came with May-ling's entourage, quietly conducted his business, then slipped away.

All this abnormal hoopla had an ulterior motive. For years, the Generalissimo had tried to get Washington to back a Nationalist invasion of mainland China. But Washington had decided long since that Chiang had no hope of winning any engagement with the Chinese Communists, and only hoped to draw America into a war with China from which Chiang hoped to emerge on top. The Generalissimo asked more than once to be given nuclear weapons "to protect Taiwan" and the China Lobby tried furiously to get them for him. Now, the United States was involved in the Vietnam War, and the shoe was on the other foot. The Johnson administration badly wanted Chiang to send Nationalist troops to fight in Indochina. The mission of CCK to Washington was to negotiate this issue, and it ended in a stalemate. America would not back a Nationalist invasion of China to please his aging father, and the

Nationalists would not send troops to help America in Vietnam. The entertainment of Madame Chiang had merely been part of the effort mounted by the LBJ administration to win her over and get her to use her influence with CCK. Of which she had none.

The consequent disenchantment of the Johnson administration with Taiwan as an ally did not produce any immediate, visible change. But, by the time the Nixon administration took office, disillusionment with Taiwan had at last become fashionable, and it was possible for Henry Kissinger to set into motion policies leading to recognition of the People's Republic and normalization of relations with Peking.

Window dressing or not, for May-ling it was a last moment of glory. While in America, she was invited to go to Wellesley to address the student body on the anniversary of Pearl Harbor. It was just like the old days, listening to her: ". . . the interstitial periods within the seasons bring forth a plenitude in natural proliferation of brilliant or subtle colors . . . within the purfled walls . . . followers of the Agiel schema . . . victims of their own web of duplicity and perdition. . . ."

This was the same May-ling Soong Chiang and the same sort of language and sentiment that had captivated audiences from the Hollywood Bowl to the U.S. Congress, but times had changed. This time the *Time* correspondent, David Greenway, grew bored, walked out, and filed a desultory summary. The Oriental fantasy, for many Americans, had become a nightmare. In South Vietnam the Diem family bore a disturbing resemblance to the Chiangs. Newsmen even called Madame Nhu the Dragonlady. There was an overwhelming sense of déjà-vu.

When her renewed celebrity turned out to be brief, May-ling gave up the Kalorama house and in April 1966 settled in Manhattan at a luxury flat on Gracie Square. Nephew Louis purchased the cooperative apartment to give her a home base in Manhattan. She had been suffering from gallstones and had surgery to remove them. She was now sixty-nine, and her health was giving out. Thereafter, all her trips to America were either for funerals or medical treatment. For decades, she had been on the list of Ten Most Famous Women, but that ended in 1967, when Henry Luce died of a coronary in his bathroom. The next year, May-ling learned positively that she had cancer and flew to New York in 1970 for a mastectomy, followed soon afterward by another hurried trip and a second mastectomy.

In American papers, stories about her had moved from page one to Society. Now they became fillers in the food pages.

There was a last splash in the press when the Generalissimo died on April 5, 1975, at age eighty-seven. Three weeks later, CCK, who was already Premier, became Chairman of the KMT. There was nothing left for May-ling to do. She went into permanent exile. She was seventy-eight years old and very sick. She became a recluse at David Kung's estate in Lattingtown, Long Island, thirty-five miles east of Manhattan. Only bodyguards and doctors were allowed inside its forbidding perimeter. She left the estate only to enter Johns Hopkins Medical Center in Baltimore under a false name for ten days of tests, and to pay visits to the Sloan-Kettering Institute. On March 28, 1983, she turned eighty-six years old. She had been living in seclusion at Lattingtown for nearly a decade. People were surprised to hear that she was still alive.

Only one Soong was left in China, where a quiet triumph came at last to Ching-ling.

On October 1, 1949, Madame Sun had been summoned to Peking to join the great celebration of the Liberation. As millions paraded down the broad boulevards in front of the Forbidden City, and Mao Tse-tung stood on the Gate of Heavenly Peace and proclaimed the People's Republic of China, Ching-ling stood at his side. She was fifty-seven years old.

As she had often put it, she was not a member of the Chinese Communist party, she was a member of the Chinese Revolution.

As a young woman, she had been enthralled by Sun Yat-sen because he thought with a "world mind." As a sexagenarian, she had learned to distrust all politicians but said: "I distrust Mao Tse-tung less than the others."

She had been a symbol in China for most of her life. Dr. Sun had had the luxury of dying while the virtuous could still be distinguished from the wicked. Ching-ling had weathered it all in solitude, as her circle of friends and supporters was reduced by torture, purge, and murder. She had bade farewell to her last intimate friend in 1931 when Teng Yen-ta had been seized by the police in the International Settlement and turned over to the Nanking regime for torture and execution. Others had been enchanted by her, among them Vincent Sheean, Harold Isaacs, and Joseph Stilwell, but she had by then become a solitary.

She was protected by her widow's weeds but imprisoned by them as well. She could take risks and speak out in a way others could not.

She inspired contemporaries but had no power to intercede when they fell under the sword. She might have lived out her life as a well-heeled exile in a city like Paris. She did not.

She did not wither into a hardened fanatic. She liked children, she liked pretty things, and she liked to dance. She could be witty, mischievous, and hilarious. She enjoyed a social drink, and when she was with friends became boisterous. She smoked Panda-brand cigarettes and liked movies and theater. (Even in austere Peking she had the privilege of a screening room, where she could see the latest Western films.)

She chose her moments, she caught her enemies off guard. She used a clever woman's guerrilla tactics in her long war with Chiang.

She spent the war years in Chungking, not under house arrest but sealed off from other Chinese by their fear of arrest and from most Westerners by the misconception that she was a "red." She staged concerts and sports events to raise money for relief to war wounded, and was condemned by gossip that insisted the relief went only to "Communist territory." She concentrated her efforts in red areas because with only a few exceptions like Operation Ichigo there was no serious fighting in areas under Chiang's control. According to U.S. army intelligence reports during the war, when she staged soccer matches, Chiang's security people warned fans not to attend, and definitely not to root for Ching-ling's team, under fear of arrest.

In August 1945, Ching-ling was dispatched with T. V. to Moscow, where they concluded the Sino-Soviet Alliance on the 14th of the month. It was the only time she had left China since 1931, except to go to Hong Kong.

The war over, she returned to Shanghai, to the Rue Molière, to carry on with the political work of the revolution that she had largely put aside during the war. Again she took up the pen to decry Chiang and America's involvement in China, but this time the Western press treated her as an embarrassingly incontinent relative of famous people.

SHANGHAI, July 23, 1946—Madame Sun Yat-sen, widow of the founder of the Chinese republic, said yesterday that "reactionaries" in America and China were working to promote a war between Russia and the United States over China's internal affairs.

Breaking a two-year silence on Chinese politics, Dr. Sun's widow, who is one of the famous Soong sisters, said in an attack on her brother-in-law Chiang Kai-shek's government, that the presence of American troops in China was not aiding the cause of peace. There would be no spreading civil war in China, she said, if the United States made it clear that munitions and military assistance will not be supplied [to either side.] . . .

"China," she said, "is threatened by a civil war into which reactionaries hope to draw America—thus involving the whole world." The purpose of such a war, she declared would be to crush communism in China. "Such a civil war—though undeclared—already has begun," she added.

Nobody in America paid attention. She became a nonentity, studiously ignored by the U.S. government.

Ching-ling sold many of her remaining possessions to support the programs of the China Welfare League she had founded. In 1948, with the Chiang regime ready to flee and the Communists on their way to victory, she took part in a last attempt to organize an alternative to both communism and fascism—a new version of the Third Force. It was called the Revolutionary Committee, and Ching-ling was named its honorary chairman. Its constituency was the powerless.

When the People's Republic came into existence, Ching-ling became one of the three non-Communist political leaders chosen as Vice Chairmen of the Central Government in Peking. She was awarded the Stalin Peace Prize, which was duly noted in her FBI dossier. In the 1950s she was named Vice Chairman of the People's Republic—ranked, in a sense, just below Mao.

She was no longer a young woman. From 1956, when she was sixty-four years old, until 1964, when she turned seventy-two, she did not leave China. The home she had shared with Dr. Sun in the Rue Molière was converted into a national shrine. She arranged to live instead in Charlie Soong's last home, the small mansion on the Avenue Joffre where she had been locked in her bedroom by Charlie just before she ran away to marry Dr. Sun.

She was also provided with a home in Peking, a stately villa on a lake beside the Forbidden City—the house where the last Emperor of China, Pu-yi, had been born. It sat near the homes of Mao and Chou En-lai, in a soft grove of trees surrounded by a high wall.

She discovered that she had leukemia. In 1960, when Edgar Snow returned to China, he tried to visit her, but was unable to because "her chronic illness had reached a critical stage." It was chronic lymphocytic leukemia, a disease some people survive for ten years or longer, although in considerable pain. One treatment includes large doses of antibiotics to boost the body's resistance to infection. Harrison Salisbury of the *New York Times,* who dined with Ching-ling in 1972, mentioned that she had recently recovered from a terrible reaction to antibiotics. She was seriously ill for the last two decades of her life.

But there was a happier side to her life. She adopted two girls, Yolanda and Jeannette. They were the children of one of her bodyguards. During the Red Guard rampages of the 1960s, the job of protecting Madame Sun became nerve-racking. Posters appeared denouncing her, and it was not safe for her to go anywhere. After one harrowing encounter with the Red Guards, Ching-ling's bodyguard drank heavily and the next morning was found dead. Although she was then nearly seventy, she was childless and without companionship. She adopted the two girls and raised them as her own.

In the summer of 1966, Premier Chou En-lai was forced to warn the Red Guards to cease their verbal attacks on Madame Sun, and to stop putting up posters accusing her of being a bourgeois reactionary. On September 21, 1966, in Shanghai where the Red Guard movement frequently got out of control, a mob stormed Ching-ling's house on the Avenue Joffre and looted it. Ching-ling was not in Shanghai at the time. She let the incident pass without public comment. Her chief adversary was the wife of Chairman Mao, who apparently resented the fact that Ching-ling was always mentioned as the woman of highest rank in China.

For the last fifteen years of her life, Ching-ling devoted her full attention to her adopted daughters. When the Red Guard movement abated, and Madame Mao and the celebrated Gang of Four were tried in a people's court as counterrevolutionaries, Ching-ling's life settled back into a tranquil twilight. She was permitted to send one of her girls, Jeannette, to Trinity College in Hartford, Connecticut. The older sister, Yolanda, became a movie actress. Fox Butterfield, Peking correspondent of the *New York Times,* saw the girl several times.

> The first time I encountered her was in the dining room of the Peking Hotel. She was dressed in a short, hip-hugging wool skirt, high brown-leather boots, and a bright-orange blouse. Yolanda was in her mid-twenties, slender, and very tall for a Chinese, about five feet eight. She had on heavy eye shadow and lipstick; not pretty, but haughty, striking, and sexy. She looked like a movie star from Taiwan or Hong Kong.
>
> Later a mutual acquaintance introduced us and I asked what she did. "I'm in movies," she said, saying she had just returned from shooting a film with an army movie production studio on location in Hunan.

On May 16, 1981, Soong Ching-ling was named honorary President of China. That same week, she was also inducted into the Chinese Communist party. But it is hard to say if she was aware of the title or consented to being given the party's last rites. She succumbed to leukemia on May 29, 1981, in her Peking home. There was no published legacy like the one prepared for Dr. Sun when he died in the same city fifty-six years earlier. But, in an interview once with writer Han Suyin, Ching-ling put into words the legacy she had learned most bitterly from the time of the Soongs: "We must learn to arm ourselves against ourselves."

May-ling Soong Chiang refused the invitation to her sister's funeral.

Epilogue

THE CONCUBINE IN THE WELL

It was late in June 1982 and the sky over Peking was beginning to clear of the yellow dust from the Gobi that usually chokes the air in April and May. I was searching the "great emptiness" of the Forbidden City for a tiny sepulcher, one that was now all but forgotten. Here and there among the pavilions clusters of tourists of different nationalities listened to guides explain the ceremonies and audiences that brought the Empress Dowager to this or that chamber at a certain hour each day. By the stone walls of the great courtyards, knots of young people, many of them Japanese, bent their heads to listen as if the rock would speak and reveal the secrets of the imperial eunuchs. Most of the tourists had already been to the Temple of Heaven, where they had been told that if they listened by the wall at one place in the courtyard they could clearly hear the words of someone whispering by the wall a hundred yards away. So they took it for granted that all stone walls in Peking whisper. Only some of them do, and the presence of a human being is not required.

The walls of the Forbidden City were all whispering to themselves as I walked by the Meridian Gate, a citadel towering beside a moat where strange legions have marched since the time of the Khans. Far up in the battlements, in the shadowy eaves, among tangerine tiles where demons live, there were sudden movements that might have been bowmen hiding from sight, but were probably birds. Across the cobblestones of a vast parade ground and the arched bridges over the Gold Water Stream, my path led (as everyone's should) by the Hall of

Supreme Harmony, around the Hall of Middle Harmony, and past the Hall of Preserving Harmony, before the Gate of Heavenly Purity, by the Nine Dragon Screen, to the Palace of Peaceful Old Age.

There, among twisted pine trees, were the secluded chambers of the imperial concubines, clustered about miniature courtyards with paving stones that still sigh from the touch of golden lotuses. In one of the smaller courtyards, near the Palace of Peace and Longevity, I found the tomb that had brought me on this uneasy pilgrimage. It was a well, shouldered with weathered stone, innocent in appearance, less than two handspans across but deeply menacing. Here in the year 1900 took place a scene of such chilling horror that it cleaves to my brain as a permanent nightmare. I came to exorcise the ghost by confronting it.

It was at the height of the Boxer Rebellion, on the 15th of August, 1900, the hour of yin in midafternoon. All Peking was in alarm as the foreign armies approached to relieve the besieged legation quarter. In the Forbidden City, the Dowager Empress decided to flee. The murderous Old Buddha, according to legend, had ordered her chief eunuch, Li Lien-ying, to obtain disguises. She put on the clothes of a peasant, and changed her Manchu hairstyle to Chinese. Carriages waited to spirit them out the back gate, the Gate of Divine Pride, to safety at Sian in the west.

Informed of her decision to take him along, the young Emperor Kuang Hsu came to plead with her, accompanied by his favorite, the Pearl Concubine. This spirited wisp of a girl, elegantly dressed in layers of embroidered silks, was devoted to the twenty-nine-year-old Emperor. But she had never toadied to gain the Old Buddha's favor. Now she prostrated herself and implored the Dowager to let the Emperor remain, to carry out negotiations with the foreign generals. The Pearl Concubine had been a thorn in the Dowager's side, interfering with palace intrigues by giving independent advice to the Emperor. It was time to dispose of her. The Dowager bellowed orders. Two eunuchs seized the Pearl Concubine. In terror, the Emperor went to his knees and begged for her life. But the eunuchs carried the struggling girl to the narrow well by the Palace of Peace and Longevity, turned her upside down in her shimmering cocoon of silks, and flung her shrieking into its maw. Because the well was so narrow, the eunuchs jumped on her to force her down.

Her spirit is still down there, like an insect in amber, adding her protest to those who whisper in the walls and rooftops. The Forbidden

City is a graveyard of souls, drowned, beheaded, throttled, flayed alive, to silence them in the interests of state. Here, murder was not an act of passion but an instrument of rule. Judicial murder. Imperial murder. Silence by assassination. To stifle those who would interfere, who would object, who would question, who would say no.

What would Charlie Soong say about how his children turned out? Ching-ling, like the Pearl Concubine, was flung down a well. But they could not jump on her enough to keep her down. She won anyway. The others passed through life like a team of pickpockets through a carnival crowd, doing what they did best, while the rubes watched geeks bite heads off live chickens.

There are those who insist that May-ling remained innocent throughout by virtue of her tunnel vision. It is not for me to say, except that these people also believe in virgin birth.

They were a family that could stand together in front of a mirror (Ching-ling missing from the group by choice), all casting reflections except Ai-ling. She cast no reflection at all. What medieval conclusion can we draw?

Of all the people who might have acted, I wondered why Harry Truman did nothing. The man who dropped the atom bomb, who fired his top general, was in the best position to act. If it was too dangerous politically or if it proved too difficult to frame legal charges, he could have found other ways to interfere with the tranquility of their retirement. At the least he could have leaked the FBI discoveries, to give the press a field day. Perhaps he concluded that so many prominent people were involved it would not be good for the nation, as they say. So nearly everyone stayed silent. Nobody spoke for the victims.

Who, then, will speak for the concubine in the well?

ACKNOWLEDGMENTS

This book was greatly enriched by the work of Peggy Sawyer Seagrave, who drew together and made sense of the conflicting source material from 1911 onward, and who did the original drafts of several chapters. As a result, the book developed a greater compass than I had originally conceived, and was more painstakingly documented.

For solving many of the mysteries surrounding Charlie Soong, I am indebted to Edward Leslie, who researched the first part of the book, covering the period from 1880 to 1911.

About Sources

This book is the result of a personal investigation that began many years ago in China. Since 1980, research has included a re-examination of all the old documents and secondary sources available in several countries, and the discovery of new documents under the Freedom of Information Act. The book benefited greatly from new work done in recent years by Asian scholars, whose insights have helped me to piece this quite different story together.

Edward Leslie traveled extensively for me through the United States, combing the National Archives, the Library of Congress, the collections of the Hoover Library at Stanford, and the libraries at Wellesley, at Harvard, at Duke, at Oberlin, and the public libraries of Boston, Baltimore, Durham, and Wilmington. To each of those institutions I am grateful for assistance and for the freedom to make use of their documents.

In Georgia, research into the education of the Soong sisters at Wesleyan was undertaken for me by writer Gail Dubroff of Atlanta, who was aided by the staff at Wesleyan's library, as well as by some of the classmates of the Soongs. Margaret Long, of the Historical Society of Summit, New Jersey, provided me with little-known material on the Soongs' time there. When I learned from declassified documents at the National Security Agency that Madame Chiang had been the subject of a stained-glass window in Massena, New York, the historian of the church, Miss Helen L. Coverdale, was kind enough to provide background and a color photograph.

A number of trips to China were involved over the years. For final touches, I visited Shanghai and Peking in 1983. Several trips to Taiwan were made for research, particularly during the 1960s and 1970s. My own interest in the Soongs and Chiangs began as a boy on the China-Burma border, and continued through a decade of the Vietnam War, while I was a correspondent based in Bangkok, Singapore, and Kuala Lumpur. I became acquainted with the extensive Soong files of Time Inc. while serving as text editor of *China-Burma-India* in their series of books on World War II, and while researching Chennault and the Chiangs for *Soldiers of Fortune,* a history of mercenary aviators, published by Time-Life Books in 1982.

The National Security Agency, the Department of State, the U.S. Army, and the Federal Bureau of Investigation produced thousands of pages of documents in response to a Freedom of Information inquiry. NSA and the FBI were especially helpful and efficient.

My special thanks go to Harold Isaacs, Jack Anderson, Stanley Karnow, Robert McCabe, Robert Shaplen, and Dennis Bloodworth, who have sharpened my interest in the Soongs over many years.

NOTES

Prologue: Shanghai Tapestry

2   Tallies of whorehouses are fanciful at best; some said one out of every twelve Chinese houses in the International Settlement was a brothel, others cited 25,000 prostitutes in the same small area, and others one out of every 130 citizens. Such things were no more certain in Shanghai than in Edwardian London. The figure I use here comes from Rhoads Murphey, *Shanghai: Key to Modern China* (1953), p. 7.

3   The Chinese view of Britain's opium trade is told in the Foreign Language Press book *The Opium War* (1976). These details are from p. 10. The American firms involved are mentioned on p. 13.

4   The lending of the national colors is from *The Opium War*, p. 33.

5   Balfour's quote came from Ernest Hauser, *Shanghai: City for Sale* (1940), p. 11.

13   A transcript of Chiang's police record is reproduced in Pichon P. Y. Loh, *The Early Chiang Kai-shek: Personality and Politics* (1971). Footnote 77, pp. 132–34.

One: A Runaway Celestial

15   These key letters, including Charlie's rendering of his original name in English and in Chinese, are from James Burke, *My Father in China* (1942), p. 7.

18   Letters between T. V. Soong and President Franklin Roosevelt, Hoover Institution.

18   The Western authority on Chinese junks is G. R. G. Worcester. For Hainan traders see his *Sail and Sweep in China* (1966), p. 39.

18   Color photos of "Big-Eyed Chickens" are in Derek Maitland, *Setting Sails* (1981), p. 61.

18   The flexible scruples and random piracy of the junk crews are attested to by Worcester, p. 39.

19   The annual trading pattern is explained by Worcester on p. 39.

19   While no definitive study of the worldwide Hakka–chiu chao opium cartel yet exists, the basic outlines can be found in Alfred W. McCoy, *The Politics of Heroin in Southeast Asia* (1973), p. 185.

21   A short summary of the triumphs and tragedies of Chinese immigrants is in Ruthanne McCunn, *An Illustrated History of the Chinese in America* (1979). This quote is from p. 32.

21   We know little about Charlie's journey, but some assumptions can be made on the basis of shipping movements at the time. See A. B. C. Whipple, *The Clipper Ships* (1980), p. 121.

21   The appearance of wealthy young Celestials in nineteenth-century America was such a novelty that it is noted by many sources. Germane here is Emily Hahn, *The Soong Sisters* (1941), p. 2.

21   Hahn gives a warm and elaborate account of New and Wen on p. 5. Contrary to what Hahn says, however, New and Wen did not attend Harvard, which has no record of them. "Harvard Letter to Author," May 20, 1983. There were other schools in the area, but it was fashionable in Asia then as now to claim Harvard credentials.

22   Hahn's account of how Charlie made his way, and how he got his name, were accepted as gospel till the last days of World War II, when a journalist serving in the Coast Guard discovered surprisingly different evidence. Unfortunately, his discoveries were given very limited circulation. See A. Tourtellot, "Charlie Soong and the U.S. Coast Guard," in *U.S. Naval Institute Proceedings,* Vol. 75 (February 1949). From Coast Guard records, it becomes obvious that Charlie got his famous name as the result of a simple mistake aboard ship, probably in a manner more or less as I have described.

24   The cozy life in Edgartown was recalled with nostalgia by young Charlie himself in an undated "Letter to His Friend Harold Wimpenny" (circa 1880). Dukes County Historical Society, Edgartown, Massachusetts. The nailhead tweed is visible in a photograph Charlie sent to his playmate.

24   Charlie's emergence in Wilmington was a big event in the life of local gentry, foremost the Moore family, who traced their line to the earliest settlement of the area. Thanks to the Moores, a few firsthand images of Charlie were preserved, including the bare details of his arrival. Louis T. Moore, *Founder of Chinese Soong Dynasty Converted to Christianity in Wilmington* (19—). Courtesy of Louis T. Moore Collection, Wilmington Public Library.

25   The pleasant but rather boring run of the *Colfax* is listed in *Information and Statistics Respecting Wilmington, North Carolina* (1883).

25   It was Colonel Moore's status as a Methodist leader in his community that actually propelled Charlie into his new life. See "Recollections of Charlie Soong," *World Outlook* (August 1938). The colonel himself described his first encounter with Charlie to his children and grandchildren. Moore and John D. Lee, Jr., "The Hand of God," *Christian Herald* (November 1941).

25   Popular accounts conflict on every detail, so I have gone to the *History of Ann Street Methodist Church, Beaufort, North Carolina* (n.d.). Courtesy Duke University Archives.

25   Unlike Emily Hahn, who was satisfied with Ai-ling Soong's version of her family history, when Elmer Clark set out to write a tiny book about the

Soong clan in the late 1930s, he went to considerable trouble to dig out actual evidence. Thanks to his enterprise, we have a fascinating picture of preacher Ricaud as a man of complex character and background, and a photograph to reinforce it. See Clark's *The Chiangs of China* (1943), facing p. 17, and Costin J. Harrell, "General Julian S. Carr and the Education of Charlie Soong," *World Outlook* (1945).

27 The eyewitness at Charlie's conversion is in "The Romance of Charlie Soong," *The Duke Divinity School Bulletin,* vol. IV, no. 4 (January 1942). See also Clark.

27 Eyewitnesses to Charlie's euphoria afterward are quoted in "The Romance of Charlie Soong."

27 The quote is from the *Morning Star* (November 7, 1880).

27 My description of the baptism is from Pauline Worthy, "When Charlie Soong Paid a Visit to Washington, N.C.," *The News and Observer,* Raleigh, North Carolina (February 28, 1943), written while some of those present were still around to be interviewed. A plaque commemorating the event can be seen in front of the Wilmington Methodist church today.

27 The christening was documented by the *Morning Star* (November 7, 1880).

28 The nonexistence of "Captain Charles Jones" was first discovered by Elmer Clark, *The Chiangs of China* (1943), footnote on pp. 16–17, but made no impression at the time. It was fortified by, but still ignored after, the discoveries of Tourtellot.

28 The minor detail about the printing shop, which had major consequences later in China, was noted by Harrell.

28 The unrestrained enthusiasm of the congregation to send Charlie to China was noted by Burke, p. 7.

28 Trinity's slim survival over the years is chronicled in *The Story of Durham* (n.d.).

28–29 Credit is given to Moore for scraping up the money, but to Ricaud for arranging Charlie's enrollment. See Braxton Craven, from the *Annual Report of Braxton Craven, President of Trinity College, to the Board of Trustees* (June 9, 1881). Courtesy Duke University Archives.

29 The flowery quote is from *Cyclopedia of Eminent and Representative Men of the Carolinas of the Nineteenth Century,* vol. 2 (1892). Courtesy Duke University Archives.

29 Carr must have been a man of rare charm and intellect, and his personal history is a story of American free enterprise at its best. But it remains untold except in Samuel Ashe, *Biographical History of North Carolina from Colonial Times to Present* (1905). I suspect that the tobacco cartel (which eventually outfoxed him and absorbed his operations) wanted Carr to be forgotten.

29 In effect, we owe the development of prefabricated cigarettes to the pressures of the Civil War. Just how can be seen in Ashe.

30 It was Washington Duke's heirs who eventually helped put Carr out of the tobacco business and into the business of making socks. Some of the story is in W. C. Dula and A. C. Simpson, *Durham and Her People* (1951).

30 The Caldwell quote is from Dula and Simpson.

30 This eloquent description of Nanny Carr is from *Cyclopedia of Eminent and Representative Men of the Carolinas of the Nineteenth Century.*

30 One of Charlie's hammocks still exists at Durham's library. They are described in Harrell.

31 The quote by a distaff admirer (Eula Bell) is from Worthy.

31 Apparently, the Southgates did not preserve their artifacts of Charlie Soong, and little is known of the Southgates themselves beyond such terse notes as made by Levi Branson, *Directory of the Business and Citizens of Durham City for 1887.*

31 The location of the original Trinity edifice is from "High Point Resident Has Cherished Photo," Greensboro *Daily News* (September 1, 1937).

31 The school enrollment is from Worthy.

31 Just how successful Charlie would be could not be foreseen even by the perceptive Craven, whose quote is in his own hand in Craven.

32 A photograph of the bearded Gannaway and other faculty members is to be seen in "The Debt of the President of China to America," *North Carolina Christian Advocate* (January 29, 1931).

32–33 I reproduce the letters from Burke, pp. 6–9.

34 Some of these juvenile episodes can be read in Roby Eunson, *The Soong Sisters* (1975), p. 9. This book is only slightly more than a recycling of Emily Hahn's *The Soong Sisters,* and contains many of the same errors and misperceptions. But there is some original material added by Eunson here and there, helping to distinguish it from Hahn's hagiography.

34 Charlie's quote is from Nora C. Chaffin, *Trinity College, 1839–1892: Beginnings of Duke University* (1950).

34 The happy scene on the porch is recalled by Eliza M. Carr Flower, *Letter to Mr. La Fargue* (January 1, 1939), courtesy Hoover Institution. Liza makes much in her letter of Charlie's devotion to her father, and the fact that Charlie always called him Father Carr. She concludes that Charlie needed Carr as a father substitute.

35 I have reproduced a portion of Charlie's comic letter intact, including spelling errors. Charlie Soong, "Letter to J. G. Hackett" (June 20, 1882). Courtesy Duke University Archives.

35 This tender scene was recalled only up to a point by Ella herself in "High Point Resident Has Cherished Photo." Interestingly, Charlie's wife also played the piano and he sat listening to her the same way, with less troublesome consequences. It is Ella also who described Charlie's expulsion.

36 These quotes are from Mike Bradshaw, Jr., "Chinese Lad Left Trinity College to Found Own Dynasty," *News and Observer* (June 28, 1936). Bradshaw's long and thorough article apparently was inspired by a visit to Duke University of the eminent Chinese philosopher Dr. Hu Shih, then China's ambassador to Washington, who had been a student of Charlie in Woosung fifty years earlier. We may therefore take Bradshaw's piece to be fairly authoritative. Dr. Hu Shih lost his Washington diplomatic post when he objected to T. V. Soong's financial manipulations of American Lend-Lease.

36 Charlie's tearful farewell scene is also from Bradshaw.

36 Regrettably, the reporter who interviewed Ella Carr Peacock was unable to draw her out beyond the admission that Charlie had been her swain briefly, and after he was driven from her door she had preserved his picture for half a century. ("High Point Resident Has Cherished Photo.")

37 Winton is quoted in Bradshaw.
37 Perhaps the Reverend Orr was being very generous. He made these remarks in John C. Orr, "Recollections of Charlie Soong," *World Advocate* (April 1938).
37 The Fink quote is from Hahn, p. 9.
37 The Wright quote is from Eunson, p. 10.
37 The Tuttle quote is from Hahn, p. 9.
38 Orr's touching anecdote is from his own "Recollections . . ."
38 The laundryman quote is from Burke, p. 3. He also tells the flatiron story.
39 The source of the burnt photo was run down by Elmer Clark, p. 21.
39 I took Charlie's letter from the *Christian Advocate* (May 13, 1889).
40 The assertion that Charlie had been graduated from Vanderbilt "with honors" and was to be a professor in Shanghai was made in "The Fortunes of a Chinese Boy," *Morning Star* (June 20, 1885).
41 The fact that Charlie never got a degree was ignored everywhere except in Clark, p. 22, who also discovered that it was McTyeire who blocked Carr's plan to finance Charlie's medical education.
41 The duplicity in the situation is obvious in the fact that McTyeire's office told the Wilmington *Star* Charlie was going to become a professor, while McTyeire himself was doing everything possible to guarantee otherwise.
42 Once again it must be noted that there was a great disparity between what was said about Charlie in public and what was being done in fact.
42 Charlie's flirtation with Rosamond was mentioned in Worthy.
43 The quote is from Charlie Soong, "Letter to Annie Southgate" (July 18, 1885). Courtesy Duke University Archives.
43 Eula Bell admits to an infatuation, nothing more, in Worthy.
43 The discomforts of rail travel in the Wild West were described at the time by the indefatigable Karl Baedeker in *The United States with an Excursion into Mexico* (1893), p. xxviii.
43 I took the day's subjects from James Trager, *The People's Chronology* (1979).
43 A hair-raising summary of white atrocities against Chinese is in McCunn, p. 22.
44 One of the better longer accounts of the anti-Chinese campaign is in Stan Steiner, *Fusang: the Chinese Who Built America* (1979), pp. 172–73. Other facts and figures follow on p. 176.
44 The "Kill 'em lots" quote is in McCunn, p. 84. She also points out that Congress singled out the Chinese for exclusion, and gives the sudden drop in immigration figures on p. 87. These brutalities, including such extremes as the castrations and beheadings, are well documented by the Chinese-American community, but have been swept under the rug by white Americans. It is only in recent years that the economic motives behind the various Yellow Peril outbreaks have become known widely; for example, the persecution of the Nisei during World War II was inspired primarily by white investors coveting Japanese farmlands in California. They were able to enlist the malicious support of the commander of U.S. army forces at the Presidio in San Francisco; he announced that the Nisei were a security risk.

Two: The Hybrid Returns

48 The tally of Methodist missionaries is from Burke, p. 30.

48 Once again, we are indebted to the tenacious Elmer Clark for rooting out this letter from Dr. Allen. See Clark, p. 32.

48 Charlie's humble assignment was described in Hahn, p. 20, and Bradshaw.

49 Bradshaw also gives us Dr. Hu Shih's anecdote about how Charlie won over his rowdy classroom. Hu Shih told the story during a visit to lecture at Duke.

50 Charlie's public ridicule in the streets is described in Burke, p. 36.

50 His aversion to Chinese food is in Howard L. Boorman, *Biographical Dictionary of Republican China* (1979).

50 The episode with Charlie Marshall is told both in Burke, p. 33, and Clark, p. 25.

50 I've taken the Marshall quote from Burke, p. 33.

51 Lockie Rankin's victory over the serpent is told in Burke, p. 33. (Chinese girls were not the only ones that missionaries sequestered; American missionary ladies signed contracts vowing not to marry for as long as five years in the field. It was believed that marriage would make them unsuited to serve their mission in any capacity, so the cost of sending them to China would be forfeited. William Burke's first wife broke her contract to marry him.)

52 Kunshan's population profile is from Clark, p. 26.

52 Charlie's disguise as an "ordinary" Chinese is from Burke, p. 30.

53 Burke relates New's marriage conspiracy, p. 36.

53 Ricci's story has been told many times, including by Vincent Cronin, *The Wise Man from the West* (1955). His relationship with New's in-laws is from Boorman.

53 The Nis' conversion to Christianity is attested to in Clark, p. 28.

53 How Mme. Ni bound all but one of her daughters' feet is from Burke, p. 37.

53 Burke also describes Miss Ni's cultivation, p. 37.

53 Emily Hahn tells us how Miss Ni was educated, and that she excelled in un-Chinese endeavors.

54 The successful outcome of the marriage conspiracy is in Burke, p. 38.

55 Burke's reunion with Charlie is from Burke, p. 30.

56 The visit to Kunshan is from Burke, p. 51.

56 I have taken the dialogue from Burke's account, p. 54.

57 Again, Charlie's quote is from Burke's recollection of the night in Kunshan, p. 54.

57 The best source for background on the secret societies is the group of essays in Jean Chesneaux (ed.), *Popular Movements and Secret Societies in China: 1840–1950* (1972).

58 For example, see the triad initiation ceremony described in Fenton Bresler, *The Chinese Mafia* (1981), p. 58. The sacrament usually consisted of chicken blood and sweet Chinese wine, into which a few drops of blood were squeezed from the fingers of the new members.

59 My authority for the economics of Bible publication, and for this quote, is *American Bible Society History*, Essay 18, Part IV. Courtesy of the American Bible Society, New York.

60 That a ripe opportunity existed for Charlie is obvious from Clark, p. 30. But Clark does not go far enough. Much more than Bibles was involved.

60 Aside from minor discrepancies, there is little argument over the dates for the children except for May-ling. In her case the different dates given range over a ten-year span. To resolve the one- or two-year ambiguity over Ching-ling, I chose to use the date given by the New China News Agency in its obituary, which I consider the most accurate. Ai-ling's age was always clear from Burke. After her marriage, May-ling claimed to have been born in 1900. I chose instead to use the date for her birth determined after some study of the matter by the faculty at Wellesley.

63 Emily Hahn, who was living in Shanghai in the late thirties, visited the house and described it.

65 If we read between the lines, it is clear both from Bishop Harrell and from Gorman that they were convinced Carr gave Charlie a large sum.

65 The chiu chao connection in Shanghai and the amalgamation of the gangs is mentioned in McCoy, p. 223.

66 We may never know to what extent Carr underwrote Charlie's investments in Bibles and noodles, but the conclusion can be drawn from Carr's own investments that he helped Charlie go after China's stomach and purse as well as its soul. For hints, see *The Story of Durham* (n.d.), and Josephus Daniels, "He Is Seventy Years Old Today" (n.d.), courtesy of the Library of the University of North Carolina.

Three: The Revolutionaries

69 One of Sun's biographers, Harold Z. Schiffrin, makes a major point of Sun's initiation into the Chih Kung Tong later in Hawaii, as though it were his first membership in a secret society. However, no boy grew up in the Pearl River delta to become a master of what we now call Kung Fu without first becoming a member of a local triad. The Three Harmonies was the parent organization of the Chih Kung Tong, and was by far the most pervasive triad in Sun's ancestral village area. It is beyond question that Sun was in its ranks as a youth. How else could he have expected to draw upon the triads when he began staging his uprisings? For background on the Three Harmonies, see Chesneaux, *Popular . . .*, p. 31.

69 His views appeared in the *China Mail* (February 8, 1887).

70 Sun's petition is from his *Collected Works*, vol. 10, p. 205. (Taipei: Chung-kuo Press, 1961.)

71 The site of the first meeting is in Lyon Sharman, *Sun Yat-sen: His Life and Its Meaning* (1965), p. 310. Also see Lo Chia-lun, *Biography of the Father of the Country* (1969); Feng Tzu-yu, *Reminiscences of the Revolution* (1947) (Feng gives 1894 as the date when Charlie first met Dr. Sun); Hahn, pp. 24–25.

72 Sun as Charlie's frequent house guest is attested to by Burke, p. 12.

72 Charlie's generosity to Sun came out of the celebrated chocolate-shop interview that Edgar Snow had with Ching-ling, described in *Journey to the Beginning* (1958).

72 See the essays in Chesneaux, *Popular . . .* for a more elaborate rendition, and McCoy for the role of the triads in narcotics and other criminal activities.

73   One of the few accounts of Coxinga available in the West is Donald
     Keene (editor), *The Battles of Coxinga, Chikamatsu's Puppet Play* (1951).
76   Charlie's letter was one of the great turning points in Sun's career, and
     attests to Charlie's influence in the revolutionary movement at that time.
     The reason his role is not more widely acknowledged is certainly because
     of their falling-out after Ching-ling's elopement. After that, mention of
     Charlie Soong became anathema in Sun's group. For citation of this
     pivotal letter, see Lo Chia-lun, p. 192.
77   Reid's facetious report is from the *China Mail* (March 12, 1895).
80   Sun's adventures in London were meticulously reconstructed by Harold
     Z. Schiffrin in *Sun Yat-sen, Reluctant Revolutionary* (1980), p. 153. I
     have the date of this organizational meeting from Boorman.

Four: The Moneyman

86   Charlie's achievements are in W. B. Nance, "Our Contribution to Chris-
     tian Literature" (n.d.).
86   His growing wealth is seen in Burke, pp. 191–92.
86   His role in creating the Chinese YMCA is in Boorman.
87   The false passport is in Burke, p. 197.
87   The journey is in "Charlie Soong Was Founder of Most Influential Family
     in Modern China" (n.d.). Courtesy Duke University Archives.
87   The Tong's address and title are from Dudley Burrows, "Chinese Masons
     Expel Sun Yat-sen as Traitor," *San Francisco Call and Post* (February 14,
     1922), from FBI archives.
87   Carr's nomination is in William S. Powell, *Dictionary of North Carolina
     Biographies* (1929).
87   Carr's extravagance is from " 'Jule' Carr, the Man," *Everywoman's Mag-
     azine* (July-August 1919). Also, "A Distinguished Son of Dixie," *The Bos-
     ton Traveler* (September 21, 1898). Courtesy of the Southern Historical
     Collection, University of North Carolina Library.
88   The Somerset link is in Mena Webb, "The House Bull Durham Built,"
     Tar Heel, vol. 7, no. 1 (January-February 1979).
88–89   Horticultural details are from "His Corner of Durham Was Full of Blos-
     soms," Durham *Morning Herald* (April 18, 1976).
89   The eagle detail is in Dula. The "most beautiful" quote and "'twixt
     heaven" are in Webb.
89   The club sessions are in "Father of First Family of China Was Trinity
     Student," *Duke Chronicle* (February 8, 1931).
89   Details of the reunion are from Bradshaw.
90   Bradshaw accepts that Charlie was obliged to raise big money.
91   Sun's comings and goings are detailed in Schiffrin.
91   See the French connection in McCoy.
92   I quote only part.
95   The quote is in Percy Chen, *China Called Me* (1979), p. 53.

Five: The Prodigies

96   Once again, Madame Chiang's age has been resolved by her alma mater,
     Wellesley, to its satisfaction. (If she had been born in 1900, as she usually
     claimed, her mother would have been pregnant with her and her

younger brother T. L. simultaneously.) See the *Memorandum on Madame Chiang Kai-shek*. Office of Publicity, Wellesley College (November 1937).

96 Even Bill Burke was intimidated by Mammy Soong's zeal. Burke, p. 193.

97 A tomboy, according to Hahn, p. 26. Others might have called it simply tough.

97 This was the most discreet, not to say economical, way to have a bodyguard. Clark, p. 38.

98 Ai-ling gave these details of dress and candy to Hahn, p. 32.

98 That Ai-ling was precocious was acknowledged by everyone. See Clark, p. 43.

98 Ai-ling's bicycle tours are noted in Hahn, p. 30.

99 A more detailed medical description of May-ling's nervous malady and its consequences are given elsewhere in this book, drawn from medical notes in the Department of State, at the National Archives; also from documents obtained from the Federal Bureau of Investigation, the National Security Agency, and U.S. Army intelligence.

100 Judge Guerry's protectiveness toward the sensibilities of his wards is reported in Burke, p. 227.

101 There was nothing illegal about opium at the time, but the missionaries aboard found it distasteful. See Burke, p. 231. Burke also describes Ai-ling's grief at parting from her father.

102 Ai-ling recounted this "dirty Chinamen" anecdote to Burke when she saw him later in San Francisco.

102 The Japanese humiliated the Russians in the war, and Jack London was defeated by them also. He hit a Japanese military groom and was only rescued by the intercession of the President of the United States. Naturally, he was glad to leave Asia after this experience. See Richard O'Connor, *Jack London: A Biography* (1962), p. 221.

103 London's remark is from Andrew Sinclair, *Jack: A Biography of Jack London* (1979), pp. 108–10.

103 Hahn never bothered to establish the identity of the woman who helped Ai-ling. The real woman was located by Elmer Clark, p. 46.

103 Clark's account of what happened to Ai-ling in San Francisco is the only one that stands up to any scrutiny. Ai-ling later made the United States government pay dearly for this shabby treatment.

104 Perhaps if Reid had not been called away, the whole saga of the Soongs would have been less vindictive. For Reid's role see Clark, p. 47.

105 Here Burke picks up the documentation from Clark. See Burke, p. 240.

106 The description is drawn from S. L. Akers, *The First Hundred Years of Wesleyan College* (1976), p. 109.

107 In one of those rare cases of a journalist who did her homework, most of the good material on the young Soong girls comes from Eunice Thomson, "Wesleyan and the Soong Girls," Chattanooga *Sunday Times Magazine* (March 13, 1938).

108 This outburst is also from Thomson. Here was one of the few recorded instances of Ai-ling's showing her teeth.

108 Hahn records the scene with Teddy Roosevelt uncritically, apparently merely transcribing Ai-ling's version. Thomson, p. 49.

109 Thomson ferreted out the brocade detail.

109 With some justice, the town of Summit, New Jersey, feels indignant. No account of the Soongs ever mentioned that two of the famous sisters spent a year there. See Anne Cooper, "World Press Failed to Mention "Summit" in Soong Sister Obit," the Summit *Herald* (August 30, 1981). Pursuing an obscure reference, I stumbled upon the Summit interlude and was given very generous help by Margaret Long of the Summit Historical Society, who provided me with answers to most of my questions, including the Potwin background.

109 A photo of the Locust Drive house is in Cooper.

109 Grant was the link to Wen and New, and thence to Charlie and the girls. Letter from Margaret Long, Summit Historical Society.

110 Charlie and B. C. Wen probably stayed in St. George's Hall while they were in town. The only reference is in "Tells of Madame Chiang's Stay Here," the Summit *Herald* (May 21, 1942).

110 All sources have the girls going straight from China to Georgia, including Clark, p. 49. In fact, they went to New Jersey and stayed for many months while their elders did business with the Chinese tongs in nearby Manhattan.

110 The quote is from Emmie [Donner] Mygatt, "Fellow Student Recalls Early School Days of Mei-ling Soong, Now Mme. Chiang Kai-shek," the Washington *Post* (September 6, 1942).

111 The librarian's remarks are from the Summit *Herald* (May 21, 1942).

111 To give the conventional flavor of her writing, I quote only a fragment of May-ling's long reminiscence, "A Letter from Madame Chiang Kai-shek," *The Piedmont Announcements* (September 1938).

113 The only accurate source here, besides college records, is Thomson.

113 Unfortunately, we learn almost nothing about Eloise even from her mother, Mrs. W. N. Ainsworth, "May-ling Soong as a School Girl," *North Carolina Christian Advocate* (undated). This young girl apparently had a major influence on May-ling, and when she died in childhood her death brought about a severe worsening of May-ling's nervous rash.

114 The Chinese fabrics are mentioned by Thomson. The way May-ling refused to wear Chinese clothes in front of American friends is also from Thomson, although Chinese makeup was not so easily removed.

114 Thomson also noted May-ling's domination of her elders, including getting her way with the faculty. The school chums are listed in Susan Myrick, "Childhood Days of Madame Chiang Recalled by Chum" (n.d.). A local newspaper columnist chatted about the girls' scandal sheet. See Harry Stillwell Edwards, "Coming Down My Creek," *Atlanta Journal* (December 4, 1936). The title of the broadsheet came from "Wesleyan Girls Make Pin-Money by Printing Daily Newspaper," *The Journal*, Macon, Georgia (March 9, 1908).

115 It is interesting that both men and women regarded Ching-ling as "radiant" and "beautiful." Her classmates are quoted by Thomson.

Six: The Fatal Euphemism

116 Wherever possible, I have relied on recent Chinese historical reevaluation, or as here deferred to the French scholar Jean Chesneaux, *China from the Opium Wars to the 1911 Revolution* (1976), p. 344.

117 For blow-by-blow accounts of these uprisings, see Schiffrin, p. 140.

117 The unvarnished account is by Wu Yu-zhang, *Recollections of the Revolution of 1911* (1980), p. 103. He tells of the bungling and treachery without coloration.

118 In this quote, Wu gives one of his rare lectures, and it is a good one, p. 89 and p. 105.

118 Most of my material from Donald is taken from the book by Earl Albert Selle, based on interviews conducted before Donald's death. *Donald of China* (1948).

119 For the role of Yuan Shih-k'ai, I have used Jian Bozan, *A Concise History of China* (1981), p. 131.

120 Yuan's treachery is remarked even by the cautious Boorman, vol. 4, p. 84.

120 Up to this point, Britain had consistently backed the Manchus, saving them from the Taiping rebels and keeping them in power fifty years longer than they could have managed on their own. Now, just by sitting on the fence, Britain doomed the Manchus, as noted by Bozan, p. 130.

120 There are various accounts of Sun's exact whereabouts. I used Boorman, vol. 3, p. 176.

120 Schiffrin describes Sun's political calculations on p. 155.

121 Schiffrin also quotes the unkind Foreign Office appraisal, p. 156.

122 Ching-ling's outburst is from Thomson.

123 Chesneaux notes Sun's attitude drily in *China from the Opium Wars . . .*, p. 375. If it had been deliberate, we can assume, it might have failed. Also Schiffrin, p. 167, and Bozan, p. 131.

123 As obvious as Yuan's ploys may seem, they worked like magic.

124 By saying this, Sun accepted as inevitable that military dictatorship was the only way out—a situation that continued for the next fifteen years. See Wu Yu-zhang, p. 136.

125 For details of the Dowager's train, see Martin Page, *The Lost Pleasure of the Great Trains* (1975), pp. 184–87.

125 Donald implies that Sun's train was a flying bordello on an endless joy ride. See Selle, p. 133.

125 Donald's madcap dialogues with Sun are from Schiffrin, pp. 170–71, and Selle, pp. 133–34.

127 The Morgan feeler is from Schiffrin, p. 171.

127 Selle mentions the deal with Pauling, p. 139.

127 The nasty scene over Ai-ling is from Selle, p. 139.

128 Boorman gives a brief sketch of Sung Chiao-jen that makes it evident he was a natural leader with tremendous potential, a figure charismatic in the same manner as John F. Kennedy, nipped in the bud by assassins. This seems to have been an almost universal appraisal.

129 Sun already had one foot out the door when he made this remark. See *The Revolution of 1911*, p. 159.

130 This settlement was an outgrowth of Japan's original effort to restrict foreigners to certain areas. The Soong home there is mentioned by Hahn, p. 89.

131 Shansi was a financial center because of its major role in the opium trade. The Kungs were rich because they turned opium revenue into far greater profit by lending it out at usurious rates through their chain of

pawnshops. In polite Western company, these pawnshops were referred to as a chain of "dime stores." This was not at all what they were. So rich did the Kungs become that the new warlord of Shansi after the Revolution of 1911, himself a member of a powerful banking clan, could not remain in power without resting one foot on the Kung pawnbrokers. For a detailed study of the warlord, and some all-too-brief glimpses of his symbiotic relationship with Kung, see Donald G. Gillen, *Warlord Yen Hsi-shan in Shansi Province 1911–1949* (1967), p. 22 et seq. Also Boorman, vol. 2, p. 264.

131 The heavily-laundered Western version of H. H. Kung's story is in Margaret Frakes, "The Story of K'ung Hsiang Hsi," *The Epworth Herald* (June 19, 1937).

132 This bloodcurdling scene is taken from Peter Fleming, *The Siege at Peking* (1959), p. 237.

133 The Kaiser's orders are from Nathaniel Peffer, *The Far East* (1968), p. 171.

133 Loti's quote is from *The Yi Ho Tuan Movement of 1900* (1976), p. 89. The Russian atrocities are cited on p. 96.

134 Unfortunately, we don't know exactly what Kung did to get this astonishing reward. Probably for very good reason. What pathetic little we know is in Boorman, vol. 2, p. 264.

134 Gillen tells us of the relationship between Kung and the warlord without ever scrutinizing it. Gillen, p. 37.

134 Again, Gillen acknowledges the warlord's avarice, without scrutiny, p. 46.

135 For the color of Ai-ling's dresses, we are indebted to Hahn, p. 91.

136 Kung's sly remark about Dr. Sun slipping away into insanity was the first calculated dig in a lifelong effort to undercut Ai-ling's sister. It is from Schiffrin, 183.

137 The only reliable account of Ching-ling's elopement is in Edgar Snow, *Journey to the Beginning,* p. 88.

138 Again, the account is from Ching-ling, through Snow, p. 89.

139 Charlie's outburst of despair is from Burke, p. 265.

139 May-ling never wrote without a dictionary in hand, and her speeches suffered as a result. For the full, tormented treatment, see "Mme. Chiang Kai-shek at Wellesley College," adapted from *The Wellesley Magazine* (February 1938).

139 These glimpses of May-ling's last days of innocence are also from *The Wellesley Magazine,* from June R. Geraghty, "Recollections of Mme. Chiang as a Student" (n.d.), and from "Memorandum on Madame Chiang Kai-shek," Office of Publicity, Wellesley College (November 1932).

140 The most interesting document in Wellesley's Soong archives was an unpublished and confidential memorandum on May-ling, written by the faculty member who ran the house she lived in at the college. The private comments it makes about May-ling's real nature, the fact that she was not really a brilliant student, and that she was essentially docile when confronted by authority, shed light on her character that is not available otherwise. Gradually, a picture emerges of May-ling as socially bright but not overly intelligent, willful in the extreme but not at all independent, and probably the lifelong pawn of her strong-willed eldest

sister. This profile fits, and helps to explain many of her actions in later years.

141 Charlie's remark—quoted in Hahn, p. 75—was probably said sadly, not frivolously.

142 The Carr quote is from Julian Carr, "Letter to the Durham Morning Herald."

142 The gift to Carr is attested to by Dr. Hu Shih, who told Mike Bradshaw about it.

Seven: The Dragon's Teeth

144 For the economic details, I drew upon the landmark study by Parks M. Coble, Jr., *The Shanghai Capitalists and the Nationalist Government: 1927–1937* (1980), p. 34.

145 For the human cost of the boom, see Lois Wheeler Snow, *Edgar Snow's China* (1981), p. 32.

145 Most Westerners managed to look the other way. This quote is from Harry A. Franck, *Roving Through Southern China* (1925).

146 The underlying corruption of decisions at Versailles is given its most thoughtful reappraisal in Charles L. Mee, Jr., *The End of Order* (1980), p. 189. The capitulation to Japan on Shantung began the process leading to World War II in Asia.

147 The blackmail quote is from Mee, p. 189.

148 For his balanced presentation of the left and right viewpoints, in the May Fourth Movement and afterward, I have leaned on Jean Chesneaux, *China from the 1911 Revolution to Liberation*, p. 68.

149 This wonderful scene at the pink schoolhouse is from Ross Terrill, *Mao* (1980), p. 55.

150 The raw details of Tu's childhood became well known to Chinese, and are summarized in English in Y. C. Wang, "Tu Yueh-sheng: A Tentative Political Biography," *Journal of Asian Studies* (May 1967). Also Boorman, vol. 3, p. 328.

150 The magnitude of Tu's monopoly is almost incomprehensible. The tip of the iceberg is in McCoy, pp. 225–27.

151 The chiu chao connection is in McCoy, chap. 6.

151 Wong Sui is identified by Jonathan Marshall, "Opium and the Politics of Gangsterism in Nationalist China, 1927–1945," *Bulletin of Concerned Asian Scholars* (July–September 1977), vol. 8, no. 3.

151 Tu either took over their organizations or set up guilds for them to join. See Wang; also Coble, p. 34.

152 The intimate brothel relationship between Tu and Chiang at this early stage is noted by Murphey, pp. 7–9.

153 For the essential details of Chiang's youth I prefer to lean on the slim but very fine psychological study by Loh, *The Early Chiang Kai-shek* (1971), from which these quotes and observations come, pp. 7–12.

153 The reference to Chiang's accent, however, is from Brian Crozier, *The Man Who Lost China* (1976), p. 3.

153 The kindling quote is in Crozier, p. 34.

153 The Pavilion is mentioned in Boorman, vol. 1, p. 319.

154 Crozier tells us of Chiang's various efforts to whip himself into shape, p. 35.

155 Chiang's life as the new-gun-in-town is from Loh, p. 22.

155 Ch'en Ch'i-mei's spectacular career is in Boorman, vol. 1, p. 164.

155 Ch'en's role as Chiang's patron is mentioned in Boorman, vol. 1, p. 164.

155 Chiang's tenacity is noted by Loh, p. 19.

156 Chiang's adventures as a gunsel are in Loh, see footnote, p. 20, also p. 133. This book is one of the few sources in English to itemize Chiang's known criminal activities, so it is invaluable. These are only his actions on public record. It is impossible not to conclude that at this time Chiang was basically a hit man for the mob running Shanghai, to whom the role of "revolutionary" was often just a convenient excuse for murder, armed robbery, and extortion.

156 See Ch'en Ch'i-mei in Boorman.

157 The murder of T'ao is also from Loh, p. 27.

157 The contemporary quotes on Chiang's debauchery are from Loh, p. 24.

158 The nightclub scene is quoted in Coble, p. 34.

158 This is a rough brothel calculation only, in order to give a sense of scale. See Murphey, pp. 7–9.

158–59 The quote on "evil thoughts" is from "À Propos d'un Ped de Chinoise," Archives d'Anthropologie Criminelle, 1898.

159 This conjecture about its origin, which seems likely, is from Levy, *Chinese Footbinding: The History of a Curious Erotic Custom* (1966), p. 30. The Manchus did not bind their women's feet.

159 That lewdness was the aspect of footbinding most often criticized suggests that lewdness was also its main objective; indeed, the idea that a girl would cripple her feet in order to excite a man was a major element in the sexual atmosphere of China. See Levy, p. 38. The incidence of masturbation from p. 31.

160 In other words, Chiang is saying that since he really did not enjoy all that debauchery it was okay. The quote is from Loh, p. 32.

161 Loh tells us they all lived together, on p. 27.

161 Crozier is the source on the concubine Yao standing in as mother, p. 44.

162 The ease with which the killers gained access to the party hideout suggests collusion on the part of Ch'en Ch'i-mei's rivals within the ranks. For the little we know, see Boorman, vol. 1, p. 165.

162 Chiang's eulogy indicates that he was in disgrace with his mentor. The quote is from Crozier, p. 45.

162 Such medical diagnoses were suspicious, at best. Was it ever possible, organically, for a Borgia to die a natural death? Details are from Boorman.

164 According to Chiang's propagandists later, he was just a poor working stiff. But there were more than a few snide rumors at the time. See "Dictator Nobody Knows," *The Literary Digest* (December 14, 1935).

164 She is mentioned in Crozier, p. 58. (Photos of a tough-looking, gaunt, and sharp-eyed lady labeled "Madame Chiang Kai-shek" appear in various books. In one she stands with Borodin and others by a train as they prepare to embark on the Northern Expedition; it is not May-ling Soong but Ch'en Chieh-ju, and she is conspicuously pregnant. What happened to the baby is not known. In 1927 Chiang tossed her out and she was sent off to the United States. This was evidently only one of two times that Chiang got her pregnant, including what seems to have been a full-term

pregnancy in 1944, according to State Department diplomatic files, and U.S. Army intelligence files mentioned later.)

164 Chiang's plaintive letter to his brother-in-law is from Crozier, p. 114.

164 A notice about a Madame Chiang Kai-shek traveling in America appeared in the *New York Times* (September 18, 1927). This was not Mayling Soong, who was at that moment preparing her trousseau for her famous wedding to Chiang three months later.

165 I doubt if Sun was entirely fooled by Chiang's protests of virtue, but the old man was clearly vulnerable to flattery. Chiang's whole purpose seems to have been to befuddle the little doctor, which, as we have seen, was not difficult. The scene is reconstructed with admirable restraint by Loh, including the quote ". . . with all my heart," p. 61.

165 The "Teacher" quote is from Hahn, p. 119.

165 Madame Sun's response is in Hahn, p. 119.

Eight: The Dancing Bear

168 The "catties" quote is in Loh, p. 70.

168 Ching-ling's magazine narrative is from Hahn.

171 "MATTERS CRITICAL" comes from Loh, p. 70. "Devilish ideas" is from p. 71. The Holmes (in Chinese translation, since Chiang never learned another language) is on p. 142.

173 "Virginal naïveté" is from Jonathan Spence, *To Change China* (1969), p. 188.

173 The historic meeting with Joffe took place on the lawn where Sun liked to play croquet, at the Rue Molière house. See C. Martin Wilbur, *Sun Yat-sen: Frustrated Patriot* (1976), pp. 135–38.

174 "Wreak mischief" is from one of the classics on China, long out of print: Harry A. Franck, *Roving Through Southern China* (1925), p. 263.

175 "Last choice" is in Edgar Snow, *Journey . . .* , p. 93.

175 Dr. Henry's remarks are from Spence, p. 188.

175 The prison records are mentioned in Dan H. Jacobs, *Borodin: Stalin's Man in China* (1981), p. 106.

176 Borodin's fine account of himself, "Snow . . . sun," is from Spence, p. 184.

176 The favorable impression on Stalin is in Jacobs, p. 19.

179 The best account of the derailing of the Chinese Revolution by Stalin and by Chiang was written by Harold R. Isaacs. His masterpiece, *The Tragedy of the Chinese Revolution* (1961), is all the more impressive for having been written with extraordinary lucidity and maturity right after the events described. Isaacs was in Shanghai as a young journalist immediately after Chiang seized power, knew Ching-ling intimately, and observed and understood the disintegration of the left. He was also one of the few to grasp the significance of the struggle between Stalin and Trotsky, as it interfered with events in China. (Isaacs, who was kind enough to read this book in manuscript in 1983 at MIT, where he was on the faculty, visited Ching-ling in Peking shortly before her death.) I have leaned heavily on Isaacs' *Tragedy* as the authority for pivotal events between 1922 and 1934, in this case for the Comintern's plans for China, and for the development of a military academy at Whampoa.

180 The scene in Canton was drily observed by Franck, p. 263. The "destructive bums" quote is from p. 223.

181 "Lafayette" is from Jacobs, p. 126.

181 From the thumbnail bio in Boorman, "Chou En-Lai."

181 Sun's strategy is from Wilbur, pp. 172–73.

182 "Satrap" is in Schiffrin, p. 241.

182 Chiang's odd love/hate flirtation with Moscow is in Loh, p. 67.

182 This body count is from John Barron, *KGB: The Secret Work of Soviet Secret Agents* (1974), p. 88, as is "merciless terror."

183 Chiang's unconvincing assertion that he once had big plans to stay in Moscow is in Loh, p. 89.

184 Chiang's real attitude toward Moscow is evident in the "sinister designs" quote from Crozier, p. 64.

184 Sun's cable to Chiang is in Loh, p. 90. Chiang's quarrel with the Russians over who would really run Whampoa is on p. 91.

186 The outcome of events in China turns so often on the teacher-student bond that it is one of the keys to understanding Chinese history. For a thorough explanation of how it worked among warlords, and between officers and their soldiers, see Ch'i Hsi-sheng, *Warlord Politics in China: 1916–1928* (1976), pp. 41–93.

186 The basic biographical materials on Mikhail Borodin were first assembled by Linda Holubnychy as her dissertation at Columbia University. She died before the dissertation was completed. As a result, she never received the acclaim she deserved for her work. All those who have written about Borodin subsequently owe a great deal to her diligence. The dissertation was published by Columbia as *Michael Borodin and the Chinese Revolution: 1923–25* (1979). The working agreement between Borodin and Dr. Sun is on p. 380.

186 Financially, Dr. Sun thereafter owed everything to Moscow and to the energies of T. V. Soong. See the memoir of the Soviet advisor Vera Vladimirovna Vishnayakova Akimova, *Two Years in Revolutionary China: 1925–27* (1971), p. 161.

186 Further elaboration of Soviet aid to Sun is from Wilbur, p. 208.

187 "A comrade . . . to impress Sun Yat-sen" is from Holubnychy, p. 381.

187 Akimova, who knew Galen, describes him, p. 339.

187 It was always believed that the leftists who went out as the first recruiters for Whampoa were murdered by various warlords. See Ch'i, p. 86. However, it was all too neat. Once the leftist recruiters were slain, Chiang Kai-shek's shadowy supporters from the Green Gang stepped in and offered to run the whole recruitment effort. They did so with a vengeance, and soon had the new military academy packed with hundreds of young Green Gang stalwarts and the children or relatives of Green Gang members. Many leftists got in through other recruiting channels, but in the long run the hard core of Whampoa was composed of men who owed allegiance directly or indirectly to the ultra-right and ultimately to Big-eared Tu. It is quite likely, therefore, that it was Big-eared Tu who arranged the killing of the original recruiters. That the suspicions of the Chinese Communist party were not aroused early on is one of the great mysteries remaining unresolved. But there were many things that should have caused alarms at the CCP, and didn't, right up to the Shanghai Massacre in April 1927.

187 The enrollment figures are from Crozier, p. 71.

188 The composition of the Whampoa faculty is from Holubnychy, p. 411.

188 Chiang's "martial qualities" are from Ch'i, pp. 98–100. Ch'i also explains why the Whampoa fighting men were radically different from anything seen in China before, on p. 141.

189 Ch'i tells how the Russians put real weapons into the hands of the Whampoa units, pp. 120–24.

189 The coming of T. V. Soong to Canton is in Boorman, "T.V. Soong."

191 The success of T. V.'s first bank is in Wilbur.

192 The fruitfulness of T. V.'s money-raising effort is from Ch'i, p. 175.

192 Vincent Sheean appraises T. V.'s advantages and disadvantages in "Some People from Canton," *Asia* (October 1927), and Ch'i, p. 176.

193 The coalescence of reaction around "snow leopard" Ch'en Lien-po is described in Jacobs, p. 158.

194 The "Save Canton" slogan is from Jacobs, p. 158.

194 Wilbur tells of the shipment of guns, p. 250. See also Isaacs, p. 68.

194 The growing Canton left-right confrontation is outlined in Wilbur, p. 251.

195 This clash is in Jacobs, p. 161.

196 Dr. Sun's inappropriate erection of the "triumphal arch" is in Jacobs, p. 162. It was in fact a tombstone.

Nine: Scramble for Power

198 Feng's offer is in Wilbur, p. 264. But Feng was a master of duplicity; attempting to make a deal with him led in the end to disaster for the KMT leftists.

199 Even Borodin was fooled by Feng when he imagined that greed and ambition were the only keys to Feng's cravings. Jacobs, pp. 168–69.

199 "Tower of strength" is in Schiffrin, p. 265.

200 "Our Generalissimo" is from Robert Payne, *Mao Tse-tung* (1950), p. 105.

200 The inside story of the bomb farce is amusingly revealed by Wu Yu-zhang, p. 100.

200 Borodin's frustration with Moscow is in Jacobs, p. 169.

201 Ai-ling's claim of a "bond" between H. H. and Ching-ling is in Hahn, p. 124.

201 Chiang's "last breath" assertion is in Schiffrin, p. 267.

201 Sun's verbal agreement is attested to by Wilbur, p. 277.

202 Sun's camp cot is from Akimova, p. 51.

202 The flag-dipping affront is from Jacobs, p. 170.

203 H. H. Kung's fatuous eulogy is in Wilbur, p. 281, as is George Hsu's eulogy.

203 The funeral voice of Henry Luce's brother-in-law is heard in W. A. Swanberg, *Luce and His Empire* (1972), p. 95.

204 Galen's lack of formal education is from Holubnychy, p. 416.

204 I take my list of candidates to succeed Dr. Sun Yat-sen from Crozier, folio.

206 The Shameen quote is from Akimova, p. 193.

207 The peril of undertaking labor agitation in gang-ruled Shanghai comes from George Moseley, *China Since 1911* (1968), p. 52.

207   One cannot be sure whether Chiang shot the man in a typical outburst of rage or to keep him quiet. The citation is in Loh, p. 128.

Ten: The Green Conspiracy

209-10   The extreme right was searching for a champion. Chiang was chosen to be it. There are only the barest of facts, but there are clues everywhere. For example, see Jacobs, p. 188.

210   Isaacs also notes these murky developments, p. 92.

210   Isaacs clearly identified Curio Chang as the mastermind of what followed, but, in the confusion of the period, nobody took note, and no study of Curio Chang's role was ever undertaken. For the quote, see Isaacs, p. 92.

211   Unless one was aware at the time that Big-eared Tu's group was behind the killings, how could anyone draw ominous conclusions from them? The numerous, strange coincidences certainly were everywhere. See Isaacs, p. 93.

211   The lame response of the CCP is in Isaacs, p. 94.

211   It was a bad moment for Borodin to be called away. But if, on the other hand, we assume that Stalin was deliberately getting Borodin out of the picture so he could not interfere, the temporary recall becomes comprehensible. The mere event is in Jacobs, p. 192.

213   These widespread denials in the international Communist press demonstrate Stalin's shell game at work. I quote them from Jacobs, p. 97.

213   A very gentle interpretation of Chiang's devious manner runs throughout Loh.

213   The naïve analysis is from George Sokolsky, *Tinder Box of Asia* (1934), p. 336. (Sokolsky was identified by one of the FBI's better-placed Asian informants as a dangerous meddler in Chinese affairs, a man who gained the ear of T. V. Soong and became T. V.'s "evil genius," until he was displaced by Dr. Rajachman and Joe Alsop in T. V.'s favor. If Sokolsky was an "evil genius" it was because his energy and pushy manner allowed him to have an exaggerated and possibly malignant influence on T. V. In this way he might have manipulated some of T. V.'s decisions in the late 1930s. However, Sokolsky was too much of an intellectual bantam to have an "evil" influence on the scale of Dr. Goebbels. Nevertheless, Sokolsky the journalist was listened to by a great many Americans in the days of radio, who took him very seriously; in the end his impact is hard to access. He was just one of many Western meddlers, but closer to the throne than most.) From FBI files.

213   The other obvious interpretation of Chiang's groveling is from Louis Fischer, *Soviets in World Affairs* (1930), vol. 2, p. 651. I contend that neither analysis is correct, and that Chiang groveled deliberately at many points in his life to throw off his adversaries and lull them back into their usual torpor.

214   The "peculiar person" quote is from Spence, p. 195.

214   The Trotsky quote is from Isaacs, p. 117.

214-15   The marriage proposal is from Edgar Snow, *Journey* . . . , p. 85.

217   For more, see Hsu Kai-yu, *Chou En-lai: China's Grey Eminence* (1968), p. 56.

217 The extraordinary situation developing in Shanghai is broken down in detail by Isaacs, p. 147 et seq. (The British troops, it appears, were there not so much to protect British property as to make certain that nobody took control who was "unfriendly" to British interests.)

218 The labor walkout is from Isaacs, p. 133.

219 "Welcome Chiang" is from Isaacs, p. 136.

219 Chiang's reward is from Isaacs, p. 135.

219 Borodin obviously sensed something very fishy going on, but did not realize the extent of Chiang's betrayal. For their confrontations, see Jacobs, p. 231.

219 Chiang's announcement is from Isaacs, p. 126.

220 Voitinsky's shrewd observation demonstrates that some Communists in Shanghai clearly saw what was happening but could not make themselves heard. For the context, see Isaacs, p. 136.

220 But communications were so bad that it was impossible for anyone to see that the collaboration between gangsters and Chiang's soldiers was going on all over the city. See Isaacs, p. 143.

221 The pact between the gangsters and Western officials is in John B. Powell, *My Twenty-five Years in China* (1945), p. 145.

222 The French involvement with Big-eared Tu is described by Jonathan Marshall.

222 Powell had a clear grasp of what was happening, but probably found it hard to believe that it was all part of a grand design. Jonathan Marshall, p. 162.

222 Powell's "the shooting began" quote is on p. 154.

223 Isaacs describes the uneven odds on p. 137.

223 I take these figures and CCP moves from Hsu, p. 57.

223 For a moment, this vanguard force, commanded by a leftist, had a chance to tip matters in the CCP's favor. See Isaacs, p. 140.

223 Compared to what else was happening downriver, the Nanking Incident was utterly insignificant. Powell, p. 156.

224 The official American inquiry is cited by Isaacs, p. 145.

224 It was only when word of the meeting with Pockmarked Huang got around that some foreign observers, like Powell and Snow, began to suspect the awful truth. Isaacs, p. 145.

225 Most observers thought this was Chiang's first real contact with the Green Gang leaders. Isaacs, p. 145.

225 "There was no split" is from Isaacs, p. 154.

226 Chiang's smokescreen summit meeting with Wang is from Vincent Sheean, *Personal History* (1969).

226 "I strongly believe" is from Isaacs, p. 154.

227 The ringleaders were all linked to Big-eared Tu and Pockmarked Huang. Isaacs, p. 151.

227 The financial details are from Coble, chap. 2; and Isaacs, p. 151.

227 "A cunning game" is from Jacobs, p. 198.

228 Hsueh Yueh's flip-flops are from Isaacs, p. 171.

228 This particularly hair-raising vignette is from Isaacs, p. 172. But it was a celebrated piece of work narrated many times elsewhere.

229 Chou's whereabouts are from Hsu, p. 57.

229 The executioners are from Isaacs, p. 177.

229 The death toll is from Lois Wheeler Snow, p. 35.
230 The body count is in Isaacs, p. 179.
230 "Pillar of society" is from Han Suyin, *A Mortal Flower* (1972), p. 62.
230 The impotent proclamation is from O. Edmund Clubb, *Twentieth Century China* (1978), p. 137.
231 Borodin's moves are from Jacobs, pp. 251-56.
231 "The only man" is in Jacobs, p. 280.
232 "Snow-white bodies" is from Isaacs, p. 149.
233 The CCK quote is from *Time* (April 25, 1927).

Eleven: All in the Family

234 The revenue percentage is from Sheean, "Some People in Canton," *Asia*, October 1927.
234 "Plight . . . is pitiable" is from the *New York Times* (May 4, 1927).
235 Fu's ransom is from Coble, p. 2.
235 Chiang's "bonds" are from Coble, p. 2.
236 T. V.'s countersigning is from Coble, p. 2.
236 T. V.'s schizophrenia is obvious in Sheean, *Personal History*, p. 194.
236 Chiang's retaliation is from Coble, chap. 2.
236 "A nervous dread" is from Sheean, *Personal History*, p. 195.
237 Chiang's love letters are from Sheean, *Personal History*.
237 "Ningpo Napoleon" is from Isaacs.
237 The evisceration of girls was something Ching-ling knew was happening and which haunted her, according to Sheean, *Personal History*.
238 "China's Joan of Arc" is from Sheean, *Personal History*, p. 209.
239 Wang's doubletalk is from Isaacs, p. 251.
239 The "ill-timed" cable is from Jacobs, p. 270.
240 The armaments are listed in Keija Furuya, *Chiang Kai-shek: His Life and Times* (1981), p. 213.
240 "Emancipation" and "consummation" are from Isaacs, p. 253.
240 "Freight cars" is from Anna Louise Strong, *China's Millions* (1928), p. 61.
241 "Wanted posters" is in Jacobs, p. 280.
242 "Conscious hypocrite" is from Strong, p. 16.
243 "I simply cannot do it" is from Sheean, *Personal History*, p. 235.
243 Expulsion of the CCP is from Jacobs, p. 283.
244 "Subtle weapons of slander" is in Strong, p. 27.
244 The message from Chiang is mentioned in Jacobs, p. 283.
245 "Not to be forgotten" is from Sheean, *Personal History*, p. 241.
245 "Not to give grounds" is in Crozier, p. 109.
245 Galen's acute indigestion is in Akimova, p. 325.
245 The hair growing is from Jacobs, p. 282.
245 The reign of terror is from Isaacs, p. 266.
245-46 "Tell the seller" is in Chen, p. 117.
246 Eugene Chen is quoted by his son in Chen, p. 117.
246 Moscow's advice to Borodin is in Isaacs, p. 267.
246 Ching-ling's broadside is from *The Nation* (September 21, 1927).
249 Fanya's escapade is in Jacobs, p. 292.
250 Description of the silver is from Chen, p. 120. He also describes it as Borodin's ransom.

250   The tragicomic farewell scene is from Chen, p. 120.
250   Feng's gratuity is from Chen, p. 128.
253   M. N. Roy's stand at the 1920 Congress is from Schwartz, *Tsars, Mandarins and Commissars* (1964), p. 99.
254   "Lick the Dust" is from Deutscher, *The Prophet Unarmed* (1959), p. 359.
254   The Sugar Palace is described by Sheean, *Personal History*, p. 268.
255   Joffe's final words are from Robert Payne, *The Life and Death of Trotsky* (1977), p. 292.
256   Ching-ling's collapse is from Sheean, *Personal History*, p. 289.
257   Chiang's proposal is from Crozier, p. 115.
257   Hu Lin's remarks are in Crozier, p. 116.
257   Tang's comment is from Han Suyin, *A Mortal Flower*, p. 71.
258   Han Suyin makes these observations on p. 71. Taken in isolation, some of these perceptions of Ai-ling would seem to have been blunt enough to alert people to her poisonous and manipulative nature. However, the effect was not so strong when the remarks were seen in context, cheek by jowl with the treacly praise most writers felt compelled to utter about Madame Chiang.
258   "Opportunism" is from Edgar Snow, *Journey . . .* , p. 85.
259   Emily Hahn, who describes the palace, is at her most fawning in these passages reciting the wealth and accomplishments of Ai-ling. See Hahn, pp. 99-100.
259   For his credentials as a "great educator" see Boorman, "H. H. Kung."
259   The private wariness of Oberlin regarding Kung is seen in the correspondence of Enoch Bell. Letter to the Reverend W. Frederick Bohn (September 17, 1926).
259   The children are listed in Boorman, "H. H. Kung."
259   "Arrogant" according to Theodore White and Annalee Jacoby, *Thunder out of China* (1946), p. 112.
259   "Sulky" according to Ilona Ralf Sues, *Shark Fins and Millet* (1944), p. 177.
260   The dinner scene is from Hahn, p. 156.
260   The description of the Kung house in Shanghai is from a Time Inc. memo by L. Borgida, "Chinese Finance Minister H. H. Kung" (November 13, 1941).
260   The Standard Oil agency is mentioned in White and Jacoby, p. 111.
260   Kung's role as interlocutor is mentioned in Boorman, vol. 2, p. 265.
261   "Real Brains" is from newly declassified FBI documents. "Memorandum to the Director" (January 9, 1943). (Obtained under the Freedom of Information Act.)
262   This anecdote of the transmitter in the closet is also from newly declassified FBI documents. (See elsewhere.)
262   Letters to James A. Thomas from Admiral Mark Bristol (January 14, 1928, and May 28, 1929), courtesy Duke University Archives.
263   May-ling's "letting it slip" is in Crozier, p. 116. John Gunther says Ai-ling actually called a press conference in her home and there presented May-ling and Chiang together, saying, "The General is going to marry my little sister." The press conference did occur and photos were taken of the happy couple seated at a table in the garden. At this point in September, the other Madame Chiang was arriving in the United States, having been paid off and ordered to get out. It is amazing that the *New*

York Times, which reported her arrival in America, proceeded to announce the Generalissimo's wedding plans without making an effort to resolve the existence of two Madames Chiang in its pages.

264 Miss Ch'en's adventures in America are summarized in Crozier, p. 59. For a detailed account of all Chiang's marriages, see Ting Yi, "A Study of Chiang Kai-shek's Marital Life," *The Perspective Monthly* (January 1973).

264 Misselwitz, choosing to ignore the existence of two Madames Chiang, made this facetious remark in *The Nation* (October 12, 1927).

265 The meeting with Curio Chang is mentioned by Clubb, p. 141.

265 "Other complications of which gossips have made much" comes from Hahn, p. 139.

265 Ainsworth's inability to marry the couple is from Clark, p. 80.

268 The manner in which Chiang's resignation caused the wheels of government to spin is from Clubb, p. 141.

288 This episode with the warlords was actually a very complicated process with a lot of rushing back and forth, but I have tried to boil it down to the essentials. For other details, see Clubb, p. 140.

269-70 The kidnapping of Madame Chiang is from Sues, p. 69.

Twelve: A Tale of Two Sisters

271 The scene at Red Square is in Chen, p. 182.

272 Sheean's comments to the Department of State are from its records in the National Archives, DOS/861.00B/522.

272 The funeral scene is in Sheean's *Personal History*, p. 301.

273 It was Sheean who tried to set up Ching-ling's U.S. speaking tour, and Sheean who ended up having to make the tour himself. What he told the embassy in Berlin is from Department of State Records, National Archives, DOS/893.00/10003.

275 "China for the Soongs" is in Eunson, p. 85, and in Clark, p. 64.

275 The Harbin news report is from "Madame Sun Says Russia Only Real Friend of China" (May 16, 1929). Courtesy Duke University Archives.

276 "No despair in my heart" is from Randall Gould, "Madame Sun Yat-sen Keeps Faith," *The Nation* (January 22, 1930).

276 A thumbnail bio of Tai Ch'i-tao is in Boorman, vol. 3, p. 203.

277 Boorman mentions Tai Ch'i-tao's extraordinary turnabout.

277 Ching-ling's full account of the conversation is from *The China Press* (November 3, 1929). I have used the high points.

280 The names of these Russian agents, except for Sorge, were known to Western intelligence circles at the time, and I have taken them from the State Department archives. Sorge was "identified" only when American Occupation Forces in Japan discovered after World War II that he had been in Japanese custody. General MacArthur's staff and the Luce press then inflated the Sorge "case" into a major spy scare as part of their postwar campaign to inflame the American public against the Red Menace. Agnes Smedley was vilified by this campaign; when she tried to fight back with lawsuits for slander, MacArthur's G-2, General Willoughby, pulled out all the stops and devoted himself full time to the concoction of his book, *Shanghai Conspiracy*, in which Smedley was unjustly portrayed as a Communist dupe. Her reputation destroyed, Miss Smedley

finally fled to England to escape the witch hunt. None of the charges against her was ever proved. Heartbroken in England, exhausted by her ordeal, and surrounded by the memorabilia of her days in China, she died in solitude, a victim of the U.S. pathology. Eventually, Smedley's ashes were taken to Peking to be buried with honors. The links between MacArthur's staff and a number of congressmen involved in the witch hunt, including Senator Joseph McCarthy, raise a number of questions that are provocative to say the least. Senator McCarthy and others joined T. L. Soong in allegedly cornering the soybean market a few weeks before the U.S. declared war in Korea and profited heavily from the consequent escalation in soybean prices.

280 Fairbank had good things to say about Smedley in *Chinabound*, p. 67.

281 For his version, see General Charles Willoughby, *Shanghai Conspiracy*. All he was ever able to charge against Smedley was that from time to time she apparently allowed various acquaintances to have some mail sent to her address, possibly including some Russians who might have been spies. Surveillance of Smedley's mail would have been quite easy since the postal employees' union in Shanghai, as we have seen, was controlled by the Green Gang.

281 There is some discussion of Powell's predicament in the State Department Records, National Archives, DOS/893.00B/655. Powell was a crusading editor with a reputation for meticulous fairness. He later rallied Chinese and American opinion against the Japanese invasion, for which he was interned in a Japanese prison camp. Both his feet were frozen during his imprisonment and were amputated after the war. His son, Bill Powell, a graduate of the University of Missouri, took over the editorship of the *Review* and continued its policies of speaking out for the underdog and printing criticism of the Chiang dictatorship. After Chiang fled to Taiwan, the *Review* continued to publish in Shanghai till 1953, often editorializing against American involvement in the Korean War. In 1953 it closed down and Bill Powell returned to America. He continued to express his unpopular views of the Chiang regime and China until, in 1959, he and his wife, and Julian Schuman of the old *Review* staff, were indicted for sedition by a U.S. grand jury. They were brought to trial in San Francisco. A week later, the judge threw the case out, announcing a mistrial. Two years later, the U.S. government quietly dropped its charges against all three. Their careers, however, were destroyed by then. (The difficulties encountered for many years by Helen and Edgar Snow are well known and require no retelling here.)

281 "Tearful Announcement" is from Department of State Records, National Archives DOS/893.00/10692.

282 I refer specifically to the afternoon of Madame Chiang's arrival in Georgia to visit Wesleyan during World War II. A hotel suite had been prepared lavishly with bouquets of flowers. May-ling ordered all the flowers removed immediately, and during the next three hours had the bed remade three times with fresh silk sheets. All this according to members of the committee organized to welcome her, who were interviewed in 1983 by my Atlanta researcher, Gail Dubroff.

283 Notes on Teng Yen-ta's life are in Boorman, vol. 3, p. 264.

284 Luce's way of bestowing nicknames is in Swanberg, p. 200.

284 "Peanut" is in Barbara Tuchman, *Stilwell and the American Experience in China* (1972).

285 May-ling's "Chinese face" quote is from Hahn.

285 The editorial is from "Chiang Kai-shek Is Baptized," *The Christian Century* (November 5, 1930).

286 "My heart bleeds" is from May-ling's "A Letter from China," *The Wesleyan Magazine* (December 1930).

287 Donald's advice is from Selle, p. 302.

287 The flag-apron incident is in Sues, pp. 62–63.

290 This figure is from Crozier, p. 159. John Gunther quotes Snow as remarking that at the going rate for the extermination campaigns, it cost Chiang about $80,000 to kill a red.

290 The missionaries' advice was reported by Jim Marshall in "China's Girl Boss," *Collier's* (April 10, 1937).

290 May-ling's "four virtues" are from Madame Chiang's own account, "New Life in China," *Forum* (June 1935).

291 "Except a man be born again" is from "Christians and the New Life Movement," *The Missionary Review of the World* (November 1937).

292 May-ling's chain smoking is from *Collier's* (August 30, 1941). When she was visited by Ernest Hemingway and his wife in Kunming during World War II, they found her smoking incessantly.

292 "Drift and insipidity" is from *The Missionary Review of the World* (July 1937).

292 "Three legs" is from Crozier, p. 167.

292 "Blue Shirts" is from Crozier, pp. 10–11.

293 Details of the organization of the Blue Shirts and Chiang's denial of their existence is in Wilbur Burton, "Chiang's Secret Blood Brothers," *Asia* (May 1936).

293 Biographical profiles of Ch'en Kuo-fu and Ch'en Li-fu are in Boorman.

293 Tai Li's profile in Boorman is sound but lacking in many of the grimmer details. For these the reader will find bits and pieces scattered through many of the books listed in the bibliography.

294 The Blue Shirt head count is from Crozier, p. 11.

294 The evolution of the Blue Shirts is best described in Burton's *Asia* article, which describes the blood oath.

294 "From the kindergarten to the grave" is from Crozier, p. 11.

294 "Frankenstein monster" is from "Calm War-Lord Chiang Decides Not to Hurry in China's Many Crises," *The Literary Digest* (October 17, 1936).

297 The live burial is from Edgar Snow, p. 87. (Another favorite treatment for dissidents was to force them to swallow a mixture of kerosene and human feces. See Spence, *Gate of Heavenly Peace*.)

297 Ching-ling's "Corinthians" remark is from Lois Wheeler Snow, p. 33; Edgar Snow, *Journey* . . . .

Thirteen: The Sugar Plum Fairies

299 T. V.'s wooing of the business leaders is from Coble, p. 49, including the quote "a step forward for democratic institutions."

299 T. V.'s opposition to the huge military budget is from John MacMurray's telegram to the Secretary of State, Washington, D.C. (August 2, 1928).

303 America's mild response to the Japanese invasion of Manchuria is in Clubb, p. 167.

303 Chiang's bland acceptance of the invasion is from Sokolsky, p. 230.

304 Sokolsky also describes Chiang's resignation maneuver, p. 243.

304 The financial subversion of the Sun Fo government, and T. V.'s sudden return with Chiang to fill the vacuum is from Coble, p. 102.

305 Sokolsky tells the effects of the anti-Japanese boycott and the punitive moves taken by the Japanese military, on pp. 247–55.

306 Chiang's withdrawal to Loyang, leaving Shanghai undefended, is from Coble.

306 The quote from Eugene Chen is from Sokolsky, p. 266.

306 How the Nineteenth Route Army was running errands for Big-eared Tu is from Jonathan Marshall.

306 The role of the Salt Tax Brigade is mentioned in *Fortune* (June 1933).

307 Fairbank's account is in *Chinabound*, p. 36.

307 Edgar Snow's description is from JOURNEY . . . , pp. 95–97.

307 The drop in trade is in Sokolsky, p. 267.

307 The interview by Karl H. Von Wiegand appeared under the headline "Chinese Prefer Communism to Military Domination," in the New York *American* (May 2, 1932).

308 Coble describes the Anti–Civil War League on p. 115.

309 Coble also tells how Chiang sent the valiant Nineteenth off as cannon fodder, p. 111.

310 T. V.'s visit to the front with the Young Marshal is from Coble, p. 122.

311 The site of the bank is mentioned in Hauser, p. 238.

312 "The trouble with Harry" is from Swanberg, p. 148; "unbribable pig-headedness," p. 152.

313 "Soong would rage and roar" is from *Fortune* (October 1933).

313 "The hero-worshipper in him" is from Swanberg, p. 71; "The moral force of fascism" is on p. 109.

313 While Soong's sacrifice in giving up the likin was heart-warming, it did not deserve such an outburst of unction from Luce. But the message was clear to readers of *Fortune:* Luce was anointing T. V. with the most sacred oil.

314 Luce's confidential memo "Going Sour on the Soongs" was quoted in Swanberg.

314 T. V.'s radio broadcast was reproduced in the *New York Times* (May 18, 1933).

316 Chiang's pocketing of $60 million while T. V. was away from China is from Coble.

316 The face-slapping incident is related by John Service in *Lost Chance in China* (1975), p. 78.

316 "Being Chiang's dog" is from Coble.

317 The economic statistics are from White and Jacoby, p. 115.

317 The disgusted observation of Cyril Rogers is from Edgar Snow's *Journey* . . . , p. 215.

317 "Pendulous flabby chins" is from White and Jacoby, p. 112.

317 "Constant state of alarm" is from Hauser's article "T. V. for Victory," in the *New Republic* (January 26, 1942).

318 T. V. and H. H. are contrasted by Coble and also by Geraghty.

318 "The Sage" is from Snow's *Journey* . . . , p. 95.

318 Kung's rewards are listed by Borgida.

318 "One picul of cotton" is from Coble, p. 152.

319 Hahn quotes Miss Thompson on Ai-ling's visit to Wesleyan, pp. 175–76.

319 Ai-ling's scholarship fund is described in her letter to Jennie Loyall, Wesleyan College (December 4, 1934), Wesleyan College Archives.

319 The Kung travels in Europe are described by Borgida.

320 "A fuss made over me" is from Hahn, p. 176.

321 "He meant well" is from Selle, p. 254.

321 Kung's inauguration is described in Coble, p. 163.

322 Kung's magic bonds are also from Coble, p. 167.

322 "Until further notice" is from Hauser, p. 231.

322 The silver export tax and its impact on Chinese currency is from Hauser, p. 232.

323 How Kung made himself an exception is from Coble, p. 170.

324 The relative size of the big banks is from Coble, p. 173.

325 How the Soong clan undermined the rival banks and took them over is from Coble, pp. 178–84.

326 The eventual self-exile of the defeated and demoralized Chang Kia-ngau in America is in Boorman.

326 The proliferation of Soong clansmen on many boards of directors is in Coble, pp. 183–92.

327 A biographical profile of Chief of Staff Ku Chu-t'ung, without the grim details and without any mention of his brother, the harbor gang boss, is in Boorman.

327 The General Motors/DuPont statement is not the sort of thing that can be investigated easily. See the FBI materials on the Soongs and Kungs developed for President Truman as evidence of the difficulty. However, the British government must have had reason to believe its information. This statement was made during an interview by *Time*'s William McHale with a senior British Foreign Office spokesman in October 1953. I take the quote from the unpublished notes of the interview, which are in the *Time* morgue. The British official said he understood that T. V. had acquired "a controlling interest" in General Motors. McHale responded that it was "understood" among Americans in the know that the company in question was DuPont.

328 The makeup of the Currency Reserve Board is in Coble, p. 194.

328 The consequences of Kung's monetary policies for China's economy through 1935 are described in Coble, pp. 202–204, and footnote 36, p. 315.

Fourteen: The High Priest

330 The extent of Chiang's dependence on opium and heroin revenues is examined in Jonathan Marshall's short study of gangster politics. Conservative estimates at the time gave 10 percent of the national budget, but the actual figure was probably more than 50 percent. It should be remembered that while general estimates of opium production in China were possible, based on known levels in the past, there was no way to calculate how much heroin was being produced by Big-eared Tu for local

consumption and export to Europe and North America. By 1935 heroin revenues may have exceeded opium revenues by a factor of ten.

332 "It would not be worthy" is also in Marshall.

332 The "prohibition" of opium was so "effective" that Chiang's regime had to import more opium tar from the Middle East to keep up with demand. The commission T. V. received for handling these imports is mentioned in Marshall.

332 The opium quote in *Time* (April 27, 1931) totally missed the point. T. V. sent agents to Formosa because that was where Japan concentrated its heroin production laboratories. What was really afoot was an attempt to negotiate a deal whereby Japan and China would stop competing for heroin sales on the mainland, but would split the market. The deal evidently fell through and cooperation thereafter occurred only on a spot basis—in deals worked out between Chinese regional military commanders and their Japanese counterparts.

333 "It was a miracle" is from the *New York Times* (July 23, 1931).

334 The great opening celebration of Big-eared Tu's temple is described in Boorman.

335 I quote the *Who's Who* from Wang.

337 As in all cases of sleight-of-hand, there were two things going on at once. Chiang's China had two treasuries—the official economic system directed by Kung and Soong, and the unofficial or black treasury that Chiang dipped into by working agreement with Big-eared Tu. It was the black treasury that enabled Chiang to make major arms purchases abroad when his official treasury was empty. The $5 million U.S. purchases are cited by Jonathan Marshall, but news stories of the day pointed out routinely that China was one of America's biggest customers for arms, particularly aircraft.

337 "Somewhat 'floored'" is from Marshall.

337 "Opium Suppression of Shanghai" is from Sues, p. 71.

337 Sues's extraordinary session with Big-eared Tu is on her pp. 68–72.

338 "A power for God" is from Sues, p. 71. Tu was always willing to start orphanages and lend them money, but he did so at exorbitant rates. As the saying goes, he was that kind of guy.

345 Wong's summit meeting in San Francisco is in Jonathan Marshall.

345 The official stamps on the confiscated five-ounce tins is in *China Weekly Review* (July 24, 1937).

345 Big-eared Tu's attendance at Kung prayer meetings is attested to by Jonathan Marshall, as is May-ling's immortal quote "Tu . . . is becoming a real Christian." Madame Chiang's astonishing naïveté was also noted by John Gunther in *Inside Asia*, p. 226, when he said, "for all her admirable capacity for administration, it seems that she lacks political sense. . . . She talks about the communists, not merely with a distaste which would be understandable enough, but with a curious glib lack of comprehension."

Fifteen: Toothless at Tiger Rock

346 Chiang's eagerness to make a deal with Japan is in Crozier, p. 174.

346 Wang's role as Japan analyst is in Boorman.

346 The Nazi arms deal is from Wu Tien-wei's dissertation, *The Sian Incident: A Pivotal Point in Modern Chinese History* (1976), p. 86. I have found this to be the only balanced and thorough account, and have relied on it for my own recapitulation.

346 Chiang's ranking as largest buyer of U.S. aircraft is in "Calm War-Lord Chiang Decides not to Hurry in China's Many Crises," *The Literary Digest* (October 17, 1936).

348 The Young Marshal's motives are explored by Wu, p. 27.

348 Chiang's plans to neutralize the Young Marshal permanently are in Boorman.

349 "We can hold the emperor hostage" is from Wu, p. 71.

351 May-ling's dead faint is from *Time* (December 28, 1936).

351 "The Generalissimo's safety" and "It gives one a pain in the heart" are both from *Time* (December 28, 1936).

352 The hint that T. V. contrived the Sian Incident is from *Time* (January 3, 1938).

352 The Young Marshal's public address is in Wu, p. 98.

352 Chiang's "blood debt as high as a mountain" is from Wu, p. 101. The response of Moscow and Tokyo are on pp. 102 and 128.

353 Chiang speechless is in Wu, p. 136.

354 The airport arrival of T. V. and Madame Chiang is from *The Literary Digest* (January 2, 1937). The presence of her chef is in a footnote to the same news story.

354-55 It is Elliston who points out that the Young Marshal had once courted May-ling. The way she palmed Chiang's spare dentures to him is from *The Literary Digest* piece.

355 The real reason Ho was replaced, as Wu demonstrates, was his eagerness to cooperate with the Japanese militarists.

356 Chiang's gratefulness to Chou En-lai is from John McCook Roots's biography *Chou* (1978), pp. 166-67.

356 Despite these positive contacts with Chou En-lai, John Gunther points out that May-ling refused ever to read Edgar Snow's *Red Star over China*, which would have given her invaluable insight into the people she railed against throughout her life.

357 "Dragon Throne," and Mao's comment "interesting specimen" are from John Paton Davies's *Dragon by the Tail* (1972), pp. 186 and 151.

357 "Seventy times seven" is also from Davies, p. 207.

358 Ching-ling's comment, "I would have gone farther," is from Edgar Snow, *Journey* . . . , p. 94.

Sixteen: On Family Business

359 Readers looking for a more elaborate account of Chennault and how the AVG ended in near-mutiny will find it in my *Soldiers of Fortune* (1981).

360 "Always be a princess" is from Moser, p. 59.

360-61 "The Italian method" is from Arthur N. Young's *China and the Helping Hand* (1963).

362 The Generalissimo continually asserted that Japan was undermining China's economy, while Madame Chiang prodded America to come to China's rescue. Meanwhile, Chinese police in Shanghai were guarding

Japanese business establishments, and high-ranking Chinese and Japanese were striking lucrative business deals under the table. Not least among these entrepreneurs were the Kungs and Soongs, who were making millions from joint ventures with Japan while supervising the Chinese economy. The quote "China looks forward" is from Chiang's "Letter to President Roosevelt" (July 20, 1939), State Department Records, National Archives, DOS 793.94/15483.

362 "We hope to be able" is from May-ling's "Letter to James A. Thomas" (November 21, 1937), courtesy Duke University Archives.

362 "Japanese are doing their best" is from Donald's "Letter to James A. Thomas" (July 31, 1937), courtesy Duke University Archives.

362 "White Man's Burden" is from *Time* (June 26, 1939).

363 "He is a converted Methodist" is from *Life* (November 7, 1932).

363 The story about T. V. trying to get the U.S. navy to smuggle him out of occupied Shanghai is in the State Department Records at the National Archives. "Japan will be on verge of bankruptcy" is from an unidentified newspaper clipping I found in the *Time* morgue, dated December 20, 1937, three months before T. V. fled.

364 Obviously, T. V. considered China to be the "family business." These quotes on his arrival are from an unpublished memo by reporter Will Lang of the *Time* Washington Bureau, dated March 7, 1944, in the Time Inc. morgue.

364 The ease with which T. V. adapted to Washington wheeling-and-dealing is described by Young, p. 133.

364 "Honey" is from the memo by Will Lang.

364 The vision of T. V. in the Shoreham pool is in Ernest Hauser's "China's Soong," *Life* (March 24, 1941).

364 It is Hauser who gives us a short list of T. V.'s powerful Washington friends and the way they played poker together.

365 Will Lang's memo tells us how T. V. now preferred to be called "Dr. Soong."

365 Young gives us the quote "nearing the breaking point" on p. 133.

365 "Star Wisconsin halfback" is from Fairbank's *Chinabound*, p. 180.

365 "Poor old T. V." and "Communist ascendancy" are from Young, p. 133.

366 Assorted gifts from T. V. and H. H. are mentioned in the "Letters to President Franklin Roosevelt" in the Soong archives at the Hoover Institution.

367 "Fantastically cheap at the price" is from Hauser's *Life* article, "China's Soong"; however, it had the ring of a line inserted at the final editing stage by Henry Luce.

369 The sorry record of State Department double dealing toward Americans wanting to fight in Spain is told in more detail in my *Soldiers of Fortune*.

370 I have this version of the origin of the shark mouth from discussions with Eric Schilling and other members of the AVG, and am persuaded that it is definitive.

372 The battle at Taierchuang is described in Chesneaux's *China from the 1911 Revolution . . .* , p. 261.

372 Tuchman quotes Chesneaux, p. 186.

372 The deliberate disaster at the Yellow River dikes is from Chesneaux, p. 261.

372 Chiang's effort to blame Japan is from Clubb, p. 224.

374 General Ku's promotion is in Boorman.

374 "Who play with fire" is from White's *In Search of History,* p. 115. "A disease of the heart" is on p. 116.

374 "Those yellow bastards" is in a memo from Annalee Jacoby to *Time* on December 8, 1944. *Time* morgue.

374 T. V.'s elevation to Foreign Minister is from the *New York Times* (December 24, 1941).

375 "The Generalissimo wants a billion" is from Young, p. 233.

375 "It was practically zero" is from Franz Shurman, *The China Reader: Republican China* (1967), p. 271.

Seventeen: Little Sister Woos America

376 "Disturbing influence" is from Davies, p. 255.

376–77 "She is just what we need" is from Clark, pp. 107–108.

378 The analysis of Willkie's odyssey is from K. C. Li's "Letter to T. V. Soong" (October 31, 1942), courtesy Hoover Library.

378 T. V.'s opposition to May-ling's visit is in Service, p. 79.

378 Crozier points out that "Darling" was the only English word Chiang used.

379 May-ling's domestic strife is from Service, pp. 92–96. The reappearance of Chambermaid Yao is on p. 94.

380 "Now come meet your new mother" is from *Time* (January 3, 1938).

380 May-ling's medical condition is described in a memo from Saint to Fuerbringer, July 20, 1945, in the *Time* morgue.

381 All three Soong sisters eventually suffered from cancer in one form or another. But it seems unlikely that Chiang would have been prescient enough to guess in 1942 that May-ling already had cancer. Years passed before it was established medically and she underwent her first mastectomy. But Chiang's prescience is attributed to him by his press chief Hollington Tong in *Dateline: China* (1950).

381 The mysterious cargo of the *Apache* is from Schleit, p. 21.

381 Pilot Shelton stayed with the Chiangs at Eagle's Nest, and his adventures with May-ling are recounted in Philip Schleit's *Shelton's Barefoot Airline* (1982), p. 25.

381 May-ling's big loan to Shelton is mentioned in Schleit; the money was used to start a Florida firm manufacturing airplane seats. Once Shelton had it going, David Kung stepped in to take over and Shelton moved on to run his airline in Central and South America. The Soong clan had a surprising number of aviation interests in Latin America.

382 The quote from Harry Hopkins is in Sherwood's *Roosevelt and Hopkins* (1948), pp. 660–61.

382 Eleanor Roosevelt's first reaction is from Tuchman, p. 351.

382 That May-ling underwent some form of treatment is mentioned by Holly Tong in an interview with *Time*'s Donohugh on February 18, 1943. *Time* morgue.

383 T. A.'s wedding was lavishly covered by *Life* on January 12, 1942. This marriage cemented the family control of the Bank of Canton in San Francisco, and made its records inaccessible to the subsequent FBI probe.

383 The Pearl Buck anecdote is from Fairbank's *Chinabound*, p. 253.
383 May-ling's manners at the White House are related by Tuchman, p. 351. So are FDR's calling Jeannette Kung "my boy" and the dinner-table throat slitting.
384 May-ling's continual rewriting is from Tong.
384 "Larger reason for her presence" is from *Life* (February 22, 1943).
384 "I was horrified" is from Fern Marja Eckman's interview with Emily Hahn headlined "China's Fabulous Soong Sisters," in the New York *Post* (September 24, 1966).
384 "Taking the country by charm" is from Clark, p. 108.
385 "Sheer hose and frivolous slippers" is from *Newsweek* (March 1, 1943).
385–86 "The lord helps those" and "Helen Hayes" are from *Time* (March 1, 1943).
386 The retrieval of May-ling's fags is from Tuchman, p. 353, as is "The President is just crazy to get her out of the country."
387 Luce's appeal to *Time* subscribers is from Helen Hull, *Mayling Soong Chiang* (1943).
387 The black-market rate is cited by Swanberg, p. 202. He also describes the New York welcoming committee.
387–88 May-ling's conduct in the Waldorf Towers is recounted by Sherwood.
388 It was reporter Helen Hull who was so deeply impressed by May-ling's ability to dress in a blackout, although she had to miss supper with her august reception committee to complete the job.
388 The impressive list of disappointed dinner guests is from Swanberg, p. 202.
388 "A soldier unafraid" is from Hull.
388 The crowd count is from Clark, p. 118.
388 May-ling's wearing of slacks at Wellesley is from Hull.
389 Tong gives a flattering account of her tour. Swanberg's is less flattering.
389 The fate of the Dowager's pearls is from Aisin Gioro (Henry) Pu-yi, *From Emperor to Citizen* (1979).
389 "Snow White" is from Kahn, *The China Hands* (1972), p. 63.
389 Tong tells of the Utah whistle stop as if it were a flattering incident.
389 The Hollywood Bowl reception was covered by *Life* (April 19, 1943).
390 Swanberg describes the extreme unction of the actors and actresses on pp. 202–203.
390 "Buried alive" is from *Life* (April 19, 1943).
390–91 "Our own quarrel would come later" is from White's *In Search of History*, pp. 144–54.
391 The off-loading in Assam is from Felix Greene's *Curtain of Ignorance* (1964), p. 21.

Eighteen: A House Divided

393 "General Cash My-check" is from Merle Miller's *Plain Speaking* (1973), p. 289.
394 Churchill's strategic concerns at the time are summarized succinctly in Moser's *China-Burma-India*, pp. 178–79.
396 Chiang's shift away from the Soongs toward the Ch'en brothers' clique was detected and duly reported by Jack Service.

397 U.S. Naval Intelligence sent Miles out to work with Tai Li, the secret police boss, at the same time it sent other agents to work with the leaders of the Sicilian Mafia. For an account of the results, see McCoy's *Politics of Heroin*. Miles's version of his assignment, including his admiration for Tai Li, is in his book, *A Different Kind of War* (1967).

397 The showdown between Donovan and Tai Li is in Dunlop's *Donovan* (1982), p. 425.

399 White's "The men walked quietly" is quoted in Moser, p. 181, which also mentions in passing that a number of Chinese generals asked for American help in staging a coup.

399 The beggar round-up is from Service.

400 "A short-term investment" is in Gary May's *China Scapegoat: The Diplomatic Ordeal of John Carter Vincent* (1979), pp. 100–108.

400 "We are fully aware" is from Moser, p. 183.

400 "Bundle of paprika" is from Moser, p. 186.

401 "Behind Chiang personally" is from May, p. 113.

401 The victim's account of how Hurley brandished the gun in his face is from Kahn, p. 145.

402 Since the Chinese consider turtles to be homosexual, the term "turtle's egg" is roughly equivalent to "latent homosexual" or "incipient fairy"— or, simply, to "faggot." Hence Mao's calling Chiang a "turtle's egg" is roughly equivalent to Hurley's calling Mao a "motherfucker." The name calling is from May, pp. 114–15, and Kahn, footnote 3, p. 139.

402 "China is in a mess" and "the popular American misconception" are from Hahn, pp. 3 and 102.

403 Chiang's habit of threatening a separate peace with Japan is from Davies, p. 266.

403 "Real Oriental," "innumerable difficulties" and "abject misery" are all from Tuchman, p. 401.

403 "The Generalissimo came up the hard way" is from Davies, p. 264.

404 FDR's confession to Edgar Snow is from Snow's *Journey . . .* , p. 347.

404 Hornbeck's career is summarized by Fairbank, p. 177.

404 Hornbeck's withholding of official cables is from May, p. 91.

406 Hornbeck's appraisal of Jack Service's reporting is from Service, p. 170.

406 "Rash, exaggerated, and immature" comes from May, p. 91.

406 "Chiang shows these traits" is from Service, pp. 91–92.

410 "The dramatic eclipse of T. V. Soong" is from Service, pp. 79–84.

410 The scandal over disappearing Lend-Lease was reiterated from time to time by Drew Pearson after the war in his column "Washington Merry-Go-Round" (July 16, 1951). Many of the later columns were written by Jack Anderson.

411 T. L.'s role as head of Southwest Transportation is from Young, p. 110.

411 The speed at which the U.S. goods moved into the black market is from George H. Kerr's *Formosa Betrayed* (1965), footnote, p. 161.

411 "If Elder Sister had been a man" is from Joseph Alsop's article in the *Saturday Evening Post* (January 7, 1950). This article is uncharacteristically revealing and not particularly charitable toward the Soongs. There is the aftertaste of spite throughout, as though Alsop felt let down by the Soongs, for reasons he did not explain, and felt impelled to air a tiny bit of their linen in public. The result is as unsatisfying as warm beer.

412 "Her head shook a bit" and the rest of the interview are from Fairbank in *Chinabound*.

412 The chilling scene of "a certain cadaverous charm" is from *Churchill, Taken from the Diaries of Lord Moran.*

413 May-ling's fall from grace was detected by Service.

413 The departure of May-ling and Ai-ling (with Louis Kung and his wife) for Brazil was kept secret but was reported by U.S. intelligence in documents provided to me by the National Security Agency following a Freedom of Information inquiry in 1983–84. I was able to trace their path as far as Brocoió Island near Rio, and to meetings with the Brazilian dictator Getulio Vargas. Brazil at the time was ruled as a personal fiefdom, and Vargas was always prepared to grant membership in his private club to anyone with adequate wherewithal. Americans with a special feeling for fascism felt very much at home in Brazil.

414 Again, the NSA intelligence files are among the very few sources to mention the breakup of the Chiangs' marriage.

414 Saint reported to the Time Inc. brass on May-ling's movements and whereabouts; the memos are in the *Time* morgue.

415 Kahn quotes Brooks Atkinson on p. 106.

Nineteen: Ashes, Ashes, All Fall Down

417 "Purely coincidental" is from David Halberstam's *The Powers That Be* (1979), p. 79.

417 White mentions "Life Looks at China" on p. 208 of *In Search of History,* and refers to his quarrels with Luce as "intellectual volleying." White is always very kind in his judgments of Luce.

417 "You have to live in Chungking" is from *Life* (May 1, 1944).

418 "Edited into a lie" is from White, *In Search . . .*

419 The starved soldiers in Chungking are mentioned in Tuchman, p. 484.

420 T. V.'s use of the nickname Ding-Ding for his wife is mentioned in files obtained from the FBI under the Freedom of Information Act.

420 The lengths to which T. V. went to obtain sprigs of dogwood for Ding-Ding are from both Greene and Tuchman.

420 T. V.'s reaction to news of the gold scandal is from the *New York Times* (May 26, 1945).

422 "Guilty parties" is from Young, p. 332. As an employee of the Chiang regime, Young gives a very naïve interpretation of these and other events.

422 The significant presence of T. L. and H. H. on the board of the bank is cited by Coble, p. 197.

422 T. V. gave his reason for wanting the two clerks executed in the *New York Times* (May 26, 1945).

422 The basic outlines of the life of "Paper Tiger" T'ang are in Boorman, vol. 3, pp. 225–30.

422 The Whampoa Clique is described by White and Jacoby, p. 177.

422 T'ang's role in the destruction of the dikes is in Tuchman.

423 "He was a pleasant man" is from White and Jacoby, p. 177.

423 The panic of T'ang's officer corps during Operation Ichigo is in White and Jacoby, p. 178.

423   T'ang's reward is in Boorman, vol. 3, p. 227.

424   "Holding jade and brocades" is in Boorman, and speaks volumes for the ambivalent attitude of some Chinese senior officers toward the Japanese during the war.

424   It is Crozier who judged T'ang to be "one of the most disreputable."

424   The relief figures are taken from Crozier, pp. 301–302.

425   Greene's tentative figure of $47 million is on his p. 147.

425   This extraordinary discussion of T. V.'s investments is so provocative that it demands the dropping of the other shoe. But, if anyone knows, nobody is talking. The tantalizing exchange is in the memo from Anatole Visson cited earlier.

425   The bootleg blood plasma is also taken from the NSA files.

425   T. V.'s staggering bill to the UN relief organization is in Kerr, pp. 158–61.

426   T. V.'s forced resignation as Premier is from the *New York Times* (March 6, 1947).

426   His consolation prize as Kwangtung governor is from Boorman.

426   "The truth can be told in one sentence" is from *Time* (March 10, 1947).

427   This figure of $800 million on deposit in U.S. banks would appear to be amazingly accurate. However, it was intended, apparently, to be regarded as a total of the U.S. deposits of all three branches of the Soong clan in exile, that is, representing the holdings of Ai-ling, T. V., and May-ling. The FBI inquiry secretly ordered by President Truman came up with the nearly identical tally of $750 million; this included—in addition to the very large holdings of H. H. and Ai-ling, and those of T. V. —a sum apparently well in excess of a hundred million held by May-ling. But the FBI inquiry failed to look into the separate holdings of T. L. and T. A. It is also worth keeping in mind that the figure of approximately $800 million apparently is intended to represent only liquid assets and portfolios, or wealth on deposit, and may not include real estate and industrial properties, whose value would have to be assessed case by case. Wholly aside from this is the question of industrial and real-estate holdings in Latin America, which may have been of equal size or greater. There were also believed to be multi-million-dollar holdings in other world financial capitals, notably Singapore, Sydney, Johannesburg, Zurich and London. Therefore, the 1950 overall or global wealth of T. V. alone was generally estimated by those who go in for such speculation to be far in excess of $1 billion U.S., and that of H. H. and Ai-ling to be approximately one billion. Hence the expression in the Encyclopedia Britannica that T. V. was "once reputed to have been the richest man in the world."

428   How times change. For the arrest of Big-eared Tu's son by Chiang Kai-shek's son, see Wang's "Tu Yueh-sheng" and Boorman on Chiang Ching-kuo.

Twenty: The Soong Legacy

429   David Kung's move to Miami Beach is from Crozier, p. 316. (Since then, he has lived in New York City, avoiding publicity of any kind. He has not been mentioned in the *New York Times,* for example, since 1950, even on the deaths of his parents. This in itself is quite a feat, since he is an

extremely wealthy man with elaborate business interests. His brother, Louis Kung, has spent much of his time in Texas and California, and dabbled in politics by backing various Republican candidates. In the 1960s he married movie actress Debra Paget. They lived near Dallas, where Louis Kung was a substantial, but nearly invisible, figure in the oil business. They were divorced in 1981.)

429 "The citizens of Shanghai" is from Boorman's profile of CCK.

430 "Nasty as a skunk" and "man of great charm" are from Swanberg.

432 "I'm not saying they bought anybody out" is from Miller, p. 287.

432 "Order of the Auspicious Star" is from Swanberg, p. 265.

432 "Chiang needed $3 billion more" is from *China: U.S. Policy since 1945* (1980), p. 84.

432-33 The Battle of Huai-hai is described in William Morwood, *Duel for the Middle Kingdom* (1980). The figures are from *China: U.S. Policy since 1945*, p. 84. The "final act of treachery" is from Morwood, p. 369. The tumblers of whiskey are also from Morwood, and are mentioned as well by Crozier.

433 "I wouldn't let her stay in the White House" is from Miller, p. 288.

434 Truman's estimate of Soong deposits is from Morwood, p. 365.

434 "Over seventy million dollars" is from FBI files, a secret memo to J. Edgar Hoover, dated September 29, 1951 (declassified in 1983 under the Freedom of Information/Privacy Act). These FBI documents number well over five hundred pages, so I am citing only a single document as an example.

435 The reluctance of the Manhattan Company to talk about T. V.'s holdings is from the same FBI files, a cable from the New York field office to FBI headquarters dated May 6, 1949, and related cables.

436 May-ling's failure to file notice of her U.S. property holdings is in a memo from the Washington field office to FBI headquarters dated May 10, 1949.

437 "They're all thieves" is from Miller, p. 289.

438 For a flattering account of Chiang's treasure house on Taiwan, and how it got there, see Arthur Zich's "Chinese Art Treasures," in GEO (September 1983).

439 Ambassador Stuart's advice is from Morwood.

440 For Chiang's last *entre-nous* with Big-eared Tu, see Wang, "Tu Yueh-sheng."

440 "Paper Tiger" T'ang's great palisade is from Crozier, p. 336. Newsman Julian Schuman looked it over and remarked, "The only plausible explanation one heard for this prodigy was that the General had relatives in the lumber business." (See Schuman's *China: An Uncensored Look* (1983), pp. 44, 780.

441 "All the gold in China" is from Noel Barber, *The Fall of Shanghai* (1977), pp. 78-79. Julian Schuman, who was also there, saw trucks loaded with war material driven onto docks saturated with gasoline and set afire; still, great quantities of arms and munitions fell into Communist hands. "It is difficult," said Schuman, "to reconcile this mass of equipment with the lamentations heard in America that we had 'lost China' by failing to supply Chiang adequately," Schuman, p. 46.

441 Chiang's praise of Tu's "loyalty and integrity" are in Boorman's profile of Tu.

441 "At 15 Bowstring Alley," the headquarters of the CCP's Social Affairs Department, headed at the time by Tsou Ta-peng.

442 T'ai Ch'i-tao's suicide is in Boorman.

443 "Tell Chiang he is finished" is from Greene, p. 43.

443 Childs is quoted by Greene, p. 43.

444 "Neither the editor . . . nor the reader" is from Greene, pp. 67–68.

445 Many Chiang supporters are listed in *China: U.S. Policy since 1945*, p. 30.

445 The Allen quote on *Time*'s Washington Bureau is from Swanberg, p. 253.

446 The Committee of One Million is from *China: U.S. Policy since 1945*, p. 117.

446 The Riverdale strategy sessions are from Greene.

447 The activities of Louis Kung were commented on by Drew Pearson in his "Washington Merry-Go-Round" (October 19, 1960). The soybean deal was just one of many activities brought to light by a study of the China Lobby in *The Reporter*. The article pointed out that Senator McCarthy was one of T. L. Soong's friends who joined in making the soybean killing. It is worth noting that General MacArthur, one of the champions of the China Lobby, who naturally knew of the decision to go to war, visited Taiwan to speak with the Generalissimo just before the declaration was made public.

448 The Cheyenne Oil Company deals were described by Drew Pearson.

448 CCK's rapid rise in status is from *China: U.S. Policy since 1945*, p. 267.

448 May-ling's bamboo painting is from an Osborne dispatch to *Time*. His unpublished notes of the interview with CCK on September 24, 1965, are in the *Time* morgue.

449 I was told the story of Mrs. Luce's shopping trip by friends of hers in Washington.

450 The scene at Sungshan airport is from the Osborne notes.

450 H. H. Kung's moist-eyed denials of great wealth are in an interview he had at Oberlin with June Faulds. The story appeared under the headline "Former China Premier Helping Oberlin Mark 50th Shansi Year," but the newspaper in which this story appeared is not identified on the 1959 clipping.

451 "Like all those Shansi bankers" is from the *New York Times*, "H. H. Kung Obituary."

451 T. V.'s absence from Kung's funeral is clear from the *New York Times* (August 23, 1967).

452 "He left Canton hurriedly" is from the *New York Times* (June 10, 1950).

452 The mysterious affair of the guns is from State Department Records, DOS 493.118/1-1250, declassified 1983.

453 The "richest man" comment is in the third edition of the Encyclopedia Britannica, vol. IX, "T. V. Soong."

454 Joe Alsop's comment to Averell Harriman is from State Department, Records DOS 793.00/1-2363.

455 CCK's discreet visit to Washington is from Boorman.

456 Louis's coop is from the *New York Times* (April 17, 1966).

456 May-ling's gallstones are mentioned by Averell Harriman in his memorandum of a conversation with T. V. Soong (September 1, 1963), in State Department Records.

456   May-ling's mastectomies are mentioned in the *New York Times* (August 24, 1976).

457   May-ling's "secret" trip to Johns Hopkins was reported by the *New York Times* (September 18, 1976).

457   Ching-ling's appearance beside Mao on the Gate of Heavenly Peace is from Dennis Bloodworth's *The Messiah and the Mandarins* (1982), p. 81.

457   "I distrust Mao Tse-tung less" is from Edgar Snow, *Journey . . .* , p. 95.

458   The secret police campaign to interfere with Ching-ling's charity soccer games is mentioned in intelligence cables from the National Security Agency.

458   Ching-ling's visit to Moscow is from Clubb's *China and Russia* (1971), pp. 343, 345.

458–59   The news story from Shanghai was printed in the Washington *Times Herald* (1946). I found it among the FBI files on Madame Sun Yat-sen.

459   Ching-ling's role in the new Revolutionary Committee is from Boorman.

459   "Her chronic illness had reached a critical stage" is from Edgar Snow's *The Other Side of the River* (1962), footnote, p. 544.

460   The storming of Ching-ling's house is from the *New York Times* (September 22, 1965).

460   Fox Butterfield's encounter with Yolanda is from his book *China: Alive in the Bitter Sea* (1982), p. 85.

461   Ching-ling was not a member of the Communist party at any point in her life until she was inducted on her deathbed, when she may not have been fully aware. They certainly had many goals in common, and a common enemy in Chiang and what he represented. My conclusion was that the destruction of the Third Force left her no alternative and she was allied with the CCP in practice, if not as a devout party member. However, others are not so charitable. This seems to turn on the fact that Ching-ling did not speak out in her twilight years against the cruelties of Mao's Cultural Revolution. This caused some of her ardent old admirers to become sharply critical. The judgment of Harold Isaacs is particularly valuable, from a letter to me written October 6, 1983: "It is no doubt true—as I can testify myself—that she had occasion to be privately critical of her CP associates. But I am not aware of any public criticism, much less attack, ever. [When she left Moscow in 1927] she went right into the network of CI propaganda activities in Europe—the League Against Imperialism was one of its most successful early examples, a creation of the CI-sympathizer system created by Willi Munzenberg out of Berlin. [Ching-ling's] statements in Shanghai—you call one of them 'Leaguespeak'—were most often pure CP-speak in style and rhetoric and it is true that those that sounded most that way were generally drafted [for her] by others. Post-1949, I am not aware that she ever publicly challenged the CP regime's violence and repressions at any stage, including the Cultural Revolution, until after it was all over. No, one can love and admire [Ching-ling], but it won't do to romanticize her way of handling her CP connection."

461   "We must learn to arm ourselves" is from Han Suyin's *Wind in the Tower* (1976), p. 426.

Epilogue: The Concubine in the Well

462 The tale of the concubine in the well is widely accepted as accurate, although the details come from the diary of the court official Ching Shan, which turned out to be largely an invention of Sir Edmund Backhouse, himself a fraud of the highest order. (See Hugh Trevor-Roper, *A Hidden Life: The Enigma of Sir Edmund Backhouse.* Macmillan, London, 1976.) The murder of the Pearl Concubine is not in question, however. As Hilda Hookham put it, while the diary proved a forgery, "the picture it conveys of the times is accurate." I have taken the anecdote from Hookham, *A Short History of China* (1972), p. 293.

BIBLIOGRAPHY

Akers, Samuel Luttrell. *The First Hundred Years of Wesleyan College.* Macon, Georgia: Stinehour Press, 1976.

Akimova, Vera Vladimirovna Vishnayakova. *Two Years in Revolutionary China: 1925–1927.* Cambridge, Mass.: East Asian Research Center, Harvard University, 1971.

Alexander, Garth. *The Invisible China: The Overseas Chinese and the Politics of Southeast Asia.* New York: Macmillan, 1973.

Baedeker, Karl (ed). *The United States with an excursion into Mexico.* New York: Da Capo Press, 1971 (originally printed in 1893).

Barber, Noel. *The Fall of Shanghai.* New York: Coward, McCann & Geoghegan, 1979.

Barron, John. *KGB: The Secret Work of Soviet Secret Agents.* New York: Reader's Digest Association, 1974.

Beers, Burton F. *China in Old Photographs: 1860–1910.* New York: Charles Scribner's Sons, 1978.

Bianco, Lucien. *Origins of the Chinese Revolution: 1915–1949.* Stanford, Calif.: Stanford University Press, 1971.

Biographies of Kuomintang Leaders. Cambridge, Mass.: Harvard University Committee on International and Regional Studies, 1948.

Bloodworth, Dennis. *The Messiah and the Mandarins.* New York: Atheneum, 1982.

———, and Ching Ping. *The Chinese Machiavelli.* New York: Farrar, Straus and Giroux, 1976.

Booker, Edna Lee. *News Is My Job.* New York: Macmillan, 1940.

Boorman, Howard L. (ed). *Biographical Dictionary of Republican China.* New York: Columbia University Press, 1979.

Botjer, George. *A Short History of Nationalist China: 1919–1949.* New York: G. P. Putnam's Sons, 1979.

Bozan, Jian, et al. *A Concise History of China.* Peking: Foreign Languages Press, 1981.

Brandt, Conrad. *Stalin's Failure in China.* New York: W. W. Norton, 1958.

Bresler, Fenton. *The Chinese Mafia.* Briarcliff Manor, N.Y.: Stein & Day, 1981.

Burke, James. *My Father in China.* New York: Farrar & Rinehart, 1942.

Butterfield, Fox. *China: Alive in the Bitter Sea.* New York: New York Times Books, 1982.

Cameron, Nigel. *Barbarians and Mandarins: Thirteen Centuries of Western Travelers in China.* New York: Walker and Weatherhill, 1970.

Chan, F. Gilbert, and Etzold, Thomas H. (eds). *China in the 1920's.* New York: New Viewpoints, 1976.

Chang Hsin-hai. *America and China: A New Approach to Asia.* New York: Simon and Schuster, 1965.

Chen, Percy. *China Called Me.* Boston: Little Brown, 1979.

Chesneaux, Jean, et al. *China from the 1911 Revolution to Liberation.* New York: Pantheon Books, 1977.

———. *China from the Opium Wars to the 1911 Revolution.* New York: Pantheon Books, 1976.

——— (ed.). *Popular Movements and Secret Societies in China, 1840–1950.* Stanford, Calif.: Stanford University Press, 1972.

Chiang Kai-shek. *Soviet Russia in China.* New York: Farrar, Straus and Giroux, 1957.

Chiang, May-ling Soong. *This Is Our China.* New York: Harper & Brothers, 1940.

Ch'i Hsi-sheng. *Warlord Politics in China: 1916–1928.* Stanford, Calif.: Stanford University Press, 1976.

Clark, Elmer T. *The Chiangs of China.* New York: Abingdon-Cokesbury Press, 1943.

Clubb, O. Edmund. *China and Russia: The Great Game.* New York: Columbia University Press, 1971.

———. *Communism in China as Reported from Hankow in 1932.* New York: Columbia University Press, 1968.

———. *20th Century China.* New York: Columbia University Press, 1978.

———. *The Witness and I.* New York: Columbia University Press, 1974.

Coble, Parks M., Jr. *The Shanghai Capitalists and the Nationalist Government: 1927–1937.* Cambridge, Mass.: Council on East Asian Studies, Harvard University Press, 1980.

Congressional Quarterly. *China: U.S. Policy since 1945.* Washington, D.C.: Congressional Quarterly, 1980.

Coye, Molly Joel, and Livingston, Jon (eds.). *China Yesterday and Today.* New York: Bantam Books, 1979.

Crozier, Brian. *The Man Who Lost China.* New York: Charles Scribner's Sons, 1976.

Davies, John Paton, Jr. *Dragon by the Tail.* New York: W. W. Norton, 1972.

Dawson, Raymond. *The Chinese Chameleon.* London: Oxford University Press, 1967.

Deriabin, Peter, and Gibney, Frank. *The Secret World: KGB*. New York: Ballantine Books, 1982.
Deutscher, Isaac. *The Prophet Armed*. New York: Oxford University Press, 1954.
———. *The Prophet Outcast*. London: Oxford University Press, 1963.
———. *The Prophet Unarmed*. London: Oxford University Press, 1959.
Drage, Charles. *Two-Gun Cohen*. London: Jonathan Cape, 1954.
Dunlop, Richard. *Donovan*. New York: Rand McNally, 1982.
Elvin, Mark, and Skinner, O. William (eds.). *The Chinese City Between Two Worlds*. Stanford, Calif.: Stanford University Press, 1974.
Eunson, Roby. *The Soong Sisters*. New York: Franklin Watts, 1975.
Evans, Les, and Block, Russell (eds.). *Leon Trotsky on China*. New York: Monad Press, 1976.
Excerpts from Three Classical Chinese Novels. Peking: Panda Books, 1981.
Fairbank, John King. *Chinabound*. New York: Harper & Row, 1982.
———. *China Perceived*. New York: Vintage Books, 1976.
———. *The United States and China*. Cambridge, Mass.: Harvard University Press, 1979.
Fehrenbach, T. R. *F.D.R.'S Undeclared War: 1939 to 1941*. New York: David McKay, 1967.
Felber, John E. *People's Republic of China*. New York: International Intertrade Index, 1974.
Fleming, Peter. *The Siege at Peking*. New York: Harper & Brothers, 1959.
Franck, Harry A. *Roving Through Southern China*. New York: Century Company, 1925.
Furuya, Keija. *Chiang Kai-shek: His Life and Times*. Anapolis, Md.: St. John's University Press, 1981.
Gasster, Michael. *Chinese Intellectuals and the Revolution of 1911*. Seattle: University of Washington Press, 1969.
Gilbert, Martin. *Winston S. Churchill: The Prophet of Truth*. Boston: Houghton Mifflin, 1977.
Gillen, Donald G. *Warlord Yen Hsi-shan in Shansi Province: 1911–1949*. Princeton, N.J.: Princeton University Press, 1967.
Goodrich, L. Carrington, and Cameron, Nigel. *The Face of China as Seen by Photographers & Travelers: 1860–1912*. Millerton, N.Y.: Aperture, Inc., 1978.
Granquist, Hans. *The Red Guard*. New York: Praeger, 1967.
A Great Trial in Chinese History. Peking: New World Press, 1981.
Greene, Felix. *A Curtain of Ignorance*. Garden City, N.Y.: Doubleday, 1964.
Gunther, John. *Inside Asia*. New York: Harper & Brothers, 1942.
Hahn, Emily. *Chiang Kai-shek: An Unauthorized Biography*. Garden City, N.Y.: Doubleday, 1955.
———. *The Soong Sisters*. New York: Doubleday, Doran, 1941.
Halberstam, David. *The Powers That Be*. New York: Alfred A. Knopf, 1979.
Han Suyin. *Birdless Summer*. New York: G. P. Putnam's Sons, 1968.
———. *The Morning Deluge*. London: Panther Books, 1976.

————. *A Mortal Flower.* London: Panther Books, 1972.

————. *Wind in the Tower.* London: Chaucer Press, 1976.

Hao Yen-p'ing. *The Comprador in Nineteenth Century China: Bridge Between East and West.* Cambridge, Mass.: Harvard University Press, 1970.

Hauser, Ernest. *Shanghai: City for Sale.* New York: Harcourt Brace, 1940.

Hobsbaum, Eric. *Bandits.* New York: Dell, 1969.

Holubnychy, Linda. *Michael Borodin and the Chinese Revolution: 1923–1925.* New York: East Asian Institute, Columbia University, University Microfilms International, 1979.

Hookham, Hilda. *A Short History of China.* New York: New American Library, 1972.

Houn, Franklin W. *A Short History of Chinese Communism.* Englewood Cliffs, N.Y.: Prentice-Hall, 1973.

Hseuh Chun-tu (ed). *Revolutionary Leaders of Modern China.* London: Oxford University Press, 1971.

Hsu, Immanuel C. Y. *Readings in Modern Chinese History.* London: Oxford University Press, 1971.

Hsu Kai-yu. *The Chinese Literary Scene.* New York: Vintage, 1975.

————. *Chou En-lai: China's Grey Eminence.* Garden City, N.Y.: Doubleday, 1968.

Hsu Long-hsuen and Chang Ming-kai. *History of the Sino-Japanese War.* Taipei: Chung Wu Publishing Co., 1972.

Hull, Cordell. *Memoirs of Cordell Hull.* New York: Macmillan, 1948.

Hussey, Harry. *My Pleasures and Palaces.* Garden City, N.Y.: Doubleday, 1968.

Isaacs, Harold R. *The Tragedy of the Chinese Revolution.* Stanford, Calif.: Stanford University Press, 1961.

Jacobs, Dan N. *Borodin: Stalin's Man in China.* Cambridge, Mass.: Harvard University Press, 1981.

Kahn, E. J., Jr., *The China Hands.* New York: Viking Press, 1972.

Kaplan, Fredric, and Sobin, Julian M. *Encyclopedia of China Today.* New York: Harper & Row, 1980.

Keegan, John. *The Face of Battle.* New York: Viking Press, 1976.

Kemp, Peter (ed.). *The Oxford Companion to Ships and the Sea.* London: Oxford University Press, 1976.

Kerr, George H. *Formosa Betrayed.* Boston: Houghton Mifflin, 1965.

Knightley, Phillip. *The First Casualty.* New York: Harcourt Brace Jovanovich, 1975.

Kubek, Anthony. *The Red China Papers.* New Rochelle, N.Y.: Arlington House, 1975.

Larteguy, Jean. *The Face of War.* New York: Bobbs-Merrill, 1979.

Levy, Howard S. *Chinese Footbinding: The History of a Curious Erotic Custom.* New York: Walton Rawls, 1966.

Leys, Simon. *Chinese Shadows.* New York: Penguin Books, 1978.

Liang Chin-tung. *General Stilwell in China, 1942–1944: The Full Story.* Annapolis, Md.: St. John's University Press, 1972.

Li Dun J. *The Ageless Chinese: A History.* New York: Charles Scribner's Sons, 1965.

Life at the Grassroots. Peking: Beijing Review Special Feature Series, 1981.

Linebarger, Paul M. A. *The China of Chiang Kai-shek.* Westport, Conn.: Greenwood Press, 1973.

Loh, Pichon P. Y. *The Early Chiang Kai-shek.* New York: Columbia University Press, 1971.

Malraux, André. *The Conquerors.* Boston: Beacon Press, 1956.

———. *Man's Fate.* New York: Random House, 1968.

Maitland, Derek. *Setting Sails.* Hong Kong: South China Morning Post, 1981.

May, Gary. *China Scapegoat: The Diplomatic Ordeal of John Carter Vincent.* Washington, D.C.: New Republic Books, 1979.

McCoy, Alfred W. *The Politics of Heroin in Southeast Asia.* New York: Harper & Row, 1972.

McCunn, Ruthanne. *An Illustrated History of the Chinese in America.* San Francisco: Design Enterprises of San Francisco, 1979.

Mee, Charles L., Jr. *The End of Order.* New York: E. P. Dutton, 1980.

Miles, Milton E. *A Different Kind of War.* Garden City, N.Y.: Doubleday & Company, 1967.

Miller, Merle. *Plain Speaking.* New York: G. P. Putnam's Sons, 1973.

Moran, Charles M. *Churchill Taken from the Diaries of Lord Moran.* Boston: Houghton Mifflin, 1966.

Morwood, William. *Duel for the Middle Kingdom.* New York: Everest House, 1980.

Moseley, George. *China since 1911.* New York: Harper & Row, 1968.

Moser, Don. *China-Burma-India.* Alexandria, Va.: Time-Life Books, 1978.

Murphey, Rhoads. *Shanghai: Key to Modern China.* Cambridge, Mass.: Harvard University Press, 1953.

National Geographic Society. *Journey into China.* Washington, D.C.: National Geographic Society, 1982.

Nee, Victor, and Peck, James. (eds.) *China's Uninterrupted Revolution from 1840 to the Present.* New York: Pantheon Books, 1975.

O'Connor, Richard. *Jack London: A Biography.* Boston, Little Brown, 1962.

The Opium War. Peking: Foreign Languages Press, 1976.

Page, Martin. *The Lost Pleasure of the Great Trains.* New York: William Morrow, 1975.

Pal, John. *Shanghai Saga.* London: Jerrolds, 1963.

Payne, Robert. *Mao Tse-tung.* New York: Weybright and Talley, 1950.

———. *The Life and Death of Trotsky.* New York: McGraw-Hill, 1977.

Peck, Graham. *Two Kinds of Time.* Boston: Houghton Mifflin, 1950.

Peffer, Nathaniel. *The Far East.* Ann Arbor: University of Michigan Press, 1968.

Powell, John B. *My Twenty-five Years in China.* New York: Macmillan, 1945.

Price, Don C. *Russia and the Roots of the Chinese Revolution, 1896–1911.* Cambridge, Mass.: Harvard University Press, 1974.

Pu-Yi, Aisin Gioro (Henry). *From Emperor to Citizen.* Peking: Foreign Languages Press, 1979.

Pye, Lucian W. *Mao Tse-tung: The Man in the Leader.* New York: Basic Books, 1976.

The Reform Movement of 1898. Peking: Foreign Languages Press, 1976.

The Revolution of 1911. Peking: Foreign Languages Press, 1976.

de Riencourt, Amaury. *The Soul of China.* New York: Harper & Brothers, 1958.

Roots, John McCook. *Chou.* New York: Doubleday, 1978.

Russell, Bertrand. *The Problem of China.* London: Allen and Unwin, 1922.

Schiffrin, Harold Z. *Sun Yat-sen and the Origins of the Chinese Revolution.* Berkeley: University of California Press, 1970.

————. *Sun Yat-sen: Reluctant Revolutionary.* Boston: Little Brown, 1980.

Schleit, Philip. *Shelton's Barefoot Airline.* Annapolis, Md.: Fishergate, 1982.

Schlesinger, Arthur M., Jr. *The Coming of the New Deal.* Boston: Houghton Mifflin, 1959.

Schuman, Julian. *China: An Uncensored Look.* Sag Harbor, N.Y.: Second Chance Press, 1983.

Schurmann, Franz, and Schell, Orville (eds.) *The China Reader.* New York: Vintage Books, 1967.

Schwartz, Harry. *Tsars, Mandarins and Commissars.* New York: J. B. Lippincott, 1964.

Scott, Peter Dale. *The War Conspiracy.* New York: Bobbs-Merrill, 1972.

Seagrave, Sterling. *Soldiers of Fortune.* Alexandria, Va.: Time-Life Books, 1981.

Selle, Earl Albert. *Donald of China.* New York: Harper & Brothers, 1948.

Service, John S. *Lost Chance in China.* New York: Vintage Books, 1975.

Seven Contemporary Chinese Women Writers. Peking: Panda Books, 1982.

Shaplen, Robert. *A Turning Wheel.* New York: Random House, 1979.

Sharman, Lyon. *Sun Yat-sen: His Life and Its Meaning.* Hamden, Conn.: Archon Books, 1965.

Sheean, Vincent. *Between the Thunder and the Sun.* New York: Random House, 1943.

————. *Personal History.* Boston: Houghton Mifflin, 1969.

Sherwood, Robert E. *Roosevelt and Hopkins.* New York: Harper & Brothers, 1948.

Shimer, Dorothy B. (ed). *Rice Bowl Women.* New York: New American Library, 1982.

Sinclair, Andrew. *Jack: A Biography of Jack London.* New York: Pocket Books, 1979.

Smedley, Agnes. *China Fights Back.* New York: Vanguard Press, 1928.

————. *China's Red Army Marches.* New York, International Publishers, 1934.

————. *Destinies: Sketches of Present-Day China.* New York: Vanguard Press, 1933.

Snow, Edgar. *The Battle for Asia.* New York, Random House, 1941.

————. *Journey to the Beginning.* New York: Random House, 1958.

————. *The Other Side of the River.* New York: Random House, 1962.

Snow, Helen Foster. *The Chinese Communists: Sketches and Autobiographies of the Old Guard.* Westport, Conn.: Greenwood Publishing Company, 1972.

————. *Inside Red China.* New York: Da Capo Press, 1977.

Snow, Lois Wheeler. *Edgar Snow's China.* New York: Random House, 1981.

Sokolsky, George. *The Tinder Box of Asia.* Garden City, N. Y.: Doubleday, Doran, 1934.

Spence, Jonathan. *To Change China: Western Advisers in China 1620–1960.* Boston: Little Brown, 1969.

——. *The Gate of Heavenly Peace.* New York: Viking, 1981.

Steiner, Stan. *Fusang: The Chinese Who Built America.* New York: Harper & Row, 1979.

Strong, Anna Louise. *China's Millions.* New York: Coward-McCann, 1928.

Sues, Ilona Ralf. *Shark's Fins and Millet.* Boston: Little Brown, 1944.

Summerville, John. *Fodor's People's Republic of China.* London: Hodder and Stoughton, 1981.

Sun Yat-sen. *Chinese Revolutionary.* New York: AMS Press, 1927.

——. *Kidnapped in London.* Bristol, 1897.

Sutton, S. B. *In China's Border Provinces.* New York: Hastings House, 1974.

Swanberg, W. A. *Luce and His Empire.* New York: Charles Scribner's Sons, 1972.

Tai Dwan. *Chiang Ch'ing.* New York: Exposition Press, 1974.

The Taiping Revolution. Peking: Foreign Languages Press, 1976.

Tang Tsou. *America's Failure in China: 1941–1950.* Chicago: University of Chicago Press, 1963.

Terrill, Ross. *Mao.* New York: Harper & Row, 1980.

Thornton, A. P. *The Imperial Idea and Its Enemies.* New York: Anchor Books, 1968.

Tong, Hollington K. *Dateline China.* New York: Rockport Press, 1950.

——. *Chiang Kai-Shek.* Taipei: Government Printing Office, 1953.

Trager, James. *The People's Chronology.* New York: Holt, Rinehart, and Winston, 1979.

Tuchman, Barbara W. *Notes from China.* New York: Collier Books, 1972.

——. *Stilwell and the American Experience in China: 1911–1945.* New York: Macmillan, 1970.

Uhalley, Stephen, Jr. *Mao Tse-tung.* New York: New Viewpoints, 1975.

The Unquenchable Spark. Peking: Foreign Languages Press, 1964.

Wei Kuo-lu. *On the Long March as Guard to Chou En-lai.* Peking: Foreign Languages Press, 1978.

Whipple, A. B. C. *The Clipper Ships.* Alexandria, Va.: Time-Life Books, 1980.

White, Theodore. *In Search of History: A Personal Adventure.* New York: Harper & Row, 1978.

——and Annalee Jacoby. *Thunder out of China.* New York: William Sloane Associates, 1946.

Wilbur, C. Martin. *Sun Yat-sen: Frustrated Patriot.* New York: Columbia University Press, 1976.

Williams, Lea E. *The Future of the Overseas Chinese in Southeast Asia.* New York: McGraw-Hill, 1966.

Wilson, Dick. *The Long March.* New York: Penguin Books, 1971.

Woo, Thomas Tze Chung. *The Kuomintang and the Future of the Chinese Revolution.* London: Allen & Unwin, 1928.

Worcester, G. R. G. *The Junks and Sampans of the Yangtze.* Annapolis, Md.: Naval Institute Press, 1971.

——. *Sail and Sweep in China.* London: HMSO, 1966.

Worswick, Clark, and Spence, Jonathan. *Imperial China: 1850–1912.* Pennwick Publishing, 1978.

Wu Tien-wei. *The Sian Incident: A Pivotal Point in Modern Chinese History.* Ann Arbor: Michigan Papers in Chinese Studies, no. 26, 1976.

Wu Yu-zhang. *Recollections of the Revolution of 1911.* Peking: Foreign Languages Prss, 1964.

Yang Shang-kuei. *The Red Kiangsi-Kwantung Border Region.* Peking: Foreign Languages Press, 1981.

The Yi Ho Tuan Movement of 1900. Peking: Foreign Languages Press, 1976.

Young, Arthur N. *China and the Helping Hand, 1937–1945.* Cambridge, Mass.: Harvard University Press, 1963.

INDEX

513

THE SOONG DYNASTY

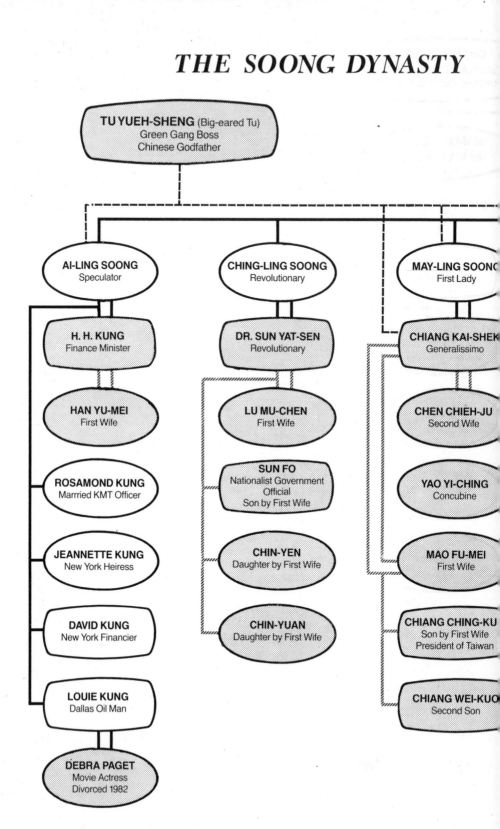